Nixon's Nuclear Specter

NIXON'S NUCLEAR SPECTER

The Secret Alert of 1969, Madman Diplomacy, and the Vietnam War

William Burr
Jeffrey P. Kimball

University Press of Kansas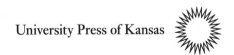

For
Linda Musmeci Kimball
and in memory of
Joan S. and John P. Burr

© 2015 by the University Press of Kansas
All rights reserved

Published by the University Press of Kansas (Lawrence, Kansas 66045), which was organized by the Kansas Board of Regents and is operated and funded by Emporia State University, Fort Hays State University, Kansas State University, Pittsburg State University, the University of Kansas, and Wichita State University

Library of Congress Cataloging-in-Publication Data
Burr, William.
    Nixon's nuclear specter : the secret alert of 1969, madman diplomacy, and the Vietnam War / William Burr, Jeffrey P. Kimball.
        pages cm. — (Modern war studies)
    Includes bibliographical references and index.
    ISBN 978-0-7006-2082-1 (cloth : alk. paper) — ISBN 978-0-7006-2083-8 (ebook)
1. Vietnam War, 1961–1975—Diplomatic history. 2. Nuclear weapons—Government policy—United States—History—20th century. 3. Nixon, Richard M. (Richard Milhous), 1913–1994—Influence. 4. United States—Foreign relations—1969–1974. 5. United States—Military policy—20th century. I. Kimball, Jeffrey P. II. Title.
    DS559.7.B87 2015
    959.704'32—dc23
                                                                                2015002802

British Library Cataloguing-in-Publication Data is available.

Printed in the United States of America

10 9 8 7 6 5 4 3 2 1

The paper used in this publication is recycled and contains 30 percent postconsumer waste. It is acid free and meets the minimum requirements of the American National Standard for Permanence of Paper for Printed Library Materials Z39.48–1992.

The main thing is . . . [we] must hold up the specter of pressures for hitting the North.

Richard M. Nixon

CONTENTS

Illustration gallery follows page 159.

ACKNOWLEDGMENTS

One of the pleasures of completing this book is that it provides us the opportunity to thank those who helped along the way and over the years. Among them are the dedicated archivists and staffers at the US National Archives, the Richard M. Nixon Presidential Library, the Gerald R. Ford Presidential Library, the Library of Congress, the History and Archives Branch of the Naval History and Heritage Command, the US Air Force Historical Research Agency, and the US Army Military History Research Collection. In particular, we thank Patricia Anderson; Edward Barnes; David Colamaria; Christine Jones; David Langbart; Abigail Malingone; Timothy Pettit; John Powers; Sam Rushay; and three archivists who have since passed on: Milton Gustafson, Sally Marks, and John Taylor. We have also benefited from the assistance of David Geyer at the Office of the Historian of the US Department of State, curator Wendy Chmielewski and Mary Beth Sigato of Technical Services at the Swarthmore College Peace Collection, and Alana Ziaya at the Marshfield Clinic Laird Collections.

Many of the documents cited in this book required declassification review, mainly through the mandatory review provisions of White House executive orders. In this respect, the Historical Records Declassification Office of the Washington Headquarters Services, then under the direction of Robert Storer, played an important role in releasing significant documents from the files of Secretary of Defense Melvin Laird. Staffers with US government archives and government agencies were tremendously helpful in making documents available and processing or otherwise facilitating declassification requests for records at the Department of State, the Nixon Library, and the National Archives. They include Jay Bosanko, David Fort, Kathleen M. Grant, Thomas Haughton, Dorothy Johnson, and Kenneth Stein.

Unfortunately, archivists could not provide access to papers of Henry Kissinger, held at the Library of Congress. This restriction is the result of Kissinger's deed of gift to the library, according to which his papers remain closed to all but privileged individuals until five years after his death—even though they include highly significant US government records that are available nowhere else. This restriction, possibly the last standing abuse of power of the Nixon era, is most likely in violation of federal records laws.

Former government officials from both sides of the Vietnam War have illuminated the archival record by providing valuable information through face-to-face and telephone interviews, postal correspondence, or e-mails. For sharing their recollections, we thank in particular: Morton Halperin, James Hoge, Melvin R. Laird, Anthony Lake, the late William L. Lemnitzer, Winston Lord, the late Luu Doan Huynh, Luu Van Loi, Roger Morris, Robert E. Pursley, Lawrence Lynn, Jr., the late Nguyen Co Thach, and the late William Watts. Daniel Ellsberg not only shared his recollections but also made helpful comments about the manuscript.

Leopoldo Nuti, Ennio di Nolfo, and Max Guderzo of the Machiavelli Center for Cold War Studies provided us with an opportunity to present some of our early findings about the October 1969 alert at a terrific conference in Dobbiaco, Italy, in September 2002. David Geyer made it possible for us to present our argument and evidence at the Department of State's Office of the Historian in December of that year, during which staff historians posed challenging questions.

Sally James made initial revisions to the map of Indochina, and Darin Franck updated it; he also prepared the maps of border base areas and the JCS Readiness Test. We are grateful to both of these graphic artists for their superb work.

We have benefited from the outstanding editorial and production process at the University Press of Kansas. Our book proposal was vetted by David Anderson, Lloyd Gardner, and Marilyn Young, and we thank them for supporting it. For their assiduous and constructive reading of the manuscript, we are indebted to Lynn Eden and John Prados. We are grateful to Editor in Chief Michael Briggs, not only for his interest in our original proposal but also for guiding the manuscript through the publication process, and to those on the UPK staff with whom we have worked: Kelly Chrisman Jacques, Rebecca J. Murray, Sara Henderson White, and Mike Kehoe.

I, Bill Burr, thankfully acknowledge the support of the National Security Archive, which provides a wonderfully congenial workplace and a matchless platform for the declassification requesting that was crucially important for this book. For encouraging this kind of history and for keeping the organization alive and well, the archive's director, Tom Blanton, and deputy director, Malcolm Byrne, deserve special thanks. The archive's nuclear project has had generous benefactors, who have contributed to the making of this book; it is a pleasure to acknowledge the support of numerous foundations, especially the Prospect Hill Foundation, the New-Land Foundation, the Carnegie Corporation, and the MacArthur Foundation, which are currently supporting the archive's nuclear weapons documentation project. The Ploughshares Fund and the late, lamented W. Alton Jones Foundation also provided important support. In the late 1980s and early 1990s, the MacArthur Foundation underwrote the Nuclear History Program, which directly supported the National Security Archive and advanced an enduring network of researchers.

I gratefully thank Ming for her patience and support. To several former teachers at Northern Illinois University, especially Carl P. Parrini and the late Martin J. Sklar, I have intellectual debts. Conversations over the years with Bart Bernstein, Lynn Eden, David Geyer, Jim Hershberg, Max Holland, Mikio Haruna, Michael Hopkins, Mark Kramer, Klaus Larres, Mel Leffler, Phil Nash, the late Anna Nelson, Leopoldo Nuti, Christian Ostermann, David Painter, John Prados, and David Rosenberg about nuclear and Cold War history have always been instructive and stimulating.

I, Jeff Kimball, express appreciation to the Miami University Libraries staff, especially Jenny Presnell, consultation librarian and bibliographer, who made it possible to get hold of almost every book and article needed; when a few items were not in the stacks or available online, the Interlibrary Loan Department came to the rescue. Ken J. Hughes of the Miller Center and Richard A. Moss shared their knowledge of Nixon tapes, as did Stephen Smith of American RadioWorks. Deborah Leff, former director of the John F. Kennedy Presidential Library and Museum, was instrumental in making possible the March 2006 conference on the Vietnam War, which brought historians and historical actors together. Professors Melvin Small and Timothy Naftali, former director of the Nixon Presidential Library and Museum, played central roles in staging the first conference of academics at the library in July 2011, where I learned more than I knew from other historians and authors about Nixon and his times. Over the years, historians Sheldon Anderson, David Culver, David Fahey, Irwin F. Gellman, Luu Doan Huynh, Stanley Kutler, George Moss, Christian

Ostermann, and Mel Small have engaged me in stimulating and informative conversations about the Vietnam War, the antiwar and antinuclear movements, Nixon, Kissinger, the Cold War, nuclear history, and history in general. Friend and former student Steve Anders, Command Historian and Professor of Military Logistics (ret.) at Fort Lee, Virginia, and former spec 5, Twenty-Fifth Infantry Division, shared his experiences in Vietnam from March 1969 to March 1970—as well as other thoughts about the war. Former high school classmate Captain James Kennedy, USN (ret.), provided information on carriers, naval aircraft, and sea mines.

I am especially indebted to Linda Musmeci Kimball, who was forever supportive, patient, and helpful with writing issues and sage with advice of all sorts. Our son, Daryl G. Kimball, Arms Control Association director, offered insightful ideas and information about the nuclear question. Our daughter, Dr. Leslie Kimball Franck, provided discerning psychological insights when asked about Nixon and Kissinger. My sister Myrna Kelt, an avid reader, was always ready with encouragement.

Both of us, Jeff and Bill, owe large debts to friends and family who have given aid and comfort over the years. We could not begin to name everyone here. Thanks to you all. None of those whom we have acknowledged, however, are responsible for any defects and errors in this book; for those, we alone are to blame.

For both of us, it was a pleasure to work with the other. We shared research and writing equitably in a cooperative project of constant and regular interaction. That it was a harmonious working relationship is demonstrated by the completion of this book—how successfully, others will judge. There is no question that our other research and writing projects delayed the completion of this book. Yet without the delays, we might not have gotten as close as we believe we have to answering the questions that had motivated us to begin this project in the first place. Over the years of this project, we have learned much from each other while forming a close association based on a shared understanding and interpretation of the events.

ABBREVIATIONS

AAF	Army Air Force
AD	assured destruction
AEC	Atomic Energy Commission
ARVN	Army of the Republic of [South] Vietnam (see RVNAF)
BMEWS	Ballistic Missile Early Warning System
CDR	commander
CIA	Central Intelligence Agency
CINC	commander in chief
CINCAL	commander in chief, Alaskan Command
CINCEUR	commander in chief, European Command
CINCLANT	commander in chief, Atlantic Command
CINCONAD	commander in chief, Continental Air Defense Command
CINCPAC	commander in chief, Pacific Command
CINCPACFLT	commander in chief, Pacific Fleet
CINCSAC	commander in chief, Strategic Air Command
CINCSTRIKE	commander in chief, Strike Command
CJCS	chairman of the Joint Chiefs of Staff
CNO	chief of naval operations
COMIDEASTFOR	commander, Middle East Forces
COMINEFLOT	commander, Mine Flotilla
COMNAVBASE	commander, Naval Base
COMSERVPAC	Service Support Command of the US Pacific Fleet
COMSEVENTHFLT	commander, Seventh Fleet
COMSTSFE	commander, Military Sea Transportation Service, Far East
CONAD	Continental Air Defense Command (preceded NORAD)

COSVN	Central Office for South Vietnam
CTF	commander, Task Force
CTG	commander, Task Group
DCI	Director of Central Intelligence
DEFCON	defense condition
DIA	Defense Intelligence Agency
DMZ	demilitarized zone
DOD	Department of Defense
DOS	Department of State
DRV	Democratic Republic of [North] Vietnam
ELINT	electronic intelligence
EMCON	Emissions Control (also known as "Electronic Silence")
FY	fiscal year
ICBM	intercontinental ballistic missile
ISA	Bureau of International Security Affairs (DOD)
JCS	Joint Chiefs of Staff
JSTPS	Joint Strategic Target Planning Staff
KGB	Committee for State Security (Soviet Union)
LOC	lines of communication
MACV	Military Assistance Command, Vietnam
MAD	mutual assured destruction
MIDEASTFOR	Middle East Forces
NATO	North Atlantic Treaty Organization
NAVORDFAC	naval ordnance factory
NLF	National Liberation Front
NORAD	North American Aerospace Defense Command
NORTHAG	Northern Army Group
NSA	National Security Agency
NSAM	National Security Action Memorandum
NSArchive	National Security Archive
NSC	National Security Council
NSSM	National Security Study Memorandum
NVA	North Vietnamese Army (also known as People's Army of Vietnam)
PACOM	Pacific Command
POL	petroleum, oil, and lubricants
PRC	People's Republic of China

PRG	Provisional Revolutionary Government (representing the NLF)
ROC	Republic of China
RVN	Republic of [South] Vietnam
RVNAF	Republic of [South] Vietnam Armed Forces (see ARVN)
SAC	Strategic Air Command
SACEUR	Supreme Allied Commander, Europe
SALT	Strategic Arms Limitation Talks
SAR	sea-air rescue
SEAGA	Selective Employment of Air and Ground Alert
SIGINT	signals intelligence
SIOP	Single Integrated Operational Plan
SLBM	submarine-launched ballistic missile
SSBN	nuclear-powered ballistic missile submarine
STRIKE	Strike Command
SVN	South Vietnam
TAC	Tactical Air Command
UN	United Nations
USAF	United States Air Force
USAFE	United States Air Forces Europe
USAREUR	United States Army Europe
USIB	United States Intelligence Board
USNAVEUR	United States Navy Europe
VC	Viet Cong (also known as People's Liberation Armed Forces)
WSAG	Washington Special Actions Group

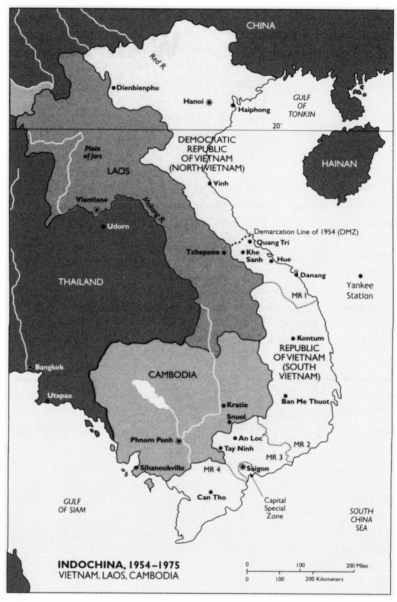

Indochina, 1954–1975.

Introduction

No one really knows . . . the secret stuff we've been doing.
Henry Kissinger and H. R. Haldeman, in conversation with Richard Nixon[1]

In October 1969, President Richard M. Nixon ordered the US high command to carry out military exercises around the world designed to be "discernible to the Soviets but should not be threatening."[2] The measures carried out between 13 and 30 October collectively constituted a worldwide nuclear alert. It was a complex military operation involving a variety of military forces, from attack aircraft and strategic bombers to Polaris submarines, aircraft carriers, and destroyers. In official circles, such operations were usually referred to by other, less ominous-sounding names—"heightened alert posture," "strategic readiness posture," "increased readiness posture," "readiness test," and similarly innocuous labels stripped of the adjective *nuclear*. In this case, the operation was officially known to insiders as the Joint Chiefs of Staff [JCS] Readiness Test. It may have been one of the largest and most extensive secret military operations in US history. The American public was not informed of its execution or purpose, and even North Atlantic Treaty Organization (NATO) allies were kept in the dark. Only President Nixon, his national security adviser, Henry A. Kissinger; Kissinger's military assistant, Colonel Alexander Haig; the president's chief of staff, Harry Robbins Haldeman; Secretary of Defense Melvin R. Laird; and his assistant, Colonel Robert Pursley, were privy to the alert's underlying policy goals and its relationship to the Vietnam War (although Kissinger and Laird shared the secret with a few others). Surprisingly, it is possible that the JCS chairman, Earle Wheeler, the top military official in the national security structure, was not officially in the loop on this matter.

The initial objective of the alert was to signal the Soviet Union, North Vietnam's major supplier and supporter, that the United States was preparing its air and naval forces around the world for any and all military contingencies that might arise should the president decide to escalate the war against North Vietnam. Since early July 1969, Nixon and Kissinger had directly and indirectly warned Hanoi's leaders that the United States would punish North Vietnam with measures of "great consequence and force" should they fail to accept US negotiating terms by 1 November 1969. The White House hoped the threat or the reality of such an attack would serve to lever Moscow's assistance in persuading Hanoi to make the military and political concessions desired by Washington and Saigon at the negotiating table in Paris. Motivating this strategy was Nixon's Madman Theory: the principle that he or any other leader could coerce an adversary by threatening to unleash extraordinary force, including nuclear force, especially if he were perceived to be unpredictable, erratic, or crazy.

This book began as an effort to chart the complex political, military, and diplomatic lead-up to the October 1969 secret nuclear alert, including the deeper background of Cold War nuclear threat making. Our exploration of new sources from the first year of the Nixon administration helped us better understand the alert in context—as part of a continuum of secret diplomatic schemes and military operations initiated by Nixon and Kissinger to bring an early end to the US military role in Vietnam. Months before the alert, they had begun applying the Madman Theory to their Vietnam policy by encouraging Hanoi and its patron, the Soviet Union, to believe that Washington would attack North Vietnam if it did not conclude an early and acceptable settlement. To fully explain the nuclear alert, we have produced the first detailed account of Nixon's and Kissinger's secret decision-making process regarding Vietnam during 1969 and the various political, diplomatic, and military elements that underlay White House threat diplomacy. As we show, both Nixon and Kissinger believed that they could use the levers of power to induce North Vietnam and the Soviet Union to take a more cooperative stance in the Vietnam negotiations. In this context, the nuclear alert was a major, even if unsuccessful, phase in the White House's secret coercive strategy.

Nixon's threat-based strategy to expedite a Vietnam settlement provided the immediate context for the alert. In September 1969, Kissinger assembled a small group of White House aides to prepare a concept plan for their so-called November Option—one that conformed to his and the president's specifications for a bombing-and-mining operation that would produce in Hanoi and North Vietnam what in a later day would be called shock and awe. Kissinger's group unofficially referred to the plan as DUCK HOOK, a code name carried over from a heretofore unknown US Navy plan for the mining of Haiphong Harbor and the blockading of Cambodia, which had been drafted in July 1969.[3] At least one of the early concept papers for the prospective November operation included options for the use of "tactical" nuclear weapons.

On Nixon's orders and in addition to the work being carried out by Kissinger's aides, an interservice group in Saigon worked on an operational plan for the November Option code-named PRUNING KNIFE. But the Saigon group's views about what targets to strike and whether the operation should emphasize military rather than diplomatic outcomes soon put the two planning groups at odds. In the end, the Joint Chiefs themselves disliked both concepts, mainly because neither met their doctrinal specifications for a sound military plan emphasizing military outcomes that would benefit the war in South Vietnam.

In early October 1969, almost a month ahead of the deadline he had set and despite Hanoi's refusal to submit to his negotiating demands, Nixon decided to abort the contemplated November bombing-and-mining offensive. Among the several reasons for his decision, the most important was probably his deep concern about possible adverse public reaction to the dramatic escalation such an operation would entail, especially given the extended length of time he and his advisers thought it would take to succeed—assuming it could succeed—and also because it would coincide with two major antiwar demonstrations scheduled for mid-October and mid-November.[4]

Instead of a bombing-and-mining campaign, Nixon went ahead in mid-October with only the JCS Readiness Test—a nuclear alert that he and Kissinger may have originally intended would precede the DUCK HOOK operation had they carried it out. They now believed or hoped there was a chance that this nuclear alert alone would jolt Moscow's leaders into pressuring Hanoi to accept Washington's terms at the negotiating table in Paris. Moscow and Hanoi might interpret it, for example, as a lead-up to the threatened November operation. In this way, it would lend temporary credibility to the threats they had made about taking measures of consequence and force after 1 November—even though Nixon was in no mood to follow through. Moscow and Hanoi might still cave in before the 1 November deadline and before it was clear that the United States was not going to attack North Vietnam within the time frame Nixon had warned. When launched, therefore, the JCS Readiness

Test was a subterfuge, a bluff, and a stopgap measure. It failed in its purpose of coercing Moscow and Hanoi, as had prior warnings and signals—notably, the secret bombing of Cambodia, launched in March, and a hitherto unknown secret mining ruse against Haiphong, carried out during the spring and into the summer of 1969.

Nixon's decision not to launch a November offensive against North Vietnam and the October alert's failure to lever Soviet diplomatic assistance marked the start of a transition in administration strategy. Unable to end the war quickly on their terms through threats and military actions, Nixon and Kissinger would now attempt to liquidate the US military role in the South by placing more emphasis on another exit strategy, elements of which had been among their several policy options in 1969. Informally referred to as the "long-route" or "long-road" strategy, it included US troop withdrawals timed to be completed more or less around the time of the 1972 US presidential election, while simultaneously strengthening South Vietnamese armed forces to compensate for the US pullout. At the negotiations in Paris, Kissinger would pursue a negotiating strategy aimed at stretching out the talks and winning a settlement that would provide the government of Nguyen Van Thieu in Saigon with a "decent chance" of surviving for at least a "decent interval" after a US exit from the war—an interval of a few years that might preserve the appearance of US honor and credibility as a military guarantor of allies and client states.[5] This approach did not mean the end of military threats and Madman diplomacy. Nixon and Kissinger still regarded those tactics as relevant, and in the years after October 1969, they continued to apply them to their Vietnam exit strategy and in other crises elsewhere in the world, notably in the Middle East.

The secret October nuclear alert and the threat diplomacy that it embodied had largely gone unnoticed by the American public and media. It remained secret until 1983, when investigative reporter Seymour Hersh published a two-page account of the Strategic Air Command (SAC) stand-down in his best-selling, award-winning book, *The Price of Power: Kissinger in the Nixon White House.* Hersh lacked documentary evidence for his account and was unaware of the other military measures taken during the eighteen-day global alert, which was then classified top secret. But drawing upon his interviews of a noncommissioned officer who had witnessed an incident during the tactical-aircraft ground alert, two of Kissinger's former aides, and a high-placed air force colonel who helped plan the stand-down, Hersh astutely reasoned that the operation was somehow linked to Nixon's and Kissinger's Vietnam War aims and the threats they had made to attack North Vietnam. Although little was known at the time about the rumored DUCK HOOK plan, Hersh implied that both it and the stand-down were examples of Nixon's Madman Theory in action.[6]

The only direct evidence for the existence of Nixon's theory at the time was H. R. Haldeman's recollection, in his 1978 memoir, *The Ends of Power*, of a conversation about the Vietnam War with Nixon during the 1968 presidential campaign. Unlike Hersh, most reporters and historians were inexplicably skeptical,[7] even though it was common knowledge that Haldeman had been a loyal member of Nixon's small inner circle of aides and advisers before, during, and after his presidency, as well as an inveterate notetaker and diarist.

During the last two decades of the twentieth century, those few researchers who were aware of the rumored SAC stand-down and did accept its historicity, including the present authors, knew little about it and next to nothing about the other readiness measures that made up the global alert. Within this small group—but excluding the present authors—the conventional wisdom about the purpose of the SAC stand-down was that it was connected not to Nixon's and Kissinger's concerns about Vietnam but to their worries about the possibility of a Soviet attack on China and what that would mean for the global balance of power. The assumption was that Nixon and Kissinger intended the October alert to deter such an attack.[8]

The authors of this volume were both skeptical of the Sino-Soviet thesis in varying degrees and in different ways. Burr thought it worth testing, and during the 1990s he made attempts to secure the declassification of source material to see what could be learned. Kimball initially thought the evidence he encountered when researching and writing *Nixon's Vietnam War* during the same period supported Hersh's thesis.[9] As bits and pieces of additional evidence in favor of the Vietnam connection began to turn up in government documents declassified after the late 1990s—further confirmed by conversations and communications with former officials—Burr and Kimball teamed up in 2001 in an effort to solve the several riddles of the readiness alert. What exactly happened? What were its constituent parts? What was its purpose? In what ways was it related to the Vietnam War?

Combining the evidence we had each collected through Freedom of Information Act (FOIA) filings, Mandatory Declassification Review

(MDR) requests, interviews with participants, and extensive research in Nixon administration papers and the Central Intelligence Agency (CIA), Department of Defense (DOD), and State Department records, we established to our satisfaction that the rumored operation had in fact taken place. We identified its constituent parts and manner of execution and, we believed, convincingly answered the question of why Nixon ordered it.

Along with other archival sources, the discovery of a file devoted to the 1969 readiness test in the records of JCS chairman Earle Wheeler and the subsequent expedited declassification by security reviewers served us well in documenting the planning process that led to the nuclear alert in its various stages, including the complex and far-flung activities that composed it. H. R. Haldeman's diary was another vital source.[10] Often overlooked by researchers, it provides information on White House thinking about the Vietnam War that either is unavailable elsewhere or assists the researcher in understanding the inner circle's state of mind and establishing the time line of decision making. One major find was a crucial sentence that had been excluded from the 13 October 1969 entry in the published print and compact disc versions of the diary. The excised sentence turned up during our search through a handwritten version held in the Nixon Presidential Materials Project (which preceded the Nixon Presidential Library), in which Haldeman had recorded that Kissinger— on Nixon's authority—had set in motion a series of worldwide military measures designed to "jar" Hanoi and Moscow. Here was clear evidence from the top that the nuclear alert was connected to the administration's strategy regarding the war in Vietnam.

In June and September 2002, we presented our findings at history conferences in Athens, Georgia, and Dobbiaco/Toblach, Italy,[11] and two months later, we were invited to make our case to researchers at the Historian's Office of the State Department. In December and January 2003, we published two articles on the subject—one in a scholarly journal, *Cold War History,* and an abbreviated version in the *Bulletin of the Atomic Scientists,* which found its way to the Associated Press and Agence France Presse. The *Bulletin* article appeared at about the same time as an online "briefing book" we posted to the National Security Archive's website on 23 December. One or the other got the attention of *NBC Nightly News* and Brian Williams, who interviewed Alexander Haig three days later about the alert and the Madman Theory.[12]

The October 1969 readiness test had also attracted the interest of other researchers. At the same June 2002 meeting of the Society for Historians of American Foreign Relations in Athens, Georgia, where we had presented our findings, for example, political scientist Scott Sagan and historian Jeremi Suri also presented theirs.[13] Although they argued in their paper that the alert was related to the Sino-Soviet crisis, they accepted our Vietnam thesis after reading our paper and considering the evidence we had accumulated. In March 2003, three months after our articles on the readiness alert had appeared, their account of the JCS Readiness Test and its Vietnam-related purpose was published in the journal *International Security*, with a focus on "political science theories concerning the role of nuclear weapons in international politics."[14]

After 2003, we two went our separate ways, each working on other historical projects. But we remained interested in the topic, kept in touch, continued to collect newly declassified top secret documents, and published additional articles on the JCS Readiness Test.[15] Even though there was and is no substantial direct or indirect evidence for the Sino-Soviet explanation of the 1969 global alert, adherents remained. As an example, the Sino-Soviet thesis inspired the document selections and editorial commentary on the JCS Readiness Test and Sino-Soviet tensions in a 2011 volume in the State Department's *Foreign Relations of the United States (FRUS)* series.[16]

One of our purposes in writing *Nixon's Nuclear Specter* was to resolve whatever uncertainty remains. Although we had previously written about this event, our acquisition of considerably more documentary evidence since 2003 has brought new information to light. It has provided us with not only a fuller and deeper understanding of this episode but also a fresh appreciation of the older evidence upon which we had based our earlier work on the subject. Particularly revealing has been declassified material from Kissinger's telephone conversation transcripts, Haig's files, the Vietnam Subject Files, and the Vietnam Country Files at the Nixon Library; mandatory review releases from Laird's top secret records at the Washington National Records Center; JCS chairman Wheeler's files at the National Archives; and the cable traffic of the Seventh Fleet in the western Pacific from the US Navy's archives. The several volumes of documents from the Nixon years published in the *Foreign Relations of the United States* series by the State Department's Office of the Historian and a special volume of every available record of the Dobrynin-Kissinger conversations prepared in collaboration with the Russian Foreign Ministry,

Soviet-American Relations: The Détente Years, were indispensable. Although the Oval Office and Executive Office Building taping systems were not set up until February 1971, we have found several conversations that have an important bearing on Nixon's and Kissinger's views about nuclear threat making and nuclear use—the central theme of our book—as well as reflective comments by these two men on the October 1969 nuclear alert and the November Option—the main topic of the book.

These cumulative declassifications and discoveries helped us draw a detailed picture of secret decision making at the Nixon White House that has not been possible before, encompassing not only the alert but also the chain of decisions and developments that led to it. Our discoveries show Nixon and his adviser, Henry Kissinger, threatening and authorizing military actions that they believed could change the course of the Vietnam War by cowing Moscow or Hanoi into acquiescence. They also confirm that Kissinger came to accept Nixon's Madman Theory during the early months of the administration and that the decent-interval strategy played a significant role in Kissinger's diplomatic forays with Anatoly Dobrynin and in Nixon's and Kissinger's exit strategy from Vietnam. Even though policymakers before Nixon and since have believed that military force is a necessary adjunct of diplomacy, he and Kissinger may have been unique in their conviction that secret threats and stealthy military operations could actually produce desired diplomatic results. Moreover, their desire for strictly compartmentalized secrecy was so absolute and their distrust of the State Department and the military leadership so great that they put themselves in what amounted to an echo chamber that was nearly impervious to advice from experts in the national security bureaucracy. Their furtive mind-set and methods would create dysfunction in government as civilian officials and top commanders puzzled over the meaning of the policies and actions that they had taken before and during October 1969.

In addition to the considerable additional documentary evidence we have gathered, interviews with and communications from participants have added to our understanding of what happened in 1969. An interview with General William Lemnitzer, who served as a Pentagon liaison officer to the National Security Council (NSC), for instance, shed light on the mining deception plan in the spring of 1969. E-mails and telephone conversations with former NSC staffer Roger Morris helped clarify the role of nuclear options in DUCK HOOK planning, options that were subsequently confirmed by declassified documents. On the question of whether the alert was related to issues concerning Vietnam or China, former secretary of defense Laird explained in a 2000 letter that the nuclear alert had nothing to do with China: "I think you will find that upon further reflection, Seymour Hersh will prove to be closer to Nixon's real reason for the low-key nuclear alert exercise. The president talked to me personally about this decision before I passed the orders on to the Chairman of the Joint Chiefs." When Kimball posed questions to Kissinger and Haig about this issue in 2006, Kissinger was evasive, but neither he nor Haig denied the Vietnam connection, and Haig positively affirmed that "readiness measures" had been launched in connection with DUCK HOOK and its cancellation. Indirect evidence came from a conversation in 2013 with Stanford University professor David Holloway: Kissinger had told him earlier in the year that the alert had been about Vietnam, not China. He did not realize at the time how worried the Chinese were about the Soviet threat. None of these and other interviews could convey the full complexity of the events of 1969, but they provided firsthand information from officials who had been there at the scene.[17]

To put the October 1969 nuclear alert in the broadest historical context, we have placed its origins and execution against the backdrop of the perilous history of nuclear threat making before 1968 and Nixon's and Kissinger's secretive direction of Vietnam War policy after 1968. Our story begins in chapter 1 with a survey of nuclear diplomacy and brinkmanship during various Cold War crises between the West and the East from 1945 to 1968. It was in this period that Nixon and Kissinger developed their worldviews about diplomacy, military affairs, and revolution— including the long-running anticolonial and then postcolonial revolution in Vietnam.

Chapter 2 explores Nixon's and Kissinger's immersion in the culture of "the Bomb" during the 1950s and 1960s—the key decades in which their strategic views about threat diplomacy originated and ripened. It was in this period and during and after his association with President Dwight D. Eisenhower and Secretary of State John Foster Dulles that Nixon developed his Madman Theory.

Chapters 3 through 5 describe the carrot-and-stick diplomacy of Nixon and Kissinger toward the Soviet Union and North Vietnam as well as the initial military measures and threat strategies they developed to solve what they called their Vietnam problem. These included early proposals for feigned nuclear attacks, a secret B-52 bombing campaign against targets along the Cambodian border with South Vietnam, and diplomatic and military schemes such as the so-called Vance Ploy and a mining deception operation against North Vietnam. Chapters 6 through 8 detail the environment of military, diplomatic, and national and international events in which the administration's prospective November 1969 bombing-and-mining operation against North Vietnam was conceived and subsequently aborted.

Chapter 9 is devoted to a description and analysis of the Joint Chiefs' implementation of the global nuclear alert and of what can be gleaned about Soviet and North Vietnamese reactions to it. The epilogue includes a discussion of the aftermath of Nixon's and Kissinger's failed threats and military measures of 1969; an analysis of their policies and strategies during the remaining years of the American war in Vietnam; assessments of their post–nuclear alert applications of the Madman Theory, especially in relation to nuclear threat making; and reflections on how the American war in Vietnam ended.

In addition to the legacy of nuclear threat making since 1945 and the wartime challenges and dilemmas Nixon and his closest advisers believed they faced in Vietnam, the complicated historical context in which the 1969 global alert evolved also involved Nixon's personality and his penchant for secrecy; Kissinger's relationship with Nixon and his affinity for compartmentalizing the work of his staff; personal and interdepartmental rivalries within the Nixon administration; electoral politics; public opinion; the administration's public relations strategies; intermediaries to Hanoi; citizen activism for and against the war; the influence of the "taboo" against nuclear use; and the policies and strategies of the Politburo in Hanoi, the Provisional Revolutionary Government (PRG) in the South, the government of the Republic of Vietnam (RVN) in Saigon, and the Soviet and Chinese governments. For all players in the drama, moreover, chance, contingency, dogmatism, doubt, and improvisation influenced their best-laid plans.

Despite the scale and scope of the secret nuclear readiness test of October 1969, Nixon, Kissinger, Haig, and Haldeman made only indirect and cryptic references to it in their memoirs. (This was even truer of the April to July mining readiness test, which none of them ever mentioned.) Perhaps they thought the October alert was too sensitive an operation, or they worried that such hastily improvised measures would not withstand public scrutiny. Or perhaps they did not want to revisit the desperate and wishful thinking that encouraged them to believe that the specter of nuclear threats exemplified by alert military forces would induce Moscow to provide greater assistance on the Vietnam problem. Whatever the reason, the nuclear readiness test demonstrated their conviction that a show of force was essential to salvaging US Vietnam policy and the credibility of American power. It failed, but it nevertheless marked a turning point in Nixon's and Kissinger's strategy to get out of Vietnam on terms they deemed acceptable. Although their strategy evolved, their faith in coercive threat making remained to the end of the American war in Vietnam.

CHAPTER ONE

Prelude: Nuclear Diplomacy and Notions about Nuclear Use from Truman to Johnson
August 1945–January 1969

> Of course we were brought to the verge of war. . . . If you try to
> run away from it, if you are scared to go to the brink, you are lost.
> . . . We walked to the brink and we looked it in the face.
> *John Foster Dulles*[1]

The strategic assumptions underpinning President Nixon's secret nuclear alert of 1969 were rooted in the "atomic diplomacy" of the recent past.[2] Even before the first nuclear test explosion at the Trinity Site near Alamagordo, New Mexico, on 16 July 1945, top government officials had become convinced that the prospective American monopoly on nuclear weapons, coupled with its ability to strike overseas targets from the air, would give the United States an enormous military and diplomatic advantage over adversaries. In May 1945, Secretary of War Henry Stimson noted in his diary that the atomic bomb would provide the United States with a "master card" in its dealings with the Soviet Union. In July, when President Harry S. Truman presided over the atomic destruction of Hiroshima and Nagasaki, his purpose was not only to force the Japanese government into an earlier surrender but also to achieve the bonus effect of intimidating the Soviets and making them, in the words of Secretary of State James Byrnes, "more manageable" in negotiations concerning the shape of the post–World War II peace.[3]

Despite great risks and mixed results, US presidential administrations from Truman on fostered the development, enlargement, or "improvement" of nuclear arsenals and delivery systems, ostensibly for the purpose of maintaining a strategic advantage in the event of war. They also practiced nuclear threat diplomacy. Especially during the Cold War era, they deployed nuclear weapons, threatened their use, and staged nuclear alerts and shows of force in order to coerce adversaries into taking more compliant diplomatic positions or dissuade them from embarking or continuing upon a course of action considered hostile or contrary to US policy.[4] Their belief in the importance of demonstrating credibility, determination, toughness, and persistence in order to deter or defend against aggression was central to their strategic worldview and public rhetoric. In practice, nuclear diplomacy was not only a deterrent strategy designed to prevent nuclear war but also a "compellence"[5] strategy designed to coerce or intimidate. Policymakers assumed that the establishment of their credibility in this regard was critical. Eventually, the Soviets, too, turned to nuclear diplomacy, as in the Suez crisis of 1956, but far less frequently than the United States. Both sides called the other's deterrence and compellence policies blackmail.[6]

Confrontations, crises, attempts at coercion, and massive buildups of tactical and strategic weapons notwithstanding, nuclear weapons were never again used after the bombings of Hiroshima and Nagasaki. Even before the Soviet Union achieved strategic parity with the United States in the 1960s, the actual use of nuclear weapons raised terrifying prospects. Ethical, bureaucratic, military, practical, diplomatic, and political prohibitions against "first use" were powerful deterrents on both sides. US policymakers sought to raise the threshold for nuclear weapons employment, even in conventional wars such as those in Korea and Vietnam, which had produced massive civilian casualties and significant losses of troops. The United States and the Soviet Union as well found that nuclear weapons were militarily useless except as instruments of deterrence.

The Truman Administration and the Emergence of Atomic Diplomacy

The principle of threatening or signaling the possible use of extreme or excessive force in order to coerce or deter appears in the earliest annals of international diplomacy and military strategy.[7] But the atomic diplomacy of the Cold War era was also the product of particular and more immediate historical lessons that American presidents and their advisers had gleaned from their experiences with the Great Depression and fascist aggression leading up to World War II. The disorder and danger of the years from 1929 to 1945 had convinced them that the future survival of representative government and capitalist political economy in the United States required a congenial, stable, and predictable global environment. In particular, they believed that these requisite international conditions

depended on preventing any unfriendly power or combination of powers from dominating the Eurasian continent. Should this circumstance
come about, they were convinced the United States would face both military threats from adversaries and restricted access to overseas markets,
investment opportunities, and raw materials.[8] Basing their strategies
on this worst-case scenario, national security planners strove to build a
global network of overseas bases that would reduce the exposure of US
territory to attack while at the same time enabling Washington to project its air and naval power abroad in the service of America's aims.[9] For
a host of reasons—not least of which were fundamental disagreements
with Moscow over the future status of Germany and Washington's concerns about Moscow's growing political influence in Western Europe—
President Truman and his advisers came to view the Soviet Union as a
serious political and military threat to the world order they envisioned.

On the cusp of the Cold War and the nuclear age, the armed services
fiercely competed for defense dollars. The US Army, US Navy, Marine
Corps, and Army Air Force (AAF) each touted the unique and indispensable contribution they could make to the nation's global needs and goals.
Within and without the AAF, airpower advocates assertively promoted
the doctrinal lesson they took from World War II; namely, that their ability to carry out strategic bombing could play a decisive role in preventing
future wars or in determining their outcome.[10] The erosion of pre–World
War II strictures against the bombing of noncombatants facilitated this
claim. The Japanese bombing of Shanghai and other Chinese cities, the
German attacks on Barcelona, Guernica, Madrid, Rotterdam, and London, the Allied fire bombings of scores of German and Japanese cities,
and the atomic destruction of Hiroshima and Nagasaki suggested that a
"moral revolution" had taken place among many military commanders,
civilian leaders, and broad swaths of the public regarding the acceptability
of bombing noncombatants in urban population centers.[11]

The moral revolution coexisted uneasily with the conscience of President Truman, who, after the bombings of Hiroshima and Nagasaki, abhorred the further use of nuclear weapons, precisely because they were
weapons of indiscriminate mass destruction.[12] Nonetheless, between 1945
and 1947, the president, his civilian advisers, Army Chief of Staff Dwight
D. Eisenhower, and the Joint Chiefs of Staff accepted the premise that a
robust US capability to wage an atomic offensive would constitute a powerful lever in the management of world affairs, a war-fighting advantage

over the Soviet Union, and the best deterrent against a possible future atomic attack by the Soviets. This belief trumped whatever concerns they had about noncombatant casualties—or thoughts about choosing alternative security measures such as nuclear arms control.[13] It was a well-established way of thinking about airpower. "In the nuclear age as in the 1930s," historian Michael S. Sherry observed, "one of the oldest temptations of air power was . . . to regard it as serving less the needs of battle than the opportunity to avoid it." Strategic bombing, whether conventional or nuclear, promised "to provide . . . a threat to an enemy's resolve and psychic stability, and a trump card in diplomatic crises."[14]

Only days after AAF B-29s dropped atomic bombs on Hiroshima and Nagasaki, senior Manhattan Project scientists and air force leaders were pondering the "establishment of an atomic bomb wing capable of delivering atomic bombs to any place in the world." Six months later, in March 1946, the AAF created the Strategic Air Command to "conduct long-range offensive operations." During the same year, the AAF also secretly began making arrangements with the Royal Air Force to prepare nuclear storage sites at two air bases in the United Kingdom to develop a capacity for deploying nuclear-capable bombers across the Atlantic.[15]

SAC would become a key element in the US nuclear force structure in the decades to come, but at the outset its capabilities were modest, reflecting its organizational infancy and the limited number of available nuclear bombs. By the end of 1947, there were only 20 SAC flight crews cleared for nuclear missions, 18 B-29s that were nuclear-capable, and 13 weapons in the nuclear stockpile of the Atomic Energy Commission (AEC). By September 1948, SAC's capabilities had increased, with 30 B-29s designed for nuclear weapons missions and 39 specially trained crews. But a significant gap still remained between plans and capabilities. Only 56 weapons were in the AEC stockpile, yet war plans drafted between 1947 and 1948 stipulated a minimum of 200 weapons to destroy Soviet industrial targets. An early intermediate proposal, DARK HORSE, brought plans and capabilities into closer balance by requiring 53 weapons and a force of 83 bombers (some of them diversionary) to destroy the twenty "most vital" targets in the USSR.[16]

With or without the capability of destroying the Soviet Union according to the standards established by nuclear war planners, US decision makers came to believe that atomic threats could be carried out through bluff. A show of force was one way of bluffing. The first such operation against the Soviet Union by SAC B-29 bombers took place in November 1946, three months after Yugoslav aircraft had shot down a US C-97 air transport aircraft flying over their country.[17] In response to the incident and against the backdrop of growing tension with the Soviet Union, air force leadership wanted to make a "demonstration of American power" by means of an around-the-world flight of B-29s. The State Department denied the request and instead approved a flight of six B-29s to the US occupation zone in Germany, which took place on 13 November, with the bombers returning to the United States on 4 December. According to SAC's brief account of this episode, "the flight . . . could not have been interpreted as a direct threat to Russia, but the implications were obvious" because the B-29s were "widely recognized as the aircraft capable of dropping atomic weapons." Although the flight's main purposes were "diplomatic," the exercise also gave the air force the opportunity to test the practicability of deploying SAC aircraft to Western Europe.[18]

A more significant demonstration of US strategic power began during the Berlin crisis of 1948, when the Soviets blocked allied access to West Berlin in reaction to allied steps to combine the western occupation zones of Germany. Worried that the blockade might foreshadow even more hostile moves, US Air Force Headquarters instructed SAC to prepare to build up its forces in Europe. On 24 June, shortly after the blockade began, and following consultations with the British, SAC deployed three bomber groups, one to West Germany and two to the United Kingdom, where they remained for the rest of the year. The objective was to raise the morale of the allies and to dissuade the Soviets from taking escalatory steps, but it was a ruse to the extent that none of the bombers deployed had been modified to carry nuclear weapons. Nonetheless, they were loaded with conventional ordnance and were combat ready. At the same time and even though they were not part of the demonstration, SAC's nuclear-capable bombardment groups went on high alert. By June 1949, the crisis had been resolved, but SAC began to deploy nuclear-capable B-29s in specially prepared bases in the United Kingdom, although the weapons themselves remained in US storage facilities.[19]

One of the lessons US civilian and military leaders drew from the Berlin blockade grew out of their anxiety that war with the Soviet Union could come about through Moscow's miscalculations. If Soviet leaders should underestimate the deadly seriousness of Washington's commitment to the defense of Western Europe, they might risk other dangerous confrontations in future policy disputes with the United States. The administration's ironic solution to this possibility was to raise the stakes in the Cold War by placing its reliance on the deterrent power of nuclear weapons. It was a step driven by the Republican-controlled Congress's funding of a larger air force than the White House had sought and its rejection of Truman's proposal for universal military training, which would have provided a conventional force for intervening in European conflicts. Previously reluctant to authorize military planning for the use of nuclear weapons, by September 1948—in the midst of the Berlin crisis—Truman relented. Planning for nuclear weapons use became institutionalized at the Pentagon, with the Soviet Union as the chief target.[20]

Even though nuclear forces had little or no relevance for more likely contingencies in Europe, such as civil wars or Communist electoral victories, the Truman administration and its successors found themselves increasingly reliant on nuclear forces and military alliances. A few months after the United States and its Western allies had formed the North Atlantic Treaty Organization in April 1949, NATO ministers approved an alliance military concept that defined strategic atomic bombing as largely a US responsibility and one that was integral to the defense of the "North Atlantic area."[21]

Atomic Diplomacy and the Korean War

The Korean War was the first Cold War confrontation in which Washington considered the military use of nuclear weapons. Believing incorrectly that the North Korean invasion on 25 June 1950 was simply the action of a Soviet puppet, Truman and his advisers worried that the Soviet Union itself would enter the war, and if that occurred, they wanted strategic forces to be prepared to act. With North Korea driving the US-led United Nations (UN) forces down the Korean Peninsula, military and civilian officials reviewed but rejected nuclear options. It was unlikely that those options would be effective, and beyond that, their use would raise an outcry around the world, especially from Asian allies and neutrals. According to an army intelligence staff report, the "use of atom bombs in this stage of the conflict would probably be interpreted as an indication of the ruthlessness of US policy and a disregard for the lives of Asiatic people, or as a 'desperation measure'; which would signify US weakness."[22] President Truman did, however, approve the deployment of nuclear weapons overseas as a demonstration of US resolve to see the conflict through. Between July and August, the administration sent weapons components and additional nuclear-configured B-29s to bases in the United Kingdom and Guam, although the fissile cores of the weapons remained in the United States.[23] During the next month, the US aircraft carrier *Coral Sea*, which was on its way to the Mediterranean, received fifteen sets of weapons components. Although the AEC retained custody of the weapons, the military was in the process of acquiring de facto control over them.[24]

The entry of the People's Republic of China (PRC) into the conflict triggered additional nuclear threats from Washington. The PRC's offensive had begun in October 1950 with the infiltration of its units into North Korea; it grew and accelerated through November, inflicting heavy casualties on US-led United Nations forces and causing them to retreat in confused haste. At the height of the crisis, Truman told reporters at a press conference on the morning of 30 November that if necessary, he would use "every weapon we have" against military and civilian targets in China and North Korea; that included the atomic bomb, which had "always been under active consideration," Truman said, adding that the "military commander in the field will have charge of the use of the weapons, as he always has." Three hours later and in the face of worldwide alarm, the White House issued a clarification, explaining that the Bomb had not been "authorized" for use.[25]

The president's atomic bluster appears to have been the product of his anxiety about the dire state of the fighting in Korea and his desire to assuage hawkish critics within and without his administration, who favored tough talk and an expansion of the air war into China. The UN commander in Korea, General Douglas MacArthur, had earlier urged the bombing of China. Some military and political advisers agreed. Others thought that nuclear weapons should only be used to prevent UN forces from being overrun. But most thought MacArthur's remarks had been imprudent and that the use of atomic weapons in Korea would not be militarily practical or efficacious. Secretary of State Dean Acheson believed that the Chinese were unlikely to act "rationally" when threatened—that is, they were not likely to back down, as some in Washington reasoned. Nuclear use could therefore lead to "incalculable consequences," including a world war with the Soviet Union.[26]

In late January 1951, UN forces launched a methodical counteroffensive, which reached the thirty-eighth parallel by 31 March. On 6 April, when Truman learned that Chinese divisions were massing for a spring counteroffensive of their own and the Soviet Union might also intervene in the fighting with planes and troops, he authorized the deployment of nine complete nuclear weapons and a SAC bomber wing to Guam as signals to deter the Chinese and Soviets. Nonetheless, the Chinese and North Koreans launched their offensive on 22 April. Truman responded by sending additional nuclear-configured bombers to Guam, ordering training flights in the western Pacific, dispatching a command and control team to Tokyo, flying reconnaissance aircraft over Chinese airfields in Manchuria and Shantung, and granting qualified authority to UN commander General Matthew Ridgway to retaliate with atomic strikes should the enemy launch air attacks from beyond the Korean Peninsula. To underline these atomic warnings, the State Department sent US diplomat Charles B. Marshall on a confidential mission to Hong Kong in order to pass a warning to Beijing through intermediaries that if the Korean conflict expanded, "the Chinese would be set back a century or more in their progress."[27]

Truman's implied threats of nuclear use may have been partly motivated by his desire to counter his hawkish critics, mostly from the Republican Party, who had been accusing him of weak wartime leadership, and supporters of General MacArthur, whom Truman had relieved from command on 11 April for insubordination. In any case, Beijing may have been unaware of Truman's deployments, and Marshall's warnings had no discernible impact on Chinese and North Korean battlefield conduct. Nevertheless, President Truman and Secretary of State Acheson persuaded themselves that their subtle use of atomic diplomacy had produced the positive result of encouraging Beijing and Moscow to support armistice talks, which began in June 1951. It was more likely that their recent gains on the battlefield had stabilized the front, and with both sides exhausted, each was in the mood for negotiation. What Acheson argued to the British was that Joseph Stalin had agreed to negotiations because he was worried that the "fighting would proceed on a larger scale which might easily spread and endanger [their] position."[28]

Truman subsequently ceased making tacit threats to use nuclear weapons in Korea. As he left the presidency, he declared it "unthinkable for rational men" to initiate nuclear war. Although he had made the critical decision to use atomic bombs against Japan and had subsequently taken major steps to expand the US nuclear stockpile, he had simultaneously placed these weapons in a category that set them apart from nonnuclear weapons and had come to see them as too horrible to use except under the most dire of circumstances. In this sense, he became an adherent of the "nuclear taboo," an informal but widely held prohibition against the use of nuclear weapons that had developed during the years after the atomic bombings of Hiroshima and Nagasaki and the onset of the nuclear arms race.[29]

The Eisenhower Administration and the Korean War

The election of Dwight D. Eisenhower to the presidency in 1953 brought a different approach to US nuclear weapons policy. As historian David Rosenberg observed, Eisenhower saw the Bomb "as an integral part of American defense and, in effect, a weapon of first resort."[30] The president and his secretary of state, John Foster Dulles, as well as his vice president, Richard Nixon, rejected the nuclear taboo. On several occasions from 1953 to 1960, during internal discussions about "peripheral" wars such as the conflict in Korea or a "general war" with the Soviet Union, Eisenhower expressed his belief in the utility and appropriateness of nuclear weapons use.[31] Nevertheless, the taboo constrained him: he understood that world opinion abhorred the use of nuclear weapons and that such use could have a disastrous impact on the US position in world affairs. There would also be practical and technical constraints. These included assessments of the inefficacy and unwanted consequences of nuclear use by military services, government departments, agencies, presidential advisers, and members of Congress, as well as the constraints imposed by a growing Soviet retaliatory capability and the risks of catastrophic global nuclear war. But during the Eisenhower administration, the taboo—whether viewed as moral, political, practical, or technical—was fragile, since it could be undermined by military planning and weapons deployments that were stimulated by Eisenhower's belief that nuclear weapons were like any other conventional weapon—like "a bullet or anything else."[32] The realities of planning and deployment could severely narrow the range of nonnuclear options available to decision makers in a crisis. The taboo, moreover, did not constrain Eisenhower and his close advisers from *threatening* to use nuclear weapons, whether as a deterrent or as an instrument of war and diplomacy. As political scientist Nina Tannenwald observed, the attitudes of Eisenhower—and Dulles—toward nuclear weapons were "complex" and often "seemingly contradictory."[33]

Elected in part because of public uneasiness over the stalemated Korean conflict, impatient with what he considered Communist recalcitrance, and professing to view nuclear weapons as just another type of armament albeit more destructive than conventional weapons, President Eisenhower encouraged his top advisers to consider military escalation in the form of expanded conventional bombing, the use of atomic weapons in Korea,[34] and the *threat* of nuclear attack to force concessions from or to defeat the Chinese and the North Koreans.

In pursuit of a favorable negotiated settlement to the war, Eisenhower authorized the transfer of nuclear weapons from the custody of the Atomic Energy Commission to the Department of Defense in April 1953. As he explained to the National Security Council, he wanted that move "handled in such a way that a foreign G-2, placing together the bits of information on the transfer, would come to the conclusion that he had pierced the screen of the intentions of the United States." In addition—and in the event that negotiations broke down—the NSC Planning Board approved a proposal in May for a major attack against China that would include the use of nuclear weapons in order to force an end to the war. Wanting to avoid provoking the Soviets in the meantime, however, Eisenhower limited his actions to those that would "impress the enemy with our determination without . . . unduly alarming our allies or our own people."[35] Eisenhower, like Truman before him, hoped that nuclear deployments would act as signals, encouraging adversaries to worry about US intentions and the possibility of nuclear attack.

The president signaled corollary threats to intimidate the Chinese. In 1955, Admiral C. Turner Joy contended that the Communist side had made concessions at the negotiating table in response to the Eisenhower government's nuclear threats against China in May 1953. In 1956, *Life,* the mass-market magazine, published a supporting story in which Secretary of State Dulles claimed to have delivered an unmistakable and effective nuclear warning to Beijing on Eisenhower's behalf in 1953. As the story goes, when Dulles traveled to New Delhi, India, in May, he told Prime Minister Jawaharlal Nehru that if the armistice negotiations failed, the United States "would probably make stronger . . . military exertions and that this might well extend the conflict"; if the fighting became more intense, he added, "it is difficult to know what [the] end might be." To underline this veiled threat, Washington apparently sent secret messages to Beijing through other intermediaries to the effect that failure to reach an armistice would lead Washington to remove constraints on types of weapons and targets.[36]

On 17 February 1965, almost a decade later, Eisenhower repeated the story about the Dulles-Nehru meeting to President Lyndon B. Johnson, who had invited him to the White House to hear his "thinking concerning the situation in South Vietnam." As summarized by State Department executive secretary Benjamin H. Read, Eisenhower told Johnson and the others in attendance that "he had sent a message to Nehru in 1953, warning that we would use nuclear weapons against China if the Korean War continued, and that he believed this warning played a decisive part in terminating the Korean War."[37]

Secretary of State Dean Rusk—probably at Johnson's or McGeorge Bundy's request—tasked Read to investigate the claim. But Read and his staff could "find no documentary support in such specific terms," except for "messages which indicate that certain signals were passed both to Nehru and to [Soviet Foreign Minister Vyacheslav] Molotov, which could conceivably have been so interpreted." According to Dulles's notes, he had told Nehru in New Delhi on 21 May 1953 that if the armistice negotiations failed, the "US would probably make stronger, rather than lesser, military exertion and that this might well extend area conflict (I [Secretary Dulles] assumed this would be relayed to Chinese)."[38]

In the course of his investigation of Eisenhower's account of the threatening signals sent through intermediaries to the Chinese, Read also found that on 27 May 1953, the White House had instructed Charles E. Bohlen, the US ambassador to Moscow, to deliver a similarly indirect signal to Molotov. Bohlen, Read wrote, "reported that he told Molotov that rejection by the North Koreans and Chinese of our armistice proposals 'would extinguish hopes for an armistice, and a failure of the present armistice talks would lead to the creation of a situation which the US government was most sincerely and earnestly attempting to avoid.'"[39]

Even if Molotov or Nehru told Chinese leaders about the Eisenhower administration's signals and interpreted them in the way the administration wanted them to be understood, the warnings were probably not critically important in ending the war. Other considerations were far more relevant to Mao Zedong's decisions. These included the high economic burdens imposed by the conflict as well as pressure from Moscow for a settlement, which increased after Stalin's death on 5 March. The full chronology of events and the evidence itself suggest a more complicated causal process leading to the armistice; namely, that it came about after war hawks on both sides had been silenced, were replaced, or had experienced a change of mind. Those whose minds were changed had responded to economic burdens, military losses, political and military pressures and constraints, the recognition of a de facto stalemate, and the insistence of allies and the international community. Both sides in the conflict had come, more or less simultaneously, to the conclusion that it was time to end this costly, deadlocked war. Moreover, the chronology of events does not seem to support Eisenhower's claims. US threats had been delivered after Communist negotiators had, several weeks previously, indicated a change in policy by accepting US general Mark Clark's proposal on the thorny issue of prisoner-of-war (POW) exchanges. In the end, both sides conceded points on the POW repatriation issue, which, though having served to prolong the war, had never been as fundamental as those issues that had already been agreed to in November 1951: a cease-fire and an armistice line, both of which acknowledged the failure of the war and the acceptance of a divided Korea. As historian William Stueck has argued, "The explicit threat of an expanded war probably was unnecessary in persuading Beijing and Moscow that the time had come for a final concession on Korea."[40]

Nevertheless, Eisenhower and Dulles drew a different lesson from the affair. Their claims about how nuclear diplomacy had worked became part of Republican Party lore and eventually the conventional wisdom in the United States about how the Eisenhower administration had brought the conflict to an end against an obstinate foe. Nixon, in particular, would take the lesson to heart. Although Eisenhower rarely included him in his meetings with senior advisers, the vice president attended National Security Council meetings, developed a close relationship with Dulles, and was an apt observer and student of Eisenhower-Dulles policymaking.[41]

Massive Retaliation and Brinkmanship

The Eisenhower presidency coincided with an immense expansion of destructive US nuclear capabilities. The Truman administration had already funded major increases in fissile material production capacity, which made possible extraordinary growth of the atomic weapons stockpile, from 169 weapons in 1949 to 298 in 1950, 429 in 1951, and 823 in 1952. But as devastating as atomic weapons were, the test of the first thermonuclear device on 1 November 1952 introduced a weapon of colossal destructive power. By 1956, hydrogen, or thermonuclear, weapons suitable for delivery by bomber had entered the nuclear stockpile. Often called an area weapon, a thermonuclear bomb could destroy an entire city and its suburbs.[42]

It was this expanded capacity that underlay the Eisenhower administration's emphasis on "massive retaliation," which, in Dulles's words, was "a great capacity to retaliate, instantly, by means and at places of our choosing." Massive retaliation was an integral part of the administration's "New Look" grand strategy, which was formally ratified in National Security Council paper 162/2 on 29 October 1953, three months after the Korean armistice, and publicly announced on 12 January 1954, when the administration's attention was increasingly drawn to a crisis in Indochina. Aimed at avoiding "military expenditures so vast that they lead to [the] 'practical bankruptcy'" of the "private enterprise" economy, the NSC 162/2 called for cuts in Truman's conventional forces buildup and emphasized greater spending on nuclear forces to avoid allegedly crippling budgetary deficits associated with Truman's projected military spending on manpower. A euphemism for nuclear attack, massive retaliation was potentially a "first-use, first-strike" nuclear strategy. In practical terms, it called for the use of both tactical and strategic nuclear weapons in local and general wars.[43]

Eisenhower endorsed nuclear planning by the armed services at all levels, from strategic use of nuclear weapons to tactical use by small army units. Nevertheless and despite his occasional loose talk about nuclear weapons being like any other conventional weapon, he insisted on strict control over any decisions to use them. Secretary of Defense Charles E. Wilson and the JCS had interpreted a key paragraph of NSC 162/2 to mean that nuclear weapons would be used "whenever it is of military advantage to do so." But by January 1954, Eisenhower had endorsed the interpretation of the State Department and the AEC that any decision to use nuclear weapons would have to take into account the risk of strategic retaliation and expanded hostilities, the danger of devastation to allies, and the possible loss of allied support. Consistent with his role as commander in chief, the president "should be in a position to consider such issues and make his decisions as each case arises." With this tight control over decisions to use nuclear weapons, Eisenhower was subtly shifting away from the view that they were weapons of first resort.[44]

Accompanying the strategy of massive retaliation, the diplomacy

Eisenhower and Dulles practiced incorporated a heavy dose of nuclear threat making. The credibility of the threat, they believed, would be based on the enemy's fear of US nuclear use—a fear that, in turn, would be reinforced by the enemy's appreciation of the nuclear superiority of the United States. By 1956, the administration's threat-making strategy became known to the public as brinkmanship, which Democratic presidential nominee Adlai Stevenson criticized as "the art of bringing us to the edge of the nuclear abyss."[45] Consistent with massive retaliation and brinkmanship and taking advantage of "nuclear plenty," Eisenhower presided over the "nuclearization" of the armed forces so that nuclear strike options could be immediately available to decision makers.[46]

After the Soviets began testing nuclear weapons in 1949, US policymakers had grown increasingly concerned with the military and economic dilemma this development posed to the United States. The Soviet Union's growing nuclear arsenal would eventually enable it to attack and destroy the US homeland, but US efforts to develop the military capability of deterring an attack would in the long term contribute to bankrupting the US economy. Before the Soviet Union had enlarged and improved its weapons stockpile and delivery capability, this dilemma led some in the Eisenhower administration to consider such extreme options as "preventive" nuclear war as a means of destroying the Soviet system and the threat they believed it ultimately presented to US security and survival.

Both Eisenhower and Dulles mused about such an option on coming to power, although the president formally ruled it out in the fall of 1954.[47] Eisenhower appears to have come to this view by at least as early as March of that year "in light of US and Soviet development of the new hydrogen-fusion weapons of mass destruction." He had grown concerned about several problems and dangers: the prospect of the chaos and destruction of a general war with the Soviet Union; the problems of occupation and reconstruction in the aftermath of such a war; the belief that US representative government could not survive the waging of a general war and out of sheer necessity would be replaced by "totalitarianism"; the negative opinion of the rest of the world toward the United States should it launch a war costing tens, if not hundreds, of millions of lives; and the waning support of NATO allies for the strategy of massive retaliation because of its consequences for Europe in the event of war.[48]

Soviet long-range air capability became a top-priority target for SAC planners. As the Soviets developed a bomber capability for the long-range delivery of nuclear weapons, SAC planners embraced preemptive action (sometimes called taking the initiative) as an essential strategy in the face of an impending threat or attack by the Soviet adversary. Under the commander in chief of the Strategic Air Command, General Curtis LeMay, SAC readied itself to launch a massive attack on Soviet nuclear targets once US intelligence received a strategic warning of an impending Soviet attack or if, somehow, "the US is pushed into a corner far enough." As difficult and dangerous as such an option was (for example, in the event of false warning intelligence or incomplete knowledge of Soviet nuclear targets), preemption became part of SAC's war planning to defeat Soviet airpower. LeMay's successor in 1957, General Thomas Power—and his successors—continued the practice.[49]

Nuclear Threats and Thoughts of Use during the Dien Bien Phu Crisis

The first test of brinkmanship and massive retaliation came in the spring of 1954 as the Communist Vietminh tightened their months-long encirclement of the outnumbered and outgunned French garrison at Dien Bien Phu, located in a remote corner of northwestern Vietnam near the Laotian border.[50] Even before the siege was in full swing, Eisenhower, Dulles, and Nixon had embarked on a campaign of rhetorical brinkmanship. In a speech Dulles delivered on 12 January 1954 to 400 attendees at a Council on Foreign Relations (CFR) dinner, which was also broadcast on radio and television, the secretary publicly rolled out the New Look policy, mentioning Indochina and warning that "the way to deter aggression is for the free community to be willing and able to respond vigorously at places and with means of its own choosing." Newspaper accounts associated that message with the president's earlier remarks in his State of the Union message that atomic weapons might be used "against an aggressor if they are needed to preserve our freedom" and other administration warnings that "open Communist Chinese aggression" in places such as Indochina might provoke massive US retaliation against the PRC.[51]

Implicit in the administration's view of the fighting in Indochina was the assumption that the Vietminh were proxies for "international Communist aggression"—that is, indicative of Soviet or Chinese support for allies and clients. Dulles's speech was a recapitulation of the message in NSC 162/2, which had described Indochina as "of such strategic importance ... that an attack ... probably would compel the United States to react with military force either locally at the point of attack or generally against the military power of the aggressor."[52] Dulles repeated these threats in other public venues at the height of the Dien Bien Phu crisis and formally elaborated on the relationship of the New Look to Indochina in an article published in *Foreign Affairs* in April, adding that in the face of Communist aggression, the United States and its allies had to be willing to use tactical and strategic nuclear weapons both inside and outside of Indochina.[53]

In his own public appearances, President Eisenhower seconded these sentiments, either by reaffirming them or by refusing to contradict his secretary of state when asked to elucidate Dulles's remarks.[54] Vice President Nixon weighed in publicly as well, most likely at the behest of the president. In a televised address on 13 March and again in a speech to a large audience at the University of Cincinnati on 20 April, he defended the appropriateness of massive retaliation in "little wars" such as the one in Indochina, citing the example of how Eisenhower had allegedly ended the Korean War by threatening nuclear attack.[55]

Verbal US warnings coincided with military measures that carried the threat of US intervention with nuclear weapons. In April, the administration sent a carrier task force capable of delivering nuclear weapons into the Tonkin Gulf and South China Sea. At alternate times, the *Wasp*, *Essex, Boxer*, and *Philippine Sea* steamed off the coast of the Indochina peninsula, and their aircraft carried out reconnaissance flights over and around Dien Bien Phu.[56] Coincidentally, on 1 March, the United States had begun a series of massive thermonuclear bomb tests at Bikini Atoll. The first, the Castle BRAVO shot, had an explosive yield of 15 megatons and spewed radioactive fallout around the world. It gravely sickened nearby inhabitants of the Marshall Islands and irradiated the Japanese crew on the fishing boat *Lucky Dragon*. Stoking world apprehensions were newspaper stories quoting AEC chair Lewis Strauss's comment that an H-bomb "can be made as large as you wish, large enough to take out a city" the size of New York.[57]

Behind the administration's rhetoric and military maneuvers was Pentagon planning for nuclear weapons use. With the French base on the verge of collapse in mid-March and after the French government requested US air strikes against Vietminh positions to force a lifting of the siege, military feasibility studies and contingency planning proceeded through late March and beyond. Consistent with White House doctrine, this included detailed reviews of the possible use of nuclear weapons against the

Vietminh—whether for the purpose of augmenting the proposed air operation VULTURE or in the event of direct US military intervention in Indochina in the near future. Pentagon officials prepared detailed plans for nuclear use by air force fighter-bombers or the navy's carrier force. One plan stipulated the use of six 31-kiloton weapons, each having the explosive yield of two Hiroshima bombs. This plan and one other suggested that the risk of Soviet or Chinese military retaliation might be minimized if the bombs were dropped by planes with French markings.[58] Douglas MacArthur II, counselor to the secretary of state, reported to Dulles on 7 April 1954 that an "advance study group" working in the Pentagon on VULTURE had concluded that "three tactical A-weapons, properly employed, would be sufficient to smash the Vietminh effort" at Dien Bien Phu. General Curtis LeMay claimed in 1957 that "he had drawn up a plan for the tactical nuclear bombardment of Dienbienphu."[59]

Although receptive to French requests for air support, Eisenhower stipulated that several conditions would have to be met before the United States intervened: the concurrence of the Congress; the collaboration of British, European, and Asian allies; and French concessions to non-Communist nationalists in Indochina regarding the training of Vietnamese armed forces and the granting of true political independence to the Indochinese states.[60] These demands underscored the policy chasm between American and French goals in Indochina. The French simply wanted air support to break the siege and save the garrison at Dien Bien Phu. That, they hoped, would enable them to negotiate a face-saving compromise at an international conference, scheduled to begin on 8 May in Geneva, and exit the war while preserving national honor and some commercial interests in Indochina. Eisenhower and Dulles, by contrast, wanted to prevent a French defeat, keep France in the war, use the Geneva Conference to partition Vietnam, and—should it be necessary—prepare the ground for possible US military intervention sanctioned by the "united action" of European and Asian allies. They were also worried about Beijing's influence in Southeast Asia and wanted insurance against the possibility of Chinese intervention.[61] Toward these ends, the Eisenhower administration considered the possibility of seeking French approval for using tactical atomic weapons at Dien Bien Phu should the United States eventually intervene with airpower or troops in the Indochina War.[62]

Dissenters in the Joint Chiefs and civilian departments argued that there were few suitable targets in Vietnam and that atomic bombs would not obviate the need for inserting US troops. In addition, they advised that nuclear use would horrify European allies, outrage and alienate Asians (who would be targeted again after Hiroshima and Nagasaki), tarnish the reputation of the United States globally, and likely provoke the Soviets and Chinese to intervene.[63] President Eisenhower was circumspect about nuclear use as well, but he did not bar planning for air operations involving the use of nuclear weapons or high-level discussions about their use.

During a private encounter with French foreign minister Georges Bidault at a NATO Council meeting in Paris on 22 April, for example, Secretary of State Dulles asked the French minister—according to Bidault's 1965 memoirs—"if we would like the US to give us two atomic bombs." Bidault claimed that he rejected the offer because it would have been disastrous politically and militarily, and he also conjectured: "I think that he [Dulles] spoke to others about this project, for he always liked to ask different people's advice, however unseemly or embarrassing."[64]

Even if Bidault misunderstood or misreported what Dulles said, a week later, on 29 April, the NSC Planning Board discussed a nuclear offer to the French in the context of considering US intervention with the participation or cooperation of allies. Questions and issues about using nuclear weapons emerged, including the possibility of "loaning" the Bomb to the French. In his memorandum of the meeting, Robert Cutler, special assistant to the president for national security affairs, substituted the euphemism "new weapons" for "nuclear weapons":

> *b.* Should decision be made now as to US intention to use "new weapons," on intervention, in Vietnam on military targets? Would one "new weapon" dropped on Vietminh troop concentrations in reserve behind DBP [Dien Bien Phu] be decisive in casualties and overwhelming in psycho effect on Vietminh opposition? (Query: could one "new weapon" be loaned to France for this purpose? Could French airmen make a proper drop? Would French Government dare take step?)
>
> *c.* If US decides that it *will* use "new weapons" on intervention (1) Should it tell its proposed associates in regional grouping at outset? Would the effect upon them be to frighten them off? (2) Will France and Britain take alarm . . . ?
>
> *d.* View was expressed that US use of "new weapon" in Vietnam would tend to deter Chinese aggression in retaliation.

e. View was expressed that neither USSR nor China wants a "new weapon" war now, a time when US had manifest superiority.[65]

At an NSC meeting the next morning, the president asked Nixon for his thoughts on using nuclear weapons at Dien Bien Phu and whether "the regional grouping should be formed without announcing our intention about the use of 'new weapons'" then or in the future. Nixon answered that it was his view that conventional bombing strikes would serve to lift the siege at Dien Bien Phu, adding that it would not be necessary to mention the possible use of nuclear weapons to allies until after they agreed on united action. According to Cutler's notes of the meeting, the president and vice president also agreed that "we might *consider* saying to the French that . . . if they wanted some [new weapons] *now* for possible use, we might give them a few."[66]

Nixon summarized the views of top decision makers, as he understood them, about using atomic weapons in Indochina in his memoir, *RN*:

> To some extent [Admiral Arthur W.] Radford did believe that the early use of tactical nuclear weapons would convince the Communists that we meant business. Dulles and I both believed that if the Communists pushed too far we would have to do whatever was necessary to stop them. Eisenhower fully agreed, although I think that Dulles and I were probably prepared to stand up at an earlier point than he was.[67]

In the end, Eisenhower decided against direct US military intervention in any form. Dien Bien Phu fell on 7 May before his key preconditions had been met: congressional approval, the formation of a united allied front, and French political concessions.[68] Paris, moreover, was not interested in the purported US nuclear offer. Discussions recorded in available documents about whether to use nuclear weapons had been based mainly on considerations of domestic and international political and moral opinion, bureaucratic and advisory assessments of feasibility and efficacy, the views of key allies, concerns about taking steps that would lead to US troop intervention, the reactions of Asians to another atomic bombing by the United States, and the diplomatic and military responses of the USSR and the PRC to nuclear use by the United States. Eisenhower, Dulles, Radford, Nixon, and some of the president's other key advisers did not appear to have had grave moral qualms about nuclear use in pursuit of what they regarded as the national interest, although they were aware of the moral qualms of others.[69]

The nuclear planning that the administration carried out during the crisis was secret. Although Vietminh leaders were aware of and took note of US threats, signals, and military maneuvers that were not secret but intended to be noticed,[70] these had no discernible influence on the strategy of the Vietminh or their Soviet and Chinese allies during the Indochina War. According to Luu Doan Huynh—a former Vietminh soldier, a DRV diplomat, and a news analyst at Hanoi's American Affairs Department during the Second Indochina War—the top leaders monitored Western news agencies and may have picked up the Eisenhower administration's signals threatening air strikes. But they were probably more concerned about the possibility of US troop intervention after a French defeat than about the possibility of nuclear attacks at Dien Bien Phu, especially since there had been no US conventional bombing raids.[71]

Coincidentally, negotiations in Geneva began the day after the fall of Dien Bien Phu and before Eisenhower's preconditions for intervention had been met. Brinkmanship having failed, US diplomacy regarding Indochina now sought and succeeded in the negotiations to bring about the temporary partitioning of Vietnam into non-Communist and Communist halves. Partition was followed by US military and economic aid and advice going to a client government of the non-Communist half—a policy that would ultimately lead to ever larger commitments of US prestige, money, and manpower, the very thing that the administration's initial brinkmanship was supposed to have prevented.

Cold War Crises, SAC Alerts, and SIOP

The "little war" crisis in Indochina was soon followed by another in Asia—one in which the United States and China directly confronted each other. Beginning in 1954, political and military tensions between the rival PRC on the mainland and the Nationalist Republic of China (ROC) on Taiwan generated a series of minor clashes over ROC-controlled offshore islands in the Taiwan Strait. When PRC leaders began shelling the islands of Quemoy and Matsu in early September 1954, they were not only responding to perceived provocations by the United States and Chiang Kai-shek's forces in the area—which included the ROC's deployment of 73,000 troops on Quemoy and Matsu in August—but also seeking to focus world attention on their claim to Taiwan. Soon after the United States and the

ROC concluded a mutual defense treaty in December 1954, the PRC then occupied one of the Dachens, a set of islands some 200 miles northwest of Taiwan that had not been included in the US-ROC pact.[72]

Although military leaders, including JCS chairman Radford, wanted to attack Chinese airfields across the strait, Eisenhower and Dulles preferred an ambiguous strategy designed to keep Beijing guessing about the next US move, in part because they did not want to lose NATO support. Their goal was to deter by means of the "uncertainty effect," which, according to Henry Kissinger, underpinned the doctrine of massive retaliation. As Dulles had phrased the matter in March 1954, "The key to the success [of threatening] massive atomic retaliation—was to keep a potential enemy guessing about the kind of action the United States might take in any particular case."[73]

In January 1955, the US government ordered a show of force in Taiwan Strait, first by rotating nuclear-capable F-86 squadrons from Japan to Taiwan and then by deploying an entire fighter-bomber wing to the island. On 16 March, when the crisis appeared to be escalating and shortly after Dulles had said in a news conference that the United States would use tactical nuclear weapons if general war broke out in Asia, Eisenhower answered a questioner on this matter at his own news conference:

> In any combat where these things can be used on strictly military targets for strictly military purposes, I see no reason why they shouldn't be used just exactly as you would use a bullet or anything else. . . . I would say, yes, of course they would be used. . . . The great question about these things comes when you begin to get into those areas where you cannot make sure that you are operating merely against military targets. But with that one qualification, I would say, yes, of course they would be used.[74]

The president's remarkable declaration was not only a ploy or stratagem by which he could send a dire signal of nuclear destruction to Beijing and keep the Chinese guessing about how far he might go. It was also a candid statement of his thinking in 1955 about the cost-effectiveness and military utility of nuclear weapons.[75] Vice President Nixon echoed the threat on 17 March, noting that "tactical atomic explosives are now conventional and will be used against the targets of any aggressive force." Unsurprisingly, his and the president's statements caused public alarm. Several days later, Eisenhower felt compelled to walk them back a little, declaring that "the concept of atomic war is too horrible for man to endure and to practice, and he must find some way out of it." Yet he could not guarantee that the horror would be avoided because "every war is going to astonish you . . . in the way it is carried out."[76]

Eisenhower's and Mao's gambits during the Taiwan Strait crisis of 1954–1955 had posed great risks, but neither man had fully understood the other's intention, much less the dangers of the game they were playing. Each had been following his own version of brinkmanship. Nevertheless, Eisenhower drew lessons that paralleled those that he had drawn from his experience at the close of the Korean War; namely, that taking a firm stand, making displays of military power, and issuing tacit nuclear threats were relevant to prevailing in a confrontation with the Communists. Eisenhower concluded his account of the confrontation in his memoir by asserting that "we refused to retreat, and the enemy, true to his formula, for a while tried harassment but refused to attack."[77]

Not to be outdone, the Soviets made their first nuclear threats during the crisis following Gamal Abdel Nassar's nationalization of the Suez Canal. In late October 1956 when the British, French, and Israelis launched plans to punish Egypt with an invasion, Soviet general secretary Nikita Khrushchev—then in the midst of his own crisis in Hungary—attempted his version of brinkmanship with atomic blackmail against the British. Though it was actually US financial pressure on London that forced an end to the British and French invasion, on 6 November Khrushchev erroneously concluded that the Anglo-French withdrawal was the "direct result" of his warnings. He continued to insist that nuclear threats had been decisive and "decided the fate of Egypt." Historian Vladislav Zubok observed that Khrushchev was "emboldened . . . to believe that nuclear power overshadowed all other factors" in world politics and soon began boasting and exaggerating about Soviet nuclear capabilities, which characterized his diplomacy until the Cuban missile crisis.[78]

As crises in the Far and Near East unfolded, US nuclear capabilities advanced significantly. In 1955, the US stockpile of nuclear weapons exceeded 2,200, and CINCSAC General LeMay claimed that his command could launch over 1,000 nuclear-capable bombers within four days for strikes against Soviet bloc targets. That same year, with intelligence estimates predicting a Soviet intercontinental ballistic missile (ICBM) threat emerging in the early 1960s, SAC planners began developing alert concepts that would make it possible to launch bombers in fifteen minutes on receipt of a tactical warning of a Soviet missile attack. Alert forces would be ready for retaliation but also for use in international crises or even preemptive strikes. They maintained that "alerts would be extremely valuable in taking the initiative because of the speed with which the force could be generated." In SAC parlance, "initiative" meant preemptive action, or making the first move. During "periods of tension," moreover, the "existence of an alert force would give SAC the facilities and support capability for expansion." After a series of tests, SAC began implementing its ground alert program in 1957. By 1960, it had 134 B-47 aircraft on thirty-minute alert in the continental United States and overseas, including bases in Guam, Spain, Morocco, and the United Kingdom.[79]

As far as SAC officers were concerned, victory meant a decisive and massively destructive strike against "every segment of the Soviet's capability to deliver nuclear weapons on Allied territory." SAC was determined to remain the principal arm of nuclear war fighting, and consistent with pre–World War II strategic-bombing doctrine, its plans for both retaliatory and preemptive attacks into the USSR were based on delivery capabilities, not specific goals in light of specific contingencies. SAC's list of Sino-Soviet bloc targets came to 2,997 in 1956 and 3,261 in 1957. In 1959, the Air Staff submitted an estimate to the president that by 1963, some 8,400 Soviet targets would require destruction. When SAC requested even more delivery capability, Eisenhower commented that "they are trying to get themselves into an incredible position of having enough to destroy every conceivable target all over the world, plus a three-fold reserve."[80]

After a November 1958 NSC briefing on the consequences of a US-Soviet nuclear war, Gerard C. Smith, director of policy planning in the State Department, wrote that "the claim that SAC plans to over-destroy targets seems to be borne out." As an example, he noted that SAC intended to target Moscow with "weapons having a total explosive yield of 100 megatons . . . the equivalent of 5000 Hiroshima-type bombs." Smith observed that because of fallout, the damage would not be limited to the USSR and the PRC and that the scenarios raised serious moral questions.[81] Others had often pointed out that war plans ignored or underestimated blast, fallout, and firestorm effects. And, of course, no one then considered the global environmental and climatic consequences of what would eventually be called a nuclear autumn and nuclear winter. If the aim was to decisively defeat the Soviet Union, the reality would be overkill and global disaster.[82]

Continuing instability in the Middle East and East Asia in 1958 provided additional occasions for SAC and other commands to experiment with alert concepts and demonstrations of military power. In response to a civil war between pro-Western Christians and Pan-Arab Muslims in Lebanon, Eisenhower sent 14,000 US Army soldiers and Marines to bolster the pro-Western government in Beirut. On 15 July, as the troops were arriving, Eisenhower met with JCS chairman Nathan Twining and approved recommendations to put air force units on an alert.[83] The backdrop to Eisenhower's actions was his concern not only about Lebanon but also about the implications of the recent coup in Iraq and fears of growing Soviet influence in the Middle East in the wake of the 1956 Suez crisis.

SAC went on a Blue Alert, generating its forces and putting them on a "full stand-down . . . alert," ready for rapid use. Of 1,213 combat aircraft available, 1,132 were taken to a combat configuration within a few days. With a one-third alert in effect, about 20 percent of the force—405 bombers and 182 tankers in the United States and at overseas bases in Morocco, Spain, Guam, Turkey, and the United Kingdom—was on runway alert. This full show of force posture lasted five days. The combat-ready forces included at least 131 of the new B-52 strategic bombers. Army and naval forces were also mobilized, including two attack-carrier strike groups in the eastern Mediterranean to back up the troops in Lebanon. Surprisingly overlooked in accounts of this crisis, the SAC alert was the largest of its kind before the Cuban crisis of 1962.[84]

Only weeks later, in late August 1958, the US launched a show of force exercise when another Taiwan Strait crisis unfolded. Just as in 1955, Eisenhower and Dulles believed that threats to the offshore islands jeopardized the stability of the Nationalist regime and the larger US position in the Pacific. With the Chinese visibly making military preparations near the islands in the aftermath of the first Taiwan Strait crisis, Secretary of State Dulles and the JCS approved steps to "improve" Taiwan's situation by measures such as augmenting the Seventh Fleet. Dulles, Twining, and others agreed that "what we did would be more important than what we said." Although Dulles knew that Chiang Kai-shek's forces had taken provocative actions that had led to a flare-up of tensions in the area, he believed it was necessary to take a tough military posture: "We should continue to look as if we would welcome a fight as this was the best stance calculated to deter." Even before this discussion on 22 August, SAC had alerted five nuclear-armed B-47s on Guam to improve the Pacific Command's capability to carry out its mission to strike coastal targets.[85]

On 22 August, the Chinese began bombarding Quemoy. Eisenhower and Dulles disagreed over how aggressive a posture the United States should take, especially the extent to which it should risk nuclear weapons use, but Eisenhower nevertheless approved additional military preparations on 25 August. While avoiding public threat making and statements about "conventional nuclear" weapons, Eisenhower approved a show of force with major deployments of nuclear-capable air and naval units into the Taiwan Strait area. This involved a massive augmentation of the Seventh Fleet with the deployment of 6 carriers, 3 heavy cruisers, 40 destroyers, and a submarine division. Of the carrier aircraft, 96 were nuclear-capable, and an additional 183 nuclear-capable fighters and bombers were deployed in the area.[86]

Eisenhower was convinced that the Chinese would not invade the offshore islands if "they were convinced that we would come to [the ROC's] aid." But if fighting broke out, he instructed the Joint Chiefs to plan for the initial use of conventional weapons. Consistent with earlier decisions about presidential control of nuclear weapons and believing that their use meant "cross[ing] a completely different line," Eisenhower refused to delegate the use of nuclear weapons, much less authorize an air attack against mainland targets, and insisted on keeping control over these momentous decisions. He was not treating nuclear weapons as conventional weapons. The president's emphasis on initially using conventional weapons perturbed military leaders, whose planning for war in the strait posited early nuclear weapons use. Nevertheless, Eisenhower took it for granted that if the Chinese invaded the offshore islands, nuclear weapons would be brought into play if conventional forces failed to repel the invasion. Before that became necessary, however, he privately considered the possibility of abandoning the islands in order to avoid nuclear weapons use with all its uncertainties, including the risk of general war.[87]

After the crisis faded away during September and October 1958, the US high command assumed that the "full-speed convergence of the 'massive Seventh Fleet' toward the Taiwan Strait and the deployment of Tactical Air Command and Air Defense Command Century fighters scored the greatest psychological impact on the Communists." Whatever US officials believed, however, Mao did not intend to land troops on the offshore islands. Instead, he had wanted to create "international tension" to make Washington nervous, drive a wedge between Eisenhower and Chiang, and protest the US intervention in Lebanon. Admittedly playing brinkmanship again, Mao wanted to avoid a direct confrontation with Washington but sought a crisis to build domestic support and get more weapons from the Soviet Union.[88]

As the Taiwan crisis trailed off during the fall of 1958, another crisis unfolded over Berlin, when Khrushchev challenged four-power control over the occupied city in November of that year. Worried about the stability of his East German ally, Khrushchev hoped that pressure tactics, backed by his vaunted nuclear power, would drive the Western powers to the negotiation table. Although he hoped to receive an invitation to the United States for negotiations over Germany and even though Eisenhower was interested in seeing him, Khrushchev's Berlin initiative made Eisenhower and Dulles worry that the Soviets might undercut allied transit rights and give the East Germans control over access to West Berlin. They wondered whether they would soon be facing a serious confrontation with military implications. Working closely with European allies, Eisenhower and Dulles sponsored intensive studies of contingency plans in the event of a crisis as well as diplomatic options and short-term measures to display resolve.[89]

To "show the Soviets that we mean business," Dulles told Supreme Allied Commander, Europe (SACEUR) General Lauris Norstad in December 1958 that he wanted military measures analogous to the deployments during the recent Lebanon and Taiwan crises. They should not be "so dramatic as to cause panic in Europe, but . . . sufficiently apparent to the Soviets to back up our hand in standing firm." In late January 1959, Dulles reemphasized this point, arguing for "military preparations, which may be detected by Soviet intelligence but which are not sufficient to create public alarm." He supported "quiet moves of increased military preparedness," including the movement of atomic weapons "into Germany as promptly as possible, believing that this would be picked up by Soviet intelligence."[90] What Dulles proposed in the way of signaling went further than General Norstad believed was necessary, but Washington had been secretly moving ahead on nuclear sharing arrangements with Bonn so that West German fighter-bomber units would be nuclear-ready.[91]

On 30 April 1959, a few weeks before the British, French, and US foreign ministers began negotiations over Berlin with Soviet foreign minister Andrei Gromyko, the US Army Europe began rotating atomic weapons delivery units, including artillery, Honest John rockets, and Corporal missiles into the NORTHAG (Northern Army Group) sector in northern West Germany. Such movements would enable the Soviet Military Liaison Mission, which monitored US, British, and French military activities in West Germany, to "become cognizant of this fact."[92]

The Soviets could not have missed another new US nuclear readiness move: the creation of airborne alert—the practice of keeping nuclear-armed bombers in the air, twenty-four hours a day, ready to strike Communist bloc targets. What made this possible was the deployment of the B-52 turbojet bomber, which was first introduced into service in 1955. With its 6,000-mile range and reduced dependence on overseas bases and refueling, it was far more capable than the smaller, shorter-range B-47. The Stratofortress could reach a maximum speed of 650 mph at cruising altitudes of 32,000 to 40,000 feet and carry up to 20 tons, thus allowing it to be armed with several thermonuclear bombs. With such a capability, SAC planners believed that the B-52 could mean the "difference between victory and defeat because of the terrible havoc which could be wrought during the first crucial days of a war."[93]

Pointing to what turned out to be inflated intelligence estimates that posited Soviet ICBM "supremacy" by the early 1960s, CINCSAC General Thomas Power, who had recently replaced Curtis LeMay, wanted to put one-quarter of the SAC bomber force on continuous airborne alert so that a surprise attack would not destroy them. Powers could not persuade the Pentagon to approve more than a one-eighth airborne alert, but no one disagreed with his argument that a capability was essential so that Washington could face Moscow "in international conferences from a position of strength and thus avoid nuclear blackmail." In 1958 and 1959, Eisenhower had approved SAC tests of the airborne alert concepts under the aptly named HEAD START exercises, which involved B-52 flights over Canadian and Danish territory (Greenland), refueled by KC-135 tankers. Senior Canadian officials approved US requests for overflights but worried that testing the nuclear-armed airborne alert while the Berlin crisis was unfolding could "mistakenly lead the Soviet Government to calculate that we are planning to take preemptive action."[94]

While SAC was testing airborne alert concepts, the Berlin crisis eased after Eisenhower and Khrushchev agreed to a summit in Paris in May

1960. But with the U-2 shootdown over the Soviet Union on 1 May 1960, a new crisis arose and the summit's prospects dimmed. On 13 May, Secretary of State Christian Herter took a page from Eisenhower and Dulles, suggesting to Secretary of Defense Thomas Gates that if the summit began to break up, it might be "desirable to institute certain measures of a character which would not be generally visible and hence alarming to public opinion but which nevertheless would readily be picked up by Soviet intelligence."[95]

Two evenings later, when it was evident that Khrushchev was going to pull out of the summit, Secretary Gates ordered the Joint Chiefs to "quietly [undertake a] state of command readiness," especially with respect to communications systems. Gates was then in Paris with Eisenhower and Herter and presumably got the go-ahead from one of them. The levels of military readiness permitted by the new defense condition, or DEFCON, system for declaring military alerts ranged from DEFCON 5 (FADE OUT), the lowest military readiness position, to DEFCON 1 (COCKED PISTOL), readiness to carry out nuclear warfare. What Gates had in mind was DEFCON 3 (ROUND HOUSE), which put US conventional and nuclear forces on a high state of readiness—making the alert measures loud and noticeable rather than quiet. Almost immediately, the fact of the alert reached the media, and it became a matter of public knowledge.[96]

During the period that airborne alert and DEFCON concepts were tested and routinized, Eisenhower presided over the creation of the first comprehensive US nuclear war plan, the Single Integrated Operational Plan (SIOP), which included the strategic and medium-range nuclear forces of all the services. Prepared by General Powers's Joint Strategic Target Planning Staff (JSTPS), SIOP-62 (for fiscal year 1962) codified basic elements of SAC nuclear planning as it had developed since the late 1940s. Under the plan, if all committed forces were available, they would use 3,240 weapons against a total of 1,060 designated ground zeroes (DGZs), an "optimum mix" of Soviet and other Communist bloc military, political control, and industrial targets, with strategic nuclear forces the priority. The SIOP could accommodate either preemptive or retaliatory options. A strike by the total force would produce an explosive yield of 7,847 megatons, killing an estimated 285 million with 40 million more injured. Among the Soviet and Chinese populations, 175 million would be killed in a strike by the alert force.[97]

Eisenhower reluctantly approved the SIOP, which he recognized involved massive overkill. Nuclear war was not war in the Clausewitzian sense of a contest in which one side could gain an advantage over the other with sustainable losses; rather, it was a contest of mutual doom. Eisenhower understood this, yet throughout his term in office, his seemingly self-contradictory positions on nuclear use appeared to have been the product of the conflict in his own mind between his military-based belief in employing all necessary means to achieve victory in war and his commonsensical and moral appreciation that victory by nuclear means was impractical and horrible. In 1956, for instance, he wrote Winston Churchill:

> I do not fully share your conclusion that an end to nuclear war will come about because of realization on both sides that by using this weapon an unconscionable degree of death and destruction would result. I do think it might tend to reduce very materially the possibility of *any* war; but I think it would be unsafe to predict that, if the West and the East should ever become locked up in a life and death struggle, both sides would still have sense enough not to use this horrible instrument.[98]

By the late 1950s, as historian David Rosenberg observed, "Eisenhower's concept of massive retaliation appears to have been reduced to a strategy of desperate resolve. . . . He could no longer see beyond the first disastrous nuclear exchange. 'All we really have that is meaningful is a deterrent,' Eisenhower told his advisers."[99] No doubt to his great relief, the president never had to face a situation in which he believed the West and the East were "locked up in a life and death struggle" in which he would have to decide whether to cross a completely different line. In practice, massive retaliation and brinkmanship turned out to be a risky strategy of bluff.

Eisenhower's ideas and policies were paradoxical. He did not abandon the idea of nuclear use against the Soviets, especially should they threaten to attack the United States or invade a NATO ally. He justified nuclear buildup by arguing that "we don't want to lose any worse than we have to," even though he knew there could be no winners in a thermonuclear war. In preparation for the contingency of general war, Eisenhower had predelegated to top military commanders the use of nuclear weapons in the event that a surprise attack on Washington cut off communication with the president.[100] He also encouraged and authorized military planning for the use of smaller, tactical nuclear weapons in "local wars," such as those in Korea and Indochina, although he insisted on tight control over their use and constrained nuclear planning during the 1958 Taiwan Strait crisis. Yet if nuclear war broke out, the US purpose was to "prevail," that is, "survive as a nation capable of controlling its own destiny" without adversaries who continued to pose a threat. The Soviet Union and Communist China would "have lost their will and ability to wage war against the United States and its allies," and the "control structure" used to "exert ideological and disciplinary authority" at home and abroad would have been "render[ed] ineffective."[101]

Shows of Force and Nuclear Threats during the Kennedy and Johnson Years

Having defeated Richard Nixon in 1960 during a presidential campaign in which he argued that the Eisenhower administration had failed to correct a supposed missile gap with the Soviets, John F. Kennedy would sustain and expand the nuclear arsenal that his predecessor had left him. Both he and Lyndon Johnson departed from the Eisenhower-Dulles doctrine of massive retaliation but agreed with Eisenhower in rejecting the notion that nuclear arms were weapons of first resort. They supported what were called "flexible response" strategies and tactics that sought to delay and even avoid the use of nuclear weapons, and they adopted tight controls over their use. Secretary of Defense Robert McNamara, who served under both presidents, agreed that the United States should never be the first to use nuclear weapons. The influence of a taboo against a first use of nuclear weapons was especially prominent in the thinking of President Johnson, who once observed that a decision to use nuclear weapons after years of nonuse "would lead us down an uncertain path of blows and counter-blows whose outcome none may know."[102]

But nuclear paradoxes lingered. Kennedy and Johnson approved steps to deploy thousands of nuclear weapons to NATO Europe. For the most unlikely contingency of all, a Soviet surprise attack on Washington, DC, Kennedy left Eisenhower's risky predelegation arrangements in place, and Johnson approved steps to update them. Horrified by the cataclysmic scale of SIOP-62 strikes, Kennedy and McNamara wanted choices for civilian authorities that avoided a holocaust. The Joint Chiefs, however, made only enough changes to give policymakers a few options, without appreciably reducing their calamitous destructiveness. The basic features of the new plan, SIOP-63, would remain in effect until the 1970s. Its attack options were either preemptive or retaliatory, involving possible strikes against Soviet nuclear capability, conventional military forces, and/or urban-industrial targets. Authorities could also withhold strikes on Warsaw Pact countries and China—and even national capitals such as Moscow or Beijing. Because the attack options would involve hundreds or thousands of weapons each, one critic later observed that the new SIOP simply represented "five choices for massive retaliation."[103]

By the first year of the Kennedy administration, high levels of alert, whether on the ground or airborne, were becoming a way of life at the Strategic Air Command—just as CINCSAC Thomas Power had envisioned. At the time the 1961 Berlin crisis was unfolding, Robert McNamara approved the first regular schedule of airborne alert flights, which in SAC parlance became known as indoctrination because of their significant training function. Code-named CHROME DOME and later GIANT WHEEL, these operations would feature eleven SAC wings that would launch streams of B-52s, totaling a dozen sorties a day (each with a SIOP mission), with four on a southern route crossing the Atlantic toward the western Mediterranean and eight flying on a northern route over the Danish territory of Greenland but around Canada, whose airspace was avoided because of policy disagreements.[104]

The Kennedy administration relied heavily on SAC airborne alert capabilities during the Cuban missile crisis of 1962. On 22 October 1962, US forces and the North American Aerospace Defense Command (NORAD) went on high alert after the president announced to the world that the Soviet Union had secretly deployed missiles on Cuban soil and that the United States would blockade Cuba until the missiles had been removed. Before the president's speech, JCS chairman Maxwell Taylor, with McNamara's assent, approved air force chief of staff LeMay's proposals for SAC to go on one-eighth airborne alert and to "generate forces toward a maximum readiness posture." Consistent with this step and after an emergency conference at the Pentagon, SAC increased its readiness level the next day to DEFCON 2 (FAST PACE), just short of full readiness for nuclear war. In addition, the Joint Chiefs declared an "A-hour" for the generation, or preparation, of maximum forces for SIOP implementation, with bombers and missiles armed with nuclear weapons and ready for launch on receipt of execution orders—their highest state of readiness short of nuclear war. The last time SAC had generated forces at comparable levels was during the 1958 Lebanon crisis.[105]

In keeping with JCS orders, SAC increased CHROME DOME airborne alert operations to sixty-six sorties daily, with each bomber carrying three or four thermonuclear weapons assigned to SIOP targets. Besides putting another 912 bombers on fifteen-minute ground alert, SAC flew about 30 B-47s to forward bases in Britain and Spain, where they assumed alert status; other bombers were dispersed to civilian and military airfields. By early November, as the crisis was ending, SAC had doubled the number of bombers on alert, from 652 to 1,479, and nearly 3,000 nuclear weapons were ready for launch, compared to 1,433 before the crisis. US air forces in East Asia and NATO Europe began to prepare Quick Reaction Alert (QRA) aircraft for immediate launch, loading them with nuclear weapons. For the first time, ICBMs went on alert, with the number ready to fire increasing from 112 to 182. Also on alert was the full force of 112 Polaris missiles.[106]

Determined to avoid nuclear war, Kennedy and McNamara generally eschewed more provocative responses to the Soviet missile deployments in Cuba. Nonetheless, they had signaled what amounted to a threat of massive retaliation, believing it essential to deter Moscow from taking dangerous countermeasures to the US quarantine or blockade of Soviet shipping heading to Cuba.[107] Yet Soviet bomber and missile forces also went on high alert several times before and during the crisis.[108]

A significant US action had taken place before the discovery of Soviet missile deployments on the island, when US forces in the area had begun to carry out what senior defense officials described as "deceptive" activities. Included among the measures was a higher tempo of training, logistics buildups, and increased naval and tactical aircraft movements. These were intended as signals to Soviet and Cuban intelligence of the US intent, "either deceptive or real," to take such military actions as an invasion of the island. These movements continued as the crisis unfolded.[109]

Although the quarantine of Cuba by US naval forces and the threat of invasion and air strikes by conventional arms played important roles in ending the crisis, the perception on both sides that conventional conflict could quickly escalate to nuclear war was fundamental in inducing Washington and Moscow to climb down from the precipice. In this context, the missile crisis was the last hurrah for threateningly massive nuclear alerts that incorporated the deployment of thousands of weapons.

In September 1963, less than a year after the Cuban crisis, President Kennedy received a briefing from the National Security Council's Net Evaluation Subcommittee (NESC) that confirmed the terrible danger of nuclear war and the irrelevance of preemption (although it would remain an option in the SIOP). The briefing estimated the results of a US-Soviet conflict in the mid-1960s. The conclusion was that whichever side initiated an attack, "neither the US nor the USSR can emerge from a full nuclear exchange without suffering very severe damage and high casualties." The NESC's director, General Leon Johnson, told Kennedy, "There is no way, no matter what we do, to avoid unacceptable damage in the US if nuclear war breaks out."[110]

Eventually, Soviet leaders at the Politburo level would also receive briefings about the catastrophic consequences of nuclear war. Recognizing the danger of confrontation and explicit nuclear threats, both superpowers would seek to avoid hostile encounters that risked spinning out of control. Nevertheless, they continued their nuclear buildups. By 1967, the United States had met its goal of having 1,000 Minuteman ICBMs and had deployed 50 Titan ICBMs, 656 Polaris submarine-launched ballistic missiles (SLBMs), and more than 7,000 tactical nuclear weapons in NATO Europe. The Soviets were not far behind in numbers of ICBMs, reaching 818 by 1967. Having backed down during the Cuban crisis, they were determined to build up a massive missile force so they would not again be caught at a disadvantage. By 1969, they had 1,274 ICBMs and 204 SLBMs. The numbers of US ICBMs and SLBMs held steady, but overall, the United States maintained a lead in the number and quality of long-range and short-range delivery vehicles, including missiles and fixed-wing aircraft.[111] By at least the mid-1960s, responsible leaders on both sides of the Cold War divide had come to understand that nuclear war between the superpowers would be catastrophic. The only practical purpose of possessing such weapons was to deter the other from attacking by maintaining "mutual deterrence."[112]

Despite this appreciation, there were those who continued to see these weapons as viable instruments of war making and threat making. In early 1968, at the height of the war in Indochina, the North Korean seizure of the US spy ship *Pueblo* prompted nuclear threat making. At the outset of the crisis, some US commanders in the region demanded a nuclear strike, and the Joint Chiefs of Staff discussed an ultimatum with an attack if the crew was not returned. President Lyndon Johnson and his top advisers rejected military action, seeking instead a diplomatic solution to the crisis. Nevertheless, to back up diplomacy, they approved Pentagon recommendations for actions that amounted to "implied threats," including deployment of a naval task force with two aircraft carriers. Moreover, to reinforce SAC bombers based in Guam and Okinawa, the White House authorized the deployment of twenty-six B-52 bombers and additional tankers. SAC had duly prepared "non-nuclear options against North Korea" in the event that military force was authorized. But no one had a convincing plan to use military force to secure the release of the crew, which only a drawn-out process of negotiation would bring about.[113]

The *Pueblo* crisis coincided with the end of airborne alerts. Secretary of Defense McNamara had been trying to cancel that program since the mid-1960s on the grounds that ICBMs and SLBMs were more versatile and effective than bombers. Moreover, he was doubtful that a show of force by nuclear-armed bombers had much value. Finally, McNamara argued that with advances in warning systems, it would be impossible to get 50 percent of the B-52 force off the ground in time. The JCS opposed McNamara's plan, but a bomber-tanker collision over the Mediterranean near Palomares, Spain, in January 1966 increased his bargaining power. The B-52 had collided with a tanker during midair refueling, causing the tanker to explode and the big bomber to break apart. Nonnuclear explosions in two of the thermonuclear bombs upon impact with the icy surface contaminated a 2-square-kilometer area near Palomares. Despite the accident, the JCS and SAC fought hard to retain airborne alert, and President Johnson approved a compromise, which gave SAC four B-52s sorties daily, including flights to monitor the Ballistic Missile Early Warning System (BMEWS) site at Thule, Greenland.[114]

A new bomber alert system was in the works on 21 January 1968 when another accident occurred. A B-52 caught fire and crashed on the ice near Thule. The four hydrogen bombs broke apart and scattered radioactive debris, creating a serious cleanup problem. The JCS complied with the Defense Department's immediate orders to remove nuclear weapons from airborne alert flights, and SAC ended the program in July.

Before this accident, SAC planners had developed a new alert concept: Selective Employment of Air and Ground Alert (SEAGA). Designed to be compatible with the SIOP, SEAGA would provide decision makers with a trained bomber force that could react promptly to tactical warning and act quickly during periods of international tensions. Although training went forward, SAC did not receive permission to use nuclear weapons for airborne alert "indoctrination."[115] (One of the components of SEAGA, which was code-named GIANT LANCE, would play a role in Nixon's secret nuclear alert of 1969.)

Going into effect in July 1968, SEAGA included three major configurations. The first was a routine ground alert with bomber and tanker forces assigned to specific target sets. The second and third were available for periods of superpower tensions. One posture was SHOW OF FORCE, designed as a "visual deterrent," in which alert forces would be launched immediately ("flush launched") and airborne and ground alert bombers would continuously switch positions at twenty-hour intervals for up to thirty days. During periods of extreme world tension, CINCSAC could employ ENDURING SURVIVAL, which provided for constant airborne coverage of targets for at least five days. SHOW OF FORCE and ENDURING SURVIVAL postures would fly aircraft in a variety of "orbits," or positions, over the Arctic Circle, the North Atlantic, the Mediterranean, and the Pacific. As Soviet urban-industrial centers (SIOP task Alpha) were the primary targets for SEAGA flights, the weapons would be used only in the worst possible circumstance of all-out nuclear war.[116]

Nuclear Threats and the Issue of Nuclear Use during the Johnson Phase of the Vietnam War

In late May 1964, shortly before the California presidential primary, Republican aspirant Senator Barry Goldwater, drawing lessons from the fall of Dien Bien Phu ten years earlier, advocated the use of tactical, "low-yield" atomic bombs in Vietnam to defoliate jungles and forests and to strike Viet Cong bases along the Cambodian border.[117] In the same year, the Joint Chiefs of Staff supported the use of nuclear weapons in the event of Chinese troop intervention in the war, recommending "an advance decision to continue military pressures, if necessary, to the full limits of what military actions can contribute toward US national objectives." Several officials within the Johnson administration—including McNamara, Rusk, McGeorge Bundy, and Henry Cabot Lodge—suggested looking into the military utility of using tactical nuclear weaponry in Vietnam and, if they were to be used, what limitations should be placed on them. On occasion, some members of the administration threatened the use of nuclear weapons against Cold War adversaries.[118]

Fear of defeat in Vietnam could, moreover, make the unthinkable appear necessary or unavoidable. In April 1964, for example, General Nguyen Khanh, then heading up the military junta in Saigon, had told Secretary of State Rusk that he had no objection to using nuclear weapons against China. Although Rusk observed that "some of our Asian allies had expressed opposition to the use of nuclear weapons," the question of nuclear use continued to be examined. A major US study of possible contingencies for nuclear use against China emphasized the severe risk of producing "an overwhelming adverse reaction from US allies, as well as the Communist world and the uncommitted powers . . . lasting resentment against the US might be generated." During a high-level meeting to discuss the study, Rusk noted that using nuclear weapons in Vietnam in the event Chinese forces entered the war would be a decision of high "gravity and difficulty" that "may affect our whole position in the world," but he expressed reluctance to surrender the option.[119]

Rusk and most other top civilian officials in the administration, however, were not in favor of following through—or at least they were wary of doing so. Most or all believed that nuclear use violated national and international moral norms, doubted their utility on the field of battle, worried about the possibility that their use in Vietnam could escalate into a general war with the Soviet Union, or were concerned about the negative political repercussions of nuclear use at home and abroad.[120]

Undersecretary of State George W. Ball addressed some of these objections in a memorandum to Rusk, McNamara, and Bundy on 5 October 1964, arguing that Washington's employment of nuclear weapons against China should they intervene in Vietnam "would inevitably be met by a Communist accusation that we use nuclear weapons only against yellow men (or colored men)." It would also "liberate the Soviet Union from inhibitions that world sentiment has imposed [and] upset the fragile balance of terror," enable the Soviet Union to claim superior "virtue in having a nuclear arsenal which it had never used," and "revive a real but latent guilt sense in many Americans" about having used nuclear weapons. The Soviet Union, moreover, "could not sit by and let nuclear weapons be used against China."[121]

Ball revisited these concerns in a memorandum to Johnson on 13 February 1965 (which also represented the views of McNamara, Bundy, and Ambassador Llewellyn Thompson): "To use nuclear weapons against the Chinese would obviously raise the most profound political problems. Not only would their use generate probably irresistible pressures for a major Soviet involvement, but the United States would be vulnerable to the charge that it was willing to use nuclear weapons against non-whites only."[122]

In the same vein, a CIA analysis in March 1966 declared that using nuclear weapons would cause a "fundamental revulsion that the US had broken the 20-year taboo on the use of nuclear weapons." It would produce a "wave of fear and anger," with allies of the United States condemning it for "having dragged the world into a new and terrible phase of history." Just as bad, some governments would see the United States as having "legitimatized" nuclear weapons, which could produce an "accelerated momentum toward nuclear proliferation."[123]

The question of nuclear use, however, continued to be examined in some government quarters as disappointment with the impact of conventional bombing upon North Vietnam grew. In the spring of 1966, one of the scientists serving in the JASON advisory group to the Department of Defense overheard a high Pentagon official say, "It might be a good idea to toss in a nuke from time to time, just to keep the other side guessing." Concerned, four of the JASON scientists, Freeman Dyson, Robert Gomer, Steven Weinberg, and S. Courtenay Wright, sought and received permission to study the consequences of using tactical nuclear weapons in Vietnam. As had Ball and the CIA, they raised moral and political objections in their report, submitted a year later, but emphasized the disutility and impracticality of nuclear use for military purposes. The scientists found that it would be difficult to detect, identify, and locate suitable targets to permit the effective employment of nuclear weapons and that to be effective, the weapons would have to be used frequently and in very large numbers. Such use would open the United States to retaliation by the Soviet Union or terrorist groups. The dangers and political costs therefore militated against their use.[124]

Despite these analyses, the issue of nuclear weapons use resurfaced in January 1968 as the North Vietnamese Army (NVA) siege around the US Marine base at Khe Sanh tightened and concerns about a repetition of the 1954 French debacle at Dien Bien Phu in 1954 deepened. On 1 February and on his own authority, Walt Rostow, Johnson's national security adviser, and his deputy Robert Ginsburgh solicited the views of Admiral Ulysses Grant Sharp, Jr., Commander in Chief, Pacific Command (CINCPAC), and General William Westmoreland, commander of Military Assistance Command, Vietnam (MACV), who then formed a secret study group on the matter. By 11 February, however, President Johnson, who was opposed to nuclear use in Vietnam and had now learned about his deputies' actions, terminated the study group while also reinforcing Khe Sanh with conventional forces. Military commanders, including General Earle Wheeler, chairman of the Joint Chiefs of Staff, followed the president's orders but never ruled out the nuclear option.[125]

By the time that Richard Nixon was sworn in as president on 29 January 1969, the military organizations that fielded US nuclear weapons and made plans for their use had developed routines that drew upon several decades of experience, including military operations during severe crises. These organizations were trained through years of practice to deliver weapons that could realize the most terrifying image of post–World War II life and culture: wholesale blast and fire devastation and irradiation by nuclear weapons. An advanced and well-organized system for deploying powerful conventional forces, making nuclear threats, and waging nuclear war was about to come under the direction of two men who believed that force and the threat of force were legitimate and effective tools for successfully managing and resolving conflict with adversaries. As a student in the Eisenhower-Dulles seminar of statecraft, Richard Nixon would bring to his presidency specific ideas about how to end wars and manage crises that drew upon his experiences with brinkmanship.

CHAPTER TWO

The Madman Theory: Mr. Nixon, Dr. Kissinger, and Dr. Strangelove
1945–1969

I call it the Madman Theory, Bob. I want the North Vietnamese to believe
I've reached the point where I might do anything to stop the war.
Richard Nixon[1]

Nixon and the Madman Theory

Richard Nixon was a war-contracts officer stationed in Philadelphia when
Japan surrendered in August 1945. In an interview forty years later, he
took the orthodox position that it was the atomic bombings of Hiroshima
and Nagasaki that had forced Japanese leaders to capitulate. The US monopoly on the Bomb, he continued, subsequently made the United States
"the most powerful nation in the world," enabling it "to play a major role
on the world's stage," and because of its nuclear lead over Moscow in the
years following, Washington "started using the Bomb as a diplomatic
stick." The strategic lesson Nixon drew was that the United States could
influence the conduct of adversaries by providing them with "incentives
on the 'negative side'": taking steps or making threats that would cause
them to wonder whether Washington would again use massive force and
even nuclear weapons.[2]

One of Nixon's favorite examples of the effectiveness of nuclear brinkmanship against the Soviet Union was Eisenhower's handling of the Berlin crisis of 1959, during which, Nixon claimed, Eisenhower had artfully
used his 11 March press conference to send a nuclear warning to Moscow, causing Soviet leaders to back down from their own threat to recognize East German authority over the city. Although acknowledging that
nuclear weapons were terrible and "could not free *anything*," much less
Berlin, Nixon said, Eisenhower had nevertheless affirmed that "we will

do what is necessary to protect ourselves," and by not ruling out the possibility of "general war,"[3] he had made sure that the Soviets thought he was accepting the irrational, self-destructive risk of a nuclear war.[4]

Nixon's selective memory of Eisenhower's atomic diplomacy during the Korean War served as his template for ending the stalemate in Vietnam. Candidate Nixon explained the strategy to southern state delegates at the Republican convention in August 1968:

> How do you bring a war to a conclusion? I'll tell you how Korea was ended. We got in there and had this messy war on our hands. Eisenhower . . . let the word go out diplomatically to the Chinese and the North [Koreans] that we would not tolerate this continual ground war of attrition. And within a matter of months, they negotiated. Well, as far as negotiation [in Vietnam] is concerned that should be our position. We'll be militarily strong and diplomatically strong.[5]

By the time of Nixon's election, however, the Soviet Union's achievement of nuclear parity with the United States had undermined a key pillar of atomic diplomacy and massive retaliation. President Nixon commented on this change to English journalist Henry Brandon in 1971:

> In the fifties, I was a strong supporter of . . . brinkmanship . . . [or] massive retaliation. . . . It was a viable policy: that when the United States had enormous nuclear advantage . . . the United States could say to the world, if in any place in the world, one of our allies, or countries whose interest is similar to ours, is attacked, we will use, we will consider the use, and might very well use our nuclear superiority to deter the attack or to answer it. . . . Today the nuclear equation does not hold.[6]

Nonetheless, Nixon retained his confidence in the viability of nuclear diplomacy and brinkmanship in part because of his faith in the power of the so-called uncertainty effect, crediting not only Eisenhower and Dulles but also South Korean president Syngman Rhee for teaching him "the importance of being unpredictable in dealing with the Communists."[7] Nixon also took inspiration from a leader on the other side of the Cold War divide, former Soviet general secretary Khrushchev. He told a

Time magazine interviewer in 1985 that he considered Khrushchev "'the most brilliant world leader I have ever met' . . . because he nurtured a reputation for rashness, bellicosity, and instability. 'He scared the hell out of people.'"[8] In his 1978 memoir, *RN*, Nixon confessed that in the 1950s, Khrushchev's bellicose manner had convinced him and many other Western leaders that he "would have no qualms about using" his supposed lead in rocketry "to unleash a nuclear war," and during the Cuban missile crisis of 1962, he "was able . . . to use the universal fear of war to put pressure on Kennedy."[9]

Eisenhower's brinkmanship had been credible, Nixon believed, not only because of US nuclear superiority during the 1950s but also because of Eisenhower's reputation as supreme commander of Allied forces on the western front during World War II. Khrushchev's brinkmanship had been credible despite Soviet nuclear inferiority because, Nixon claimed, he had portrayed himself as a "madman." Drawing lessons from this, Nixon apparently reasoned that the projection of madness would therefore make the incredible credible in the new age of superpower nuclear parity as well in peripheral wars in which nuclear threats would seem to exceed all proportionality, thus lacking the necessary credibility required by the dedicated revolutionary who has been fighting in the jungle, rice paddies, mountains, or urban slums.

Fittingly, Nixon gave his own version of coercive nuclear diplomacy the sinister-sounding name of Madman Theory. It consisted in threatening an adversary with the use of extreme or excessive force—force that normal people would consider disproportionate to the issues in dispute and, beyond that, senselessly dangerous because it risked a larger conflict that would also imperil the vital interests and security of the threatener. Adversaries would or might assume that the threatener was genuinely crazy—even though he was not—and therefore capable of irrational, imprudent, unpredictable acts. During his 1968 campaign for the presidency, Nixon told H. R. Haldeman—his political consultant, confidant, and soon-to-be presidential chief of staff—that the credibility of such a threat rested on his reputation for impulsive anger and ruthless vindictiveness against foreign enemies and domestic opponents. Implicit, too, was his reputation for having threatened nuclear use against Communist states in the 1950s and 1960s. Thus, leaders in Moscow and Hanoi, he claimed, feared him more than any other American politician.

They'll believe any threat of force that Nixon makes because it's Nixon. . . . I call it the Madman Theory, Bob. I want the North Vietnamese to believe I've reached the point where I might do *anything* to stop the war. We'll just slip the word to them that, "for God's sake, you know Nixon is obsessed about communism. We can't restrain him when he's angry—and he has his hand on the nuclear button" . . . and Ho Chi Minh himself will be in Paris in two days begging for peace.[10]

Nixon had said much the same thing in 1967 to Richard Whalen, one of his speechwriters in the presidential campaign. At the time, he was considering a proposal for ending the war that retired air force general Lauris Norstad had put forward: the United States should call a thirty-day halt in the bombing of North Vietnam; issue an ultimatum; make an all-out effort to bring about negotiations; and, if these steps failed, "apply whatever level of military force, particularly bombing, proved necessary to end the war." When Whalen pointed out that the only persuasive threat would be nuclear strikes, Nixon replied, "Well, if I were in there, I *would* use nuclear weapons." Paraphrasing Nixon's other remarks, Whalen wrote: "He explained at once that he did *not* mean that he would use them in Vietnam, only that he would be as willing as John Kennedy to threaten their use in appropriate circumstances."[11]

Other aides attested to Nixon's faith in irrational unpredictability and excessive force. Herbert G. Klein, President Nixon's communications director, wrote in his memoir: "One of the assets he coveted was that the international opposition was never quite certain how he would react. They only knew he would not back away from confrontation." William Safire, a presidential speechwriter, remembered that at least as early as March 1968, "the essence of the Nixon position was to . . . put diplomatic heat on the Soviets and the Chinese . . . [and] to sharply increase the bombing and naval blockading of the North Vietnamese, thereby forcing an early end to the war." Leonard Garment, a special White House consultant, recalled in 1997 that

> Kissinger . . . briefed me on what I should and should not do in my meetings with Soviet officials [in Moscow in July 1969]. . . . If the chance comes your way, Kissinger told me, convey the impression that Nixon is somewhat "crazy"—immensely intelligent, well organized, and experienced, to be sure, but at moments of stress or personal

challenge unpredictable and capable of the bloodiest brutality. Today, anyone familiar with Nixon's foreign policy knows about the "madman" strategy.[12]

Although Nixon's Madman Theory did not require that he make overt nuclear threats or actually use nuclear weapons, the encouragement of the enemy's belief in the possibility of his using such weapons would, he asserted, enhance his coercive leverage. Winston Lord, a top aide to Henry A. Kissinger—the president's national security adviser and special negotiator —affirmed after the war that both Nixon and Kissinger were "quite serious" about communicating irrationality through the threat of massive military force. In Indochina, this meant such measures as resuming the bombing of the far northern part of North Vietnam; carpet bombing its villages and cities; destroying its dikes; blockading or mining its ports; and invading Cambodia, Laos, or North Vietnam. But Lord mistakenly maintained that contingency planning did not include consideration of the use of nuclear weapons—although that was, he said, "the kind of thing that if they ever thought about, probably only three people would know about it," and in any case, Nixon and Kissinger were not averse to having the Vietnamese believe that nuclear weapons might be employed.[13]

Nixon saw nonnuclear options as dramatic escalatory outbreaks that would hurt North Vietnam militarily and also send a signal with a psychological message—one that would cause Hanoi to fear that he possessed the will and ability to disregard domestic and international constraints in order to deliver more devastating destruction in the future, even to the point of destroying the North and risking conflict with the Soviet Union and China. Nixon had long criticized the gradual-escalation bombing strategy of the Johnson administration, in which each incremental turn of the screw of torture was intended to inflict graduated increments of damage and pain upon North Vietnam, at some point compelling Hanoi to yield. Kissinger described this strategy in 1975 as the "McNamara syndrome," suggesting that it had lacked the coercive power of sudden and dramatic escalatory "ferocity"[14] or what would later be called, by the time of the George W. Bush administration, "shock and awe."[15]

The main purpose in Nixon's Madman Theory, which included the notion of sudden ferocity, was not so much the rational military purpose of inflicting damage on key military targets in proportion to one's goals but the instilling of fear in the enemy about an irrational or unpredictably ruthless opponent and the likely possibility of incurring incomprehensibly greater and more widespread destruction and pain in the future. Implicit signals of possible nuclear use were intended to enhance this threat. Indeed, Nixon hoped that threats to bomb and mine North Vietnam would have an impact on the Soviet Union. Given Moscow's close relationship with Hanoi as a supplier of economic resources and war matériel, Nixon wanted the Soviets to worry about escalation and the risks of a wider conflict. None of this was particularly new or noteworthy in the several thousand-year history of statecraft or in the recent history of the Cold War, except for Nixon's strong attraction to and belief in the efficacy of the strategy—and his emphasis on conveying the danger that he could act irrationally or, as he and Kissinger sometimes said, "crazy."[16]

When Nixon coined the name Madman Theory for his version of the principle of threatening and signaling the use of excessive force, he did not have to look far for the title. The words *mad, madness,* and *madman* in reference to nuclear policy and strategy were commonplace in the world of the 1950s and 1960s. Critics of a nuclear deterrent strategy based on massive retaliation or flexible response often used the word *mad* or similar language to describe the international arms regime. These included moviemakers, novelists, and scientists, as well as grassroots activists in the disarmament movement who opposed the nuclear arms race, nuclear testing, and massive retaliation for impoverishing economies, causing cancerous radioactive fallout, and risking global doom.[17]

Ironically and paradoxically, the practitioners of nuclear deterrence also invoked madness in reference to the system. Eisenhower referred to a US-USSR nuclear war as "insane" in correspondence with Winston Churchill in 1956.[18] Admiral Arleigh Burke, chief of naval operations under President Eisenhower and an advocate of "minimal deterrence" based on submarine-launched ballistic missiles, said in 1957 that the United States had to be prepared "to counter any madmen who would resort" to all-out nuclear war.[19] Robert McNamara, President Kennedy's secretary of state, used the word in 1967 in describing the "mad momentum intrinsic to the development of all new nuclear weaponry."[20] On the other side of the Cold War divide, Soviet general secretary Khrushchev regularly claimed that "some madmen in the camp of the imperialists threaten the world with their atomic and hydrogen bombs. . . . Only a madman would want war." Yet at other times, he could issue mad warnings of his own: "Should any madman launch an attack on our state or on other Socialist states we would be able literally to wipe the country or countries which attack us off the face of the earth."[21]

Reinforcing the meme of madness during the 1960s was "assured destruction" (AD), a strategic doctrine that Secretary McNamara formulated in late 1963 to describe "an actual and credible second-strike capability" (a retaliatory ability to destroy at least 50 percent of the Soviets' industrial capacity, 30 percent of their population, and 150 of their cities).[22] As the term became public, many observers regarded assured destruction as yet another name for mutual deterrence.[23] Skeptics, such as journalist Tom Wicker, voiced their objections to the "Strangelovish world of megatonnage and 'assured destruction'" and the surrealistic, rationally irrational logic of "the terrible balance that renders both Soviet and American nuclear power useless for anything but mutual destruction."[24] By at least 1968, McNamara was publicly referring to assured destruction as "*mutual* assured destruction*,"[25] although it was apparently not until May 1971 that Donald G. Brennan, former president of the Hudson Institute and an advocate of missile defense, coined the satiric acronym MAD in *New York Times* op-eds. Brennan strongly criticized the concept as "one of the few instances in which the obvious acronym for something yields at once the appropriate description for it; that is, a Mutual Assured Destruction posture as a goal is," he wrote, "almost literally, mad." But others, including McNamara, doubted that missile defense was any more reasonable.[26]

"Nixinger" and the Madman Theory

From the moment of his appointment as special assistant to the president for national security affairs, Henry Kissinger played a fundamental role in developing and implementing the administration's plan for the Vietnam War—as well as plans for other foreign policy matters. So close was their collaboration on foreign affairs that observers found it difficult to discern whether it was Nixon or Kissinger or both who made the administration's policy. Some pundits referred to them collectively as "Nixinger,"[27] which to admirers and critics alike represented either a creative and constructive symbiosis or a Jekyll and Hyde, good/evil duality—or both (although the term obscured or oversimplified some aspects of the complex relationship).

Regarding the Madman Theory, Nixon told an interviewer in the late 1970s that when president, he had "discussed the concept or principle of threatening to use excessive force . . . in connection with employing

Kissinger in the role of the 'good messenger' to play off against his own well-known anticommunist views when negotiating with communist nations." Although he denied having used the *term* Madman Theory, Nixon confessed that he had indeed spoken regularly about the ideas that constituted the *concept* behind the theory. These included the threat of excessive force in tandem with diplomacy and the reinforcing tactic of good messenger/bad messenger—or, more aptly in the case of dealing with "outlaw" movements such as communism, good cop/bad cop.[28]

Nixon may have assimilated this ploy into his foreign policy views while serving as vice president as he observed President Eisenhower cultivating the persona of a peace-loving, avuncular, but tough-minded good cop and as Secretary of State Dulles enthusiastically played the role of the crusading, tough-talking, nuclear-threatening bad cop. In any case, Nixon would reverse these roles in his own administration: Kissinger-the-negotiator would often act as the good cop pleading for cooperation so that he could protect the criminal enemy from Nixon, the presidential bad cop—the supervising officer who was capable of acting violently, excessively, angrily, or irrationally.[29]

As President Nixon's national security adviser, special negotiator, and (in his own words) "a good courtier," Kissinger fully embraced this strategy and on many occasions was also an enabler, advising or encouraging Nixon to threaten the North Vietnamese with excessive violence as though he were "going crazy."[30] Some who have written about the Nixon-Kissinger collaboration have even argued that it was Kissinger, not Nixon, who invented the term *Madman Theory* and the concept behind it.[31] Others have suggested that the different but parallel backgrounds and experiences of the two men led them simultaneously to endorse and practice the Madman Theory.[32] Haldeman claimed in a 1990 interview, however, that "Henry bought into the Madman Theory"[33]—becoming a convert only after Nixon appointed him to be his national security adviser. The record of Kissinger's strategic thinking during the fifteen years before his appointment in 1969 appears to confirm Haldeman's testimony.

In his first major article on security affairs in April 1955, Kissinger had criticized the Eisenhower administration's doctrine of threatening massive retaliation as an "all-or-nothing military policy" that could "paralyze" the US ability to defend the "grey areas" in Southeast Asia and the Middle East, which lay on the periphery of the geopolitical centers of the rival Western and Sino-Soviet coalitions. Massive retaliation was fraught with paradox and dilemma: "The increasing Soviet nuclear capability undermines our willingness to run the risk of a general war. . . . The destructiveness of strategic nuclear weapons has made them useless. . . . The Sino-Soviet bloc will consider it [that is, the threat of massive retaliation] a bluff and thus confront us again with the dilemma of Dienbienphu." A more realistic alternative to this dilemma, Kissinger argued, was a strategy of "limited war" that was suited to fighting "little wars" in the grey areas. Its key elements could include economic assistance to the Third World, political programs to gain the confidence of "indigenous peoples," and the training of local forces capable of fighting "delaying actions" until the arrival of reinforcements supported by carrier-based airpower and the possible use of tactical nuclear weapons.[34]

Two years later, Kissinger added a new wrinkle to his critique of the doctrine of massive retaliation in *Nuclear Weapons and Foreign Policy,* his first major book on nuclear strategy. The core psychological element in brinkmanship, he pointed out, was "deliberate ambiguity," which combined "political, psychological, and military pressures to induce the greatest degree of uncertainty and hesitation in the minds of the opponent." Although the designers of the "strategy of ambiguity" believed it was "in itself a deterrent because the enemy can never be certain that military action on his part may not unleash all-war," this "uncertainty effect," Kissinger complained, "may have precisely the contrary effect; it may give rise to the notion that we do not intend to resist at all and thus encourage aggression," or the aggressor may interpret localized "resistance . . . as a prelude to all-out war."[35]

He called instead for a nonambiguous strategy, one that would present the enemy with "an unfavorable calculus of risks" by having the United States conduct military operations that at each stage forced the adversary to assess "risks and possibilities for settlement" before Washington began the next phase of operations. His proposal for "graduated deterrence" required a military and diplomatic capability for fighting limited wars with smaller-yield (500 kilotons or less) nuclear weapons, which he saw as falling below the threshold of general, all-out nuclear war (Kissinger apparently overlooked the reality that weapons in the 500 or less kiloton range were tremendously destructive). By contrast, he suggested that the use of conventional forces would be less stable than limited nuclear war and would invariably raise the risk of full-scale war. But limited nuclear war also involved the danger of "miscalculations and misinterpretations," which could develop into a wider war. Thus, even as a critic of massive retaliation, Kissinger exhibited a willingness to take the grave risk of nuclear war, and as one critic observed, he failed to "consider the precedent-setting effects of initiating the use of nuclear weapons and . . . the impact upon allied and neutral nations of our having taken this fateful step." Unsurprisingly, Kissinger argued that above all, a strategy of limited nuclear war "requires strong nerves. . . . Its effectiveness will depend on our willingness to face up to the risks of Armageddon."[36]

In a 1961 book, *The Necessity for Choice*, Kissinger conceded a point critics had made of his and others' discussions of limited nuclear war; namely, that lacking definable and workable control mechanisms, a so-called limited nuclear war could quickly escalate into Armageddon—all-out nuclear war. He acknowledged that a "firebreak" should be created between the use of conventional and nuclear weapons, but like many defense intellectuals of those days, he insisted that the *capability* to wage limited war with conventional and nuclear weapons would serve as an effective deterrent against Sino-Soviet aggression. A doctrine of limited war remained preferable to that of massive retaliation because "as long as we rely on the threat of all-out war as the chief deterrent we will condemn ourselves to the dilemma that in order to avoid [Soviet] blackmail we must be able to act irrationally with conviction."[37]

Believing Soviet leaders to be less responsible than US leaders and therefore more willing to take risks, Kissinger argued that they would not likely "credit our threat of [massive] retaliation" but would instead be tempted to make their own irrational threats of full nuclear war. Khrushchev's threatening antics at the United Nations General Assembly in 1960 implied, Kissinger noted, that the Soviets were capable of deliberately using irrationality with conviction as a device in their own coercive strategy. If international relations turned "into a series of threats and counter-threats, a premium will be placed on irresponsibility. . . . We, not only the Soviets, would have to be ready to act like *madmen*."[38] "Deterrence," Kissinger observed in a 1965 book, "is as much a psychological as a military problem. It depends on the aggressor's assessment of risks, not the defender's. A threat meant as a bluff but taken seriously is more useful for purposes of deterrence than a 'genuine' threat interpreted as a bluff."[39]

Kissinger's complex thoughts and sentences about the paradoxes of the doctrine of massive retaliation drifted "across ideas like a thick fog," as biographer Walter Isaacson aptly noted,[40] and they often seemed paradoxical themselves. Nonetheless, it is clear from a careful reading of his words that he believed graduated nuclear deterrence was a more predictable and, therefore, more rational and viable deterrent strategy than massive retaliation—despite the continuing risk of all-out nuclear war. But committed to deterrence and forceful coercion, Kissinger, too, had been unable to resolve the very paradoxes he had perceived to be plaguing nuclear strategy.

In his effort to resolve the strategic dilemmas of the nuclear age, Kissinger was not unlike other mainstream nuclear strategic thinkers, who had also recognized that the uncertainty effect was a central element in the Eisenhower-Dulles strategy of brinkmanship and Khrushchev's blustering behavior—and that the nuclear balance of terror had made both possible and both seem necessary. In 1959, Oscar Morgenstern critically noted, for instance, that "the time is with us when even a moderate [nuclear weapons] edge gained by one side over the other, coupled with a will to exploit it ruthlessly, creates new possibilities of threats, ultimatums, blackmail: open and veiled."[41] In the same year, Daniel Ellsberg, examining Adolph Hitler's policy of unpredictability, delivered two lectures on the uses of blackmail and madness before Kissinger's Harvard seminar on defense and international issues. He followed these with a series of public lectures and radio broadcasts in Boston on the topic of "The Art of Coercion." Specific lecture topics included "The Theory and Practice of Blackmail," "Presidents as Perfect Detonators," "The Threat of Violence," "The Incentives to Preemptive Attack," and "The Political Uses of Madness."[42]

In a game-theory study of bargaining published in 1960, Thomas C. Schelling—one of Kissinger's Harvard colleagues—explained the strategy of "uncertain retaliation," pointing out that in a competitive situation, whether it had to do with economics or national security, one agent's framework for rationality is not always necessarily another's. If, for example, agent A does not act according to agent B's conventional assumptions about the rules of the game, B will consider A's behavior irrational. During the game, B will be uncertain about the trajectory of A's behavior. From B's point of view, A's behavior is ambiguous and unpredictable. Thus, A's irrationality might result in A winning the competition. If agent A is not truly irrational—or mad—but is using unconventional behavior as part of a conscious bargaining or competitive strategy, then A's so-called irrationality is functionally rational in relation to the game's payoffs.[43] Writing about purposeful and successful madness in a different context in the eighteenth century, François-Marie Voltaire phrased this thought more obliquely: "Be sure that your madness corresponds with the turn and temper of your age. Have in your madness reason enough to guide your extravagancies; and forget not to be excessively opinionated and obstinate."[44]

Kissinger told Ellsberg in 1970 that he had learned more from his Harvard lectures "about bargaining than from any other person."[45] Even if Kissinger meant to flatter Ellsberg, his praise was important because it reinforced Haldeman's claim that Kissinger had bought into the Madman Theory: the principle of coercion and compellence based on apparently irrational, unpredictable threats, which was what Ellsberg believed Kissinger meant in 1970. It remains true, however, that in 1959 and until late 1968, neither Kissinger nor the other strategy intellectuals with whom he had associated at Harvard, Yale, and RAND and from whom he had borrowed ideas had endorsed massive retaliation, the uncertainty effect, or any other strategy of ambiguity. These thinkers had instead advised against it and argued in favor of seemingly rational deterrent strategies.

Ellsberg told Seymour Hersh sometime before 1983 about a Vietnam strategy meeting he had with Kissinger and Schelling on 26 December 1968 in New York (see chapter 3), during which Schelling commented that the study Ellsberg had submitted to Kissinger did not "lay out a strategy that you think would win" the war in Vietnam. Ellsberg replied, "I don't believe that there *is* a way to win," and he thought at the time that Kissinger "had reached that same conclusion himself years earlier." After some discussion of what Ellsberg considered the impracticality of sending more US troops or invading North Vietnam or using nuclear weapons to "win" the war, Schelling made another criticism: "You don't have a threat tactic." Ellsberg responded, "It's hard for me to believe that new threats of escalation could have any effect on them." Finally speaking, Kissinger said: "How can you conduct diplomacy without a threat of escalation? Without that there is no basis for negotiations."[46] Ellsberg did not explain what exactly Kissinger meant by escalation. Although Kissinger had never been opposed to making threats of force to facilitate diplomacy or even threats of escalation, what he had previously opposed were "irrational" threats. But by the time of this meeting with Ellsberg and Schelling, Kissinger had not only been talking with President-elect Nixon but had also been discussing Vietnam strategy with him. Perhaps by that point, he and Nixon had some ideas about "excessive" or "irrational" threats.

Constraints on US Power

Despite their emphasis on the utility of force in diplomacy, Nixon and Kissinger realized by 1969 that in exercising US power in world affairs, they would be facing new constraints. International balance-of-payments considerations had already shaped the Johnson administration's decisions on Vietnam in 1968 and would continue to constrain the ability of the United States to operate as a global policeman. The rise of new centers of power in world affairs, such as the emerging European community and Japanese industrial power, also complicated US decision making. Nixon and Kissinger were acutely aware that the domestic situation placed important limits on the White House's freedom of action. The Vietnam War was shattering the Cold War consensus in favor of military intervention in the Third World, and an emerging sociocultural-political revolution at home gave them great concern. Both men worried about the "slothfulness" of youth, the "detachment" and effeteness of intellectuals, the "civil war" conditions within the body politic, and the "general moral decay" of the American people. In particular, Nixon complained in 1971 that "homosexuality, dope, and immorality are the basic enemies of a strong society, and that's why the Russians are pushing it here, in order to destroy us." Even more worrisome, Nixon believed that the nation, overall, was politically "very, very, very heavily liberal."[47]

The USSR's attainment of strategic nuclear parity with the United States was another constraint on US power. During the 1968 presidential campaign, Nixon would assert that the United States had to regain nuclear superiority, but he no doubt recognized that the Soviets would not let that happen and that the United States could not do much better than maintain "sufficiency"—enough power to threaten a devastating blow to the Soviet Union.

Thus, when the Nixon administration came into office in 1969, the new president and his national security adviser were concerned that in the era of Vietnam, the credibility of American power was in doubt. Kissinger, like Nixon, believed that credible military threats were necessary to deter conflict and to strengthen US power in world affairs. He was also worried that US nuclear war plans did not serve useful political purposes. Early in the administration, a briefing on such plans would show that the execution of the SIOP would be a catastrophic event. Kissinger later characterized the war plan as a "horror strategy." Possibly following the emphasis of the Madman Theory on threats of disproportionate force,

Kissinger believed that US presidents needed more plausible threats than a nuclear holocaust to manipulate the Soviet Union or China. He wanted the Pentagon to develop plans for limited nuclear options to deter war and strengthen US diplomacy and, if war could not be averted, to control nuclear escalation. In the era of parity, Kissinger believed, nuclear war might be controllable because neither side would take the horrible risk of launching "everything." His assumption that presidents needed credible military threats to strengthen US diplomacy showed that he, like his fore-runners in earlier Cold War administrations, believed Washington might have to run risks in diplomatic crises by raising the level of danger to an adversary. Kissinger, no less than Dean Acheson or John Foster Dulles, saw nuclear weapons and risky threats of nuclear use as providing neces-sary and powerful support for US foreign policy. For Kissinger, the pros-pect of limited nuclear use would pose one of those acceptable risks that might keep an opponent from a given course.[48]

Mr. Nixon, Dr. Kissinger, and Dr. Strangelove

With his proposals for graduated deterrence and limited war, Kissinger had sought to develop a rational, calculable strategy of deterrence and coercion—that is, a process by which American and Soviet or Chinese leaders could rationally calculate the risks. But even though Kissinger and the other "wizards of Armageddon," as Fred Kaplan observed, thought of themselves as "rational analysts" who wanted "to impose a rational order on—nuclear war," many other intellectuals and much of the rest of the citizenry believed that any talk of nuclear use, whether in an all-out or a limited war, was "inherently irrational."[49] Portrayals of nuclear strategy and nuclear war in popular culture often took this view.

An immigrant intellectual who advised the government on national security matters, spoke with a thick German accent, seriously discussed the advisability of actually using nuclear weapons, and calmly supported the strategic value of risking the end of the world, Dr. Kissinger became by the mid-1960s one of the prime models for the popular culture character Dr. Strangelove in Stanley Kubrick's 1964 movie *Dr. Strangelove or: How I Learned to Stop Worrying and Love the Bomb*. Others who may have inspired Strangelove's character were rocket scientist Wernher von Braun, nuclear strategist Herman Kahn, physicist John von Neumann, and H-bomb "father" Edward Teller.[50] But Kubrick and his co-scriptwriter, Terry Southern, probably created Dr. Strangelove as a composite of all these men.

The dark satire of the motion picture captured many of the elements of the nuclear culture of the time: faith in but also fear of the revolutionary power of technology; psychological numbing to massive destruction; deranged morality; generalized anxiety; political rancor;[51] anticommunist hysteria; Cold War paranoia in the United States and Soviet Union; and, of course, the strange, paradoxical, but esoteric and euphemistic "nukespeak" vocabulary and logic of those specialists who strategized about nuclear war.[52] With the prime exception of the crazed movie character General Jack D. Ripper—who had ordered B-52s of the 843rd Bomb Wing participating in a practice nuclear alert to attack the Soviet Union—the other main characters, including Dr. Strangelove, were not clinically insane individuals in control of the nuclear arsenals of the United States and the Soviet Union. They were "normal" representative leaders caught up in the institutional madness of what "experts" had once called the balance of terror—whether it be brinkmanship, all-out war, or limited nuclear war. A few years earlier, sociologist C. Wright Mills had labeled them and others like them "crackpot realists."[53]

Sometime between 1956 and 1957, about the time Mills was writing, the US Air Force (USAF) produced a training film for SAC officers entitled *The Power of Decision*. It depicted the USAF's implementation of the war plan QUICK STRIKE in response to a Soviet surprise attack against the United States and its European and East Asian allies. The narrator, Colonel Dodd, asserted that "nobody wins a nuclear war because both sides are sure to suffer terrible damage," including millions of deaths. Despite acknowledged catastrophic devastation, one of the film's operating assumptions was that national defeat was avoidable as long as the Soviet Union could not impose its will. The last few minutes of the film suggested that the United States would prevail because of its successful nuclear air offensive. One of the characters, General Pete Larson, optimistically asserted that the Soviets "must quit; we have the air and the power and they know it." It was the Soviets, not the United States, who were sending out pleas for a cease-fire. The relatively unruffled demeanor of the film's performers was perhaps intended to serve as a model for SAC officers.[54] Whether the US Air Force personnel who made the film matched C. Wright Mills's criteria for crackpot realists or not, their training film depicted a surreal scenario in which "victory" would be possible in a cataclysmic nuclear war.

Nixon and Kissinger may not have fit the crackpot realist, Strange-lovian mold precisely, but what seems clear is that it was Nixon who, drawing on his life's experiences, put the principle of the threat of excessive force at the center of his Vietnam policy, and it was Kissinger who, drawing on his own theories about the role of force in diplomacy, made himself the indispensable adviser to the president by supporting Nixon's use of this principle when others might have opposed it. Although Kissinger was ten years younger than Nixon, his foreign policy outlook had been formed, like Nixon's, during World War II and the Cold War crises and seminal strategic debates of the 1950s and 1960s. Even though he appeared in his publications to prefer supposedly rational strategies of deterrence, his proposal for implementing nuclear deterrent strategies required that American leaders demonstrate their ability and willingness to fight limited nuclear war and *risk* escalation toward general nuclear war. Underneath it all, Kissinger, too, was willing to think the unthinkable. It was not too far a leap from the thoughts Kissinger had expressed during his pre–White House years about nuclear strategy to Nixon's claim that threats of extreme or excessive force were more credible when made by a national leader who possessed a reputation for or who could project an aura of unpredictability, erratic behavior, and ruthlessness—all forms of madness in the nuclear age. Hanoi regarded Nixon at the time of his election to the presidency as more bellicose than Johnson, a perspective that would be reinforced by his public and private threat making in the months and years to come. Vietnamese Politburo documents, resolutions, and press commentaries would describe Nixon's war efforts as *dien cuong*, which translates into related meanings of madness: rabid, frenzied, violently angry, and crazed.[55]

CHAPTER THREE

The "Big Game" and the Bombing of Cambodia
December 1968–March 1969

> The single most important problem in [the] present mix is public opinion pressure, which undermines [the] intended US carrot-stick strategy.
> *Henry Kissinger*[1]

> The big stick and the carrot, what is it?
> Fighting and talking. . . . It is the same.
> *Nguyen Co Thach*[2]

Ending the war was President Nixon's most urgent priority. "I'm not going to end up like LBJ," he had declared after his electoral victory, "holed up in the White House afraid to show my face on the street. I'm going to stop that war. Fast."[3] By fast, he meant within six months to one year but perhaps at most two years, and the way he and Kissinger were going to end it on terms they could accept was by using the carrots of diplomacy and the sticks of military pressure.[4] Even though they believed that negotiations with Hanoi might work, negotiations alone, Kissinger observed, were "also a very time-consuming strategy, and time is not on our side"[5]—especially since they were putting forward demands that the other side firmly opposed. Negotiations with Hanoi would have to be facilitated, they believed, by other methods. With the Soviet Union, they would link progress on trade, arms control, and the Middle East negotiations with Moscow's cooperation in persuading Hanoi to make concessions in negotiations with Washington on the Vietnam War. Force and the threat of more force would underpin diplomacy, providing bargaining leverage with Moscow and Hanoi. Among other measures, nuclear options—at least as threats—were among the military measures Nixon and Kissinger were considering. Proposals for an actual or feigned nuclear escalation in Vietnam appeared in some of the very first planning papers of the administration in February 1969, but the road to the secret nuclear alert of October would nonetheless be long and tortuous, passing through Cambodia, Laos, North Korea, Subic Bay, Moscow, and Haiphong.

On coming to office, Nixon and Kissinger had yet to select the specific military and diplomatic measures they would use against their Vietnamese adversaries, decide when to implement them, and coordinate the disparate elements of what they called their "big game" of simultaneously withdrawing US troops, making war in Indochina, negotiating with Hanoi and Moscow, and placating US and international public opinion.[6] Battlefield realities, the politics and costs of the war at home, disagreement within and between the national security agencies, and decisions made in Hanoi, Moscow, and other capitals influenced the choices they made in ways they could not completely foresee or control.

The RAND Options Paper and the Big Game

The specific elements of the administration's strategy for Vietnam grew out of a RAND survey of US national security bureaucracy views on the current realities of the war and the future prospects for victory in South Vietnam. With President-elect Nixon's authorization, Kissinger had commissioned the survey early in the presidential period. Daniel Ellsberg and Fred Iklé, who led the RAND team, met with Kissinger at President-elect Nixon's preinauguration headquarters in the Pierre Hotel in New York after Christmas Day 1968 to deliver their findings.[7] Initially entitled "Options Paper" and later "Vietnam Policy Alternatives," Ellsberg's written report of the RAND survey delineated the alternative strategies that agency heads and staffs favored. In this context, the words *options* and *policies* were interchangeable with *strategies*: these words referred to alternative methods, schemes, and procedures in pursuit of high national policy goals.

The paper opened by defining what victory in South Vietnam would entail: "the destruction or withdrawal of all NVA units in South Vietnam, the destruction, withdrawal, or dissolution of all (or most) VC [Viet Cong] forces and apparatus, the permanent cessation of infiltration, and the virtually unchallenged sovereignty of a stable, non-Communist regime . . . , with no significant Communist political role except on an individual, 'reconciled' basis."[8]

But Ellsberg and Iklé reported finding a "distinct cleavage in opinion" between two groups about the prospects for victory. Designated Group

A and Group B in the RAND report, each included subsets of officials who recommended variant military and diplomatic strategies. In general, Group A optimistically favored military measures aimed at "Communist 'fade-away' or negotiated victory" resulting in the "assured control" of South Vietnam by the Saigon government. Group B was less optimistic about achieving victory through military means and favored a "compromise settlement" comprising a coalition government, the *mutual* withdrawal of US and North Vietnamese armed forces, or a cease-fire—or all three.

Group A was composed of officers and officials at the highest levels in the JCS; the Military Assistance Command, Vietnam; the State Department; and the American embassy in Saigon, as well as some CIA analysts. To achieve victory, they recommended that Washington maintain a large military presence in South Vietnam and avoid putting destabilizing pressures on the Saigon government until victory was assured. To ensure a swifter and more complete victory, they proposed escalations in US operations beyond pre-Tet 1968 levels: air and ground operations in Cambodia and Laos, unrestricted bombing and mining of the Democratic Republic of Vietnam (DRV, or North Vietnam), limited invasion of North Vietnam and Laos, full-scale invasion of North Vietnam, or any combination of those measures.

Depending on the option chosen, the majority of Group A members argued that US force levels would have to be increased and the reserves mobilized, there would be higher casualties and greater dollar expenditures, and the Soviets and Chinese might take countermeasures. Rather unrealistically, they maintained that the American public would accept the costs and that there would be only a small risk of a strong Soviet or Chinese response. Dissidents in Group A doubted that the old American military methods of big-unit operations and bombing would succeed, and they recommended stepped-up counterinsurgency activities. In any event, it was likely that none of the options mentioned would be necessary because—as they claimed in a recommendation that resembled the Madman Theory—"the credible threat, explicit or tacit, of unrestricted bombing or limited invasion of the DRV might well cause the Politburo in Hanoi to accept our conditions for victory immediately."[9] To enhance threat credibility, Group A argued that the United States should not offer compromises in negotiations.

Group B, which included the secretary of defense and most of his staff, a minority at high levels in the State Department, and some CIA analysts, believed that a return to pre-Tet operations or a resort to one or more kinds of escalation would lead to military failure and unacceptable risks and costs, in the process triggering even greater domestic opposition to American policy in Vietnam. Expanded counterinsurgency would also fail. Hanoi would be encouraged to hold out, and the United States would eventually have to withdraw without winning concessions.

Members of Group B were convinced that Group A's strategy was bankrupt and would result in crisis or defeat. Although uncertain of Hanoi's motives, they did not believe that Hanoi was in Paris to negotiate from weakness or desperation. Group B was less sanguine about the length of time required to reach an agreement or terminate US intervention—two to three years compared with Group A's one to two. They recommended that the United States seek a formal or tacit diplomatic compromise, namely, "a coalition government> . . . [and] mutual withdrawal [of US and NVA forces] or cease-fire . . . as part of an agreed overall settlement."[10] A formal settlement was preferable to a tacit one, for "there would be a clear expression, politically useful both for the Republic of Vietnam (RVN, also known as South Vietnam) and the United States, that the main purpose of the US involvement had been accomplished— hence US withdrawal was appropriate."[11]

Group B's strategic recommendations were diverse. They included the continuation of current military operations and the negotiation of both a mutual withdrawal from and a coalition government for South Vietnam; a tacit or explicit mutual de-escalation and the negotiation of mutual withdrawal only while the United States encouraged the RVN to assume a larger burden of the war; a substantial initial withdrawal of American troops combined with the building up of the Army of the Republic of Viet Nam (ARVN) while seeking a compromise settlement; or variants of the last two recommendations. Whether in favor of mutual withdrawal only or a more comprehensive settlement that included a political compromise in South Vietnam, Group B's members were more willing than those in Group A to pressure the RVN into making an accommodation with non-Communist political elements in the South, refraining from obstructing bilateral talks between Hanoi and Washington, and negotiating in good faith with the National Liberation Front (NLF, also known as the Viet Cong).[12]

At Key Biscayne on 28 December, President-elect Nixon approved

Kissinger's distribution of the RAND paper to the National Security Council, whose first meeting was to take place on 25 January 1969. The paper also served as the basis of President Nixon's first National Security Study Memorandum, NSSM 1, a compendium of questions on war strategy that Kissinger sent to key national security agencies on 21 January, the day after Nixon's presidential inauguration. The questions focused on topics Nixon and Kissinger wanted addressed: the negotiating environment, enemy capabilities, South Vietnamese military capabilities, the progress of "pacification," political prospects in South Vietnam, and the effectiveness of US military operations. The RAND study was more important to the development of their plan for Vietnam than NSSM 1, however, for it provided Nixon and Kissinger during the transition period and the first two months of the administration with a timely assessment of the difficulties they faced in Vietnam and also of the range of options available. Agency responses to NSSM 1 were received in early to mid-February, but a summary was not prepared and circulated to the NSC Review Group until 14 March, and it was revised during the next week in preparation for a 28 March meeting of the NSC. Typically assigning such studies to the bureaucracy in order to keep it busy and out of their hair, Nixon and Kissinger had already begun to consult with the JCS on military options and to piece together and implement parts of their paradoxical Vietnam strategy of fighting and threatening while talking and withdrawing.[13]

Although surprised by the diversity of views reported in the RAND survey, Kissinger and his staff had begun before Nixon's inauguration to cherry-pick those portions of the agency-proposed options identified in the RAND report that conformed to the broad strategic ideas Nixon had announced piecemeal during the 1968 campaign. On 21 January, two days into Nixon's presidency, Kissinger asked General Earle G. Wheeler, chairman of the JCS, for his ideas on "contingency planning."[14] On 25 January the National Security Council convened to discuss in a general way the options that Nixon and Kissinger had been developing during the transition period. Following presentations by the CIA, the Joint Chiefs of Staff, and others, Nixon commented that he thought it "could take two years to settle" the problem of the war, which he wanted everyone to "approach . . . without inhibitions as to where we've been" and to "seek ways in which we can change the game." But it quickly became apparent that he already had some game-changing ways in mind when he turned the meeting over to Kissinger, who called the group's attention to Ellsberg's RAND paper.[15]

Following Kissinger's presentation and more group discussion, President Nixon summarized his and Kissinger's emerging scenario for action:

We might end up with a [diplomatic] settlement of some type without a formal agreement, a sort of mutual accommodation in which either side is not deprived of the hope of ultimate success. . . . The mix of actions should be something like this. We talk hard [with the Communist Vietnamese side] in private but with an obvious peaceful public stance, seeking to gain time, initially giving the South Vietnamese a chance to strengthen the regime and add to the pacification effort while punishing the Viet Cong. Within three or four months, bring home a few troops unilaterally as a separate and distinct action from the Paris negotiations and as a ploy for more time domestically, while we continue to press at the negotiating table for a military settlement.[16]

Nixon added later that he would try to force Hanoi to change its policy and enlist Soviet assistance with a "carrot and stick approach," offering deals on nuclear arms control to the Soviets but also undertaking actions toward the Democratic Republic of Vietnam that, as Kissinger put it, "look threatening . . . but actually may not occur"—a reference to the principle of threatening but not necessarily using excessive military force.[17] That had been on Nixon's mind before the inauguration.

Current levels of ground operations were to be stabilized or gradually reduced; it was also clear that withdrawals of US troops were to be made, even if slowly.[18] Consequently, it was not likely that US soldiers would be engaged in big-unit operations in South Vietnam on the scale of those before Tet 1968 (except for those already planned for early 1969), nor would they participate in large-scale invasions of North Vietnam, Laos, and Cambodia—although these latter operations in scaled-down form were probably considered possible alternatives. The remaining options were to strengthen the Republic of [South] Vietnam Armed Forces (RVNAF); shift the role of US troops at some point to a greater emphasis on small-unit operations; accelerate counterinsurgency pacification; and resume and expand aerial bombing in Indochina, including the North.

As time passed and circumstances dictated or warranted, Nixon and Kissinger modified particular options and gave priority to one option or combination of options over others. In January and February 1969, however, their strategic plan was still a work in progress, with many of the details of implementation (including the negotiating strategy) yet to be devised and decided upon. Kissinger was still working on what he called "an overall 'game plan'" in March.[19]

Talking while Fighting

Considering the difficult circumstances of the war in Indochina and on the home front, Nixon and Kissinger did *not* believe that a military victory was possible in Vietnam. They understood that they would have to negotiate with their Vietnamese enemy. After learning on 29 March 1968 that the "Wise Men"—key leaders of the northeastern internationalist establishment who had served and advised presidents since World War II—had recommended to President Johnson that he should begin to disengage from the war, presidential candidate Nixon had told his speechwriters, Richard Whalen, Raymond Price, and Patrick Buchanan: "I've come to the conclusion that there's no way to win the war. But we can't say that, of course. In fact, we have to seem to say the opposite, just to keep some degree of bargaining leverage." It was a restatement of his assessment in the autumn of 1967 that the war was deadlocked—now reinforced by a greater sense of the political mood of the nation's electorate and its elites, the erosive impact of the war on the global economic and military posture of the United States, and the post-Tet realities of the war on the ground in Indochina.[20] For his part, Kissinger, like Nixon, had supported military escalation in Vietnam during the Johnson era. But he also came to the conclusion that the war was militarily stalemated after the Viet Cong launched its Tet Offensive on 30 January 1968. "No matter how effective our actions," he wrote in late 1968, "the prevalent [US] strategy could no longer achieve its objectives within a period or with force levels politically acceptable to the American people. . . . This made inevitable an eventual commitment to a political solution."[21]

After the presidential election and into the first year of the new administration, Nixon's and Kissinger's preelection assessments of the dim prospects for military victory were reinforced by those of Kissinger's aides, Secretary of Defense Melvin Laird, and the commander of Military Assistance Command, Vietnam, General Creighton Abrams. In a report to Nixon on 20 March 1969, for example, Kissinger wrote:

The situation in South Vietnam which we inherited on 20 January is well described in Secretary Laird's memorandum to you: "General Abrams has made remarkable progress in achieving a measure of military superiority throughout South. . . . But none of our officials, either military or civilian, is under any illusion that the battle in South Vietnam can be brought to a military conclusion within six months, a year or even several years. Options, over which we have little or no control, are available to the enemy for continuing the war almost indefinitely, although perhaps at a reduced intensity."[22]

Weeks later, in May, Nixon recalled this report in a telephone conversation with Kissinger about their strategy: "In Saigon the tendency is to fight the war to victory. It has to be kept in mind, but you and I know it won't happen—it is impossible. Even Gen. Abrams agreed." In *White House Years*, Kissinger wrote that even though he disagreed with Laird on policy, he knew that the secretary of defense was "also a realist who understood that the prospects . . . to win the war . . . were problematical at best."[23]

From the outset of the administration, US officials' maximum or most "desirable" objective—as Kissinger explained to the meeting of the NSC on 25 January 1969—was one that would enable the government of Nguyen Van Thieu in Saigon to survive into the indeterminate future after a negotiated settlement that would provide it with something close to assured control, which had been previously described in the RAND report. But Nixon, Kissinger, and others in the administration understood that the political, economic, military, and international costs of the war and the length of time it would take to achieve such an outcome were too great (even assuming doing so were possible). Their alternative "formulas, which include risks," as Kissinger noted in January, were to seek what they considered a compromise negotiated agreement with Hanoi for the mutual withdrawal of US and DRV armed forces and "leave the political side to the Vietnamese," or to see a compromise political solution to which Saigon, Hanoi, and the NLF, as well as Washington, would be parties. The risks were that Thieu could lose the battle in a military or political struggle with the Southern NLF following a mutual US and NVA withdrawal, unless Washington increased Saigon's chances for survival by stretching out US troop withdrawals while strengthening South

Vietnamese armed forces and weakening those of the VC/NVA through stepped-up US military measures on the ground and in the air.[24]

In 1969, the long-term goal of Nixon and Kissinger was to provide Thieu's government with a "decent chance" of surviving for a "decent interval" of two to five years after a US and NVA exit from South Vietnam. They would have preferred that President Thieu and South Vietnam survive indefinitely, and they would do what they could to maintain South Vietnam as a separate political entity, but they were realistic enough to appreciate that this goal was unlikely and beyond their power to achieve by military or diplomatic means. In this sense, the decent-interval solution could be considered a stopgap or fallback option, but at this stage of the war, it was just as much a recognition of what was pragmatically possible if the goal was to preserve US honor and credibility, which Nixon and Kissinger believed it was.

The phrases "decent interval," "reasonable interval," "healthy interval," "respectable interval," "suitable interval," "sufficient interval," "reasonable period," "time interval," and "reasonable time" were Nixon's and Kissinger's private nomenclature during the war for a war-exiting scenario by which the period of time between US withdrawal from Indochina and the Saigon government's possible defeat would be sufficiently long that when the fall came—if it came—it would mask the role their policies had played in South Vietnam's collapse. The interval varied from two to five years depending on the starting point from which Nixon and Kissinger counted, the particular nature of the settlement they proposed, whether US "residual" troops and airpower were left behind after a diplomatic settlement, and the audience with whom they talked. In the months and years ahead, Nixon and Kissinger would discuss or hint at this strategic policy option with North Vietnamese, Soviet, and Chinese diplomats, often using these very phrases: a "decent chance" for Thieu and a "decent interval" for the Nixon administration.[25]

In his 1985 book *No More Vietnams*, Nixon maintained that before his inauguration, some hawks had proposed he adopt a decent-interval solution to the problem of the war but that he thought it to be the "most immoral option of all."[26] Despite his claim of considering it immoral, he had much earlier agreed with Johnson's Wise Men that the war could not be won militarily, and the record suggests that he was in a receptive frame of mind in regard to other solutions after his narrow election victory on 5 November 1968. By that date, Kissinger was close to completing an article in which he advocated or at least hinted about a proto–decent-interval option. Two days after meeting with President-elect Nixon at his transition headquarters in the Pierre Hotel in New York on 25 November, Kissinger learned that he was Nixon's choice to be special assistant to the president for national security affairs. The article was published in the January 1969 issue of the journal *Foreign Affairs* but distributed to subscribers in late December 1968.[27]

Kissinger presented arguments that must have appealed to the president-elect: US credibility as a world power was at stake, but the war could not be settled by military force alone; a negotiated solution had to be sought, in which North Vietnam would have to give ground and America's honor would be preserved. Although Kissinger did not mention it by name, what he described in the article matched the reality of what would become known as the decent-interval solution. His prose, as usual, drifted "across ideas like a thick fog":

As for the United States, if it [the negotiating process] brings about a removal of external forces and pressures, and *if it gains a reasonable time for political consolidation, it will have done the maximum possible for an ally*—short of permanent occupation. . . . If Hanoi proves intransigent and the war goes on, we should seek to achieve as many of our objectives as possible unilaterally. . . . We should continue to strengthen the [South] Vietnamese army to permit a gradual withdrawal of some American forces, and we should encourage Saigon to broaden its base so that it is stronger for the *political contest* with the communists which sooner or later it must undertake. . . . A new [US] administration must be given the benefit of the doubt and a chance to move toward a peace which grants the people of Viet Nam what they have so long struggled to achieve: *an opportunity to work out their own destiny in their own way.*"[28]

The last sentence of this paragraph was a high-sounding but opaque and elastic formulation that would reappear in Nixon's and Kissinger's public pronouncements between 1969 and 1975. But when talking in this way about the "people of Vietnam," Kissinger was implicitly including both the supporters of the Saigon government and its opponents, who would work out their own destiny after a US withdrawal. In *White House Years*, he phrased this sentiment slightly differently: "We had to give the South

Vietnamese time to replace American forces without catastrophe."[29] In Nixon's and Kissinger's private conversations and memos, however, such wording would appear alongside the admonition that a decent, reasonable, or sufficient interval would have to pass before the possible catastrophe in order to preserve US credibility.

The exit options Kissinger was advocating in the article were similar to those circulating within officialdom. In particular, these included mutual US and DRV troop withdrawals; increased training, equipping, and strengthening of South Vietnamese armed forces (Vietnamization); and territorial and political accommodation (similar to a cease-fire-in-place). These would be accompanied by a dual-track negotiating process, in which the United States and the DRV would talk about the mutual withdrawal of their forces while the Government of [South] Vietnam (GVN) and the NLF would negotiate the political issues, the most important being which groups would make up the government of South Vietnam. Meanwhile and even before a diplomatic settlement, the United States might unilaterally withdraw some forces.[30]

Kissinger's ideas about the negotiating process had been long in the making. According to his account in *White House Years*, by at least 1967 he believed that the war was unwinnable militarily and, therefore, that negotiations were necessary to bring about an end to the fighting, US disengagement, and an "honorable outcome." But he also believed the United States should not overtly negotiate the dissolution of the Saigon government. Such assumptions required a face-saving solution for America's Vietnam dilemma.[31]

During a three-year period before Nixon's presidential election victory, Kissinger had been privy to the views of many high- and midlevel American policymakers and planners in Washington and Saigon. As consultant to Henry Cabot Lodge and later Averell Harriman, he had visited South Vietnam three times in 1965 and 1966 and was an intermediary in Operation PENNSYLVANIA, an unsuccessful Johnson administration diplomatic effort in 1967 to open negotiations between Washington and Hanoi. In 1968, he corresponded with David Davidson, an aide to Harriman, who headed Johnson's negotiating team in Paris. Kissinger was also in touch with lower-level planners, advisers, and consultants, such as Daniel Ellsberg and Morton Halperin, who served as deputy assistant secretary of defense in the Johnson administration. Halperin had drafted policy options papers, including a 1968 plan in which he proposed a mutual-withdrawal, dual-track formula for negotiating a settlement that could result in a graceful US exit accompanied by a Vietnamese political solution worked out between the GVN and the NLF, allowing Washington to avoid blame if the final outcome in South Vietnam were unsatisfactory: "The US would be free of the criticisms that would be directed at us if we used our position to negotiate concessions on political matters over the objections of the GVN, and we would avoid receiving a major share of the blame if the eventual evolution of South Vietnam turned out to be less than satisfactory to our allies."[32]

Almost four years earlier, as the Johnson administration prepared to commit more troops, key US policymakers and staffers from several agencies serving in the NSC Working Group realized that even after incurring the domestic and international costs and risks associated with a much larger US commitment of forces, the GVN "might still come apart." Washington's fallback objective should therefore be "to hold the situation together as long as possible so that we have time to strengthen other areas of Asia" and thereby maintain the standing of the United States as the "principal helper against Communist expansion" and simultaneously preserve "our will and ability" to intervene militarily in other troubled nations—"in Asia particularly." Failure could be blamed on "special local factors that do not apply to other nations."[33]

Ellsberg reported in his published memoirs, *Secrets*, that in private conferences on the war in 1967 and 1968, Kissinger had "argued that our only objective in Vietnam should be to get some sort of assurance of what he called a 'decent interval' between our departure and a Communist takeover, so that we could withdraw without the humiliation of an abrupt, naked collapse of our earlier objectives."[34] Nixon and Kissinger tenaciously concealed their true motives, goals, and strategies from the public, Congress, cabinet heads, and even their staffers—with the occasional exception of such trusted, like-minded aides as Alexander Haig and H. R. Haldeman. But according to some of Kissinger's aides, the decent-interval solution had been "in the air" and part of general conversation about Vietnam options among staffers since the 1968 presidential transition period and through the late winter of 1969, when, according to Roger Morris, there was "wide-ranging" discussion and "unique openness" within and among White House NSC staff about such options.[35]

Few readers among the wider public or even the foreign policy cognoscenti seemed to have penetrated the veil of Kissinger's oblique linguistic evasions in his *Foreign Affairs* article to understand that one of the options he was proposing amounted to a deceptive feint, which had the disguised purpose of masking the administration's role in Saigon's possible military and political defeat—even if it left the GVN with a decent chance to survive. Readers in the United States interpreted Kissinger's proposals as constituting a brilliant and reasonable negotiating scenario that promised a graceful exit from a hopelessly stalemated tragedy.[36]

Saigon officials had a different perspective on this or any negotiated scenario:

> We do not want a less costly war; we want an end to the war, and this will only come when Hanoi withdraws its forces and we are strong enough to keep them north of the DMZ [demilitarized zone]. We do not want a political struggle with the Communists; we want the Communists to leave South Vietnam alone, and this will only happen when we have destroyed their infrastructure. . . . These goals cannot come through negotiation. In negotiation you have to compromise.[37]

In contrast, the Communist side was wary of negotiations that prolonged the war, sidestepped US-DRV talks on the key question of a political settlement, demanded the withdrawal of the NVA, failed to provide for the prompt withdrawal of all US forces, permitted the strengthening of the GVN, and called for a postsettlement electoral process that Thieu's government would largely control.[38]

Perhaps because of these concerns, South and North Vietnamese readers of Kissinger's *Foreign Affairs* article seem not to have made that final leap of logic necessary to grasp fully that the incoming US administration was prepared to make the decent-interval solution—as it then stood—one of its exit options; namely, that the United States would promise not to interfere or militarily reintervene in the event the NLF would somehow come to power after a US withdrawal and a period of political and/or military struggle in South Vietnam. The GVN may have come closest to suspecting the truth, given its precarious situation. But Nixon and Kissinger deflected these suspicions by repeatedly offering assurances to the South Vietnamese that even after the departure of US and DRV forces, the United States would continue to provide political, economic, and military support to the GVN and perhaps even to keep residual forces in South Vietnam. The DRV and the NLF were focused on Washington's demand for the withdrawal of NVA troops and its refusal to negotiate a political settlement that included Thieu's ouster from power and the creation of a transitional coalition government leading to a permanent South Vietnamese government and the reunification of the nation. Even if they surmised that the decent-interval solution was a component of Kissinger's mutual-withdrawal proposals, the leaders in Hanoi mainly understood the proposals as the Nixon administration's plan to "settle the war through negotiations on conditions favorable for them"[39]—that is, they saw the American position as it stood then more as a decent chance and, indeed, a better than even chance for South Vietnam to endure.

For Nixon, however, Kissinger's article addressed the president-elect's self-imposed Vietnam paradox: how could they exit the war gracefully or honorably—how could they avoid the appearance of defeat without being able to win the struggle militarily? Kissinger's tactical ideas about negotiating procedures and ways of talking about it—in addition to his well-known realpolitik belief in the efficacy of coupling force with diplomacy—complemented Nixon's inclinations to use carrot-and-stick diplomacy vis-à-vis Moscow and Hanoi in order to force the DRV and NLF into making concessions in negotiations. Kissinger had also demonstrated his skill in tactical maneuver and verbal circumlocution and particularly in his willingness—indeed his preference—to say one thing in public while meaning another in private. The two men also found common ground in their proclivity for secret diplomacy.[40]

From the outset, Nixon and Kissinger believed that this solution would serve to extricate US forces from South Vietnam even as it provided President Thieu with a reasonable chance of surviving, thus avoiding the reality or perception of US defeat. They had split the difference between the negotiated victory advocated by Group A in the RAND survey and the compromise settlement proposed by Group B. What Nixon and Kissinger wanted to avoid was a negotiated defeat, which they understood as an agreement whose terms included the removal of Thieu from power, provided for a coalition government that included the NLF, or sanctioned postsettlement political and military conditions that could lead to Thieu's downfall and Vietnam's reunification too soon after US forces completely exited South Vietnam. The Communists' understandings and goals were precisely the opposite: they wanted unilateral US withdrawal as soon as possible, Thieu out of power, and a transitional coalition government or "peace cabinet" in Saigon that did not include Thieu but did include only those parties committed to Central Office for South Vietnam (COSVN) Resolution no. 9, calling for "independence, sovereignty, unity, and territorial integrity."[41] Between the two major parties—the United States and the Democratic Republic of Vietnam—there was maneuvering room, but with the war stalemated in 1969, neither side was ready to make key concessions. Both would continue fighting while talking in order to alter the balance of power in their favor.

President-elect Nixon had endorsed the four-party negotiations arranged during the last months of Johnson's presidency, in which US, RVN, DRV, and NLF representatives were to meet at the International Conference Center on avenue Kléber in Paris. These meetings, which began on 25 January 1969, were variously known as the Kléber, plenary, or public talks. The public format immediately proved unworkable. Rather than engage in the give-and-take of real negotiation, the parties took propagandistic positions intended for national and international audiences—feigning goodwill but denouncing their counterparts' motives and solutions while putting forward their own demands for ending the war. In addition, the RVN did not want to talk to the NLF and the NLF did not want to talk to the RVN because the war was essentially about their competing claims of political legitimacy. In deference to their junior partners and in recognition of the political issues, the DRV would not talk to the RVN and the United States would not talk to the NLF, although the US and DRV delegations met privately—that is, "backstage"[42]—when opportune or possible.

The Johnson-appointed delegates, led by W. Averell Harriman, continued to represent the United States until Nixon's representative, Henry Cabot Lodge, took over in early March. Meanwhile, Nixon and Kissinger planned on winning the consent of the other delegations in Paris for a dual-track process consisting of two sets of private two-party negotiations, in which the United States and the DRV would discuss the military issues and the RVN and NLF would separately discuss the political issues. The primary military issues included a cease-fire-in-place and mutual US-DRV troop withdrawals. The primary political issues included the political status of the RVN and NLF and the timing and nature of Vietnam's reunification. This arrangement would shield the US administration from having to take responsibility for compromising the political viability of the RVN and also make it easier for Washington to reach a settlement on a matter the American people cared most about: the military issue of US troop disengagement from the fighting in South Vietnam. Nixon and Kissinger realized, however, that they had to "at some point be prepared to discuss a political settlement"—as Kissinger reminded the president on 20 March.[43] The DRV also favored secret two-party talks but opposed the dual-track procedure of separating military and political issues, arguing that they were inextricably intertwined—as in the case of troop withdrawals and a cease-fire-in-place, which would require both military and political understandings.[44]

Although Nixon and Kissinger hoped that the formalization of two-party talks would be advantageous to them because "it would . . . split up the NLF and Hanoi,"[45] the reality was that the advantage was Hanoi's. The Politburo had comparatively more leverage with the NLF than the White House had with the RVN, and the fundamental interests of the DRV and NLF were more closely aligned than those of the United States and RVN. Nixon felt hamstrung because, as he put it, "we can't twist Saigon's arm"[46]—although as Kissinger later pointed out, "at some point we will have to engage in arm twisting the GVN."[47] Thieu's "firm conditions" were: mutual withdrawal, no NLF politically controlled areas, no suspension of pacification and counterterrorism, no infiltration from the North, and the restoration of the DMZ.[48] He would vehemently oppose a negotiated US-DRV political settlement for South Vietnam that he deemed disadvantageous to himself, thereby posing a major domestic political problem for Nixon with hawks on the home front and a perceived credibility problem abroad with both client governments and anti-US nationalist revolutionaries. Nixon and Kissinger also feared that if they abandoned Thieu, the non-Communist South Vietnamese political structure would tumble like falling dominoes. All parties understood, however, that within certain limits, the DRV and the United States would lead the way in the negotiations, with the NLF and RVN "tagging along."[49]

An informal private meeting between Henry Cabot Lodge and Xuan Thuy, titular leader of the DRV delegation, took place on 8 March, when Lodge paid an introductory visit to the North Vietnamese residence at 11 rue Darthé in suburban Paris. The second private meeting between delegations was on 22 March. At both, Lodge repeated the US demand for the mutual withdrawal of DRV and US armed forces from South Vietnam, complained about the current Communist offensive, warned of US retaliation, and insisted that the DRV talk with the RVN. Thuy complained about escalated US military operations, repeated the DRV's demand for the unilateral withdrawal of US and non-Vietnamese coalition forces, urged direct US talks with the NLF, and called on the United States to abandon the Thieu regime. The two sides remained at loggerheads in large part because both of them continued to pin their hopes on battlefield developments. One of Kissinger's remarks to Nixon about the 8 March meeting was: "The more reasonable we sound, the worst [sic] off we are."[50]

For the American side at least, the first two private meetings were pro forma, since it was not until 1 April that President Nixon officially approved his administration's own negotiating strategy. Priority objectives for the next several months would be mutual withdrawal, the reestablishment of the demilitarized zone and the restoration of the seventeenth parallel as a provisional boundary line, the release of US and allied prisoners of war, and an eventual cease-fire with international guaranties and supervision.

Nixon's and Kissinger's design for mutual withdrawal was tied to a timetable and verification conditions that would stretch out the American troop withdrawal and create a pretext for possibly leaving residual US combat forces behind. In order to avoid political fallout on the home front, the Nixon administration would not publicly repudiate the Johnson administration's position that American forces would complete their withdrawal within a six-month period following the completion of the North Vietnamese pullout. But as Kissinger reminded Nixon in late March, Washington would "in practice" control the timing of the completion of the US withdrawal because it was contingent on Hanoi's compliance with the conditions the United States set for DRV withdrawals: the international verification and supervision of the withdrawal of its forces, the removal of its forces from Cambodia and Laos as well as South Vietnam, and guarantees from Hanoi and an international entity that the withdrawals would be permanent. The White House game plan for achieving its priority objectives in Paris was to pursue a dual-track negotiating procedure; assume a posture reflecting a "sincere desire for progress" but not "over-eagerness"; place early emphasis on the mutual withdrawal of US and DRV forces; and discuss de-escalation only if the other side brought it up—and then only in the context of mutual withdrawal.[51]

Both the administration's priority objectives and its game plan for the negotiations, however, were patently unacceptable to the other side. Washington's call for the release of US POWs was a humane gesture, but as the other side pointed out, prisoner releases usually take place after a settlement on ending hostilities is reached. From the point of view of the DRV and NLF, moreover, reciprocity demanded that VC prisoners also be released, but the RVN opposed such a move. The White House position on the DMZ and seventeenth parallel was tantamount to calling for the semipermanent, Korea-like division of Vietnam into North and South. The timetable for withdrawal from the DRV/NLF's point of view was too long and too obviously designed to keep residual US forces in South Vietnam. (The concept of residual forces more often than not referred to those US forces remaining in South Vietnam or Indochina during the process of troop withdrawal but before a negotiated settlement.)

The administration's demand for the withdrawal of DRV forces from South Vietnam was also a nonstarter. The Politburo did not accept the US position that NVA troops in South Vietnam were "foreign"—as though they were the equivalent of coalition troops from the United States, Australia, and South Korea. Hanoi also opposed Washington's demand because the withdrawal of North Vietnamese personnel would leave VC forces and NLF political cadres vulnerable to Saigon's reprisals, especially since the settlement sought by the United States and the RVN called for the disarming of the VC/NLF and its transformation into a political party within the framework of a Thieu-led government. Meanwhile, the United States would covertly continue to fund the building of a Thieu-led national political alliance to compete with the Southern Communists.[52]

Détente, Linkage, Triangular Diplomacy, and the China Card

Nixon and Kissinger viewed the war in Vietnam within a particular global context. Although Nixon had used the term *revolutionary war* to describe the long conflict in Indochina, what he meant was not domestic social and political transformation in Vietnam but a conflict in which the "foreign" regular army of North Vietnam had invaded the South, where it controlled its guerrilla fifth columnists, the Viet Cong. In his view, the Viet Cong force was created to serve as an auxiliary of the North Vietnamese army and would not have existed without its instigation and support. Vietnam, he asserted in 1968, was a testing ground of Mao Zedong's "wars of liberation," which served both Chinese and Soviet interests. Hanoi, which he claimed controlled the Viet Cong, was not a "puppet," he conceded, but it had to remain a "respectful client" of the Soviet Union "in order to keep Soviet aid flowing and to balance the influence of nearby Peking." The war, he maintained, was not "an isolated trial, a war in a vacuum":

> Beneath the struggle among Vietnamese lies the larger, continuing struggle between those nations that want order and those that want disorder; between those that want peace, and those that seek domination. It is this larger conflict which gives the war in Viet Nam its importance far beyond Southeast Asia. . . . We must recognize if we are to restore a realistic perspective on the war . . . the deep and direct involvement of the Soviet Union.[53]

This was a perspective that Kissinger shared. Both he and Nixon saw the war more in terms of great-power rivalry in the global Cold War than as a Vietnamese war of national liberation and social revolution that doubled as a civil war.[54] As Nixon had explained to the NSC on 25 January 1969, he put considerable faith in the prospect of indirectly levering Hanoi's compliance by means of carrot-and-stick measures directed at Moscow. At the outset, however, and judging by his comments in his *Foreign Affairs* article, "The Viet Nam Negotiations," Kissinger apparently did not initially believe that Moscow had sufficient influence over Hanoi to give Washington hope that the Soviet Union could be persuaded or coaxed into levering Hanoi's cooperation in negotiations with the United States.[55] As he had won Kissinger over to the Madman Theory, Nixon may have also converted him to a carrot-and-stick approach to Moscow.

Earlier, in his acceptance speech for the Republican nomination on 8 August 1968, Nixon had argued that a US president had to "negotiate with the leaders of the Soviet Union because in today's nuclear world there is no alternative to negotiation." But he insisted that negotiations had to occur in ways that preserved American power: the "United States must be strong. We've got to make sure that our president will always be able to negotiate from strength." Quoting an unnamed leading European statesman, he added, "Genuine détente presupposes security; it does not replace it." Such considerations would shape Nixon's and Kissinger's understanding of détente in 1969 and beyond. Though Nixon would later speak of détente as a policy aimed at building a "structure of peace," in his and Kissinger's hands it was primarily an instrumentalist strategy designed to achieve their pragmatic goals in Vietnam and around the world.

As historian-diplomat Raymond Garthoff has pointed out, Nixon and Kissinger privately saw détente less as an idealistic end in itself than as a "strategy to contain and harness Soviet use of its increasing power" by ensnaring the Soviet Union in "a web of relationships with . . . the United States, a web that he would weave." In this way, they hoped détente would serve to stabilize the arms race, channel US-Soviet rivalry, and prevent crises or at least make them manageable. At the same time, détente was a means by which they thought they could encourage and coerce Soviet acceptance of the existing world order, offering incentives for cooperation and penalties for noncooperation on terms favoring the United States. Although not a coherent, grand vision for Nixon or Kissinger at the beginning of 1969, if ever, détente was for them a strategy to preserve a central place for the United States at a time when its principal adversary, the Soviet Union, posed a formidable nuclear threat and a diplomatic obstacle to America's foreign policy aims. Although their version of détente embraced some degree of coexistence and even cooperation, it was also another form of containment.[56]

"Linkage" was one of the tactics Nixon and Kissinger planned to use in carrying out the deal-making, web-weaving aspect of détente. Embodying the traditional stratagem of carrots and sticks, linkage was, in Garthoff's words, a "governing device for applying the incentives and penalties that they placed at the center of their concept of diplomatic strategy."[57] The carrots were offers of deals on issues dividing Moscow and Washington—such as strategic arms, the Mideast Arab-Israeli conflict, Berlin, Germany, European security, and US credits and trade—in exchange for Moscow's cooperation regarding Nixon's most immediate concern: the Vietnam War. Regarding economic agreements with the Soviet bloc, Nixon, who wanted the other side to pay a price, argued that the "Soviets must give first" before expanded trade would be possible: "I do not accept the philosophy that increased trade results in better political relations. In fact just the converse is true."[58] The sticks of linkage included the denial of such agreements in the event of Soviet noncooperation, various military measures and threats against the Soviets and North Vietnam, and triangular diplomatic ploys such as the "China card." Nixon and Kissinger would raise these issues and deploy these tactics at virtually every meeting they would have with Soviet officials.

Even before Nixon's inauguration, Kissinger invoked linkage in a 2 January 1969 meeting with Boris Sedov—a KGB officer serving as counselor at the Soviet embassy in Washington—in connection with nuclear arms control, an issue central to the achievement of détente and one he and Nixon knew the Soviets were eager to discuss. Linking the Vietnam War and Middle East instability to arms control, he told Sedov that it was necessary to "see more progress" in those two areas before Washington could engage in strategic arms negotiations. "As long as American soldiers continue to be killed in Vietnam with Soviet weapons," he said, "it was difficult to speak of a real relaxation of tensions." It would be much easier to communicate with the Soviet Union, Kissinger explained, if "Moscow showed some cooperativeness on Vietnam."[59]

Kissinger also brought up the decent-chance/decent-interval solution at this meeting. Responding to questions from Sedov, Kissinger told him that the mutual withdrawal formula he had put forward in his *Foreign Affairs* article should take as long as three to five years to implement, subject to negotiation, during which time the NLF would have to abstain from "violent upheaval." Kissinger's comments to Sedov revealed that the mutual-withdrawal/decent-interval formula, as it stood in 1969, was designed to encourage Hanoi to accept a negotiated settlement that would provide Washington with a graceful exit from the war while on balance favoring Saigon in the struggle ahead. When Sedov asked whether this formula was the policy of the incoming administration, Kissinger replied that "we were studying all realistic options."[60]

In a meeting with Kissinger on 14 February, preparatory to his first meeting with President Nixon, Soviet ambassador Anatoly Dobrynin complained that Kissinger's "linkage" of issues suggested that "Washington was preparing for a lengthy bargaining process, a political game, for pressuring the USSR." He cautioned that their talks on issues as serious as strategic arms, the Middle East, and Vietnam on such a basis would not serve to "build constructive relations." It was also at this meeting that Kissinger proposed, on Nixon's behalf, that he, Kissinger, and Dobrynin establish "a confidential channel" between themselves in readiness to meet "any time, any place." Dobrynin agreed.[61]

In Nixon's first meeting as president with Dobrynin, on 17 February 1969, he pressed forward with the linkage tactic when discussing the prospects of strategic arms limitation talks (SALT). Telling Dobrynin that he wanted to clarify his views about the relationship between these and progress on "political issues," Nixon observed that both nations recognized that the principal purpose of strategic arms talks is peace, but there is no guarantee that freezing strategic weapons at the present level alone would bring about peace. History makes clear that wars result from political differences and political problems. It is incumbent upon us, therefore, when we begin strategic arms talks to do what we can in a parallel way to defuse critical political situations such as the Middle East and Vietnam.[62]

During a follow-up meeting between Kissinger and Dobrynin on 21 February about the range of global topics discussed in recent conversations, Kissinger moved beyond linkage to military threat making. Raising the issue of Vietnam, he issued a thinly veiled warning, saying—according to Dobrynin's report—that "the president will evidently face the need to make an appropriate decision regarding the subsequent course of US actions" should the "present impasse in the Paris negotiations" continue; the president "'cannot wait a year for Hanoi to decide to take some new step and . . . a more flexible position.'" Understanding the hint, Dobrynin remarked that "the views of those who would like to continue talking in terms of ultimatums and . . . re-escalate the war" would only cause them to suffer the same fate the Johnson administration had experienced.[63]

Kissinger denied having issued an ultimatum, then shifted the conversation from sticks to carrots, outlining the "two main principles" on which the United States "is prepared to resolve the Vietnam issue." The first was mutual withdrawal. According to Dobrynin's notes, Kissinger acknowledged that "the president is in fact prepared to withdraw U.S. troops . . . , but there must be some sort of linkage here with the withdrawal of DRV troops." Kissinger's second main principle was the decent-interval solution. He told Dobrynin that the administration

cannot accept a settlement that would be followed *immediately* . . . by a replacement of the South Vietnamese Government and a drastic change in the entire policy of South Vietnam, for that would be regarded in the United States and throughout the world as an outright defeat of the United States or as a backroom deal by Nixon—the United States "handing over" the Saigon Government to the tender mercies of its enemy. However, the United States would have no objections if . . . events in Vietnam were to take their own "purely Vietnamese" course.

Dobrynin concluded from such remarks that "the main yardstick" for Nixon on "the matters of war and peace in Vietnam" was his primary concern "about his own political reputation and . . . political future."[64]

Kissinger had not mentioned the decent-interval option by its name at this meeting but eventually did do so on 14 May 1969 at another meeting with Dobrynin. According to the ambassador's notes, Kissinger said: "Nixon is even prepared to accept any political system in South Vietnam, 'provided there is a fairly *reasonable interval* between conclusion of an agreement and [the establishment of] such a system.'"[65]

In addition to these early examples of linkage, military threat making, and the carrot of the decent-interval solution, Nixon and Kissinger used the prospect of restored Sino-American relations as a means of levering Moscow's cooperation in settling their Vietnam problem. Nixon had written and spoken since 1967 about the need for slowly moving toward the normalization of relations with China—as had elements of the Democratic Party. Alexander Haig, Kissinger's aide, noted in his postwar memoir that a surprised Kissinger had told him that Nixon made a basic decision in the first weeks of his presidency to seek rapprochement with the PRC.[66]

A collateral benefit of edging toward normalization of relations with the PRC or even simply talking about such a step was that it enabled the administration to play a China card in its poker game with Moscow. In a 1 February 1969 memo, Nixon wrote Kissinger that in US dealings with Soviet allies in Eastern Europe, "I think we should give every encouragement to the attitude that this administration is 'exploring possibilities of rapprochement with the Chinese.' This, of course, should be done privately."[67] The expectation clearly was that such hints would filter back to Moscow. The timing of this effort coincided with the continuing deterioration of Soviet-Sino relations in 1969 over ideological and border disputes. As Kissinger remarked in his memoir, "The maneuver was intended to disquiet the Soviets, and almost certainly . . . to provide an incentive for them to help us end the war in Vietnam."[68]

In early March, Nixon and Kissinger may have been further encouraged to press on with the China card tactic when Xuan Thuy warned Lodge in Paris that the United States "should not take advantage of the differences between the socialist countries"—and in particular the Sino-Soviet conflict—"to protract its war of aggression in Vietnam."[69] The available evidence is inconclusive, but it seems fair to say that in spite

of these concerns about Sino-Soviet frictions and US triangular diplomacy, leaders in Hanoi acted mostly in response to their assessment of
the balance of forces in South Vietnam, which would favor them after a
US withdrawal, and also to their assessment of American political and
economic conditions, which limited Nixon's options and exerted pressure
on him to compromise in the negotiations.

In any case, rapprochement with China was a diplomatic course the
White House could not control. The best ways and means of reaching
this goal and the chances of achieving it were imponderable at this early
stage, since much depended on Beijing's reciprocation. The White House,
therefore, moved slowly and gingerly during 1969, attempting to discover
which intermediary—France, Romania, or Pakistan—could best assist in
communicating with China.[70]

But Washington played the China card anyway. Kissinger apparently
made the administration's first such gambit at his meeting with Dobrynin
on 21 February, telling him that the United States was "prepared to conduct an exchange of views with Peking for the purpose of promoting US-
Chinese relations." He disingenuously added that the move "is not based
on any unfriendly designs" against the Soviet Union. Raising the China
question again in his meeting with Dobrynin on 11 March in relation to
recent Soviet-Chinese clashes on their border, Kissinger pointedly denied
that the White House sought to "somehow capitalize on the friction in
Sino-Soviet relations." But Dobrynin thought otherwise, telegramming
Moscow on 13 March that Washington sought a "relationship with Beijing
. . . to more effectively exploit Soviet-Chinese differences." He further
argued that the Nixon administration was interested in the "idea of 'containment' of the Soviet Union by reinforcing . . . pressure on it from two
flanks—the West German (NATO) and the Chinese." By 2 April, however, Dobrynin was less alarmed, telling Moscow that "for the time being
one has the sense that they [Nixon and Kissinger] are taking a wait-and-
see attitude" because "relations with Moscow remain more important to
Washington than relations with Peking."[71] The Soviet ambassador was
right on both counts.

Jarring North Vietnam's Leaders with "Indicator Actions"

Kissinger's warnings to Dobrynin about turning to "other means" flowed
from planning and thinking that was already under way in the White
House. From the first weeks of 1969 through much of the rest of the year,

Nixon and Kissinger extensively considered how they could apply "maximum pressure" on North Vietnam and the VC/NLF in South Vietnam, which would have the goal of altering the military situation in their favor, enable them to bargain from a position of strength, and persuade the other side to concede key terms to the US and RVN in negotiations.[72] To this end, they thought it necessary not only to escalate the fighting in Indochina but also to threaten the use of excessive military force against North Vietnam.

The subject came up early into the new administration, at a 27 January late luncheon meeting in the Pentagon dining room between the president, Kissinger, JCS chairman General Earle Wheeler, and Secretary of Defense Melvin Laird. The current comprehensive US nuclear war plan, the SIOP, was a major topic on the agenda, but someone in the group—probably Nixon or Kissinger—turned the discussion to "the possibility of working out a program of potential military actions which might jar the North Vietnamese into being more forthcoming at the Paris talks." The Joint Staff of the JCS soon set about the task of preparing a set of "*indicator actions*" designed "to create fear in the Hanoi leadership that the United States is preparing to undertake new highly damaging military actions against North Vietnamese territory, installations, and interests."[73]

A few days later, on 30 January, Kissinger met with Laird and Wheeler at the Pentagon for discussions on a range of global military issues, including contingency plans to deal with a possible Communist attack on Saigon and indicator actions against North Vietnam. The latter, as Kissinger phrased it, were to "convey to the North that there is a new firm hand at the helm" and "signal . . . that we might be considering a step-up or escalation of operations." Kissinger was particularly interested in the possibility of stepping up in-country ground operations and B-52 air strikes. Wheeler, however, saw no real hope of significantly escalating US operations in South Vietnam because ground forces were fully committed and B-52 units were operating at maximum capacity. Nonetheless, he suggested that a shift in some operations from South Vietnam to the southern portion of the DMZ, air strikes in Laos, and the resumption of air and naval attacks against North Vietnam between the seventeenth and nineteenth parallels might achieve the desired result of signaling "change in US leadership."[74] With these recommendations, Wheeler was passing on proposals that the commander of MACV, General Creighton Abrams, had made in the last week of January in response to Nixon's expressed desire for more aggressive actions with the resources available to MACV. After Laird reminded Kissinger that public and congressional opinion favored de-escalation, the discussion turned to alternative measures. The group put forward proposals that included reinitiating surveillance flights over China and increasing aerial reconnaissance over North Vietnam, assembling amphibious shipping at a South Vietnamese port, and moving carriers and other vessels from YANKEE STATION (16° N/110° E) in the South China Sea north into the Gulf of Tonkin. Wheeler, however, held out for additional offensive operations, including troop forays and covert attacks into Cambodia and Laos, and he repeated these and previous suggestions for aggressive action when Kissinger turned the discussion to possible US responses to the contingency of renewed enemy attacks on Saigon. The meeting concluded with a decision to prepare a "menu of pressure tactics" to be presented at a meeting with President Nixon on 11 February.[75]

Wheeler's call for escalating US operations in Cambodia and Laos was already on President Nixon's mind. In November 1967, when former President Eisenhower had advocated "hot pursuit" of the enemy into Cambodia and Laos, presidential aspirant Nixon publicly called it an unsound step—but with the qualification, "at this time."[76] In the December 1968 RAND survey, Group A recommended air and ground operations in Cambodia. By 8 January 1969, President-elect Nixon believed the time was ripe for developing military options that had long appealed to him, and he ordered Kissinger to begin the process, especially regarding Cambodia: "I want a precise report on what the enemy has in Cambodia and what, if anything, we are doing to destroy the buildup there. I think a very definite change of policy toward Cambodia probably should be one of the first orders of business." The administration's NSSM 1 directive included questions about the importance of Cambodia and Laos as conduits for enemy supplies to South Vietnam, which elicited JCS recommendations to bomb Cambodia.[77]

On 1 February, two days after Kissinger had met with Laird and Wheeler at the Pentagon to discuss Vietnam War contingency plans and indicator actions, Nixon told Kissinger to tell Wheeler that he thought it "urgent" to "increase as much as we possibly can the military pressure on the enemy in South Vietnam . . . without going to the point of breaking off negotiations. . . . I believe that if any initiative occurs it should be on our part and not theirs."[78] A message from General Abrams a few days later provided Nixon and Kissinger with the proposal they had in mind. Abrams cabled Wheeler on 9 February that "recent information, developed from photo reconnaissance and a rallier [a VC/NVA defector] gives us hard intelligence on COSVN HQ facilities in Base Area 353." The elusive headquarters of the Central Office for South Vietnam directed Viet Cong and North Vietnamese Army (VC/NVA) operations in the South, and Abrams argued that a large, concentrated B-52 attack on COSVN would ensure its destruction and disrupt future offensives the enemy might be planning. Passed on to the president, these recommendations, Kissinger recalled, "fell on fertile ground."[79]

When Nixon met with Laird and air force chief of staff General John P. McConnell on 11 February, they discussed US responses to possible enemy attacks on Saigon and other population centers in South Vietnam and the issuance of presidential authorities for conducting operations in Laos and Cambodia.[80] A two-man military team from MACV in Saigon briefed Kissinger, Secretary of Defense Laird, General Wheeler, Deputy Secretary of Defense David Packard, Colonel Robert Pursley (Laird's military assistant), and Colonel Haig about a prospective B-52 bombing operation along the border in Cambodia at a breakfast meeting in Laird's office on 18 February. At this time or shortly afterward, the code name of BREAKFAST was given to the operation in probable recognition of this initial breakfast planning meeting. Later, Kissinger tactlessly punned that the code name was "tasteless." Reporting to the president that day, Kissinger recommended against unprovoked bombing, suggesting instead a review of the military and diplomatic situation at the end of March. On 22 February, as he was preparing to depart Washington the next day to meet with West European heads of state, Nixon approved Kissinger's recommendation for the deferment the Cambodian decision.[81]

The day before—in what may have been an effort to collect information about additional military options before Nixon headed for Europe—Kissinger asked Laird for a progress report on the Joint Staff's work concerning his and Nixon's proposed indicator actions. Laird replied the same day, enclosing a working copy of the Joint Staff's proposed "dramatic steps," which could take the form of either actual or feigned operations—"each developed over an adequate period of time to be picked up by the communists":

a. A combined airborne/amphibious operation against several objectives in NVN.

b. Punitive airborne/airmobile expeditions against enemy lines of communications (LOC) and base areas in Laos and Cambodia.

c. Renewed and expanded air and naval operations against NVN to include closure of Haiphong and the blockade of NVN.

d. Subversion of the population and preparation for active resistance by the people against the Hanoi regime.

e. A *technical* escalation.[82]

Each of the proposed military measures was keyed to political and diplomatic maneuvers designed to increase the potential for a jarring impact. The proposal for a technical escalation, the most startling of them all, amounted to a threat to use atomic and/or biological or chemical weapons and included a "visit" by chemical-biological-radiological weapons experts to the Far East. Haig's paraphrase of the fifth (e) option, however, focused on a *nuclear* escalation: "A plan for actual or feigned technical escalation or war against [the] North (nuclear)." The visit by weapons experts would be accompanied by political moves such as a US diplomatic hint of a "possible technical escalation of the war" and a statement by a senior military official that the "Pentagon periodically examines moves by which new and more modern weapons" could be introduced into the Vietnam conflict.[83]

Laird had dutifully passed on the Joint Staff's proposals to Kissinger, but he disassociated himself from them in his cover memorandum. Not only was this paper "preliminary," he observed, but General Wheeler and other members of the Joint Chiefs had not reviewed it, nor had Laird's staff. Moreover, Laird suggested his own skepticism toward the paper when he wrote, "I must confess to you being more impressed . . . with the potential disadvantages of the proposals than with the possibility of achieving movement in Paris by such means."[84]

No record has yet surfaced to indicate when the nuclear option had first been introduced and by whom—whether, for example, Nixon, Kissinger, Laird, and Wheeler had discussed it in Laird's Pentagon dining room on 27 January or whether the Joint Staff had subsequently initiated the proposal.

Post-Tet

On the following day, Saturday, 22 February (US time), before Kissinger could respond to the Joint Staff's proposals for dramatic steps against the North, the VC/NVA launched attacks against targets near Saigon and Da Nang. Because the offensive had begun several days after the start of the 1969 Vietnamese lunar new year on 17 February, American officials labeled the attacks the Post-Tet Offensive.[85]

DRV sources indicate that Post-Tet was part of a general strategy fashioned in Hanoi in November and December 1968 to maintain an offensive posture in the wake of the mixed gains and losses in the aftermath of the Tet Offensive of 1968. By 1 January 1969, DRV planners had examined the fundamental dilemmas facing the new US president and inferred the probable choices he would have to make in order to resolve them.[86] Their inferences were close to the mark, concluding that Nixon would want to negotiate from a position of strength but that he might think it politically necessary to withdraw a portion of US forces unilaterally. In order to compensate for US withdrawals and resolve the contradictions in his position, the US president would likely set out to strengthen Saigon's army. Even though this policy of de-Americanization would take time, Hanoi was aware that US/RVN forces remained "numerous and did not resign themselves to remaining passive." If, however, the VC/NVA could inflict sufficient additional casualties on US forces during Post-Tet and follow-on offensives, Nixon might feel compelled to negotiate an end to the war by means of a compromise political solution. If, however, the VC/NVA offensive fell short of its goals—as it did—Nixon might seek to prolong the war by resuming the bombing of the North or expanding the war into Cambodia and Laos—which he would.[87]

Nixon's interest in bombing Cambodia predated Post-Tet. It was on his mind at least as early as his inauguration, and soon after that, the Pentagon also launched over a dozen American ground operations. These coincided with the continued growth of US troop strength (which would peak at 543,482 on 30 April 1969) and changes in ground, air, and pacification tactics developed during the previous year in response to the VC/NVA's 1968 Tet Offensive. The "clear and hold" strategy included ground, artillery, and air operations that incorporated accelerated pacification, population relocation, aerial defoliation, and relaxed restraints on the killing of civilians. The central purpose of the strategy was yet another attempt to bleed the "fish"—the guerrilla infrastructure—and also drain the "water" in which they swam—the civilian population, villages, crops, trees, and foliage.[88]

The Post-Tet campaign of 22 February to 30 March was intermittent and small by comparison. Both MACV and COSVN described it as a "non–all out" campaign. Kissinger's own 6 March assessment of Post-Tet for the president was that "the attacks have had relatively limited impact on the pacification program and the stability of South Vietnam." VC/NVA forces attacked 125 targets with sappers and 400 others by rocket and artillery shelling. Two attacks were carried out by regimental-sized units, sixteen by battalion-sized units. Casualties were another matter. Kissinger reported to the president that the enemy had been "able to achieve a relatively high casualty rate among US and South Vietnamese forces while not exposing their own main units"—1,140 American and over 1,500 South Vietnamese soldiers were killed during the first three weeks of fighting, by the time Nixon launched bombing strikes into Cambodia. VC/NVA casualties cannot be definitively known, but in this war, they were usually greater than US and RVN losses.[89]

In hopes of depriving Nixon of an opportunity for retaliation, the Politburo had timed the start of the offensive to coincide with his scheduled departure to Europe on Sunday, 23 February.[90] Post-Tet's timing did serve to delay a US response but probably made Nixon even more determined to strike a blow. According to Kissinger, the president was "seething" about the attacks as he read stacks of briefing books in preparation for his European journey. "All his instincts were to respond violently," Kissinger claimed. But the president was in a quandary: US reprisal attacks on targets outside of South Vietnam would, he believed, provoke antiwar demonstrations in Europe and spoil his goodwill visits with other leaders. For the time being and before leaving Washington the next day, he settled for having Kissinger make a midafternoon Saturday telephone call to Soviet ambassador Dobrynin, warning of strong retaliation should Post-Tet "turn into a general offensive or attack on major population centers."[91]

The Decision: On-Again, Off-Again, On-Again

Still angry during the transatlantic flight on Sunday, Nixon suddenly decided while aboard *Air Force One* to order the bombing of Cambodia. Kissinger concurred but advised a forty-eight-hour postponement of the "execute order" because, he argued, a step of this magnitude required consultation with relevant officials and "a detailed plan for dealing with the consequences," which could include negative domestic and international reactions.[92] Kissinger wired his military assistant, Haig, to join him in Belgium and to bring along Colonel Ray B. Sitton of the JCS Current Operations Branch, who had been working on Cambodian bombing options and was known in the Pentagon as "Mr. B-52." Haig was an ardent advocate of bombing; Sitton was the B-52 operations expert who would know how to carry it out secretly.[93]

On Monday morning, 24 February, they met with Kissinger and Haldeman on *Air Force One*, parked at the Brussels airport. Kissinger had just returned from a NATO convocation he had attended with Nixon. To avoid attracting attention to the deliberations on the plane, the president had chosen not to be present but to carry on with his schedule of wreath laying at the Tomb of the Unknown Soldier and lunching with the Belgian king and queen. Later in the day, Nixon boarded the plane for the flight to London, near the end of which he went to the briefing room where the planning session was still in progress, apologized for not having attended, and said that he would discuss the matter with Kissinger.[94]

With Haldeman looking on during the meeting on Nixon's behalf and at Kissinger's request, Kissinger, Haig, and Sitton developed, as Kissinger put it, "both a military and a diplomatic schedule as well as guidance for briefing the press."[95] In the process, they prepared their scheme of dual reporting and disingenuous public announcements designed to reduce the chances of Nixon's and Kissinger's greatest worry, "the dormant beast of public protest," as Kissinger phrased it—the possibility that the press, Congress, the general public, and especially the antiwar movement would learn about and react negatively to the raids and their rationale. "My administration was only two months old," Nixon wrote in *RN* years later, "and I wanted to provoke as little public outcry as possible at the outset."[96] A large segment if not a majority of the public was against the intensification or expansion of the war in Indochina. A Gallup Poll conducted between 12 and 17 March 1969 found that 21 percent of those surveyed were in favor of a "pull out, let South Vietnamese take over"; 15 percent were for continuing present policy, which Gallup described as "work for a cease-fire in Paris, stay as long as necessary"; and 15 percent wanted to "end the war as soon as possible." Though 25 percent were in favor of escalating or going "all out," 52 percent believed it had been a "mistake" to send US troops to fight.[97]

Although their BREAKFAST plan called for a public announcement of the operation, Nixon and Kissinger would not describe it as a retaliatory measure in response to Post-Tet but as a "normal B-52 operation against targets along the Cambodian border"—targets that "would not be specifically identified" as within Cambodia. Even though Hanoi would likely recognize the operation as Washington's response to Post-Tet (thus serving the White House's purpose), the absence of a public announcement of purpose would be less likely to "induce retaliatory actions by Hanoi, a major protest by Cambodia, a Soviet protest, and major domestic criticism in the press." If, nonetheless, Cambodia lodged a major protest, apologies and monetary compensation would be offered. If the Soviets privately made a major protest, the administration would "point out the military reasons for the action" but counterbalance it with an assurance that the administration was simultaneously initiating a request for private talks between the United States and the DRV in Paris to resolve the problem of the war.[98]

In their attempt to ensure that the press, the public, and Congress were kept in the dark, a covert dual-reporting system for targets bombed would bypass normal air force requirements for recording flight plans, targets struck, fuel consumed, and bomb tonnage dropped.[99] But in the event that journalists might still ask questions about any rumors and reports of bombs falling and exploding in Cambodia, the administration would refer them to the Saigon press spokesperson, who would be instructed to say that targets had routinely been bombed near the border. If the press persisted or the government of Cambodia protested, the administration would neither confirm nor deny reports but say that the matter would be investigated.[100]

Long contemplated by Pentagon military planners as a proactive military and coercive measure, the bombing of enemy base areas in Cambodia was now in part motivated and rationalized by a desire for retaliation in response to the previously awaited provocation. "We started thinking of this [bombing of Cambodia] well before the offensive," Nixon told Kissinger, but after Post-Tet, "it's really the right thing." Nixon and Kissinger also worried that a failure on their part to respond swiftly and forcefully would undermine Saigon's confidence in their resolve and the credibility of the threats they had signaled to Hanoi and Moscow—what Nixon called their "specter of pressures for hitting the North."[101]

Neither Secretary of State William Rogers nor Secretary of Defense Laird was initially privy to the onboard decision. Even though Rogers was traveling with the president on the plane, Nixon did not inform him until their arrival in London and then, according to Kissinger, only with "a cryptic account of his thinking but no details." It was not Nixon or Kissinger but Haig who, on his return to Washington, briefed Laird.[102]

Having decided to bomb Cambodia, the president, however, deferred the operation again on 1 March. Another two weeks would pass before Nixon issued an execute order for the operation on 15 March. During this two-week period, Nixon would twice again decide to go ahead with the operation only to defer both times until his final decision. His vacillation after the initial decision on 23 February was the product of his concerns about possible negative public reaction, antiwar demonstrations in the United States and Europe, possible North Vietnamese and Soviet responses, the impact of such a major step on bringing about private Paris negotiations between the US and DRV delegations, and the reservations Laird and especially Rogers and the Department of State expressed. The secretary of state and department officers had questioned the need to make any response to Post-Tet and voiced concern about the probable negative impact of the bombing on the negotiations in Paris. Nixon and Kissinger, too, had initially been concerned about the impact of bombing Cambodia on the private meetings but decided to gamble that the operation was less likely to derail them if launched before rather than after the talks began.[103] Although Laird supported the bombing, he doubted that it could be hidden from the American public, warned that the attempt to do so could backfire, and argued that if COSVN was a legitimate target, then the operation could probably be defended publicly. Initially, he advised "delay to a moment when the provocation would be clearer"—as Kissinger paraphrased him.[104] Despite Nixon's tough talk, he often wavered when confronted with a dramatic military decision against which large segments of Congress and the public would object or about which some of his aides had reservations. It would not be the last time.

Indicator Actions and Retaliatory Options

Meanwhile, discussion and planning for other operations went forward, with the result that a de facto process of merging initiative-seizing indicator actions with reactive retaliatory options, already in evidence with BREAKFAST planning, gained additional momentum. On Monday, 3 March, the day after Nixon and his entourage returned from Europe, Kissinger belatedly replied to Secretary of Defense Laird's 21 February memorandum on indicator actions, in which the secretary had enclosed the JCS's working paper on proposed options for dramatic steps against the North. Kissinger now replied that "the plans are well conceived and the risks involved in their implementation are precisely enumerated." Nevertheless, he stated, "the 'realities' of the current domestic and international environment do not lend themselves to an acceptance of these risks at this time. . . . For example, expanded air and naval operations" against the DRV would create an international uproar. So would an "actual or feigned technical [nuclear] escalation." Kissinger suggested instead that there might be "some less elaborate actions which could be initiated" that would be "more subtle in nature" and "might be undertaken with reduced risks of news media recognition." He had "in mind such measures as the selective implementation of indicators which might signal force buildup, increased planning, etc."[105]

On a separate but related matter, Secretary of Defense Laird in turn replied on Tuesday, 4 March, to Kissinger's earlier request for military options in response to Post-Tet—responses beyond the bombing of Cambodia. The enemy offensive was insufficient provocation for several reasons: the principal aim of Post-Tet, he wrote, was psychological, not military, and US commanders were "confident that they can deal with the military aspect of this campaign," which may itself have been provoked by US operations in South Vietnam that were designed "to apply maximum possible pressure against enemy forces." Laird expressed doubt that any US measure could prevent the other side from initiating attacks and repeated his refrain that the best route toward the reduction of hostilities and casualties would be mutual de-escalation. Urging circumspection in considering proposals for retaliation, he disputed the efficacy of a recommendation from CINCPAC Admiral John S. McCain, Jr., and Saigon ambassador Ellsworth Bunker for a ninety-six-hour air and naval campaign in North Vietnam south of 19° N latitude. Citing a CIA analysis, he warned that such escalations against Northern territory could result in domestic and international criticism and a disruption of the negotiation process in Paris. Laird also questioned the wisdom of a JCS request for authority to reinitiate large-scale military operations in and around the DMZ. He urged patience until he returned from a fact-finding trip with General Wheeler to South Vietnam from 5 to 12 March, which would put him in a better position to make specific recommendations.[106]

As an alternative to military escalation, Laird recommended a show-of-force indicator action with "nominal military importance" but "psychological impact" on the enemy: the movement of "naval gunships or a carrier task force into the Gulf of Tonkin" for the purpose of encouraging a diminution of enemy activity in the South.[107] The secretary's proposal on Tuesday was consistent with Kissinger's suggestion on Monday for more subtle indicator actions that could still signal force buildup and increased planning but with reduced risks of news media recognition.

Despite Laird's call for patience and restraint, on the same day, 4 March, Nixon ordered the Cambodian strikes to begin five days in the future.[108] Later, at a 9:00 p.m. prime-time press conference, the president delivered several public warnings to Hanoi and Moscow as he answered questions about events in Vietnam and relations with the Soviet Union. In response to one about whether he considered the bombing of North Vietnam to be an appropriate response, Nixon answered:

I will only say . . . we have several contingency plans that can be put into effect. I am considering all of those plans. . . . We will not tolerate a continuation of this kind of attack without some response that will be appropriate. . . . I will not indicate in advance, and I am not going to indicate publicly, and I am not going to threaten—I don't think that would be helpful—that we are going to start bombing the North or anything else.[109]

On Friday, 7 March, Nixon again rescinded a decision to implement BREAKFAST in the face of Rogers's objection that it would damage the prospect of starting private talks in Paris.[110] But the president did implement measures resembling the recommendation Laird had submitted on Tuesday. He ordered increased aerial reconnaissance flights over North Vietnam "for the purpose of leading the North Vietnamese to the conclusion that the action was preparatory to a resumption of bombing of NVN [and] to see if such action would elicit a lessening of combat activity in SVN," as well as naval ship movements into the Gulf of Tonkin "for psychological purposes and to test NVN reaction."[111]

At 5:30 p.m., as the president was leaving Washington for his vacation residence on Key Biscayne, Florida, Kissinger talked by telephone to the chief of naval operations, Admiral Thomas H. Moorer, informing him that another BREAKFAST decision might be made at 9:00 p.m. that night and that the operation should be "kept on a short fuse." He also confirmed Moorer's understanding that the ships Nixon ordered to the Tonkin Gulf should sail beyond 20° N latitude and "closer to NVN territory" than the 12 nautical miles Hanoi claimed as their territory.[112] These were two or three carriers from Task Force 77, along with ships for sea-air rescue (SAR) and frigates with search radar for identifying aircraft in the area. They were to remain at their northern stations for a short period, then repeat their movements at frequent but irregular intervals.[113]

The stepped-up aerial reconnaissance flights began on 8 March. The ships reached their northern stations in international waters one day later. Such deployments would have been routine in the event that the YANKEE STATION aircraft carriers were about to launch bombing raids against the DRV. The destroyers had been removed from the Tonkin Gulf after President Johnson had canceled bombing operations against the North on 1 November 1968, after which they had operated south of and up to 20° N latitude.[114]

With US planes and ships on the move in the skies over North Vietnam and in the Tonkin Gulf but with BREAKFAST still on hold, Nixon and Kissinger reviewed their strategic options in two telephone conversations on Saturday, 8 March—between Nixon's boating and sunning excursions on Biscayne Bay. The president expressed continuing concern about the possibility that if he bombed Cambodia, the secret might leak out and cause a public uproar, especially if Rogers and the "little State boys" started "squealing." Although Kissinger assured the president he had "made the right decision . . . to defer" BREAKFAST, he expressed the view that "if the war is settled in a year, it doesn't make any difference if you get attacked now. So the really key question is, how can one bring it to a conclusion more quickly?" If the bombing became public knowledge, he added later, "we have to step up and say what we did." It was a topic they had discussed before. Nixon agreed with Kissinger's logic but continued to delay the decision: "I don't mind making a decision, but if we can bring Rogers along, it would be infinitely better."[115]

When and if launched, the two main purposes of BREAKFAST, Kissinger reiterated, were to strike at the VC/NVA infrastructure in Cambodia and "to influence the Soviets. . . . We still have a chance—six months—to get them moving in a qualitative direction." Kissinger was referring to their emerging game plan of launching damaging military operations; signaling even greater future military threats in order to move the Soviets and North Vietnamese in the direction of US negotiating terms; and thereby shoring up Saigon's morale while simultaneously building up their military and police forces—all by the second half of the year. By this time they would have announced the first unilateral US troop withdrawals and have another six months to negotiate a settlement on terms acceptable to Washington and Saigon. But the operation had to get under way soon in order to lend credibility to the warnings they had already broadcast and before formal private talks between the four parties in Paris began—talks they expected would soon be agreed upon and would possibly begin as early as Friday, 14 March.[116]

Sometime later in the night, Nixon gave the go-ahead for the bombing of Cambodian bases, only to postpone it again the next day, 9 March, because of Rogers's continuing objections and momentary concerns about the impact of bombing Cambodia upon US-Soviet relations in connection with continuing low-level East-West tensions related to the status of Berlin.[117] Deputy Secretary of Defense Packard was "very disturbed" about the cancellation, and Kissinger's state of mind was that he thought it was better to be "clobbered now" by the "establishment press" than to extend the delay—according to what he told Haldeman.[118]

Midafternoon on 15 March, Nixon ordered the "immediate implementation of the BREAKFAST plan," telling Kissinger by phone that "State is to be notified only after the point of no return. . . . The order is not appealable." Rocket attacks had resumed on 11 March and included Saigon. The initial informal private meeting between the US and DRV delegations had taken place on 8 March and produced only confusion about the prospect, timing, and form of formal private talks between the four parties. The impasse in the negotiation process deprived Rogers's reservations of practical significance; the renewed attacks angered Nixon and also provided him with a provocation for reprisal. In what was undoubtedly a disappointment to the White House, moreover, Moorer had reported to Kissinger on 11 March that there had not been "any noticeable reaction to US ship movements in the Gulf of Tonkin."[119]

After all these days of indecision, the president and his assistant were frustrated with the NSC decision-making process, in which so many contrary voices could be heard. Nixon was ready to bomb Cambodia despite caveats, and he shared the sentiment Kissinger expressed on 8 March that "our military effort leaves a great deal to be desired, but it remains one of our few bargaining weapons."[120] On 12 March, Laird had returned from his trip to South Vietnam recommending US withdrawals and still holding the same reservations about BREAKFAST he had mentioned earlier. But according to his biographer, Laird wanted "to support the Joint Chiefs in this first test of their authority" under him, and because this would mean they "owed him," Laird did not stand in the way of the operation.[121]

Yet there was to be one more discussion of the bombing. After church services on Sunday, 16 March, Nixon met with Kissinger, Rogers, Laird, and Wheeler in the Oval Office. Kissinger claimed in his memoirs that he had recommended the meeting to Nixon, arguing that "such a decision should not be taken without giving his senior advisers an opportunity to express their views—if only to protect himself if it led to a public uproar." In any case, it would take at least twenty-four hours for the bombing order to be executed. But Kissinger probably had an additional motive: to expose those who disagreed with the president, alienating Nixon from them. Kissinger had already learned enough about Nixon to know that when he arrived at a firm decision, as he now had about this matter, he nonetheless wanted to pretend that the issue was still open until his advisers voiced their opinions. Such sessions "led to hours of the very discussion that he found so distasteful," Kissinger wrote, "and that reinforced his tendency to exclude the recalcitrants from further deliberations." Kissinger's main target was Rogers, the only one of the group who persisted in objecting to the raids and who, as secretary of state, was the main threat to Kissinger's growing influence over foreign policy. Just one week before this Oval Office meeting, Kissinger had accused Rogers of "self-interest . . . so paramount that he can't adequately serve the P[resident]," and he had recommended that Rogers be fired and made chief justice of the Supreme Court. Kissinger was already seen within Nixon's inner circle as the czar of foreign policy, but his predominant influence on the president was not yet solidified.[122]

Launched on 17 March (US eastern time), the bombing of Base Area 353 in the Fish Hook region of Cambodia was accompanied, according to White House planning papers, by "maximum possible aerial reconnaissance over North Vietnam . . . , increased naval activity in international waters adjacent to North Vietnam," and air attacks on "NVN military concentrations in the DMZ . . . 12 hours prior to Breakfast Plan."[123] BREAKFAST was in part a response to Post-Tet, but President Nixon would have bombed Cambodia without it—although the enemy offensive provided him with a public justification should he need it. As Kissinger had reminded Nixon on 8 March, the decision to bomb was "quite independent . . . ; we started thinking of this well before the [VC/NVA] offensive." Even though the CIA doubted that COSVN or VC/NVA troop concentrations were in the targeted areas, Nixon's view was "that doesn't bother me too much . . . ; we'll hit something."[124]

The main purpose of bombing bases in Cambodia was to threaten North Vietnam indirectly with excessively brutal force and influence the Soviets into pressuring Hanoi into yielding on some of their demands. Kissinger explained to his White House NSC aide for East Asia, Richard L. Sneider—who doubted the cost-effective military value of bombing the bases and scoffed at the likelihood of destroying COSVN—that military usefulness was secondary to the psychological principle of "always keeping the enemy guessing," which was, of course, the uncertainty effect inherent in Nixon's Madman Theory.[125]

Kissinger's planning paper for BREAKFAST described officials' "reasons for action" as "political/psychological." The operation was mainly a "signal to the Soviets" of the administration's "determination to end the war" on terms acceptable to the White House and also "a signal that things may get out of hand."[126] Even though it was not the direct escalation against North Vietnam that had earlier worried Dobrynin, Kissinger nevertheless regarded the bombing of Cambodia as a stick accompanying the carrots of détente in their diplomacy of linkage vis-à-vis the Soviets. Their expectation was that Soviet leaders would be so concerned about the war spinning out of control, with a consequent deterioration in US-USSR relations, that they would put pressure on Hanoi to compromise at the table in Paris.

The bombing of Cambodia, Nixon and Kissinger believed, would additionally encourage Thieu's government to agree to begin private talks with the DRV and/or the NLF—talks that the RVN had opposed, instead calling for retaliatory strikes against North Vietnam in response to the VC/NVA shelling of Saigon. On the other side of the coin, Nixon and Kissinger thought that a "failure to take action" via the bombing of Cambodia in response to enemy shelling and rocket attacks "would have appeared to Hanoi as a demonstration of weakness," thus encouraging them to use additional military pressure to force concessions at the negotiating table—especially in light of Nixon's repeated public and private, direct and indirect warnings that he would retaliate.[127]

Nixon recorded in his historical memoir, *RN*, that BREAKFAST "was the first turning point in my administration's conduct of the Vietnam War."[128] Originally proposed by MACV as the logical next step in military strategy—the destruction of enemy troop concentrations, the interdiction of supply lines and bases, a deterrent against attack, a counterweight to the impending withdrawal of American troops—Nixon had, with Kissinger's assistance and encouragement, transformed the bombing of Cambodian sanctuaries into an indicator action, a retaliatory measure, and a demonstration of his determination. He had sent a threatening signal to Moscow and Hanoi, disregarded Department of State objections, and bypassed Congress and the citizenry. Yet Nixon and Kissinger were not done. They continued to search for other measures that would "jar" their adversaries into compliance.

The poker-playing Nixon considered airpower his "hole card"[129]—a decisive resource in his deck of options to win peace on terms he and Kissinger and most of his government wanted. It not only served to damage VC/NVA capabilities and benefit US/RVN ground operations but could—as he and Kissinger firmly believed—also benefit his diplomatic strategy because it served as an indicator of dramatic future escalation against North Vietnam. For the time being, however, North Vietnam was off-limits, and the air offensive would be confined to Cambodia and Laos, where Congress and the public were less likely to take notice. Nevertheless, Nixon and Kissinger were considering ways and means to threaten North Vietnam and how to link that effort to a peace settlement.

CHAPTER FOUR

The Vance Ploy and the Mining Ruse
March–April 1969

We should . . . develop alternate plans for possible escalatory military actions with the motive of convincing the Soviets that the war might get out of hand.
Henry Kissinger[1]

Target Haiphong

During and after the period of President Nixon's uncertainty about bombing Cambodia, he and Kissinger continued to evaluate attack options against North Vietnam itself. With or without BREAKFAST, they were no less determined to demonstrate resolve in the face of the Post-Tet offensive, eager to seize the strategic initiative, intent on intimidating Hanoi, and convinced of the possibility of persuading Moscow to cooperate. Even though they judged domestic and international conditions unsuitable for direct and dramatic military steps against North Vietnam in March and into April, planning went ahead for possible escalatory measures in the near future. Their preparation and review of options soon produced a threatening military scheme for a mining ruse—or feint—against Haiphong in conjunction with a diplomatic maneuver aimed at Moscow that Nixon dubbed the Vance Ploy. Grounded in the assumption that Moscow could render significant help, this was Nixon's and Kissinger's first major attempt at linkage concerning Vietnam.

Located in the Red River delta at 20°51′22″ N latitude on the coast of the Gulf of Tonkin 70 miles east of Hanoi, Haiphong was, as it is now, North Vietnam's major seaport and transshipment center, with road, rail, air, and water connections to the interior and other points along the coast. In 1968, approximately 90 percent of North Vietnam's ocean-borne imports had passed through the city—most from the Soviet Union and China. The Joint Staff described Haiphong as "by far the most important and critical war-supporting logistic installation in North Vietnam."[2]

Nixon had been a longtime advocate of targeting the North, especially Haiphong. As a presidential aspirant in 1967, he had pressed the Johnson administration not only to bomb Laos, Cambodia, and North Vietnam more heavily but also to mine and impose a naval blockade of the port of Haiphong. Nixon had additionally advocated trade reprisals against foreign shippers and the curtailment of foreign aid to allies supplying North Vietnam.[3]

The Johnson administration had investigated the pros and cons of a bombing-and-mining interdiction campaign against Haiphong and its lines of communication after the president had imposed restrictions upon Operation ROLLING THUNDER on 31 March 1968.[4] A CIA study, completed in May 1968, of the advisability of such a campaign was largely negative, citing its likely adverse impact on negotiations; potential international and domestic objections; strong defenses in the area; and North Vietnam's ability, with its allies, to compensate over a relatively short period of time for the closure of the port.[5] Nonetheless, there continued to be those within the national security bureaucracy, including the Joint Chiefs, who strongly favored mining and blockading Haiphong—as evidenced in the responses of Group A in the RAND survey Kissinger had commissioned on Nixon's behalf during the presidential transition period.[6]

After Nixon's inauguration on 20 January and into the month of March, his National Security Study Memorandum 1 (of 21 January), his directive to the JCS to develop indicator actions (on 27 January), and the White House's desire to launch retaliatory measures in response to the Post-Tet offensive (after 22 February) generated additional recommendations from the JCS for attack options against North Vietnam. All of these included proposals for mining Haiphong and other ports in North Vietnam.

In its January 1969 working paper for indicator actions, the Joint Staff explained that mining operations were particularly well suited to the purpose of jarring Hanoi's leaders: "The naval buildup for a blockade will provide the opportunity to extend military preparations over a substantial period of time, thus providing more flexibility to this approach"—that is, one with a better chance "over sufficient time to affect . . . [Hanoi's] negotiating posture" by signaling to North Vietnam's leaders "the picture of a hardening United States Government resolve."[7] Military planners also considered mining to be one of the most feasible and effective ways of rendering the enemy "incapable of continuing the war" or causing "him to recognize the inevitable destruction of his capability to continue the war." Thus, mining could additionally serve as a means of bringing about the attrition of VC/NVA forces—a goal Kissinger had identified in NSSM 1 —and as retaliation for Post-Tet or future and more significant attacks on South Vietnamese cities.[8]

But bombing still had its advocates at high levels. On 7 March, the day after Laird and Wheeler left for South Vietnam, Kissinger discussed "attack options for the application of military force against North Vietnam" with Assistant Secretary of Defense David Packard, Deputy Assistant Secretary for East Asia and Pacific Affairs Richard C. Steadman, and John McConnell, acting chairman of the JCS.[9] An air force general and strong advocate of airpower, who in Laird's view "could not conceive of fighting a war in which victory was not the goal,"[10] McConnell submitted six JCS-recommended options to Packard five days later, on 11 March, the day before Laird and Wheeler returned from South Vietnam. All six called for air attacks on selected military and logistics targets in North Vietnam: strikes in and around the DMZ, up to the nineteenth or twentieth parallel, or throughout North Vietnam.[11]

Neither Laird nor Steadman nor Kissinger favored such dramatic and public steps against North Vietnam at this time. Laird and Steadman thought air strikes against the North to be disproportionate and unnecessary retaliatory responses that also risked significant US losses. On 4 March, the day before leaving for Vietnam, Laird had recommended a naval show of force in the Tonkin Gulf and advised against attacks on the North. On 6 March, Steadman had recommended another form of gunboat diplomacy: sending the battleship *New Jersey* opposite a North Vietnamese coastal target north of the DMZ but south of 19° N latitude. Then, if Post-Tet attacks continued, the United States should respond with a "proportional" two-hour naval bombardment and also "go . . . to the Russians and tell them that . . . [we] mean business."[12] Kissinger favored BREAKFAST as a clandestine alternative to striking the North and as an appropriate and effective retaliatory and initiative-taking operation, as did Packard. Wanting to retaliate for Post-Tet but reluctant to go ahead with BREAKFAST in the face of State Department opposition, "Nixon's resentments and impatience increased," as Kissinger recalled," but he wanted to do "something."[13]

In Kissinger's late-afternoon conversation with Admiral Moorer on 7 March—the same one in which he had affirmed the president's order to move naval ships into the Gulf of Tonkin north of 20° N latitude

—Kissinger asked the admiral to "look at the situation and see what we can do with minimum loss of lives in [the] shortest period." Kissinger wondered "whether it was possible to sink a ship in the harbor." He may have raised this possibility in hopes of developing a less drastic alternative to other JCS recommendations for striking the North.

Moorer replied that planners in the past had "looked at several possibilities—even [sinking] submarines—and it turns out to be difficult because they [the cargo ships to Haiphong] lighten [their] load and then go in." But "it could be done with mines," he added. Kissinger's misgiving was that mining would have to be kept going, but Moorer thought that would be no problem if aircraft laid the mines. Kissinger asked whether there had been any opposition to these plans in Moorer's "shop." Moorer replied that he could brief him "about what could be done in this area." Kissinger affirmed that he would like to have a briefing "fairly soon."[14]

In his morning telephone conversation with Kissinger the next day, Nixon—now at Biscayne Bay and in a belligerent mood—expressed his intention to "crack the North and crack it good" if the Post-Tet attacks continued or escalated and if Moscow continued to go along with Hanoi. Kissinger deferentially reminded the president of their agreed-upon strategy of retaliating against VC/NVA attacks and influencing the Soviets with BREAKFAST—but holding out the direct threat of major or drastic escalation against the North at a later date. "My feeling is we lean over backward not to hit the North," Kissinger explained. After BREAKFAST, he said, "I would keep taking things [from the other side in a low-key manner] for a long time and then do something very drastic . . . Haiphong is the only target worth doing it to."[15] Kissinger's mention of Haiphong suggests that he and Nixon had previously discussed the targeting of the port city.

Near the end of the conversation, Nixon came around to their original strategy. "I don't want to hit the North, but I'm going to do something. . . . This is not the time to hit the North: I think we've got to threaten it by physically having a movement," which was a reference to the movement of ships into the Gulf of Tonkin. "But if we hit the North we have to hit something worthwhile"—his reference to Kissinger's remark about Haiphong. The conversation ended where it had begun, with Nixon wanting Packard to convince Rogers of the crucial place of BREAKFAST in "the specter of pressures for hitting the North."[16] Later in the night,

Nixon decided to go ahead with BREAKFAST, then retracted the order the next day (see chapter 3). But Haiphong was also on their minds—and especially on Kissinger's mind.

Contingency Plans

The declassified record of early White House communications and discussions with the Pentagon about blockading and mining Haiphong is spotty,[17] in large part because of the sensitive nature of the planning, which Nixon and Kissinger wanted to keep secret even from the various departments and agencies of the national security apparatus.[18] Available documents reveal, however, that the Joint Staff responded to White House interest by dusting off and updating several 1967–1968 plans for impeding North Vietnam's imports.[19]

On 13 March, General Wheeler sent Kissinger two plans: one to block a main channel to the harbor by sinking a submarine, the other to mine deepwater and close-in approaches to the harbor. The blocking plan required US Navy SEALs to perform a secret hydrographic survey of the Nam Trieu Channel, a major approach to the Maritime Canal, in order to determine the worth of a blocking operation. Then, a submarine could be covertly "scuttled athwart the channel," with another submarine waiting nearby to collect the crew. An aerial mine-laying operation could then funnel "all traffic into the main ship channel" while foreign governments were warned about the blockage and hazard. To prevent dredging operations from opening up a new channel, harassing air strikes would be necessary. The Joint Chiefs deemed this plan feasible.[20]

The other plan, the mining plan, was based on concepts developed when Admiral Moorer had been commander in chief of the Pacific Fleet and unsuccessfully lobbied the Johnson administration to mine the harbor.[21] It called for the laying of four minefields by twenty-two A-6 Intruder carrier aircraft in three deepwater areas and a narrow close-in passageway through the Maritime Canal. The minefields would include bottom mines, which were difficult to sweep, and Destructors, which operated at all depths, including shallow waters, and were therefore effective against the lighterage craft (sampans, junks, and other small boats) used by the North Vietnamese to off-load cargo from merchant vessels anchored offshore. According to planners, the operation would be "almost 100 percent effective against deep draft ships" and would further "indicate US resolve to pursue the war." But there were disadvantages and shortcomings to the plan. Aerial mining, for example, would "provoke a cry of unwarranted escalation by Hanoi and its allies" and also "endanger foreign shipping which might venture into the minefield." Moreover, although mining would "exact the maximum hardship on NVN and would be a determining factor in shaping Hanoi's reaction toward the war," Hanoi could adjust by using alternate harbors and lighters for off-loading merchant ships anchored outside of minefields—"unless the plan is carried out in concert with an intensive air campaign against NVN."[22]

Kissinger read the plans and asked Wheeler for additional analyses of their military and diplomatic pros and cons, for suggestions and analysis of other options to limit North Vietnam's imports, and for JCS assessments of their comparative effectiveness. On or before 19 March, he also created a task force to review contingency operations in the Haiphong area. It was headed by his aide Richard Sneider and included representatives from the Joint Staff, DOD's International Security Affairs (DOD/ISA), and CIA. They were warned of "the extremely sensitive nature of this study and . . . directed to hold the matter closely to avoid any implication within the departments that such studies are underway."[23]

This heightened interest of the White House in Haiphong mining options was fundamentally the product of Nixon's and Kissinger's staunch faith in military escalation as a crucial means by which they could advance their Vietnam strategy. The main difficulty they were facing, however, was that the multiple players—the secretary of defense, the Joint Chiefs, MACV, the State Department, CIA, and the Paris negotiating delegation —continued to offer conflicting advice about how to proceed. Some wanted dramatic and sustained escalation, and others wanted none; there were also disagreements about how to handle the negotiations in Paris.

Laird and Wheeler had returned from South Vietnam and submitted their reports to the president on 13 March. Although willing to acquiesce in BREAKFAST, Laird opposed military escalations generally and instead advocated US troop withdrawals and the strengthening of ARVN— otherwise known as Vietnamization. Wheeler recommended major military escalations across the board: preemptive ground and air raids against enemy base areas in Laos, as well as in Cambodia; naval and/or air attacks against targets in North Vietnam; and air and ground attacks in the southern DMZ. The view of Wheeler and the JCS was that escalation should be aimed at achieving concrete military objectives in preference to political, diplomatic, and psychological results. In particular, they were not optimistic about the lower-profile indicator actions the Joint Staff had assembled in mid-March after Kissinger had observed that their initial proposals risked provoking domestic and international unrest. The Joint Chiefs concluded that "it is unlikely that any one of the 'indicator' actions alone would cause a reduction of NVN combat activity in South Vietnam or produce a more forthcoming attitude at the Paris negotiations . . . even in combinations." Laird agreed with the JCS assessment. He had never been in favor of indicator actions anyway because he believed they could escalate into more dramatic military steps against North Vietnam—which he thought would turn out to be politically, diplomatically, and militarily counterproductive.[24]

Meanwhile, Daniel Ellsberg and Winston Lord had finished collating and summarizing agency responses to the questions posed in the January NSSM 1. Kissinger's staff then produced a preliminary summary for the NSC Review Group on 14 March, followed by a revised summary on 22 March, just ahead of the 26 March meeting of the NSC.[25] The document revealed "agreement on some matters" but also "substantial differences . . . within the US Government on many aspects of the Vietnam situation." The last paragraph of the revised summary, for example, noted agency agreement "that Chinese and Soviet aid has provided almost all the war material used by Hanoi" but disagreement on "whether alternative military courses of action could reduce the flow enough to make a difference in South Vietnam." MACV and the JCS believed that "if all imports by sea were denied and land routes through Laos and Cambodia attacked vigorously, . . . NVN could not obtain enough supplies to continue." The State Department and CIA, however, disagreed, arguing that overland supply could make up the difference and enable North Vietnam "to continue the war."[26]

On the diplomatic front, even though informal private talks had taken place in Paris on 8 and 22 March, the administration was unsure about what steps to take next. Nixon and Kissinger had to decide whether to push for private negotiations on a regular schedule or only when necessary. The DRV delegation, moreover, did not accept the US position that political and military discussions should be separated, which meant that Washington had to find the means to persuade them. Nixon and Kissinger were inclined to put their faith in military threats and linkage diplomacy. Moscow would have to be pushed in the direction of using its presumed clout with Hanoi to leverage the North Vietnamese Politburo into negotiating on US terms. On this matter, the White House view ran counter to that of the national security agencies, all of which agreed in their NSSM 1 responses to the question about Moscow's and Beijing's influence in Hanoi that "neither . . . had exerted heavy pressure on Hanoi and . . . are unlikely to do so." In their competition for influence on Hanoi, they "tend to cancel out each other," and "the Hanoi leadership is attempting to chart its own independent course, despite its reliance on its allies for supplies."[27]

A related matter that especially worried Kissinger was that the Soviets would have to be disabused of the notion planted by Secretary of State Rogers in his talk with Dobrynin on 8 March that US negotiators would be willing to combine political with military issues in their discussions with DRV representatives. Kissinger had complained to Nixon about Rogers later that day.[28] On 10 March, Haldeman had suggested that Kissinger try to turn Rogers's blunder to their advantage "by a maneuver designed to totally confuse the Soviets." Kissinger thought it possible.[29] What Haldeman specifically recommended, if anything, is unknown, but at this juncture, Kissinger was coming to the view that an operation against Haiphong could be the sword that would cut the Gordian knot of the military and diplomatic impasse at home and abroad. He had previously raised the possibility of a blocking operation in Haiphong Harbor with Moorer on 7 March as a viable indicator action. Kissinger now proposed joining a threat against Haiphong to a stratagem of diplomatic linkage aimed at Moscow, which would speak to Nixon's inclination toward coercive diplomacy.

The Vance Ploy

Kissinger later wrote, in *White House Years*, that during this March to April period, he had "concluded that time was working against us and that we should find some means of bringing matters to a head. I sought to involve the USSR in a complex maneuver and recommended Cyrus Vance as the ideal man for the mission."[30] Vance was a corporate lawyer who had served Presidents Kennedy and Johnson in high-level defense positions and had recently been cochairman of the US delegation in Paris. Kissinger had begun to consider the maneuver sometime before 18 March—which was the day after BREAKFAST got under way and the same day he and Nixon met with Vance to elicit his impressions of the Paris negotiations, North Vietnamese goals, and his "evaluation of the Soviet role . . . and how we might best utilize them."[31]

This new effort was to be their first attempt at establishing a secret contact with the DRV separate from the Paris negotiations. It would be, as Kissinger thought of it, a new "framework" for negotiations.[32] To arrive at a Vietnam agreement, Kissinger suggested, Vance was to be authorized to undertake a "mission . . . to Moscow," where he would begin talks on strategic arms limitation and, linking these with Vietnam, also meet secretly with a "senior North Vietnamese representative." In these latter discussions, he would be empowered to negotiate both political and military issues—a departure from the previous dual-track tactic but one that Kissinger believed Secretary of State Rogers had already compromised in statements he had made to Dobrynin on 8 March.[33] A timetable for talks would be set, backed up by military threats and stepped-up military action, which included mining Haiphong Harbor. Drawing upon the president's assumptions about SALT and the Moscow-Hanoi relationship, Kissinger constructed the proposal in a way that would appeal to Nixon. Sending Vance to Moscow on a SALT mission could garner the Soviets' cooperation because of their supposedly greater interest in reaching an arms control agreement. Moscow would become more amenable on the Vietnam issue and use its sway to assure a more compliant attitude on Hanoi's part.

The next day, 19 March, Kissinger told Vance by telephone that the scheme he was proposing had originally been his "personal idea," but he had had "a very full discussion with the president since then, and the more they kicked it around, the more attractive it looks." Vance expressed some perplexity about the plan: "How do you spend time on 'a' aspects of it without 'b' group knowing what is going on?" Vance might have meant that if he were to lead a secret SALT-Vietnam initiative in Moscow, how could it be kept secret from the US negotiators in Paris or SALT experts in Washington? There were related objections from Kissinger's associates. An unsigned memo in Haig's files characterized the Vance Ploy as "bold but extremely risky." When Saigon and other allies found out about it, there could be "serious domestic and international repercussions." Congress would be in the dark, and because "certain administration officials" were opposed to the proposed talks and terms, it "could lead to deep divisions in the government."[34] Whether Nixon learned of those concerns is unknown.

Despite these difficulties, Kissinger laid the groundwork for winning Nixon's approval for the ploy in a memorandum that was probably drafted by Morton Halperin and sent to the president on 22 March concerning "where we stand . . . on Vietnam" and "where do we go from here." In it, he summarized the diplomatic and military situation and their options and also recommended the choices that he thought should be made "for action in the next several months." He argued against de-escalation, as proposed by Laird and Rogers—a position he had taken with Nixon in the preceding days. Instead, he reiterated their original strategy of synchronizing military and diplomatic moves in order to "play our hand" in a way that increased the time they had available to reach a settlement; build up the confidence and armed forces of Saigon; pace and delay the negotiations to suit their own timetable; focus on military and not political issues in the talks (even though "we must at some point be prepared to discuss a political settlement"); and escalate militarily for the purposes "we are trying to achieve."[35]

These purposes, Kissinger emphasized, were mainly political vis-à-vis the US citizenry, the North Vietnamese, and especially the Soviets, whom Nixon and Kissinger regarded as central to progress in the negotiations. "Our escalatory moves," Kissinger wrote, "would not have primarily a military objective. Our concern would be the political effect of our actions." By that, he meant effecting changes in Soviet and North Vietnamese policy while remaining sensitive to public opinion in the United States. The "sustained resumption of the bombing of the North would not now be justified," Kissinger noted, in consideration of the likely "loss of domestic and international support of the American [i.e., the administration's] position." The bombing of Cambodia, he argued, had for the time being "conveyed the appropriate message." But in the weeks and months to come, "the only credible objective we could have in escalating would be to give the Soviets concern."[36]

The Soviets "would like the war to end," he affirmed, and "could play a major role in bringing the war to an end if they decided to put pressure on Hanoi"; but, he added, "we have not yet found the leverage to get them to act on that desire." Though some in the administration argued that a show of good faith would yield Soviet assistance, Kissinger thought otherwise, arguing that "the Soviets will put pressure on Hanoi only [when] they [have] decided that it is in their interest to do so," which was a conviction often voiced by Nixon. Indirectly referring to the linkage tactic, Kissinger declared that "we must find a way either within the Vietnam context or beyond it to change the current Soviet calculation of gains and risks." In that connection, "possible escalatory steps" were relevant. "We must worry the Soviets about the possibility that we are losing our patience and may get *out of control.* . . . We have just begun to give imaginative thought to this problem."[37]

In the concluding summary section of the memo to Nixon, Kissinger recommended that "we should begin immediately to develop alternate plans for possible escalatory military actions with the motive of convincing the Soviets that the war might get *out of hand.* (At your direction, work is underway on this question.)"[38] This was most probably a reference to the mining plans Kissinger had requested from the JCS and for which the NSC task force had been formed. At the same time, military planners were also working on additional Cambodian operations beyond the initial BREAKFAST bombings. (On 31 March, Kissinger advocated bombing the triborder area of Cambodia, Laos, and Vietnam.)[39]

With *out of control* and *out of hand,* Kissinger was using phrases that both he and Nixon had voiced in the past and would again in the future in connection with their Vietnam strategy—phrases whose meaning in this context were consistent with the Madman Theory.[40] Their aim was to alarm the Soviets, worrying them that US escalation against North Vietnam would not only expand the war but endanger North Vietnam's survival as a nation, perhaps requiring the Soviets to step up their support of the North. At a minimum, US escalation could undermine hopes for détente. At a maximum, American escalation in the form of a mining operation, for example, could cause the destruction of a Soviet ship with loss of life, creating the risk of political if not military confrontation.[41]

When Kissinger submitted a formal plan for the Vance mission to Nixon on 3 April, he recapitulated his concerns about the current state of diplomatic, military, and bureaucratic affairs. The Paris delegation was divided, and some members, he charged, were "undisciplined," often leaking statements to the press, which deprived "our policy of flexibility and coherence." The split between the State Department (which favored military de-escalation and the combining of military and political issues in the negotiations) and MACV and the JCS (which favored escalation) was "so great that it will be very hard to present a coherent approach in Paris." Public pressures to end the war, he continued, might cause negotiators to "squeeze" Saigon into making concessions, reducing the White House's minimum terms of today to the maximum ones of tomorrow. All of these problems, he argued, conflicted with the administration's desire to convince the US public that the administration was eager to settle but also persuade Hanoi that it could not "afford to outwait us"; to apply sufficient military pressures against Hanoi to achieve the settlement they sought; and for the administration "to speak with the same voice."[42] In sum, the rest of the administration was out of sync with the Vietnam strategy they had brought to the White House in January.

In the proposed discussions, Vance would also call for mutual withdrawal, offer the NLF "freedom from reprisals and the right to participate fully in the political and social life" of South Vietnam if they and the DRV agreed to forego force and violence, and insist on "mechanisms for supervision and verifying the carrying out of the agreement." In addition, South Vietnam would be "separate and independent for at least 5 years." If Vance got "an agreement in principle, the negotiations would shift back to Paris for final implementation."[43]

"Not sure the Vance Ploy will work" and believing that the US delegation in Paris was "piddling around" and that Hanoi intended "to wait us out," President Nixon thought it preferable to "hit them again" in Cambodia. Talking by telephone to Kissinger on 5 April, he argued that "it will worry them a little—that was the purpose of the other one [BREAKFAST], wasn't it?"[44] Nevertheless, Nixon approved the Vance Ploy after the two had several more discussions of the matter between 5 and 11 April. He may have been persuaded by his own belief that the Soviets were very interested in SALT negotiations; that they had considerable influence over Hanoi; and that, according to Kissinger's claim regarding recent talks with Dobrynin, the ambassador "seemed very insecure when speaking about Vietnam," which implied that "maybe the Vance mission is our best hope." In making the proposal to the Soviets, Kissinger was to explain it to Dobrynin and link US cooperation on strategic arms control to their help in reaching an acceptable settlement of the Vietnam problem —"the key to everything."[45]

Kissinger recommended that the effort to bring about talks in Moscow be given six weeks to succeed. He optimistically predicted that if Moscow and Hanoi agreed to these negotiations, "the whole process should be completed before the end of August." But recapping what he and the president had previously discussed, he reminded Nixon that he should "be prepared to take tough escalatory steps if Moscow rejects the overture (*mining Haiphong, bombing Cambodia, etc.*)"—adding that "to fail to do so would be to risk your credibility." The threat of reprisal was implicit in the six-week deadline—and also in the many hints Nixon and Kissinger had previously dropped and would continue to drop in conversations with Dobrynin and other Soviet officials between 17 February and 14 April. Nixon believed, however, that a two-month deadline was more realistic. When Kissinger had discussed the Moscow mission with Vance, he had omitted telling him that the administration would force a military show-down with Hanoi if the diplomatic gambit failed.[46]

A Mining Ruse

During the late March period in which Kissinger's Vance plan took shape, the Joint Chiefs had been working on Kissinger's request for additional options to limit North Vietnam's imports and for a more thorough analysis of these and previous plans. On 28 March, Laird forwarded their partially repackaged compendium of Haiphong contingency plans to Kissinger's NSC task force on Haiphong alternatives, which was now called the "NSC ad hoc committee." According to Laird's aide, Colonel Pursley, "the papers are responsive to the questions posed—remarkably so."[47]

Hanoi's capability for adjusting its import delivery system led the Joint Chiefs to conclude that mining by itself would not bring enough hardships to the economy. Thus, JCS chairman Wheeler recommended a "large scale sustained air campaign" that would include lighterage, alternate ports, and "all military targets in the area."[48] In addition to providing more details on the earlier plans for mining Haiphong and the submarine scuttling operation, the compendium included a plan for a blockade of North Vietnam designed to "effectively halt all seaborne imports to NVN." The blockade would encompass the DRV's entire coastline, with twelve destroyers available to enforce it (even to the point of attacking vessels attempting to run the blockade), two aircraft carriers providing air support, and twelve patrol aircraft available for spotting ships.[49]

The compendium also included the JCS's analysis of the plans and their advantages and disadvantages, including political and legal considerations. All three plans were "feasible low-risk courses"—although the blockade had a "latent potential of provoking a direct confrontation [with] a third-country ship." The Joint Chiefs did not expect Beijing or Moscow to confront Washington over a blockade or mining, since the Soviets were unlikely to "martyr premeditatedly" one of their ships. It was possible, however, that any of the options could lead Hanoi to suspend the Paris talks, if not break them off altogether. Yet carrying out the plans would indicate US resolve, which "could cause [the DRV] to strive for a settlement."[50]

A key international legal requirement for mining operations was to provide sufficient warning to "neutral shipping before mines are armed" and to confine minefields to DRV territorial waters. The Joint Chiefs judged the blockade plan consistent with this requirement. Even though Hanoi and Washington were engaged in an undeclared war, the JCS pointed out that US actions to defend South Vietnam were lawful under Article 51 of the UN Charter, which "authorized hostilities in collective self-defense."[51]

For the Joint Chiefs, the main problem with all three plans was that Hanoi could accommodate to them by using road and railway routes to China, from which it could "import all essential military and economic materials." Even if the mines prevented deep-draft ships from entering the harbor, moreover, Hanoi had sufficient numbers of lighters to off-load their average monthly cargo of 165,000 metric tons. For these reasons, the Joint Chief's "preferred course of action" for substantially reducing DRV imports was aerial mining "in concert with naval bombardment and an intense air campaign" targeting rail lines, rolling stock, the road network, lightering operations, and alternate port facilities.[52]

The Joint Chiefs were not the only ones recommending bombing. In late March, Kissinger sought the advice of General Maxwell Taylor, the former chairman of the JCS under President Kennedy and ambassador to Saigon under President Johnson, who was soon to end his terms as chair of the President's Foreign Intelligence Advisory Board and president of the federally funded, nonprofit Institute for Defense Analyses. Kissinger asked Taylor what he thought should be done to minimize the danger of protracted war stemming from the ongoing controversy in Paris over mutual troop withdrawals, which could "exhaust our patience and lead us to a unilateral withdrawal of American forces—and perhaps to other ill-advised actions." Taylor saw nothing but stalling ahead in Paris because, he said, DRV leaders were accurately "convinced that time *is* on their side,> . . . [but] time is a commodity which is running out for our side."

Taylor viewed "our bombing weapon [as] the only instrument available to us which . . . offers the hope in the short run of getting things moving in Paris in a direction favorable to us." He recommended that the threat to resume bombing "if substantive negotiations do not begin" should be used explicitly in the negotiations and more subtly in public discussion.[53]

Nixon's and Kissinger's specific reactions to Taylor's proposal or to the JCS arguments for an intense bombing-and-mining campaign have not yet surfaced, but they were no doubt influenced by their continuing concern about the strong likelihood of public, congressional, and international protests against such an escalation and expansion of the war. Moreover, if it was indeed the case that current planning for mining Haiphong was related to their Vance Ploy—which is highly likely—what Nixon wanted when Kissinger presented the two-month deadline to the Soviets was only "a little war of nerves"; namely, an operation that signaled their intention to lay mines when and if the deadline expired.[54]

For a fresh approach to the Haiphong problem—the "imaginative thought" he had mentioned to Nixon on 20 March—Kissinger once again turned to the navy: Admiral Moorer and Captain Rembrandt C. Robinson, then the admiral's man in the White House who served on both the JCS Chairman's Staff Group and the JCS liaison staff to the National Security Council. Robinson would quickly become one of Kissinger's idea men for Vietnam military operations and contingency plans.[55]

Moorer's first proposal came on 8 April, delivered to Kissinger through the NSC ad hoc committee. He suggested a "subterfuge plan" to deceive Hanoi into believing that the United States had laid a live minefield near the approaches to Haiphong Harbor. The mines would be inert, but there would be enough to "represent a credible attrition minefield" and give the appearance of a real threat to ships entering and leaving the harbor.[56] A few days later, on 11 April, Kissinger told Laird by telephone that Moorer's proposal "wasn't exactly what the President had in mind,"[57] perhaps because actual mine laying was too close to an actual attack or perhaps because the deception would have been discovered sooner or later, which would have put the White House in a diplomatic and political bind.

By 11 April, Robinson had come up with a more elaborate ruse: a "mining feint of Haiphong Harbor" that would become known as the "mining readiness test." Following Nixon's and Kissinger's wishes, Robinson sent the new plan from his office at the JCS directly to Laird and Kissinger, bypassing the vetting process of "the whole [NSC] machinery." Robinson's four-part scheme laid out a series of naval actions that "separately or collectively [would] create the impression that the US is making plans for or giving consideration to the mining of Haiphong." Although these military actions would have a "cover story," they were designed to "come to the attention of the Hanoi government through the communist intelligence and espionage system." The actions would be "relatively low key" and mostly deniable, but at the same time, they would be credible enough that their cumulative effect would supposedly "create indecision within the [DRV] with regard to intended US military action." Although Robinson's proposal focused specifically on Hanoi's potential reactions, it is likely that Kissinger wanted the operation to influence Moscow, especially in light of imminent discussions with Dobrynin about the Vance Ploy.[58]

The plan that Rembrandt Robinson devised was entirely in the spirit of the administration's notion of indicator actions. To trick Hanoi into believing that the United States was going to mine Haiphong Harbor, he proposed a series of steps to "provide an increasing order of activity." The naval signals would begin with small moves, such as taking inventory of mines, putting 150 mines at the Subic Bay Naval Base in the Philippines on a high state of readiness, and then airlifting them to Subic and to attack carriers. The navy would transition toward measures with an increased threat potential, shifting from conducting mine-planting exercises in Subic Bay to loading mines on an ammunition ship in the bay that would sail to the Tonkin Gulf. Various unscheduled activities in part four included more severe threat measures, such as dropping "empty mine drogue parachutes in areas of ostensible minefield approaches to Haiphong" and positioning a squadron of destroyers off Haiphong to "simulate threat of blockade."[59]

The assumption that "the communist intelligence and espionage system" would become aware of the US Navy's actions in the western Pacific was an important one. Officials in the Pentagon and the White House staff took it for granted that Soviet or Chinese intelligence was closely watching US military activity, as were harbor workers, and that the information gathered would ultimately reach Hanoi. The assumption must have been that stevedores at Subic Bay would take notice of the loading of mines and would talk to others about what they had seen.

US bases in Japan would also play a role in the exercise. Yokosuka Naval Base, a major US installation in Japan, employed thousands of Japanese workers, and Yokosuka itself was a busy commercial harbor. Base workers belonged to the Zenchuro, the Japan Garrison Forces Labor Union (GBFLU), and longshoremen belonged to the Zen-nihon-kaiin-kumiai, the Japan Seamen's Union (JSU). Both organizations were in the orbit of the Japanese Socialist Party, which was then highly militant, critical of US policy, and close to the Soviet Union. Another member of the JCS liaison staff to Kissinger's NSC, Colonel William Lemnitzer, characterized the Japanese harbor workers as "communist." The assumption of the plan was that worker observations of US military operations would find their way to Soviet intelligence operatives and eventually to Moscow.[60]

Commenting on the proposed mining ruse, General Wheeler observed that it was feasible and "nothing [was] wrong with it militarily," but he thought the bombing of Cambodia was "more meaningful." Secretary of Defense Laird, however, expressed serious reservations, telling Kissinger in an 11 April telephone conversation that he "didn't see where the plan leads." He immediately followed up that remark with the words, "unless you are willing to go all the way." Because a mining ruse alone lacked credibility, Laird may have suspected that it was preparatory to an actual mining operation—the sort of attack on the North that he had previously advised against. The ellipses in the transcript of the conversation suggest that Kissinger interrupted Laird in midsentence in order to deliver a denial: "We are not going anywhere beyond the point mentioned. The whole thing should be very closely held. The point is to underline something to indicate we are thinking of certain things, and it will not go any farther than this. This is it!" Kissinger underlined his point by mentioning that Nixon "was anxious to get something started on this." Laird was doubly suspicious and bothered because Kissinger had bypassed his office in dealing directly with Admiral Moorer, even though Kissinger had assured him that he "wasn't working directly with the Navy on this."[61]

Kissinger had protested too much. It was on this very day that he met again with Nixon to discuss the Vance Ploy, which the president approved. The scheme was to be backed up by the mining of Haiphong should the diplomatic mission be rejected by the Soviets or North Vietnamese or should the mission fail in Moscow if carried out. With or without the Vance Ploy, moreover, Nixon and Kissinger intended to do something "drastic" against the North sometime in the future if the other side did not cooperate, and they believed that Haiphong was "the only target worth doing it to."[62]

Persuaded that the president wanted it carried out and despite his own reservations, Laird authorized the Haiphong mining ruse after he met Kissinger the next day to discuss the plan in more detail. Moorer immediately began issuing orders to the commanders in chief of the Pacific and Seventh Fleets to begin the first steps of the mining readiness test: placing 150 mines at Subic Bay on "Configuration Charlie," higher operational readiness. The whole operation appears to have been closely held within a small circle who knew what the objectives were: Nixon, Kissinger, Haig, Laird, Moorer, Wheeler, and a few aides (Pursley, Robinson, and Lemnitzer). Likely, none of the navy's commanders in the Pacific had the big picture.[63]

Channeling the Threat

Nixon's chief of staff, Haldeman, referred to these developments in a brief diary entry of Monday, 14 April: Kissinger, he noted, was "about to launch another project," which had "started last Friday [11 April]" when the president decided to proceed with a "program of *mining Haiphong* to look tough." In his meeting that evening with Dobrynin, Kissinger would tell the ambassador that Washington would make one more try to reach a settlement, and failing that, "[we will] have to move." Nixon was "putting a two-month deadline on results." According to Haldeman, Kissinger was very impressed with Nixon's "guts in making this hard decision." Indeed, Kissinger was "so pleased with this plan, like the earlier one [BREAKFAST], that he can't resist telling someone outside his shop, so he goes over it with me."[64]

With the mining ruse in motion, Kissinger met with Dobrynin the evening of 14 April to explain the Vance initiative. Deploying one of his favorite tactics to underline the military threat he was also about to deliver, he showed Dobrynin a copy of his talking points, which Nixon had signed. The president had also written marginal notes extending the military escalation deadline from six weeks to two months and adding the carrot of US trade-restriction relaxation with the Soviet Union to the list of Vance's bargaining points.[65]

Another carrot was to propose a postwar South Vietnam in which the NLF could operate as a "normal political party" and become part of the government via elections. If that led to the end of the current Saigon government in the future, Kissinger said that Washington would not object. "We are not committing ourselves to preserve the present Saigon administration forever," but a negotiated agreement should stipulate that South

Vietnam would be "a separate and independent [entity] for at least five years." If Hanoi accepted the possibility of this negotiated and formalized decent-chance-with-a-stopgap-decent-interval solution (terms he did not use on this occasion), it could avoid the prospect of US escalation. The White House, Kissinger claimed, felt "growing pressure" to use "more forceful measures," but that could be avoided only if Hanoi agreed with Washington to withdraw forces from South Vietnam. What the Soviets should understand, he informed Dobrynin, was that the United States would not support a settlement that could be seen as surrender, which threatened a loss of prestige. Kissinger argued that Americans were growing more impatient with the prospect of a long, drawn-out war and wanted to end the conflict as quickly as possible, even if it meant using even greater military force. He warned that if the Vietnam War was not settled, the administration was prepared "to take measures which might create a complicated situation."[66]

Apparently inferring that Kissinger was talking about an operation directed against Haiphong, Dobrynin "then asked whether these new measures might involve Soviet ships," to which Kissinger evasively responded that "many measures were under intensive study" and that the president "never threatened idly." On the one hand, the guarantee of five years of independence for South Vietnam, combined with the withdrawal of the NVA, gave South Vietnam a decent chance at permanent independence; on the other hand, there was still a chance of a Northern invasion or internal revolution after five years, but by that time, a decent interval would have passed. To Hanoi, this looked like a plan for a Korea-like solution.[67]

Dobrynin took note of Kissinger's references to linkage, repeated the Soviet rejection of the principle, and argued that this American policy could only serve Chinese interests in Indochina. He expressed a desire to continue talks with Washington on strategic arms control and the Middle East and agreed to pass on Kissinger's Vietnam proposal to Moscow, but he criticized Saigon's intransigence at the negotiating table, as well as US tactics in the negotiations in support of Saigon's stance, and he warned of "the possible serious consequences if the US should attempt to escalate the war in Vietnam."[68]

The EC-121 Shootdown and Operation LUNCH
The same 14 April night that Kissinger met with Dobrynin, North Korean MiG interceptors shot down a US Navy Lockheed EC-121

electronic-surveillance plane with a thirty-one-man crew aboard at 11:50 p.m. (Washington time). There were no survivors. The plane had been flying a "routine" mission over the Sea of Japan off the coast of North Korea, outside its territorial waters. Nixon's immediate "feeling" was that "they're testing us," and his "instincts" told him that "we need to show [a] strong reaction." Whether from sincerity or a desire to impress the president with his own toughness, Kissinger concurred: "To let this one go . . . will be taken very seriously." Nixon and Kissinger, as well as Laird, Haldeman, and others, thought of the shootdown as the administration's first major international crisis.[69]

Nixon and Kissinger believed that a failure to respond forcefully would signal US weakness to Communist and non-Communist opponents, great and small alike.[70] As information dribbled in on Tuesday and over the following days, Secretaries Laird and Rogers argued that this was an isolated incident and urged restraint. Having seen sensitive intelligence, Laird informed Nixon "that the decision to shoot down the EC-121 was probably made by a jittery pilot who had not sought approval up the chain of command."[71] CIA tea-leaf readers speculated that the shootdown was Prime Minister Kim Il-sung's gruesome birthday present to himself at a time when US military resources in Asia were concentrated in Indochina.[72] The US ambassador to Seoul, South Korea, William Porter, warned that too strong a response might play into the hands of North Korean extremists who wanted to provoke a crisis on the Korean Peninsula.[73]

Nixon ordered three aircraft carriers to redeploy from Vietnamese to Korean waters while reprisal options were developed and discussed. In the absence of contingency plans for the shootdown, the JCS hastily prepared, by 9:55 a.m. Tuesday, a "rough-cut" concept paper of possible air attack missions against North Korean air bases by carrier-based aircraft, land-based tactical fighter-bombers, or B-52s.[74] Other proposals from aides and agencies included an air and naval show of force outside North Korean waters; a naval bombardment of the North Korean coast; the resumption of EC-121 reconnaissance flights with combat escort; high-speed, high-altitude reconnaissance flights over North Korean territory; ground incursions across the DMZ; and diplomatic protests.[75]

Kissinger advocated a carrier-based retaliatory air strike against the departure airfield of the attacking MiGs. During the day and into the evening, Nixon floated other "symbolic" reprisal options: seize a North Korean ship on the high seas; attack a North Korean vessel with submarine-fired torpedoes; impose a naval blockade of Wonsan Harbor; or launch a new B-52 bombing operation in Cambodia and "get caught" doing it, thereby publicly signaling a tough, although indirect, response. Code-named LUNCH, the prospective B-52 operation would strike VC/NVA Base Area 609 at the triborder corner of Cambodia, Laos, and Vietnam. It had originally been planned as a follow-up to BREAKFAST in the event the Soviets rejected the Vance Ploy.[76] Nixon and Kissinger now assumed that Communist leaders in Moscow, Beijing, Hanoi, and Pyongyang would also interpret such a blow against Communist troops in Cambodia as a reciprocal response to the shootdown of an American surveillance plane off the coast of North Korea.

Between Tuesday and Thursday, Nixon and Kissinger whittled the choices down to four: (1) bomb one or more airfields; (2a) resume EC-121 surveillance flights with fighter escorts; (2b) carry out the escorted surveillance flights but couple them with operation LUNCH; or (3) "do nothing but protest." "Option 1," an attack on North Korean airfields, their preferred choice, would be risky, but as Haldeman characterized White House thinking, it would back up the warnings Kissinger had given to Dobrynin on Monday night and be "potentially very productive toward ending the Vietnam War."[77] Intelligence analysts pointed out, however, that the risks were adverse public and international reactions and, more seriously, North Korean counterblows by air or on the ground across the Korean DMZ, which could draw the United States into another Asian war, while draining military resources from Indochina. Although supportive of Option 1, Laird and Haig called attention to the seriousness of the risks. Rogers and the State Department favored diplomatic measures.[78]

Kissinger, too, was concerned about the risks but nonetheless argued that the administration was being tested and that a tough move would serve the purposes of the Madman Theory, particularly with regard to Vietnam: "If we strike back . . . they will say: 'This guy is becoming irrational—and we'd better settle with him.' But if we back down, they'll say, 'this guy is the same as his predecessor, and if we wait he'll come to the same end.'"[79] By Wednesday, 16 April, Kissinger believed Nixon's choice would be to bomb the North Korean airfield on Monday, 21 April. When he consulted with Haldeman and John D. Ehrlichman (the president's domestic affairs assistant) on that day about possible domestic reactions to an air strike against the MiG base, Ehrlichman asked, according to Haldeman's account, "What if they knock out something of ours?"

"Then it could escalate," Kissinger replied.

"How far?"

"Well, it could go *nuclear.*"

This over-the-top assertion confirmed Ehrlichman's suspicions about Kissinger's Strangelovian inclinations. At the same time, the risk-taking approach followed the Joint Staff logic that a nuclear response was unavoidable if North Korean conventional forces swept across the DMZ, overwhelming US and South Korean forces.[80]

By the evening of Thursday, 17 April, however, the president was wavering. Nixon agreed with Kissinger's argument that "a really strong overt act on the part of [the] P[resident] is essential to galvanize [the] people into overcoming slothfulness and detachment arising from general moral decay" and that Option 1 would serve that purpose. Nevertheless, he was concerned that his other advisers were either opposed to or unenthusiastic about the air strike and that prominent domestic opponents such as Senator Edward Kennedy (D-MA), as well as the antiwar movement, would be strongly against him. Also concerned about adverse Soviet responses to Option 1, Nixon consoled himself that the Russians would "have their hands full for a few weeks" in Czechoslovakia putting down popular riots against the additional steps hardliners there had just taken against the remaining reforms of the Prague Spring of 1968.[81]

Kissinger answered these concerns with tough talk about the need to bite the bullet. If the president chose Option 1, the White House would have to be prepared "to go very very far in case it leads to ground action." Nixon would face criticism that he was preparing the way for another ground war in Asia, and he would have to say that he would not tolerate one. To avoid that, it might be necessary to use "*tactical nuclears*" [*sic*] in order to "clean it up." Then, "all hell would break loose for two months"— a reference to a massive domestic and international uproar over the first use of nuclear weapons since 1945. But the outcome would be good, Kissinger predicted: in the end, "there will be peace in Asia."[82]

The president returned to his earlier theme of US domestic perceptions of his actions, complaining that Option 2(a)—the resumption of EC-121 surveillance flights with fighter escorts, *without* coupling these with LUNCH—did not address the issue of public confidence in his toughness. But Kissinger undermined the forceful alternative, Option 2(b), arguing that he had come "to feel that Option 2[a] with LUNCH (2[b]) is not feasible" because the other side would have no incentive to make the Cambodian bombing public. Remaining secret from the public, LUNCH would do nothing to improve Nixon's public image as a strong president. (This assessment, however, overlooked the possibility of the White House itself making LUNCH public if the public's confidence in his toughness was the real issue.)[83]

Nixon accepted Kissinger's logic, replying, "That leaves Option 2 without LUNCH"—a response to the shootdown that he thought was "a piddily [sic] thing." Kissinger now offered another choice: "Yes, and then do that [LUNCH] two weeks after"—with the purpose of impressing the Soviets. But perhaps Kissinger's focus had been on impressing the Soviets all along, and perhaps he had been trying to steer Nixon in this direction by talking tough but warning Nixon of dire consequences from Option 1. He then added that with Option 2, "[you] will not lose much, if anything" and "will not be significantly worse off" vis-à-vis the enemy, especially the Soviets. Nixon agreed that "with Option 1 the gains are great and the risks very great," but "with Option 2 there are no gains and no risk except down the road. . . . Every time [the] US fails to react, it encourages some pipsqueak to do something." Kissinger agreed.[84]

Sometime the next day, Friday, 18 April, Nixon decided to go with the resumption of surveillance flights, Option 2(a), as soon as possible, followed *later* by LUNCH, Option 2(b), which would be preceded by two additional BREAKFAST raids, Bravo and Coco.[85] Considering the relatively mild public and congressional reactions to the incident, he had inferred that neither expected "hard retaliation" and the consequent "risk of a second war, which [the] public wouldn't buy." No longer feeling comfortable in advocating Option 1—or no longer feeling it necessary to pose as the tough guy toward North Korea—Kissinger announced that he had changed his mind, telling Nixon that although he was "determined to make a big positive move," he was "*not* convinced this is the best time and place for *us*."[86]

On 22 April, Nixon approved the JCS plans. Time over target (TOT) in the Fish Hook region was the morning of 24 April for BREAKFAST Bravo and the evening for BREAKFAST Coco. TOT for LUNCH in the triborder region was the morning of the following day. The White House's official but secret rationale for the plan was that it was a "strong military blow," manifesting White House "resolve to end [the] conflict." It signaled that the EC-121 shootdown did not divert US attention from the Vietnam War; it was an effective follow-up to Kissinger's recent talk with Dobrynin; and it could complement the president's overall plan.[87]

In his memoir, *RN*, Nixon explained his relatively tepid response to North Korea as the product of limited options, domestic political factors, and divided counsel. Privately, he accused Ehrlichman in particular of having "sold out to the doves too."[88] Kissinger made essentially the same argument in *White House Years* but was also critical of Nixon's supposed indecisiveness, the Pentagon's obstructionism, and the unwieldiness of the NSC advisory structure.[89]

The response of Nixon and Kissinger to the shootdown exposed a pattern of behavior in which they would bluster during crises to one another and to Dobrynin, threatening to use excessive force, but then in practice vacillate or back down out of concern for possible adverse reactions from the American and international publics, Cold War allies, the North Vietnamese, the Soviets, or in this case North Korea. The EC-121 decision-making process led Nixon to withdraw even more into himself and nurse an inclination to make future decisions within the smallest possible White House circle. Taking advantage of the president's mood, Kissinger, with Nixon's approval, strengthened his control over the advisory process by forming a new committee called the Washington Special Action Group (WSAG), consisting of the second-ranking officers from the other national security agencies, which he would chair.

On 26 April, Nixon issued NSSM 53, calling for the preparation of "a full range of military contingency plans . . . in the event of future provocations by North Korea." WSAG reviewed the several plans prepared by the JCS at the end of June. These included a nuclear-bombing plan code-named FREEDOM DROP, which incorporated three options, each with differing military targets, delivery vehicles, and explosive kiloton yield.[90]

"If in Doubt, Bomb Cambodia"—and Laos and South Vietnam

The North Korean crisis proved to be a temporary distraction from the war in Indochina. The administration's military response to the EC-121 shootdown had been indirect, taking the form of reprisals in Indochina for the purpose of signaling continuing US determination to Moscow and Hanoi. In recompense for their inaction against North Korea in April, Cambodia had again become the target of Nixon's and Kissinger's displaced fury. As Kissinger phrased it a month later at a time when Hanoi and Moscow had apparently frustrated the administration's diplomatic strategy, "If in doubt, we bomb Cambodia."[91] Bombing Cambodia was not only conveniently kept secret from the American public but was also consistent with the Nixon-Kissinger strategy of signaling threats to Hanoi and Moscow, substituting airpower for boots on the ground in Indochina, and damaging enemy logistics bases. It was habit forming. BREAKFAST and LUNCH, which had begun in March and April 1969, were succeeded by SNACK (Base Area 351), DINNER (352), SUPPER (740), and DESSERT (350)—becoming collectively known as operation MENU, which ended in May 1970. But the bombing of Cambodia continued to August 1973, now going deeper into the interior. Official figures reported to Congress at the end of the war put total tonnage delivered by US fighter-bombers between March 1969 and March 1973 at 155,247 and by B-52s at 383,851, with 31 additional tons dropped by fighter-bombers during the Johnson administration in 1968.[92]

Laos was another target of opportunity. B-52s and fighter-bombers that were no longer permitted to strike North Vietnam after President Johnson's 31 October 1968 bombing halt were diverted to neighboring Laos, where they augmented preexisting air campaigns against villages and Communist military units in the Plain of Jars and against the complex of logistics highways and jungle paths known as the Ho Chi Minh Trail. During 1969, the number of combat sorties in Laos increased by 60 percent over the previous year. Between 20 January 1969 and 1 May 1970, tactical aircraft dropped 476,571 tons of bombs on Laos; B-52s dropped 244,586. American planes also pounded South Vietnam even more heavily than in the past. B-52 sorties increased threefold over the rate in 1967, from 1,000 to 3,000. Compared to the period 1965 through 1968, the total expenditure of munitions deployed by airpower across all of Indochina from the beginning of 1969 through 1972 increased dramatically, from 3,190,458 to 4,213,073 tons, even though the number of combat sorties declined, from 1,765,000 to 1,687,000. A sharp rise in B-52 sorties accounted for the rise in tonnage dropped: from 36,809 in Johnson's final term as president to 75,539 in Nixon's first term.[93]

In the spring of 1969, however, the target Nixon and Kissinger most wanted to attack was North Vietnam—especially Hanoi and Haiphong, to which their attention returned in late April as LUNCH got under way and Kissinger awaited news from the Soviets concerning his Vance Ploy.

CHAPTER FIVE

The Mining Ruse, Threat Diplomacy, Peace Plans, and Withdrawals
April–July 1969

> We might try a little war of nerves.
> *Richard Nixon*[1]

H. R. Haldeman noted in a 15 April diary entry that on first hearing of the EC-121 shootdown, Kissinger "worried that this louses up our mining operation temporarily, because it will look like [a] reaction to this."[2] But preparations for the mining readiness test against Haiphong, the initial military stage of the Vance Ploy, went forward despite the North Korean crisis. The minor delays and problems encountered were the product of the usual frictions of war and divisions within the administration. Each preparatory step followed the scenario, if not the exact schedule, that Captain Robinson had previously drafted for the White House. But as signaling ploys, the Vance initiative and the mining readiness test would come up empty. The failure of Nixon's first attempt at linkage induced Kissinger to deliver more threats to Moscow and Hanoi, although he honeyed them with decent-interval language. Moreover, domestic political pressures and the adept maneuvering of Secretary of State Rogers and Secretary of Defense Laird caused Nixon to announce troop withdrawals from South Vietnam while also stepping up his diplomatic strategy of simultaneously talking tough and talking peace.

The Mining Ruse Begins

On 12 April, two days before the EC-121 crisis broke, Admiral Moorer took the first step in Robinson's scenario by ordering a survey of the Seventh Fleet's supply of sea mines. The CNO's message was unclassified, but to "raise interest in the field," he informed the Pacific Fleet the next day that the message's classification was secret. On 14 April, the CNO, at the White House's behest, asked for more information, in addition to the inventory: estimates of the time needed to "ready all mines with everything" short of readiness for actual combat use (such as arming devices and flight gear), "verification of MK-36 destructors on components" already deployed on aircraft carriers, and appraisals of the "mining proficiency of deployed carriers."[3]

On 15 April, the navy's Service Force Command began to meet these requests with an inventory of mines held at bases and facilities in Guam; Subic Bay; the Philippines; and Atsugi, Japan. Most were air-dropped bottom mines operable at depths of 18 to 600 feet, including the 500-pound MK-50, 1,000-pound MK-52, and 2,000-pound MK-55.[4] The MK-50 was an acoustic mine; the MK-52 and MK-55 came in acoustic, magnetic, and pressure varieties. At Subic and Atsugi and on ships and aircraft carriers at Yankee Station in the Tonkin Gulf, the NSFC also identified thousands of the recently developed 1,000-pound MK-36 and MK-42 Destructor mines, which were effective at all depths, including shallow waters. Following Robinson's scenario, Moorer also ordered the assembly of 150 MK-50 and MK-52 mines at the US Naval Magazine at Subic Bay in "configuration Charlie." That was naval code for a higher state of combat readiness but still short of readiness for combat use.[5]

These instructions went out around the same time that a North Korean fighter jet shot down the US EC-121. On 15 April, Robinson asked Kissinger if he wanted to make any changes in the mine readiness test. According to Robinson, Kissinger "still has strong hopes that the mining exercise will transmit a signal to Hanoi," and he wanted to go ahead. The next step would be instructions to the Pacific Fleet's commander "to prepare to move the mines" to aircraft carriers. Robinson was not so sure that Hanoi would get the message in the short term because "increased mining activity in Japan and Okinawa will read out as intended actions against North Korea—particularly with the carrier task force moving north." Nevertheless, Communist perceptions could change "when mines actually go south to the Philippines," as the carriers would stay in the Tonkin Gulf.[6]

The navy sent instructions for preparations to move the mines around 15 April. A week later, on 21 April, Kissinger requested that the navy airlift to Subic Bay 150 "prereadied" MK-52 mines from Naha (Okinawa), Iwakuni (Japan), and Yokosuka (Japan) Naval Bases to Subic Bay. The airlift by C-130s began rapidly the next day and was completed by

26 April. No doubt Robinson believed that Communist agents would detect the loading of the mines on the massive C-130s and then the off-loading in the Philippines. So that the CIA could catch "any indication of communist knowledge" of the "increased mine posture," Kissinger had told the director of Central Intelligence (DCI), Richard Helms, about the operation.[7]

The next move envisaged by Robinson was delivering mines and specially trained personnel to attack carriers in the Gulf of Tonkin. But before orders went out and the mine airlift got going, Kissinger met with Dobrynin at his White House office on the evening of 24 April for the purpose of delivering military threats. According to Dobrynin's report to Moscow—the only known record of the meeting—Kissinger opened their discussion by informing the ambassador that the US fleet then concentrated in waters off North Korea would "for the most part" be withdrawn in a few days, partly in response to Soviet calls for US "prudence and restraint." But he warned that a repetition of the North Korean attacks on US armed forces would be "met with immediate US retaliatory measures, with no additional warnings or negotiations." Turning to the war in Vietnam, Kissinger asked Dobrynin whether he had received any response from Moscow concerning their 14 April conversation about the Vance mission. Dobrynin answered that he had not but added that "if one is received, I will then get in touch with . . . [you] directly."

According to Dobrynin, Kissinger then "launched into a vague discourse" to the effect that "the administration cannot wait forever until Hanoi becomes convinced that US public opinion does not want to, and cannot force, the president, to undertake a full and unconditional withdrawal of US troops . . . without any reciprocity from the DRV." Criticizing North Vietnam's "delaying tactics" and "active military operations," Kissinger declared that Washington wanted to negotiate but was "'prepared simultaneously to accept the enemy's challenge in the military arena as well.'" If North Korea's actions had in any way emboldened Hanoi, Kissinger warned, that would be a mistake on their part because Washington "'will not sit around twiddling its thumbs'" while Hanoi and NLF troops attacked US forces. Repeating arguments he had made on other occasions, Dobrynin cautioned Kissinger that "US efforts to achieve a military solution to the Vietnam problem were futile and involved the risk of seriously complicating the entire international situation should Washington pursue such a course." In response to a question from Dobrynin about whether the United States was planning "any major operations against North Vietnam," Kissinger said that Washington was "not planning 'qualitatively new actions'" in the near term, but it could take a "'harder line'" depending on the circumstances. Dobrynin reported to Moscow that the references to a harder line could be seen as a "veiled hint directed at us."[8] Although not "qualitatively new actions," US B-52s were then bombing Cambodia and the White House was moving forward with additional measures in the mining-ruse scenario.

By the end of April, with the air delivery of the mines to Subic Bay completed, Robinson reported to Haig and Kissinger that the operation "was one week behind the original scenario." Some slippage had occurred because carriers assigned to Task Force 171, such as the *Ticonderoga*, had to return from Korean waters before they could participate in the mining readiness test. Robinson suggested two more actions to be taken in the short run: delivering mines to carriers and beginning "pilot, aircrew, and mine personnel training." Noting that these steps would require more time and expense, Robinson proposed that mine training exercises begin on 30 April. Mine delivery would commence on 2 May with the *Ticonderoga* at Subic, and thirty mines would be airlifted to each carrier at Yankee Station on 4 May. Kissinger signed off on Robinson's proposals, except directing that the training exercises begin three days later, on 3 May.[9]

Why Kissinger wanted to postpone crew training exercises by a few days is unknown. The White House may have wanted to separate and extend the timing of the several indirect and direct threats the administration was then signaling, thus giving the Soviets and North Vietnamese an opportunity to recognize and assimilate each. Robinson's recommended date for the commencement of crew training, for example, would have soon followed BREAKFAST Bravo/Coco and LUNCH, which had begun on 24 and 25 April (Vietnam time).

Following Robinson's scenario and with Kissinger's approval, Admiral Moorer ordered the loading of thirty mines along with the deployment of "mobile mine assembly teams" on the *Ticonderoga* at Subic Bay. The mines were to be brought to "increased condition of readiness." Moorer also sent instructions for the Seventh Fleet to airlift thirty mines with their parachute packs to Task Force 77 carriers then deployed at Yankee Station: the *Bon Homme Richard* and the *Kitty Hawk*. The navy high command wanted this mission to receive "maximum effort," instructing personnel at Subic to give it "priority over all . . . other commitments." In a follow-up readiness measure, the naval air station at Cubi Point received orders to send the mine assembly teams to nearby Subic Bay Naval Base for transfer to the carriers at Yankee Station. The air station was to treat this action as "imperative."[10]

The assembly teams received orders to deploy to the *Oriskany* and *Enterprise*, which had also received thirty mines each when they arrived at Yankee Station. The three teams assigned to the four carriers would rotate from ship to ship so that their presence at Yankee Station would be continuous. The loading of mines on the *Ticonderoga* at Subic and the airlifting of mines to the carriers were activities that presumably would have been visible to observers, but whether and to what extent anyone other than US Navy personnel paid close attention to the exercise is unknown.

The next step was more likely to be noticed. With procedures established and "drill mines" (dummy weapons) in place, on 9 May 1969 Moorer ordered mine-laying training to begin during the period from 15 to 20 May, when the *Enterprise*, loaded with thirty mines in configuration Charlie, was due at Subic Bay. This was several days past Kissinger's amended schedule, probably the result of routine slippage in orchestrating military operations. Other carriers would participate in mine training exercises when they arrived for regular "in port" operations. Detailed instructions for the training exercise recommended that it be as realistic as possible. All squadrons of A-4 Skyhawks and A-6 Intruders assigned to the carriers were to participate, with each carrier delivering thirty mines. Instructions were that there should be a minimum of two aircraft per mission flying at "maximum airspeed and minimum altitude" laying "one-one" minefields consisting of at least four mines per line. To the extent possible, the mines were to be recovered from the bay once the exercise was completed.[11]

Because of scheduling snafus, the *Enterprise* was unable to participate and was replaced by the *Bon Homme Richard*. The revised plan called for the *Bon Homme*'s A-4s to deliver twenty-three mines in six missions, dropping them in a single line in a field located near Port Binanga on the southeastern end of the bay. The half-hour exercise in the morning of 24 May was deemed "satisfactory," even though the accuracy of delivery was only "fair." Some of the mines, however, could not be recovered because of float and parachute malfunctions and the pilfering of floats by local fishermen.[12]

The Vance Ploy Fizzles

Meanwhile—and unbeknown to Washington—Moscow had forwarded the administration's Vance mission proposal to Hanoi's Politburo soon after Kissinger had presented it to Dobrynin on 14 April. The Politburo turned it down. On 5 May, Premier Pham Van Dong informed Moscow that the issues separating Hanoi and Washington could better be settled between the two sides at the Paris negotiations.[13] Hanoi's leaders were opposed to third-party international involvement in negotiations, especially considering their experience at the multinational talks in Geneva in 1954, when Moscow and Beijing had pressured Vietminh negotiators to make more concessions to the French and United States than they thought warranted by the military and political situation on the ground in Indochina.[14] Moscow did not inform Washington about Hanoi's response.

Kissinger again raised the matter of the Vance initiative with Dobrynin on 14 May, when he repeated the administration's offer "to meet with representatives of the other side in a different location [other than Paris] for confidential talks" as the Soviet ambassador was leaving the White House after his conversation with the president in Nixon's study. Although Dobrynin understood this to be a reference to the Vance proposal, he offered no response about its status in Hanoi or Moscow. Nixon and Kissinger interpreted Dobrynin's silence as indicative of a deliberate pattern of Soviet stonewalling on the issue.[15]

In a related exchange concerning the broad context of US-USSR relations, Soviet premier Alexei N. Kosygin replied on 27 May to Nixon's letter of 26 March. In his letter, the president had reaffirmed his desire to improve relations with the Soviet Union but repeated his intention to link US-USSR détente with progress on problems having to do with Vietnam, the Middle East, Berlin, and nuclear arms competition—a linkage concept he had explained to Dobrynin on 14 February. In his 27 May response, Kosygin used what Kissinger later called "reverse linkage," rejecting the administration's logic and repeating the Soviet position that each problem between the US and the USSR could better be resolved on its own merits. He argued that Nixon's linkage approach would "lead to the emergence of a vicious circle and would in no way facilitate the solving of problems which have become ripe for this." Regarding the Vietnam War, Kosygin expressed Moscow's willingness to facilitate a settlement but chastised Washington for its "unrealistic" support of the Thieu government and for opposing a political solution that "reflects the actual disposition of political forces in South Vietnam," which was, of course, the DRV/NLF negotiating position. In a cover memo to Nixon, Kissinger wrote of Kosygin's comments on Vietnam that he saw "nothing particularly hopeful in this." About Kosygin's letter, Nixon noted: "A very shrewd and depressingly hard-line letter. There is *no* conciliation in it except style!"[16]

In an address at a September 2010 conference about the history of the Vietnam War sponsored by the Historian's Office of the State Department, Kissinger told the audience that the proposal to the Soviets and North Vietnamese involving Vance "was never answered. The Russians never answered; the Vietnamese never answered. We then sort of dilatorily studied enhanced military action." Kissinger had previously written, in his 1979 historical memoir, that planning "proceeded in a desultory fashion."[17] But there was little that was dilatory or desultory about the administration's planning for escalation. Although Nixon and Kissinger had not yet directly commissioned attack plans, they had been reviewing JCS contingency planning, had expanded the bombing of Cambodia, and had set the mining ruse in motion.

Absent a direct, formal reply from Moscow about the Vance overture by the end of May, Nixon and Kissinger surmised that the North Vietnamese were unwilling to cooperate and the Soviets were being evasive. The Vance Ploy had come to a dead end. Believing their threat-making credibility was on the line and putting their faith in the coercive power of military force, Nixon and his adviser began to consider the tougher escalatory steps they had discussed in prior planning.[18]

Their timetable held to the end of May, six-week deadline they had set for Soviet acceptance of the Vance initiative but also conformed to their timetable for the overall game plan that Nixon had outlined to the NSC at its 25 January meeting, the details of which they continued to refine or develop. The goal was still that of bringing about a negotiated settlement with the DRV/NLF by the end of the year—one that provided for the mutual withdrawal of US and DRV military forces, yet one that also stretched out the withdrawal period and allowed so-called residual or advisory US forces to remain as the RVN negotiated with a disarmed NLF to settle political issues and US aid continued to flow to Saigon. But while pursuing a hard line in the negotiations, Nixon's home front political strategy was to take a "peaceful public stance" and "within three or four months bring home a few troops unilaterally as a separate and distinct action from the Paris negotiations and as a ploy for more time domestically." Because unilateral US troop withdrawals would have the effect of weakening allied ground operations, signaling inconstancy, and endangering the survivability of the RVN, time was needed to strengthen the Saigon regime by expanding and improving its armed forces. Escalated military and political pressure on the enemy by means of enhanced counterinsurgency/pacification efforts, stepped-up bombing of Indochina, and a mining operation against Haiphong (all backed by a rhetorical strategy of threatening excessive force) would not only help to sustain the Vietnamization effort but also coerce the enemy into accepting the administration's indispensable negotiating terms—or so they believed. Their triangular diplomacy would aim to get Moscow and Hanoi "moving in a qualitative direction" by August 1969.[19]

Dueling Public Peace Plans

Consistent with the game plan, Kissinger had directed the interdepartmental Ad Hoc Group on 10 April to analyze the modalities of the administration's priority negotiating objectives. Two weeks later, he presented the president with a draft outline for a peace plan speech, reminding Nixon that the administration needed to publicly "elaborate a clear-cut position of our own" instead of being "whipsawed" between congressional, citizen, and media demands. In an effort to nudge the president in this direction, Kissinger informed him the next day, 25 April, that Xuan Thuy had recently taunted the American delegation in Paris in saying that "if the Nixon administration has a great peace program, as it makes believe, why doesn't it make that program public?" Nixon hesitated—he was waiting for a Soviet reply to the Vance proposal, and beyond that, he was not in the mood to battle the national security bureaucracy or Saigon on the details of a plan.[20]

The other side beat the administration to the punch. On 8 May, the NLF delegation in Paris announced its Ten-Point Overall Solution, whose key proposals called for the unilateral withdrawal of all US forces and war matériel from South Vietnam without conditions; the dismantling of US bases; democratic elections preceded by a provisional coalition government that would exclude Thieu, Ky, and Huong but include other representatives from the Thieu camp, NLF representatives, and a third party "supporting peace, independence, and neutrality" for South Vietnam; reunification of the south and north zones; and negotiated releases of prisoners of war. All but the last demand were diametrically opposed to US demands, which President Johnson had enunciated in the "Manila communiqué" of 25 October 1966 and which Nixon had continued to support after his inauguration: the cessation of "aggression" by the DRV and the mutual withdrawal of US and DRV forces, with American troops remaining in South Vietnam for six months after all NVA forces were confirmed to have withdrawn. The RVN would continue as a separate state until reunification elections involving "all Vietnamese" could be held—elections in which the Saigon regime, remaining in power, would have the upper hand over a disarmed NLF. The most objectionable demands in the NLF's Ten-Point proposal from the point of view of the Nixon White House were those calling for the withdrawal of US forces only; interim and permanent coalition governments, each of which would exclude Thieu and consist of Communists and those sympathetic to the Communist side; US reparations; and international supervision of US force withdrawals only.[21]

The NLF plan nonetheless received considerable attention in the United States and sparked calls for the administration to avoid passing up an opportunity for peace. This pressure apparently spurred Nixon to read and make notes on Kissinger's speech draft on the same day of the NLF's Ten-Point announcement. On the evening of 11 May, he finally decided to go ahead with the speech—but only after vetting it through Rogers, Laird, Lodge, Bunker, Thieu, the CIA, and allied governments of Southeast Asia. When Nixon met with Dobrynin shortly before he was to address the nation at 10:00 p.m. on 14 May, the president gave the ambassador a text of the speech, commenting that it "is a sincere attempt . . . to get out of the current impasse," which, "given good will on both sides, can be used to find an equitable political solution."[22]

But from the point of view of Hanoi and Moscow, his eight-point plan was uncompromising, even though it departed from Johnson's Manila formula on some key points—particularly the Manila stipulation for a US withdrawal *after* a DRV withdrawal. In an attempt to mollify those in Congress and around the nation who wanted to end the war as soon as possible, Nixon sandwiched within his long address to the nation language about the need for mutual, phased withdrawals of the "major portions" of US and DRV forces over a period of twelve months, with remaining forces moved to designated noncombat base areas. International bodies would verify withdrawals and supervise the release of POWs and the other terms of the agreement, including the arrangement of a cease-fire. There was no provision in the plan for negotiating a political settlement or reunification other than a vague call for the oversight of "elections" by an international body. Elsewhere in the speech, Nixon made it clear that though Washington would be willing to discuss the political issues, its participation in such talks would depend on Saigon's concurrence, which, of course, was not likely. Indeed, Saigon itself was unwilling to discuss political questions.[23]

Although Nixon and Kissinger had removed "some of the threatening stuff" in the semifinal draft of Nixon's address in response to State Department objections, they had retained a not-so-subtle warning to Hanoi in the final version: "I must also make clear, in all candor, that if the needless suffering continues, this will affect other decisions. Nobody has anything to gain by delay."[24] (Meanwhile, B-52s continued to bomb Cambodia, and the night before his speech, he told Kissinger to go ahead with a bombing operation in the DMZ.)[25] Nixon had also made threatening remarks to Dobrynin at their meeting at the White House on the night of the speech. Arguing that Hanoi was mistaken in its presumed assumption that "he will ultimately have to give in, mainly owing to pressure from public opinion," the president declared that he could persuade the US public to accept "other measures and support for those measures" once it understood that Hanoi was blocking an "honorable settlement." Knowing that the phrase "other measures" was a reference to the use of additional force, Dobrynin countered that "military means" could not solve the Vietnam conflict. But Nixon persisted in warning that he would have to think about "alternatives" if Hanoi did not cooperate.[26]

Nixon held a joint meeting of the NSC and the cabinet the next day in order to encourage members to tout the plan publicly, including the need to use force if necessary. The president insisted that his proposals were reasonable and "offered the enemy a way out." What was on the line, he maintained, was not only the loss of South Vietnam but also "the balance of Asia . . . if we fail to end the war in a way that will not be an American defeat." For that reason, he continued, "we need to threaten that if they don't talk they will suffer. . . . We have an option, which is military action not only at the present level but at an expanded level."[27] Kissinger echoed the president's remarks during a press backgrounder that same day. Responding to a question from a reporter about whether the president's speech had contained an "implied . . . threat of greater military activity," he said, "It stands to reason that if this proposal is not accepted that we will have to make other decisions," which amounted to an implied threat. Laird, who favored a Vietnamization strategy, dutifully followed the White House line. On 18 May, he told the press that he "wouldn't want to rule out any military activity. I think it would be a mistake . . . to rule out the various options that could be used. We must remain strong."[28]

The purpose of the military option was not military victory, since Nixon and Kissinger did not consider such an outcome achievable. The president had reaffirmed his long-held belief about this question on 12 May, while discussing with Kissinger Thieu's suggested revisions of the semifinal draft of the speech: "In Saigon the tendency is to fight the war to victory. It has to be kept in mind, but you and I know it won't happen— it is impossible. Even Gen. Abrams agreed."[29] Instead, the purpose of the military option Nixon mentioned to the cabinet was leverage—enough leverage to persuade the DRV/NLF to accept a negotiated settlement that would either achieve a two-state solution in Vietnam (which is what Saigon and American hawks wanted and which would have constituted a political or policy "victory") or more probably provide Thieu with a rea- sonable chance of staying in power for at least a decent interval. Just two weeks before Nixon's national address, Kissinger told a trusted reporter, Murray Marder: "The only basis for us taking [US] troops out is a belief that the South Vietnamese can take up the slack. . . . There is a big dif- ference between South Vietnam going Communist in two years after we leave and ten years, the difference between giving them a reasonable and an unreasonable chance of survival." But Kissinger quickly followed that comment, saying that if North Vietnam would give up on uniting "all of Vietnam in one cave-in [and] accept an interim division of Vietnam [for] two or three years" by means of a negotiated settlement, then Washington and Hanoi could work out an agreement "in three months."[30] The two or three year figure was closer to what Nixon and Kissinger had said about their decent-interval solution in private conversations during 1969 in the Oval Office and the Executive Office Building—as well as with Soviet representatives and US allies—when they defined the best reasonable in- terval they could hope for as five years or less.[31]

A compromise resembling the negotiated agreement that would be struck four years later, in January 1973, was not, however, in the cards in 1969 as long as the White House was unwilling to withdraw US military forces unilaterally within a period shorter than twelve months and as long as Hanoi and the NLF were unwilling to compromise on the political question of Thieu's exclusion from a coalition.[32] Nixon and Kissinger were placing their bets on the threat and use of greater force, the strengthening of the Saigon regime and army, and the future possibilities of triangular diplomacy. Aware of the administration's strategy and belatedly recognizing the dangers of extending their offensive operations, the DRV/NLF prepared for a prolonged war—and even escalation—on the military, diplomatic, and political fronts. According to a COSVN analysis:

> US imperialists . . . hope to de-escalate in a strong position so they can settle the war through negotiations on conditions favorable for them. . . . They will strive to consolidate and strengthen the puppet army and administration, and as an immediate objective, they will . . . go on with their "clear and hold" strategy; . . . accelerate the pacification program . . . [and] seek all means to weaken our military and political forces. . . . The Americans may, in certain circumstances, put pressure on us by threatening to broaden the war through the resumption of bombing in North Vietnam within a definite scope and time limit, or the expansion of the war into Laos and Cambodia.[33]

On the home front, the president's speech received a tepid reception from the American press. Reading the Sunday papers on 18 May, Nixon found that "all comments were either neutral or negative." He assumed most reporters were prejudiced against him: "If JFK had made the speech" he complained, "they would have all been ecstatic." Haldeman agreed with Nixon that what was needed was a PR plan and a special staff to build up the president's image. Kissinger's analysis focused on rhetorical technicalities. On the afternoon of 14 May, even before Nixon had delivered the speech, Kissinger realized that it was "too complex with too many nuances that are totally unintelligible to the ordinary guy." He concluded that the plan should have been presented as a diplomatic white paper and summarized on television in a brief inspirational talk.[34]

Bringing Home Some Troops Unilaterally

Concerning another part of the overall game plan, US troop withdrawals, Nixon had understood at least as early as 1968 that even as he would escalate the fighting, he could possibly appease a sizable portion of the American electorate by gradually drawing down US forces—even without a negotiated agreement. On 13 March, three days before his final decision to proceed with BREAKFAST, he had met with Secretary of Defense Laird to receive his recommendations for the unilateral withdrawal of American forces from South Vietnam.[35] Laird had just returned with General Wheeler from Saigon, where they had discussed the matter with General Abrams and his MACV staff. Although commanders in South Vietnam had for some time expected that there would be troop withdrawals, they had not begun to plan for it because they had not received specific guidance from Washington and assumed that reductions would take place as part of a negotiated mutual withdrawal of American and North Vietnamese forces. In lieu of an agreement, Abrams argued that US withdrawals would only be feasible if three "indicators" were favorable: progress in pacification, improvements in the RVNAF, and the strength of the enemy threat.[36]

Though approving these conditions in principle, Laird put greater priority on the political need to make plans for withdrawals before Nixon's honeymoon period expired—"before the time given to the new Administration runs out," he told Abrams, "be it three, six, or nine months, but probably with[in] the next three or four months."[37] Laird was not a dove on the war, but neither was he a hawk—even though he supported US goals in Vietnam and often favored strong military measures. He was, however, an astute observer of home front political and economic winds. Perhaps above all he worried about the high costs of the war, its destructive impact on the US military, and its adverse impact on the global US economic and strategic position. He knew that most of the hawkish options floated in Washington and Saigon would not fly politically and could not produce a military victory in Vietnam anyway. Nixon's plan of action—as Laird understood it—would bring about a negotiated mutual withdrawal, and Vietnamization would enable South Vietnamese forces to take the place of US forces.[38]

The White House designed each policy for different audiences: friends and foes at home and abroad. De-Americanization—the unilateral withdrawal of US forces from Vietnam—was mainly put in place to assuage the American electorate. Among the factors influencing Nixon's intention to withdraw troops were events on the battlefield in South Vietnam. On 10 May, for example, the US 101st Airborne Division (Airmobile) engaged the NVA Twenty-Ninth Regiment at a small mountain named Dong Ap Bia (Hill 937) on the Laotian border near the A Shau Valley in an operation called APACHE SNOW. B-52s and US artillery bombarded the mountain with 3.5 million pounds of munitions in the next nine days. But when allied troops launched twelve assaults on entrenched enemy positions, they lost fifty-six US and five RVN troops killed, with over 400 US wounded, before capturing the hill on 20 May. Confirmed dead were 633 NVA soldiers, and there was no telling how many others had been killed or wounded. After all this, on 7 June US commanders decided to abandon the hill.

The US press had been covering the battle, posing questions that GIs had been asking about the purpose of repeated futile, bloody assaults. Drawing heightened criticism from the press and dovish US senators, the battle had come to be called Hamburger Hill. As the battle continued to be fought, the controversy focused more attention on the figures for US troops killed in action throughout South Vietnam. The total was 430 for the period 10–17 May—the highest since the week ending 1 March, and that did not include the figures for Hamburger Hill, where fighting continued for another three days.[39]

On the last day of the battle, Kissinger told Laird by telephone that the president "would like to find out why we kept attacking the hill on [the] Laotian border." The next day, Laird reported that General Wheeler did not explain why it had been "conducted or considered necessary in the broad context of the overall military effort in Southeast Asia," except that it was consistent with the search-and-destroy strategy. "Our commanders, both here and in South Vietnam," Laird explained, "are unanimous in the assertion that immediate pressure . . . on the enemy keeps friendly casualties lower overall." But he added, "I am convinced there is no way to ascertain the validity of this thesis." On 26 May, Nixon told Kissinger to go ahead with the press backgrounder on the issue. When he met with reporters later in the week, Kissinger tried to defuse concern by talking about the administration's policy of de-escalation and the general reduction in casualties since November. But public controversy swirled for weeks. On 20 June, for example, CBS TV presented a filmed interview with a US soldier, who commented that the battle had been a "turkey shoot . . . and we were the turkeys"; many of his buddies, he said, had been badly wounded in the "seemingly senseless exercise." It was one of the press stories that got the administration's attention. Nixon thought it effective because the soldier was "just an average young guy" in favor of the war and "no hippy or peacenik." The only comment that the president wanted to pass on to Laird and Kissinger was that the story was "a pretty sad commentary on our public relations effort."[40]

The day before, Nixon had ordered General Abrams to alter US strategy in order to conduct the war with minimum casualties. From now on, Nixon would be keen on holding down US losses. Eleven days earlier, on 8 June, he had announced forthcoming troop withdrawals from South Vietnam along with reductions in personnel in Thailand and the redeployment of naval vessels off the coast of Vietnam—all justified, the release claimed, by progress in the Paris talks and Vietnamization, but political concerns played a key role.[41]

As with all White House policies and strategies, Vietnamization had several aims and audiences. The major purpose, of course, was to compensate for the withdrawal of US forces by turning the war over to a reformed Saigon government and a strengthened, better-trained, better-equipped, better-led RVNAF. But Nixon, Kissinger, and Laird also thought that it, along with de-Americanization, would provide positive and negative incentives for Saigon to hold on and for Hanoi to negotiate.[42] The positive incentives would be to encourage the GVN in the belief that the process of Vietnamization would result in the strengthening of its armed forces, whereas de-Americanization would signal to the DRV that the US was exhibiting good faith in unilaterally withdrawing its forces. The negative incentives were that de-Americanization would frighten the GVN into reforming itself and strengthening its political base, whereas the prospect of a strengthened RVNAF and a simultaneously broadened Saigon government would pressure the DRV into compromising at the negotiating table.[43]

Laird, however, was dissatisfied with the doctrinal orientation of MACV, which placed more emphasis on military operations than on preparing the South Vietnamese to fight alone. Skeptical of the possibility of rapid progress in the Paris negotiations and of the political and military efficacy of sustained escalation, he was determined to initiate the process of American troop reductions independent of Kissinger's negotiations and Abrams's conditions. In his 13 March report to Nixon, Laird had recommended the withdrawal of 50,000 to 70,000 American troops in 1969 and the drafting of a long-range, comprehensive plan as soon as possible. At the same time, his advocacy of de-Americanization was not as vigorous as that of Secretary Rogers and the State Department, who were in favor of more rapid withdrawals.[44]

When asked at a press conference the next day about rumors of forth-coming withdrawals, the president responded that "in view of the current offensive on the part of the North Vietnamese and the Vietcong, there is no prospect for a reduction of American forces in the foreseeable fu-ture."[45] He then cited three conditions that would have to be met before withdrawals took place. Although phrased differently than Abram's con-ditions, they were compatible: "the ability of the South Vietnamese to de-fend themselves," progress in the negotiations, and the level of the enemy threat. He was dissembling, however, for at that moment, he was prepar-ing to give the order for withdrawals before any of these conditions had been fully or adequately met.

Two weeks after receiving Laird's report, the president brought up the matter of US troop withdrawals and compensatory stepped-up training and equipping of the RVNAF at a 28 March NSC meeting: "We cannot sustain this [war] at current rates for two years. The reality is that we are working against a time clock. We are talking 6 to 8 months. We are going to play a strong public game but we must plan this. We must get a sense of urgency in the training of the South Vietnamese." Laird unsurpris-ingly supported Nixon's argument but suggested a verbal sleight of hand for home front political reasons: "I agree, but not with your term 'de-Americanizing.' What we need is a term [such as] 'Vietnamizing' to put the emphasis on the right issue." Attuned to the importance of words in matters of public relations, Nixon agreed.[46]

As a policy, it was not a new idea. Colonial powers throughout history had raised native forces to assist them in suppressing rebellion. Funded by US aid, France adopted such a policy during the First Indochina War, calling the program *le jaunissement*—the "yellowing" of their forces fight-ing the Vietminh. In the Second Indochina War, it was the so-called Wise Men—senior advisers to President Johnson—who had recommended at the onset of the 1968 Tet Offensive that the administration should step up efforts to raise and train South Vietnamese troops in order to lessen the burden on US forces, arguing that high toll of US troop casualties was "the most serious single cause of domestic disquiet." Soon thereaf-ter, Johnson's new secretary of defense, Clark Clifford, began developing plans for Vietnamization. Meanwhile, the American anti-Vietnam War movement from its beginnings in the early 1960s had called for and dem-onstrated in favor of bringing US troops home. At least as early as 1967, some began using the terms *de-Americanize* and *de-Americanization* in referring to the withdrawal of US forces. During 1968, the words entered the wider public discourse about the war in the United States and South Vietnam, each carrying dual meanings: either US troop withdrawals alone or US withdrawals accompanied by the buildup of South Vietnamese forces.[47]

As used by the Nixon administration, the word *Vietnamization* could apply either to the training and expansion of South Vietnamese forces and the reform of Saigon's government or to US troop withdrawals—or both. Vietnamization had the public relations purpose of emphasizing the positive implication of building up the South Vietnamese armed forces and government over the negative implication of de-Americanization, withdrawing US troops. The administration viewed the word *de-Americanization* as negative insofar as it signaled to American hawks and Hanoi's leaders that the United States was unilaterally withdrawing (albeit slowly). In theory, US troop withdrawals were supposed to be linked to the buildup of South Vietnamese forces. In practice, however, unilateral US withdrawals would proceed with or without significant progress in reforming the Saigon government or in the training and buildup of the RVNAF.

On 10 April, the White House issued NSSM 36, instructing the JCS and DOD to prepare specific alternative timetables for US withdrawals in coordination with the Department of State and CIA. The goal was to bring about "the progressive transfer . . . of the fighting effort" from US to RVN armed forces, leaving only a support and advisory mission in place at the end of the process. Although the withdrawals were to be unilateral, their pace was supposed to vary according to circumstances, which included progress in Vietnamization, political factors, and other indicators and conditions previously listed by Abrams and Nixon. Troop reductions were to begin on 1 July 1969, with options to complete them on 31 December 1970, 30 June 1971, 31 December 1971, or 31 December 1972.[48]

Submitted in early June, the Laird-endorsed JCS/DOD plan recommended a "tentative" withdrawal goal of 50,000 troops by 31 December 1969, with the first increment of 20,000–25,000 to begin on 1 July. The Department of State, by contrast, recommended a total of 85,000 by the end of 1969—"depending on further consideration after the initial withdrawal." The JCS warned that US troop withdrawals up to 290,000 "could result in [the] interruption of pacification progress," whether they were completed in December 1970 or December 1972. In part because of this danger, the JCS/DOD recommended keeping 260,000 to 306,000 residual US troops in South Vietnam.[49]

Nixon decided on an initial 1 July withdrawal increment of 25,000. He informed Generals Wheeler and Abrams and Admiral McCain of the decision at a meeting with them and Rogers, Laird, Bunker, and Lodge in Honolulu on 7 June. Kissinger recalled that the military commanders accepted the decision with a "heavy heart."[50] The president and Kissinger had stopped in Hawaii on their way to Midway Island, where Nixon was to confer with Thieu on 8 June. In a joint statement after their meeting, the two presidents publicly announced the imminent troop withdrawal.[51]

Instead of confiding in the public about the purposes shaping the troop withdrawal decisions, Nixon told the press that the proposal came from President Thieu and General Abrams, but that was far from true. Indeed, Kissinger had asked Thieu to treat it as his initiative in order to counter news reports that the purpose of the Midway meeting was to "remedy" US-GVN disputes as well as to dispel rumors about a rift in relations between Saigon and Washington and about Nixon administration efforts to pressure Thieu into accepting a coalition government. To help meet Nixon's "domestic problem," Kissinger wanted Thieu to act as if the withdrawals were his idea. Thus, during the private meeting, Nixon approached the troop withdrawals gingerly. When the discussion reached the problem of troop "replacements" (avoiding the word "withdrawals"), Thieu, playing the game, made a proposal on specific US units.[52]

According to a South Vietnamese source but not the US record, Nixon made an important commitment and Thieu made a significant request. After the meeting, Thieu told Chiang Kai-shek that Nixon had promised four years of military aid to support Vietnamization and, in his second term, four years of economic assistance. Moreover, Thieu asked that as part of a settlement, the United States leave behind two residual divisions of American troops to serve as a deterrent to a North Vietnamese invasion. Apparently, he was thinking in terms of a South Korean–type solution. Any notion of a long-term US presence in Vietnam, however, would have been politically and diplomatically impossible. Hanoi would never have accepted it, and it would have been inconsistent with Nixon's long-range goal of liquidating the US presence.[53]

Trying to make the best out of the situation, Thieu asked Nixon to commit funds and equipment for special provincial and regional military units so he would have better control over the rural population. Thieu accepted the idea of a "negotiated peace" and free elections with international observers, but he thought about the Vietnamese adage "*dau xuoi duoi lot*" (if the head slides through easily, the tail will follow). He was plainly concerned about the political impact of withdrawals, mentioning the low morale of urban middle classes and intellectuals who worried that Washington would withdraw support and were keeping their options open to support a coalition government. Nixon was noncommittal about Thieu's military proposals, and the latter could do little to alter the course of events. He even acquiesced when he learned that the White House wanted to keep open the possibility of secret, direct talks with Hanoi, with Nixon promising him that he would be informed of the results.[54] For the time being, American relations with the Saigon regime had proved manageable.

Those on the Communist side took heart from their understanding of the "objective contradictions" in the predicaments of Nixon and Thieu, especially on the question of US troop withdrawals. If conditions in Vietnam were such that Nixon could not withdraw troops without producing a sudden collapse of Thieu's government, they hoped or expected that the internal conflicts between him and the American people and the Saigon regime would increase. But if he did withdraw troops, it would undermine American military strategy, accentuate the demoralization of US and RVN forces, and lead to the "political isolation, . . . decay, and ineffectiveness" of Thieu's administration. This predicament, centering on the troop withdrawal question, they believed, was "the *greatest weak point* of the Americans."[55]

Reflecting on Nixon's words and actions, Nguyen Co Thach, DRV vice minister of foreign affairs and aide to Le Duc Tho, noted after the war that at this time, "Nixon on the one hand was threatening bombing and on the other withdrawing troops. That means . . . [his signal] was very vague. The question for us was not [the threat of] bombing or any kind of force. We should have been able to survive, to stay on. But for the Americans, in any case, they must leave. That was their problem."[56]

Coincident with the Midway meeting between Nixon and Thieu, representatives of the NLF and other anti-Thieu nationalist groups met in the "liberated zone" of Tay Ninh Province near Saigon from 6 to 8 June to form the Provisional Revolutionary Government (PRG). The PRG claimed recognition as one of the two "coexisting" administrations in

South Vietnam—the other being the RVN, or the government of President Thieu.[57]

New Mine Readiness Measures

Perhaps because of Nixon's and Kissinger's long-shared concerns about Laird and Rogers, not to mention their lack of faith in the State Department negotiators in Paris, the president and his national security assistant had begun in May to think about making a transition from their ongoing mining ruse to an actual mining operation. With the impending expiration of their end-of-May deadline for the Vance Ploy, a mining operation would be consistent with their initial game plan, as well as the diplomatic-military stratagem, and it had long been one of Nixon's and Kissinger's preferred military options should circumstances, in their estimation, call for it. As Nixon had told his cabinet on 15 May: "If they don't talk they will suffer. . . . We have an option, which is military action not only at the present level but at an expanded level."[58] But it was one thing to have an overall game plan option—that is, a general inclination to do such a thing as mining—and another to have an operational plan and to carry it out.

As a step preliminary to developing an operational plan, Kissinger had asked DCI Richard Helms on 21 May to task CIA analysts with estimating the feasibility of a "quarantine" against North Vietnam. In using the word *quarantine*, the Nixon White House was borrowing a page from the playbook of the Kennedy White House, which had applied the euphemistic term to its blockade of Cuba during the 1962 missile crisis. In both cases, no internationally recognized state of war existed; the United States had not declared war against its adversaries, and therefore a blockade would have been considered an act of aggression under the terms of the UN Charter. The Nixon administration's quarantine of North Vietnam, however, would include the added dimension of mine laying.[59]

On 20 May, as the CIA was considering the quarantine option, Robinson informed Kissinger that "we have reached one of the final steps in the planned schedule" for the mining readiness test. The mining exercises in Subic Bay were part of Step Three, but there were two other measures that remained to be implemented: the shipment of 1,000 mines from Yokosuka to Subic and the assignment of Marine Corps A-6 pilots from Da Nang, South Vietnam, to Cubi Point, Philippines, for training. Those measures, Robinson wrote, would "increase our 'visibility' to a limited degree," but he recommended continuing the training activities to bring the "fleet in a constantly improving mine warfare posture."[60]

Robinson also raised the question of the Step Four measures that would require coordination between the Joint Chiefs and CINCPAC. He did not think they were "useful or necessary until such time as an actual feint or planting operation is initiated." In other words, they could be a prelude to military escalation. Robinson then enumerated a number of Step Four measures, all of which could be studied further. They included increased reconnaissance of coastal approaches to Haiphong using P-3 and antisubmarine warfare aircraft for "continuous and intensive surveillance of sea approaches to Haiphong," efforts to "simulate threat of blockade" by stationing destroyer squadrons in an area 20 miles off Haiphong, and the release of mine drogue parachutes in areas near Haiphong to imitate mining operations. Moreover, tracking aircraft and specialized search-and-rescue ships, which had been pulled back from waters near North Vietnam when the bombing halt began, would be restored to their earlier positions.[61]

On 25 May, Helms submitted the CIA's report. Its main finding cast doubts on the value of a mining operation, much less threats or feints that one was imminent: a naval quarantine unaccompanied by the air interdiction of rail and road lines to China would fail to prevent the North from making "adjustments and alternate arrangements" to prevent the loss of Soviet or Chinese support. Beijing and Moscow could provide aid overland by trucks or railway—a conclusion that was consistent with earlier studies (see chapter 4). Moreover, the CIA analysts argued that imposing a quarantine "after so many signs that the Nixon administration is interested in a negotiated settlement" would probably cause Moscow to rethink its advice to Hanoi to support a negotiated settlement. Kissinger's handwritten comments on the report indicate his irritation with the analysis: "Why did CIA believe that there was enough rolling stock to make greater use of railroads possible?" He also complained in general that "all this [the CIA analysis] assumed that negotiating is not consistent with pressure."[62]

While waiting for Nixon to read the CIA report, Kissinger met with Moorer on 29 May to discuss naval activities around the Korean Peninsula and the continuing mine readiness test. Their meeting took place despite the assurance he had given Laird on 11 April that he "wasn't working directly with the Navy" on the mining ruse. On the agenda were questions about how long the test should last and whether the navy was ready to take any of the more threatening Step Four measures "to provide further signaling to Hanoi." Deciding that Step Four was premature, they approved one of the last Step Three measures: moving 1,000 mines from Yokosuka to Subic. As Robinson later noted, "This [would] increase both the visibility of western Pacific mine activity and the level of actual fleet mine readiness."[63]

The merchant ship conveying the mines, SS *Durango Victory*, delivered its cargo around 18 or 19 June, a few days behind schedule. It is likely that Japanese dockworkers at Yokosuka base helped with the heavy lifting and possible that others in touch with Soviet intelligence observed the transfer of the mines to the ship, whether from afar or close in. In any event, the delivery significantly increased the mine inventory at Subic. The current contingency plans for mining operations in Southeast Asia required 800 mines, so Subic now had plenty, including the 180 kept at configuration Charlie.[64]

As these exercises were taking place and a few days after meeting with President Thieu at Midway, President Nixon read the CIA report on mining Haiphong and was as deeply dissatisfied as Kissinger had been. He told Haig that the CIA's analysis "is really loaded in the sense it prejudged the effect the action would have on the Communists." Although it was not uncommon for agency analysts to "prejudge," predict, or guesstimate the consequences of prospective actions and possible contingencies, Nixon was unhappy with the report's implication that the blockade would not cause Hanoi's leaders to "back off the war or modify their negotiating line." Long a believer in the doctrine that coercive measures could have a significant impact on adversaries, he rejected the "logic of [one] paragraph which assumes that negotiations are not related to pressure." Moreover, the CIA's position that the "closing of Haiphong would be interpreted as a reversal of the US government's present policy, especially in light of his recent speech," contradicted Nixon's conviction that his warning in the 14 May speech "was quite explicit" in signaling that "the failure of Hanoi to negotiate" would trigger a US "reevaluation of other decisions."[65] Displeased that the CIA had devalued the mining option, Nixon wanted the agency to take another look.

Kissinger tasked the CIA with recasting its original analysis about the efficacy of quarantining North Vietnam and mining Haiphong Harbor. The deputy CIA director, Robert Cushman, who was working with

George Carver, Helm's special assistant on Vietnam and the officer assigned to write the reevaluation, then asked Kissinger what his and the president's objections were to the May paper. But Kissinger declined to explain on the grounds that "he did not want to be in [the] position of telling [the] Agency what to write" or "what he wants."[66] What Nixon and Kissinger wanted, it seems, was information that would affirm or at least not contradict their strategic notion that even without supporting air strikes, the mining of Haiphong would impair North Vietnam's war effort and intimidate the Politburo into yielding on key issues at the negotiating table.

More Warnings to Moscow via Dobrynin

During this period, on Friday, 11 June, three days after Nixon's troop withdrawal announcement at Midway Island and as the mining feint continued, Kissinger met again with Dobrynin. The Soviet ambassador was scheduled to leave for Moscow on Saturday for his summer holiday. Kissinger's purpose was to remind him of the US position that the settlement of such issues as US-USSR trade, strategic arms control, Middle East peace, and the status of Berlin was linked to Soviet cooperation in stopping "the Vietnam conflict as soon as possible." Complaining that the Soviet Union had left the negotiations "entirely to the discretion of the Hanoi leadership," he urged Moscow to assist "in overcoming the existing dead end in Paris." It was "evident from everything," Dobrynin commented in his report to Foreign Minister Andrei Gromyko, that "the Vietnam question . . . occupies the main place in the minds of the president and his most important advisors."[67]

Kissinger also brandished threats. His first was to suggest indirectly that Nixon might play the China card, insinuating that "there are people who think that the USA and China can somehow come to an understanding in opposition to the USSR," even though it "would not satisfy the interests of the US itself" to do so. Instead, the United States and the USSR, which were the only powers capable of confronting one another in "different parts of the world," needed "to conclude concrete agreements" and "follow appropriate parallel courses in the most important and dangerous questions."[68]

Proceeding to defend "Nixon's program to settle the Vietnam conflict," Kissinger then explained that the American side was willing "to discuss 'any suggestions and to look for compromises.'" But he insisted that, among other things, Hanoi could not be allowed to "reject Thieu, because that would represent . . . a political capitulation" by the United States and South Vietnam. He then made his second threat: if the DRV continued to "obstruct" the negotiations in Paris, the administration would consider "other alternatives," which led Dobrynin to comment in his report that

> this sufficiently firm sounding theme of "other alternatives" in talks with both Nixon and Kissinger cannot but be noted. Although at the current stage these comments carry, evidently, more the character of attempts to blackmail the Vietnamese and in part the USSR with hints that upon expiration of a certain period of time Nixon might renew the bombing of the DRV or take other military measures, it is not possible to entirely exclude the possibility of such actions by the current administration if the situation, in Nixon's opinion, will justify it.

Kissinger, Dobrynin noted, also "threw out a comment" that if the US administration turned to these other alternatives, the administration hoped that "Soviet-American relations do not fall any further than a 'dangerous minimum.'" It was necessary, the ambassador suggested to Gromyko, for the Soviet government "to be ready" for developments, "especially if Beijing's provocative course against the USSR will gather strength, and, if in Washington they start to believe that the situation in this sense may be unfavorable for Hanoi."[69]

In reply to Kissinger, Dobrynin reaffirmed Soviet policy concerning the Vietnam War:

> There cannot be any other alternatives to peaceful negotiations and a peaceful settlement. . . . Any attempt of the USA to solve the Vietnam question by forceful means unavoidably is destined to fail and that such a course . . . undoubtedly will bring in its train a general increase in international tension, which could not but touch on our relations with the USA.

Matching Kissinger's irony with satire, Dobrynin told him that Nixon should not repeat Johnson's mistakes, the consequences of which were made "sufficiently clear by the example of the previous owner of the White House."[70]

If the Soviets passed on any of Kissinger's messages and warnings to the DRV/PRG, they had little effect on them except to reinforce their stance and perhaps even harden their negotiating position. In Paris on 19 June, Le Duc Tho told the press that "no settlement in Vietnam was possible as long as the Thieu-Ky-Houng administration is in power, because the Provisional Revolutionary Government would never accept them."[71] At the time, Nixon was preparing to meet with Henry Cabot Lodge, the chief US negotiator, on 24 June to discuss the Paris negotiations. Kissinger told him that Lodge would probably recommend greater flexibility in the talks. The ambassador favored private meetings with the other side and a policy of responding to any North Vietnamese probes on political issues, but Kissinger advised that the president should take the position "that we must play a harder line in Paris for the present."[72] This advice was not only a reaction to Tho but also representative of a shift by the administration to a harder line, both at the talks and militarily.

Stretch-Out of Mine Readiness

Despite his warnings to Hanoi and Moscow through Dobrynin, Kissinger had nothing to back them up except implied threats. The administration did not yet have a credible China card to play, and the mine readiness exercises and continuing bombing of Cambodia, Laos, and South Vietnam did not threaten North Vietnam directly or immediately, much less the Soviet Union. Nonetheless, Nixon and Kissinger considered the possibility of prolonging and stepping up the ongoing mining ruse as they pondered the impact of Kissinger's latest meeting with Dobrynin. Even though the CIA had tacitly questioned the value of mining threats, Kissinger remained committed to them and found it useful to approve a "stretch-out" of mining readiness operations. In the short term, however, he had a greater worry: Nixon seemed to be edging toward a strategy of precipitate withdrawal.

A few days after his meeting with Dobrynin, Kissinger became concerned about what he perceived as the waning resolve of the other members of the administration, including the president,[73] who, Kissinger believed, had made some "startling" statements in a 19 June press conference. Asked about comments by former secretary of defense Clark Clifford concerning his schedule of troop withdrawals, Nixon said that he would make another withdrawal decision in August and added that he hoped he could beat Clifford's proposed timetable of having 100,000 troops out by the end of 1969 and all troops out by the end of 1970. When asked whether he was "wedded" to the Thieu regime, Nixon responded: "I would not say that the United States, insofar as any government in the world is concerned, is wedded to it in the sense that we cannot take any course of action that that government does not approve."[74] In context, it could be seen as a measured statement because in his next sentence he made a point of affirming the commitment of the United States to the Saigon government.

But Captain Robinson wrote to General Wheeler to say that "an aura of gloom prevailed outside Dr. Kissinger's office today, attributed to the president's statements on 'force withdrawals' during yesterday's press conference."[75] Haldeman noted in his diary that "all this shook K pretty badly" because he feared that Thieu would "consider it a betrayal, as will all South East Asia, and it will be interpreted as unilateral withdrawal." Haldeman told Kissinger that the president had probably wanted to "hit back" at Clifford and had simply overplayed his hand, but Kissinger nonetheless thought that it would be extremely difficult to shore up their tough line. Kissinger had been pushing for an approach opposite that of Laird and Rogers, but now he feared that Nixon had, like them, decided to pull out of Vietnam.[76]

Haldeman's view was that Kissinger was overreacting. Yet at the same time, he felt he had good reason because of his disappointed expectations. In the "last few days," Haldeman recorded, Kissinger had become "deeply discouraged" that their "Vietnam plans aren't working out right." He conjectured that the president also believed things were not working out as originally planned and had reacted accordingly in the press conference; that is, politically, by trying to counter critics, assuage the public, and gain time for his policies to work.[77]

Mining Feint Decisions

Meanwhile, to continue the visible level of activity sought by the White House, in early June the Task Force 77 commander ordered a "mine warfare training program" that would include giving navy personnel practice in assembling and loading mines and in acquiring proficiency in delivering them under combat conditions. All of these measures would ensure that personnel at Subic NAVMAG, carriers at Yankee Station, and aircraft crews could implement the mining contingency plan if it were ordered. In addition, the *Oriskany* conducted its Subic Bay mining drill in

June and was scheduled for another one in early July; the *Kitty Hawk* was slated for one in mid-July.[78]

Even before the *Kitty Hawk* exercise, Admiral William Bringle had reported that the Seventh Fleet possessed "satisfactory" mine readiness. Each of the carriers at Yankee Station was carrying thirty mines in configuration Charlie, and mobile mine assembly teams were maintaining a "continued presence" on the ships. The sixty mines could be dropped within twenty-four hours of an order, and the 150 Charlie-configured mines at Subic Bay could be quickly transported. Another 500 mines could be placed in Charlie configuration within ninety-six hours. Although the admiral believed that the mine assembly teams needed relief because they had been at work since early May, the exercises had disclosed "no problem areas," he observed, and the "present mine readiness can be maintained indefinitely."[79]

At the same time, the navy was looking at ways to sustain the activities that comprised the mining feint. In early June, while keeping Kissinger abreast of the plans to move the 1,000 mines to Subic Bay, Robinson mentioned that the navy was "developing a new action which offers promise." The idea was to stretch out the mining readiness program by directing a "team of outside mine experts" to carry out an "operational readiness inspection at each major mine facility in the western Pacific." The inspections, which would take up to two weeks, could involve checking inventories, mine publications, test and handling equipment, storage facilities, safety procedures, personnel readiness, and mine settings. Robinson saw an overall benefit because the activity would "stimulate virtually every aspect of our mine posture, yet [be] attributable to normal Navy business." Not only would it "add a new sense of realism to all that has gone on before," it would also "fit logically" between the transfer of 1,000 mines to Subic and the shipment of mines in an ammunition ship to Yankee Station.[80]

Kissinger agreed with the stretch-out concept, and Robinson drafted for Wheeler's use a 23 June memorandum to Secretary Laird in which Wheeler reported to Laird that all of the measures he had authorized in April had been taken, except for greater threats such as loading mines on an ammunition ship for "operations in the Gulf of Tonkin." That step would be "directed in the near future." According to Wheeler, Kissinger wanted to find ways to stretch out the mining readiness activities. One more possibility was carrying out "on-site operational readiness inspection[s]" of major mine facilities located in the western Pacific. Such inspections would make it possible to "test current Navy readiness in the light of activity" since the mining feint began in April.[81]

Kissinger's support was hardly decisive for Laird, and he did not at first sign off on the stretch-out concept. He had been unenthusiastic about the mining readiness test in the first place, and his military assistant, Colonel Pursley, sent him some probing questions in response to Wheeler's memorandum. Pursley asked, for example, what portions of the readiness test "have been achieved," "what can/or will be gained by 'stretching out' the present increased mining posture," and "what costs or risks are involved, if any, which might offset any expected benefits from prolonging the increased mining posture?" It is not clear whether Laird had seen the CIA analysis questioning the impact of a quarantine, but it *is* clear that he thought that skeptical questions were worth asking, and he told Pursley that Wheeler had some questions about the exercise as well. Nevertheless, Laird had spoken with Kissinger, who told him that Nixon wanted to keep the plan "very much alive." According to Kissinger, Laird reported, Nixon supported the on-site operational readiness inspection plan to keep this option open. Thus, Laird duly approved Wheeler's request but nonetheless sent him the questions.[82]

The role of the Joint Chiefs was to provide independent military advice to the president, but the White House was compromising that independence. Working closely with Haig, Captain Robinson, who as a member of the chairman's Staff Group drafted papers for Wheeler, wrote the response to make sure that Laird got the answers the White House wanted. Whatever Wheeler's private doubts were, he knew Nixon's and Kissinger's preferences, and he signed the response on 1 July. Recognizing that the procedure was somewhat irregular, Haig advised Kissinger that "Laird should not know you've seen" the Wheeler paper.[83]

The memo that Haig and Robinson drafted and Wheeler signed included arguments in favor of the stretch-out—with no evidence that the mining ruse had had any impact. According to the original concept behind the mining readiness test, the United States had wanted to "create indecision" in Hanoi about the possibility of the mining of Haiphong Harbor. Many of the readiness measures taken were "visible at both waterfront and depot locations," where it was anticipated that "Communist agents would detect and report this activity." The United States had not intercepted any communications indicating any reactions to the measures, but "it is reasonable to assume that the enemy is aware of the increased activity and readiness." Thus, the stretch-out was necessary to show Hanoi that should the negotiations fail to make progress, the United States was prepared to mine Haiphong.[84]

Also according to the Haig-Robinson memo, rejecting the stretch-out could have led foreign intelligence to draw the unwanted conclusion that Washington had rejected "this credible military option." Implementing the on-site inspection plan would sustain the "outward visibility" sought while also giving the navy an opportunity to "assess [mining] readiness." The risks and costs were low; financial costs were "minimal"; and if adversaries deployed a "propaganda reaction," the Pentagon could easily deploy a cover story about a "routine Pacific-wide test of mining plans."[85]

Within days after Laird signed off on Wheeler's request for a stretch-out of mining readiness activities, a twelve-man team began to assemble in Honolulu to start carrying out the operational readiness test.[86] During the weeks that followed, various mine warfare units in the western Pacific went through the detailed inspections that Nixon and Kissinger had requested.

By late June, however, it had become clear to both men that the mining ruse had failed to intimidate Hanoi. It and the other coercive military measures and threats that they had already put into motion had not forced Hanoi into compliance with their demands or succeeded in winning Soviet cooperation—warnings they had signaled in public statements or through Dobrynin, continuing ground operations in South Vietnam, stepped-up pacification, and expanded bombings in Cambodia and Laos. The timetable they had set at the outset of the administration for "moving" the North Vietnamese and the Soviets in a favorable direction by August and achieving an acceptable negotiated agreement by December was now in jeopardy.[87]

SAC Underground Command Post II, Offutt Air Force Base, Omaha, NE, ca. February 1961. Large screens could show weather conditions, deployments of aircraft and missiles, and other information requested by SAC's commander in chief. (Box: Still Pictures Division, RG 342B, NARA)

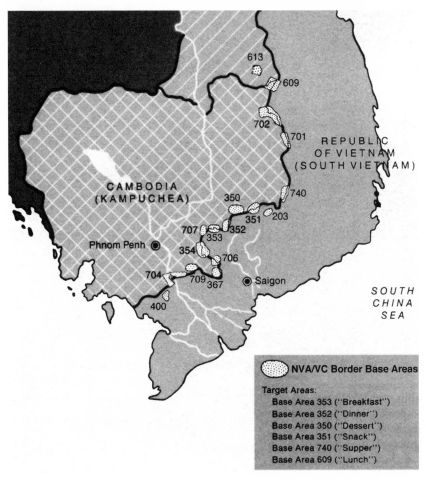

NVA/VC Border Base Areas.

Luncheon meeting during Nixon's first official visit to the Pentagon, 27 January 1969. Later, Nixon received a briefing on US nuclear war plans. From left to right: General Earle Wheeler, President Richard Nixon, Secretary of Defense Melvin Laird, and National Security Adviser Henry Kissinger. (Historical Office, Office of Secretary of Defense)

NSC meeting on 12 September 1969 to discuss Vietnam War policy. Clockwise from left: National Security Adviser Kissinger; Attorney General John Mitchell; Vice President Spiro Agnew; Admiral John McCain; General Creighton Abrams; CIA Director Richard Helms; the US delegate to the Paris talks, Philip Habib; the US ambassador to South Vietnam, Ellsworth Bunker; Secretary of State William Rogers; President Nixon; Secretary of Defense Laird; and General Wheeler. (RNPL)

Laird and his aide Robert Pursley. (Laird Collections, Marshfield Clinic, Marshfield, WI)

Rogers, Nixon, and Kissinger on *Air Force One*. (RNPL)

The Joint Chiefs of Staff, 31 December 1969. From left to right: Air Force Chief of Staff John D. Ryan, Navy Chief of Staff Thomas Moorer, Chief of Staff Earle Wheeler, Army Chief of Staff William Westmoreland, and Marine Corps Commandant Leonard F. Chapman, Jr. (Historical Office, Office of Secretary of Defense)

Alexander Haig receiving his general's star in the Oval Office, five days after the JCS Readiness Test ended; he had been promoted to brigadier in September 1969. Left to right: Helms, Laird, Haig, Nixon, and Kissinger. (RNPL)

Captain Rembrandt C. Robinson, June 1969. Robinson worked closely with Kissinger and Admiral Moorer in planning the mine readiness and DUCK HOOK contingency plans. (No. 85525, Robinson Folder, Photo Archive, Naval History and Heritage Command)

H. R. Haldeman and Nixon on the presidential campaign plane in 1968. (RNPL)

President Nguyen Van Thieu and President Nixon, Midway Island, 8 June 1969. (RNPL)

Anatoly Dobrynin and Kissinger in the Map Room, their most frequent meeting place in the White House, 17 March 1972. (RNPL)

Soviet merchant freighter *Vysotsk* near Haiphong Harbor, 8 September 1969, carrying trucks and vans. US reconnaissance aircraft took the photo as part of the BUMP ACTION project to gather information on targets in North Vietnam. (Box 63, Wheeler Records, RG 218, NARA)

DUCK HOOK

20 JULY 1969

Office of Chief of Naval Operations

Cover to the July 1969 DUCK HOOK plan booklet for a mining-only operation.
(Department of Defense Mandatory Declassification Review Release)

13 September 1969

VIETNAM CONTINGENCY PLANNING

Concept of Operations

U. S. military forces will conduct operations against North Vietnam in order to demonstrate U. S. resolve to apply whatever force is necessary to achieve basic U. S. objectives in Southeast Asia.

Such operations will be designed to achieve maximum political, military, and psychological shock, while reducing North Vietnam's over-all war-making and economic capacity to the extent feasible. The campaign will be conducted in a series of separate and distinct actions, each signalling an increasing or escalating level of military intensity.

Domestic and international pressures, and the possibilities of Soviet or Communist Chinese reaction, will be important factors, but will not necessarily rule out bold or imaginative actions directed toward achievement of the primary objective.

In undertaking actions to achieve these objectives, military forces will be employed in periodic, short but intensive military operations of 48-72 hours each during a period of approximately six months. Continuous military actions, such as armed reconnaissance over North Vietnam, or naval blockade of Haiphong, are not envisioned except to substantially maintain the effects achieved by the previous operation(s).

Subsequent to each phase of this campaign, North Vietnamese military and diplomatic responses will be evaluated before initiating the next major military action.

The initial campaign of military action against North Vietnam will be commenced on order and no later than 1 November in order to take maximum advantage of the transition period between the Northwest and Northeast monsoon seasons. Thereafter, operations

---

probably will be conducted with reduced visibility because of deteriorating weather conditions. Initial actions will include, but not be limited to, the mining of Haiphong, Hon Gai, and Cam Pha, and a major anti-war campaign to reduce the enemy ability to resist further military actions against NVN. In addition and to the maximum extent possible, enemy supply operations in support of VC/NVA activities in SVN will be degraded. Thereafter, subsequent operations will include consideration of the following military actions, as well as others which may be applicable:

Possible Washington Decision Points	Possible Action
1	Mine NVN ports (complete and long duration closure).
1	Conduct major air strikes against NVN air order of battle, imposing collateral damage as practicable against NVN airfields.
1	Conduct selective anti-SAM/AAA operations south of 19 degrees N.
1	Attack military supplies south of 19 degrees N.
1	Conduct ground sweep in DMZ south of Ben Hai River.
2	Reseed NVN minefields.
2	Conduct major air strike against Haiphong port complex.
2	Remove B-52 attack restrictions on certain supply concentrations/sanctuaries in Laos.
2	Attack military supplies and LOCs in North Vietnam.

Possible Washington Decision Points	Possible Action
2	Conduct ground sweep across the Ben Hai River within the limits of the DMZ.
2	Quarantine or mine Sihanoukville (with permissive channel).
2 or 3	Partial destruction of Red River dikes (or during period of optimum flooding).
3	Conduct major air strikes against high value targets in Thanh Hoa and Vinh.
3	Conduct ground sweep through the DMZ into NVN, employing reinforced ARVN division, supported by U.S. air.
3	Cross border operations (brigade size) into Laos and/or Cambodia.
3 or 4	Complete breaching of dike system.
4	Conduct major air strike against high value target systems (electric power, war supporting industry, transportation support facilities, military complexes, POL and air defense).
(4)	Clean nuclear interdiction of three NVN-Laos passes.
(5)	Nuclear interdiction of two NVN-CPR railroads.
5	Amphibious landing near Vinh, draw NVA forces, and generate killing zone.

This 13 September 1969 "concept of operations" paper outlined an early version of what was known within the White House NSC September Group as the DUCK HOOK bombing-and-mining plan. Probably drafted by Captain Robinson, this maximal planning concept included ground incursions into North Vietnam and the use of tactical nuclear weapons. The inked-in marks on p. 3 could be Kissinger's. (RNPL)

US soldiers carrying a wounded comrade. From the late 1950s to the end of 1968, 37,726 US armed forces personnel died in Vietnam, most during the Johnson presidency. During the Nixon presidency, 9,414 more had died by the end of 1969, slightly exceeding the total for 1967. The total of US deaths from January 1969 to the end of 1973 came to 21,885. (Department of Defense)

USS *Bon Homme Richard,* or "Bonnie Dick," with A-4s, F-8s, and other aircraft on deck, 17 June 1969. In May 1969, during the period when it was assigned to Yankee Station, the *Bon Homme Richard* participated in mining readiness test exercises in Subic Bay. (Bon Homme Richard CV-31 folders, CVA-31–0636–6-69, Naval Subject Collection, Photo Archive, Naval History and Heritage Command)

USS *Ozbourn*, off the Vietnam coast, 27 February 1965. On 23–24 October 1969, as part of the JCS Readiness Test, the *Ozbourn* tracked the *Uzhgorod*, a Soviet POL ship, on its way to Haiphong. (Ozbourn DD-466 folder, no. 111898, Photo Archive, Naval History and Heritage Command)

B-52s on the line, armed with AGM-28 Hound Dog Missiles, 1967. (Still Pictures Division, NARA)

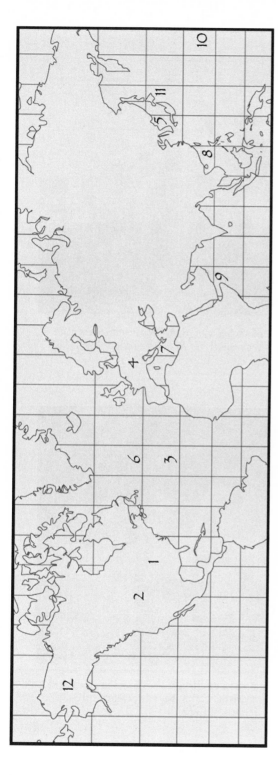

The JCS Readiness Test: Major Measures

1. Heightened alert and stand-down at SAC bases in the United States, 13–18 and 25–30 October

2. Stand-down at Tactical Air Command, Alaskan Command, and Continental Air Defense Command bases in the United States, 14–18 and 25–30 October

3. Emergency movement by aircraft carriers in the northern and western Atlantic, 18–20 October

4. Stand-down by US air forces in Europe, 15–18 and 25–30 October, and heightened surveillance and intelligence gathering, beginning 18 October

5. Task Force 71 deployment in Sea of Japan extended until 24 October

6. Stand-down of CINCLANT air assets, 25–30 October

7. Sixth Fleet, EMCON, ca. 15–30 October

8. Seventh Fleet trails Soviet merchant ships headed toward Haiphong, 20–29 October

9. Increased ship activity in Gulf of Aden, ca. 19–27 October

10. Enhancement of SIOP naval forces at sea, ca. 19–30 October

11. Stand-down by Pacific Air Forces in Japan and Korea, 14–18 and 25–30 October

12. SAC nuclear-armed airborne alert flights over northern Alaska, 27–30 October

At a meeting in Washington, DC, 1 October 1969, Sam Brown and colleagues plan Moratorium activities. (*U.S. News and World Report* collection, Library of Congress)

One of the events of the Moratorium was a candlelight march on the grounds of the Washington Monument, led by Coretta Scott King, on 15 October 1969. (*U.S. News and World Report* collection, Library of Congress)

Antiwar demonstration on the Mall, 15 November 1969. Haldeman remarked in his diary, "It was really huge." (Photographer Theodore B. Hetzel, Theodore B. Hetzel Photograph Collection, Swarthmore College Peace Collection, Swarthmore, PA)

At the initialing of the Agreement on Ending the War and Restoring Peace, 23 January 1973, Paris. Right to left: Kissinger, Le Duc Tho, Nguyen Dinh Phuong (interpreter), Xuan Thuy, and Nguyen Co Thach. (NARA)

CHAPTER SIX

The First DUCK HOOK Plan, the "Nixon Doctrine," and a Deadline
July–August 1969

> The president has not excluded the possibility that he could take
> the option to the right in order to wind up the war quickly.
> *Henry Kissinger*[1]

Concerned that their "plans for ending [the] war aren't working fast enough," as he put it to Haldeman on 7 July,[2] Kissinger, like the president, believed that more dramatic military steps might be necessary to force Hanoi into making concessions in the Paris negotiations. In preparation for this contingency and at Kissinger's request, US Navy planners secretly began preparing a mining plan code-named DUCK HOOK, which would soon evolve into a larger scheme to mine *and* bomb North Vietnam. Meanwhile, Nixon and Kissinger amplified their campaign of threat making against Hanoi, hoping to coerce concessions from the North before having to face the difficult and fateful decision of expanding and intensifying the war.

Kissinger may have been more hawkish than Nixon at this juncture, if only because the president worried more about the political, congressional, and international fallout should he launch highly visible attacks against North Vietnam. Roger Morris, a former NSC staffer, reported in 1982 that he thought Alexander Haig was egging Kissinger on. In 2006, Haig told Kimball that though Nixon often "baited" Kissinger by taunting him about his preference for diplomacy over force, "Henry was the real hawk during this period."[3] Perhaps both stories are true.

Laird and Rogers favored a policy of accelerated troop withdrawals over military escalation, although Rogers advocated a faster rate of withdrawal than Laird. Haldeman noted in his diary that Kissinger—aware of Nixon's hesitancy to confront Laird and Rogers and knowing that Haldeman favored escalation too—complained to him that Rogers and Laird "are constantly pushing for faster and faster withdrawal." It would lead, he felt, to a "'cop out' by next summer." If this were going to be the policy, Kissinger grumbled, the administration might as well "cop out now."[4] Nixon's support of US troop-withdrawals, albeit at a slower pace than advocated by Laird and Rogers, would make it necessary for him to assure President Thieu and other Southeast Asian allies of his continuing commitment to their internal security during an around-the-world trip in July.

The Meeting on the *Sequoia*

On the evening of 7 July, the president chaired a four-hour Vietnam War policy meeting of what Kissinger called the NSC executive committee aboard the presidential yacht *Sequoia* as it cruised up and down the Potomac River. In attendance were Kissinger, Laird, Rogers, Wheeler, Attorney General John Mitchell, and CIA Deputy Director General Robert E. Cushman. Although no official record of the gathering has been found, other sources indicate that the main topics on the agenda had to do with what the lull in ground fighting in South Vietnam portended for DRV/PRG military and diplomatic intentions, the degree of progress thus far achieved in Vietnamization, and the balance to be struck between de-Americanization and military escalation—the most contentious issue.[5]

Before the meeting, Kissinger had told Haldeman that he would "push for some escalation, enough to get us a reasonable bargain for a settlement within six months." But the record of what was said on the *Sequoia* that night is spotty, and it seems the issue of a military escalation option did not come up. What *is* known is that Nixon placated Laird and Rogers with a presidential commitment to make additional troop withdrawals in September (beyond the initial June increment) and to order a change in MACV's mission statement from defeating the enemy and forcing the withdrawal of the NVA from South Vietnam to providing maximum assistance to the Saigon government. Nixon had apparently been unwilling to inform Laird and Rogers about his and Kissinger's thoughts on escalation; he was also disinclined to confront them face-to-face and reject their calls for stepping up the pace of troop withdrawals.[6]

Despite gaps in the record, however, available sources indicate that the president and his national security assistant were seriously but privately considering military escalation. Nixon had chosen to keep his options open. As he had since January, he would simultaneously continue Vietnamization, apply military pressure, and issue threats against Hanoi. But he would also explore the necessity and desirability of embarking on new and dramatic military escalations.

Nixon noted in his memoir, *RN*, that he came out of the *Sequoia* meeting planning to "'go for broke' in the sense that I would attempt to end the war one way or the other—either by negotiated agreement or by an increased use of force." In "several long sessions" from July into October, Nixon wrote, he and Kissinger "developed an elaborate orchestration of diplomatic, military, and publicity pressures we would bring to bear on Hanoi."[7] Their purpose was to build greater momentum behind their negotiating strategy before Congress resumed work and students returned to their campuses in September. These coming events, they feared, would lead to a "massive new antiwar tide" during the fall and winter. Moreover, other threats to their plans and timetable loomed: the possibility of a VC/NVA offensive during the post–February 1970 dry season and the long political lead-up to the November 1970 midterm elections, during which Nixon expected increased public and congressional pressure for more troop withdrawals.

But the decision for an increased use of force had not yet been made; it was still only an option. At the time of the *Sequoia* meeting in early July, Nixon and Kissinger were transitioning from a mining ruse stretch-out to the serious consideration of actually mining Haiphong Harbor and blockading the coast of North Vietnam, which was the response they had earlier agreed upon should the Vance Ploy fail—and it had failed.

On Monday 7 July—even as George Carver worked on refashioning the CIA's "Haiphong paper" and before the *Sequoia* meeting was to take place—Kissinger requested through Captain Robinson that Admiral Moorer prepare "an updated plan . . . for the actual mining of Haiphong," including "ancillary actions," with a "target date for the operation on or about 1 September." Because of the sensitive nature of the operation, Kissinger also indicated to Robinson that the White House wanted the navy to prepare the plan unilaterally, and he asked "that no discussions be initiated in other channels at this stage." Robinson later wrote Wheeler that he thought "a [White House] decision to mine Haiphong is a distinct possibility on about 1 September."[8]

But if 1 September was indeed the potential target date Nixon and Kissinger originally had in mind, within a week they would move it forward to 1 November. The September deadline fell closely on the heels of President Nixon's recently scheduled around-the-world diplomatic trip from 23 July to 5 August, whose purpose was to give Thieu the bad news about more US withdrawals and reassure Asian allies of US commitments, as well as to prepare the way for his and Kissinger's Madman Theory scheme of escalating the naval and air war. A November target date would allow more time for JCS and NSC contingency planning, interdepartmental discussion, and White House decision making, especially since Nixon and Kissinger were privately thinking about adding a bombing campaign to the mining operation. They may also have wanted to provide sufficient time for Moscow and Hanoi to respond to the threats they were about to signal and for Vietnamization to strengthen RVN forces in the event Hanoi agreed to a negotiated settlement.

The 1 November date marked the first anniversary of President Johnson's 1968 bombing halt, and Nixon might have seen it as a more fitting deadline for Hanoi to comply with Washington's demands or else face the possibility of a blockade and the resumption of bombing. In addition, the early November date fell during the transition between the southern and northern monsoon seasons, when the winds are light and variable and more suitable—though not ideal—for mining *and* bombing.[9] Average rainfall amounts during the southeast monsoon in September are over five times greater than in November. (However, the JCS would argue that the northeast monsoon brings low cloud cover and light rain to northern Vietnam from October to April—poor conditions for offensive air operations.)

In July, however, Nixon's and Kissinger's focus was on mining alone. During the morning after the *Sequoia* meeting, Kissinger gave Robinson more details about what he wanted included in the mining and blockading plan: an analysis of shipping not only into North Vietnam ports but also Sihanoukville, Cambodia, on the Gulf of Siam; an "explicit concept" of blockading operations against these ports; and an assessment of possible Soviet reactions. When Kissinger repeated the need for security during the planning stages, Robinson reassured him that "the channel would be limited to CNO-CJCS-SecDef-Kissinger." Because Kissinger was mildly surprised by this chain-of-command formality of including Laird, Robinson had to remind him that it met his original requirement for navy-only planning, that is, it "did not constitute full-fledged 'joint staffing,'" which, Robinson later told Wheeler, is what Kissinger "obviously wishes to avoid." Robinson's explanation of the makeup of the secure channel awakened Kissinger to the realization that he had been mistaken in thinking he had successfully cut Laird out of the loop. But given Laird's statutory authority and responsibility, he could not legally be kept out. This prompted Kissinger to telephone the secretary of defense immediately with excuses.[10]

Kissinger told Laird that "the press of business" during the *Sequoia* meeting had caused him to forget "to inform [Laird] of a special plan which the president was eager to get and which should be prepared 'outside official channels.'" He said he was phoning now because "he thought [the secretary] would want to know" that the president wished to have it "for his own private use"; that it "would have no official status and will be just a Navy staff study"; and that he, Kissinger, had "already discussed [the matter] with Capt. Robinson." Laird responded that he already knew about the study and promised to keep it confidential. Kissinger further explained that "the president has not excluded the possibility that he could take the option to the right in order to wind up the war quickly." This information, he emphasized, was for Laird's *"own* use." Laird agreed that the president "had to be in that position."[11] The phrase *option to the right* was Oval Office vernacular for military escalation, which Nixon linked with hawkish, right-wing ideas about what should be done in Vietnam.

A Warning to Hanoi

On Kissinger's recommendation and consistent with their post-*Sequoia* intention to escalate threat making, President Nixon met with Jean Sainteny on 15 July to ask him to undertake a mission to Hanoi. A former French Resistance fighter and military planner in World War II, Sainteny had represented France in negotiations with the Vietminh during the First Indochina War and had subsequently maintained contacts with DRV officials. He was also Kissinger's friend. Nixon and Kissinger hoped he could meet with President Ho Chi Minh and carry out three tasks, which together would convey a carrot-and-stick message from Nixon to North Vietnam's leaders. Because the DRV refused to grant him a visa, however, Sainteny was limited to delivering Nixon's message to Mai Van Bo, one of Hanoi's representatives in Paris, on 19 July.[12]

Nixon's letter included entreaties for peace:

I realize that it is difficult to communicate meaningfully across the gulf of four years of war. But precisely because of this gulf, I wanted to take this opportunity to reaffirm in all solemnity my desire to work for a just peace. . . .

There is nothing to be gained by waiting. . . .

The time has come to move forward at the conference table toward an early resolution of this tragic war. You will find us forthcoming and open-minded in a common effort to bring the blessings of peace to the brave people of Vietnam. Let history record that at this critical juncture, both sides turned their face toward peace rather than toward conflict and war.[13]

A second but essential task for Sainteny was to deliver an *unwritten* warning from Nixon, which incorporated an indirect reference to the mining and blockading operation Nixon and Kissinger were now considering:

He has decided to hope for a positive outcome from the conversations at Paris by 1 November, and he is prepared to show good will by some humanitarian gestures, which Mr. Kissinger will be prepared to discuss in detail. But if, however, by this date—the anniversary of the [Johnson] bombing halt—no valid solution has been reached, he will regretfully find himself obliged to have recourse to measures of great consequence and force.[14]

Sainteny's third assignment was to set up a meeting between Kissinger and DRV representatives for 4 August, when Kissinger would be in Paris at the tail end of Nixon's round-the-world trip. He was to tell Bo that Kissinger would like "to learn of Hanoi's reaction to the message of the president."[15]

Carver's Reevaluation

Meanwhile, on 2 July and before the *Sequoia* meeting, Kissinger had phoned Deputy Director Cushman to ask about the "Haiphong paper" that his special assistant George Carver was working on, saying that "the president is very interested and keeps asking him about [it]." When Kissinger mentioned his earlier conversation with Carver, Cushman—who apparently understood what Nixon and Kissinger wanted—volunteered that he had already given Carver "some methods on presenting facts, etc."[16]

On 16 July, Carver sent Helms a fifty-page report entitled "The Effects of the Imposition of a Quarantine on North Vietnam." Kissinger received a copy directly from Helms the next day. He and Nixon held the study closely, probably sharing it only with Haig and Mitchell.[17] Carver must have learned from Cushman that Kissinger wanted plenty of "facts," and he provided lots of them: 125 paragraphs' worth on North Vietnamese trade, Hanoi's economic relations with Beijing and Moscow, and an assessment of the impact of a blockade.[18]

His answer to the question of the probable impact of mining or blockading Haiphong Harbor upon the DRV's economic and military capabilities—one of the key points of interest to Nixon and Kissinger—dovetailed with the analysis that the CIA had provided in June, which Nixon had found wanting. A blockade unaccompanied by air attacks on inland transportation, he argued, would cause a "severe" disruption of Hanoi's "import patterns," but only a few months of adjustments would be necessary to ensure that Chinese and Soviet supplies flowed through overland routes instead of from shipping. The leaders of North Vietnam were "shrewd improvisers," and furthermore, the DRV had plenty of capacity to expand the use of roads, railroads, and inland waterways so that goods could move from China and the Soviet Union. In addition, photographs taken by US spy planes showed a "continual and large . . . buildup of [military] supplies" at storage areas in Hanoi and elsewhere. Even with a quarantine blocking Soviet shipping, "the great bulk of North Vietnam's requirements of [nonmilitary supplies] could be supplied from China." North Vietnam's economy would remain viable, and Hanoi would be able to continue the war. This was the same assumption that underlay the JCS's long-held views in favor of coupling bombing-and-mining operations.[19]

The CIA report also addressed the question of possible Soviet, Chinese, and North and South Vietnamese reactions to a US quarantine. Perhaps to avoid irritating Nixon, Carver shunned "summary judgments" and provided instead a detailed exposition of the political considerations that could shape responses in Beijing, Moscow, and Hanoi. He argued that Chinese and Soviet reactions would be particularly significant because they would heavily influence "Hanoi's range of options." Beijing, a key DRV ally, would find it essential to come to Hanoi's rescue rather than let US actions drive it "to the wall." In light of their rivalry with Moscow, the Chinese would find an opportunity to increase their influence with the DRV, while attacking the Soviets for "being too cowardly to contest" the blockade. In general, Beijing was likely to wage a "high-decibel propaganda campaign" against Washington, rather than sending warships or taking any other confrontational action, although mine-sweeping assistance was possible.[20]

The Soviets were also unlikely to confront the United States, but, as Carver explained, they would feel pressure to stand by the DRV. Determined to sustain its policy of containing China, its major national security priority, Moscow would feel compelled to maintain a presence in the DRV. If the United States blockaded Haiphong, the Soviet Union would want to "keep in step" with North Vietnam. Moreover, as the chief user of the port of Haiphong, Moscow would not allow the United States to cause it a loss of face as a "great power." Yet even if the "odds [were] heavily against [a] physical challenge" by the Soviets, a quarantine would confront them with "most difficult decisions." They would "certainly issue grave warnings and attempt to create the impression that a major world crisis could soon result if the US quarantine was not speedily lifted." The Kremlin, for example, could make implied threats that if Washington sustained its aggressive approach, "critical situations would inevitably be generated at points of confrontation in other areas." Soviet-instigated "countercrises" could not be ruled out, but Moscow was more likely to reap benefits in "demonstrating that the US move would not bring Hanoi to its knees and in stimulating political pressures . . . to impel the US Government to desist."[21]

According to Carver's analysis, as long as the DRV could bank on Chinese and Soviet aid, political considerations, not supply problems, would determine its response. Based on long-standing assumptions that domestic pressure in the United States would "make continuation of the struggle . . . politically unsalable," as it had for France in 1954, Hanoi believed that as long it "sits tight and more or less stonewalls on its present political posture," Washington would be forced to make "major concessionary gestures." Although a US blockade would come as a surprise to Hanoi, the leadership would assume that the action would spark protests in the United States that could reverse it. Therefore, the DRV was likely to "wait to see how events unfolded." Soviet support would enable Hanoi to gamble that Washington would find it difficult politically to prolong the blockade. Simultaneously, the DRV would probably wage a "strident propaganda campaign" and suspend the Paris talks with Washington.

On the other issue that most concerned Nixon and Kissinger—whether a blockade would influence Hanoi's negotiating position—Carver again carefully calibrated his analysis to avoid annoying the White House. The blockade, he wrote, would "certainly not induce Hanoi to opt promptly for a negotiated settlement," but

> if the US Government turned what appeared to be a deaf ear to the criticisms the quarantine would inevitably provoke at home and abroad and persisted in the quarantine through a period of weeks stretching into months, the arguments within Hanoi would become increasingly nervous and sharp. . . . Persistence in the quarantine . . . would—at a minimum—almost certainly compel Hanoi to review its basic strategy and the political calculations on which that strategy is based.

This alone, however, would not necessarily determine Hanoi's conclusions. Other determinants—in addition to the DRV's estimate of the political situation in the United States—included levels of Soviet and Chinese aid and developments in South Vietnam. Indeed, the CIA's economic analysis suggested that as long as Beijing and Moscow were willing to help, Hanoi could tough it out.[22]

Carver was probably sincere in giving this balanced assessment in the report, but he also recognized that Nixon's and Kissinger's opposition to the coupling of bombing to mining stemmed primarily from their (or at least Nixon's) considerable concern with the probable home front and international reactions to the renewal of bombing in North Vietnam. Carver's implicit message was: it's up to you; if you are willing to ignore protests for weeks and months and stick with it, mining alone could possibly work.

Nixon and Kissinger no doubt welcomed the CIA's assessment that a sustained blockade could make the DRV leadership "nervous" and compel it to "review its basic strategy," but the agency's political analysis brought out other complicating elements. The Saigon regime, for instance, would be surprised and delighted by the blockade, yet at the same time, the improvement in its morale would make it less interested in negotiations or in "set[ting] its house in order to gird for a period of political competition." If, however, Washington lifted the blockade without forcing concessions from Hanoi, Saigon would interpret this development as "a major US political defeat." As for US allies in Asia, "few would expect the US move to effect decisively Hanoi's will to continue the war, or, at least in the short term, its ability to do so," and they would find the possibility of a US–Soviet confrontation to be "particularly unnerving."[23]

Carver's equivocal analysis of the risks and limits of a blockade or quarantine probably had a significant influence upon White House thinking about the pros and cons of mining alone versus mining and bombing, inasmuch as Kissinger would urge the latter during the next several weeks, and Nixon would ultimately scuttle both options by October.

DUCK HOOK

DUCK HOOK, the navy plan for mining Haiphong and blockading North Vietnam and Cambodia that Kissinger had requested on 7 July, arrived at the White House and the office of the secretary of defense on 21 July, one day before the "suspense date,"[24] or the deadline Kissinger had set, and two days before Nixon and Kissinger set out on their globe-circling diplomatic journey. The mining and blockading schemes against North Vietnam and Sihanoukville had the common purpose of being "shows of determination" to induce Hanoi and Moscow to cooperate on a Vietnam settlement. Drafted by Robinson and sent to Kissinger and Laird under Moorer's signature, the detailed, fifty-page document was divided into a summary, an intelligence appraisal, mining plan concepts and options, rules of engagement, potential world reactions, and implications for international relations. Its basic premise was that imports through Haiphong were a major "prop" to the DRV economy, and transshipments of supplies out of Sihanoukville were critical to the DRV/NLF effort in the South. The closing of the Haiphong port complex and the quarantining of Sihanoukville, the authors argued, "will have a major effect on the North Vietnam economy and the ability of the North Vietnamese to support the war in the south." This assessment diverged markedly from the special analysis that the CIA had provided the White House.[25]

The mining operation against Hanoi included three options. Option Alpha involved three aircraft carriers, Bravo two, and Charlie one. With each option, the purpose was to block large merchant ships from access to Haiphong Harbor as well as to disrupt any attempts by Hanoi to use lighterage craft to off-load merchant ships anchored past the minefields. The extensive use of Destructor mines in shallow waters would make such disruption possible. If one of the carriers happened to be at port, Alpha could take more time to implement, but Robinson saw it as the most advantageous option because it "provides the most complete and effective mining of the Haiphong Complex and accomplishes the mission in one launch." Using 605 Destructors and 154 MK-50, -52, and -55 mines carried in eighty-seven sorties, DUCK HOOK provided for the simultaneous mining of fifteen fields around Haiphong and the coastal cities of Hon Gai and Cam Pha. This was twelve times as many Destructors and a third more MK mines than the previous JCS plans had called for. DUCK HOOK was also more comprehensive, especially in seeking to foreclose attempts by Hanoi to use small ships to elude the minefields.[26]

To minimize political problems, automatic timing systems would ensure that the MK mines used in all three options would not be armed for seventy-two hours after the fields were laid. Destructors, unlike the other mines, could remain disarmed for only twenty-four hours and, therefore, had to be laid forty-eight hours after the first group of mines. Such arrangements would ensure that Russian, Chinese, and other freighters would have safe passage to leave the area.[27]

Robinson and Moorer maintained that international law imposed no restrictions upon the mining of Haiphong Harbor. Although the Hague Convention of 1907 had prohibited the use of mines against commercial shipping and stipulated that a state of war had to already be in effect before mines were used, the authors of DUCK HOOK argued that "revolutionary" changes in warfare during the Cold War had "rendered obsolete" the pre–World War II international laws of war. They argued that with South Vietnam's "national right of self-defense," its ally, the United States, had the right to use a "reasonable method" to help repel aggression from North Vietnam. Not only was such action necessary, it was also proportional because mining was a "passive, not aggressive measure." Other countries would receive advance notice, the area of mining was limited, and "this defensive measure will reduce loss of life and material elsewhere in the zone of hostilities."[28]

The authors also tried estimating world reactions to a mining operation and came up with more optimistic assessments than the CIA analysts had, especially on Soviet reactions. Believing that global "uneasiness" about the war had somewhat subsided, Robinson suggested that public opinion would be manageable: the world would see the mining operation as a show of determination, whereas a year earlier, it would have condemned it as a reckless move. As for North Vietnam, with its highly limited ability to counter mining operations, it would probably undertake major efforts to use smaller boats to move goods around the minefields and attempt to compensate for the disruption of supplies by relying on overland and coastal-water shipments from China. The navy planners were not worried about Beijing's reaction, which would be mostly propagandistic, although they expected Hanoi to ask for more aid. Even if the Soviets lost some ships and reacted adversely—for example, by freezing arms control talks—they might become more "disgusted" with the war and press the North to settle. This estimate conflicted markedly with the CIA's view that Moscow would want to "keep in step" with Hanoi.[29]

None of the anticipated adverse reactions would be enough to deter US mining operations, Robinson argued. The United States could counter them all. On the propaganda front, Washington could argue that the mining was a "low order response" to Hanoi's "complete lack of cooperation." If the Soviets lost some ships, the United States could simply lay the blame on Moscow for "callously sacrific[ing] the loss of their men and matériel in spite of all US attempts to protect third nation shipping." If the Soviets anchored ships past the minefields and off-loaded supplies to DRV lighterage, the navy could seed the routes with Destructors and launch aerial attacks against DRV ships (far from Robinson's "passive measures"). The diversion of North Vietnamese resources into a lighterage operation and the delays in imports "would have a cumulative effect on the North Vietnamese economy and their ability and willingness to continue the war effort in the South." Again, this differed from the CIA's analysis that, with Chinese and Soviet aid, the DRV could stay in the war.[30]

Intelligence community opinion had been divided on the role Cambodia played in supplying the DRV/NLF forces, but by mid-1969, new information from sources in Hong Kong and elsewhere produced a consensus view that significant amounts of matériel were reaching VC/NVA forces out of Sihanoukville.[31] For Robinson, this justified an interdiction plan to surveil ships approaching that port. If they lacked a Certificate of Clearance issued by the State Department at ports of departure, the US Navy, he argued, could use force to stop, seize, and even destroy the ships once their crews had debarked.[32]

Robinson estimated that the interdiction of Sihanoukville would not be as controversial as mining Haiphong because a "quarantine would clearly discriminate between ships carrying contraband and those which do not." Moscow was not likely to contest the operation because it would be significantly less of a direct challenge than mining Haiphong, but he thought it politically useful all the same. The Soviets were likely to "recognize the quarantine as a demonstration of US resolve and might," which could lead them to "put more pressure on Hanoi to reach a speedy settlement." Such action, Robinson argued, was consistent with international law because it was defensive and met the "twin tests of necessity and proportionality."[33]

Around the World with More Threats

On 23 July, two days after the White House received the DUCK HOOK plan, Nixon and Kissinger flew out of Washington on the first leg of their global mission. Aside from the public relations boost he hoped to receive from the whirlwind trip, the president intended it to serve several purposes, most of which were related to his Vietnam game plan. Years after the war, he wrote that the trip provided "perfect camouflage" for Kissinger's secret meeting on 4 August with Xuan Thuy in Paris that Sainteny had arranged. In keeping with other secret steps Nixon and Kissinger were taking, Laird and Rogers were not informed of the meeting.[34]

The president's entourage landed at Johnston Island in the mid-Pacific, then steamed across the international date line on the USS *Arlington* to rendezvous with the aircraft carrier *Hornet* on 25 July. From its bridge, Nixon watched the splashdown and recovery of the *Apollo 11* space capsule, which returned to earth from its moon-landing mission. After a greeting ceremony for the triumphant astronauts, an exuberant Nixon flew on to Andersen Air Force Base in Guam.

In the evening, he held a press backgrounder at the Officers' Club, which he opened by telling reporters that before he took their questions, he wanted to give them his "perspective" on the US "role in Asia and in the Pacific" because Asian leaders were wondering whether Americans' "frustration over the war in Vietnam" would cause the United States to "withdraw from the Pacific and play a minor role" in the future. He assured them that the United States would continue to play a significant role in Asia-Pacific affairs and stand by its military commitments. But even though America would not retreat from Asia, it had to be sensitive to nationalist sentiment. Americans, he observed, also wanted to avoid turning their security commitments into another frustrating Vietnam quagmire. Hence, the administration was in the process of reevaluating its policies to see if and how all this could be accomplished. These remarks were reminiscent of what he had written in an article for the October 1967 issue of *Foreign Affairs* entitled "Asia after Vietnam," but as in that piece, his comments lacked specificity about how to solve the paradox of commitment without war.[35]

Reporters followed with several questions about how he would assure an Asian leader who was now receiving US military aid but was concerned about de-Americanization in Vietnam that the United States would "remain to play a significant role . . . in security arrangements in Asia." And if the United States continued to provide security support, how could it avoid "a Vietnam-type situation" from developing in the future? Nixon's answers again indicated that his thinking on the subject had not yet been put into the form of actual policy and that, in any case, he certainly did not intend his incipient policy to become a rigid doctrine: "I would simply say we are going to handle each country on a case-by-case basis." He added that he was just "attempting to avoid that creeping involvement which eventually simply submerges you—incidentally, I don't say that critically of how we got into Vietnam, but I do know that we can learn from past experience, and we must avoid that kind of involvement in the future."[36]

Had Nixon concluded the conference at this point, reporters and pundits might not have been inclined to view his expressed intention of avoiding creeping troop involvement in future crises as a turning point in policymaking. But the president continued with additional extemporaneous remarks that may have made his incipient policy sound more like a doctrine.

> I recall in 1964 some advice that I got from Ayub Khan . . . of Pakistan. . . . He said: "The role of the United States in . . . any of those countries which have internal subversion is to help them fight the war but not fight the war for them." Now, that, of course, is a good general principle, one which we would hope would be our policy generally throughout the world.

When a reporter asked whether Nixon's message was "no more Vietnams," the president repeated his desire "to avoid another war like Vietnam any place in the world. . . . I realize it is very easy to say that. . . . But what we can do is to learn from the mistakes of the past."[37]

Almost immediately following the backgrounder, the press began referring to Nixon's comments on Vietnam as the Guam Doctrine, a term that remained in use in some newspapers at least as late as September 1970. Yet almost as quickly, editorialists and reporters had also begun using the term Nixon Doctrine, placing Nixon in the pantheon of other presidents who had announced doctrines. Incongruously, the press continued using the appellation even when they noted contradictions between Nixon's rhetoric and his actions.[38] This practice, which journalists and historians would soon follow, may simply have been the result of groupthink and stylistic convenience. Even if the Nixon Doctrine was not a true doctrine, everyone seemed to be calling his "new" Asian policy a "doctrine." Perhaps it was easier to write or say Nixon Doctrine than to try to describe, explain, or encapsulate the ambiguous statements Nixon had uttered in Guam or to discover and explain what lay beneath the rhetoric.

As with other presidential doctrines, repetition caused the verbal abstraction of the Nixon Doctrine to acquire a life of its own, partially or wholly detached from material existence. In addition, Nixon had told reporters at the outset that his remarks were "for attribution but not direct quotation, and for background"; no one besides those in attendance could review, study, and parse his comments carefully. Complicating matters further, the White House did not release the transcript of the press conference until 1971.

Another reason for press and public misunderstanding and mischaracterization was that Nixon's words were intentionally imprecise. His purpose was not only to make policy but also to project an image of a foreign policy leader who was experienced, nuanced, farsighted, comprehensive in his thinking, and a moderate regarding the Vietnam War.[39] Above all, he was walking a fine line—needing to assure voters and European allies that he intended to withdraw from Vietnam and avoid future Vietnams while also reassuring Asian and other allies and clients in the capitalist-leaning developing world that he was not abandoning US commitments to their regimes' security. In July 1969, Nixon was still stuck in Vietnam, trying to uphold his and previous administrations' commitments to the Saigon government in the name of preserving his and the government's honor and credibility.[40] To this end—the end of avoiding defeat or the appearance of it—he was paradoxically considering military escalation in Vietnam with operation DUCK HOOK and issuing secret and dire threats to Hanoi as he was simultaneously embarking on de-Americanization and Vietnamization.

Haldeman described the so-called doctrine in his diary entry for the day of the Guam backgrounder as one designed to "supply arms and as-sistance only to those nations that would supply their own manpower to defend themselves. No more automatically rushing in our men."[41] But that was exactly how the United States had walked into the quagmire of Viet-nam: initial US arms and assistance in the late 1950s; then a dribble of US advisers into the 1960s; and then a rush of US troops in 1965, when the earlier commitment of men, aid, and credibility was perceived as failing. Haldeman's diary comment, which reflected Nixon's thinking, was clearly in reference to the Johnson escalations, not to Eisenhower's provision of money, advice, and men to Ngo Dinh Diem in the late 1950s, which had initiated the commitment of US prestige and credibility.

Before the trip, Nixon had given some thought to the danger of walking into additional quagmires, but there was as yet no administration policy or doctrine to address the problem. On 18 July, during a brief discussion of global hot spots, Nixon offhandedly commented to Kissinger that "we might get into the idea of developing policies now so we don't get bogged down in another Vietnam. In every one of these countries, there is the potential."[42]

Days before, a personal account by former secretary of defense Clark Clifford about US involvement in Vietnam had appeared in the July 1969 issue of *Foreign Affairs*. Clifford had earlier sent offprints to Kis-singer, Laird, and Rogers, and Nixon may have read the article before his around-the-world trip and his comment to Kissinger about developing new policies to avoid other Vietnams. Reviewing the drip-by-drip process of US involvement in Vietnam over the decades, Clifford made a strong case for de-Americanization and argued that the South Vietnamese and other Southeast Asian allies must in the end fight their own battles. If Nixon did read the article, Clifford's arguments probably reinforced his own misgivings about the prospects for victory in South Vietnam. They also represented the widespread sentiment in the American public and foreign policy establishment for an end to the war and no more Vietnams in the future. Clifford's article followed the public comments he had made in mid-June, to which Nixon had responded (see chapter 5). In a private interview with Carroll Kilpatrick, the former secretary of defense went further, telling Kilpatrick that the outcome of the war was likely to be a "mess" and would "leave the American people with a sense of dissatisfac-tion." With Nixon's and Kissinger's fixation on credibility, they thought it was better to have the mess after a decent interval.[43]

In any event, Kissinger seems not to have taken Nixon's remark about developing new policies seriously, and the president had prepared his opening statement at the press backgrounder in Guam without Kissinger's knowledge or the assistance of Kissinger's staff—an unusual step but one indicating that his intention had not been to make a serious, formal announcement of a new doctrine. Years later, Kissinger commented that he did "not think that Nixon intended a major policy pronouncement in Guam: his original purpose had been to make some news because of the empty period produced by the crossing of the international dateline. That a formal pronouncement was not at first on Nixon's mind is indicated by the fact that his remarks were made on background."[44]

Initially surprised by Nixon's impromptu remarks and the press reaction to them, Kissinger later tasked Winston Lord, one of his aides and a specialist on Asia, with examining the policy implications of what the press was now calling the Guam Doctrine. In January 1970, Lord's study noted that "there is no such thing as a grand strategy for Asia" and that the "proposed policy is not all that different from the rhetoric of past policy."[45] By then, however, Nixon and Kissinger had embraced the label Nixon Doctrine because it had been praised by prominent politicians and pundits and accepted by much of the public. It served their political purposes on the home front, implying that the administration had a middle-of-the road, pragmatic grand design for dealing with the Vietnam problem and foreign policy in general.[46]

The day after the press conference, the presidential party flew on to the Philippines, Indonesia, and Thailand, ruled by rightist dictatorships that had security agreements with the United States. Nixon offered President Ferdinand Marcos, General Suharto, and Field Marshal Thanom Kittikachorn the requisite assurances of the steadfastness of American commitments despite the looming, although gradual, disengagement of the United States from South Vietnam. In Saigon on 30 July, however, Nixon gave President Thieu unwelcome news: additional American troop withdrawals would take place in phases according to an American plan whose timetable was supposed to be contingent on the circumstances of the war but would in practice prove to be contingent as well on political and economic circumstances in the United States. Nixon tried to soften the blow by assuring Thieu that he was taking steps to strengthen South Vietnam's military while hinting that he would also back up the de-Americanization process with dire threats and military escalations against the enemy. As paraphrased in the record of the meeting, President Nixon said

> that he wished to say something to President Thieu in the utmost confidence and asked President Thieu not to discuss this with any other individual. He said that he had in mind that it might be highly desirable to issue a warning in the near future to Hanoi about the course they were following, but he wanted President Thieu to know that this will be done in an unorthodox way. He wanted President Thieu to know that he was not discussing this at present with anyone in the US Government, and that it should be held strictly between the president and President Thieu.[47]

In Lahore, Nixon succeeded in persuading President Yahya Khan—who needed little persuading—to serve as an intermediary with the Chinese leadership. Stopping in Bucharest on 3 August before heading home to Washington, Nixon told President Nicolae Ceauşéscu that he was prepared to resume the bombing of North Vietnam unless there was progress in the negotiations—a message he expected Ceauşéscu to pass on to Hanoi. Aiming to win Romanian assistance in persuading Hanoi to make concessions, Nixon also offered some carrots, telling Ceauşéscu that North Vietnamese cooperation in ending the war on a "fair basis . . . will make possible the many Romanian-US [trade] actions we talked about, could make possible US-Chinese relations, and would help relations with the Soviet Union."[48]

Flying from Romania to England, Nixon stopped at Middenhall Air Base, where he had a short meeting with Prime Minister Harold Wilson. Nixon did not much like Wilson, but they had a mutually respectful relationship. The British were a major ally, and the prime minister generally supported the Vietnam War—even if he had displeased Lyndon Johnson by not providing material aid. By meeting Wilson, Nixon had an opportunity to pass the same message that he had given Ceauşéscu, telling him that Washington had offered free elections to the other side but that they had offered really nothing in the way of diplomatic concessions. As a consequence, his advisers were "working out a timetable program," according to which, "if there had been no real sign of movement" from Hanoi by 1 November, "he might have to take very serious decisions." Invoking John

Foster Dulles, Wilson commented that Nixon would be making an "agonizing reappraisal"; Nixon replied that this was "just what he meant."[49]

Wholly out of sync with the left wing of the Labour Party, which was strongly opposed to the Vietnam War, the prime minister expressed sympathy with Nixon's reluctance to withdraw suddenly from Vietnam. Wilson supported a version of the domino theory that maintained that precipitate US withdrawal would cause "consternation" in a number of countries such as Singapore and India beyond "predictable" ones such as Thailand. He commented that he would understand if Nixon "felt it right to resume bombing or otherwise to seek to redress the military balance." Although asking that Nixon consult with him on what he intended to do, the prime minister nevertheless assured the president that whatever course in Vietnam the United States took, he "could count on us going with him all the way."[50]

Perhaps wanting to avoid an uncomfortable confrontation, the president did not bring up another Vietnam War matter that had bothered the US government since the Johnson administration and regarding which Nixon wanted Wilson's active help: ending Hong Kong trade with Hanoi. In prior years, Washington had pressed a number of countries, including close allies such as the United Kingdom, to end their maritime shipments to North Vietnam. London had been cooperative, but British flag merchant ships chartered out of Hong Kong, which was then a British colony, remained the largest group of "free world" ships calling at North Vietnam ports. Seventy percent of the vessels, however, were contracted to or under the control of Chinese interests in Hong Kong; their cargoes were foodstuffs, cement, fertilizers, and other nonmilitary but important supplies from China and North Korea. The indirect British role (and the lesser role of other countries such as Cyprus and Somalia) elicited letters from irritated US congressmen, but it also annoyed Nixon. This had led Haig, a few days before the Nixon-Wilson meeting, to ask the State Department to make recommendations on measures to "stop or . . . reduce this traffic."[51]

These officials understood, however, that the British had scant leeway in the matter because Hong Kong authorities lacked legal power over the shipping companies and their cargoes. Any attempt to restrict them would result in a "loss of face to Peking," and the Chinese government, the officials predicted, would "certainly call for retaliation in some form against the British and/or Hong Kong." What made retaliation likely was "the failure of communist activists to bring the colony to its knees last year, and because of Chinese sensitivity on the subject of aid" to Hanoi. Tolerating shipping to North Vietnam was the price that the British had to pay "for the continued existence of their colony." In light of this, State Department officials could not have been surprised when, on 1 August 1969, Minister Edward Tomkins told them that "HMG [Her Majesty's Government] has no legal power to interfere." All Tomkins could do was ensure that no British ships were sold to Hanoi and remind the Foreign Office that "the US still takes seriously the problem of shipping to North Vietnam."[52]

Even though Nixon had not raised the Hong Kong issue with Wilson in their London meeting, he did not give up on it, and he soon asked Kissinger for a report on the matter. On 8 August, Kissinger responded with a summary of the facts of the case, concluding with a comment that the issue should be taken up with Wilson: "If you agree I will talk to the British Ambassador about the problem." Nixon sent a note saying, "See if they won't do something for just 60 days (i.e., the critical period ahead before Nov 1.)"[53] The first of November was, of course, the deadline for Hanoi's response to Nixon's warnings to Hanoi.

Meanwhile, Kissinger had a chance to convey the deadline message directly to North Vietnamese diplomats. When Nixon left for Washington, Kissinger slipped away from the presidential party and headed for Paris, where he, his assistant Anthony Lake, and the US military attaché in Paris, General Vernon Walters, met secretly with Xuan Thuy, Mai Van Bo, and their assistants on 4 August in Sainteny's apartment on the rue de Rivoli in Paris.[54]

Kissinger began by asking Thuy whether there had been an answer from Hanoi to the letter from Nixon that Sainteny had delivered two weeks earlier. Thuy's only reply was that the letter had been forwarded. Kissinger then extended carrots and brandished sticks, telling Thuy and Bo that President Nixon was "ready to open a special and secret channel of contact" if "negotiations are serious," and if such talks did come about, he added, "the president is prepared to adjust military operations in order to facilitate negotiations" and appoint him, Kissinger, to negotiate. However, Kissinger said, the president had instructed him to inform them "in all solemnity that if by 1 November, no major progress has been made toward a solution, we will be compelled—with great reluctance—to take measures of the greatest consequences."[55]

Kissinger also admonished the Vietnamese for claiming in their propaganda that the conflict was "Mr. Nixon's War," and he warned them that "if it is Mr. Nixon's War, he cannot afford not to win it." He added: "You are a courageous, indeed a heroic people, and no one knows what the final result would be of such a sequence of events. We believe that such a tragic conflict to test each other can be avoided." Xuan Thuy replied in kind: "If the war goes on, or is expanded, . . . [we] would be forced to continue fighting in order to reach [our] . . . objectives," but we are "also rich in goodwill" and prefer peace. When Thuy asked what the United States had in mind for a settlement, Kissinger answered: "We are not saying that we insist on any particular government being maintained after a settlement. But we will not—because it is beyond our power and for other reasons—replace Thieu and Ky and Huong. We want the people of South Vietnam to choose their own government after a settlement . . . and a free political process." For his part, Thuy stood by the Ten Points.[56]

The encounter with Thuy must have rankled Kissinger, who found an opportunity that same day to convey another warning. At a meeting with French Foreign Ministry officials, he remarked that "in the conduct of long range American policy throughout the world it was important that we not be confounded by a fifth rate agricultural power. . . . It was unthinkable for a major power like the United States to allow itself to be destroyed politically. . . . The North Vietnamese and the NLF should have no illusions about what is ahead." Kissinger may have been blowing off steam but also hoping that the French would convey his comments and emotions to Hanoi's representatives in Paris.[57]

Before and after the presidential around-the-world trip, Kissinger encouraged or maneuvered others into delivering similar warnings on their behalf, among them presidential counsel Leonard Garment, who had made plans to attend a film festival in the Soviet Union in July and would also meet with Georgi Arbatov and other experts from the USA Institute in Moscow. Kissinger advised Garment to convey to the Soviets the impression that Nixon was "somewhat 'crazy'—immensely intelligent, well organized, and experienced . . . but at moments of stress or personal challenge unpredictable and capable of the bloodiest brutality." Garment later recalled in his memoir *Crazy Rhythm* that his Soviet interlocutors busily took notes when he observed that Nixon was "capable of barbaric cruelty to those who engage him in tests of strength." Moreover, the president was "full of complex contradictions, a strategic visionary, but when necessary a cold-hearted butcher." On his return from Moscow, Garment told Kissinger that he had been sure to tell the Soviets that when Kissinger speaks, "he is speaking for the president" and that he had "conveyed as clearly as possible what [Kissinger] wanted him to say" to the Soviets.[58]

Senate Discovery of the Mining Ruse

In the first week of August—around the time Nixon and Kissinger returned to Washington—the USS *Oriskany* was scheduled to participate in another mining exercise at Subic, while naval technicians overhauled and reworked mines onshore and on carriers in Tonkin Gulf. This left but one final step in the program: the loading of mines aboard an ammunition ship in Subic Bay for movement to Yankee Station. With that shipment, the mining ruse was slated to end on 17 August. But on 8 August, Captain Robinson proposed a delay in the transfer of mines and yet another stretch-out of mine readiness training in anticipation of actual mining operations against Haiphong. The navy, he argued, could improve readiness for carrying out DUCK HOOK by adapting the composition of mines on each carrier in the western Pacific so that they could, if ordered, implement the Alpha option, the maximum plan for mining Haiphong's harbor.[59] The White House apparently accepted Robinson's proposal for a stretch-out. The navy carried on with mine readiness inspections and considered formalizing them, and exercises continued in Subic Bay into October, one involving the USS *Hancock* and the other the USS *Coral Sea*.[60]

Soon after Robinson made his proposal for a stretch-out, the White House encountered an unexpected political danger with the discovery of the mining drills by two Senate staffers, Walter Pincus, a former *Washington Post* reporter, and Norman Paul, a Washington, DC, lawyer. In early August, they happened to be looking into US military activities in the western Pacific at the direction of Senator Stuart Symington (D-MO), who was chairman of the National Security Commitments Abroad subcommittee of the Committee on Foreign Relations. While in Japan, they learned about the shipment of 1,000 mines to Subic Bay. Pursuing the matter at Subic Bay, they found that the chief of the naval magazine was unable to explain the purpose of the shipment or why the mine inventory was larger than usual. On visiting the USS *Oriskany*, Paul learned from its commanding officer that his pilots were engaged in training exercises. Asked about the nature of the training, the officer told Paul that it was an "aerial mine-laying exercise." Pincus and Paul then interviewed the captain in charge of the Mine Readiness Test Team, who explained that the navy's Service Force Command had directed the mine shipments; that his team was at Subic to conduct an "annual inspection on a surprise basis"; and, misleadingly, that the mines were in "normal configuration 'Charlie.'" He assured them that the exercise was routine: the training of the carrier crews was "not unusual" and was taking place in connection with programs for the "general improvement in mine warfare readiness."[61]

Pincus and Paul were unconvinced and "repeatedly demonstrated" their concern to a US Embassy officer about the possibility of "military actions that could increase our . . . level of involvement in Vietnam." As if to lend credence to their concerns, Pincus and Paul noted that during the presidential campaign, Nixon had discussed the mining of North Vietnamese ports, especially Haiphong Harbor, as a means of wringing concessions from Hanoi.[62]

They also informed Foreign Relations Committee chairman Senator J. William Fulbright (D-AR) about their discovery. It worried Fulbright, who wrote to Laird on 13 August that if the purpose of the mine shipments was "to prepare to mine the harbor at Haiphong, it would appear to me such action would be directly contrary to the announced policy of President Nixon with regard to withdrawal of United States forces from Vietnam." He demanded that his committee "be informed as to the purpose of this movement of sea mines."[63] The Foreign Relations Committee's concerns had already been heightened after members had recently learned about the existence of a secret 1965 agreement with Thailand that provided for US troops to assist the Thais in the event of a Communist invasion. Arguing that such an agreement could lead to another Vietnam, committee members publicly demanded to see it.[64]

Word of Pincus's and Paul's discovery spread, and interest in contingency plans to mine Haiphong grew in the Senate and at high levels of the State Department. Rogers wanted to see the plans, and apparently, Fulbright did as well. In a telephone conversation with Kissinger on 18 August, Laird remarked that "everyone knows we have them in the JC[S]." Kissinger replied that "we can't get into the business of revealing our contingency plans." Laird agreed, commenting that "the only one they can see is the [one about] Thailand." Kissinger suggested the explanation should be that the training exercises in the Philippines were simply part of "a Navy readiness test," which was true, though not the whole story.[65] Neither Pincus's and Paul's suspicions nor Fulbright's concerns about the purpose of mining exercises at Subic reached the public; the Haiphong issue soon faded, although the possibility of escalation remained very much on the minds of Nixon and Kissinger.

CHAPTER SEVEN

Toward the November Option:
DUCK HOOK and PRUNING KNIFE
July–September 1969

> If [the] USSR thinks [the] president is a madman, then they've
> driven him to it, and they'd better help calm him down.
> *Henry A. Kissinger to "trusted aides"*[1]

Sometime before, during, or after their around-the-world trip, Nixon and Kissinger decided that planning for their go-for-broke strategy should include a bombing component to supplement the mining operation. Recently declassified documents have thrown more light on the decision-making process leading to this step, but some parts of the story remain murky. The White House taping system did not exist, and except for abbreviated entries in Haldeman's diary and meeting notes, no other records are available of the "several long sessions" to which Nixon referred in *RN*. In these, he and Kissinger "developed an elaborate orchestration of diplomatic, military, and publicity pressures we would bring to bear on Hanoi." The extant documentary record for the period suggests that even with their strong interest in the original DUCK HOOK mining plan, they were also thinking about launching a corresponding bombing campaign as early as the latter part of June, if not before. During the following weeks, civilian and military planners produced new contingency plans that spoke to Nixon's and Kissinger's interest in coercing Hanoi with punishing blows. Two competing concepts emerged: PRUNING KNIFE and an expanded DUCK HOOK, whose earlier iteration included proposals for the use of tactical nuclear weapons on selected logistics targets. Despite Kissinger's strong interest in escalation, however, Nixon continued to weigh alternatives to a November escalation option because of his concerns about the international, intragovernmental, and domestic political climate.

An Expanded DUCK HOOK Concept

During the week before the *Sequoia* meeting, Kissinger again sought General Maxwell Taylor's advice on military options. Taylor conjectured that the onset of de-Americanization had probably encouraged Hanoi to stand pat in the negotiations and "hope for the US withdrawal momentum to accelerate." Hanoi's reasoning, Taylor argued, was that "Washington—before Nixon's inauguration—had already spent most of its 'blue chips,' i.e., the bombing of the Hanoi/Haiphong area, the air/sea interdiction of the southern NVN panhandle, operations in the DMZ, and non-recognition of the NLF." Following this logic, Taylor recommended a scenario of reescalation. The president, he suggested, should explain the Vietnam situation "to the American people in a major TV appearance, and . . . announce the initiation of actions which would lead to the mining of Haiphong and, perhaps in addition, resumption of full-scale bombing of NVN."[2] Taylor's scenario, with some targeting revisions, would be the one Kissinger embraced and advocated between July and October: warnings to Hanoi of US reprisals should the Politburo fail to cooperate, an explanation to the American people of the reasons for escalation, and the launching of a military operation that combined mining with bombing.

At the time of Kissinger's meeting with Taylor, the strategy of the administration—as described in its "Policy Alternatives" paper of 3 July—was not military victory or military escalation but "military pressure." Its aim was "to keep 'maximum' pressure on the enemy to induce them to negotiate and to minimize our casualties to buy time at home." Morton H. Halperin, the primary drafter of options papers during this period, apparently placed the word *maximum* in quotation marks to suggest a flexible meaning: it represented the level of military pressure the White House thought possible or prudent in the circumstances.[3] These were defined by "three key factors . . . : US public opinion, the other side's willingness to negotiate seriously, and the political and military situation in Vietnam."[4]

But Halperin expressed uncertainty about the prospects for success in Vietnam despite the "maximum" military pressure that had been and was being applied; namely, the bombing of bases in Cambodia, air operations in South Vietnam and Laos, robust ground operations, enhanced pacification, the mining ruse, and *threats* of escalation directed at North Vietnam. Kissinger's consultation with Taylor might have been an attempt to find an escalatory path that would enable the administration to escape the current impasse—a qualitatively different kind of maximum pressure to bring about a settlement that met US conditions.

The mining of Haiphong and the bombing of targets in northern North Vietnam were the top candidates for the task, but in July, Nixon was not prepared to launch either. The proponent of the Madman Theory, he was intellectually and emotionally open to both courses of action. But he was ambivalent about going ahead with either because of his worries about popular and congressional reactions and in consideration of Laird's and Rogers's preferences for de-Americanization and Vietnamization.[5] Although he had accepted Kissinger's recommendation to dispatch Jean Sainteny to Paris with a warning to Hanoi's representatives and followed up that gambit with additional threatening warnings in the following weeks, Nixon continued to equivocate, while weighing his options for or against military escalation.

During their late July to early August, two-week around-the-world journey, Nixon and Kissinger probably discussed the DUCK HOOK mining and Sihanoukville quarantine plans, copies of which Kissinger had taken with him,[6] along with Carver's reassessment of the impact of mining. Kissinger may also have presented Nixon with a memorandum outlining a "conceptual plan for implementation of operation DUCK HOOK," which placed the operation into a broader context of force, diplomacy, and politics and may have been prepared by his own staff. The operation, Kissinger began, "would not be approached as a purely military action but instead as a combined military and diplomatic operation intended to produce both military and political results with minimum adverse reactions at home and abroad." The diplomatic part of the scenario would begin a week before the military operation by calling in Ambassador Dobrynin to tell him in "strong terms" that "our patience with Hanoi had been strained to the breaking point" by its "intransigence at Paris" and its "actions in South Vietnam . . . and Cambodia." If Hanoi did not reverse its course, Washington would "be obliged to take some form of action to show Hanoi that it could not escape the consequences of its behavior." Ambassador Lodge would deliver the same message in Paris. "If Hanoi should not respond," the military action would begin. It would include not only the aerial mining of the Haiphong port complex and the interdiction or quarantine of Sihanoukville but also B-52 raids in Laos and Cambodia.[7]

According to the scenario, one hour before the attacks, US allies and other interested parties, such as the government of Cambodia and "ambassadors of all friendly countries with ships in or en route to Sihanoukville and the Haiphong complex," would be informed. Dobrynin would be assured that it "was not anti-Soviet but only against Hanoi." Washington would make the same points to Moscow one-half hour later by the Moscow/Washington Emergency Communications Link (MOLINK)—informally known as the Moscow/Washington hotline. Nixon would brief congressional leaders, and the White House would hold a "locked-door press briefing." At the time of the launch of the attack, the president would make an announcement to the nation via television and radio, and the White House would request a special meeting of the UN Security Council.[8]

In addition, US forces would *"assume a heightened PACOM and SAC alert posture militarily to show our resolve and to respond to whatever contingencies arise."* The latter step amounted to a nuclear readiness alert. On Wheeler's copy of the memo, the reader, probably Wheeler himself, placed a question mark in the margin next to that sentence. Favoring concrete measures over psychological threats, he may have thought that a SAC and PACOM alert was pointless and wasteful.[9] Nevertheless, according to Robert Pursley, military aide to Secretary Laird, Nixon's and Kissinger's interest in nuclear readiness measures "began not terribly long after Midway [Nixon's 8 June meeting with Thieu] but certainly before September 1969."[10]

Nixon's and Kissinger's discussion of the mining of Haiphong Harbor and quarantining of Sihanoukville in light of Carver's assessment of these naval operations appears to have caused them to also consider adding air operations against North Vietnam to the mix—and to reconsider their strategic options concerning the Vietnam problem. This is suggested by Kissinger's request of General Wheeler to provide a "concept plan" for an aerial military operation that would implement Nixon's threat to take measures of great consequence and force against North Vietnam after 1 November should Hanoi remain "intransigent" in the negotiations. While abroad, Kissinger also instructed Halperin in Washington to prepare another paper on "Vietnam Policy Alternatives."[11] Both papers were to be ready for Kissinger when he returned to the capital on 5 August, the day after having repeated Nixon's threats of dire reprisal against North Vietnam to Xuan Thuy.

Wheeler's concept plan was based on an operation carried out during the

ROLLING THUNDER bombing campaign of the Johnson era. It proposed a series of intensive, four- to five-day bombardment attacks by tactical aircraft and naval vessels against two military logistics complexes at Thanh Hoa and Vinh—85 and 205 miles from Hanoi, both south of 20° N latitude. A week later, on 13 August, G. Warner Nutter, assistant secretary of defense for international security affairs and DOD representative on Kissinger's Ad Hoc Vietnam Advisory Group, informed Laird— presumably on behalf of the group—that the plan would "neither be a wise nor effective course of action at this time." But, he added, it could be "one of the many options to be considered" should the North Vietnamese launch a major attack.[12]

Even though Wheeler's plan incorporated the administration's desired concept of carrying out short-duration air attack "packages," it did not measure up to Nixon's warning to Hanoi about taking measures of great consequence and force after 1 November. He and Kissinger, moreover, did not want a bombing plan modeled on ROLLING THUNDER; namely, an operation that was designed to be the start of a gradually escalating bombing campaign over a sustained period of time, whose main objective would be to erode North Vietnam's military capabilities and thus assist the US/RVN military effort in the South. Instead, they wanted a concept plan that emphasized psychological and political aims. Its purpose would not necessarily be to destroy North Vietnam or its war-making capacity but instead to produce shock and awe: sudden and dramatic military pressure on Hanoi to yield in the negotiations. The nature of the operation would be defined by the targets chosen and the weight of the initial attacks, all divided into phases or stages that would force Hanoi to assess the risks and possibilities of continued war versus a negotiated settlement. It was a concept that resembled Kissinger's discussion of a "calculus of risks" in his 1957 book, *Nuclear Weapons and Foreign Policy*. In addition, the successive short-duration attack packages of the Nixon-Kissinger concept of carrying out the principle of threatening excessive force would supposedly better enable Washington to gauge Hanoi's reaction to each package and also cope with unfavorable domestic and international protests should these materialize, as Nixon and his advisers expected they would.[13]

Such a concept was contained in the 5 August policy alternatives paper drafted by Halperin and Winston Lord. It began by identifying several evolving circumstances that a revised administration strategy should take into account. The most important of these were the continuing lack of movement in the negotiations, the uncertainty about whether the other side's current military "lull" would continue or transform into fighting of "fresh intensity," and the expectation that US public pressure on the administration to make progress in the negotiations would increase. This was likely because the American citizenry would again turn its attention to Vietnam after having been distracted by the *Apollo 11* moon landing and the president's world trip. Moreover, the return of students to their campuses in September would "certainly raise the level of controversy over the war. . . . We are torn between the impatience of war-weary Americans and a commitment to reach a just settlement."[14]

Halperin and Lord were correct in anticipating renewed protests by students and other Americans dissatisfied with what they considered the Nixon administration's token troop withdrawals and the prospect of a perpetual war. By July 1969, separate groups of activists in the liberal and leftist camps of the antiwar movement—who only sometimes cooperated in planning and staging demonstrations—had begun to organize two events for the fall. The first, the Moratorium to End the War in Vietnam, was a liberal-led action scheduled for 15 October in cities and on campuses across the country. It combined countrywide teach-ins with a call for Americans to suspend business as usual that day in order to reflect on or protest the war, with the aim of persuading the Nixon administration or the Congress to set a fixed timetable for US withdrawal from Vietnam. The second action combined demonstrations organized by the Moratorium and the New Mobilization Committee to End the War in Vietnam (New Mobe). These were scheduled for 13–15 November in Washington, DC. The New Mobe called for the immediate withdrawal of the United States from Vietnam.[15]

In consideration of this eventuality and the other evolving circumstances of the war at home and abroad, Halperin and Lord explained that US strategy was "aimed at three basic audiences: the enemy, the GVN, and the American people." The purposes of the administration were to: "convince the *enemy* that they have nothing to gain by waiting; reassure the *GVN* that we will negotiate and disengage at a pace that should allow it to compete politically and militarily with the other side; maintain the support of the *American people* for an honorable outcome to the war." In support of these objectives and reflecting the views of Kissinger and the NSC staff, Halperin and Lord proposed four alternative strategies. The first, Option A, "Pursue Our Current Strategy," was the starting point: "Keep two options open: negotiation of a political settlement in Paris and gradual, flexible Vietnamization of the war to permit US disengagement in the absence of a settlement. Our military tactics are designed to keep pressure on the enemy to induce them to negotiate and to minimize our casualties to buy time at home."[16]

The other three options were variations on the theme: Option B: "accelerate negotiations" and seek a cease-fire-in-place and political compromises while "moderating . . . military tactics" but continue current de-Americanization policies; Option C: accelerate de-Americanization while moderating military tactics but continue the current negotiating approach; and Option D: "*escalate* militarily" while continuing the current negotiating approach but halting the de-Americanization process.[17]

The military escalation option, they wrote, "would be used as a *means* to a negotiated settlement, not as an *end*, since we have ruled out military victory. We would halt escalation as soon as it produced diplomatic results." The military tactics employed

> would not repeat the process of slow escalation designed gradually to increase the pressure on the enemy to negotiate. . . . Instead we would move decisively to quarantine North Vietnam through such actions as blockading Haiphong Harbor, resumption of bombing in the north (including close to the Chinese border), and stepped up pressures against third-country trade with Hanoi. We would simultaneously pursue the war in the South with maximum air and ground efforts. We might move into Laos and Cambodia.[18]

Not long after Lord and Halperin wrote this, the White House resumed pressure on one "third-country" trade issue that continued to preoccupy Nixon: the Hong Kong shipping problem. During August and September, Kissinger and then Haig pressed Undersecretary of State Elliott Richardson and his assistant Morton Abramowitz to bring the matter up again with the British and to apprise them of Nixon's threat to Hanoi. In accordance with White House instructions, on 11 September Richardson told John Freeman, the British ambassador to the United States, of a "new factor" that "warranted further discussion of the subject" of British shipping to North Vietnam. This new factor, Richardson told Freeman, was the State Department's "belief that the next sixty days or so might represent a critical period in moving toward a settlement of the Vietnam problem." In that connection, Richardson suggested that if the British could take action that led to a "a reduction, slow-down, or preferably stoppage in Hong Kong/North Vietnam shipping," it could help induce Hanoi to "move in the desired direction." Nixon had already told Prime Minister Wilson about the possibility of military action against Hanoi on a November deadline, but now the White House wanted to see if the British could help turn the screws on the DRV. Although Ambassador Freeman explained why this was a difficult problem, Richardson asked that London try to find a way. The British, however, were not going to jeopardize their position in Hong Kong. There was another flurry over British shipping to Hanoi in early 1970, but this problem in Anglo-American relations gradually faded away.[19]

Catch-22

White House officials understood the limits of military threats. According to Halperin and Lord, the "rationale" for military escalation would come into play if the White House became convinced that its *threats* of escalation had not and would not "induce the other side to negotiate or erase their impression that time is on their side." Halperin and Lord warned, however, that "if we embark on this course we must be prepared to follow through with it." To "be caught bluffing" would undercut "not only our Vietnam policy but our across-the-board relationship with the Soviet Union."[20]

But there was a catch-22 in this rationale: if the administration's threats of escalation failed to achieve results, Halperin and Lord observed, the escalation option itself was also "very likely to fail." Failure could result, in large part, because the "option would require the enemy to compromise in the face of all-out offensives against the North and in the South. Determined resistance is at least as probable as a cracking of will." The choice seemed to be one of either bluffing and losing credibility or choosing military escalation and upholding credibility but failing to move Hanoi.[21]

Halperin and Lord saw other risks associated with the escalation alternative, comparing them to "many of the dangers and costs of seeking a military victory"—an objective the administration had dismissed. The "uproar" in the United States and around the world "would be tremendous" and "dwarf past efforts." The administration would lose "domestic support not only on the Vietnam issue but also on a range of other issues."

Hanoi might respond to the US escalation by "overrunning all of Laos and attacking US air bases in Thailand." Progress with Moscow in negotiating nuclear arms control agreements, moderating Mideast frictions, and coming to grips with other major issues would grind to a halt. More likely, the Soviets might launch "counter thrusts" elsewhere in the world and also succeed in improving their relations with China. There would also be a risk of the Soviets and/or Chinese being sucked into the Indochina war, at which point, they said, "we [would find] ourselves on the edge of World War III." There would be other dangers and problems that "one can speculate at length on."[22]

The warning Halperin and Lord raised about the strategic penalties in being caught bluffing echoed the views Kissinger had expressed in his published writings during the 1950s and 1960s.[23] They had no doubt read these, and perhaps they hoped to dissuade their boss from choosing the escalation option by reminding him of his own caveats. Each had serious doubts about this fateful course of action and preferred other alternatives. Halperin favored putting US troop withdrawals on a fixed schedule; Lord preferred a de facto political settlement by means of a cease-fire with territorial accommodation.[24]

If Nixon read the policy alternatives paper or was briefed on it by Kissinger, its warnings about the twin risks associated with either being caught bluffing or following through with his threats must have been sobering, since he had already embarked on a course of escalated threat making. He now faced the dilemma of deciding whether to escalate or not. To Kissinger's chagrin, Nixon remained undecided about going ahead with the gambit. The president and his national security assistant gave themselves four weeks to choose either the option of military escalation or one of the three other options enumerated in the 5 August paper. The choice would depend, in large part, on whether there would be "movement at Paris" or whether Kissinger would hear directly from the North Vietnamese about revisions in their negotiating position.[25]

Surveying Public Opinion

American public opinion was one of the other considerations that would influence Nixon's decision on escalating. Sometime during the first part of July, the White House commissioned a confidential national survey, paid for by the Republican National Committee, to try to get a better sense of what the public thought about Nixon's handling of the war and the military and diplomatic options that he and Kissinger had in mind. David R. Derge, a political scientist who was then vice president and dean at Indiana University, designed and managed the survey. He had directed a previous poll for the administration in May.[26]

Derge met with Nixon and Kissinger at the White House on 16 July to run some things by them. Almost a week later, on 22 July, the day before he and the president were to begin their around-the-world trek, Kissinger phoned Derge with suggestions for changes in the wording of three survey questions. Two of his recommendations had to do with the public's views on imposing a coalition government upon Thieu. His other recommendation was about the phrasing of a question concerning the blockading and bombing of North Vietnam. Kissinger's proposal for revised wording suggests that before their trip, he and Nixon were focused more on mining and blockading North Vietnam and less on sustained, heavy bombing. The transcript of the telephone conversation reads: "K suggested leaving out heavy bombing [from the question] and focus on blockade— something to [the] effect 'as last resort selective bombing.'"[27]

Between 28 July and 4 August, the Opinion Research Corporation of Princeton, New Jersey, carried out 1,579 nationwide personal interviews in the homes of respondents who were twenty-one years of age and older. On 11 August, Derge submitted his fifty-four-page report to the president, who two days before had flown to the "Western White House" in San Clemente for a month-long working vacation. The survey results were mixed.[28]

Among the key questions and responses, a majority continued to view President Nixon as "supporting some kind of middle position . . . between an immediate withdrawal and a complete military victory." Only 17 percent, however, thought the administration was "telling the American people most of the facts" about the war. The results were better when respondents were asked whether they would support an administration strategy "that would decide to end the war in Vietnam with a compromise settlement within six months," during which "we would take necessary military actions, such as [a] blockade of the port of Haiphong and, as a last resort, selective bombing of North Vietnam," with no additional US troops sent. "Strongly in favor" garnered 24 percent support, and "somewhat in favor" 42 percent. The survey did not specifically mention mining as a means of blockading North Vietnam, however, and in any case, only 47 percent favored "closing" the port of Haiphong. A slim majority

of 51 percent believed "we should resume the bombing of military targets in North Vietnam," but only 35 percent supported the bombing of
"enemy sanctuaries . . . in Cambodia and Laos," whereas 46 percent were
"against" and 19 percent had "no opinion." The public still did not know
that the Nixon administration had been and was currently bombing targets in Cambodia and Laos.[29]

A narrow majority of 51 percent favored a US "withdrawal over a two-
year period while negotiations are continued" and the United States
"would continue the level of military operations as it is now"; 30 percent
favored a "withdrawal in six months, agreeing to anything to end the war";
and 37 percent favored "a military victory." The survey did not, though,
spell out what constituted a military victory or raise the issue of how to
achieve it, except that it would *not* entail the invasion of North Vietnam
or the use of nuclear weapons. Only 7 percent thought the administration was "doing a good job in handling the war in Vietnam"; 55 percent
thought the administration was doing "as well as can be expected." But
59 percent thought the administration "should be more actively seeking
some way to stop the fighting."[30]

According to the survey, the issue of how the administration could
manage to stop the fighting implicitly hinged on some combination of
military action, US troop withdrawal, and a negotiated compromise. In
practice, military escalation—the action Nixon and Kissinger were now
contemplating—might eventually have stopped the fighting but only after
much more combat. The White House was already withdrawing troops.
But without a negotiated end to the fighting, Nixon and Kissinger were
only prepared to withdraw all troops and forces as a last resort, with a
completion date extending beyond the November 1972 presidential election. What constituted a negotiated solution was not made clear by the
questions in the survey. Yet what was clear was that most respondents
were against imposing a "coalition government" on President Thieu, even
though (and somewhat contradictorily) they believed that no Saigon government could be "representative" without the participation of the Provisional Revolutionary Government.[31] In mid-1969, the DRV and PRG were
opposed to any political settlement that failed to provide for a coalition
government that would include the PRG but exclude Thieu's participation in it.

One of the more significant findings was that compared to Derge's May
survey, the July–August poll provided "evidence of some movement of

public opinion toward the 'dovish' position both with respect to how the public views themselves and how they perceive the position of President Nixon." This survey result probably deepened Nixon's quandary about military escalation.[32] If the public was more dovish than it had been at the outset of his administration and, moreover, if he was now perceived as being more dovish than he had been previously, then a military escalation of the conflict might possibly produce a strong public backlash against him for having acted too hawkishly. In any case, even though the survey results suggested that a majority would support military escalation under certain circumstances and with particular restrictions, it remained to be seen whether Nixon could hold that support for the time required for escalation to work—assuming that mining and bombing could force Hanoi to give in.

Pondering Alternatives

President Nixon may not have read the survey results until 18 August, when, as Haldeman noted in his diary, he met with Kissinger, Haldeman, and Ehrlichman—his "hard-core inner circle"—for an hour and fifteen minutes at the Western White House to discuss "Vietnam alternatives." It was "obvious," Haldeman observed, "that we have to end it [the war] in six to nine months."[33] The Vietnam alternatives discussed at the meeting were DUCK HOOK—at least in its mining-only form—and most probably the alternatives outlined in Halperin's and Lord's paper of 5 August. Outside Nixon's office in San Clemente, Kissinger lobbied Haldeman, Ehrlichman, and Mitchell to help convince the president to support military escalation, arguing that the president had "to make [a] total commitment and really be prepared for the heat." Haldeman thought that the president "realizes this and is getting ready," and he believed this was the reason Nixon was pushing hard for a "better PR capability and also . . . the reason he's really taking a vacation."[34]

On 28 August, Haldeman recorded in his diary that Nixon "reviewed K's contingency plan for Vietnam tonight," although he did not specify what contingency document Nixon examined. Whatever it was, the conceptual plan for the implementation of the DUCK HOOK mining operation, the diplomatic and PR concept associated with it, and the 5 August policy alternatives paper would have served as the starting points for any operational concept designed to smite North Vietnam. Kissinger had spoken with Nixon by telephone for a few minutes in the morning. He may also have talked with Haldeman, who observed that "K feels strongly that he, E[hrlichman] and I, plus Mitchell, must hang tight and provide the backup," along with "a domestic [PR] plan to go with it, covering actions and reactions here" on the home front. "If we go to" the contingency plan, there "will be a tough period ahead."[35]

Two days later, on 30 August, Kissinger informed President Nixon that President Ho Chi Minh's reply to his letter of 15 July had been delivered to the White House through Sainteny in Paris. Ho's letter was dated 25 August. It was both conciliatory and defiant. Ho opened by saying that he had "the honor" of acknowledging Nixon's letter, but he accused the United States of waging a "war of aggression . . . against our people" and said that it "continues to intensify military operations, the B-52 bombings, and the use of toxic chemicals." He expressed indignation at the "losses and destructions caused by the American troops to our people and our country" and voiced sympathy for US military casualties, saying that he was "deeply touched at the rising toll of death of young Americans who have fallen in Vietnam." But he added, perhaps with intended sarcasm, that US troops had fallen "by reason of the policy of American governing circles." Acknowledging Nixon's need for Hanoi to "allow the United States to get out of the war with honor," Ho closed with a conciliatory sentiment: "With good will on both sides we might arrive at common efforts in view of finding a correct solution of the Vietnamese problem."[36]

It is not known with certainty whether Ho actually wrote the 25 August letter, which is doubtful, or whether it was the product of a joint effort by the collective leadership of the DRV, perhaps led by First Secretary Le Duan, a longtime activist in the Communist Party from Quang Tri Province in northern South Vietnam. The NSC White House staff and US intelligence services saw him as one who "enjoyed a close personal relationship with Ho," who was "known for his policies of sacrificing everything for the struggle in the South," and who after Ho's death "would consolidate his power position."[37] But whether the letter to Nixon was written by Ho, Le Duan, or others, neither North Vietnamese nor National Liberation Front leaders saw anything in the US position that amounted to meaningful concessions or compromises that would justify the abandonment of their long battle to end the foreign occupation of South Vietnam and bring about national reunification under Communist leadership.[38]

In his cover memorandum to Nixon, Kissinger tried to turn Ho's message into grist for the mill of a mighty US military blow against North Vietnam. Describing the letter as "tough" and "insolent" in making "demands but no concessions," Kissinger took umbrage with Ho's use of the term *governing circles* in referring to Nixon's presidency. He also disparaged the last paragraph as "rather conciliatory, although probably for the sake of symmetry." In the careful language that usually went into official documents, Kissinger concluded with a plea for escalation: "The letter is disappointing in content but does have the virtue that it can help demonstrate the necessity of whatever actions are taken in November."[39]

Nixon underlined the words *intensify military operations* and *B-52 bombings* in Ho's letter, but what he thought about these words or the letter as a whole is unknown. Was he encouraged that Hanoi had taken note of these military operations or disappointed that these operations had not yet persuaded Hanoi to yield? In his 1978 memoir, *RN*, he characterized Ho's message as a "cold rebuff" because the DRV president had called for a negotiated solution based on the PRG's Ten Point plan without even mentioning the US plan. Yet in his own letter to Ho in July, Nixon had expressed a willingness "to discuss any proposal or program that might lead to a negotiated settlement," including the other side's Ten Point proposal. But he had belittled its importance by equating it with the "other proposals" put forward by other groups and individuals, while identifying his own proposal as the fairest of all. Ho had reversed this hierarchy of peace programs, and even though he had called for goodwill on both sides, he had made it clear that his government would not yield in the face of US threats no matter how dire. On 2 September, only four days after the White House had received Ho's letter and on the twenty-fourth anniversary of Vietnam's independence, Ho Chi Minh died of heart failure at the age of seventy-nine. This led the US administration to speculate on the implications of unsubstantiated rumors that a power struggle had broken out in the Hanoi Politburo, which might possibly produce enemy concessions.[40]

Nixon knew that he would soon have to make a decision about which course of action he would pursue. At the moment, he was not as convinced as was Kissinger about the necessity or practicability of military escalation and had probably hoped that what he had regarded as Madman threats would have been sufficient: the bombings in Cambodia and Laos, the mining feint, and his warnings about launching devastating strikes against North Vietnam. He might have thought there was another way out of Vietnam without having to lose face.

In addition to DUCK HOOK and the military escalation option in Option D of the 5 August alternatives paper prepared by Lord and Halperin, Nixon was also considering Options B and C. Both called for moderating military tactics and putting more emphasis on de-Americanization. Option B accented negotiations with the aim of bringing about what US planners considered a compromise solution to the political dilemma: a "mixed electoral commission" that would include PRG, GVN, and third-party representatives but would fall short of constituting a coalition government. Should the other side reject this solution, US negotiating tactics would shift to a search for a settlement based on a cease-fire and political accommodation; that is, a cease-fire-in-place, which would leave the GVN and PRG with political and military control over the territories they each occupied and controlled. The major problem with this approach, Lord and Halperin maintained, was that it was "ambiguous and risky—if it turned sour we would be all the more responsible for engineering a fake peace," which was another name for the decent-interval solution. By "turning sour," they meant that it could result in renewed civil war between the parties and, eventually, Thieu's defeat.[41]

Option C accented de-Americanization. In contrast to Option B—which called for a flexible approach to troop withdrawals keyed to the level of violence—Option C called for a specific or fixed timetable, attempting "to strike a balance in our withdrawals between enough speed to satisfy American opinion and enough deliberateness to allow a reasonable chance for GVN survival." The main problem with this approach was that "the Saigon regime's strength might quickly unravel once our policy is made known."[42]

President Nixon would eventually be drawn to particular elements in Options B and C, specifically, the negotiating strategy of Option B coupled with the steady, unilateral withdrawal of US troops—but on a secret timetable to be completed shortly before or shortly after the 1972 presidential election. This he would soon dub the "long-road" or "long-route" strategy. It would bring about what the administration considered an honorable political settlement in three more years, while giving Thieu a reasonable chance to survive and providing the Nixon administration with a decent interval between US withdrawal and Thieu's possible collapse.

During the period of US withdrawal, variants of the military measures proposed in Option D would be used in response to real or perceived military moves of the NVA/VC and in support of the American withdrawal and Thieu's government.[43]

At this moment, however, Nixon was uncertain about his future course, not only because of his own doubts and concerns about the risks of military escalation measures but also because of the views of those advocates within the administration in favor of accelerated troop withdrawals, notably, his secretary of defense and secretary of state. On 4 September, for example, Laird recommended giving "the highest priority to Vietnamizing the war" while looking "for ways to accelerate the Vietnamization program. . . . Not only should the concept of Vietnamization be broadened to include non-military areas, but the options in the military field on force levels, force composition, and potential budgetary savings incident to all our operations in Southeast Asia should also be vigorously examined."[44]

By this time, the term *Vietnamization* had become the byword for both the withdrawal of US troops (de-Americanization) and the US-assisted strengthening of the South Vietnamese army and government. The JCS conceded that a thirty-month schedule for withdrawing half of the US forces then in Vietnam could be "accomplished with acceptable risk" but favored a forty-two-month timetable "for military purposes." The withdrawal of half of the US troops would leave behind a force of 267,500 to 285,000 men "to support the RVNAF, protect American units, and provide an emergency reinforcement capability." Laird, by contrast, was advocating a twenty-four-month timetable and leaving fewer residual troops behind—225,000.[45] In preference to military escalation, Rogers also favored withdrawals but on an eighteen-month timetable, and he additionally advocated a cease-fire-in-place, which was one of the proposals in Lord and Halperin's Option B.[46]

Public opinion was also very much on Nixon's mind. The proposals within the government for "accelerated" US troop withdrawals—even those from Laird and Rogers—would still have stretched out US troop participation in the war beyond what the majority of the public wanted. The Derge survey of July–August, for example, had found that 51 percent favored a complete US withdrawal within a two-year period, with 30 percent favoring withdrawal within six months. Independent polls in September and October supported these earlier findings.[47]

Two Contingency Groups Formed

Despite his doubts and concerns, Nixon was still open to the option of military escalation. Kissinger and others in the inner circle were also in favor of escalation because they believed the United States was withdrawing troops too rapidly to pressure Hanoi into concessions but not rapidly enough to please the American public. Contingency planning went forward. On the morning of 9 September, Colonel Haig reminded Kissinger that in his meeting with Nixon that day, he was to tell the president that he, Kissinger, was scheduled to meet with General Wheeler at 5:00 p.m. "to discuss military planning for the DUCK HOOK operation . . . and would like to convey to him the president's personal mandate that planning be held strictly in *military* channels" in order to "preclude discussion of the plan and the ongoing detailed planning with even the Secretary of Defense." Haig added that "you may mention to the president that it would be additional insurance if he could convey these instructions personally, although briefly, to Wheeler."[48] Nixon took the advice, meeting at 5:10 p.m. with both Kissinger and Wheeler for ten minutes.[49] Wheeler subsequently ordered the formation of a "planning group" composed of members drawn from MACV, the Seventh Air Force, and the Seventh Fleet to rendezvous at the MACV compound in Saigon for the purpose of designing an operational plan for attacks against North Vietnam, which was supposed to be based on the White House concept of a sharp and sudden blow over a limited period of time. Their plan in the making would be code-named PRUNING KNIFE.[50]

In the White House Situation Room the next day, 10 September, Kissinger held his first meeting on the military escalation option with his own "trusted group" of NSC aides, but whether he met with the whole group, a smaller working group, or a set of working groups is still a mystery. He would meet again with some or all of them on 12, 20, 24, and 29 September. Who was in attendance at these meetings is unknown. Known to be associated with having worked on the escalation option in one capacity or another were Alexander Haig, John Holdridge, Richard Kennedy, Anthony Lake, Winston Lord, Laurence Lynn, Roger Morris, Peter Rodman, Helmut Sonnenfeldt, William Watts, Colonel William Lemnitzer, and Captain Rembrandt C. Robinson. Morris referred to this group as the September Group, which was divided into working groups, but whether all members were trusted by Kissinger is also unknown. His so-called trusted group may have been a smaller set of aides who supported escalation. Lake, Lord, Lynn, Morris, and Watts, for example, had reservations about many of the escalation measures proposed and discussed. Lord, with Halperin, had voiced these reservations at least as early as July. Kissinger referred to them as his "bleeding hearts." In early September, Halperin—who had played a key role in writing earlier options papers but who was now, unjustly, under a cloud of suspicion of having leaked information to the press—resigned from Kissinger's staff soon after coauthoring a 10 September memo with Lord about their preferred policy alternatives, which diverged from those of Nixon and Kissinger.[51]

Kissinger charged individuals and his working groups with different and apparently separate and isolated tasks: preparing a concept of operations; examining the military, diplomatic, political, and legal consequences of the operation; drafting a presidential speech in which Nixon would announce and defend the attacks against North Vietnam should he decide to go ahead with military escalation; and designing a scenario for what they hoped would be postattack negotiations with Hanoi. He initially met with each staffer individually to give them their assignments. Robinson and Lemnitzer were responsible for drafting the details of the military strike, although Robinson seems to have been the main figure in this regard. Lake, Morris, and Kennedy prepared legal and diplomatic assessments of the attack plans. Lake and Morris also worked on the presidential speech, as did Rodman. Bill Watts handled public affairs issues, and Holdridge, Lord, and Sonnenfeldt assessed Soviet and Chinese reactions to reescalation. Lynn analyzed North Vietnamese targets. Haig was apparently not involved in planning or drafting but was, as Morris put it, "Henry's scribe and enforcer."[52]

The left hand, however, may not have known what the right hand was doing; the analyses made by each working group or individual may have been wholly or partially unknown to other groups and individuals. In 2007, for instance, Lemnitzer said that he did not remember anything about a *group*, and the only DUCK HOOK plan he recalled was the original mining-only plan. In 2005, Lake said that although he remembered being aware at the time that there was an escalation planning group, he was not familiar with the name September Group and did not consider himself part of a working group but was instead collaborating with Morris on specific tasks and busy with other issues; he was also unaware of the code name PRUNING KNIFE.[53]

This Kafkaesque environment—in which work was compartmentalized, aides were isolated from others, and some were kept in the dark about the real purposes and constituent parts of a common plan or strategy—was not unusual in Kissinger's NSC. When Ellsberg's release of the Pentagon Papers almost two years later triggered a discussion in the Oval Office about the possibility of staffer leaks of Nixon papers, Kissinger tried to reassure Nixon and Haldeman that "our bureaucratic papers are different anyway; we are forcing them [the aides and bureaucrats] to write [mere] options, so no one really knows . . . the secret stuff we've been doing [and what our purposes and decisions are]." With Nixon's concurrence, Kissinger—as Bill Watts put it—was the "juggler," keeping all in motion to reach a desired end. This "bureaucratic" philosophy extended to the cabinet and the rest of the government. In *White House Years*, Kissinger referred to it as a "chess game whereby Nixon, with my assistance, moved toward a foreordained decision while confusing his Cabinet as to his plans."[54]

Some members of the amorphous so-called September Group, along with Kissinger, would contemporaneously or retrospectively refer to the concept plan they worked on as DUCK HOOK—the vestigial code name of the navy plan originally drawn up in July but which would now include bombing as well as mining operations. This unofficial, informal code name may have lingered because its "basic military action"[55] remained that of mining Haiphong and five other deepwater ports. Or the name may have been in circulation among some members of the September Group simply because its civilian members were unaware of the PRUNING KNIFE code name, DUCK HOOK was the only name they encountered, and it was a convenient shorthand reference. When Bill Watts was given a stack of attack plans to examine at Key Biscayne in early October, for example, the only one that carried a code name was the original DUCK HOOK mining-only plan, but it was mixed in with other apparently unnamed plans to mine and bomb North Vietnam—plans that probably came from the JCS PRUNING KNIFE group in Saigon.[56]

The crux of the code-name muddle was that Nixon and Kissinger wanted a plan that emphasized shock and awe for the purpose of bringing about diplomatic concessions from the Soviet Union and North Vietnam. The template for the White House September Group was the Nixon-Kissinger-Robinson concept for an assault on the North that was associated with the Vance Ploy, the mining ruse, the original DUCK HOOK mining plan, and Option D of the Halperin-Lord policy alternatives paper of 5 August (which no doubt reflected Kissinger's views), as well as an identical paper with a slightly revised introduction that Kissinger gave to Nixon on 11 September.[57] The DUCK HOOK label was applied to the November operation desired by the White House, but it was a phantom code name for what was in fact, from September to November, a *concept of operations*, not an operational plan.

The PRUNING KNIFE group was supposed to work from the template Kissinger had communicated or supplied to Wheeler, but those in this group favored what they thought of as a "sound military concept,"[58] as did Wheeler and the Joint Chiefs. Apparently working from previous plans on the shelf (see chapter 8), they wanted an operation that would produce military results in North Vietnam in support of the US war effort in South Vietnam—a plan, in other words, that was a "doctrinally pure" concept, representing military principles.[59] However, their instructions from Kissinger were to follow the concept he proposed, apparently causing the group to deviate somewhat from pure doctrine, which eventually displeased even the JCS.[60]

Regardless of nomenclature, both concepts were works in progress that were never completed. A more convenient but informal name for the prospective operation sometimes used within the White House and the JCS regarding the prospective escalation was the November Option, after the name of the month in which reescalation was to begin.[61]

Key documents on Kissinger's highly secret discussions with the September Group remain closed at the Library of Congress. According to Roger Morris, however, Kissinger told the group that the negotiations were not going well. With the bureaucracy endemically incapable of coming up with fresh initiatives, he, Kissinger, would "have to do it" and take the president, Congress, and the people along with him. Journalists Tad Szulc and Seymour Hersh later reported that their sources said Kissinger did not rule out the use of tactical nuclear weapons, possibly "a nuclear device" to block a key railroad pass to China if that should prove the only way of doing it. Charles Colson, special counsel to the president, who was not a member of the special group but who asked Haldeman about the affair in 1970, claimed that Haldeman said, "Kissinger had lobbied for nuclear options in the spring and fall of 1969." Morris told the authors that the subject "surfaced because the use of nuclear weapons to close off main supply routes at the Mu Gia Pass [a choke point on the Ho Chi Minh Trail] and elsewhere had been raised in a larger options paper, put there by the military liaison members of the group, Robinson and Lemnitzer (on the authority of the JCS, I am certain)."[62]

Morris's and Colson's recollections were on the mark. Significant evidence has surfaced at the Nixon Presidential Library that Kissinger and his aides were looking at specific nuclear options in September. A staff report entitled "Vietnam Contingency Planning: Concept of Operations," dated 13 September—the day after Kissinger's second meeting with "trusted members" of the so-called DUCK HOOK September Group— laid out, among other strike options, *"clean nuclear interdiction of three NVN-Laos passes"* and *"nuclear interdiction of two NVN-CPR [PRC] railroads."*[63] The NVN-Laos passes mentioned in this concept paper presumably included the Mu Gia Pass.

In 2007, Morris said that since the Johnson administration there had been factions in a "corner of the JCS" who had advocated using nuclear weapons against important logistics targets, including the Mu Gia Pass. He added that Robinson and Lemnitzer, perhaps representing this "corner," had introduced the nuclear issue into a "larger options paper" (which may have been the 13 September concept plan but which the authors did not have at the time of this interview), causing him and Lake to comment on it orally and textually. They commented because, according to Morris, they thought the idea of nuclear use "appalling." Morris said that he and Lake addressed the matter in the 29 September memo to Robinson and also in other analytical papers about the November Option as a way of "getting their ideas [against nuclear use] across"—ideas and objections they also voiced orally. It was a way of making sure that Nixon and Kissinger would confront beforehand the possibility that the president might eventually have to make a decision on nuclear use should conventional military measures fail to persuade Hanoi to yield—especially since this possibility had been floated in discussions of attack concepts.

Lake independently confirmed Morris's account, explaining that their comments about nuclear use in the 29 September memo and other memos *did not* constitute their advocacy or preference for nuclear escalation but were attempts to head off a slide down a slippery slope—a "warning [that] if you are going to do it, know what you're doing, . . . make sure you've thought of everything." It was only in this sense "analytical." He added that he and Morris had been told that to be successful, the operation would have to be "brutal and sustainable" and that this requirement might include or have to include the possible use of tactical nuclear weapons, although decades later, he "did not remember specifics."[64]

Lake had written a slippery-slope warning to Robinson in an earlier, 17 September memo analyzing the DUCK HOOK concept of operations; it was presumably Lake and Morris who would again comment in a 2 October version of the operations concept on nuclear use. Even though the extant versions of this paper do not contain recommendations for nuclear use, their remarks regarding "nuclear weapons" imply that the matter of nuclear use had remained in circulation, if not in play, up to early October —the period when Nixon finally decided against the November Option (see chapter 8).

None of this thinking ever reached the office of Secretary of Defense Laird, who in any event rejected the idea of nuclear use in Vietnam. Robert Pursley, Laird's aide, said in 2001 that he had never seen any such documents at the time: "My hunch is that . . . this is just something internal that they'd ginned up and they want to see how far they can take it analytically."[65] Laird recalled that the "NSC suggested all sorts of things," but not everything was taken seriously. Kissinger's approach toward Vietnam was that "nothing was out of consideration" and nuclear-weapons threats were "always to put it there as an option." The whole question of nuclear use and nuclear threats with respect to Vietnam during the Nixon phase of the war, Laird added, "comes from the Korea analogy" and Eisenhower's use of threats in the Korea settlement, but that was "not my approach." Laird's reaction to using nuclear weapons in Vietnam was that it was a "laughable thing," and his attitude at the time was "just forget it." When asked about Laird's statement, Lake answered, "That would be true enough"[66]

In *White House Years*, Kissinger provided a suggestive explanation of how the nuclear and ground invasion options became conceivable. He reported that among other things, he told the group that the president was not willing to "capitulate" but had "lost confidence" in the current strategy of walking a fine line "between withdrawing too fast to convince Hanoi of our determination and withdrawing too slowly to satisfy the American public." What was needed was a "military plan designed for maximum impact on the enemy's military capability" in order to "force a rapid conclusion" to the war. He asserted that he and Nixon had offered "concessions which have been unrequited." Therefore, options were now needed. "I refuse to believe that a little fourth-rate power like North Vietnam does not have a breaking point. . . . It shall be the assignment of this group to examine the option of a savage, decisive blow against North Vietnam. You start without any preconceptions at all."[67]

All the same, Kissinger had preconceptions from the start. On 12 September, for example, he told the September Group that the purpose of the operation was not only to intimidate Hanoi but also to influence the Soviet Union to put pressure on North Vietnam to give in. According to his own memorandum for the record, Kissinger's words were: "If [the] USSR thinks [the] president is a *madman,* then they've driven him to it [military escalation], and they'd better help calm him down."[68]

For Kissinger, the most important ideas in the original DUCK HOOK mining plan and the bombing-and-mining scheme in Option D of the August and September options papers were that military escalation had the political, psychological, and diplomatic purpose of persuading Hanoi to negotiate on terms favorable to Washington and Saigon but not the purpose of achieving military victory in the South. The actions taken would include mining Haiphong Harbor and bombing North Vietnam, even up to the Chinese border; the initial attacks would be powerful and sudden, avoiding the Johnson-era pattern of piecemeal, gradual escalation.

Kissinger versus Laird and Rogers

By the time Kissinger brought the group together, he had become increasingly concerned about the influence of Laird and Rogers upon Nixon as well as the president's own deepening state of uncertainty about how to resolve their Vietnam problem. He recalled in *White House Years* that it was during this period when he began composing "quixotic" memoranda to persuade the president to approve the November Option.[69] On 10 September, for instance, two days before an important meeting of the NSC, Kissinger wrote a long memo to Nixon, explaining that he had "become deeply concerned about our present course in Vietnam." Their strategy of "attempting to solve the problem of Vietnam on three highly interrelated fronts" was failing regarding the first two: "within the US" and "in Vietnam." This had the effect of undermining their strategy on the third front, "diplomacy." He told the president that he was writing the memo "to inform you of the reasons for my concern," not to discuss the alternative options, about which "you know my recommendations."[70]

Acknowledging that polls indicated citizen satisfaction with the administration's handling of the war, he also reminded Nixon what all in the White House believed: home front public pressure to bring the war to a swift conclusion would increase. The antiwar demonstrations planned for October along with the increasingly strong opposition of "moderate" opinion makers would polarize public opinion, putting the president in the position that Lyndon Johnson had found himself in—"caught between hawks and doves." These circumstances would confuse Hanoi but also "confirm it in its course of waiting us out." Kissinger further argued that the administration could not win the war with current military operations and pacification within the two years some advisers had predicted, although "success or failure in hurting the enemy remains very important." Vietnamization/de-Americanization likely would not succeed because the RVNAF was fundamentally incapable of assuming the full burden of the war, and the "withdrawal of US troops will become like salted peanuts to the American public." Serious consequences would follow: the DRV/NLF would be emboldened to protract the war; the American public would be encouraged to demand continued disengagement that could lead to de facto unilateral, complete withdrawal; and the morale of US soldiers who were among the last to leave would decline. President Thieu, Kissinger argued, was chronically unwilling and inherently incapable of broadening the base of his government, and he lacked the full confidence of even non-Communist elements in the South Vietnamese body politic. Concerning the strategy of the DRV/NLF, Kissinger's estimation was that they were prepared to "wait us out" unless there were "some break like Sino-Soviet hostilities." Characterizing their diplomatic policy as one of intransigence, he predicted that they were not likely to make concessions in Paris. He concluded: "I do not believe we can make enough evident progress in Vietnam to hold the line within the US (and the US government). . . . Hence my growing concern." Nixon underlined Kissinger's sentences about the inability of their current strategy to win the war, the forthcoming antiwar demonstrations, Saigon's political weaknesses, and Hanoi's strategy of protracted conflict.[71]

The meeting of the NSC on Friday, 12 September, was a long, four-hour affair. Initially, its purpose had been to discuss the political landscape in Hanoi after Ho's death, the military and political situation in South Vietnam, and the status of the Paris negotiations. But just before the meeting was to begin, Kissinger recommended to the president that there should also be a "far-ranging, . . . full, frank, and open exchange of views" on Vietnam, with emphasis on two issues: the next increment of troop withdrawals and the option of a cease-fire-in-place. Kissinger was apparently concerned that Nixon would favor larger rather than smaller troop reductions and that he was also considering the possible benefits of a cease-fire. He perhaps assumed that a frank discussion of these issues would serve to dampen the president's interest in both. The option of military escalation was not on the agenda. During the meeting, there was a brief exchange on the issue of the bombing of the North, but it came up for discussion only in the context of retaliating against a possible yet then unlikely North Vietnamese strike into the South. The response of Abrams and Wheeler to the question, however, had indirect bearing on the DUCK HOOK and PRUNING KNIFE concepts, inasmuch as they expressed the view that even if all targets were in play, US bombing "would be no fatal blow" against the North if only carried out for a short period of time. This view resurfaced later as Kissinger's DUCK HOOK team and the JCS PRUNING KNIFE group sparred over the question of how to implement the military escalation warnings that Nixon and Kissinger had delivered to Hanoi. Most of the discussion at the NSC meeting, however, centered on the issues of a cease-fire and the pace of troop withdrawals. Kissinger was perturbed. His last words were: "We need a plan to end the war [on our terms], not only to withdraw troops. This is what is on people's minds."[72]

Nonetheless, Nixon came out of the meeting prepared to make a 40,000-man reduction in the US troop ceiling authorization by 15 December, which was 15,000 more than Wheeler had recommended. In addition, the cease-fire proposal was to be brought up for discussion with the GVN but without "any hint of pressure" by the White House on the Thieu government. Nixon announced the troop ceiling reduction on 16 September, aiming it at two audiences—the US public, whom Nixon hoped to appease, and Politburo members in Hanoi, whom Nixon thought would be impressed by this gesture of de-escalation and by his apparent seriousness in seeking a settlement. He reported in *RN* that he wanted "the new leaders of North Vietnam to know that I was not assuming that they were bound by Ho's reply to my letter."[73]

Nixon was hopeful. In a telephone conversation with Kissinger the night before his troop-reduction speech, he opined that his "hunch may be correct"—that is, "they can't simply ignore it." Kissinger chose that moment to make a case for military escalation by appealing to Nixon's ego: "If they do, then they really show they are completely rigid or they have no respect at all." He also repeated one of the points in his argument against de-Americanization: "Once we are down to lower [US troop] figures, we will lose our combat effectiveness and they will hit us." Nixon ended the conversation saying, "We'll see," by which he apparently meant that time would tell whether Hanoi would respond favorably to his gesture of additional troop withdrawals.[74]

In Nixon's view, it was a game of carrots and sticks. But Kissinger thought the rate of US withdrawals was too rapid, impairing the effectiveness of the sticks they wielded. Kissinger was right insofar as troop withdrawals did serve to undermine Nixon's Madman threats. When asked about this by one of the authors in 1994, Nguyen Co Thach, vice minister of foreign affairs in 1969 and soon to become a top aide to Le Duc Tho in the private negotiations with Kissinger in Paris, answered: "He [Nixon] would like to show to the Vietnamese that he was an unpredictable person, that he can surprise—how to say, a big stick surprise. But this backfired on Nixon, because we saw that Nixon could not have a big stick, because of the step-by-step withdrawal of American forces. That means that the stick becomes smaller and smaller."[75] At the same time, Hanoi's leaders thought the pace of US troop withdrawals was too sluggish anyway to warrant major diplomatic concessions at that point. As a gesture of diplomatic conciliation, moreover, de-Americanization was contradicted by Vietnamization, the military measures Nixon had been using in Indochina since January, and the threats he had made against them about taking coercive measures of great consequence should they fail to yield in Paris. This, at least, is what they told two of Kissinger's unofficial envoys in early September, professor Joseph R. Starobin and Kissinger's friend Jean Sainteny.

Reading Tea Leaves

Starobin had once been a member of the Communist Party; was formerly the editor of the *Daily Worker*; and, in Kissinger's words, "had been in the jungle with Xuan Thuy in 1953." Leaving the Communist movement in 1957, Starobin turned to academic pursuits and became a professor of political science at York University in Toronto, Canada. He had recently published articles in *Foreign Affairs*, which impressed Kissinger, who described him to Nixon as "perceptive." In Paris on 26 July 1969, Starobin had renewed his acquaintance with Thuy, and believing he had new information to convey about the negotiations, he described the conversation to Kissinger at the Western White House on 12 August. Before returning to Paris in late August for a meeting with Thuy on 1 September, he contacted Kissinger again, asking "for suggestions . . . about what he might do to further the possibilities of peace." Kissinger supplied these suggestions but instructed Starobin to "put it forward as his own judgment of what Mr. Kissinger had said, and not as a message from Mr. Kissinger."[76]

In Washington, DC, on 10 September, Starobin reported to Kissinger that, as advised, he had told Thuy that "the basis for peace lay in understanding what could and could not be done," especially in light of "powerful right-wing" forces in the United States. As Kissinger had observed, Hanoi and Washington could work out the "details relatively easily," but the problem of a negotiated political solution should be left "to the chances of the political process" for a five-year period. This was another of Kissinger's oblique references to the decent-chance/decent-interval solution as it stood in 1969, by which the United States was prepared to stand aside if Thieu's government fell after a period of at least five years had elapsed following a US withdrawal, during which Communist forces could not "reorganize." Kissinger had also told Starobin to tell Thuy the White House thought that the Politburo in Hanoi wanted to "break the president" and that if there were "no improvement [in the negotiations] bad developments could occur"—that "serious events were to happen if there were not movement toward a settlement." Along these lines, Starobin then "told Thuy of his own impression of the potential effect of the powerful right wing in the US,"[77] the influence of which could bring on US military escalation.

Starobin thought it significant that Thuy had informed him that before his death, Ho had commented that he believed "Kissinger wants peace." However, Starobin and Kissinger noted that Thuy stood by the terms of the DRV/PRG's Ten Points and said that Hanoi would only agree to private talks between Hanoi and Washington "on the condition of evidence of the possibility of a rapid settlement within one to five months." According to Starobin, Thuy also "argued that US actions have not added credibility to its stated desire for peace." In this regard, he complained about "US 'maximum military pressure,' . . . the US failure to reduce the number of . . . B-52 raids . . . [and] also attacked the US piecemeal withdrawal, referring to the next withdrawal of another 25,000 men." (Nixon had not yet announced the 40,000 troop reduction increment, and as Kissinger wrote the president on 11 September, the day before the big NSC meeting, "this [25,000] was all they expected.")[78]

The DRV Foreign Ministry's brief notes of the meeting singled out what the ministry officials believed to be the most important points Starobin had transmitted to Thuy on Kissinger's behalf: there should be a "five-year political process for the question of government in South Vietnam; prolonged negotiations will invite the right-wing's hostility (*resumption of bombing or mining of ports*); the US dislikes the present Saigon government but does not want a complete rupture."[79]

Ten days later, on 20 September, Kissinger received a letter from another back-channel contact, Jean Sainteny, who reported on his conversation with Premier Pham Van Dong in Hanoi on 9 September, the day of Ho Chi Minh's state funeral. Like Xuan Thuy with Starobin, Dong made a point of distinguishing words from deeds. When Sainteny told him that he believed Kissinger wanted to "find . . . a solution acceptable to both parties," Dong replied, "I see that they have convinced you, but we, we are not able to take them at their words: only acts will convince us." Dong also stood by the Ten Points.[80]

In his memo to Nixon, however, Kissinger put a positive gloss on the meeting, characterizing Dong as "un-vituperative" and arguing that his most significant remarks in response to Sainteny's questions had to do with the mutual withdrawal of US and DRV armed forces. Sainteny had quoted Dong as saying that "in the case where [US] forces would retire outside of their territory, [NVA] units would themselves fall back beyond the actual line of demarcation. . . . Accordingly, an end would be put to infiltration." But as Kissinger pointed out, Dong's comment left open the question of "who would withdraw first or if we would withdraw together, and whether they would withdraw from Laos and Cambodia." Also attached to Kissinger's memo to Nixon was a cable from the American embassy in Paris, dated 19 September, which, among other things, noted that "little new had emerged" from Sainteny's meeting with Dong. Nonetheless, Kissinger concluded: "The letter indicates that we are fortuously [*sic*] getting to them. . . . I believe that this letter makes it all the more important that we show discipline in the coming months to demonstrate that we are not on the skids."[81]

What Kissinger meant by his cryptic use of the words *fortuitously, discipline,* and *not on the skids* is not entirely clear. But because he still favored the military escalation option over the long-route strategy, he may have been suggesting that whatever little diplomatic movement by the DRV/PRG that he or Nixon gleaned from Sainteny's letter had been fortuitous in the sense of being unexpected and indirect—discovered only through chance meetings in Paris and Hanoi. They, Nixon and Kissinger, were "getting to them" not by gestures of peace but by their tough stand, their signals and threats, and their military actions to date. Therefore, as he told Nixon, "we should not appear anxious" to make peace. Instead, they should be disciplined and play out the string. While waiting for Xuan Thuy to return to Paris and hoping for a diplomatic concession from Hanoi, they should continue to plan for the November Option and follow through with mining and bombing in case Hanoi refused to change course in the next few weeks.

In *RN*, Nixon emphasized Pham Van Dong's remark about wanting the proof of the administration's deeds over the administration's words, commenting: "Since this conversation had taken place before my mid-September troop withdrawal [announcement], I felt I had supplied the deed to prove our words. Once again the choice lay with Hanoi."[82] Nixon wanted to sound diplomatically flexible as well as tough in this 1978 historical memoir of his presidency. But in mid-September 1969, Kissinger may have felt that the president was sliding on the matter of military escalation—that he might be "on the skids." What happened in the following weeks confirmed his worries.

CHAPTER EIGHT

To Escalate or Not to Escalate?
September–October 1969

> Trouble is there whatever we do.
> *H. R. Haldeman*[1]

> Should we alert our strategic and/or the various theater forces?
> *DUCK HOOK concept plan*[2]

Nixon continued to trust in the power of threat making, but he had yet to decide whether he would follow through on his November ultimatum if Moscow refused or failed to pry concessions from Hanoi. Between mid-September and early October, he first convinced himself that domestic and international circumstances were compelling him to go ahead with a bombing-and-mining operation, but he soon changed his mind in the other direction, believing that circumstances were forcing him to abort the prospective operation. His resoluteness in favor of dramatic military escalation had been tentative from the outset—especially if it was to be public and not secret, as the bombing of Cambodia and the mining readiness test had been. Political circumstances, significant political and bureaucratic opposition, and possible concern about the diplomatic fallout of escalation drew Nixon away from the precipice.

DUCK HOOK versus PRUNING KNIFE

On 16 September, Kissinger tasked Tony Lake to comment on the DUCK HOOK "Concept of Operations" paper. Judging from remarks in Lake's assessment memo to Kissinger, dated 17 September, the version of the concept he was given to appraise appears to match the 13 September staff report on the concept (first mentioned in chapter 7). Consonant with the rationale of the original DUCK HOOK mining-only plan of July and Option D of the 5 August "Vietnam Policy Alternatives" paper, the 13 September concept recommended that operations against North Vietnam should be designed "to demonstrate US resolve to apply whatever force is necessary to achieve basic US objectives in Southeast Asia." Targets would be selected to "achieve maximum political, military, and psychological shock, while reducing North Vietnam's overall war-making and economic capacity to the extent feasible."[3]

The United States would wage the campaign "in a series of separate and distinct actions [or "packages" of distinct actions], each signaling an increasing or escalating level of military intensity." These intensive but "short-duration" packages of forty-eight to seventy-two hours would be carried out south and north of 20° N latitude, including around Hanoi and up to the Chinese border, with additional "packages of more intense operations planned and available for later use if necessary." After each attack, the United States would evaluate North Vietnamese responses to determine whether to initiate the next round. The operation would begin "on [presidential] order around 1 November in order to take maximum advantage of the transition period between the Northwest and Northeast monsoon seasons."[4]

The nineteen "possible action[s]" were organized into five attack packages, each consisting of several "decision points." Each action requiring a decision raised the ante by "signaling an increasing or escalating level of military intensity." The first decision point included the mining of North Vietnamese ports, major air strikes against North Vietnam's air order of battle and airfields, attacks on surface-to-air missile (SAM) and antiaircraft sites, and a "ground sweep" into the DMZ. The second included a "major air strike against Haiphong Harbor," the removal of B-52 restrictions on bombing supply concentrations in Laos, and attacks on lines of communication and military supplies in North Vietnam. The third included the partial destruction of the Red River dikes, a ground sweep by a South Vietnamese division—supported by US airpower—across the DMZ into North Vietnam, and brigade-sized cross-border operations into Laos and Cambodia.[5]

Decision point four consisted of two elements. One incorporated "major air strikes against high value target systems," such as electric power facilities and air defenses. The other was a *"clean nuclear interdiction of three NVN–Laos passes."* What was meant by "clean" very likely was a nuclear weapon that did not have dirty, fallout-producing effects. The aide or aides who drafted the concept of operations—Robinson perhaps—may simply have had in mind an airburst of a low-yield tactical nuclear weapon, so as to minimize fallout effects but kill soldiers, truck drivers, and other logistics personnel in the area through immediate radiation effects. The classic, so-called clean nuclear weapons that had been discussed since the late 1950s were not in the US weapons inventory, although scientists at Lawrence Radiation Laboratory had been working on "neutron," or enhanced and suppressed-radiation, weapons for years. In any event, the concept of a so-called clean nuclear weapon was partly designed to reduce the political opprobrium that would result from using nuclear weapons, but that was probably wishful thinking.[6]

Decision point five also had two elements: One was *"nuclear interdiction of two NVN–CPR railroads,"* which had also been a favored target at the Pentagon. Presumably, the weapons would be used to destroy significant parts of the track on the two railroad lines that carried the most tonnage between the DRV and China: the Hanoi–Dong and the Kep–Thai Nguyen–Yen Vien. "Clean" was not mentioned, so the weapons probably could have enough "dirty" effects to disable railroad operations and much more in the area. The other action was an "amphibious landing near Vinh" to draw in North Vietnamese forces and create a "killing zone." On the declassified copy of the report, the two nuclear options were circled in ink by hand and had check marks next to them, possibly put there by Henry Kissinger.[7]

The "Concept of Operations" paper included no further discussion or elaboration, but it was evident that some of the actions in points three, four, and five were especially fraught with danger. The Johnson administration had previously rejected an invasion, especially an amphibious landing, because such action infringed on the territorial integrity of the DRV and increased the danger of direct confrontation with China and the Soviet Union. Even on the smallest scale, nuclear weapons use, moreover, would violate the de facto nuclear taboo and very likely expose the Nixon administration to international condemnation and isolation. It would also increase the peril of confrontation between the great powers.

In all likelihood, each of the specific decision points and proposed actions were discussed at Kissinger's meetings with this trusted group of aides, but *direct* mention of the most controversial actions—the two nuclear use proposals and the two options for ground invasion—disappeared from the remaining extant record. Tony Lake and Roger Morris, however, raised red flags about the nuclear proposals when analyzing the evolving DUCK HOOK concept papers through the month of September and into October.

When Lake offered his "initial comments on the concept of operations" on 17 September, he cautioned that the opening attack would have to "be as tough as possible to gain as much psychological effect as it can," since the reception on the home front to "each 'package' will be politically more difficult." He also questioned the efficacy and wisdom of three of the proposed actions: ground incursions into North Vietnam; the bombing of dikes; and a "permissive channel" into Sihanoukville—that is, allowing only those ships with a US-issued Certificate of Clearance to enter the port. Ground operations into North Vietnam, he argued, would run the risk of provoking a Chinese response and, moreover, could not be carried out "on a scale which would pose much threat to Hanoi," especially considering the White House policy of withdrawing troops from South Vietnam. The bombing of dikes would pose a political problem in the United States, and he suggested that the administration could instead "somehow imply its possibility" during the initial attacks. The permissive channel in Sihanoukville "could face us with the daily decisions we wish to avoid," and the Soviets might also choose "to force the issue."[8]

Referring to the nuclear attack recommendations, as well as to the overall operation itself, Lake went on to raise questions that signaled danger but would also have a bearing on the strategic alert measures Nixon and Kissinger launched in mid-October:

— What would be our concurrent movements of ships to the area, our state of strategic readiness, our posture in Korea and Berlin?
— If we go as far as the interdiction measures in (4) and (5) [the nuclear measures], what other actions would we take at this very high level of escalation once the precedent is established?
— What would we do if these actions fail?
— What counter-actions should we take in various contingencies?[9]

By *state of strategic readiness*, Lake meant the alert posture of US nuclear forces and the extent to which they were poised for rapid use in a crisis. Perhaps he did not know that the late July to August conceptual paper for the implementation of the mining-only version of DUCK HOOK included "a heightened PACOM and SAC alert posture militarily to show our resolve and to respond to whatever contingencies arise" (see chapter 7). In that scenario, an alert posture would have had the purpose of signaling determination of purpose. But Lake intended his question about an alert to ring an alarm bell regarding the recommended use of tactical nuclear weapons—mentioned as possible actions in the latest DUCK HOOK concept.[10]

Meanwhile, on 15 September, as members of Kissinger's September Group discussed and debated these and related issues in Washington, DC, the Seventh Air Force and Seventh Fleet contingents of the PRUNING KNIFE group were on their way from Hickam Air Force Base in Hawaii to Clark Air Base in the Philippines. Their final destination was Saigon, where a MACV delegation would round out the group. Having been given a paper on the White House's operational concept or been briefed by Wheeler—who had met with Nixon and Kissinger on 10 September—the PRUNING KNIFE group had already begun to formulate what they considered to be a "sound *military* concept," which went in a direction different from White House planning concepts (although how much of that was by design is unclear). It is quite possible that Wheeler had encouraged them to take this course. In the first status report from the PRUNING KNIFE group, for example, Rear Admiral Frederic A. Bardshar wrote to Wheeler that "plans already in existence or parts thereof will be a basis for this" military concept. "We recognize," he continued, "that this approach may not be acceptable at certain levels but suggest that a completely sound and agreed military proposal should be stated clearly and supported as the basic JCS proposal."[11] "At certain levels" was most likely a reference to Kissinger and perhaps Nixon as well.

On 25 September, Admiral Bardshar cabled a draft of the PRUNING KNIFE group's formulation of the prospective operation to General Abrams and General Wheeler, who sent it on to Kissinger. It had not yet been reviewed by the Joint Chiefs of Staff or Secretary of Defense Laird.[12] After the JCS made "some modifications," Admiral Moorer sent the revised version to Laird and to Kissinger as well, on 1 October.[13] Like the initial plan drafted by the Saigon-based PRUNING KNIFE group, the JCS version called for two attack phases. Phase I was designed to be "an integrated package of three attack modules": the neutralization of the North Vietnamese air force, the closure of North Vietnam's ports, and the destruction of high-value targets. Concentrated attacks would be launched against North Vietnam's air force and surface-to-air missile sites to suppress its air defenses and gain US air superiority. These attacks would be carried out in coordination with the aerial mining of Haiphong and other ports; US surface-ship attacks against coastal shipping; the interdiction of the northeast railroad line from Hanoi to China; and the bombing of industrial installations, power plants, communications facilities, railroad and truck marshaling yards, key bridges, and important governmental and military control centers in and around Hanoi and Haiphong.[14]

The Joint Chiefs predicted that Phase I would "have a severe psychological impact on the North Vietnamese government"—which was what the White House wanted. Their plan, moreover, proposed the "employment of B-52s in selected areas," which, they argued, would "provide additional shock effect, add to the total weight of effort, and enhance round-the-clock impact." Depending on weather conditions, Phase I operations would require nine to twenty-one days to complete. The purpose of the PRUNING KNIFE plan, however, was not only to produce maximum psychological shock but also to achieve maximum military results. Thus, air and naval operations in Phase II would continue to target the Northeast Rail Line, coastal craft, and port facilities as well as additional "war-supporting facilities," including "military logistics facilities, supplies, vehicles, and equipment . . . primarily within the Hanoi-Haiphong area." In contrast to Phase I, Phase II would have to continue "for as long as it takes to achieve the desired result."[15]

Warnings, Politics, and Wavering Presidential Resolve

Meanwhile, during the last week of September, the White House once again turned to threat making. At Camp David for the weekend, Nixon emphasized his interest in a tough approach to the Soviets on Vietnam. Meeting with Nelson Rockefeller to discuss Latin American policy, the president addressed "mistaken views of Soviet intentions" early in the conversation. Dismissing what he saw as the State Department view that the "Russians want to see the Viet Nam war end," Nixon argued that Moscow had different interests and that it was "perfectly prepared to see us bogged down in Vietnam." With some admiration, he observed that the "Soviets are tough, they know what they want and they proceed to go after it." Therefore, if the United States had a "certain goal," it had to make "clear to the Soviets that it is in their interest to do whatever it is." The implication was that Washington also had to be tough and go after what it wanted so that Moscow accepted US thinking and encouraged Hanoi to accept US negotiating positions.[16] This could require a complex diplomatic strategy for identifying and pursuing mutual interests, but Nixon was then more interested in threats.

Simultaneously, he tried to shore up support among his allies on the political Right, who—according to Pat Buchanan, speechwriter and special assistant to the president—were apprehensive about the "long-run success of this troop withdrawal and Vietnamization program."[17] The first occasion was a political strategy meeting from 2:15 to 4:30 p.m. on Saturday, 27 September, at Camp David with thirteen House and Senate leaders, whips, campaign chairs, and White House staffers concerning a range of domestic and foreign policy issues. Early in the meeting, according to Buchanan's notes, the president told them that "he did not intend to be 'the first American president to lose a war.' . . . If we lost the war in Vietnam or pulled an elegant bug out, the United States would 'retreat from the world.' . . . By [the] 1970 elections . . . , one way or the other, it is going to be over with; we are going to be able by then to 'see the light at the end of the tunnel.'"[18] *Bug out* was an oft-used White House idiom—along with terms such as *cop out* and *flush it*—that referred to an accelerated unilateral US withdrawal without a satisfactory negotiated settlement that provided Thieu with a decent chance for survival.[19]

Later, at 3:15 p.m., in midmeeting and with the senators and congressmen within earshot, Nixon placed a prearranged two-minute telephone call to Kissinger, who was in a separate meeting with Anatoly Dobrynin. According to Kissinger's transcript of the president's words:

> The president . . . said he had been thinking. It is very important to leave no illusions on the decision he made on the whole Southeast Asian area. It is very important that everybody realize the whole situation is changed. *We would be delighted to have nice personal relations, but the boat has gone by now, and that is that.* He wants to be sure that is understood; and we reached this conclusion reluctantly. K said he understood.[20]

Both meetings ended at 4:30 p.m. Ten minutes later, Nixon phoned Kissinger for a report on his conversation with Dobrynin. After discussing what the Soviet ambassador had said regarding Berlin, the Middle East, Strategic Arms Limitation Treaty talks, and Vietnam, Nixon asked Kissinger whether "you have no doubt but that he is reminded of the fact we are going the hard route" on the Vietnam issue. Kissinger answered, "Yes"—he had been "very tough on" the ambassador. "I believe," Kissinger added later, "that the Soviets are concerned and now more clearly understand that we mean business."[21] Whether this was actually the case is uncertain. If Dobrynin made a record of the conversation, Russian archivists did not find it when they compiled documentation on the Dobrynin-Kissinger exchanges.[22]

In his follow-up memorandum to Nixon about his conversation with Dobrynin, Kissinger recounted that after the president had phoned, he had reminded the Soviet ambassador that "the Soviet Union should not expect any special treatment" from Washington on the global issues dividing Moscow and Washington until the Soviets assisted the US administration in solving the Vietnam problem. He added that "the president had told me in his call that *the train had left the station and was now headed down the track.* Dobrynin responded that he hoped it was an airplane and not a train and would leave some maneuvering room. I said the president chooses his words very carefully and that I was sure he meant train."[23] The president had actually said "boat," but in their memoirs, Nixon and Kissinger repeated the railroad version of the military escalation warning as the one the president issued over the phone.[24]

Based on what was to follow in US-USSR relations regarding Vietnam, Kissinger's claim in his telephone conversation with Nixon on Saturday about their having convinced Dobrynin that Washington "means business" is highly suspect. Politically, however, Nixon may have achieved his purpose with regard to Republican conservatives—if only for the time being. Pat Buchanan, for example, liked Nixon's remarks about Vietnam, especially his tough-sounding comments to Kissinger by telephone. Regarding Nixon's comments on Vietnam in general, Buchanan remarked that "the president seemed throughout the meeting as confident about his direction and the efficacy of what he was doing as this observer had seen in some time." Soon, though, Haig would remind Nixon that "a large majority of the Right has been thoroughly disenchanted with what they have seen" about administration policy and strategy regarding Vietnam.[25]

Even so, antiwar challenges to Nixon's Vietnam policies caused most conservatives to continue their support of the president despite their misgivings about troop withdrawals. Furthermore, although Nixon was indeed worried about a counterreaction from the Right regarding his handling of the war in the long run, he was even more concerned about the antiwar movement and the opinions of the majority of Americans in the short run.[26] The politics of the war were complicated.

Kissinger—wanting to go ahead with the November Option—tried to use the public's impatience with the war as an argument in his favor. In his telephone conversation with Nixon right after the 27 September meeting with Republican political strategists, he made the case that the "events of the last two or three weeks show the long-route [strategy] can't possibly work." At the time, Nixon agreed, complaining that "the doves and the public are making it impossible to happen."[27] Two days before the meeting, for instance, Senator Charles Goodell (R-NY) had put forward a resolution in the Senate for the withdrawal of all US troops by the end of 1970 and a prohibition of the use of congressionally appropriated funds in Vietnam after 1 December 1970. Although the resolution failed, equivalent resolutions would be offered by Democrats in the Senate and the House. In mid-September, Kissinger had been sent to the House in a futile attempt to dissuade representatives Donald Riegle (R-MI) and Pete McCloskey (R-CA) from introducing proposals similar to the Goodell resolution. At the same time, mainstream civil rights, labor, and religious organizations, along with prominent intellectuals, academics, Democratic lawmakers, and the liberal Republican Ripon Society, endorsed the Moratorium. CIA infiltrators reported that the Moratorium was "shaping up to be the most widely supported public action in American history."[28]

These developments led Nixon to believe more than before that the majority of the public would not patiently wait until 1973 for him to end American troop participation in the war. Thus, he thought he needed to go through with "the tough move"—the November Option—in order to end the war successfully as early as possible. If his support for the November Option had been on the skids in mid-September, as Kissinger had feared, he appeared resigned to its necessity by late September and into early October.[29]

Eager to persuade Hanoi and Moscow to change their diplomatic stance before having to launch his threatened bombing-and-mining operation, Nixon found another occasion to transmit a tough message. In an Oval Office meeting in the late afternoon of 30 September with Republican congressional leaders, he "planted a story" that members of the group would likely leak to the press. His purpose—as he explained in his 1978 memoir, *RN*—was to "attract some attention in Hanoi" and turn up "the pressure . . . a notch."[30] But he probably also wanted to hold the support of conservatives and counter the peace signals that doves in and out of Congress were sending. After Nixon told the group that he would never "bug out" of Vietnam, one of the senators asked why the United States had not sufficiently used its military power to win the war. When Nixon replied that the military option was still open, another senator asked what he meant by "military option"—the bombing of the North, including Hanoi and Haiphong, or the invasion of North Vietnam? Nixon replied that the military option might include both.[31]

The story did leak to the press a week later in the form of a commentary by syndicated columnists Rowland Evans and Robert Novak—but perhaps not with the message Nixon wanted to send. Although observing that "Mr. Nixon was conveying a calculated message of his growing impatience in a way that would carry more conviction than a public statement," Evans and Novak interpreted the president's effort as one designed to warn "restive Republican politicians" to support his "Vietnamization plan" lest he and they repeat President Johnson's experience of "finding it impossible to pacify South Vietnam and his own country at the same time."[32]

The actions of the antiwar movement along with the current and prospective mood of the general public regarding the war cut both ways: if citizen impatience with the war suggested the need to end it quickly by means of military escalation, as Kissinger argued, it also caused Nixon to worry that he would lose additional public support should he carry out the November Option. Recent polls had indicated slippage in public approval for his handling of the war, an uptick in disapproval, and a rise in support for accelerated troop withdrawals.[33] As a consequence, Nixon began to vacillate on the question of when or whether to proceed with the military escalation strategy.

Should he decide to attack North Vietnam, the forthcoming Moratorium and New Mobe demonstrations produced other concerns about the signal that would be sent to Hanoi by the coincidental timing of the bombing-and-mining operation scheduled to begin soon after 1 November and the demonstrations scheduled for 15 October and 13–15 November. In a 29 September telephone conversation with Kissinger, Nixon explained that he did not "want to appear to be making the tough move after the 15th just because of the rioting at home"—that is, the Moratorium. Moreover, although he thought Secretary Laird might have been right in predicting that for about three months after the operation began, "it [would] have relatively high public support," with most Americans taking a "dimmer view" of the protesters, Nixon said he "would like to nip it before the first demonstration, because there will be another one on 15 November." He believed there was a possibility that in the days following the launching of the military operation in early November and leading up to the second Moratorium and New Mobe in mid-November, "horrible results" might be produced by the buildup of "a massive adverse reaction" among demonstrators.[34]

Nixon asked Kissinger whether "in his planning, he could pick this up so that we make the tough move before the 15th of October." Kissinger answered yes, but he cautioned that if the D-day for the operation were moved up to a time before 15 October, it would "confuse" the North Vietnamese and "look as if we tricked them." He recommended that the president might instead consider holding a press conference or giving a television report on criticizing the demonstrators for "dividing the country and making it impossible to settle the problem [of Vietnam] on a reasonable basis."[35]

Two days later, Nixon was leaning toward the notion of holding a press conference ahead of the Moratorium and setting in motion other PR counteractions. These included putting pressure on TV network executives; organizing a national "day of prayer" for peace, led by Rev. Billy Graham; and unleashing prowar labor unions, military veterans, Rotarians, Kiwanis members, and women's groups to speak out in favor of the administration's Vietnam policy. As part of this campaign, Nixon would act presidential by making "non-political appearances."[36]

As the president plotted his PR strategy, the September Group worked on preparing a revised version of DUCK HOOK. It and the JCS plan, PRUNING KNIFE, were completed in time for the group's one-hour morning meeting with the president at the White House on Thursday, 2 October. The agenda of the meeting has not been disclosed, but it is possible that DUCK HOOK and PRUNING KNIFE were discussed. Kissinger may have given copies of the papers or executive summaries to Nixon at or before this meeting in preparation for discussions about Vietnam during a forthcoming three-day weekend at the presidential compound in Key Biscayne, Florida. The subject heading of the September Group's paper read "Contingency Military Operations against North Vietnam," but Kissinger's copy also carried a handwritten notation at the top of the first page reading "DUCK HOOK Plan." This latest version incorporated and reaffirmed core principles of the NSC group's earlier concepts and included additional details about the prospective operation and its chances of success, among them assessments of proposed military actions and targets; the diplomatic and military scenario; and possible North Vietnamese, Soviet, and Chinese responses. It also included a draft of a presidential speech to the public announcing the operation.[37]

Nixon left Washington, DC, on Thursday at 6:00 p.m. on *Air Force One* with a retinue of aides and guests for a two-hour flight to Homestead Air Force Base. From there, the president, Kissinger, and a smaller group went by helicopter and automobile to one of several houses Nixon was then renting and borrowing on the bay side of Key Biscayne. By 10:00 p.m. during a stormy night, the president, the First Lady, and Nixon's friend and confidant Charles "Bebe" Rebozo watched *The Guns of Navarone*, a 1961 movie about an Allied commando unit during World War II that sets out to destroy a seemingly impregnable Nazi fortress. The political and moral choices leaders faced in World War II seemed simpler and more righteous to Nixon than those he faced in Vietnam.[38]

Early the following morning, 3 October, Nixon called in Haldeman and Ehrlichman for what Haldeman described in his diary as one of those "mystic sessions, which he had obviously thought through ahead of time." Dressed in swim trunks and a sport shirt, the president told them that for the next six weeks, they would have to handle "most of the domestic matters without him." The staff would have to understand that he "wants large chunks of scheduled time to work on Vietnam decisions." The three men then spent the rest of the two-hour meeting reviewing plans and ideas "about the need to game-plan Vietnam alternatives and start [the] buildup for whatever actions he decides to take."[39]

The president next met with Kissinger to discuss those alternatives, including his "contingency plans."[40] By this time, Nixon had probably read the 2 October version of the DUCK HOOK plan or a summary of it, as well as the 1 October JCS version of PRUNING KNIFE. If not, Kissinger may have already briefed him or did so at this or other meetings in Key Biscayne. In any one of these cases, he would have learned or been reminded that according to the 2 October memorandum, the DUCK HOOK version of the operation would seek to "impose a substantial physical isolation of North Vietnam and destroy vital targets sufficient to confront Hanoi with military and economic disruption and deprivation, involving costly and time-consuming restoration or countermeasures." At the same time, the objective would be to strike a balance between, on the one hand, signaling Hanoi that the United States would "go to almost any length to end the war quickly" by inflicting significant damage on North

Vietnam "as a society" and, on the other hand, conveying to Hanoi, Moscow, and Beijing that the US goal was "*not* the total destruction of the country or the regime." This balance would presumably avoid a confrontation with the Soviets and Chinese while also having the potential of persuading Hanoi to cooperate. Weather permitting, the operation would involve "intense" attacks carried out in "short-duration" phases of four days each against targets of "a more general strategic importance" than those of past campaigns, whose purpose had been to reduce Hanoi's capacity to support the war in the South. These had required "continuous" but "spasmodic" follow-up bombing. The targets attacked in the DUCK HOOK plan, however, would serve to bring about "lasting military and economic effects" without the need for follow-up attacks.[41]

Dropped from the concept plan were the controversial options to invade North Vietnam and to control shipping to Cambodia. Nor were there recommendations for possible nuclear options in the extant copies of the document. The "basic military action" would consist of the aerial mining of Haiphong Harbor and five other deepwater ports as well as the interdiction of the Northeast Rail Line to China. Other targets in and around Hanoi and Haiphong during Phases I and II would include four military airfields; six key electric power stations; three bridges and two rail yards; five major storage facilities; three manufacturing plants (cement, machinery, and coal processing); five petroleum, oil, and lubrication (POL) facilities; and "the breaching of the levee system in the Red River Delta." The fait accompli produced by these measures, planners argued, would "cause a deep psychological impact on the Hanoi leadership," forcing them to decide between "unacceptable damage to their society" or compromise at the negotiating table.[42]

The settlement sought by the White House would be based on Nixon's eight-point proposal of 14 May, which retained the mutual-withdrawal formula and the long-standing US demand for such provisions as a cease-fire without a political solution having been negotiated or agreed upon— except for the vague US proposal for internationally supervised elections sometime in the future. The DRV/PRG demand for a coalition government was not part of the Nixon-Kissinger plan. The US troop pullout would extend over a twelve-month period yet leave tens of thousands of US troops in South Vietnam, who would leave only by 1972 or 1973, if then. President Thieu would remain in power, backed by US residual troops and airpower, a strengthened RVNAF, and Thieu's police forces.

Vietnam would stay divided. The DRV and PRG did not consider the US proposal a compromise, although they might have accepted some version of these withdrawal provisions had Washington and Saigon agreed to the formation of a coalition government with or without Thieu as a member of it. But a coalition government or any other power-sharing solution was unacceptable to President Thieu and the Nixon administration. With both sides unwilling to compromise on the basic military and political issues at this time, Nixon and Kissinger believed that military escalation was necessary to compel the other side to give in—to "compromise"— before the public turned against the administration.

Aborting the "Tough Option"

Nixon approved the DUCK HOOK goal of signaling Hanoi's leaders that he would "go to almost any length to end the war quickly," since it conformed to his own oft-repeated attraction to and faith in the Madman Theory. But it was one thing to issue threats and prepare detailed attack plans, and it was another to follow through. By the first week of October, if not before, Nixon's resolve in favor of the November Option operation began to fade in the face of several considerations.

One had to do with doubts about the efficacy of the November Option concept in either version, whether DUCK HOOK or PRUNING KNIFE. Several of the planners in the September Group had expressed reservations about the prospects for achieving its military goals. They cautioned, for example, that "the probability of success is heavily dependent on the weather. . . . Thus, for . . . Phase I we could expect a high probability of partial success—i.e., the establishment of the sea quarantine—but questionable prospects for accomplishing the desired effect on all targets." In addition, US military actions in both phases of the operation ran the risk of incurring US aircraft losses, including some of their crews, of up to 5 percent, "as well as inflicting considerable NVN civilian casualties." As Tony Lake and Roger Morris had cautioned back on 17 and 29 September, the proposed attacks on Red River dikes in particular were likely to cause considerable collateral civilian casualties and provoke strong protests at home and abroad. Even though Kissinger had criticized the JCS PRUNING KNIFE plan because some of its recommended military actions increased the chance of producing civilian casualties, the plan's only solution to the problem of public and intragovernmental disapproval was to recommend a policy that Nixon did not believe was sustainable: "To strike and maintain a political posture clearly immune to all likely pressures against continuing the action so long as Hanoi refuses to compromise."[43]

Reactions and counteractions by North Vietnam and its allies, moreover, could reduce the operation's impact and undermine its purpose. Hanoi's leaders might misconstrue the purpose of the operation, uncertain whether it was an "act of desperation or the beginning of a long and persistent campaign." In either case, they could take retaliatory steps, such as threatening to expand the war in Cambodia and Laos, breaking off Paris talks, and calling for foreign "volunteers" to fight in Indochina. Moscow's counteractions might assume the form of taking steps to undercut or mitigate the US sea quarantine and also replace North Vietnamese aircraft destroyed in the US attacks. The Soviets might supply personnel for certain North Vietnamese operations, such as air defense, and they might respond diplomatically or military in areas outside of Indochina. Another risk was that the United States would have to "be prepared to spill Soviet blood and to inflict damage to Soviet ships, if this proves necessary." In any event, there was only a fifty-fifty chance that Moscow would pressure Hanoi to change its negotiating position in response to DUCK HOOK. For its part, Beijing might respond to the US operation with an intensive propaganda campaign, encourage anti-US guerrilla movements in other parts of the world, reintroduce previously withdrawn Chinese "volunteers" to Vietnam, and open South China ports and lines of communication for the transport of supplies to North Vietnam. However, the DUCK HOOK group did "not anticipate that the Chinese will try to prevent Hanoi from seeking an accommodation with us if and when Hanoi decides to do so."[44]

The 2 October DUCK HOOK paper concluded with a list of "important questions" for which the administration "should have a very good idea of the answers . . . before adoption of the action." These may have been written by Lake and Morris as a way of issuing a warning about a slippery slope. What, for example, were the prospects for success and how could it be measured? What were the consequences of succeeding or failing in this manner? How "hard-hitting" should the first phase be? Should the second and third phases be equal in strength or "stepped-up in overall impact"? How would warnings affect loss of surprise? What should be the US diplomatic stance before and during the operation? What signals from Hanoi would persuade Washington not to proceed? How should the administration "relate" the vagaries of the weather and political and diplomatic considerations to the decision to proceed? How should US officials determine how long each phase should last? How would they deal with likely domestic reaction?[45]

Also included were comments about nuclear use, which suggests that for Robinson, Kissinger, and perhaps the president, the nuclear options were still on the table:

> To what limit of force should we be prepared to go in order to spur meaningful negotiations? *Should we be prepared to use nuclear weapons?* . . . Should we make any major adjustments in our current military posture? . . . *What military actions should we undertake concurrently, e.g., should we alert our strategic and / or the various theater forces?*[46]

These questions may have been prompted by Lake's and Morris's prior recommendations, on 29 September, for a reworking of an earlier version of the November Option draft paper. The two aides had argued or warned that for the operation to succeed, the president should be prepared to accept two operational concepts:

— The action must be brutal and sustainable. Brutal, because of the proven tenacity of NVN in the face of actions which did not strike at their existence in society. Sustainable, because we must assume that even in this extreme case they will be evasive and rely on pressures in this country to deflect our action, and that later packages will be required.
— The action would be self-contained. The president would have to decide beforehand, *the fatal question of how far we will go.* He cannot, for example, confront the issue of *using tactical nuclear weapons* in the midst of the exercise. He must be prepared to play out whatever string necessary in this case.[47]

The possibility that the initial strike against North Vietnam might be insufficient and that the necessity for intensified military escalation might require a decision on whether to use nuclear weapons must have troubled not only Lake and Morris but also, in the end, Nixon, since he would have to make the decision. Moreover, there was the risk—as planners pointed out—that the Soviets might take counteractions in response to a US assault on North Vietnam with or without the US use of nuclear weapons. This had not been in Nixon's game plan. Up to that point, the North Vietnamese had seemed impervious to his military threats, and he had been banking on the Madman notion that Moscow's fear of his getting out of control would cause them to lever Hanoi into making concessions at the negotiating table rather than running interference for them militarily.

Perhaps because of dilemmas such as these, Nixon's resolve in favor of the operation began to falter. According to Haldeman's diary, Kissinger had made the case at his 3 October meeting with the president in Key Biscayne that there were no good choices, repeating what he had previously argued concerning the hard decision Nixon would have to make between the two major alternatives: an escalation or a bug out. Kissinger's position was that "we must escalate or [the] P[resident] is lost" politically and militarily. Nixon believed, however, that he was "lost anyway if that fails, which it well may." Kissinger's counter was that the "main question is whether [the] P[resident] can hold the government and the people together for the six months it will take" to succeed. But that was precisely the rub, since "it's obvious from the press and dove buildup," Haldeman noted, "that trouble is there whatever we do."[48]

On top of Nixon's and the September Group's reservations about the plan, the Joint Chiefs had spurned the DUCK HOOK concept and tendered their own plan, PRUNING KNIFE. It emphasized the achievement of military goals in support of the US/RVN war effort, whereas DUCK HOOK emphasized the achievement of military goals in support of the US diplomatic effort. Laird and Rogers, however, continued to support speedier troop withdrawals over military escalation, and Laird's severe critique of the PRUNING KNIFE plan, which he sent to the White House on 8 October, raised questions about its military efficacy as well.

Although Laird never got to see the DUCK HOOK scheme, many of his criticisms of PRUNING KNIFE applied to it as well. His memorandum included a key argument: the Joint Chiefs had failed to demonstrate that PRUNING KNIFE would produce "conclusive" or "decisive results." Laird included the CIA's analysis of PRUNING KNIFE, which had identified a number of problems. He argued that the plans for blockading North Vietnam, for instance, would only produce a temporary disruption and that by "drawing down present reserves and maintaining present imports overland," Hanoi could sustain its economy. Through river, railroad, and highway connections with China, Hanoi could sustain the flow of supplies at "twice the present daily volume." Moreover, a bombing-and-mining campaign carried potentially "significant liabilities"; foreign ships could be damaged or sunk and "create new risks of a Soviet-US confrontation." If Hanoi became more dependent on Chinese supply lines, that could strengthen "Chinese political influence."[49]

Laird pointed to other difficulties, including the possible loss of over 100 bomber aircraft within five days, "high" civilian casualties in North Vietnam, the risk of stepped-up DRV attacks in the South, and North Vietnam's development of "sanctuary air bases" in China for its aircraft. Moreover, Laird argued, once the campaign began, the US military command might request additional "operating authorities," such as a quarantine or blockade of Cambodia; "ground incursions into Cambodia, Laos, and NVN"; and "B-52 raids into NVN," which presumably would be mass-scale attacks. Sensitive to the domestic implications in the United States, Laird anticipated a "devastating" public reaction if US casualties grew. In any event, "demonstrations would have to be expected" around the world and at home.[50]

Kissinger would soon register his disagreements with Laird's analysis, but the secretary of defense was a political and bureaucratic force, and his critique of the efficacy of escalation and its domestic ramifications carried weight with the president. Nixon's political capital had dwindled: press editorials were more critical of his presidency, congressional opposition to his court nominees and legislative proposals was on the rise, and public opinion polls about the war indicated opposition to military escalation and support for faster troop withdrawals. Coincidently, reduced NVA/VC–initiated fighting in South Vietnam appeared to indicate that Vietnamization—the alternative to the November Option—might be making progress.

Nixon was concerned about holding public and congressional opinion in his favor for an extended period after launching the November Option; beyond that, he worried that the three major antiwar actions scheduled for mid-October and November would erode confidence in his leadership and blunt the impact of military escalation upon Hanoi. Haldeman noted in his diary entry for Wednesday, 8 October, that the president was concerned about the rise in "domestic dissatisfaction with the ongoing 'impossible' war." Nixon had complained to Haldeman that the main cause of his declining popularity with the press and public was Vietnam. Even though he had "bought" a nine-month respite from strong criticism and protest, he "can't expect to get any more time." So far, he had "kept the doves at bay," by which he meant the antiwar movement and dovish senators and representatives. But now he thought he had "to take them on," especially in light of the forthcoming Moratorium and New Mobe demonstrations. He would first unleash Vice President Spiro Agnew against them, but "then later the P" would have to do it himself. The political "problem," he knew, was that "this does make it his war" and no longer Johnson's.[51]

It was probably just coincidence, but Nixon made this remark on the eve of the one-year anniversary of his having said to antiwar hecklers, while campaigning for the presidency in Santa Monica, California, on 9 October 1968: "Those who have had a chance for four years and could not produce peace should not be given another chance. We will take that chance."[52] After his electoral victory in November 1968, he had told Haldeman, "I'm not going to end up like LBJ, Bob, holed up in the White House afraid to show my face on the street. I'm going to stop that war. Fast. I mean it!"[53] Nixon believed, as did Kissinger, Laird, and other White House advisers, that his honeymoon with public opinion would last only six to nine months. In October 1969, his nine months were almost up. He had three years remaining in which to end the war. The uncertain prospects of achieving the military goals of either DUCK HOOK or PRUNING KNIFE, the planners' forecasts of possible counteractions by the other side, and the likely adverse reactions of the American public to the operation had given the president pause.

On 9 October 1969, Kissinger came out of a forty-five-minute meeting with Nixon around midday and told Haldeman that he believed the president "has decided finally against his plan for Vietnam."[54] Soon after, Nixon had a late lunch with Haldeman, who later wrote in his diary that they had a "long talk about things in general," which included the "whole Vietnam program." Nixon told his chief of staff that "he still is pondering the course" [in Vietnam] and "does *not* yet rule out K's plan [DUCK HOOK] as a possibility, but [he] *does* now feel [the] Laird-Rogers plan [of stepped-up Vietnamization and de-Americanization] is a possibility, when he did not think so a month ago." The president, however, had "ruled out the dramatic cop out" while "blaming the dove senators," even though that would be "a great way out for him." As for the other alternative,

"K's plan," the "worry . . . is that it will take six to eight months and [the president] fears [he] can't hold the country that long at that level, where he could hold for some period of withdrawals."[55]

Haig left additional evidence of the probability of an 8 or 9 October date for Nixon's decision to sideline the November Option. Writing to Kissinger on 9 October, Haig used mixed metaphors in criticizing Nixon's change of mind, linking the cancellation to the inception of the nuclear alert.

I personally believe that we would have had to ferret out the meaning of the lowered activity in Vietnam before the first of November. However, professional poker players play their cards with far greater finesse. Certainly our cards should have been played after 15 October unless we believed serious upheavals were going to come on the 15th here at home. I do not believe this and would have far preferred our playing the game at least to the 25th of October. Obviously the fat is now in the fire and the game has started but our chips are already considerably lower than they might have been.[56]

Haig's mixed metaphors were esoteric but decipherable. "Lowered activity in Vietnam" probably referred to reduced NVA/VC military activity, which Nixon—perhaps grasping at straws—was beginning to believe indicated Hanoi's willingness to scale down the war and negotiate, thus negating his felt need to escalate the war by means of the November Option. It also meant there would be fewer US casualties than if the fighting had picked up and therefore less public anxiety about the war. "Poker players" was Haig's reference to President Nixon, who, since his money-making, poker-playing days in the navy during World War II, had often touted his bluffing skills and their applicability to threatening force in order to get one's way in international diplomacy. "The game" was likely the administration's game of threat making associated with the 1 November ultimatum to Hanoi, along with its entreaties to Moscow. "The 15th" and "15 October" were shorthand for the Moratorium action. "Our cards" and "our chips" were cryptic allusions, but they probably represented Haig's preference for holding onto the military cards or chips that comprised DUCK HOOK at least until 25 October. Such language was reminiscent of General Taylor's comment ahead of the fateful 7 July meeting on the *Sequoia* about how, in his and the military's view, the Johnson administration had already bet and lost most of America's military and diplomatic "blue chips" in its deadly game with Hanoi. The remaining but "lower" stack of "chips" in the present game the Nixon White House was playing was probably Haig's code for launching the JCS Readiness Test without following it up with the November Option, and by "fat in the fire," he may simply have meant that the cards had been dealt and the game was in play. In other words, the administration had issued its ultimatums and would soon have an answer in one form or another to the question of whether Moscow and Hanoi would—in poker lingo—either call the bluff or fold.

During another crisis of decision making two and a half years later, Nixon explained his theory of bluffing to Kissinger:

> You ought to remember, if you ever talk about my [playing] poker, I didn't win by bluffing. . . . I very seldom lost a pot when I was called, because I knew pretty well when I was going to be called, [and] I always had the cards. . . . You've got to have a little bluff in your game, but the key to my success in poker was playing a very different kind of a game. I would bluff at times, but then when I knew that I didn't have the cards I got the hell out. But whenever I was called in the game, I usually won. That's why I won $10,000 when I was in the service. Not bad![57]

The available documentary evidence strongly suggests that by 8 or 9 October 1969, President Nixon had come to believe that he did not have the cards and was ready to get the hell out of this year's poker game— namely, the November Option scenario. He may not have finally decided to quit the game, but he was on the verge of doing so and was definitely thinking about withholding his bombing-and-mining chips in order to play a different game instead.

Nixon's own account in *RN* of the causes and timing of his cancellation of the November Option is unclear.[58] But in 1978, the same year in which *RN* was published, he gave a more coherent explanation to the Oxford Union Society about his reasons for not going ahead with strong military measures in 1969: a "military solution" to the war would have made it difficult for him "to hold the country together"; it was also "imperative" that the United States remain in Vietnam long enough to provide President Thieu with the wherewithal to defend his government; and he feared that "strong action" against North Vietnam would snuff out the chances for détente with the Soviet Union and rapprochement with China.[59]

Yet there were surely additional and related causes. Among these were his concerns about his ability not only to hold the country together but to hold the government together as well, especially considering the opposition of Laird, Rogers, the State Department, and members of Congress to the sort of military escalation he and Kissinger were contemplating. Moreover, both Kissinger's aides and the Joint Chiefs were skeptical about the prospects of such escalation, and Hanoi seemed unwilling to negotiate in the face of his threats.

One of the most critical of his reasons for sidelining the November Option was his concern about the forthcoming antiwar demonstrations on 15 October and 13–15 November. Sandwiched between the October and November actions, the prospective bombing-and-mining operation, he claimed, would lose its "credibility," by which he meant its power to convince Hanoi that he, President Nixon, would be able to sustain the attacks for as long as necessary.[60] In contrast, the other strategic alternative—the long-road option—had become comparatively more attractive because he believed that the death of Ho Chi Minh had created opportunities for a settlement, and lower American casualty figures implied that the prospects for Vietnamization were more promising. As with most complex events, the causes of Nixon's irresolution in this case were also complex.[61]

In any case, in early October 1969, as Kissinger and Haig believed, neither PRUNING KNIFE nor DUCK HOOK was in the cards—except for the global nuclear alert. By the afternoon of 9 October, Nixon was appraising other Vietnam alternatives. These included the question of how quickly or slowly to withdraw US troops, how he should explain to the Joint Chiefs that he was retreating from their PRUNING KNIFE version of the November Option, and the wording of the message to be communicated to the public in his address to the nation.

The Speech Announcement and the "Special Reminder"

Nixon and his inner circle of advisers had long believed that a public relations campaign should precede and accompany the bombing and mining of North Vietnam, should these operations be launched. The PR campaign would include a televised speech to the nation in which the president would announce the start of the offensive and make a case for its necessity. This idea had been proposed as least as far back as July, when General Taylor had described to Kissinger his scenario for reescalating the war.[62]

As a member of the DUCK HOOK planning group, Tony Lake—

perhaps with the collaboration of William Watts—wrote at least one and perhaps as many as three presidential speech drafts between mid-September and early October.[63] The 2 October version—which was included in the DUCK HOOK concept plan discussed at the Key Biscayne meeting—began with a laudatory history of Nixon administration attempts to find a negotiated solution. It extolled the president's patience and reasonable proposals as well as his good-faith withdrawals of US troops. At the same time, this account castigated Hanoi's "savagery on the battlefield," rejection of compromise, insolence, and disrespect for US diplomats. According to the argument advanced in this speech, the only alternatives left were escalation or rapid US withdrawals, the latter of which would subject South Vietnam to "terror and barbarism" and cause "the collapse of our friends' confidence in America and . . . the loss of America's confidence in herself." The "choice is clear," the speech draft read; "our responsibility is to demonstrate our unflinching resolve to end this war now." This language was followed by an announcement of the launching of US attacks against North Vietnam and a brief statement about their purpose, which, the president would say, was the achievement of a peace based on a "compromise," ending in "true independence" for South Vietnam.[64]

Nixon, however, was probably reluctant to give such a speech, as he would be three years later, in December 1972, when launching the LINE-BACKER II bombing operation against North Vietnam. His solution at that point would be to go ahead with the operation without explaining it to the American people in a presidential address.[65] Whether Nixon considered such an option in 1969 is unknown. Nevertheless, he was loath to appear on television in order to announce to the American people a major escalation of the war, and that was probably one of the reasons he rejected the November Option but launched the JCS Readiness Test. Disinclined to deliver a televised presidential address announcing a major escalation of the war, the president chose instead to make a case for his handling of the war and its continuance into the unforeseeable future. Haldeman—who was privy to most of Nixon's private thoughts about policy matters and almost all of them about scheduling—predicted correctly on 9 October that the president would go on TV on 3 November after a PR buildup to the speech and "enumerate secret moves made for peace."[66]

The next day, 10 October, Kissinger volunteered advice for the speech, recommending that it "should be a factual listing of what the president has done" to bring an end to the war. Nixon replied he would do that but in "a simple, uncomplicated, and very brief" form. Earlier in the conversation but also on the issue of addressing the nation, he had remarked that "by '72 the war is going to be over, and [I am] going to be the man who ended it."[67] He was clearly no longer hoping to end the war in 1969 or 1970 by means of military escalation. On 13 October, the same day the JCS readiness alert began, the White House publicly announced the date of the forthcoming speech: 3 November. During the next two weeks, Nixon solicited the advice of aides and members of his cabinet, including Laird and Rogers. In a memo to Kissinger on 21 October, Nixon said he wanted a rewrite of the speech to include more specific language about Communist "bloodbaths" and also to emphasize the "silent majority" theme. Two days later, he received another, but by now different, draft of the speech, and he set out to try his own hand at revising and improving it.[68]

Kissinger claimed in *White House Years* that the public announcement of the speech, coming more than two weeks ahead of the 1 November deadline for Hanoi to give some sign of its willingness to comply with the administration's negotiating demands, was "a daring decision, because it compounded uncertainty and encouraged pressures to sway whatever decision he might be announcing."[69] It was an enigmatic comment. Kissinger seemed to be saying that the 13 October announcement would compound Hanoi's nervousness about the possibility of a November attack. But if Hanoi's leaders assumed that the speech was to be Nixon's announcement of the start of an offensive against North Vietnam, it would mean that they had been forewarned two weeks ahead of the specific date of a major military operation against them; this might have undermined the credibility of the threat in their minds. One of the reservations that some DUCK HOOK planners had expressed about the efficacy of the plan had to do with this very issue of forewarning.[70]

What Kissinger probably meant but did not want to reveal in his memoir was that the date of the announcement was connected to the start of the secret global alert—that he and the president were hoping the announcement would lend credibility to the alert, instilling fearful uncertainty in the minds of North Vietnamese and Soviet leaders about what the *alert* portended for the future. On 23 October 1972, three years later, as Nixon, Kissinger, and Haldeman were reminiscing in the Oval Office about those crucial weeks of October 1969, Kissinger remarked: "Most people didn't know the game you were playing . . . , but you were announcing three weeks ahead of time that you were going to speak on November 3rd while all the riots were going on. . . . But the reason you did it was because we were running that, that big flap on the, on the mining and alerting all our aircraft."[71]

Still, the announcement was a forewarning, and it did not make military sense. Just as plausibly, if not more so, Nixon could have been hoping that the anticipation engendered by the announcement of the speech date might divert public attention from the antiwar message of the 15 October Moratorium and allow him to withhold further public comments on the war until the night of the 3 November speech. But if the latter was true and if the North Vietnamese and Soviets saw it that way too, Hanoi and Moscow might have interpreted it as a sign that the alert meant nothing and that the November attack was probably a bluff.

Having decided against a November bombing-and-mining campaign, Nixon settled on the JCS Readiness Test. With regard to his strategy in Vietnam for the future, he was now disposed to accept some version of a troop withdrawal–and–Vietnamization option backed up by a military attack option that would be launched only in response to a major North Vietnamese offensive. In this context, the October nuclear alert was an expedient—a stopgap operation in place of the now-aborted November Option. Nixon explained his reasoning in his memoir, *RN*: "It was important that the Communists not mistake as weakness the lack of dramatic action on my part in carrying out the ultimatum. We would be able to demonstrate our continuing resolve to the North Vietnamese on the battlefield, but I thought that the Soviets would need a special reminder."[72]

The special reminder to which he referred was most probably the worldwide nuclear alert. It had been part of the DUCK HOOK concept from the beginning. Its purposes were to persuade the Soviets and North Vietnamese that the November attacks—should they be launched—could include the use of nuclear weapons and also to signal Moscow that Washington was ready for any contingency.[73] Beyond that, it was intended to cause the Soviets and North Vietnamese to fear that it was a lead-up to the now-canceled November Option. It was a bluff, but one he hoped would jar the Soviets into levering Hanoi's diplomatic cooperation.[74]

Laird understood that the proposed operation was tied to Nixon's concept of the Madman Theory. He recalled in 2001 that "Nixon did it because of Soviet aid to North Vietnam—to alert them that he might do something. This was one of several examples of the Madman

Theory. . . . He never used the term 'madman' but he wanted adversaries to have the feeling that you could never put your finger on what he might do next. Nixon got this from Ike, who always felt that way."[75]

Laird's military aide, Robert Pursley, agreed: "Nixon had this idea, and Kissinger and Haig were supporting it, that getting the Soviets to worry that there was a madman [in the White House] who could create enough uncertainty would cause them to cave in on their aid to DRV. Even Al Haig said that this was exactly what they wanted to do."[76]

Whether Nixon and Kissinger intended the Soviets or Vietnamese to interpret the readiness measures as preparation for a major conventional bombing campaign against the North or as preparation for the actual use of nuclear weapons in Vietnam is unclear. But that is the interpretation Hanoi could have made, as suggested by Le Duc Tho's defiant comments to Kissinger in 1972 about Nixon administration threat making:

> You made statements amounting to threats. . . . We foresee that if the war is not settled the war will be very ferocious. Maybe you would even use massive B-52 bombing raids, perhaps even to level Hanoi and Haiphong. *We also sometimes think that you would also use atomic weapons,* because during the resistance against the French, Vice President Nixon proposed the use of atomic weapons. . . . But . . . no matter what destruction is brought to our country we will continue the struggle.[77]

Luu Doan Huynh—a Vietminh soldier and DRV diplomat, news analyst, and historian—told Kimball it was his view that early on, "the Vietnamese top leadership thought Nixon was more bellicose than Johnson, and some of the measures that were taboo for Johnson (no intensive air escalation, no operations in Laos and Cambodia, no attacks against dikes, no nuclear attacks) might be undertaken by Nixon." Nixon's ultimatum to Ho Chi Minh in July 1969 reinforced this view. The DRV leaders' analysis of the "danger" was that Nixon would mine the coast and launch bombing attacks against dikes and cities, including Hanoi and Haiphong. But they anticipated that he might also use nuclear weapons, although this was more unlikely than conventional bombing. Whatever concerns Hanoi's leaders had about the launching of nuclear attacks by Nixon against North Vietnam, they were tempered by their belief that US and international opinion, especially opinion in Asia, would restrain him, and they thought the bombing of dikes a more likely drastic move by

Nixon.[78] They may also have been skeptical, believing they were covered by a Soviet nuclear umbrella.

Meanwhile, in another move that was not formally part of the JCS Readiness Test but complemented it as a threatening signal to Hanoi and Moscow, Nixon once again authorized B-52 raids into Cambodia; they began on 10 October with an all-day attack on what Kissinger told the president was a "new area, just north" of previously bombed targets. The raids, he recommended, should continue through the rest of October and only "stop . . . as we get closer to the first [of November]." Nixon was pleased by the day's raid, remarking that he was "convinced that this is more important than anything else." He was pleased mainly because "we are hurting them and they don't get anything out of it," by which he meant PR benefits. In other words, Hanoi's leaders could not complain because they did not acknowledge that their forces were in Cambodia, and the American public would not learn about the secret raids unless news of them somehow leaked to the press.[79] Renewed bombing in Cambodia leading up to the November deadline had been proposed in the DUCK HOOK concept plan. That plan had been aborted, but paralleling the worldwide alert, the secret bombing in Cambodia had resumed. It was a tested method by which Nixon "would be able to demonstrate our continuing resolve to the North Vietnamese on the battlefield" without drawing public or congressional attention.

Informing the Brass and Changing the Game

Before deciding to abort the November Option, Nixon and Kissinger had scheduled a meeting with the JCS for Saturday, 11 October, to discuss the November Option and alternate Vietnam strategies. Shortly before the meeting was to be held—but unaware of Nixon's decision to cancel the November operation—General Wheeler asked for assurance that the president would have read the entire plan before the conclave. On Friday, he received that assurance from Haig through Robinson.[80] But whether Nixon actually read the plan or not, Kissinger, with assistance from staff, prepared an appraisal of it and talking points for the president, as well as critical remarks about Laird's own assessment of PRUNING KNIFE. Kissinger's critique of the plan laid bare the fundamental conceptual differences between it and the DUCK HOOK concept concerning the objectives sought by the White House and the methods to be used in the prospective November operation.

Kissinger argued that the PRUNING KNIFE plan had "several serious shortcomings." In general, it did not reflect the "strategic criteria" and "political requirements" that he and his team believed were essential to the success of the operation. In particular, the two-phased JCS plan did not incorporate the White House's original strategic requirement that "the operation should involve a series of *short, sharp military blows of increasing severity,* holding out to Hanoi the prospect of a long and increasingly disabling siege if they failed to come to an agreement." Nor did it include priority targets Kissinger considered strategic; namely, those whose destruction would result in a *"sudden and significant disruption of the economy"* of North Vietnam and whose restoration "should be costly and time-consuming, so that their *destruction achieves a lasting military and economic effect* and continuous follow-up bombing is unnecessary." Additionally objectionable, the JCS concept did not provide for a "mining operation sufficient to seal off the sea approaches to North Vietnam, thereby *stopping her supply of waterborne imports.*" Kissinger was also critical of what appeared to be the plan's "routine use of our attack resources," limiting Thai-based aircraft, for example, to only one sortie per day.[81]

Concerning the White House's political requirements, a "large number" of the sensitive targets in Hanoi that the JCS had identified would, Kissinger warned, "maximize adverse domestic and foreign reactions to the operation." The sensitive targets on the JCS list included the Ministry of Defense, the telephone and telegraph office, the Air Force and Army Air Defense Command Headquarters, and the civilian airport. Striking government offices would send the wrong signal—that the administration's goal was "the destruction of the country and the regime, thus inviting major outside intervention" (from the Soviet Union and China). Moreover, Hanoi was also where the North Vietnamese and international press, the foreign diplomatic corps, and foreign businesses were concentrated; civilian casualties would be extensive; and because Hanoi was strongly defended, US crew and aircraft losses would be "disproportionately heavy."[82]

Aside from its strategic, tactical, and political shortcomings in relation to the objectives of the White House, Kissinger was concerned that "the JCS concept Plan is in effect the first step toward what they hope will be a sustained and unrestricted bombing campaign. If we proceed in their way, the logic of events will probably impel us towards continuous, no-holds-barred attacks. If the plan fails, the alibi will be that the nation's leaders failed to take all required military steps to make it succeed."[83] In a nutshell, the JCS plan was focused on military rather than diplomatic and psychological results; as such, it did not meet the core Madman Theory criteria desired by Nixon and Kissinger.

Kissinger then took issue with Laird's argument against PRUNING KNIFE, most probably because Laird's criticisms also applied to the DUCK HOOK concept Nixon and Kissinger had wanted from the start. The secretary of defense, he told Nixon, maintained that the JCS plan "would involve the US in expanded costs and risks with no clear resultant military or political benefits." The risks included possible confrontations with the Soviet Union and China, negative reactions from "Free World maritime states," possible losses of naval ships, and probable aircraft losses of up to 100 planes. Rejecting these claims, Kissinger asserted that Laird's analysis was but a "smorgasbord of speculations, assertions, and evidence" aimed at making the point "that nothing at all" could be done militarily to convince Hanoi to negotiate on US terms.[84]

According to Admiral Moorer's memorandum of conversation, the president opened his midmorning meeting on Saturday with the Joint Chiefs saying that their purpose was to "evaluate what we could do if it became necessary to take more military action against North Vietnam." But before exploring that issue, Nixon meandered. He first posed questions to the group about the progress of and prospects for Vietnamization, the military intentions of the other side, the military situation in Laos, and the meaning and significance of the "lull" in fighting. Although pleased that the lull had resulted in fewer US casualties, Nixon wanted the group's views on whether "the enemy was deliberately effecting the lull for political reasons." Kissinger chimed in, saying that "the North Vietnamese were trying to put us into a position where we cannot act," by which he meant launching a bombing-and-mining operation against North Vietnam. Attorney General Mitchell expressed support for Kissinger's sentiment. Nixon then mentioned a related political concern of his: "[We] . . . must not let the enemy take credit for reducing the tempo of operations."[85]

Having made the point that the public was leaning toward de-escalation and against escalation, Nixon turned the conversation to a discussion of three Vietnam options other than bombing and mining: "get out now; negotiate a settlement; [or] go the long road, which also carries with it a risk of failing."[86] He was less interested in the first two than in the third option because he regarded an immediate or rapid withdrawal without a satisfactory settlement as cutting and running, or, as he put it on other occasions, a bug out. Although he did want a negotiated settlement of the war, he knew that he could not presently achieve one on his terms. Indeed, that was why he and Kissinger had been considering an attack on North Vietnam. But by now, he had rejected the November Option and was exploring the pros and cons of the long-road option, which relied on de-Americanization and Vietnamization—Laird's priority.

In November, the secretary of defense would recommend a target date of July 1973 for the complete withdrawal of US troops, leaving "a small advisory mission" behind.[87] Nixon and Kissinger's concept of the long-road strategy was compatible with Laird's but more likely consisted of two options that at that point resembled Option B of the July and September alternative policy papers: couple negotiations and military force with the steady, unilateral withdrawal of US troops—but on a secret timetable to be completed soon before or soon after the 1972 presidential election, with or without residual troops left behind. The aim would be to provide Thieu with a decent chance to survive after an American exit.

At the same time, the Nixon administration would try to ensure that a decent interval would pass between the US pullout and Thieu's possible or even likely demise by weakening DRV/VC forces through US military measures and strengthening Thieu and his government through the Vietnamization program. The possible collapse of Thieu's government was what Nixon had meant when he said that the long-road option carried with it "a risk of failing." Even so, the strategy could succeed politically for Nixon if a reasonable interval passed before the fall—one long enough to blur any causal connection between Thieu's fall and Nixon's Vietnam policies.[88]

For now, however, Nixon thought the long-road option was almost as problematic as the escalation option. He told the assembled group that "if we hold the line politically, Vietnamization will work, provided we have time to do it deliberately. . . . The people will stand still for support [of Saigon?] but will not stand still for a long drawn-out ground action." But with or without protracted ground action, he said he had been told by some congressmen that he would "'catch hell' from the hawks as well as doves if we followed the long road." In addition, "the student uprising will get more violent," and the pollsters who measured public opinion would continue to skew their questions in such a way as to bias the results against him. The "real question," however, was "whether the US, after all this effort, should make a withdrawal and accept a coalition [government in Saigon]. It will be very detrimental to our long-range interests." This was the fundamental issue—the casus belli. A unilateral US withdrawal without a negotiated agreement would bring about Saigon's collapse, but the success or failure of a negotiated withdrawal would depend on the terms of the agreement.[89]

Because Laird, along with Rogers, was the main proponent of a unilateral withdrawal, Nixon asked him whether "we can hold [public and congressional opinion] that long" or whether we are "going to lose 10,000 men this year for nothing and then have a new Congress stop the appropriations?" The secretary of defense answered that the main political problem was the wrongheaded interpretation within the United States of "what's going on" in Vietnam. Predicting that "18 months from now no US forces will actually be engaged," he recommended getting "a vote now from the Congress" in support of Vietnamization. "Anything else done in Vietnam" would "take at least a year" anyway, he argued, so the administration "should game-plan progress for Vietnamization," and "it will work if we stick to it."[90]

Laird's focus was on winning congressional approval for a strategy of getting US armed forces out of Vietnam during the next thirty-six to forty-two months while building up South Vietnamese armed forces. But Nixon was not as confident as Laird about this plan. He observed that if the 1970 congressional "election results in doves coming in we are in trouble." And there was another problem. If the enemy launched a military campaign on the scale of the 1968 Tet Offensive, the American public would blame the administration for misleading them about progress in Vietnam, as they had blamed Johnson in 1968, and Nixon would have to "react" with counterattacks anyway. "The real question," he repeated, "is how long we can hold public opinion. . . . We could sustain current efforts for a year and take a look. If between now and next September we haven't made progress then we must act—we cannot sit still." The disagreement between Nixon and Laird was not over whether US forces should be withdrawn by or in 1973 or even over the question of how many, if any, residual US troops should be left behind; instead, it was over the issue of whether, when, and how to attack North Vietnam.[91] (By spring 1971, the number of residual troops Nixon had in mind was 50,000; by spring 1972, the number was to be reduced down to virtually zero; and in any case, the residuals to be "left" in Vietnam would be there only until a negotiated settlement was concluded.)[92]

At this point in the conversation, Admiral Moorer returned the discussion to the issue of Hanoi's motives behind the lull in NVA/VC military operations, seconding the view that it was a political move. He further argued that the other side held the military initiative and could increase the "tempo of operations . . . at will." Nixon chose the moment to call on General Wheeler for his assessment of PRUNING KNIFE, which was the main purpose of the meeting. Since no one else but Kissinger was as yet informed of Nixon's decision to abort the November operation, Wheeler's explanation of why he and the Joint Chiefs "did not think" PRUNING KNIFE "was a sound *military* plan" was based in part on his assumption that the attack was to be launched in November, when the weather over northern Vietnam is not optimal for aerial bombing. Wheeler noted that one of the problems with the plan was that bad weather would mean "it would take at least a week to get five days of operations." And there were other "problem areas": moving an aircraft carrier from the Korean area to the Tonkin Gulf and coping with improved North Vietnamese air defenses. Moreover, the Joint Chiefs believed that the prospective duration of the operation would be too short to be effective.

The crux of the matter was that the Joint Chiefs were displeased with the DUCK HOOK criteria developed in the White House and upon which the PRUNING KNIFE plan was partially but imperfectly based. As Moorer observed in a parenthetical note in his memorandum of conversation, the PRUNING KNIFE plan "was a political and not a military plan and was not intended to have full-scale military objectives"—even though it was more military in its design than the DUCK HOOK concept. The Joint Chiefs preferred that a bombing-and-mining campaign continue for as long as it took to destroy Hanoi's capacity and will to keep fighting, but they had been constrained to plan military operations whose main purpose was to persuade Hanoi to make concessions at the negotiating table..[93]

Nixon nonetheless followed Wheeler's remarks with a call for the PRUNING KNIFE plan to be "refined" along the lines of the DUCK HOOK concept—without using that code name. He said it should be designed "in terms of maximum shock impact, with limited civilian casualties" for the purpose of reducing North Vietnam's "capacity to wage war" by impairing its economy. Kissinger joined in to accentuate Nixon's comment, saying that "we should use as target criteria high economic value targets and bottleneck areas" and noting that "it doesn't mean much to strike at supplies distributed on trails" to the South. Nixon drove home the point, saying that "the objective was not to stop support of the war in the South."[94]

Then the president finally dropped his own bombshell, so to speak, ordering the drafting of refined plans for possible execution *in the future* but not in November. He wanted "two plans of 7 and 14 days' duration for both the wet and dry seasons with reduced follow-on sorties to re-seed minefields and hit [the] Northeast railroad," and he added that "we should not be concerned about degrading SIOP," which was apparently a reference to JCS concerns about using B-52s in such operations. Nixon explained that US attacks on the North would be his *response* to a North Vietnamese "provocation," which he predicted would come in April.[95]

In the middle of much back-and-forth about targeting issues, Hanoi's intentions, the situation in Cambodia, political and budgetary concerns, the importance of electing supporters of Nixon's policies to Congress in September, and of holding public opinion, Nixon remarked, perhaps for Laird's benefit, "We must keep the Air and Navy forces available. The North Vietnamese may decide to talk now and fight later." As the meeting drew to a close, Laird had apparently gotten the message that there would be no attack on North Vietnam unless there was a provocation because he understood what Nixon's preference now was. Laird put it this way: "We should continue along [with] the present [withdrawal] plan," which "is working," and "a date on withdrawal should not be given since it, in effect, stops negotiations." Nixon soon added: "If there is a chance that Vietnamization will work we must take this chance. . . . If the North Vietnamese try to break us with an offensive then we must hit them—and I do not mean tit for tat. [I] want the military to think differently than the previous policy of tit for tat. . . . A great power must go on [the] basis of: 'Don't strike a king unless you intend to kill him.'"[96] Nixon's equation of himself with a stricken king revealed, moreover, the great extent to which he took Hanoi's and Moscow's defiance personally. As he said on other occasions, he believed they were trying to break him, as though the war was more about that than about the clash of real or perceived national interests.[97]

The discussion at this meeting encapsulated the reasons for Nixon's decision to cancel the November Option: his concerns about holding public and congressional support should he attack North Vietnam; his uncertainty about the probable success of such an offensive; his worries about how the Moratorium and New Mobe demonstrations would play out; Laird's opposition to the November Option; the irreconcilable differences between White House and JCS views concerning a bombing-and-mining offensive against North Vietnam; and the lull in fighting, which helped to persuade Nixon that the long-road strategy, combined with negotiations and diplomacy, might work out. If Moorer's memorandum of the conversation of the meeting is complete and accurate, the matter of the secret global readiness alert did not come up. On it, however, rested Nixon and Kissinger's last remaining hope of making Hanoi and Moscow cooperate for fear of retribution before the year 1969 came to an end.

CHAPTER NINE

The Secret Nuclear Alert
October 1969

The Soviets would need a special reminder.
Richard M. Nixon[1]

When Nixon and his party returned to Washington from Key Biscayne late Sunday morning, 5 October, several domestic and international issues filled his presidential agenda. But his focus remained on Vietnam—his "overriding major challenge."[2] Just before noon the next day, Nixon and Kissinger began to cobble together a set of military exercises that would soon be officially referred to as the JCS Readiness Test, or Increased Readiness Posture—the equivalent of a worldwide nuclear readiness alert. It was intended to signal Washington's anger at Moscow's support of North Vietnam and to jar the Soviet leaders into using their leverage to induce Hanoi to make diplomatic concessions. Carried out between 13 and 30 October, it involved military operations around the world, the continental United States, Western Europe, the Middle East, the Atlantic, the Pacific, and the Sea of Japan. The operations included strategic bombers, tactical air, and a variety of naval operations from movements of aircraft carriers and ballistic missile submarines to the shadowing of Soviet merchant ships heading toward Haiphong.

Although the alert was held secret from the American public and most of the government, some elements of the readiness test were noticed around the world, including in neighborhoods near SAC bases and at ports in the Pacific and in Western Europe. Within the US government, secrecy created moderate confusion, since such activities as the sudden departures of ships at port were unusual and unexplained. Moreover, top US military commanders had no idea what was behind their instructions and found them perplexing. As Nixon and Kissinger hoped, the Soviets took note of the unusual US military activity and responded with precautionary actions, but it remains to be learned what exactly Moscow made of the situation, especially the extent to which Soviet leaders understood the message that Nixon and Kissinger intended to send.

Planning the Global Alert

On Monday, 6 October, five days before the JCS meeting and twenty-four hours after returning from Key Biscayne, Nixon had instructed Kissinger to "have the Secretary of Defense initiate a series of increased alert measures designed to convey to the Soviets an increased readiness by US strategic forces."[3] Since the available evidence suggests that Nixon did not firmly or finally decide against launching the November bombing-and-mining operation against North Vietnam until 9 October, the 6 October date of his instruction to Kissinger to initiate the readiness alert suggests that it was intended to precede a possible November attack, one that had yet to be finally decided upon. A nuclear readiness alert had been part of the original "conceptual plan for implementation of operation DUCK HOOK" submitted to Nixon by Kissinger in August. As envisioned then, it would include "a heightened PACOM and SAC alert posture militarily to show our resolve and to respond to whatever contingencies arise."[4] But because Nixon had serious doubts about going ahead with the November Option by the time of the meeting at Key Biscayne, it is just as likely that Nixon and Kissinger at that point thought of the alert in both ways: either as a prelude to the bombing and mining of North Vietnam or as a substitute for such an offensive should the president decide against it. In the end—and as it turned out in practice—the latter was the case.

Speaking with Laird by telephone just before noon on 6 October, Kissinger told him he had noticed there was a SAC exercise scheduled for October. "I'm all for it," he said, "but I just want to know what it is. Has it been announced?'" When Laird answered that it had not been announced, Kissinger asked, "Will the other side pick this up? We want them to." Laird responded, "They will pick it up" because of "the fact that we are exercising our bombers." Kissinger added, "Could you exercise the DEFCONs for a day or so in October? I'll give you a brief as to why." Laird answered, "We can." Kissinger replied, "The president will appreciate it very much." Nixon spoke to Laird about the matter sometime that evening.[5]

On Tuesday morning, 7 October, Kissinger asked Laird to send him a paper on the SAC exercise; Laird said he would.[6] That same day, Laird's military aide, Colonel Pursley, called Kissinger's aide, Haig, who was now a brigadier general, to inform him that Defense was sending over a plan for an "increased SAC alert." But when it arrived, the White House learned that "it was merely a résumé of an already scheduled East Coast continental air defense exercise" (CONAD) code-named SNOW TIME, which Kissinger and Haig thought "was not responsive to the president's instruction."[7]

Meeting with Pursley later in the day, Haig provided detailed guidance so that the Pentagon would be more responsive. Haig asked for more impressive military measures based on several criteria: "Be discernible to the Soviets and be both unusual and significant; not threatening to the Soviets; not require substantial funding or resources; not require agreement with the allies; not degrade essential missions; and have minimum chance of public exposure."[8] To be "not threatening to the Soviets" suggests that although Nixon wanted something big and unusual, signifying (as Laird said about Nixon and the Madman Theory) that "you could never put your finger on what he might do next,"[9] he did not want it to appear that he was preparing to make a move against the Soviet Union.

Pursley responded on Wednesday with a list of seven actions: communications silence, increased reconnaissance operations around the Soviet periphery, increased ground alert rates for SAC bombers and tankers, dispersal of SAC aircraft with nuclear weapons to designated military bases, the alerting and sending to sea of ballistic missile submarines (SSBNs), a stand-down of combat aircraft, and increased surveillance of Soviet ships en route to Vietnam. Pursley may have made the last recommendation in recognition of Nixon's irritation over Soviet aid to Hanoi. He suggested that this measure, as well as the other six proposed measures, could be easily detected by the Soviets without being noticed at home, could be executed beginning 13 October (the following Monday), and could last "sufficiently long to be convincing." Pursley also informed Haig that he had asked the Joint Staff to develop detailed plans for each of the proposals.[10] He had made no recommendations to raise the alert level of the US intercontinental ballistic missile force, since it was routinely on a high state of alert, ready for launch on warning.

The stand-down of military air activity was one of Pursley's chief recommendations because Nixon wanted a show of force that Moscow would notice. SAC bombers were one of the few instruments of strategic nuclear power that could be used for signaling purposes, for the reason that their alert status and flight activity could be visibly changed. Doing so involved taking maintenance personnel, pilots, crews, and aircraft off their routine training and surveillance duties and placing the aircraft on runways in take-off positions—armed, fueled, and ready to fly attack missions. Pursley later observed that they were sure to be noticed as long as enough forces were included to make it meaningful. Standing down bomber forces and putting them on higher alert was a traditional form of signaling activity by both sides in the Cold War since at least the time of SAC's Blue Alert in 1958 during the Lebanon crisis and SAC's larger stand-down in 1962 during the Cuban missile crisis.

The Soviets, too, had staged stand-downs. As recently as August 1969, US intelligence had become aware of a "continued lull in Soviet air operations," which caused enough concern that CINCSAC general Bruce Holloway proposed alert measures if the situation continued. According to a CIA report on the lull: "A stand-down in military air activity is one of the classic indicators of preparations to initiate hostilities," if not a "conclusive sign." The CIA was not sure what had caused the Soviet stand-down, but one explanation had to do with continuing Sino-Soviet border tensions. The Soviets were already conducting large-scale military exercises on the border, among other "unusual" activity, and the lull may have represented signaling to make Beijing wonder and worry what might happen next.[11]

On Wednesday, 8 October, Haig and Kissinger were paring down Pursley's list of seven recommendations to five, selecting radio silence, aircraft stand-down, increased surveillance of Soviet shipping, higher alert rates for SAC aircraft, and dispersal of bombers "phased appropriately through the week." Off the list were increased aerial reconnaissance operations and raised alert levels for ballistic missile submarines. The readiness exercise would begin by 13 October and end on 25 October. Later in the day, Pursley sent Haig an analysis of the pros and cons of the measures on his original list, perhaps to expose the White House to their downside. Some proposals, such as increased reconnaissance sorties, were clearly risky because of a greater chance of provoking a Soviet shootdown, and others, such as relocating SAC aircraft to military dispersal bases, "could be publicly alarming." Less provocative measures, such as a stand-down of combat aircraft and an increased ground alert rate for SAC bombers, would be considered significant by the Soviets. On the con side of things, they could have a disruptive impact on routine US Air Force operations. It would be difficult, for example, to maintain an increased ground alert "for weeks without strain on air crews." Increased surveillance of Soviet ships en route to Vietnam would be a "significant departure from current operations," but it raised the risk of a collision at sea and "could provoke Soviet charges to interference with shipping."[12]

Pursley's evaluation may have had an impact, but the White House did not look back. During the evening of 9 October, Nixon signed off on Kissinger's recommendations, initialing the memo Kissinger gave him, to which was attached Pursley's list. Haig then informed Pursley and requested a detailed plan with implementing instructions.[13] No more was heard in the White House about going ahead with DUCK HOOK. And regarding PRUNING KNIFE, Nixon and Kissinger were preparing to tell the Joint Chiefs at the NSC meeting on Saturday, 11 October, that the attacks would not go forward in November but only at some time in the future under special circumstances.[14]

Haig's phone calls to the Pentagon brought the JCS into planning for the alert on 9 October. William Lemnitzer, one of the Joint Staff liaison officers to the White House and a member of the DUCK HOOK group, sent Pursley's list of measures to Wheeler, telling him that the president had approved "five major actions" and that Laird had approved "execution as directed by the White House." What Kissinger wanted, Wheeler learned, was *"an integrated plan of military actions to demonstrate convincingly to the Soviet Union that the United States is getting ready for any eventuality on or about 1 November 1969. . . . Rather than threatening a confrontation (which may or may not occur), the objective of these actions would be a demonstration of improving or confirming readiness to react should a confrontation occur."* Lemnitzer presented Wheeler with a directive authorizing the Joint Staff to prepare plans based on the approved five actions so they could be sent to the White House by the close of business on 10 October.[15]

Kissinger did not expect or want a confrontation with the Soviets, but language about "getting ready for any eventuality" was consistent with the White House's purpose of signaling the Soviets that the United States was preparing for any contingency that might develop in connection with a US attack against North Vietnam sometime after 1 November. The attack had been aborted, but presumably, neither the Soviets nor the North Vietnamese knew that. Indeed, at this point, Laird did not yet know. Wheeler never learned officially or directly what the specific objectives of the readiness test were beyond getting ready to react to some Soviet response, but this left him unsure about how to assess Soviet military reactions, apart from reporting them to the White House.[16] The White

House purpose was political, not military; that is, it was to elicit Moscow's help in persuading Hanoi to yield diplomatically. But neither Wheeler nor Laird knew this at the time.

That same day, 9 October, but before he made his recommendations to Nixon, Kissinger had met with Dobrynin, very likely to help set the stage for the alert. Although it covered China and the Middle East, the discussion began with recriminations over Vietnam. Signaling the resentments that underlay the forthcoming readiness measures and reminding the Soviets that Nixon had not given up on linkage, Kissinger told Dobrynin that the "Vietnam issue inevitably has an effect on the creation of a general climate that is of great importance for progress on other issues." Stressing that his remarks were unofficial, he emphasized his and Nixon's disappointment that Moscow had not supported earlier White House initiatives, such as the proposed Vance mission. "We expected the Soviet leadership to provide us—through the same confidential channels—a detailed commentary on this matter, which might allow us to search together for constructive approaches." Yet the president had "never received a direct reply to this from the Soviet leaders." According to Dobrynin's report, Kissinger restated that point in a "vexed tone." Acknowledging that these complaints might be creating a "problem," Kissinger asked the ambassador to "forget his personal comments" and not report them to Moscow. Dobrynin nevertheless did that, no doubt just as the White House had expected.[17]

Around noon the next day, Friday, 10 October, Laird phoned Kissinger with three concerns. The first was about presidential approval for the readiness measures. He wanted reassurance that he correctly understood that the president had approved "the exercises that are to be laid on for 13 and 14 October and running through that week." Kissinger answered, "Yes, . . . the president went over them last night" (9 October). Soon after, he said, "Go ahead and execute this," adding that "he has a signed paper from the president that he wants it."[18]

Laird's second concern was about the standing requirement that allies were supposed to be notified about DEFCONs. He asked, "We will not be contacting our allies (Canada or NATO) on any of these?" Kissinger answered: "That is what we want. We were worried about getting the allies involved. All of these activities will get [give?] some sort of signal—they will get the word [out], but there will be no DEFCON. There is no military significance to this." For the benefit of the cost-conscious secretary of defense, Kissinger quipped, "It won't cost much money."[19] What Kissinger meant with these responses was than the White House wanted to send nuclear-readiness signals for political rather than military purposes. In order to preserve the operation's secrecy and keep its purpose from the public and allies, the signals should not be designated a DEFCON, even though the intention was for Soviets and North Vietnamese to take notice of the readiness measures and worry about their portent.

Laird's third concern was whether the alert was connected with or "contingent in any way on the other operation that is going to be discussed on Saturday." His reference was to the scheduled morning meeting between Nixon, Kissinger, the Joint Chiefs, Attorney General John Mitchell, and Laird himself on Saturday, 11 October, in the president's Executive Office Building office. The main topic on the agenda was a discussion of the latest version of PRUNING KNIFE. Knowing Laird's reservations about the plan, Kissinger assured him that "it has nothing to do with that." Later he emphasized, "it is independent." Kissinger then added that the alert was, "frankly, an attempt to prevent our having to face a thing like tomorrow," by which he meant the PRUNING KNIFE plan—thereby affirming that the alert was a substitute for military escalation, whether in the form of PRUNING KNIFE or DUCK HOOK. He prefaced this remark by citing Laird's own critique of the JCS plan as "a powerful case" against it and noting that "the thinking" at the White House "is much more on . . . [your] line" than the JCS line.[20]

Technically, Kissinger had answered truthfully. The strategic readiness measures, strictly speaking, had not been and were not contingent on, related to, or part of the PRUNING KNIFE concept. But Kissinger had dissembled nonetheless. Laird had asked whether the alert exercises were contingent "in any way" on PRUNING KNIFE. The way they *were* contingent was that they had been related to and part of the DUCK HOOK concept—in other words, related to the November Option, which was what was on Laird's mind when he asked his question. Although Kissinger was making an effort to camouflage the purpose of the alert, Laird no doubt understood that it was related to Vietnam—however vague this purpose seemed and however extravagant the alert appeared to be as a means of accomplishing the purpose. Wheeler probably understood as well as most that the purpose was Vietnam related, but his main interest was in understanding its military objectives so that he could better design readiness measures and assess Soviet reactions. It was likely that neither

Nixon nor Kissinger were themselves clear on what to expect or require of the Soviets, other than some sign that Moscow would push Hanoi in the direction of a diplomatic settlement acceptable to Washington.

Meanwhile, the Joint Staff quickly prepared a plan that Wheeler sent to Laird on Friday but that went to the White House later, apparently on Saturday morning, 11 October. Wheeler told Laird that he had already sent cables to the commanders in chief (CINC)s that would be summarized in a memorandum for the president. The key element of the plan was a "stand-down of flying training activities in selected commands, and for the development of increased readiness." The CINCs would be asked for recommendations for "additional actions."[21]

The cables that Wheeler sent on Friday, 10 October, notified the CINCs of seven unified and specified commands that "higher authority" had "directed that we test US capability to respond to a possible confrontation with the USSR," explaining that "implementing actions should be discernible to the Soviets but should not be threatening." The commanders in chief had the following commands: Strategic Air Command (CINCSAC), European Command (CINCEUR), Pacific Command (CINCPAC), Southern Command (CINCSO), Strike Command (CINCSTRIKE), Alaskan Command (CINCAL), and North American Air Defense Command (CINCONAD). Each CINC received specific instructions to stand-down military training flights and to "increase the readiness" of their forces to the "highest state that can be attained consistent with no change in DEFCON status."[22]

The instructions each of the CINCs received were tailored to their roles and missions and their importance for strategic signaling. Thus, the Strategic Air Command was to go first, beginning with a stand-down of bomber flights (excluding forces with Vietnam War assignments) and increased ground alert levels beginning at 8:00 a.m. local time on 13 October. As a SAC historian later observed, suspension of training flights was necessary to "beef up [SAC's] ground alert" status by increasing the number of nuclear-armed bombers available for alert operations. To give the appearance of an "intensification of US readiness," the other commands would follow by beginning operations on 15 October. The Pacific Command stand-down included air force, army, and navy air units in the Korean Air Defense Identification Zone as well as Japan and Okinawa. The European Command would supplement the stand-down of training flights and higher readiness levels for combat aircraft with "emissions control [EMCON]"—or communications silence for the Sixth Fleet—thus complicating Soviet efforts to track fleet movements.[23]

On 10 October, Wheeler also sent a separate message to the same CINCs and also to CINCLANT (commander in chief, Atlantic Command), informing them that the readiness test would take place between 13 and 25 October. Besides the stand-downs, higher readiness, and radio silence in selected commands, measures could include "increased surveillance" of Soviet ships bound for North Vietnam and an increased ground alert rate for SAC. Wheeler did not have a plan, however, so he asked the CINCs to "nominate further actions compatible with the guidance," taking into account local conditions and military budget cuts. The proposals should arrive no later than late in the day on 12 October.[24]

What Wheeler had done so far was crucial for starting the signaling process that Nixon and Kissinger wanted, but it was less than what they had asked for, despite Lemnitzer's emphasis on "five major actions." The White House would soon notice but Wheeler did not instruct SAC to disperse bombers and tankers to other bases or the Pacific Command to surveil Soviet ships. Wheeler had decided to hold these measures "in abeyance" because they would raise costs (which Haig's original criteria had enjoined) and because of their "political implications."[25]

Exactly what Wheeler had in mind is unclear, although the points that Pursley had made about risks—for example, that dispersal of nuclear-armed bombers could be "publicly alarming"—may have been telling. Moreover, Wheeler may already have understood what SAC generals would tell him the following week. They recommended against significant dispersal because of the "serious shortage of aircraft crews." The shortage was such that if a major international crisis broke out, SAC would have to choose between dispersing bombers or putting them on airborne alert.[26]

While the CINCs were digesting their instructions and sending out action messages to units in the field to begin the stand-down on 13 October, Laird reported to Nixon on plans and schedules. Without mentioning bomber dispersal or the surveillance of Soviet ships, he pointed out that measures that would raise costs or degrade forces had been excluded. He also informed Nixon that the "stand-down posture will continue until US intelligence indicates [the] Soviets have become aware of the increased readiness." Toward that end, "a special intelligence watch has been established."[27]

Deep Secrecy and the Naming of the Alert

As with the bombing of Cambodia, secrecy veiled the worldwide readiness exercise. Haig's guidance to Pursley included the admonition to ensure "minimal chance of public exposure." Nixon and Kissinger took it for granted that if the press and public learned about the alert, the reaction would be hostile. Unwilling to go ahead with the November Option in large part because he believed he could not hold public opinion for the time it would take to work—if indeed it could have worked—Nixon thought it imperative to keep the readiness measures out of the public eye.

Public apprehension about the administration's saber rattling would have raised additional questions about Nixon's Vietnam policy, strengthened the Vietnam War protests, and further diminished his standing in the polls. Press reports about the operation, moreover, could have caused Soviet leaders to regard their own superpower prestige and credibility as being at risk, thus raising the chances of confrontation. As they had when deciding to bomb Cambodia secretly, Nixon and Kissinger may have reasoned that if the alert measures leaked, Moscow would have thought it necessary to react with countermeasures of unpredictable consequence. In this sense, secrecy was necessary to prevent serious instability in US-Soviet relations.

Given the emphasis on secrecy, only a few individuals in the US government knew about the alert measures and why Nixon wanted them. At the White House, the circle of knowledge seems to have included only Nixon, Kissinger, Haig, and Haldeman. It is not clear how much, if anything, NSC staff experts on Vietnam and Soviet affairs knew about Nixon's decision, although watch officers in the White House Situation Room may have been clued in.

At the Pentagon, only Laird and Pursley had the full picture of the readiness test and its purposes. Laird, the secretary of defense, had to know, even though he doubted that the alert would have any impact on Moscow's relationship with Hanoi. Further, Pursley recalled that Laird believed "an alert posture would only cause consternation" in Moscow. "It was wrong to push sticks through the bar at a caged animal; that was not in our strategic interest."[28] JCS chairman Wheeler had a complete picture of military activities, but he later wrote that he had not been told about the readiness test's objectives—although Laird may have provided some clues.[29]

Secretary of State Rogers and Undersecretary Richardson would not learn about the alert measures until they were already under way. Haig had recommended to Kissinger that they be told even although they "will most probably strongly object." He argued that unless Rogers and Richardson were informed, "feedback will most certainly come immediately through State channels"—that is, a government, perhaps a NATO ally, was likely to notice the heightened military posture and raise the issue with a US ambassador. Haig further observed, "I do not believe Rogers or Richardson will forgive our failure to keep them informed," and in addition, the White House would face criticism should the press learn that State had been shut out.[30] Rogers was already on record as opposing escalatory military measures in Vietnam and may have objected to the readiness actions had he been consulted in advance. Aside from his continuing competition with Rogers for influence with the president, Kissinger might have expected that Rogers would argue that the readiness test was unlikely to influence Moscow's Vietnam policy and, if anything, could confuse the Soviets about US intentions and perhaps spark a confrontation. Laird's aide, Robert Pursley, later recalled such concern at the time.[31]

Reflecting the degree of secrecy surrounding the exercise, Wheeler did not explain to the CINCs why "higher authority" had described the alert's purpose as a "test of US capability to respond to a possible confrontation with the USSR." Perhaps because the Joint Chiefs, Laird, or the White House decided that talk of confrontation raised too many concerns and questions, Wheeler sent a message to the CINCs on 11 October rescinding the first paragraph of the initial message, which had implied the possibility. He substituted language stating simply that "higher authority has requested that as a test, we take certain actions which would increase our readiness and would be discernible but not threatening to the Soviets." From then on, the series of readiness actions requested by Nixon became known as the JCS Readiness Test, or Increased Readiness Posture.[32]

"Tail Twisting" at the Pentagon

On the evening of 13 October, just as SAC was beginning to stand down, Laird told Kissinger that the test would interfere with a nuclear command post exercise code-named HIGH HEELS, slated to begin on 14 October. "We should cancel one or the other," he advised, or postpone the readiness test. An annual exercise that had begun in the early 1960s, HIGH HEELS was a worldwide operation that involved the Defense Department, the Joint Chiefs of Staff, the CINCs, and the State Department, among other agencies. Prepared long in advance, HIGH HEELS 69 posited the "exercise" of US war plans in response to a Soviet preemptive nuclear strike.[33]

Wheeler, who wanted to carry out HIGH HEELS, recommended that Laird agree to postpone the readiness test until 24 October. Planning for HIGH HEELS had already involved "considerable" expenditures, the activation of field command posts, and Weapons System Evaluation Group (WSEG) analysts already in place to observe exercise procedures. Nevertheless, a few of the CINCs had recommended simply canceling HIGH HEELS in order to "enhance" or "bring attention to actions being taken" under the readiness test.[34]

When Laird spoke with Kissinger, he mentioned that US military intelligence saw a conflict between HIGH HEELS and the readiness test. He did not describe the nature of the conflict, but officials from the National Security Agency and Defense Intelligence Agency thought there was the potential for a US-Soviet crisis. The message traffic produced by HIGH HEELS would slow down the transmission of information from intelligence collectors "containing the real intelligence we are looking for regarding Soviet reaction to our military readiness test." Moreover, the Soviets would detect the high volume of HIGH HEELS message traffic, and "we have no way of knowing how their analysts will read, or misread, the traffic levels." Dangerous circumstances could emerge because, inevitably, as shown by the "history of exercises," messages will be "inadvertently transmitted without the prescribed prefix or on the wrong circuit." A "hazardous situation" could emerge if the Soviets read a message that included "threatening material" at the same time they were observing "actual US movements, radio silence, and stand-down activities." Thus, to avoid sending confusing signals, military intelligence thought it better to cancel HIGH HEELS and even to announce cancellation. That would "contribute to the objectives of the 'real' operation," which was, in any event, "a more realistic test" for detecting Soviet reactions.[35]

The advice from military intelligence did not persuade Laird. When he spoke with Kissinger, his concern was that top commanders, including General Andrew Goodpaster, commander in chief, European Command, were concerned that the alert activities could damage relations with US allies. In messages to the Pentagon, the CINCEUR observed that NATO officials would inevitably notice and raise questions about the US readiness operations. This would put US diplomatic representatives to NATO in a difficult position, in light of the Nixon administration's emphasis on "full and timely consultations." Unless Goodpaster could tell NATO officials something, the "possibilities for disarray, resentment, and embarrassment for the US seem extreme." Wheeler shared Goodpaster's concern about information sharing and hoped that the disclosure policy could be modified "as we get deeper into this test." CINCONAD general Seth McKee made a similar point: Canadian military officials working at NORAD would become aware and ought to be told that a readiness test was under way.[36]

Agreeing with Wheeler that the alert should be postponed for the sake of HIGH HEELS, Laird said as much to Kissinger, which got the latter quite exercised. Anxious to begin the signaling that Nixon had sought on Vietnam, Kissinger exclaimed: *We really needed this, this week.* He further complained, "Why is it that anytime you want something done, the military have 50 bureaucratic reasons why it can't be done?"[37]

Not taking no for an answer, the White House prepared to push back. The next morning, Tuesday, 14 October, Haig stopped by the Pentagon to investigate and then met with Kissinger at the White House to prepare for their meeting with Laird. Haig reviewed with Kissinger the controversy over HIGH HEELS, concerns over informing allies, and Pentagon inaction on SAC dispersal and surveillance of Soviet shipping. On these issues, Haig argued, Laird's objections were "not overriding." In particular, the proposal to postpone the readiness test did not take into account the problem of time sensitivity related to Nixon's forthcoming Vietnam speech. Haig believed that *"it was necessary to have the measures completed sufficiently before 3 November for the president to ascertain beyond a doubt whether or not the signals have been effective."* In other words, before giving his speech, Nixon wanted to know whether the alert had made an impression on Moscow concerning Vietnam.[38]

As for the problem of consultations with NATO and the Canadians in NORAD, Haig recommended that Goodpaster and McKee could tell any inquisitive allies that a stand-down was an "additional aspect of the HIGH HEELS operation." He also advised that Kissinger "encourage" Laird to implement the other measures that Nixon had approved. That would take "tail twisting," Haig observed, and Kissinger needed Nixon's support to override the JCS and such a powerful figure as the secretary of defense.[39]

After meeting with Nixon, Kissinger went to see Laird. No record of these conversations have surfaced, but Kissinger must have received authority from Nixon to twist Pentagon tails because Laird dropped the idea of postponing the readiness test and agreed to modify HIGH HEELS so that it would not complicate the readiness test. For the first time, the Pentagon limited the exercise to government officials in the "Washington area alone," leaving the CINCs free to concentrate on readiness measures.[40]

At Kissinger's meeting with Laird, a decision about the duration of the readiness test was apparently made because that same day, Wheeler instructed the CINCs that instead of 25 October, the alert would last until 30 October. Kissinger probably imposed that schedule because of Nixon's strong interest in knowing whether the readiness test had an impact on Moscow before his November speech. Four more days might be needed to produce a Soviet reaction. Apparently, the readiness test would terminate if the Soviets reacted before the designated end point, although this was not spelled out.[41]

Also settled was the problem of consultations with allies. Reflecting the understanding that Laird apparently reached with Kissinger, Wheeler sent General Berton Spivy, the top US representative at the NATO Military Committee, a message on 14 October designed to help him "ward off speculation and concern of our allies." In that message and a parallel one to Goodpaster, McKee, and the other CINCs, Wheeler instructed them that if national authorities detected "elements of the test" and made inquiries, "to maintain good relations" the CINCs response should be consistent: "This is a unilateral action to test . . . operational readiness," and once the "readiness test [is complete] we will return to normal operating condition."[42]

The CINCs themselves could only puzzle over why the White House wanted the exercise. When CINCSAC General Holloway called the Pentagon for more information regarding his instructions, he learned nothing. Although SAC officers had orders not to discuss the readiness posture or even to speculate about it, speculation was hard to suppress. Correctly believing that Henry Kissinger was involved in the operation, senior officers at SAC headquarters suspected a possible connection to the Vietnam negotiations in Paris, noting the return of US negotiators to Washington for consultation as well as Nixon's announcement on 13 October that he would make a major address on Vietnam on 3 November.[43]

On the additional measures that the White House sought—increased surveillance of Soviet shipping, dispersal of SAC bombers, and higher alert rates—General Wheeler gave some ground. He acquiesced in the matter of a close watch of Soviet shipping en route to Vietnam. By 18 October, instructions to that effect had gone to the Seventh Fleet in the western Pacific. On SAC dispersal and higher alert rates, Wheeler drew on proposals from General Holloway and offered a substitute that the White House accepted: SAC would stage a "small airborne/ground alert."[44]

While Kissinger, Laird, and Wheeler settled disputed issues, the State Department leadership was only partially brought into the great secret. When Kissinger asked Laird whether he had told Rogers, for example, Laird said that Pursley would tell Theodore L. Eliot, Jr., the State Department's executive secretary, that a "routine SAC exercise" was under way and that Nixon was aware of it. The next morning, 14 October, Laird informed Kissinger that he had "played it low key with State." Having been told about the SAC exercises, Theodore Eliot had briefed Elliot Richardson, Rogers's deputy. But when Eliot and Richardson asked Laird about the purposes of the exercise, the secretary of defense told them it was only a "training exercise" and that "they would have to ask the highest authority about it." Years later, however, Laird recounted that he had personally told Rogers about the alert. Indeed, Wheeler's schedule indicates that on the morning of 17 October, as the readiness test was expanding, Rogers had met with Laird at the Pentagon.[45]

Readiness Test Activities by the Various Commands

The first phase of the readiness test emphasized stand-downs and a higher alert status, with SAC taking the lead. Following Wheeler's orders, on 12 October, CINCSAC Holloway instructed over forty SAC commanders to begin the stand-down the next day. Following instructions, he ordered them to reinstate "degraded aircraft alert sorties"—that is, to raise the number of bombers and tankers on ground alert. Under procedures that had been in effect since the early 1960s, SAC was to maintain 40 percent of each squadron (six aircraft for each fifteen) on ground alert and ready to strike SIOP targets. Yet shortages of bomber crews (largely because of Vietnam War commitments) had forced SAC to reduce or "degrade" the number of bomber and tanker alert sorties. Thus, even though the latest revision of the SIOP required a ground alert force of 202 B-52 and B-58 bombers and some 182 KC-135 tankers, actual ground alert bomber and tanker forces as of 1 September totaled 110 and 130, substantially below requirements. Only by canceling flight training was it possible to increase the numbers of aircraft on ground alert.[46]

After SAC began the stand-down, it increased forces on alert to 176 strategic bombers and 189 KC-135 Stratotankers in the continental United States (excluding unaffected B-52s stationed in Guam). That involved meeting SAC's SIOP commitment at Goose Air Base in Labrador, Canada, where a KC-135 was deployed from Plattsburgh Air Force Base, with two crews, to "insure that no alert degrade occurred" there. Cumulatively, the SAC actions put ground alert not quite at the 40 percent requirement but substantially higher than routine conditions.[47]

Commands in the continental United States and overseas with nuclear-capable air forces expanded the geographic scope of the readiness test. Beginning on 15 October, air forces assigned to CINCEUR, including USAFE, the US Army Europe (USAREUR), and US Navy Europe (USNAVEUR), participated in the readiness test. Following Goodpaster's orders, US forces tightened security around bases and stood down the flying activity of air units. USAFE had a formidable force of nuclear-armed and nuclear-capable tactical aircraft, including F-4 Phantoms, deployed at bases across Europe from the United Kingdom to Turkey. By 19 October, with the stand-down in effect, those forces had obtained an average operational readiness rate of 94 percent. In addition, as already noted, Goodpaster ordered the Sixth Fleet in the Mediterranean to "expose minimum communications/radiation profile commensurate with safety."[48]

Key units of Strike Command—a predecessor of Central Command—participated in the readiness test, even though the commander of its air force units had sought an exemption on the grounds that a stand-down would disrupt Southeast Asia training. Wheeler did give exemptions for a few important scheduled operations, such as CORNET BARE, which involved the Eighty-Second Airborne, but he had ruled that no other exceptions could be granted. The Tactical Air Command (TAC) began a stand-down of flying operations on 14 October. Pilots at TAC bases around the country stopped flying nuclear-capable aircraft—F-105 Thunderchiefs and F-4 Phantoms—as well as C-130s used for tactical airlift operations. During the stand-down, TAC canceled 4,216 scheduled sorties, using the spare time to raise the combat-ready status of aircraft.[49]

Also joining the stand-down of training flights were the forces of the Alaskan Command and the Continental Air Defense Command. Like other commands participating in the alert, these were ordered to bring about the "maximum state of readiness." Their forces included Bomarc nuclear surface-to-air missiles and interceptor aircraft armed with Falcon and Genie nuclear air-to-air missiles.[50]

SAC commanders took it for granted that the Soviets would notice the stand-down straightaway. According to an internal history, "By virtue of their own monitoring procedures of our military actions [the Soviets] would know nearly immediately that SAC was not flying." This may have been a reference to the "spotters" that the Soviets were suspected of having assigned to communities near SAC bases, although details about such activities have not come to light.[51]

Not long after the readiness test had begun, US intelligence picked up signs of what may have been a reaction by Soviet forces in the Far East. According to a declassified CIA report, the Soviet action "occurred less than two hours after the . . . stand-down began and . . . was extremely localized." Unfortunately, the specific nature of the action has been excised from the report. Kissinger mentioned it elliptically during a 14 October telephone conversation with his former patron, New York governor Nelson Rockefeller, who was now a member of the President's Foreign Advisory Board. Speaking of the readiness test, Kissinger said that "they [the Soviets] had already picked some of it up and it will build." Despite Kissinger's prediction, a few days later, JCS chairman Wheeler reported that US intelligence had seen "no significant" reaction by Soviet military forces to US operations. Later in the month, the CIA concluded that "we [now] doubt that . . . [the Soviet action in the Far East] was a reaction to the US readiness test."[52]

But there *was* another Soviet reaction in the Far East that began early in the readiness test and continued to the end. The DIA described it as "increased sensitivity to US aerial reconnaissance activities . . . over the Sea of Japan near the Soviet coast." On 12 October, the day the SAC stand-down started, Soviet air defense units in the Vladivostok area began to exhibit "an increased level of reaction," which may have taken the form of more message traffic, air patrols, and the interception of the flights. Pursley had proposed increased reconnaissance flights as an element of the readiness test, but such flights were not part of Wheeler's instructions to the CINCs. Nevertheless, US reconnaissance flights increased, perhaps as part of the effort to collect intelligence on Soviet reactions.

In the context of an upswing of US readiness activities, Moscow wanted Washington to recognize that its watchers were being watched.[53]

Expanding the Scope and Increasing the Intensity of Nuclear Alerts

As military intelligence searched for Soviet reactions to US signals, Wheeler's staff investigated other military readiness measures that could be taken by way of implementing White House instructions. By 15 October, the Joint Staff had prepared a package of actions. Two days later, after the White House approved them, Wheeler sent a message to the CINCs instructing them to implement new air, ground, and sea-based readiness measures around the world. At the same time, he allowed a temporary relaxation of the stand-down to meet concerns about flight training.

Four days earlier and soon after the CINCs had received Wheeler's initial action messages on the readiness posture, they had forwarded the "nominations" he had requested from them for additional actions. Lack of knowledge about the alert's purpose, however, made it difficult for operational planners at SAC to frame suggestions on possible actions for the readiness test; they could only wonder whether their proposals were even relevant.[54]

It is hard to generalize about the CINCs' recommendations because they were so varied. Suggestions from CINCPAC, CINCONAD, and CINCSAC paralleled the actions taken in the first phase of the readiness test: stand-downs, higher readiness for combat aircraft, and higher alert levels for air defense deployments. But with naval forces in the Persian Gulf and North Atlantic, commanders in chief of Strike Command and the Atlantic Command recommended ship diversions as a way of giving "high visibility to some unknown operational matter." Each CINC suggested measures US forces could take to attract Moscow's attention by drawing upon resources at hand. CINCLANT Admiral Ephraim Holmes, for example, proposed "emergency" maneuvers by US aircraft carriers in the North Atlantic, an "emergency backload" of an amphibious squadron undergoing jungle training in Panama, and measures to reinforce Guantanamo Bay. Holmes also included a "fortuitous situation," in which Polaris submarines were scheduled to deploy on normal schedules during mid-October from bases at Charleston, South Carolina; Holy Loch, Scotland; and Rota, Spain.[55]

CINCPAC Admiral John McCain recommended a variety of measures, some involving nuclear weapons. These, unfortunately, have been excised from declassified messages. His other suggestions included increased surveillance of Soviet shipping to the DRV and "Soviet shipping world-wide"; active prosecution of "submarine contacts"; increased EC-121 (COLLEGE EYE) flights in the Sea of Japan; "increase[d] counterintelligence measures to inhibit Soviet collection efforts," such as jamming of Soviet electronic intelligence (ELINT); and the unannounced recall of personnel "during non-duty hours." McCain also suggested "increased intelligence watch," expanded local security, and antisabotage at military facilities. He observed that rescheduling "world-wide reconnaissance . . . along the Soviet periphery" would be "most discernible" to Moscow but that a stand-down of combat aircraft, among other considerations, would make it difficult to execute. Therefore, he did not recommend it.[56]

Some of McCain's suggestions, such as jamming Soviet ELINT and worldwide surveillance of Soviet shipping, were provocative, but he was not the only CINC who proposed such measures. CINCSAC Holloway proposed "increase[d] peripheral reconnaissance," and CINCAL general Robert G. Ruegg suggested that if HIGH HEELS were canceled, it would be necessary to take "real-world" military measures so that the Soviets would not conclude that the cancellation had been a cost-saving action. He therefore proposed aerial operations in Bering Sea waters: "modest" deployments of KC-135 tankers and F-106 fighters, a "small number of EC-121 reconnaissance aircraft," and "increased air surveillance of the large Soviet trawler fleet." The latter action (and some of the others) would "suggest an increased US concern with warning and Soviet intelligence efforts." With "communications security, blackout, and deception" measures taken, Moscow would see "an interesting US attempt to conceal actual military movements."[57]

The Joint Staff may have seen General Ruegg's suggestions as too "interesting" because they did not survive the Pentagon's review process; neither did McCain's more aggressive proposals or SAC suggestions on reconnaissance. Consistent with White House instructions, Wheeler and his staff avoided measures that the Soviets might have deemed threatening and provocative. "Unusual and significant" was enough. By 15 October, the Joint Staff had digested the suggestions and prepared lists of measures that each CINC would take. The next day, the package went to the White House, which approved it on 17 October. Later that day, Wheeler cabled the instructions to the CINCs.[58]

Wheeler's directive included a modification of the stand-down, apparently because of the burden it had imposed on flight training. He authorized the CINCs with combat air forces to relax the stand-down during the period 18–24 October. They could resume "selective" flying training, although flights were to be held to "the minimum commensurate with critical requirements." This applied to SAC, USAFE, TAC, CONAD, the Alaskan Command, the European Command, the Strike Command carrier aircraft in the Atlantic, and US air forces in Europe and East Asia (Japan, Okinawa, and South Korea). They would resume the stand-down on 25 October.[59]

When SAC returned to a stand-down status, it was to place additional aircraft in the "highest state of maintenance readiness." They would be "EWO [Emergency War Order] Configured"; that is, equipped with nuclear weapons but not on ground alert status or assigned with crews with combat mission folders (target lists). Maintenance readiness would raise SAC's alert posture without further straining the crew-shortage problem, thus meeting the White House goal of a larger-scale alert.[60]

Besides ordering increased maintenance readiness, Wheeler approved Holloway's recommendation for an airborne alert action by SAC bombers. This would be a GIANT LANCE show-of-force operation, one of the nuclear alert options available under SAC's Selective Employment of Air and Ground Alert [SEAGA] program. It would begin on 26 October and continue "until further notice." SAC bombers and tankers would fly the "Eielson East orbit," over the Arctic Circle—a reference to Eielson Air Base in east-central Alaska. Airborne alert of nuclear-armed bombers was exactly the type of "unusual and significant" action that Nixon and Kissinger sought in order to get Moscow's attention.[61]

In addition to calling for the temporary TAC respite from stand-down, Wheeler ordered CINCSTRIKE General John L. Throckmorton to return "selected units to their home stations," which was a reference to a proposal for that action by US Special Forces units and a brigade of the Eighty-Second Airborne. Moreover, a number of ships assigned to CINCSTRIKE's Middle East naval arm, Middle East Forces (MIDEASTFOR), would make unscheduled departures from port visits in Bahrain, Djibouti, and Mombasa, and sail into the Gulf of Aden for "multiple ship exercises." Commander, Middle East Forces (COMIDEASTFOR) Rear Admiral Walter Small could cancel a planned visit to Pakistan and Afghanistan at his discretion.[62]

Ship diversions on a larger scale, mostly those under emissions control

[EMCON], or radio silence, would take place in the North Atlantic. Wheeler instructed CINCLANT to order the heavy cruiser USS *Newport News*, and a hunter-killer antisubmarine warfare group led by the aircraft carrier USS *Yorktown*, which was then on stopover at Rotterdam, to rendezvous in the North Atlantic with EMCON in effect. Moreover, two other aircraft carriers, the USS *Forrestal* and the USS *Franklin D. Roosevelt*, were to leave ports in Virginia and Florida, respectively, and steam at high speed to points in the western Atlantic. CINCLANT would also stand down air patrol and carrier air operations in the North Atlantic between 25 and 30 October.[63]

In Western Europe, a focal point of the readiness test was to be the West German–East German border. CINCEUR General Goodpaster was to order an increase in surveillance and intelligence gathering, beginning 18 October, followed by a closer watch of the Soviet Military Liaison Mission (SMLM) that monitored US forces in West Germany. US units would also establish a "temporary restricted area" along the border that the SMLM could not inspect. Beginning 21 October, USAFE and USAREUR units were to raise "readiness tests" at their bases but with no increase in DEFCON levels—although they were to stand down "communications transmissions" for training activities. CINCEUR's other air forces were to continue their participation in the stand-down (except for temporarily allowed training activities).[64]

Wheeler's instructions to Admiral McCain included a number of measures for the Pacific Command, all of which were to begin immediately. One objective was to "enhance naval SIOP forces at sea," that is, submarines and aircraft carriers assigned to nuclear war missions were to assume a higher profile. Thus, McCain was to put to sea as many nuclear missile submarines as feasible (one of Pursley's original suggestions), although other actions remain classified, such as measures by nuclear-capable carrier air. Besides the PACAF stand-down, units in the area were to raise the readiness of conventionally armed tactical and air defense aircraft and missile systems and to boost local security and antisabotage surveillance at bases in Japan and Korea. Consistent with Pursley's initial suggestion and White House preferences, the Seventh Fleet would increase surveillance of Soviet ships headed for North Vietnam. In addition, forces assigned to PACOM were to increase their "intelligence watch" of Soviet forces through the region.[65]

One proposal involving Pacific Command forces came from Henry

Kissinger, who suggested that the Seventh Fleet send the Yankee Station carrier task force farther north into the Tonkin Gulf, no doubt as a warning to Hanoi. But JCS chairman Wheeler advised against the move, observing that it would not produce a "significant response." Moreover, moving the carriers would complicate bombing operations in Laos and South Vietnam, and if air strikes against North Vietnam became necessary, the redeployment would not facilitate them.[66]

The Alaskan Command and the Continental Air Defense Command were to keep forces on high alert. Despite General Ruegg's ambitious suggestions, Wheeler informed him that the Alaskan Command would take only "limited actions." Besides the stand-down, the general was to order increased deployments of air defense interceptors to two western Alaska air bases from 18 through 23 October. That would be followed by "maximum ground alert" by air defense forces at all bases. CINCONAD General McKee would put his air defense forces on 100 percent alert of one hour or less and also order the deployment of additional interceptors to two bases in Missouri and New York from 27 to 30 October. This deployment was carried out under the command's College TAP program for deploying training aircraft to augment air defense forces in special circumstances. Selective flight training for "critical requirements" only could occur during 18 to 24 October.[67]

Probably to "focus the intelligence watch," Wheeler would order some actions to stop if a Soviet action suggested a specific reaction to them; otherwise, they were to continue. CINCPAC, for instance, was to keep "maximum feasible SSBNs at sea" unless the Soviets reacted by 23 October. Similarly, the Sixth Fleet was to maintain electronic emission controls with a possible stop date of 24 October. In the Mideast, the destroyer USS *Rich*, part of Strike Command's forces, was to steam in the Gulf of Aden unless Moscow reacted by 22 October. For CINCONAD, 25 October was a possible stop date for a number of actions, including "15-minute" alerts for interceptors and Air National Guard air defense attachments and "20-minute" alerts for Nike-Hawk missiles. Other elements of the test could be canceled at any point if the Soviets made an "unusual response."[68]

A Last-Ditch Meeting with Dobrynin

On 17 October—as the Pentagon was preparing to expand the scope of the JCS Readiness Test—Kissinger came to believe that Moscow had taken notice of the operation. Soviet ambassador Anatoly Dobrynin phoned Kissinger in late afternoon to say that he had received a message from Moscow about the strategic arms limitation talks. He told Kissinger that he wanted President Nixon to read the message, adding, "There may also be some further discussion on Soviet/American relations." Persuaded that Dobrynin's call was a response to the alert, Kissinger told Laird the next day that "the game plan seems to be working" and that there might be a "little payoff." Coincidentally, a possible Soviet military reaction to the readiness test had also taken place around 17 October. Records about the specific nature of the reaction remain classified, but the CIA opined that it may have been a response to the SAC or CINCEUR stand-downs.[69] In any case, Kissinger and Nixon quickly scheduled a meeting with Dobrynin for 20 October.

Kissinger also expressed optimism that day in a conversation he had with White House Chief of Staff Bob Haldeman, who recorded Kissinger's sentiments in his diary—an entry that also made the connection between the readiness alert and White House policy regarding the Vietnam War: "*K has all sorts of signal-type activity going on around the world to try to jar Soviets and NVN.* Appears to be working because Dobrynin asked for early mtg, which we have set secretly for Monday. K thinks this is good chance of being the big break, but that it will come in stages. P is more skeptical."[70]

On the same day, Kissinger and Nixon met with British counterinsurgency expert Sir Robert Thompson to discuss the latter's "plan for ending [the] Vietnam [war]." Nixon told Thompson that he "felt that the USSR was not presently exercising its influence but, as in the case of the Korean War, might possibly do so if there were incentives on the 'negative side'"—an allusion to Eisenhower's nuclear threat against China in 1953. Throughout the discussion, Nixon and Kissinger argued that the Soviets did not want and had a fear of confrontation, which suggested that they believed or hoped they could impose a negative incentive—such as a "bold strike" against North Vietnam or perhaps a nuclear alert—without fear of Soviet counteraction.[71]

A talking points memorandum that Kissinger sent to Nixon on 18 October in preparation for the forthcoming 20 October meeting with Dobrynin further confirmed the link between the global alert and their Vietnam policy. Kissinger reminded Nixon that Dobrynin's request for a meeting "comes against the background of several developments, including . . . Moscow's undoubted awareness of unusual military measures on our part, preceded by the stern comments made to Dobrynin on September 27." He added:

> *Your basic purpose will be to keep the Soviets concerned about what we might do around 1 November.* . . . You should . . . not enter into an argument about the catalogue of our sins which Dobrynin will probably recite (Romanian trip, flirting with China, no East-West trade legislation, hostile press treatment, Safeguard [antiballistic missile] decision, etc.); tell him that our main concern with the Soviets at present is their support of Hanoi's intransigence and their heavy strategic weapons program.

If Dobrynin raised the subject of current US military measures, Kissinger recommended that the president should simply answer that they were "normal exercises relating to our military readiness."[72]

During telephone conversations with longtime colleagues near midday on 20 October, Kissinger expressed his hope for a "big break" to come out of the Nixon-Dobrynin meeting. Speaking with Nelson Rockefeller a few hours before that meeting, Kissinger remarked that "the thing they had discussed the other day—it's gotten down to producing little twitches." He added that "there's now a 30 percent chance—it would be sheer gold if we could get away with it." In a conversation about an hour later with Fritz G. A. Kraemer—who had a formative influence on Kissinger's career and was now serving as senior civilian adviser to the US Army chief of staff—he was more cautious. Kissinger told Kraemer that there was a "10 percent chance" of success and admitted that "it has no business succeeding, but it may." Perhaps Kissinger was more careful when speaking with Kraemer because he felt that his former mentor was savvier than Rockefeller about military matters or because by this time, a week into the alert, Kissinger himself understood that the chances of the Soviets falling for the administration's bluff were remote.[73]

With Kissinger sitting quietly in attendance, the meeting in the Oval Office between Nixon and Dobrynin began at 3:30 p.m. with a report by the Soviet ambassador about Moscow's perceptions of the state of USSR-US relations on a range of issues, including European affairs, a Middle East settlement, China, and Vietnam. The message from Moscow was that the administration's habit of evading discussion of these issues had made the Moscow leadership uneasy and distrustful about its claims of wanting to settle "major international problems fraught with dangerous crises." Among the critical remarks was a sweetener: the Soviet leaders' suggestions for a date and place for prospective SALT talks between the United States and the Soviet Union. After some discussion about the scheduling of these talks, the president "immediately" handed Dobrynin one of his ubiquitous yellow writing pads, suggesting that "you'd better take some notes" and "write down in detail" what he had to say to Soviet leaders.[74]

Nixon then spoke for half an hour about his own "disappointment in US-Soviet relations." Dobrynin wrote to Moscow later, noting that Nixon "rambled" at first but then "seemed to pull himself together and began speaking more calmly and clearly" about the Middle East, trade, European security, Berlin, China, and Vietnam. About the question of Washington's outreach to Beijing—which Moscow correctly believed was Washington's way of exploiting the Sino-Soviet rift—Nixon tried to deflect the accusation by explaining that in twenty-five years, "China will be in a position of immense power and we cannot have it without communication." Assuring the Soviet ambassador that his remarks were not directed against the USSR, he observed that "within 10 years, China will be a nuclear power, capable of terrorizing many other countries. The time is running out when the Soviet Union and the United States can build a different kind of world. The only beneficiary, then, of US-Soviet disagreement over Vietnam is China. And, therefore, this is the last opportunity to settle these disputes."[75]

Having played his China card, Nixon turned to the Vietnam War, reminding Dobrynin of the approach of the anniversary of President Johnson's 1 November 1968 bombing halt, which was also the impending deadline of Nixon's ultimatum to Hanoi. The United States, he added, had halted its bombing, but "the Soviet Union has done nothing. . . . All conciliatory moves for the past year had been made by the United States." Dobrynin recorded in his notes that Nixon complained that Hanoi— believing he cannot "manage" antiwar sentiment—wanted to "break" him. "If the Soviet Union would not help us to get peace," Nixon warned, "the US would have to pursue its own methods for bringing the war to an end. It could not allow a talk-fight strategy without taking action." He assured Dobrynin that while he recognized that Soviet leaders were tough and courageous, "so was he."[76]

With the stick of military escalation brandished, the president then extended a carrot of diplomacy: "If the Soviet Union found it possible to do something in Vietnam, and the Vietnam War ended, the US might do something dramatic to improve Soviet–US relations, indeed something more dramatic than they could now imagine. But until then, real progress would be difficult." Asked by Dobrynin whether no progress would take place in US–Soviet relations without a Vietnam settlement, Nixon repeated his refrain that though "he wanted nothing so much as to have his administration remembered as a watershed in US–Soviet relations, . . . we would not hold still for being 'diddled' to death in Vietnam."[77]

In the memorandum of the meeting that Dobrynin sent to Moscow, he noted that "during the conversation Nixon kept returning time and again to the Vietnam issue, regardless of what other issue or problem we were discussing." In response, Dobrynin repeated what Soviet leaders in Moscow had said in their message to Nixon:

> Due note has been taken in Moscow, of course, of the hints by American representatives about the possible use by the United States of some "alternative" methods to solve the Vietnam question. Such hints cannot be regarded in any other way but as a rather open threat addressed to the DRV and the Provisional Revolutionary Government of South Vietnam. If that is so, Moscow feels that the president should be frankly told that the method of solving the Vietnam question through the use of military force is not only without perspective, but also extremely dangerous.[78]

Dobrynin recapitulated the Soviet Union's own position about settling the Vietnam issue, telling the American president that the USSR also wanted a speedy and peaceful negotiated agreement but supported the program put forward by the DRV and PRG: "a coalition government in South Vietnam based on consideration of the actual alignment of political forces there." Washington's "stubborn resistance" to such a solution, he continued, raises "questions regarding statements about the US desire to end the war in Vietnam and achieve a political settlement of that conflict. These questions also arise because the United States is simultaneously conducting negotiations in Paris and making extensive preparations to continue the war in Vietnam."[79]

At several points in the memorandum to his superiors in Moscow, Dobrynin remarked on what he called Nixon's nervous responses to his statements about Moscow's "assessment of the situation regarding the Vietnam issue." It is not clear whether by the word *nervous* (the US State Department translation from Russian to English) Dobrynin meant that the president was nervous in the sense of being jittery or apprehensive or whether he meant Nixon was excitable, spirited, or perhaps even erratic—considering the circumstances of a meeting in the Oval Office between a president and an ambassador. Perhaps he meant Nixon was all of those things. At one point in his memcon, for instance, Dobrynin commented: "I must say that Nixon was displeased and agitated by our position on Vietnam as set forth above, and he did not try to hide that. He reacted very nervously and went into a long-winded monologue." Elsewhere in the memcon, Dobrynin remarked that Nixon's behavior appeared to confirm reports that he was angry because advisers hostile to the Soviet Union were "whispering to him that the Soviet leadership wants nothing to do with Nixon and therefore does not respond to his 'personal messages'" (a reference to the White House view that Moscow had not replied promptly, directly, and formally to Nixon's overture regarding Kissinger's Vance Ploy). Nixon, Dobrynin added, had "articulated" such sentiments himself, asserting "that the Soviet leadership is apparently trying to 'break' him."[80]

Was Nixon nervously apprehensive or nervously angry? In either case, his appearance of instability, agitation, and anger failed to frighten or intimidate the veteran statesman Dobrynin, who regarded the president's demeanor as lacking emotional self-control. He attributed Nixon's state of mind to his concerns about the next election. To Moscow, Dobrynin wrote that no matter what the issue, Vietnam, China, Europe, or the Mideast,

> the recurring theme underlying all his remarks was . . . the same: the main thing now for him, Nixon, is to end the war in Vietnam, everything else is secondary. . . . It was perfectly clear from the conversation with Nixon that events surrounding the Vietnam crisis now wholly preoccupy the US president, and that to all appearances the fate of his predecessor Lyndon Johnson is beginning to really worry him. Apparently, this is taking on such an emotional coloration that Nixon is unable to control himself even in a conversation with a foreign ambassador.[81]

Dobrynin reported to Moscow that he repeatedly assured Nixon that Soviet leaders wanted to normalize and develop relations with the United States toward "the establishment of proper businesslike personal relations between the leaders of the two countries." Toward the end of the conversation and in part because of the ambassador's assurances, Nixon, according to Dobrynin, "evidently felt he had gotten too worked up . . . , and the president . . . cooled off a bit, . . . saying he should not be taken literally. Not everything, he said, looks only negative in our relations."[82]

Nixon's change in demeanor must have served to undermine his pose of toughness, especially when he began to talk about the lull in fighting in Vietnam. Dobrynin wrote: "The only thing noteworthy was the interest shown by Nixon in the fact that recent US losses in Vietnam were the lowest in three years. If that is the manifestation of some sort of policy on Hanoi's part, he remarked it merits attention. *If it is a coincidence and the Vietnamese resume large-scale military operations, the United States will be forced to take countermeasures.*" In effect, what Nixon had said was that the United States would attack North Vietnam only if the NVA/VC resumed "large-scale military operations." In other words, for the time being, he was standing pat on the hand he was dealt: the military and diplomatic status quo. There would be no US offensive against North Vietnam in November. "In this connection," Dobrynin wrote, "Nixon advised me to pay close attention to his upcoming 'important speech' on television about the Vietnam issue on 3 November."[83]

Despite Nixon's upbeat assessment of the meeting in his postwar memoir, *RN*, it was a disappointment for him and Kissinger. Dobrynin had said nothing about the alert—unless his comment about the United States "making extensive preparations to continue the war in Vietnam" was a reference to it (or the earlier mining ruse). In addition, Nixon had given the game away at the end of the meeting in his remark about taking US "*counter*measures" in *response* to an NVA/VC military initiative. With this remark, he had undermined the purpose of the nuclear alert: a bluff meant to suggest that the November attacks would follow. Apparently disappointed in his own performance, Nixon told Kissinger by telephone four hours after the meeting had ended that he should meet again with Dobrynin in the morning of 21 October and engage in Madman playacting. In the transcriber's words, Nixon said:

If the Vietnam thing is raised (try to get it raised), the P wants K to shake his head and say "I am sorry Mr. Ambassador, but he is out of control. Mr. Ambassador, as you know, I am very close to the president, but you don't know this man—he's been through more than any of the rest of us put together. He's made up his mind and unless there's some movement," just shake your head and walk out.[84]

Kissinger told Nixon that "he might type up everything the P said on a plain slip of paper" with the implication that he would give it to Dobrynin the next day. But in *White House Years,* Kissinger confessed that he ignored Nixon's directive, believing—as he wrote in his memoir—that with this instruction, "Nixon sought to compensate for his unwillingness to face down his old friend," Dobrynin. (Perhaps Kissinger as well did not want to face down his friend Dobrynin.) Kissinger also conceded that he thought Dobrynin had succeeded in applying "reverse linkage" at the 20 October meeting by extending a Soviet carrot that Nixon could not refuse: an offer to move up the opening date for SALT talks to mid-November. The Soviets had thus deftly neutralized Nixon's big-stick diplomacy, and in any case, the president had already sidelined the November Option. Big-stick diplomacy was left to depend on the ongoing readiness alert.[85]

Kissinger had praised Nixon's performance to Haldeman right after the meeting, telling him that the president "had the guts of a riverboat gambler" and had "played it *very* cold with D—giving him one back for each he dished out." But Haldeman wrote in his diary that "K was, I think, disappointed that D had not come in with something specific." Kissinger's written assessment of the meeting the following day, on 21 October, revealed his veiled disappointment. He wrote the president that "the main point here is Soviet acknowledgment of our allusions to possible military actions," about which, he said, "they are concerned, and your comments might just give them ammunition to use in Hanoi in lobbying for a more flexible position." Referring to the readiness alert, he advised, "In any event, it will be essential to continue backing up our verbal warnings with our present military moves." Commenting that he "could find nothing new in Dobrynin's presentation," Kissinger suspected that "*Dobrynin's basic mission was to test the seriousness of the threat element in our current posture and to throw out enough inducements (SALT, Berlin, direct informal contact with you) to make it politically and psychologically difficult for you to play it rough over Vietnam.*"[86]

Here, Kissinger had explicitly linked the JCS Readiness Test—the "threat element in our current posture" and "present military moves"— to the Vietnam problem. Notably, nothing said at the hour-long meeting indicated that the US military posture, preparations, and moves had anything to do with an attempt by the United States to exploit Sino-Soviet friction or defend China against Soviet threats. It was all about Vietnam.

Expanding the Alert

Meanwhile, when the second round of readiness test instructions went out on 18 October, the commander in chief of the Pacific Fleet (CINCPAC-FLT) had already directed Task Force 71—the nuclear-armed aircraft carrier USS *Constellation* and a number of destroyers—to conduct antiaircraft warfare and strike force exercises in the Sea of Japan from 17 to 20 October. On 18 October, the Seventh Fleet's commander, Admiral William F. Bringle, ordered these operations to continue until 24 October to meet the demands of "higher authority." The task force also put its conventionally armed tactical and air defense aircraft and missile systems on an "increased readiness posture." To improve the antiaircraft warning posture against possible Soviet overflights, Air Reconnaissance Squadron One provided electronic early warning surveillance. In addition and possibly in conjunction with the readiness test, on 17 October the Seventh Fleet's commander ordered picket ships to "conduct surveillance of Soviet combatants in the Sea of Japan."[87]

The Seventh Fleet also carried out orders from the Pacific Fleet to monitor Soviet ships heading toward North Vietnam. It was a measure that Kissinger and Haig had directed Wheeler to implement, probably to signal Nixon's anger over Soviet economic and military aid to the DRV or perhaps as a sign that something big was about to happen. Admiral Bringle informed the fleet task groups that he would "direct surveillance of specific Soviet vessels en route [to North Vietnam]."[88] Within a few days, naval intelligence had detected two Soviet ships that were apparently heading toward Haiphong, either the *Uzhgorod*, an oil tanker, or the *Vitim*, a cargo ship. On 20 October, Bringle instructed the destroyer USS *Ozbourn*, which was on its way to Vietnam from Yokosuka, to attempt to rendezvous and conduct surveillance. Providing the coordinates for the two ships, Bringle asked the *Ozbourn*'s commander to monitor one of them to within 60 nautical miles of Haiphong. The *Ozbourn* was to conduct the "surveillance . . . from [a] safe distance [and] not so close as to be interpreted as harassment." If, however, the Soviet ships "harassed" the *Ozbourn*, it was to follow unspecified instructions, which are not available. By remaining 12 nautical miles from North Vietnam, the *Ozbourn* was to avoid incidents. To help find the ships, Bringle directed Task Force 72, the Seventh Fleet's patrol-reconnaissance force, to send out aircraft to locate them.[89]

Task Force 72 located the *Uzhgorod* within a day or two but was also trying to find other ships in the area, the *Vitim* and the *Virsk*. By 22 October, the USS *Orleck*, a ship routinely involved in Vietnam missions, was "shadow[ing]" the *Virsk* on its way to Haiphong. While monitoring the ship, at one point getting as close as 1,500 yards, *Orleck*'s crew members took "Snoopy videotape" (apparently by the QH-50 drone reconnaissance helicopter) and twenty-two intelligence photos to document what could be seen of the *Virsk*'s communications systems. No cargo on the deck could be identified, and no "unusual activity" or "deviations from rules [of the] road" were detected. A number of Soviet crew members were on the deck; whether they had already been on deck or whether the intelligence-gathering piqued their interest is unclear.[90]

On 23 October, the *Ozbourn* was shadowing the *Uzhgorod,* at one point within 500 yards. As expected, the *Uzhgorod* was a POL tanker, which appeared to be carrying a full load. Because the *Ozbourn* had a military assignment on the South Vietnamese coast, it headed down the Gulf of Tonkin on 24 October, and the *Orleck* took over the surveillance, completing it later that day.[91]

The next day, 25 October, Bringle sent out instructions to the naval bombardment group operating off Vietnam, Task Force 70, advising that two more "candidates for surveillance" were approaching: the merchant ships *Iman* and the *Ivan Moskvin.* This time, however, the surveillance was discretionary and only as long as it was "consistent with other [scheduled] operations." No further details on any shadowing of those ships have surfaced, but within a few days, on 29 October, aircraft operating from the Task Force 77 battle group at Yankee Station "located and maintained . . . surveillance" of another Soviet merchant ship, the *Spassk Dalniy,* then heading toward Haiphong. Moreover, a destroyer, *Everett F. Larson,* heading toward Yokosuka, received orders to track Soviet ships as part of the readiness test, but the special surveillance operations that it conducted (tracking a Soviet ship, the USSR *Sirn*, in the East China Sea on 26 October and intercepting other ships that were serving a surfaced *Zulu*-class submarine a few days later) may have been unrelated to the test.[92] During the readiness test, the Seventh Fleet shadowed at least three Soviet merchant ships. What the Soviets made of it and whether they saw it as part of a pattern reflecting White House anger over Moscow's Vietnam policy is unknown.

Cracks in the Wall of Secrecy

Nixon had wanted the readiness test kept secret from the public and much of the US government, with a minimum chance of public exposure. None of its elements were supposed to alarm the public. Some of the measures, however, could not avoid detection and did cause local excitement, but no one who noticed particular measures could put all the pieces of the puzzle together.

On 20 October at 6:10 a.m., less than two hours before the end of the graveyard shift, State Department watch officers received word from their representative at the Pentagon National Military Command Center (NMCC) about "CODEWORD traffic of potential importance." They soon learned additional details about the mysterious activity. The command center's operational summary described an exercise involving military aircraft (which was most probably associated with the SAC bomber stand-down). Wondering whether a crisis was brewing, the watch officers discussed the information with staffers at the White House Situation Room and kept in touch with the NMCC in order to prepare themselves for "upward alerting": informing State Department officials higher up in the chain of authority. By 7:15 a.m. they learned that "all US aircraft [were] accounted for." Without having received a "firmer indication of crisis" by 8:00 a.m. and with senior watch officials entering the building at the end of the shift, the watch officers decided against issuing "phone alerts."[93] Had the watch officers taken their information to midlevel echelons in the State Department, the secrecy that Nixon and Kissinger sought might have been compromised. This could have led to the kind of intragovernment feedback Haig had warned about, even though by this time (and unbeknown to the watch officers), the White House had previously informed Rogers, Richardson, and Eliot that SAC was to be part of a readiness test.

Outside government offices, ordinary citizens, reporters, foreign governments, and diplomats also got glimpses and took notice of some of the measures associated with both the stand-down and the naval readiness exercises. Joseph P. Urgo, who had served his one-year tour in Vietnam and was now an air force security sergeant assigned to guard four F-106 Delta Dart interceptors detached to the Atlantic City airport, was one of those who took notice. He told Seymour Hersh during the 1970s that he had been "freaked out" when leaves were canceled for an extended period and two of the F-106s were parked at the ready at the end of the runway armed with tactical nuclear weapons. Believing the United States was "in some sort of a real situation," he scanned newspapers for information. But finding none, he "telephoned a wire service desk in New York, got some guy on the phone, and told him, 'there is something going on. We're on nuclear alert!' The guy was sleepy. I asked if there was anything to justify it. . . . He said no. We went on and on and he didn't pursue it. He didn't even ask my name."[94]

On the Pacific coast, residents in Riverside, California, noticed that SAC aircraft had stopped flying at nearby March Air Force Base, which supported SAC operations in the Far East and Southeast Asia. According to the official history, the base information office "was flooded with phone calls from local civilians who did not understand why they had not seen or heard jet aircraft activity for some time." On 14 October, Laird told Kissinger that a reporter near March was asking "why there were no planes flying" and that SAC headquarters was also receiving inquiries. When Laird volunteered that the Pentagon would tell reporters that "we do not discuss readiness tests," Kissinger asked him to hold off until the next day, 15 October. The first Moratorium against the Vietnam War was scheduled for that day, and Kissinger said that he "would hate to see the peaceniks worked up about this."[95]

The "do not comment on/discuss readiness tests" line became standard operating procedure during October 1969. It represented a considerable softening of even more restrictive guidance by the assistant secretary of defense for public affairs Daniel Z. Henkin, who wanted to forbid answers to any question about the readiness test unless specifically permitted. That may have been the most logical position to take, since most Pentagon officials had no idea why the White House wanted the exercise.[96]

In the midst of the alert, CINCLANT admiral Holmes said in a speech indirectly referencing the alert that "at times the events which are making history at sea are not visible, are not reported, and so in a sense become unsung, untold, and recorded too late to affect a timely impression."[97]

Nevertheless, some naval readiness measures were quickly noticed by reporters, foreign governments, and diplomats, even if they did not know
how to interpret them.

Nothing received as much notice as the sudden departure of aircraft
carriers and other ships from home ports and "goodwill missions" in the
North Atlantic and the Pacific. According to press reports, on 18 October,
the *Yorktown*, at Rotterdam for an official visit, suddenly left port four
days ahead of schedule. That left stranded 200 crew members who had to
be returned to the ship on an improvised basis thanks to a "heroic job" by
the US Defense attaché. The same day, only a few hours after returning
from maneuvers in the Atlantic, the *Franklin D. Roosevelt* sailed out of
Mayport, Florida, near Jacksonville, while the *James Forrestal* abruptly
left Norfolk (both returned two days later). Navy combat aircraft also flew
out of Cecil Field near Jacksonville, but "officials declined to say whether
the planes would rendezvous with the *Roosevelt* as they have in the past."
Also noticed was the unscheduled departure from Guam of the *Proteus*,
a Polaris submarine-tender. Before the *Proteus* sailed, "emergency messages over local radio and television stations" ordered the crew to report
back immediately.[98] Except for the *Proteus*'s sudden departure, however,
the other readiness actions taken by the Pacific Fleet went unreported and
unsung.

But reporters regarded the ship movements that were noticed as unusual. One wrote from Norfolk that "no one around can recall a time,
at least in the last fifteen years, when American ships were ordered to
recall their crews and put to sea immediately unless there was a clearly
discernible international incident in the making." Unsurprisingly, reporters for the *Washington Post* and the *New York Times* got no explanation
beyond the rote response that a "readiness test" was occurring. The State
Department and the Pentagon refused to comment, although one official
observed that he had been trying to ascertain if there was a trouble spot
somewhere but found that nothing was occurring, "except usual things."[99]

The unscheduled carrier movements disturbed US diplomats in Rotterdam and other ports, such as Casablanca, who expected a visit from
the *Newport News*, part of the *Yorktown* group. For the diplomats, the
problem was not the readiness test itself but that no one had given them
a "suitable cover story" they could use to "dampen lurid speculation as
to reasons for departure" or to explain a delayed ship visit. This was the
price for the State Department's initial exclusion from the White House

decision. CINCLANT Holmes, at least, was allowed to tell NATO admirals something before they started asking questions: "This is a unilateral action to test . . . operational readiness."[100]

Resumption of the Stand-Down and Launching GIANT LANCE

On 25 October, the respite from stand-down was over for air units in the United States, NATO Europe, and the Pacific and elsewhere. USAFE, Pacific Air Force, SAC, TAC, and other air forces stopped flight training and went back to stand-down to increase local readiness. General Holloway sent instructions to SAC commanders on 23 October to resume the stand-down in a few days. But it would be a stand-down at a higher level. The CINCSAC ordered commanders to generate additional bomber and tanker aircraft over and above those on ground alert to the "highest state of maintenance readiness." The nuclear-armed aircraft would have "adequate supervision" and undergo daily inspection, with tires rotated and engines and other systems checked at regular intervals. They would not, however, have crews assigned to them. This action was to begin no later than 8:00 a.m. local time on 25 October and would last "through the first week of November and possibly longer."[101]

Also to increase the intensity of the readiness test, CINCSAC instructed the commanders of the Twenty-Second and Ninety-Second Strategic Wings to implement the SEAGA show-of-force posture "with weapons" in the Eielson East orbit. "Implementation," or "I" Hour, would be at 19:13 Zulu time on 26 October. In keeping with the effort to avoid steps that could compromise secrecy, the bomber wing commanders were told that the I Hour "would not be accompanied by [a] declaration of DEFCON 3," which was the usual procedure for a SEAGA show-of-force operation. As with the maintenance measures, the alert could continue into early November. What SAC commanders did not know was that under White House orders, SAC maneuvers could end sooner, depending on when the Soviets were known to have reacted to the readiness test.[102]

Several days later, SAC units began the next phase of the readiness test. The generation of maintenance steps that began on 25 October assured that a large portion of the SAC nonalert bomber and tanker force—about 65 percent—was loaded with weapons, although crewless. Designated crew chiefs would conduct daily "walk-around inspections" to look for fuel leaks and other problems. Besides the alert force of 144 bombers, another 170 or so B-52s were nuclear armed.[103]

More dramatically, at about 8:00 a.m. on 27 October—twenty hours after the I Hour—the SAC's Twenty-Second and Ninety-Second Wings began the SEAGA show-of-force operation, GIANT LANCE. Morning fog delayed the first sorties launched from March and Fairchild Air Force Bases in Washington State. After flying adjacent to the Canadian coast, six B-52s flew in the Eielson East orbit over northern Alaska. As part of the operation, "mated" KC-135 air tankers flew to Eielson Air Force Base for deployment. The sorties, lasting eighteen to twenty-four hours each, kept B-52s flying continuously "over the frozen terrain of the Arctic." With each bomber carrying four or more nuclear weapons, this was the first time that SAC had flown a nuclear-armed airborne alert since the January 1968 B-52 crash at Thule Air Base, in Greenland. Soviet warning systems no doubt detected the activity.[104]

During the last week of the readiness test, and apparently before resuming the stand-down, the Pacific Air Force took a variety of alert actions at base installations in Japan and South Korea, including scrambling fighter jets, testing reconnaissance aircraft, flying to verify weapons systems, and flying aircraft in to "increase strength in Korea." In addition, the US CINC for UN forces in Korea conducted an "expanded command post exercise," which created "additional activity," such as intelligence message traffic and the activation of air control units. Finally, on 30 October, as the readiness test ended, the Fifth Air Force initiated a "SIOP forces alert exercise." Coincidentally, the SAC stand-down enabled PACAF to increase the number of aircraft slated for the SIOP alert.[105]

Military Perspectives on the Readiness Test

Within days after the readiness test's conclusion, the Joint Chiefs asked the major commands for their assessment of the operations. These varied, but there were common themes. CINCEUR Goodpaster saw benefits in "crisis management" and "unit reaction time," and he noted that the Seventh Fleet units in the Mediterranean had useful experience from conducting operations under EMCON. Nevertheless, the stand-down had a "significant" negative impact for US air forces in Europe: "Curtailment of flying resulted in immediate regression in air crew proficiency." Colonel Richard MacDonald at SAC's Current Plans branch made the same point using similar language (speaking of "deterioration" instead of "regression"). CINCONAD saw important benefits ("excellent test of unit's ability to achieve maximum readiness") but indirectly referred to problems created by the stand-down: the need for an "intensified flying effort to enable pilots to meet crew requirements." CINCLANT avoided negative comments, rating the test "beneficial from an operational readiness [viewpoint]," but he noted that the lack of "suitable cover stories" for abrupt changes in visits by aircraft carriers and other ships had caused problems. That was an area for future improvement.[106]

A number of the commanders commented on the problem of secrecy. CINCONAD could not report on the test's "overall effectiveness" because, he said, "I was not privy to the overall purpose." He also noted that most of the instructions "bore an overall classification of top secret," which "created substantial delays in passing instructions to subordinate units." Although pleased that SAC fulfilled its mission without a hitch, Lieutenant Colonel MacDonald pointed to the gap between the secret decision-making process in Washington and military operational planning. SAC, he stated, "is not fully capable of evaluating whether or not actions taken were appropriate." The command had made proposals to upgrade combat-ready status, such as a higher state of maintenance readiness, but its leaders could not be sure whether they related to the readiness test's goals.[107]

Planners at TAC also had significant reservations. Fighter units, airlift units, and headquarters staff felt "confusion" about the purpose of the readiness test: "Much conjecture resulted from everyone not knowing 'why.'" Suggesting that confusion about the mission was inconsistent with good planning, TAC's deputy chief of staff for operations recommended that "mysteries . . . not be allowed to persist unless explanations must be withheld for the purpose of security." Poignantly, Chairman Wheeler made the same point to Laird, remarking that his lack of knowledge about purposes made him unable "to furnish the CINCs with more definitive guidance as to the objectives and goals of the operation." It is likely that this problem, among others, raised pressure for intelligence on the intentions of the Kissinger NSC. This may have been one of the roots of the JCS spying operation uncovered in early 1972.[108]

General Wheeler raised broader issues. Because President Nixon had wanted to keep the readiness test out of the public eye and also avoid a confrontation with the Soviets, Wheeler, on instructions from higher authority, had ordered no change in DEFCON status. Any change, especially a heightened status, would have involved a host of complex security measures that would have made the readiness test even more visible to the public and would have also increased the risk of a Soviet overreaction. But as Wheeler pointed out, there was a drawback: divorcing the global exercise from DEFCON status protocols imposed a degree of "artificiality" upon it, which might have caused the Soviets to take it less seriously than otherwise. If the alert measures had been truly necessary to meet an international contingency that could rise to the level of a confrontation with the Soviet Union—such as a major escalation against North Vietnam that threatened its economic viability—Pentagon leaders would not have hesitated to recommend the appropriate increase in DEFCON status.[109] Wheeler's criticism was reminiscent—though not precisely the equivalent—of the line in the 1960s movie *Dr. Strangelove* when Strangelove tells the Soviet ambassador, "The whole point of the Doomsday Machine is lost if you keep it a secret."

Moreover, the DEFCON status issue—along with budgetary limits—meant that the test could not be seen "in any way . . . as a vehicle permitting an evaluation of US forces' ability to respond to a threat by increasing readiness." However, Wheeler saw a "degree of success" in the "unusual or unexplained Soviet actions observed by the intelligence community." Indeed, the chairman believed that the test gave US intelligence "a unique opportunity to test their procedures under realistic conditions."[110]

Colonel Ray Sitton, who had participated in planning for the secret bombing of Cambodia and was also involved in planning the SAC standdown, had a completely different take on the repercussions of secrecy. After the war, he told Seymour Hersh: "The guy on the other side [the Soviets] saw what looked like a DEFCON I, but it wasn't announced. They saw something that would make them say, "What the hell is he doing?" . . . As far as I know, the other guy didn't come up to alert status. All we know is that he did notice, and he wondered what we were doing."[111] In this regard, secrecy conformed to the uncertainty effect inherent in the Madman Theory. Whether this, along with Nixon's concern about public discovery, was one of his motives for secrecy is unknown, but it probably was not.

Looking for Reactions from the Soviets

When the readiness test began, DCI Richard Helms initiated an intelligence watch to monitor Soviet reactions. Military intelligence scoured reports for signs that the Soviets had responded to the alert, in part because significant reactions could lead to a decision to terminate the operation. Moreover, some specific actions were to end if Moscow reacted to them. One activity that the Soviets did notice was stepped-up US destroyer movements in the Gulf of Aden. According to Wheeler, this "caused a change in [their] naval posture in that area." Late on 20 October, two Soviet missile ships were sailing in the Red Sea for a scheduled visit to the Egyptian port of Safaga from 24–31 October. On 21 October, however, they reversed course and headed toward the Gulf of Aden and sailed southeast, where "they subsequently rendezvoused with several other Soviet ships near the Island of Socotra off Somalia." General Wheeler had previously chosen 22 October as the date to evaluate Soviet reactions to the Gulf of Aden exercises, but the Joint Chiefs decided to continue them until 27 October while continuing to monitor Soviet naval actions.[112]

The Chinese and the North Koreans probably noticed US naval operations in the Sea of Japan, but only the Soviets reacted to them. On 21 October, several Soviet Badger medium bombers flew in the vicinity of the *Constellation,* possibly on photographic or electronic intelligence missions. US aircraft intercepted them, but the Badgers nonetheless flew across "the Connie's" port bow. US military intelligence could not discern whether the Soviets had interpreted American naval operations in the Sea of Japan and the Gulf of Aden as local activities or elements of a global operation. Overflights of US naval activity were routine, so these were not necessarily a reaction to the readiness test as such, but Moscow may have wondered why the task force was lingering in the Sea of Japan.[113]

One development surely took the White House and the Pentagon by surprise. On October 21, Laird informed Kissinger that the Chinese "have gone on alert." The next day, they discussed an intelligence memorandum on the Chinese alert that Laird had forwarded. Kissinger said that he "didn't know whether it was a reaction to us or what the Soviets did in reaction to the US." Laird said "he didn't know either."[114]

CIA analysts speculated a few days later that the PRC alert could have been a reaction to Soviet military measures they had deemed to be aimed at them. The CIA analysis alluded to some sort of Soviet action that "cover[ed] the opening of Sino-Soviet border talks on 20 October," but the description of this action has been excised from the declassified report. However, CIA analysts also conjectured that the Chinese alert could have been a response to either US naval operations in the Sea of Japan or to press stories about US readiness test activities in the North Atlantic.

Alternately, they proposed, China's alert could be a response to *both* Soviet and US actions or "the result of considerations of which we are not yet aware."[115]

The conjecture about the relationship of the alert to Sino-Soviet talks appears to have been correct. China specialists Roderick MacFarquhar and Michael Schoenhals argued in their 2006 book about the Cultural Revolution that the alert had to do with tensions between Beijing and Moscow and Chinese suspicions about Soviet intentions—even though tensions appeared to be easing by this time. With border talks scheduled for 20 October in the wake of premier Alexei Kosygin's September meeting with Zhou Enlai at the Beijing airport on his way back from Ho Chi Minh's funeral, Mao Zedong worried about the possibility of a Soviet surprise attack when the October talks would begin. Overreacting to Mao's concern, Defense Minister Lin Biao ordered the evacuation of the leadership from Beijing and planned full-scale military alert measures by the People's Liberation Army (PLA). On the evening of 18 October, the PLA's chief of staff then sent the alert directive to military units, which soon "galvanized the whole PLA" to disperse combat-ready aerial, ground, and naval forces. The alert lasted only for a day or two because Mao, incensed over Lin's order, had it brought to an end.[116] Chinese alert activities may have been ending by the time of the Kissinger-Laird conversation on 21 October, but exactly what US intelligence picked up remains classified.

Toward the end of October, as the US global alert continued and SAC was preparing to implement GIANT LANCE, the DIA, NSA, and CIA continued to search for signs of Soviet reactions. During the final phase of the readiness test, as noted, the commands were to shut down specific activities if the Soviets had reacted to them but to continue them if the intelligence system did not pick up feedback. The European Command and the North American Air Defense Command, for example, were to stop certain actions on specific dates during the third week of October if a Soviet reaction had been detected. Among the measures in progress was the Sixth Fleet's EMCON and the US Army in Europe's occupation of observation posts on West Germany's border with East Germany. CONAD and Air National Guard interceptors were on fifteen-minute alert, nuclear-armed Bomarc missiles were on a high alert status, and one launch section for each Nike-Hawk unit was on twenty-minute alert. By 25 October, US intelligence had not picked up a Soviet reaction to any of these activities, so Wheeler issued instructions to modify them: Sixth

Fleet EMCON was to continue, and the observation posts on the German border were to remain occupied. But the Nike-Hawk and the interceptors were to go on one-hour alert, and the Bomarc units were to stand down.[117]

The Pacific Command was also engaged in activities that the Joint Staff had slated for special assessment on 23 October. In Japan and South Korea, US bases had increased security and antisabotage measures. Moreover, the command had boosted naval forces slated for SIOP missions, with "maximum feasible" deployments of Polaris submarines. So far, "no increased Soviet reaction" to any of these measures had been detected, and Wheeler recommended that they continue.[118]

Kissinger was beginning to receive special intelligence reports from the Defense Intelligence Agency specifically geared to the readiness test, but an early one, dated 22 October, did not identify any unusual reactions. On 25 October, however, Kissinger received a report on the detection of a "possible large-scale Soviet strategic exercise." CIA officer David McManis, a staffer at the White House Situation Room, informed Kissinger that the exercise may have begun on 10 October (just as JCS instructions on the SAC stand-down and other activities were going out), so it was "not a reaction to our readiness activities." McManis's report remains partly classified, but he suggested that the exercise was complex enough that some of its specific features could have been implemented "in reaction to our operations."[119]

Two days later, the CIA sent Kissinger a fuller report on the results of the "all-source watch" that it and the DIA had maintained to detect Soviet military activity. The CIA's report on "Possible Communist Reactions to US Readiness Tests" remains heavily excised. Its classification as "top-secret UMBRA" denotes the use of highly classified communications intelligence, but its basic conclusions are clear enough. A few military reactions, all classified, were "unusual" enough to be possibly connected to the readiness test, but only one action, also classified, "seems clearly related." Nevertheless, the analysts were not so sure and suggested that the action, whatever it was, "might be directed less at the worldwide US posture than at the specific operations of HIGH HEELS, the NATO DEEP FURROW exercise in the Eastern Mediterranean, Task Force 71 [exercises] in the Sea of Japan, and the tensions in the Middle East." Other Soviet actions, such as the naval activity in the Gulf of Aden and the aerial monitoring of Task Force 71, "seem best explained by other considerations." In addition, the Soviets had done nothing to show any "acute concern" such as "a nationwide military stand-down or general alerts."[120]

Some clues on the "clearly related" action have been declassified. It could be a reference to a component of the previously mentioned "large-scale Soviet strategic exercise." Or it could be a reference to another phenomenon that US intelligence was detecting: by 15 October if not earlier, the Soviets had increased "military signal collection activity." This development was cited in a report prepared by the DIA a week or so later.[121] Increased Soviet signals intelligence (SIGINT) activities makes sense because, as noted, CIA analysts thought it might be a reaction to various military exercises that were separate from the readiness test, such as HIGH HEELS and DEEP FURROW.

Of Moscow's reactions that have been declassified, one type involved the increase in Soviet responses to US aerial reconnaissance flights in the Far East. By 29 October, the Soviets had reacted to thirty-one of thirty-three US flights, intercepting ten of them. According to the DIA, "This reaction was well above what might normally have been expected."[122]

US intelligence detected another Soviet reaction that took place before 27 October, the day of the CIA report. Military intelligence may have detected it by then, although more information is needed to be certain. According to a DIA report, on 23 October, "general staff communications to selected headquarters utilizing a probable primary alert system indicated increased concern." The National Security Agency spotted message traffic identified with particular units and the frequencies used for particular communications systems. Even if the NSA could not decipher the messages, significant changes in the volume of traffic could indicate states of greater "concern." To what the Soviets were reacting remains unknown, although it could have been the increased activity by the Pacific Command or the Pacific Air Force.[123]

On 27 October, the same day that Kissinger received the CIA report, additional Soviet responses took place, although when US intelligence detected them is unclear. The DIA later reported that on 27 October, "some military staff elements were apparently moved to alternate command posts." In other words, Soviet concerns about the security of the main military command post—the Soviet equivalent of the Pentagon War Room at the National Military Command and Control Center—led the high command to staff backup command centers. Also on that same day, the Soviet high command conducted "a communications test with tactical air force headquarters" from Moscow.[124]

The next day, 28 October, Kissinger received the latest DIA report, "Summary of Soviet Reactions to US Operations." It is heavily excised, with some implication that the Soviets' "read-out" of information collected from their KOSMOS reconnaissance satellite may have produced some reactions. Nevertheless, for the various categories listed in the report, including strategic rocket troops, tactical air forces, air defense, military air transport, ground forces, naval fleet air forces, diplomatic, and reconnaissance, Soviet activity was "normal." A "normal status" for tactical air forces suggests that the communication test on 27 October may not have been assessed. In any event, the category for the Soviet long-range air forces is excised from the report, so the DIA may have reported on unusual bomber activity. Perhaps this was a reference to the "large-scale Soviet strategic exercise." The DIA described a wide range of Soviet naval activities in the Indian Ocean and the Mediterranean, but nothing pointed to a connection to the readiness test.[125]

Military intelligence continued searching for Soviet reactions to specific US military operations in the North Atlantic and Western Europe. Acting JCS chairman Westmoreland informed Laird on 28 October that US intelligence had not detected any Soviet reaction to several actions: the increased surveillance of the Soviet Military Liaison Mission to West Germany and the stand-down of test and training communications in the CINCEUR area and of training flight operations by VP-16 air patrol aircraft based in Argentia (Canada), Iceland, and the Azores. Westmoreland recommended continuing these activities.[126]

In the same memorandum, General Westmoreland advised Laird that the readiness test would end as scheduled at the first hour of 30 October GMT. Perhaps Westmoreland and his colleagues were eager to conclude an exercise that had taken so much time and effort. Laird's deputy, David Packard, signed off on the proposal, and a JCS message to that effect went out to the CINCs that afternoon. Late in the evening of 28 October, SAC units received notice that they would "return to normal alert and training the following midnight."[127]

The White House and Pentagon high command had assumed it would be the discovery of a Soviet reaction to the readiness test that would bring it to an end, but Westmoreland's memorandum only mentioned the lack of response to several ongoing actions. Nevertheless, years later, former Secretary of Defense Laird recalled that the readiness test ended when US intelligence picked up Soviet communications expressing "concern" about US military operations. He did not specify but may have had in mind some of the indicators discussed earlier, such as the use of the "primary alert system" and alternate command posts. Perhaps enough Soviet responses to other elements of the test had been detected and Westmoreland believed that it was time to bring it to a close.[128]

On 6 November, almost a week after the readiness test ended, Kissinger received the DIA's "Final Summary of Soviet Reactions to US Operations," covering the entire 13–30 October 1969 period. Originally classified "Top Secret UMBRA," it is massively excised, but its opening sentence remains, summarizing the DIA's findings: "The Soviets were apparently aware of a change in the readiness posture of US forces." It was a cautious assessment but clear enough. Kissinger sent the report to Nixon a month later, with a cover memorandum abstracting its findings. The "significant Soviet responses" included increased signal intelligence collection activity, general staff communications to selected major headquarters, the movement of "staff elements" to alternate command posts, and "sensitivity" to US aerial reconnaissance flights in the Far East. Kissinger concluded: "The above measures, along with others contained in the report, indicate that Moscow was aware of US activities and took some defensive precautions."[129]

The Soviets and Chinese gave regular briefings to the North Vietnamese on affairs related to the war, which included information about the movements of US carriers in the Tonkin Gulf and US air operations originating in Guam, thus augmenting North Vietnam's own intelligence capabilities.[130] But what or when Hanoi learned about Nixon's nuclear alert is still a mystery.

Almost half a century later, significant information on what US intelligence agencies detected about Soviet, Chinese, or Vietnamese knowledge and reactions remains classified. So far, the Interagency Security Classification Appeals Panel has refused to declassify National Security Agency reports on Soviet reactions. Perhaps the reason is that information from the highly classified GAMMA communications intelligence program that the United States directed against the Soviet Union is involved, including the GAMMA GUPPY radio messages intercepted from limousines carrying Soviet leaders.[131] In any event, the relatively low-key Soviet reactions did not alarm the Pentagon leadership, whose concern had been that Soviet responses might bring on a military crisis.

Despite unusual defensive precautions taken by the Soviets, the readiness test had failed to evoke suitable Soviet and North Vietnamese diplomatic responses that would have helped Nixon and Kissinger resolve their Vietnam dilemma. The strategy they had pursued through most of the year 1969—and with which they had optimistically expected to coax or force Hanoi to yield—had ended with a whimper.

Aftermaths and Assessments

The Protests and the Speech

On Moratorium Day, hundreds of thousands of Americans across the country participated in suspensions of business as usual, teach-ins, memorial services, and other nonviolent actions in opposition to the war. Well received by many among the nondemonstrating public, the event did not, however, fulfill the dire expectations of the White House. Nixon's inner circle breathed "a great sigh of relief because it wasn't nearly as bad as everyone feared." Yet they continued to worry about the impact of antiwar movement actions and, in particular, the upcoming New Mobilization demonstration scheduled for mid-November. Haldeman noted in his diary entry for 16 October that "great debates rage [within the White House] on the tactics for the future [responses to demonstrations] and analysis of how this one [the Moratorium] was handled."[1] Although hopeful that Nixon's televised speech on 3 November "would clearly state the case and . . . under normal circumstances be very effective, . . . probably buy[ing] us another couple of months," they also knew that the circumstances were not normal. The demonstrations might grow in the ten days following the speech and produce adverse results.[2]

The protesters did not realize at the time how much of an impact they had on the White House's calculations and that they had helped head off a dramatic escalation of the war. With DUCK HOOK abandoned, Nixon's November threat had turned out to be an empty one, a fact Moscow and Hanoi must have perceived as well. Even the October alert could not compensate for this underlying problem of credibility. Although Nixon and Kissinger had tried to alarm the Soviets into extracting concessions from Hanoi, they had secured little in the way of Vietnam accomplishments after months of highly secret contingency planning and White House–directed measures that included the bombing of Cambodia, diplomatic ploys, threat diplomacy, a mining ruse, and the October nuclear readiness alert. All that the administration felt free to discuss publicly was US troop withdrawals and Vietnamization. The unspoken and secret Madman Theory propelled the military and diplomatic measures, and though these had not succeeded, it would continue to motivate Vietnam War strategy as well as US conduct in the Middle East. This was business as usual as long as Nixon and Kissinger took it for granted that threats of force were effective tools in international diplomacy.

Nixon and his aides had originally envisioned the 3 November speech as an announcement and defense of the bombing and mining of North Vietnam, but it was now an explanation and defense of his Vietnam policies in the past and into the future. The president argued that he had inherited the war from the previous administration but insisted that it remained his responsibility to uphold the nation's foreign policy commitments. In an outline of the steps he had taken in pursuit of "America's peace," he maintained that North Vietnam had caused the war and had refused to cooperate in finding a solution, thus delaying an end to the war. Warning of "bloodbaths" in Vietnam and a "collapse of confidence" abroad if the United States were to withdraw precipitously from Vietnam, the president explained his own plan for the future, which he promised would ultimately succeed: de-Americanization, Vietnamization, the search for a negotiated settlement, and the determination to take "strong and effective [military] measures" should the other side increase its violence. Concluding, he returned to his original premise about the critical need for national unity and for confidence in his government. To achieve unity behind his policies, he appealed to the "silent majority" to support the war until an honorable peace through negotiations could be achieved, but he rebuked the "vocal minority," which, he claimed, had caused division at home with its criticisms of the war. North Vietnam could not "defeat or humiliate the United States," he proclaimed—"Only Americans can do that."[3]

Vocal critics of the war had disputed the wisdom of sacrificing American lives and taxpayers' dollars in a faraway war fought by immoral means in defense of dishonorable globalist goals and a corrupt and inefficient regime in Saigon, while militarism and social injustice persisted at home. The president's focus in the speech on credibility and its domino theory implications echoed the arguments his predecessors had used in justifying the war, but he reframed these ideas by portraying the conflict as a struggle for personal and national self-respect, patriotic loyalty, bringing home American POWs, and preventing a purported Communist bloodbath should South Vietnam fall.

Gathering for the events of the November Moratorium and the New

Mobilization, antiwar critics also had a nationwide impact, which was well captured on nightly TV news. Thousands of protesters silently filed across the Arlington Memorial Bridge from the National Cemetery to the Mall in the cold wind and rain, from the night of Wednesday, 12 November, through the morning of Friday, 14 November, as drummers beat a somber funeral roll. Each marcher carried a lighted candle and a poster bearing the name of one of the 45,000 Americans who had died in Vietnam or a destroyed Vietnamese village. On 15 November, this March against Death was followed by the largest single demonstration against the war. Perhaps as many as 500,000 people gathered near the Washington Monument, in song, speech, and silent witness calling for American withdrawal, peace in Vietnam, and justice at home.[4]

The protests shaped the public's evaluation of the president's 3 November speech. Nixon had won the support of 77 percent of Americans polled, who disagreed with the tactics of the antiwar movement by a margin of 51 to 36 percent. But as wide as this margin was, support for the war was relatively shallow: some 81 percent believed the demonstrators were raising important questions that should be answered, and 50 percent thought the war was a mistake and morally indefensible. By the end of November, public approval of Nixon's management of the war rose 5 percent compared to figures in September, but by a ratio of 55 percent to 33 percent respondents rejected the president's characterization of protesters as "hippie, long-haired, and irresponsible young people." In addition and more important than a temporary poll advantage, Congress was deeply divided on the war, and the press was skeptical of Nixon's claims.[5]

Nixon's commitment to the principle of US credibility would prolong the war, eventually weaken his domestic support, and damage his presidency. But in the years ahead, he would publicly characterize the speech as his "most significant" and "effective" because it had garnered popular support.[6] As Haldeman noted in mid-December 1969: "Seems that P[resident] has pretty thoroughly gotten into the position of calming down the war opposition, killing the mobilizations and assuring the people that he has a plan and that it's working. Can probably keep it that way for a while. Problem will be if Viet Cong mounts a big offensive, or some other turnaround."[7] Privately, however, Nixon also thought of the speech as the culmination of an ordeal, remarking to Kissinger in March 1971 they had "gone through hell" with "the run up to November 3rd [and] demonstrations."[8] This reference to demonstrations no doubt was meant to include not only those in October and November 1969 but also those that followed in the wake of his invasion of Cambodia in 1970.

Strategic Transition

President Nixon's November 1969 address to the nation marked a turning point in the way he and Kissinger prosecuted the war. Although they continued to carry out threat diplomacy toward Hanoi, by 3 November they had begun to transition to a different endgame strategy with a more extended timetable: the so-called long-road or long-route strategy. As President Nixon explained in his speech, his plan for exiting Vietnam was to place emphasis upon US troop withdrawals and the strengthening of South Vietnamese armed forces. He would also be more aggressive in assailing his opponents on the home front, as indeed he had been in the speech itself. He would also revise his strategy regarding the Soviets. Although he would continue to practice coercive diplomacy, he would put more emphasis on extending the carrots of détente in order to induce their assistance in pressuring North Vietnam. In addition, he would now redouble his efforts to bring about rapprochement with Beijing in order to foster its cooperation vis-à-vis Hanoi and also to play the China card against Moscow with enhanced emphasis. In South Vietnam, the RVNAF would be expected to do more of the fighting, and more stress would be placed on counterinsurgency and pacification efforts. Military operations in this scenario did not have the main purpose of winning the war but facilitating the endgame instead.

The administration's priority of de-Americanizing the fighting virtually dictated such a strategy. At the beginning of 1970, however, the pace of US withdrawals had yet to be determined. Withdrawal rates would depend on the degree of progress or regress in Vietnamization, the military conditions on the ground in South Vietnam, the status of negotiations with Hanoi, and the extent to which the USSR and—should US-PRC rapprochement become possible—China could or would assist the United States in achieving a satisfactory negotiated solution.

After consultations, studies, and deliberations, some involving the president, Kissinger summarized the administration's two major strategic alternatives in a memo on 20 July 1970: (1) withdraw American forces at the administration's own pace until all combat units were out, leaving the political solution of the war to the Vietnamese, or (2) offer the other side a more rapid US withdrawal as an incentive at the negotiating table in an effort to entice them into agreeing to a political settlement acceptable to the Thieu and Nixon governments.[9] The first alternative amounted to unilateral withdrawal followed by continued civil war in South Vietnam. The second would consist in a negotiated political compromise and a cease-fire-in-place. The compromise would provide a measure of political recognition to the PRG but leave Thieu in power. This was the course Kissinger advocated, even though he conjectured that it, like the first option, would also lead to civil war. But he argued that the route of pursuing negotiation and more rapid withdrawals was preferable not only for Thieu but also for Nixon. US troop withdrawals could be calibrated at a pace that would allow Vietnamization to strengthen the RVNAF and pacification operations designed to weaken the Viet Cong. They, along with a negotiated end to the war, would politically assist Nixon at home.[10]

A negotiated political compromise for South Vietnam would then give Thieu "the potential for eventual national control and leave the US with a reasonable period after its extrication, during which the final outcome is at least in doubt." What Kissinger meant was that even if the Communist side won national control in the long run—which was the most likely outcome—this decent-chance/decent-interval scenario would serve to disguise the role the Nixon administration's policies had played in South Vietnam's collapse.[11]

Kissinger recommended that, for the time being, they continue on course; that is, keep both options in play. He advised the president, however, that a choice of one or the other alterative would have to be made by April 1971, when they would reach a "fork in the road": American troop strength on that date would stand at 284,000, down from the peak of 550,000 in June 1969. Reductions in the six months beyond April would total another 100,000, seriously eroding their bargaining position in negotiations.[12]

Regardless of the option chosen—either a unilateral US armed forces withdrawal without a negotiated settlement or a somewhat quicker withdrawal associated with a negotiated agreement—the process would not be completed before the November 1972 US presidential election. Although Nixon was committed to this timetable, his patience occasionally faltered, and he was tempted in frustration to scuttle either option and, as he put it, "bug out"—that is, to withdraw remaining troops as soon as possible, trying to get US POWs back in the process, but leave Thieu to his fate, which meant without a decent chance of surviving. At the same time, however, Nixon would bomb the "bejeezus" out of North Vietnam.[13] At other times, he was fearful of abandoning Thieu because of credibility considerations and adverse political repercussions at home. But helped along by Kissinger, he stayed on track: the choice would be either a stretch-out of unilateral US withdrawals or a negotiated settlement brought about through selective negotiated concessions backed by military force. This was their long-term strategy and the only "honorable" way out, as they saw it, of what Nixon and Kissinger regarded as their "nightmare."[14] On 21 December 1970, for instance, Haldeman noted in his diary that Kissinger argued against a premature

> commitment to withdraw . . . all combat troops because he feels that if we pull them out by the end of '71, trouble can start mounting in '72 that we won't be able to deal with, and which we'll have to answer for at the elections. He prefers, instead, a commitment to have them all out by the end of '72, so that we won't have to deliver finally until after the elections and, therefore, can keep our flanks protected. This would certainly seem to make more sense, and the president seemed to agree.[15]

The Decent Interval Solution

A few weeks after delivering the November 1969 speech and as he was beginning to transition to the long-road strategy, President Nixon told Kissinger: "I get the rather uneasy impression that the military are still thinking in terms of a long war and eventual military solution. I also have the impression that deep down they realize the war can't be won militarily, even over the long haul."[16] His and Kissinger's recognition that the war was militarily unwinnable and that there were limits on what could be done to protect the Saigon regime in the future informed their continued interest in the decent-interval solution. As they approached and then passed their April 1971 fork in the road and having chosen to follow the strategic option of negotiated compromise, they touted the decent interval as a positive incentive in their talks with the Soviets and Chinese, fully expecting and wanting their views to be passed on to the Communist Vietnamese.

Dobrynin noted in his journal, for example, that on 9 January 1971, Kissinger made the "rather curious remark," among several others, that "it will no longer be their, the Americans', concern but that of the Vietnamese themselves if some time after the US troop withdrawal they start fighting with each other again."[17] Moscow dutifully informed Hanoi about Kissinger's comments, emphasizing the decent interval: "The North Vietnamese should undertake to respect a cease-fire during the US withdrawal plus a certain period of time, not too long, after the US withdrawal; that is the important point."[18]

For Kissinger's meetings with Prime Minister Zhou Enlai in July 1971, his staff prepared a background paper in which they referred to the decent interval in indirect diplomatic terms of assurance:

> On behalf of President Nixon I want to assure the prime minister solemnly that the United States is prepared to make a settlement that will truly leave the political evolution of South Vietnam to the Vietnamese alone. We are ready to withdraw all of our forces by a fixed date and let objective realities shape the political future. We recognize that a solution must reflect the will of the South Vietnamese people and allow them to determine their future without interference. We will not re-enter Vietnam and will abide by the political process.

In the page margin next to this paragraph, Kissinger scrawled a more blunt formulation, which clearly affirmed what the elastic diplomatic words meant: "*We want a decent interval. You have our assurance.*"[19]

Months later, Nixon reminded Kissinger in a 30 April 1972 memorandum: "Our long-range goal" is to "give the South Vietnamese [a] reasonable chance" (but not a guarantee) to meet future attacks. "In effect we have crossed the Rubicon and now we must . . . , if possible, tip the balance in favor of the South Vietnamese for battles to come [after a settlement and US withdrawal] when we no longer will be able to help them with major air strikes."[20] Along these lines, Nixon observed in a 29 September 1972 conversation with Kissinger, at a critical moment in the Paris negotiations: "Well, by next summer [1973], you have to—Christ, by next summer, Henry, we have to get out. I think that by then you'd have to announce it. . . . I'd just announce it, get it—and get it done with, I mean. But, I think—you know what that means? Get the air [forces] out, too."[21]

As much as Nixon wanted to get out, he worried that the Vietnam situation and his personal credibility could unravel. On 3 August 1972, for instance, as he weighed the political and international costs and benefits of a preelection deal in Paris, he was prepared to be "perfectly cold-blooded about it" with Thieu. He told Kissinger: "If you look at it from the standpoint of our game with the Soviets and the Chinese, from the standpoint of running this country, I think we could take, in my view, almost anything, frankly, that we can force on Thieu. . . . I look at the tide of history out there; South Vietnam probably can never even survive anyway." Hamlet-like, however, he asked: "Winning an election is . . . terribly important this year . . . , [but] can we have a viable foreign policy if a year from now or two years from now North Vietnam gobbles up South Vietnam?" No doubt keeping in mind that DRV forces in the South were a great vulnerability to Saigon and that a North Vietnamese invasion of the South was a future possibility, Kissinger answered by once again reminding Nixon of their decent-interval ruse: "If a year or two years from now North Vietnam gobbles up South Vietnam, we can have a viable foreign policy if it looks as if it's the result of South Vietnamese incompetence. . . . So we've got to find some formula [in the negotiations] that holds the thing together a year or two, after which—after a year, Mr. President, Vietnam will be a backwater."[22]

On 23 October 1972, at the time Kissinger had struck a deal with Le Duc Tho and was trying to win Thieu's approval for the agreement, Nixon told the hawkish Haig, who was skeptical of Kissinger's negotiations: "Call it cosmetics or whatever you want. This has got to be done in a way that will give South Vietnam a chance to survive. It doesn't have to survive forever. It's got to survive for a reasonable time. Then everybody can say 'goddamn we did our part.' . . . I don't know that South Vietnam can survive forever."[23] Nixon and Kissinger knew the war could not be won militarily, yet they wanted to exit with "honor" and "credibility," and so they put their faith and hopes in the decent-interval solution.

Neither Nixon nor Kissinger publicly acknowledged that the decent-interval concept underlay their Vietnam policy and diplomacy. In 2010, however, Kissinger conceded several points on the matter in answer to a question about the policy at a State Department conference. He admitted that historical documentation confirms that the administration made "statements" about the decent interval; that the Paris settlement "was a precarious agreement"; that the administration was "willing to abide by the outcome of . . . [a postsettlement] political contest" between the warring Vietnamese parties; and that "we could not commit ourselves for all eternity to maintain a government against all conceivable contingencies. . . . So in that sense, the decent interval phrase has a meaning."[24]

Continuing Military Operations

Despite the administration's new emphasis on troop withdrawals and Vietnamization after November 1969, the option of military escalation would remain central to Nixon's thinking. Complaining to Kissinger about the status of the Paris negotiations in late June 1971, for example, Nixon had a flashback. He recalled that during the October–November 1969 period, he had perceived his choices to be either escalating militarily to force a favorable negotiated agreement (the purpose of the 1969 November Option) or "escalating for the purpose of accelerating the [US unilateral] withdrawal and to protect the Americans when you're getting out." In either case, he exclaimed, "we'll bomb the bastards." Perhaps wanting to needle the president about having jettisoned the short-route November Option, Kissinger, responded: "You remember, we had a plan for that in '69 ready."[25]

Although Nixon had not followed through with the 1969 November Option, military force continued to play a critical role in his prosecution of the war. So-called protective reaction air strikes against targets in the panhandle of North Vietnam began in early 1970 and extended into 1973. The secret and devastating bombing of Laos and Cambodia persisted through 1972 and 1973. At the end of April 1970, GVN and US forces invaded the Fish Hook region of Cambodia northwest of Saigon, withdrawing two months later. In early February 1971, US-supported GVN units entered southern Laos, leaving in disarray in late March. In early spring 1972, Nixon launched POCKET MONEY, a mining operation, and LINEBACKER, a bombing operation—both aimed directly at North Vietnam. The bombing continued until October of that year but was followed during the last two weeks of December by LINEBACKER II, which was focused on targets in and around Hanoi and accompanied by the reseeding of mines. POCKET MONEY and the two LINEBACKER operations included many of the measures recommended earlier in the PRUNING KNIFE and DUCK HOOK concept plans.[26]

These operations had multiple contributory causes, reasons, and purposes, some of which were veiled by official secrecy and obfuscation. The professed military purpose of the invasion of Cambodia was to destroy COSVN headquarters and supply depots, and that of the invasion of Laos was to destroy or damage NVA units and supplies building up along the Ho Chi Minh Trail west of the DMZ. But the underlying policy purpose of both invasions was most likely preserving the Vietnamization strategy and preventing or postponing potential NVA/VC offensives, thus protecting the progress of de-Americanization and Vietnamization while preserving the decent-chance/decent-interval strategy. Beyond that, the Madman Theory was also a motive. In May 1970, an unnamed White House official, who was probably Kissinger, told *Washington Post* reporter Murray Marder that the invasion of Cambodia should make Hanoi become aware that "the United States, if pushed beyond a certain point, can take actions that are unpredictable."[27] Although POCKET MONEY and LINEBACKER I were military responses to the NVA's 1972 Easter Offensive, they served other purposes: demonstrating Nixon's resolve to make good on his threats to retaliate against North Vietnamese offensives, damaging North Vietnam's ability in the immediate present and near future to invade South Vietnam, and satisfying his longtime and oft-expressed desire to "bomb the bastards."[28]

These military operations were not launched, however, to win the war by military means, since Nixon did not believe that military victory was possible. He had followed his own belligerent instincts and had also been responsive to the military preferences of the JCS. Commenting to Kissinger in March 1971, he noted, "We've tried everything, we've done everything the military wants."[29] He said this even before the POCKET MONEY and LINEBACKER operations were launched but after the protective reaction strikes and the Cambodian and Laotian invasions had been carried out—measures that had long been advocated by the military as well as civilian hawks.

Nuclear Weapons and Vietnam, 1972

Nuclear weapons had also been on Nixon's mind when he was working his way toward a decision about how to respond to North Vietnam's Easter Offensive. With his anger boiling over, Nixon told Kissinger on 19 April 1972:

> I'll destroy the goddamn country . . . if necessary. And let me say, even the nuclear weapon if necessary. It isn't necessary, but you know what I mean. What I mean is that shows you the extent to which I'm willing to go. By—a nuclear weapon, I mean that we will bomb the living

bejeezus out of North Vietnam, and then if anybody interferes we will threaten the nuclear weapon.[30]

It was not the first time Nixon had threatened the use of nuclear weapons in Vietnam.[31] Nor would it be the last. What is especially interesting and puzzling is the recurring pattern of speech and thought inherent in these remarks, for which there are several recorded instances.[32] Nixon first impulsively states or warns that he *would* use one or more nuclear weapons, then—as though suddenly realizing that his words might surprise and shock others—he immediately retracts the remark and substitutes words to the effect that what he really meant to say was that he would either threaten nuclear use or devastate North Vietnam by means of conventional bombing to such an extent that it would be or seem to be the equivalent of a nuclear attack. Also remarkable was Nixon's warning that he would threaten nuclear weapons if other countries "intervened"— presumably a reference to the Soviet Union or China.

Nixon continued along the same lines a few days later, on 25 April 1972. In a taped conversation with Kissinger in the Executive Office Building, the president wondered whether the purpose of their forthcoming LINE-BACKER operation was more psychological than military. He appeared to favor the former goal. When Kissinger listed the targets that were to be attacked, Nixon suggested they should also "take the dikes out now." Kissinger, who seemed to have favored such attacks in November 1969, now demurred, complaining, "That will drown about 200,000 people." Nixon interjected, "Well, no, no, no, no, no, no, I'd rather use a nuclear bomb. Have you got that ready?" Kissinger muttered, "Now that, I think, would just be, uh, too much, uh—." Nixon interrupted, "A nuclear bomb, does that bother you?" Kissinger's retort is barely understandable, but he seemed to say, "A nuclear bomb, you wouldn't do it anyway." Nixon gruffly ended the conversation on this topic, saying, "I just want you to think big, Henry, for Christ's sake!"[33]

What is to be made of this and similar conversations? Nixon's tone of voice on tape sounds as though he was initially serious about using a nuclear weapon rather than just taunting Kissinger, who may have advocated nuclear use in 1969 but now seemed opposed to the idea. At the same time, Kissinger's retort to Nixon, "You wouldn't do it anyway," sounds sarcastic as well as critical of Nixon's habit of talking tough and then backing down in the face of the nuclear taboo: moral considerations (even though these might be the moral considerations of others), the opposition to nuclear use by cabinet members and advisers, negative domestic political repercussions and international reactions, the possibility of a dangerous Soviet response, and other such factors that made up the taboo.

As callous as Nixon seemed to be, he recognized that nuclear weapons use was not feasible. Indeed, as the 1972 North Vietnamese offensive unfolded, both Rogers and Laird had publicly stated that nuclear weapons should not be used in Vietnam, perhaps because they were not so sure about Nixon's intentions and wanted to constrain him. Nixon plainly disliked those statements because they undercut his freedom of action. On 8 May, after he had made the decisions to launch the LINEBACKER I operation, he told top officials at an NSC meeting, including Laird and Rogers, that "we must always avoid saying what we're not going to do, like nuclear weapons." He soon explained that it was obvious that "we are not going to use nuclear weapons" against North Vietnam, but he wanted to leave the nuclear threat "hanging over them."[34] What Nixon meant by "hanging over them" he did not need to explain to his small audience. But he may have had in mind a somewhat more subtle point than the existence of the US nuclear arsenal as a basic threat (even if an incredible one). Nixon may have assumed that the various threat statements he had made and Kissinger had passed on to Hanoi directly or indirectly since 1969 were open-ended enough to be interpreted as ultimate threats.[35] In any case, whatever Nixon meant, his Madman threats would not induce Hanoi to change its negotiating position.

Threat Diplomacy, the Madman Theory, and Misconceptions about the War's Ending

The December 1972 LINEBACKER II operation, widely known as the "Christmas bombing," was Nixon's final implementation of the Madman Theory in Vietnam. He later claimed that he had aimed at breaking Hanoi's supposed intransigence in the Paris negotiations, but the copious documentary record from both sides calls that assertion into question.[36] Only a few issues remained to be resolved by mid-December 1972. Kissinger and Le Duc Tho had reached an agreement on 22 October, and the next day, Washington closed down LINEBACKER I.[37] Both sides had made key political concessions: Hanoi dropped its demand for Thieu's outright removal from power; Washington affirmed the territorial integrity of Vietnam (as acknowledged in the Geneva Agreements of 1954) and recognized the de facto political authority of the PRG in the territory it controlled in South Vietnam. Also included in the October agreement was a provision for the formation of the Committee of National Reconciliation with PRG and Thieu-government membership, which represented a compromise for both sides. Regarding military issues, Washington agreed to withdraw all of its ground, air, and naval forces from Indochina, but the old US demand for the withdrawal of North Vietnamese troops from South Vietnam was absent from the settlement.

President Thieu rejected the October agreement because of these political and military concessions. Additional negotiations between Kissinger and Tho took place in late November and again in early December as Nixon sought revisions that would please Thieu in Saigon and the Right at home. As he told Kissinger in a 1 December telephone conversation: "It must be a settlement that . . . the Right Wing . . . will not be let down. . . . The hell with the Left and the Democrats and the rest. . . . Our concern now is the Right here. It's a real problem."[38]

Hard bargaining at the December round of talks resulted in the resolution of all issues but two: how the final documents should be signed by the four parties (the United States, the DRV, the PRG, and the RVN) and the phrasing of language on civilian and military movement across the DMZ. The first issue grew out of Thieu's reluctance to recognize the PRG as a legitimate political entity. For Saigon, the second issue had to do with maintaining the DMZ as a de facto border between the North and the South; for Hanoi, such a border violated the principle of Vietnam as one nation. Le Duc Tho's view was that other members of the Hanoi Politburo should not hold firm on the DMZ question because it was mainly a matter of symbolism and not the most important issue in the talks. Tho thought the US stance was ultimately futile in any case, inasmuch as NVA forces controlled the DMZ. Thieu of course wanted to maintain the DMZ as a boundary between North and South. In the end—that is, in the armistice agreement signed later in January 1973—both sides found compromise language that blurred the DMZ issue, overcoming Thieu's objection to signing and satisfying the PRG. Helping Thieu make up his mind, Nixon threatened to go ahead without him.[39]

A key bone of contention for Saigon had been the question of North Vietnamese forces occupying significant positions in South Vietnamese territory. Determined to settle the war by the 1972 elections, however,

Nixon and Kissinger had already conceded as early as 1971 that the with-drawal of "outside" forces would not be reciprocal. Despite all of the pun-ishment meted out by Washington upon North Vietnam and the NVA during the 1972 fighting, their spring offensive had been a strategic suc-cess because it lodged greater numbers of DRV forces (albeit damaged) even more securely in the South and aided the reconstitution of some VC forces. Thieu was constrained to accept a settlement that left the NVA in place. That was Saigon's "nightmare," according to Kissinger aide John Negroponte.[40]

While trying to manage relations with Thieu, in early December Nixon and Kissinger had been debating whether, when, and how to break off the negotiations yet make it appear that the other side was responsible for doing so.[41] On 12 December, Tho had informed Kissinger that he would have to return to Hanoi to consult with his government, citing disagree-ment within the Politburo concerning some of the changes demanded by the United States. On 13 December, Kissinger recommended a recess until after Christmas.[42] In his farewell to Kissinger, Tho suggested fur-ther exchanges between Hanoi and Washington and expressed confidence that the remaining issues could be resolved. Kissinger, however, appeared irritated.[43]

Kissinger may have been irritable because he was tired but also because he and Nixon had been at odds about how and on what terms they could settle with North Vietnam and about how they could win Thieu's accep-tance of an agreement. He also needed to appease the president. He was aware of Nixon's mistrust of his toughness in negotiations—as well as of Nixon's belligerent mood at this time. Thus, Kissinger's characterization to Nixon of the attitude and demeanor of Tho and his entourage in the last round of talks appears to have been harsher than was warranted. On 13 December, as he prepared to return to Washington, Kissinger reported to Nixon that the negotiations were deadlocked, leaving them with their old dilemma: "Hanoi is almost disdainful of us because we have no ef-fective leverage left, while Saigon in its shortsighted devices to sabotage the agreement knocks out from under us our few remaining props." Kis-singer outlined two options. The first was to "turn hard on Hanoi and in-crease pressure enormously through bombing and other means . . . [and] concurrently, . . . try to line up Saigon." The second was to hold back on bombing and resume talks in January, which would still require an effort to persuade Saigon. If the North Vietnamese "once again stonewalled in

January," Washington would place major blame on them but also fault Saigon for the collapse of negotiations. Bombing would be expanded against the North as the United States sought a bilateral agreement with Hanoi on the military issues.[44]

Nixon quickly decided on the first option. What remained to be resolved was the nature of the air campaign. Kissinger had initially recommended an escalation of bombing south of the twentieth parallel only, but the president, supported by Haig, believed that "if we want to step it up, we've got to make a major move and go all out." He considered Kissinger's suggestion another sign of "insubordination." Kissinger quickly came around, supporting what Nixon wanted—the reseeding of mines and "massive" B-52 strikes in the Hanoi-Haiphong area in operation LINEBACKER II.[45]

Considering this background, LINEBACKER II's most likely purposes were to provide Thieu with incentives to cooperate by giving him a lease on life while also signaling him and Hanoi that Washington might intervene with airpower in the conflict that lay ahead. A related benefit of the operation would be to once more damage North Vietnam's war-making capability and facilitate the decent-interval solution. Not least of all, the renewed bombing and mining was also the product of Nixon's political calculations, as well as his temperament and views regarding coercive diplomacy. As a forceful, symbolic closure to the American war in Vietnam, it would fulfill the promise Nixon had often made to himself and his inner circle that he would not go out of Vietnam whimpering. The operation also had the potential of convincing hawks that he had been tough, whereas in fact he had negotiated a settlement that included a problematic cease-fire-in-place and an ambiguous political compromise. Considering Nixon's rigid doctrinal concerns about credibility and his firm belief in Madman stratagems—and factoring in Kissinger's, Haig's, and Haldeman's reinforcement of the president's intellectual bent—LINEBACKER II had an element of ineluctability about it.[46]

The operation was clearly founded on the Madman Theory and attendant coercive diplomacy. In the belief that "bombing and mining is what [had] made the difference" since the previous spring and convinced that any breaking off of the talks by Hanoi was a sign of intransigence, Nixon told Haig, "If they don't settle, then bomb the hell out of them." Back from Paris, Kissinger supported Nixon's approach. On 14 December

1972, a few days before LINEBACKER II began, he advised Nixon that Hanoi would return to Paris by New Year's Day only "if they get a terrific shock, now." Soon, Haig chimed in: "Yes, if they get a good kick in the ass." Kissinger added, "They are scared out of their minds that you'll resume bombing." Hanoi would have returned to Paris, shock or no shock, but Nixon was eager to resume the bombing. Yet he recognized that resuming air strikes was difficult to justify publicly: "Stepping up the bombing for the purpose of getting them to talk is not going to be [laughs] a very easy one to wheel." That public relations problem meant that "we are not ever going to announce the bombing."[47]

If, as part of this stratagem, Nixon and Kissinger also intended to signal a willingness to bomb North Vietnam should it invade South Vietnam sometime after the United States pulled out, it was a bluff. With the Paris agreement, *all* US forces exited Vietnam and the Indochina region. The return of air and naval units to the battle would have been politically and logistically difficult and costly. In any event and as noted previously, this was not Nixon's intention in 1972 and 1973.

The Endgame

Months before the Saigon regime collapsed in 1975, Nixon was out of the picture, having resigned the presidency in order to avoid impeachment. The Watergate story is plainly outside the scope of this book, but it should be noted that Nixon's confidence in secrecy and secret operations as routine adjuncts of presidential power created the conditions for the abuses of power that were at the heart of the proposed articles of impeachment. Nixon's resignation meant that his successor, Gerald R. Ford, would preside over the Vietnam endgame.

As North Vietnam's 1975 spring offensive unfolded, Secretary of State Henry Kissinger briefly raised, in Nixonian fashion, the issue of military reintervention, but neither he nor anyone else was seriously prepared to follow through.[48] The US exit policy had been set earlier: get out and hope for a decent interval and then blame the Democrats and the antiwar movement for the collapse if and when it came. In July 1974—a year and a half after the Paris agreement and five months before VC and NVA fighting would begin to build up to the 1975 spring offensive that would overrun South Vietnam by April—Ambassador to Saigon Graham Martin told Kissinger and his aides, Lawrence Eagleburger and W. R. Smyser:

"Militarily, they [the South Vietnamese] are holding. Politically, they are more solid than I had the right to hope." Kissinger replied: "When I made the [January 1973] agreement, I thought it might be a two-year thing."[49]

About Saigon's prospects, Martin was wrong and Kissinger was mostly right. The South Vietnamese government and army were not as strong as Martin believed, but Kissinger was close to the mark about the decent interval extending two years. Thus, when Saigon's collapse was imminent, he was resigned to its fate, telling his special action group: "We got out. Now let the situation be settled locally."[50]

Spinning the Story

One of the enduring myths about Nixon's and Kissinger's handling of the war, however, is the claim that US mining and bombing in 1972, coupled with their masterful management of war and diplomacy, had made it possible to bring US POWs home and honorably end a long and tortuous American war against a devious and determined enemy. All this gained currency despite the opposition and obstruction of the press, Congress, and the antiwar movement—which opposition, they would charge, resulted in Saigon's collapse two and a half years later.[51]

This initially private narrative had its inception within the White House inner circle at least as early as 1971.[52] It was often accompanied by Nixon's and Kissinger's assertion that had such brutal force been used earlier—that is, in 1969 and 1970—it would have ended the war sooner. On 8 May 1972, for example, when debating whether to mine and bomb North Vietnam in response to its Easter Offensive, Nixon reviewed the history of strategic "mistakes" that he had made since 1969. In 1969, these included his failure to bomb North Korea during the EC-121 shootdown crisis and to "go hard" against North Vietnam in November.[53]

Followed by the Paris agreement, the LINEBACKER bombings gave these claims about earlier "mistakes" more traction. When, for instance, Nixon speechwriter William L. Safire asked Kissinger in early 1973, "What should we have done if we had the four years to live over?," Kissinger answered by lamenting the decision to abort the 1969 November Option: "We should have bombed the hell out of them the minute we got into office. . . . The North Vietnamese started an offensive in February 1969. We should have responded strongly. We should have taken on the doves right then—start bombing and mining the harbors. The war would have been over in 1970."[54]

But even though Nixon had been a firm believer in threat diplomacy and Kissinger a strong advocate of mining and bombing in 1969, it is doubtful they truly believed their own assertions about the folly of aborting the 1969 November Option. In his 1978 memoir *RN*, to cite one example, Nixon defended his decision: "I underestimated the willingness of the North Vietnamese to hang on," he wrote. Although he had "wanted to orchestrate the maximum possible pressure on Hanoi," he could not "depend on solid support at home" if Hanoi "call[ed] my bluff."[55] In *No More Vietnams*, published seven years later, he confessed that he thought at the time "it would be very hard to hold the country together while pursuing a military solution." Nixon also wrote that bombing and mining "would have been more than the traffic could bear." Reflecting the criticisms by the Joint Chiefs and some of Kissinger's aides regarding the DUCK HOOK concept, he added that such an operation would have offered only "a temporary respite from enemy actions," which "would not by itself guarantee South Vietnam's survival"; moreover, the chances of détente with the Soviets and Chinese would have been "snuffed out."[56] The Moratorium in particular, he wrote in *RN*, "had undercut the credibility of the ultimatum." Like the analysis given him in October by guerrilla warfare analyst Sir Robert Thompson, Nixon explained that a dramatic escalation of the war would have "risk[ed] a major American and worldwide furor and still not address[ed] the central problem of whether the South Vietnamese were sufficiently confident and prepared to defend themselves against a renewed Communist offensive at some time in the future."[57] These published remarks are consistent with the available record of what happened at the time—discussed in previous chapters of this book—and they cast doubt on the parallel but contrary narrative that the November Option would have ended the war to Nixon's and Kissinger's satisfaction by 1970.

As inevitable as the POCKET MONEY and LINEBACKER operations were in Nixon's presidency, no conclusive evidence has turned up to prove that they compelled Hanoi to sign the 1973 agreement—upon which also rest claims touting the potential efficacy of the earlier but aborted 1969 November Option. The 1972 mining and bombing unquestionably damaged North Vietnam's war-making capability and increased pressure from allies to settle—and it may also have raised the level of war weariness. But the weight of evidence linking mining and bombing to Hanoi's position on signing an agreement in Paris by January would have to come from Hanoi, Moscow, and Beijing, not from assertions made by self-interested former US policymakers. Unfortunately, the declassification of vital Vietnamese, Russian, and Chinese records bearing on this question has yet to occur.[58]

If there are any lessons to be learned from the LINEBACKER II experience and the history of Nixon's Vietnam threat making generally—including the 1969 Cambodian bombings, the spring and summer mining ruse, the 1 November deadline warnings, and the October nuclear alert—one may be that Madman diplomacy is not likely to succeed even against a small nation-state such as the DRV when its leaders and a sizable proportion of its population are motivated by dynamic anticolonial and revolutionary nationalism that draws upon a long tradition of resisting foreign invaders. Nguyen Co Thach, aide to Le Duc Tho, encapsulated this mentality in a statement made to delegates at the Paris negotiations. His intention was to "tease" Kissinger after he had made one of his many threats while criticizing the North Vietnamese about their own threats:

It is Kissinger's idea that it is a good thing to make a false threat that the enemy believes is a true threat. It is a bad thing if we are threatening an enemy with a true threat and the enemy believes it is a false threat. False or true, we Vietnamese don't mind. There must be a third category for those who don't care whether the threat is true or false.[59]

The Madman Theory and Nuclear Threat Making beyond Vietnam

Even after the failure of nuclear threat making in 1969, Nixon and Kissinger continued to apply the Madman Theory and make implied threats of nuclear use in their conduct of diplomacy—with regard both to the war in Vietnam and to crises elsewhere. Only eleven months after the October 1969 alert, Nixon and Kissinger deployed their Madman Theory nuclear threat diplomacy in the Middle East. After members of the Popular Front for the Liberation of Palestine hijacked several airliners and flew them to Jordan in September of that year, a civil war broke out that threatened King Hussein's rule and raised questions about possible intervention by Soviet clients Syria and Iraq, which were on the side of the Fedayeen. To demonstrate US support for the Jordanian state, Nixon ordered US forces to reach maximum readiness in the region. The entire Sixth Fleet assembled in the eastern Mediterranean. It was a substantial force that included two aircraft carriers, a cruiser, fourteen destroyers, and supporting ships with an embarked marine battalion; a third carrier was on its way as well. US carriers routinely carried nuclear weapons, but they were not directly part of the threat to Syrian and Iraqi intervention. Carrier air would have used conventional weapons to bomb Syrian or Iraqi armor or whatever other forces intervened. If, however, Soviet forces had interceded, the two great nuclear powers would have been confronting one another, which would have raised the risks considerably. In addition to naval movements, a US airborne brigade in West Germany went on alert, and the Eighty-Second Airborne Division went on the highest alert possible without it becoming publicly known.[60]

With these measures, Nixon intended to convey a threatening message, and he soon reinforced it with a rhetorical allusion to the Madman Theory. As the Sixth Fleet was steaming toward the eastern Mediterranean, he was in the American Midwest for speeches and had an off-the-record meeting with editors of the *Chicago Sun-Times*. At a private briefing on the morning of 17 September 1970, President Nixon discussed the crisis, and in its first two late-afternoon editions of the day, the *Sun-Times* printed a report written by veteran journalist Peter Lisagor about Nixon's startling comments. He quoted Nixon as having said: "If Syria and Iraq invade Jordan, it may be necessary for US and/or Israel to intervene. It is very important that we never create the impression with the Russians that the US will always act rationally. The real possibility of irrational American action is essential to the US/Soviet relationship."[61] Nixon clearly intended that the rapid introduction of major naval forces during the crisis would make the Soviets think that he was a madman and therefore refrain from intervening themselves to avoid escalating the crisis. The Voice of America broadcast the report to the world, and Soviet and Arab sources expressed displeasure about US military deployments to the region and Nixon's threat to intervene.[62]

Later that evening, Nixon was back in Washington, reflecting on developments with Kissinger by telephone. Referring to the impact of the naval movements upon the Soviets, Kissinger said that the United States "might as well let them know what chips are in the pot." Nixon responded that it was necessary to handle the Soviets with "cool detachment" and to avoid overt warnings because they will "think you are bluffing." US forces should "just move [in]" and "they will know that we are ready to do something." This was in keeping with Nixon's desire to project an image of unpredictability and an ability to move suddenly and without warning; then the adversary might think it was a real threat, not a bluff.[63]

Kissinger's use of a poker metaphor presaged a statement he made in August 1972 during a conversation with a senior Pentagon official, Gardner Tucker, assistant secretary of defense for systems analysis. The Pentagon had completed a study on limited and selective nuclear strike options as a way for US presidents to limit escalation in a crisis and have available less catastrophic alternatives to massive and cataclysmic uses of nuclear weapons. During the discussion, Kissinger commented on Nixon's conduct during crisis situations, observing that "the president's strategy has been (in the Mid East crisis, in Vietnam, etc.) to 'push so many chips into the pot' that the other side will think we may be 'crazy' and might really go much further."[64] The Middle East and Vietnam references no doubt included the Jordanian crisis and the October 1969 nuclear alert as well as Nixon's general threat posture during 1969 and the years leading up to the 1972 bombing-and-mining campaigns against North Vietnam.

The alerting of US forces during the crisis in Jordan caught the attention of US intelligence officials, who apparently then carried out a study of White House decision making. In 1973, Andrew W. Marshall, a RAND Corporation official who worked for Kissinger's office, summarized the conclusions of the intelligence study in a report to the NSC Intelligence Committee Working Group. Among the study's findings was one that identified a pattern of thinking about coercive diplomacy and threat making that shaped White House decision making. Marshall's summary read: "The policymakers believe that changes in deployment and levels of alert of US forces can be used to influence foreign decision makers' perceptions of the consequences of their actions, US level of concern, etc., and to improve the outcome from the USG's [US government's] point of view." This generalization about Nixon's and Kissinger's threat-making outlook may also have been reinforced by the experience of October 1969, when some of the same intelligence analysts may have been tasked to assess the Soviet response.[65]

That the Madman strategy remained in Kissinger's playbook even after the US exit from Vietnam was evident in one of the most famous nuclear alerts of the Cold War: the DEFCON III alert during the October 1973 Arab-Israeli War. Kissinger took from the Vietnam experience the lesson that force or threats of force should be used sooner rather than later, although what he did in 1973 demonstrated his faulty recollection of the events of October 1969. As the Arab-Israeli war unfolded, Moscow and Washington engaged in rivalrous activities, such as shipping arms to support their regional clients. At the same time and consistent with the purposes of détente, they tried to contain the conflict by arranging a cease-fire. But Israeli violations of the cease-fire and their success in encircling Egypt's Third Army on the Sinai Peninsula made Leonid Brezhnev believe—and he was not altogether mistaken—that Kissinger had encouraged Israel. In this context, Brezhnev felt angry and betrayed, and in a moment of stress, he warned Nixon and Kissinger that Moscow might unilaterally deploy Soviet forces to implement the cease-fire in the absence of joint US-Soviet measures.[66]

Taking Brezhnev's message as a serious threat and not a bluff that exploited Nixon's Watergate-induced vulnerability, Kissinger—who had become secretary of state only weeks earlier—argued during a WSAG meeting in the overnight hours of 24–25 October 1973 that "we must prevent them from getting away with this." No doubt worried that Soviet intervention would upset the balance of power, harm extensive US interests in the Middle East, and complicate his plans to establish US control over the peace process, Kissinger supported a show of force. WSAG members signed off on a series of measures, including alerting the Eighty-Second Airborne Division and establishing a DEFCON III for all US forces worldwide, both nuclear and conventional.[67]

When WSAG was shaping its response to Brezhnev's message, Nixon was out of action. Despondent and apparently intoxicated because of the forced resignation of Vice President Spiro Agnew and the Watergate-related Saturday night massacre, Nixon was disengaged from the DEFCON III decision. But Kissinger made a Nixonian decision for him: harkening to a basic tenet of the Madman Theory—the threat of excessive force—he told the group that he "had learned, finally, that when you decide to use [or threaten?] force you must use plenty of it." The idea of making the adversary worry that the president was getting "out of control" was hardwired into Kissinger's thinking: for him, the "Dulles ploy" (as he called it) of threatening nuclear force was a lesson of history—and so was the assumption that threats and shows of force would produce favorable results diplomatically.[68]

Partly in light of the experience of the October 1969 alert, Kissinger had wrongly expected the DEFCON III alert to stay relatively secret, noticeable mainly to the Soviets. He told the *Washington Post*'s Murray Marder a few weeks later: "We did not think it would become public," but news of the alert quickly leaked and spread to the front pages and national TV news. This created a difficult problem, Kissinger told Marder, because "I wanted to avoid a situation in which we had confronted the Soviets and (faced?) [*sic*] them down." Referring to the events of October 1969, he informed Marder—who kept this secret—that the White House had once ordered a "SAC alert which didn't get into the press at all." Kissinger may have forgotten that the 1969 alert stayed secret in part because it was not a DEFCON, precisely because of the noise level problem. In any event, from his perspective, he said, "I had in the back of my mind that the practical consequences would be like" the military measures that Washington had ordered during the September 1970 Jordan crisis. "People would see the 82nd Airborne go on alert . . . , but I did not think we'd be hitting the newspapers the next morning with a global alert." A DEFCON alert, however, was a global action involving a formal process of notifying military forces down to the level of individual pilots, who received messages to hurry to their bases. As the word spread, the possibility of leaks and public awareness increased.[69]

A DEFCON III that alerted US commands around the world to heighten their readiness raised troubling questions about credibility and danger. It was potentially dangerous because it raised the level of threat to the Soviet Union, and an accident, a mistake, or a misunderstanding could have unintentionally produced a superpower conflict. In addition, alerting all US forces, including strategic bombers, was out of proportion to the apparent dangers unfolding in the Middle East. Washington was threatening Moscow with nuclear retribution even if it only deployed small conventional forces to the Sinai Peninsula. The DEFCON response also lacked credibility because, consistent with the purposes of détente, Washington and Moscow had been working together to cool temperatures in the Middle East to prevent the conflict from getting out of control. Indeed, senior Soviet officials were astonished and puzzled by the alert and were incredulous that Brezhnev's reference to possible Soviet unilateral action had triggered it, especially because he had no intention to send troops to Egypt, even though a healthy, but overruled, minority in the Politburo thought otherwise and favored intervention despite the risks.[70]

The 1973 DEFCON III was a singular moment in the history of Cold War crises. Although it was Kissinger, not Nixon, who had set this nuclear readiness condition in motion, he had long before embraced the outlook that Nixon had absorbed during his association with Eisenhower and Dulles—namely, the supposed diplomatic value of nuclear threats and alert actions during Cold War crises. Kissinger had been persuaded or found it expedient to believe that Madman threats were potentially effective for settling diplomatic crises and resolving intractable problems such as the Vietnam War in his favor. He had carried out DEFCON III despite the failure of the October 1969 alert to sway Moscow.

Both decisions involved risks that Nixon and Kissinger had not acknowledged. Fortunately, the Soviets, who were invariably puzzled by US maneuvers during the October 1969 alert and other alert activities, had made relatively minor, nonperilous responses to the 1969 secret alert, possibly because they did not see the point of US actions and regarded them as hardly credible. After several Nixon administration threats and alerts, Foreign Minister Andrei Gromyko observed that the "Americans put forces on alert so often that it is hard to know what it meant."[71] For all of Nixon's and Kissinger's concerns about the credibility of American power, their use of nuclear alerts for signaling purposes on occasions when there was no threat or when the action was far out of proportion to any possible danger raised the level of risk to global security and undermined the credibility of the decision makers themselves.

The most extreme threats—nuclear threats—are unlikely to succeed when the side threatened possesses its own nuclear weapons, when a non-nuclear state such as the DRV is presumably under the protection of a nuclear state such as the Soviet Union, or when the threat is disproportionate because it is aimed at a small country.[72] Threats did not end the Vietnam deadlock, in part because Moscow had achieved nuclear parity with Washington, which meant it was becoming dangerously anachronistic to brandish nuclear weapons. It was also becoming impossible to threaten nuclear destruction secretly. Kissinger apparently came to understand this. In 1977, with several alerts under his belt, he told NSC consultant Samuel Huntington that he had concluded that the United States could not "afford to repeat the rapid escalation gambit."[73] This made the October 1973 DEFCON the last stand of the Eisenhower-Dulles, Cold War style of nuclear manipulation, but it did not necessarily mean the end of nuclear threat making altogether. Today, the operative phrase is "all options are on the table." The extreme degree of secrecy that characterized the Nixon White House did not, however, fade away. The methods used by Nixon and Kissinger had distinctive characteristics based partly on personal factors, but subsequent presidents would sometimes also find it expedient to centralize national security decision making in the White House behind a wall of secrecy and to conduct secret military operations that would not withstand public scrutiny.

NOTES

Introduction

1. Oval Office Conversation 527-16, Nixon, Haldeman, Kissinger, and Ehrlichman, 9:14 a.m.–10:12 a.m., 23 June 1971, White House Tapes (hereafter WHT), Richard M. Nixon Presidential Library (RNPL), Yorba Linda, CA. Unless noted otherwise, taped conversations cited here and after were transcribed by Jeffrey Kimball.

2. Msgs, CJCS to CINCS, 10 October 1969, subj: Increased Readiness Posture, box 109, Records of Chairman Earle Wheeler, Record Group (RG) 218, National Archives and Records Administration (NARA).

3. Whatever the code name signified to planners, in golfing parlance a "duck hook" is a swing that produces a sharp and unintended downward hook of the ball. Alternatively, "hook-a-duck" is a traditional American game found at fairground stalls.

4. The influence of these demonstrations on Nixon's decision to abort the November Option has long been part of the antiwar movement's conventional wisdom. Probably the first historian to systematically examine this question was Tom Wells, *The War Within: America's Battle over Vietnam* (Berkeley: University of California Press, 1994), 328–338. Also see Melvin Small, *Johnson, Nixon, and the Doves* (New Brunswick, NJ: Rutgers University Press, 1988), 163; Charles DeBenedetti and Charles Chatfield, *An American Ordeal: The Antiwar Movement of the Vietnam Era* (Syracuse, NY: Syracuse University Press, 1990), 248–274.

5. Daniel Ellsberg was probably the first author to introduce the public, the news media, and historians to the term *decent interval*, in "Laos: What Nixon Is Up To," *New York Review of Books*, 11 March 1971, http://nybooks.com/articles/10633 (accessed 31 January 2008).

6. Seymour Hersh, *The Price of Power: Kissinger in the Nixon White House* (New York: Summit Books, 1983), 124–125.

7. The best-known scholarly skeptics were Fred I. Greenstein and Joan Hoff. See Greenstein, "A Journalist's Vendetta," *New Republic*, 1 August 1983, 29–31; Hoff, "Richard M. Nixon: The Corporate Presidency," in *Leadership in the Modern Presidency*, ed. Fred I. Greenstein (Cambridge, MA: Harvard University Press, 1988), 185–189; Hoff, *Nixon Reconsidered* (New York: Basic Books,

1994), 173–181. However, Kimball, in *Nixon's Vietnam War* (Lawrence: University Press of Kansas, 1998), and *The Vietnam War Files: Uncovering the Secret History of Nixon-Era Strategy* (Lawrence: University Press of Kansas, 2004), documented Nixon's and Kissinger's embrace of this threat strategy, traced its origins in history, and explored its links with nuclear diplomacy. Burr, in "The Nixon Administration, the 'Horror Strategy,' and the Search for Limited Nuclear Options, 1969–1972: Prelude to the Schlesinger Doctrine," *Journal of Cold War Studies* 7, no. 3 (Summer 2005): 34–78, linked it to Kissinger's notions about limited nuclear war.

8. Scott D. Sagan, "Proliferation, Pessimism, and Emerging Nuclear Powers," *International Security* 22, no. 2 (Fall 1997): 197. Previously, Bruce G. Blair, *The Logic of Accidental Nuclear War* (Washington, DC: Brookings Institution, 1993), 180 and 339n15, broached the Sino-Soviet crisis theory and other possible explanations, citing declassified military information about the operation. Both have since changed their minds. A former bomber pilot during the Vietnam War and later SAC commander in chief, General Eugene Habiger (ret.), has also taken the view that the Sino-Soviet crisis was the motivation for the alert; conversation with Habiger at "The Bulletin of the Atomic Scientists' Third Annual Doomsday Clock Symposium," 9 January 2012, Washington, DC.

9. See, e.g., Kimball, *Nixon's Vietnam War*, 164.

10. Journals and Diaries of Harry Robbins Haldeman (HRHD), RNPL. Haldeman handwrote these diaries from 18 January 1969 to 30 November 1970 but recorded them on tape afterward. *The Haldeman Diaries: Inside the Nixon White House—The Complete Multimedia Edition* [compact disc] (Santa Monica, CA: Sony Electronic Publishing, 1994), contains more entries than the book version published in the same year by G. P. Putnam's Sons. Unfortunately, this CD is not compatible with Windows versions after XP. Moreover, some entries were not declassified until after the publication of the diaries but can be found, of course, in the original handwritten and taped records.

11. William Burr and Jeffrey Kimball, "Nixon's GIANT LANCE: Atomic Diplomacy, the Vietnam War, and Détente, October 1969," paper presented at the Society for Historians of American Foreign Relations 2002 Conference, 23 June 2002, University of Georgia, Athens; Burr and Kimball, "Nixon's Secret Nuclear Alert: Vietnam War Diplomacy and the Joint Chiefs of Staff Readiness Test, October 1969," and "NATO, the Warsaw Pact, and the Rise of Détente, 1965–1972," papers read at a conference on 28 September 2002, Dobbiaco, Italy.

12. William Burr and Jeffrey Kimball, "Nixon's Secret Nuclear Alert: Vietnam War Diplomacy and the Joint Chiefs of Staff Readiness Test, October 1969," *Cold War History* 3 (January 2003): 113–156; Burr and Kimball, "Nixon's Nuclear Ploy," *Bulletin of the Atomic Scientists* 59, no. 1 (January–February 2003): 28–37 and 72–73; Burr and Kimball, "Nixon's Nuclear Ploy," National Security Archive Electronic Briefing Book no. 81, 23 December 2002, http://www.gwu.edu/~nsarchiv/NSAEBB/NSAEBB81/index2.htm (accessed 3 December

2014). Also see the "Nuclear Notions" section in Kimball, *Vietnam War Files*, 110–120. In 2002 and 2003, we had been unaware of a recently declassified air force official history published three years earlier in which the author, Wayne Thompson, chief of analysis at the Air Force History Support Office, included a brief, two-paragraph account of the SAC stand-down and the nuclear-armed airborne alert over Alaska; Thompson, *To Hanoi and Back: The United States Air Force and North Vietnam, 1966–1973* (Washington, DC: Air Force History and Museum Program, 2000), viii, 167–168. He, too, had linked them to the Vietnam War, explaining that these measures were an attempt by Nixon "to underline the seriousness of his ultimatum to Moscow and Hanoi." Thompson, however, had not used documents from the files of Nixon, Kissinger, Laird, the Joint Chiefs of Staff, or the relevant military commands but had instead drawn upon "older official histories."

13. Scott Sagan and Jeremi Suri, "The Secret Nuclear Crisis of October 1969: Instability amidst Strategic Parity," paper presented at the SHAFR 2002 Conference, 23 June 2002, University of Georgia, Athens.

14. Scott Sagan and Jeremi Suri, "The Madman Nuclear Alert: Secrecy, Signaling, and Safety in October 1969," *International Security* 27, no. 4 (Spring 2003): 151.

15. William Burr and Jeffrey Kimball, "New Evidence on the Secret Nuclear Alert of October 1969: The Henry A. Kissinger Telcons," *Passport: The Society for Historians of American Foreign Relations* 36, no. 1 (April 2005): 12–14; Burr and Kimball, "Nixon's Secret Nuclear Alert," *Cold War International History Studies* 2 (June 2006): 34–78; Burr and Kimball, "Nixon White House Considered Nuclear Options against North Vietnam, Declassified Documents Reveal: Nuclear Weapons, the Vietnam War, and the 'Nuclear Taboo,'" National Security Archive Electronic Briefing Book no. 195, 31 July 2006, http://www2.gwu.edu/~nsarchiv /NSAEBB/NSAEBB195/index.htm (accessed 3 December 2014).

16. See, e.g., Editorial Note, *Foreign Relations of the United States: National Security Policy* (hereafter *FRUS*), *1969–1976*, vol. 24, doc. 59, pp. 230–233. The editor did not directly state a position but strongly leaned toward the Sino-Soviet thesis, despite scant documentation for it and the weight of evidence and argument in favor of the Vietnam War thesis, which he did not cite or acknowledge.

17. William Lemnitzer, telephone interview by Burr, 27 March 2007; Roger Morris, telephone interview by Kimball, 19 February 2007; Letter, Laird to Burr, 12 January 2000, held by the authors; Kissinger and Haig, responses to question by Kimball, 11 March 2006, John F. Kennedy Library, Boston; Haig, conversation with Kimball, 10 March 2006, Kennedy Library; Kissinger, conversation with Holloway, 15 January 2013, as reported to Burr by Holloway, 18 October 2013, Austin, TX. Kissinger's and Haig's responses to the Kimball-Burr question at the Kennedy Library conference can be viewed at about 2:09 hours into the C-SPAN video of the conference on 11 March 2006, at http://www.c-spanvideo .org/program/PresidencyW. See also Kissinger conversation with Jeremi Suri,

2007, New York, reported in Suri, "The Nukes of October: Richard Nixon's Secret Plan to Bring Peace to Vietnam," *Wired Magazine* 16, no. 3 (25 February 2008): 5.

Chapter 1. Prelude

1. Quoted in *Life*, 16 January 1978.

2. Historian Gar Alperovitz either coined the term *atomic diplomacy* or at least was one of the first to use it in his book *Atomic Diplomacy: Hiroshima and Potsdam —The Use of the Atomic Bomb and the American Confrontation with Soviet Power* (New York: Simon & Schuster, 1965).

3. Sean Malloy, *Atomic Tragedy: Henry L. Stimson and the Decision to Use the Atomic Bomb against Japan* (Ithaca, NY: Cornell University Press, 2008), 84 and 95. For "bonus," see Barton J. Bernstein, "The Atomic Bombings Reconsidered," *Foreign Affairs* 74, no. 1 (January–February 1995): 142 and 150.

4. Daniel Ellsberg was the first or one of the first to explain that "again and again, generally in secret from the American public, nuclear weapons have been used" to threaten adversaries; Ellsberg, "Call to Mutiny," *Monthly Review* 33, no. 4 (September 1981): 1–26, also reprinted in E. P. Thompson and Dan Smith, eds., *Protest and Survive* (New York: Monthly Review Press, 1981), i–xxviii. For extended discussion of the role of nuclear threats and alerts during the Cold War, see Sean M. Lynn-Jones, Steven E. Miller, and Stephen Van Evera, eds., *Nuclear Diplomacy and Crisis Management* (Cambridge, MA: MIT Press, 1990).

5. Not found in most standard dictionaries, the word *compellance* is, however, often used in strategic writings.

6. As political sociologist and RAND researcher Hans Speier observed, "A government that is exposed to atomic threats in peacetime readily regards them as 'blackmail' whereas the threatening poser is likely to call them 'deterrence'"; quoted in Richard Betts, *Nuclear Blackmail and Nuclear Balance* (Washington, DC: Brookings Institution, 1987), 4. In *Arms and Influence* (New Haven, CT: Yale University Press, 1966), 69–73, Thomas C. Schelling attempted to distinguish between compellence, coercion, and deterrence.

7. E.g., demanding the return of a hostage, the second millennium BCE Hittite king Mursili sent a clay-tablet cuneiform message warning a hostage-taking vassal, "I will come and destroy you along with your land"; Hittite tablet archives, quoted in Trevor Bryce, *The Kingdom of the Hittites* (Oxford: Clarendon Press, 1998), 232. For ancient "ferocity," also see Robert Drews, *The End of the Bronze Age: Changes in Warfare and the Catastrophe ca. 1200 B.C.* (Princeton, NJ: Princeton University Press, 1993), 45–47.

8. As Eisenhower would put it in 1951 when he was NATO commander: "If other countries of the free world . . . fall under the domination of Russia, we will finally get to the point where we have no friends with whom to trade, and after that, it would only be a short distance to economic disaster for us and consequent regimentation of some kind"; Letter, Eisenhower to his brother Earl, 5

October 1951, in *The Papers of Dwight D. Eisenhower: NATO and the Campaign of 1952*, vol. 12, ed. Louis Galambos (Baltimore, MD: Johns Hopkins University Press, 1970), 619, and for related thinking, see 37–38, 391, 430, 756–757, 794, and 819–820. Interpretations of national security policy at the close of World War II exhibit considerable variance; for example, compare William A. Williams, *The Tragedy of American Diplomacy* (Cleveland, OH: World Publishing, 1959); Gabriel Kolko, *The Politics of War: The World and United States Foreign Policy, 1943–1945* (New York: Random House, 1968); John Lewis Gaddis, *Strategies of Containment: A Critical Appraisal of Postwar American Security Policy* (Oxford: Oxford University Press, 1982); Melvyn P. Leffler, *A Preponderance of Power: National Security, the Truman Administration, and the Cold War* (Stanford, CA: Stanford University Press, 1992); and Odd Arne Westad, *The Global Cold War: Third World Interventions and the Making of Our Times* (New York: Cambridge University Press, 2005).

9. For wartime and early postwar thinking about air bases, see Michael S. Sherry, *Preparing for the Next War: American Plans for Postwar Defense, 1941–1945* (New Haven, CT: Yale University Press, 1977), 42–47 and 203–204; Leffler, *Preponderance of Power*, 56–59.

10. See, e.g., George F. Lemmer, "The Air Force and Strategic Deterrence, 1951–1960," US Historical Division, Liaison Office, December 1967, p. 35.

11. For the "moral revolution," see Ronald Schaffer, *Wings of Judgment: American Bombing in World War II* (New York: Oxford University Press, 1985). Regarding Hiroshima and Nagasaki, also see Robert C. Batchelder, *The Irreversible Decision, 1939–1950* (Boston: Houghton Mifflin, 1962), 211–222; Nina Tannenwald, *The Nuclear Taboo: The United States and the Non-use of Nuclear Weapons since 1945* (New York: Cambridge University Press, 2007), 81–89; Malloy, *Atomic Tragedy*, 50 and 169.

12. Tannenwald, *Nuclear Taboo*, 88 and 98–99.

13. See, e.g., Lemmer, "Air Force and Strategic Deterrence," 35. Regarding arms control, see Lawrence S. Wittner, *The Struggle against the Bomb*, vol. 1, *One World or None: A History of the World Nuclear Disarmament Movement through 1953* (Stanford, CA: Stanford University Press, 1993), chaps. 4 and 14.

14. Michael S. Sherry, *Rise of American Air Power: The Creation of Armageddon* (New Haven, CT: Yale University Press, 1987), 358; Leffler, *Preponderance of Power*, 111–112 and 210.

15. Letter, Norman L. Ramsey to Oppenheimer, n.d. [mid-August 1945], box 60, J. Robert Oppenheimer Papers, Manuscript Division, Library of Congress, Washington, DC; Walton S. Moody, *Building a Strategic Air Force* (Washington, DC: Air Force History and Museums Program, 1996), 63–66; Ken Young, "US 'Atomic Capability' and the British Forward Bases in the Early Cold War," *Journal of Contemporary History* 42, no. 1 (January 2007): 117–136.

16. L. Wainstein, C. D. Cremeans, J. K. Moriarty, and J. Porturo, *The Evolution of US Strategic Command and Control and Warning, 1945–1972*, Institute for

Defense Analyses Study S-467, June 1975, document NH00039, pp. 14–18, 34, and 72, *Digital National Security Archive/ProQuest* (*DNSA*) (Washington, DC, and Ann Arbor, MI). In his valuable study of nuclear nonuse, T. V. Paul mistakenly suggests that these early plans were for "preventive war," but it is more accurate to consider them as the early stages of what would become routine nuclear war planning by the US military establishment; Paul, *The Tradition of Non-use of Nuclear Weapons* (Stanford, CA: Stanford University Press, 2009), 41–42.

17. Five American crew members died in the shootdown. The Truman government chose to interpret the incident as a Soviet-inspired provocation, although the affair could best be understood in its local context as a Yugoslav controversy over air traffic rights and overflights.

18. Strategic Air Command, *The Strategic Air Command, a Chronological History, 1946–1956* (Offutt Air Force Base, NE: Historical Division, Strategic Air Command, ca. 1957), 49–50. For details of the shootdown, see Lorraine M. Lee, *Keeping Tito Afloat: The United States, Yugoslavia, and the Cold War* (University Park: Pennsylvania State University Press, 1997), 14–17. Some have claimed that a flight of six B-29s to Uruguay in early 1947 was another occasion for US nuclear weapons threats, but that also is a misunderstanding. The B-29 flight was a goodwill mission in honor of the inauguration of the new president on 1 March 1947. Major General Charles F. Born led the flight and represented the air force at the ceremony; Strategic Air Command, *Strategic Air Command*, 69. For the claims, see Peter Kuznik, "The Decision to Risk the Future: Harry Truman, the Atomic Bomb and the Apocalyptic Narrative," *Japan Focus*, http://japanfocus .org/-Peter_J_-Kuznick/2479, n. 90 (accessed 5 December 2014).

19. Simon Duke, *US Defense Bases in the United Kingdom: A Matter for Joint Decision?* (New York: Macmillan, 1987), 29–34; Strategic Air Command, *Strategic Air Command*, 208; Wainstein et al., *Evolution*, 31 and 75; Young, "US 'Atomic Capability'"; Leffler, *Preponderance of Power*, 220. That the aircraft did not carry "bombs" was public knowledge at the time, but there was no implication that they were not nuclear capable. See "60 B-29s Ordered to Fly to Britain," *New York Times*, 16 July 1948.

20. Lynn Eden, "Capitalist Conflict and the State: The Making of United States Military Policy in 1948," in *Statemaking and Social Movements*, ed. Charles Bright and Susan Harding (Ann Arbor: University of Michigan Press, 1984), 247–254; David Alan Rosenberg, "The Origins of Overkill: Nuclear Weapons and American Strategy, 1945–1960," *International Security* 7, no. 4 (Spring 1983): 13.

21. Leffler, *Preponderance of Power*, 202–203 and 208–218; Irwin Wall, "France and the North Atlantic Alliance," in *NATO: The Founding of the Atlantic Alliance and the Integration of Europe*, ed. Francis H. Heller and John R. Gillingham (New York: Palgrave Macmillan, 1992), 45–55. For NATO's defense concept and a comprehensive study of US nuclear strategy and NATO during its formative

period, see Robert Wampler, "Ambiguous Legacy: The United States, Great Britain, and the Foundations of NATO Strategy, 1948–1957" (Ph.D. diss., Harvard University, 1991), 13–16. Also relevant to NATO's founding was an interest in propitiating French concerns that a revived Germany might become a military threat; see John Lamberton Harper, *American Visions of Europe: Franklin D. Roosevelt, George F. Kennan, and Dean G. Acheson* (New York: Cambridge University Press, 1996), 282.

22. Matthew Jones, *After Hiroshima: The United States, Race, and Nuclear Weapons in Asia, 1945–1965* (New York: Cambridge University Press, 2011), 68–70.

23. For a detailed account of the deployments, see Roger Dingman, "Atomic Diplomacy during the Korean War," *International Security* 13, no. 3 (Winter 1988–1989): 56–65. Also see Tannenwald, *Nuclear Taboo*, 117–120.

24. Wainstein et al., *Evolution*, 312–332.

25. Quoted and paraphrased in the *New York Times* and *Washington Post*, 1 December 1950.

26. Tannenwald, *Nuclear Taboo*, 123–124.

27. Dingman, "Atomic Diplomacy," 72–77; Memorandum of Conversation (hereafter MemCon), Marshall et al., 9 May 1951, *FRUS, 1951*, vol. 7, pt. 2, p. 1659.

28. Dingman, "Atomic Diplomacy," 77–79; MemCon, US-UK Foreign Ministers, 11 September 1951, *FRUS, 1951*, vol. 7, pt. 1, pp. 897–898; Jeffrey P. Kimball, "The Panmunjom and Paris Armistices: Patterns of War Termination," in *America, the Vietnam War, and the World: Comparative and International Perspectives*, ed. Andreas W. Daum, Lloyd Gardner, and Wilfried Mausbach (New York: Cambridge University Press, 2003), 107–113.

29. For definitions of the taboo, see Tannenwald, *Nuclear Taboo*, 10–17, and for Truman, see chaps. 3 and 4.

30. Rosenberg, "Origins of Overkill," 68.

31. See, e.g., Tannenwald, *Nuclear Taboo*, 148–149.

32. News Conference, 16 March 1955, *Public Papers of the Presidents of the United States: Dwight D. Eisenhower, 1955* (Washington, DC: Government Printing Office, 1959), 332.

33. Regarding the taboo and Korea, see Tannenwald, *Nuclear Taboo*, 140–153, who links moral and political factors with the taboo, and Lynn Eden, "The Contingent Taboo," *Review of International Studies* 36, no. 4 (October 2010): 831–837.

34. Tannenwald, *Nuclear Taboo*, 142–146.

35. Ibid., 140–147; William Stueck, *The Korean War: An International History* (Princeton, NJ: Princeton University Press, 1995), 306 and 329; Rosemary Foot, *The Wrong War: American Policy and the Dimensions of the Korean Conflict: 1950–1953* (Ithaca, NY: Cornell University Press, 1985), 206–209; Memo, S. Everett Gleason to Dulles, 29 April 1953, subj: Transfer of Custody of Atomic

Weapons, folder: Miscellaneous NSC Memoranda, box 123, Lot 66D148, Records Relating to Participation in the Operations Coordinating Board and the National Security Council, 1947–1964, General Records of the Department of State, RG 59, NARA.

36. C. Turner Joy, *How Communists Negotiate* (New York: Macmillan, 1955), 161–162; James Shepley, "How Dulles Averted War," *Life*, 16 January 1956, 70–80. An earlier story in *Look* was more skeptical of Dulles's claim; see Fletcher Knebel, "We Nearly Went to War Three Times Last Year," *Look*, 8 February 1955, 27. See also Edward Keefer, "President Dwight D. Eisenhower and the End of the Korean War," *Diplomatic History* 10 (1986): 267–268 and 280; Dingman, "Atomic Diplomacy," 50–51; Daniel Calingaert, "Nuclear Weapons and the Korean War," *Journal of Strategic Studies* 11 (June 1988): 177–202; Dwight D. Eisenhower, *Mandate for Change, 1953–1956* (Garden City, NY: Doubleday, 1963), 181. In 1985, Nixon claimed that Dulles had made his threats through Krishna Menon, Indian ambassador to the United Nations, not Nehru; see "What the President Saw: A Nation Coming into Its Own," *Time*, 29 July 1985, 50.

37. Memo of Meeting with the President and Others, 17 February 1965, 10:00 a.m., box 1, Meeting Notes File, Lyndon Baines Johnson Library (LBJL), Austin, TX, and Memo, Read to Rusk, 4 March 1965, subj: Threat of the Use of Nuclear Weapons against China in Korean War, folder: Def 12 US, box 5, Formerly Top Secret Foreign Policy Files, 1964–1966, RG 59, NARA.

38. Memo, Read to Rusk, 4 March 1965. Nehru claimed many years later that Dulles had not mentioned a nuclear threat at their meetings, adding that had Dulles done so, he would not have relayed it to the Chinese; see Mark A. Ryan, *Chinese Attitudes toward Nuclear Weapons: China and the United States during the Korean War* (Armonk, NY: M. E. Sharpe, 1989), 64 and 156. This denial, however, is ambiguous, since he may have relayed the *indirect* warning to the Chinese.

39. Memo, Read to Rusk, 4 March 1965. Molotov replied on 3 June 1953, telling Bohlen that "the Soviet government has taken note of the information"; records of exchanges with Molotov and Nehru are in *FRUS, 1952–1954*, vol. 15, pt. 2, pp. 1068–1069, 1071, 1103–1104, and 1108–1111.

40. Ryan, *Chinese Attitudes toward Nuclear Weapons*, 156; Stueck, *Korean War*, 148–165, 172–177, and 329. On Chinese resolve regarding US bombing, see Mao Zedong to Joseph Stalin, 18 July 1952, doc. 108, in "New Evidence on the Korean War: New Russian Documents on the Korean War," introduction and translations by Kathryn Weathersby, *Cold War International History Project Bulletin*, no. 6–7 (Winter 1995–1996): 78; Lt. Gen. Du Ping, "Political Mobilization and Control," in *Mao's Generals Remember Korea*, trans. and ed. Xiaobing Li, Allan R. Millett, and Bin Yu (Lawrence: University Press of Kansas, 2001), 63–64. On economic issues in North Korea and China, see, e.g., Ciphered telegrams, Mao to Stalin, 31 January and 8 February 1952, docs. 100 and 102, in "New Evidence

on the Korean War," 74–76. For an analysis of how the Korean War ended in mutual compromise in relation to war termination theory, see Kimball, "Panmunjom and Paris Armistices," 107–113; Elizabeth A. Stanley, "Ending the Korean War: The Role of Domestic Coalition Shifts in Overcoming Obstacles to Peace," *International Security* 34, no. 1 (Summer 2009): 42–82.

41. For one of the more recent books about the Eisenhower-Nixon relationship, see Jeffrey Frank, *Ike and Dick: Portrait of a Strange Political Marriage* (New York: Simon & Schuster, 2013).

42. RAND Corporation, "Implications of Potential Weapon Developments for Strategic Bombing and Air Defense," 10 July 1952, doc. NH00048, p. 7, *DNSA*.

43. For background on massive retaliation and the New Look, see Report to the National Security Council, 30 October 1953, *FRUS, 1952–1954*, vol. 2, pt. 1, pp. 577–596, esp. pp. 583, 591, and 595. The key phrases used in NSC 162/2 are "adequate offensive retaliatory strength and defensive strength" and "massive atomic capability." Maintaining the "free world" coalition was, of course, the goal, but it was also necessary in order to provide military bases for massive retaliation; ibid., 591. Dulles claimed to have "originated the concept of 'massive retaliation' in 1950 when it was impossible for the Free World to match the conventional strength of the Soviet Union"; MemCon, Dulles and representatives of the State and Defense Departments, 7 April 1958, doc. NH00099, *DNSA*. But within the Truman administration government, others had advocated "counterattacks of utmost [atomic] violence"; Lemmer, *Air Force and Strategic Deterrence*, 35. For public statements by Dulles, Eisenhower, and Nixon on massive retaliation, see *New York Times*, 13 and 14 January and 14 March 1954; John Foster Dulles, "The Evolution of Foreign Policy," *Department of State Bulletin* 30 (January 1954): 107–110; Dulles, "Policy for Security and Peace," *Foreign Affairs* 32, no. 3 (April 1954): 353–364.

44. Robert R. Bowie and Richard H. Immerman, *Waging Peace: How Eisenhower Shaped an Enduring Cold War Strategy* (New York: Oxford University Press, 1998), 197–198.

45. Adlai Stevenson, quoted in *New York Times*, 26 February 1956.

46. *New York Times*, 26 February 1956.

47. Rosenberg, "Origins of Overkill," 34.

48. For a documentary sampling of Eisenhower's and Dulles's changing views on nuclear use, see MemCon, 190th Meeting of the National Security Council, 25 March 1954, *FRUS, 1952–1954*, vol. 2, pt. 1, pp. 640–642; MemCon, Dulles and representatives of the State and Defense Departments, 7 April 1958, FOIA release, available at *The Nuclear Vault* on the National Security Archive (NSArchive) website, http://www2.gwu.edu/~nsarchiv/nukevault/ (accessed 5 December 2014).

49. Lemmer, "Air Force and Strategic Deterrence," 35; Rosenberg, "Origins of Overkill," 34–35; David Rosenberg, "'A Smoking Radiating Ruin at the End of Two Hours': Documents on American Plans for Nuclear War with the Soviet

Union, 1954–1955," *International Security* 6, no. 3 (Winter 1981–1982): 27 (see 36–37 for the difficulties of the preemptive option); Scott Sagan, "SIOP-62: The Nuclear War Plan Briefing to President Kennedy," *International Security* 12, no. 1 (Summer 1987): 30–31.

50. On this point, see, e.g., Lloyd Gardner, *Approaching Vietnam: From World War II through Dienbienphu, 1941–1954* (New York: W. W. Norton, 1988), 185.

51. *New York Times*, 13 January 1954. At a press conference on 13 January, Eisenhower touted the deterrent value of instant retaliation against a surprise thermonuclear attack on the United States, and in answer to questions, he did not reject Dulles's remarks about the utility of massive retaliation in local wars; *New York Times*, 14 January 1954.

52. Report to NSC, 30 October 1953, *FRUS, 1952–1954*, vol. 13, vol. 2, pt. 1, p. 584. The wording of NSC 162 is unclear as to whether Indochina was seen as of "vital strategic importance" or "strategic importance," but because policymakers believed that US credibility was on the line, their consequent domino theory made this peripheral area of vital interest.

53. John Foster Dulles, "Policy for Security and Peace," *Foreign Affairs* 32, no. 3 (April 1954): 358–360.

54. See, e.g., *New York Times*, 14 January 1954.

55. "Formosa Encouraged," "Chiang's Stock Rises," "Peiping Sees War Threat," and "Nixon Clarified Position on Asia," *New York Times*, 2, 4, and 21 April 1954; Toshihiro Higuchi, "Radioactive Fall-Out, the Politics of Risk, and the Making of a Global Environmental Crisis, 1954–1963" (Ph.D. diss., Georgetown University, 2011).

56. Jeffrey Barlow, *From Hot to Cold War: The US Navy and National Security Affairs, 1945–1955* (Stanford, CA: Stanford University Press, 2009), 385–391; Edward J. Marolda, *By Sea, Air, and Land: An Illustrated History of the US Navy and the War in Southeast Asia* (Washington, DC: Department of the Navy, 1994), 5. Also see earlier sources: Joseph Buttinger, *Vietnam: A Dragon Embattled*, vol. 2, *Vietnam at War* (New York: Praeger, 1967), 819; George Bidault, *Resistance: The Political Autobiography of Georges Bidault*, trans. Marianne Sinclair (1965 [in French]; repr., New York: Praeger, 1967), 196; Townsend Hoopes, *The Devil and John Foster Dulles* (Boston: Little, Brown, 1973), 214; Herbert S. Parmet, *Eisenhower and the American Crusades* (New York: Macmillan, 1972), 364; Ronald H. Spector, *Advice and Support: The Early Years, 1941–1960*, United States Army in Vietnam series (Washington, DC: Center of Military History, 1983), 200; *The Senator Gravel Edition, The Pentagon Papers: The Defense Department History of United States Decisionmaking on Vietnam*, vol. 1 (Boston: Beacon Press, 1971), 100.

57. William Burr, "60th Anniversary of Castle BRAVO Nuclear Test, the Worst Nuclear Test in US History," NSArchive Electronic Briefing Book no. 459, 28 February 2014; see also "The H-Bomb," *New York Times*, 4 April 1954.

58. Spector, *Early Years*, 192–194 and 200–201.

59. Memo, Douglas MacArthur II to Dulles, 7 April 1954, *FRUS, 1952–1954,* vol. 13, pt. 1, p. 1271. LeMay made his claim to Robert McClintock, former counselor to the US Embassy in Saigon and chair of an interdepartmental working group on Indochina; see McClintock, *The Meaning of Limited War* (Boston: Houghton Mifflin, 1967), 166–168. Also see Jules Roy, *The Battle of Dienbienphu* (New York: Harper & Row, 1963), 203 and 211–212; Bernard Fall, *Hell in a Very Small Place: The Siege of Dienbienphu* (Philadelphia: J. B. Lippincott, 1967), 299; Robert McClintock, *The Meaning of Limited War* (Boston: Houghton Mifflin, 1967), 166–168; Richard Nixon, *RN: The Memoirs of Richard Nixon* (1979; repr., New York: Simon & Schuster, 1990), 150–155; John Prados, *The Sky Would Fall: Operation Vulture, the Secret US Bombing Mission to Vietnam, 1954* (New York: Dial Press, 1983), 145–156; Betts, *Nuclear Blackmail,* 48–54; Paul, *Tradition of Non-use,* 52–53 and 111–112.

60. See, e.g., Eisenhower's comments in MemCon, 194th Meeting of the NSC (extracts), 29 April 1954, *FRUS, 1952–1954,* vol. 13, pt. 2, pp. 1431–1445.

61. There is a large literature on the diplomacy and politics of the Dien Bien Phu crisis; for good accounts of the complex purposes of and relationships within the Eisenhower administration and between it and the French government, see Gardner, *Approaching Vietnam,* esp. chaps. 5 through 8; Hoopes, *Devil and John Foster Dulles,* chap. 14; and Fredrik Logevall, *Embers of War: The Fall of an Empire and the Making of America's Vietnam* (New York: Random House, 2012), chap. 19. Also see Diary entries, 22 and 26 March, 22 May, and 23 June 1954, Nixon's Platters (transcripts of Nixon's occasional Dictaphone notes transcribed by Rosemary Woods), courtesy of Irvin Gellman.

62. Memo, MacArthur II to Dulles, 7 April 1954, *FRUS, 1952–1954,* vol. 13, pt. 1, pp. 1270–1272; Memo, Robert Cutler to W. B. Smith, 30 April 1954, subj: Draft of formal record of action of the NSC Meeting, 29 April 1954, *FRUS, 1952–1954,* vol. 13, pt. 2, pp. 1445–1449; Nixon, *RN,* 154–155.

63. Spector, *Early Years,* 201; *Pentagon Papers* (Gravel ed.), 1: 92–93.

64. Bidault, *Resistance,* 196. Policymakers and historians have taken diverse positions on whether Dulles really did offer atomic bombs, as Bidault claimed. In any case, the dispute comes down to Bidault's account of what Dulles said versus Dulles's own recollections. Historians Laurent Césari and Jacques de Folin take Bidault's account more seriously. They point out, for example, that Jean Chauvel mentioned the reputed offer in his memoirs, and Paul Ély noted it in his diary; "Military Necessity, Political Impossibility: The French Viewpoint on Operation *Vautour,*" trans. Mark R. Rubin, in *Dien Bien Phu and the Crisis of Franco-American Relations, 1954–1955,* ed. Lawrence S. Kaplan, Denise Artaud, and Mark R. Rubin (Wilmington, DC: Scholarly Resources, 1990), 113–114; Logevall, *Embers of War,* 497–499. George C. Herring and Richard H. Immerman cast doubt on Bidault's account in "Eisenhower, Dulles, and Dienbienphu: 'The Day We Didn't Go to War' Revisited," *Journal of American History* 71, no. 2 (September 1984): 343–363. For another skeptical view, see Jones, *After Hiroshima,* 212–213

and 234. Messages between Dulles and the US ambassador to France, C. Douglas Dillon, 9 and 10 August 1954, *FRUS, 1952–1954,* vol. 13, pt. 2, pp. 1927, 1928, and 1933, do not confirm or confute the offer. Often lost in the debate is the context: the many other occasions when the Eisenhower administration either considered nuclear use or threatened use.

65. Memo, Cutler to Walter Bedell Smith, 30 April 1954, subj: Draft of formal record of action of the NSC Meeting, April 29/54, *FRUS, 1952–1954,* vol. 13, pt. 2, pp. 1445–1449. One of the participants or an observer wrote a marginal note in this record about a basic problem that appears not to have been discussed explicitly. Next to the words *give them a few* is a comment that a "question of law" was involved. This was almost certainly a reference to the 1946 Atomic Energy Act, then still in effect, which made it illegal to transfer nuclear materials to other countries. Moreover, the AEC still had custody over nuclear weapons, and it would be interesting to know whether AEC chairman Lewis Strauss had been consulted on the possibility of lending or giving the weapons; ibid., 1447.

66. Ibid., 1447. The delaying tactic was one Admiral Radford had proposed; Douglas MacArthur II to Dulles, 7 April 1954, *FRUS, 1952–1954,* vol. 13, pt. 1, pp. 1270–1272.

67. Nixon, *RN,* 155, taken from Diary entry, 30 April 1954, Nixon's Platters, courtesy of Irvin Gellman.

68. David L. Anderson, *Trapped by Success: The Eisenhower Administration and Vietnam, 1953–1961* (New York: Columbia University Press, 1991), 38.

69. On this point, also see Tannenwald, *Nuclear Taboo,* 140–181. Regarding possible post–Dien Bien Phu and post-Geneva nuclear use upon US intervention, the NSC by 1955 began to consider the creation of "highly mobile" US forces for "flexible" operations in Indochina, with a full range of capabilities. NSC 5501 (6 January 1955) and NSC 5602/1 (15 March 1966), for example, called for units "equipped for local war, including atomic capability but not dependent on [the] use of atomic weapons for effective action"; Memo, Robert Bowie, Dept. of State Representative on the NSC, to Dulles, 6 June 1956, subj: Defense Presentation: "Capability to Deal with Local Aggression in Vietnam"—NSC Agenda, 7 June 1956, *FRUS, 1955–1957,* vol. 1, pp. 694–695; see also Memo from the JCS to Secretary of Defense, 9 September 1955, *FRUS, 1955–1957,* vol. 1, pp. 539–540.

70. General Vo Nguyen Giap mentioned the implied US threats of using an atomic bomb in *Dien Bien Phu,* 6th ed. (Hanoi: Thê´Gió Publishers, 1999), 155.

71. E-mail message, Luu Huynh to Kimball, 19 September 2009.

72. For background on the course of the 1954–1955 crisis, see Gordon Chang and He Di, "The Absence of War in the US-China Confrontation over Quemoy and Matsu in 1954–1955: Contingency, Luck, Deterrence?," *American Historical Review* 98, no. 5 (December 1993): 1500–1524; Ronald W. Pruessen, "Over the Volcano: The United States and the Taiwan Strait Crisis, 1954–1955," in *Reexamining the Cold War: China Diplomacy, 1954–1973,* ed. Robert S. Ross and

Jiang Changbin (Cambridge, MA: Harvard University Asia Center, 2001), 77–105. See also Chen Jian, *Mao's China and the Cold War* (Chapel Hill: University of North Carolina Press, 2001), 167–169; H. W. Brands, "Testing Massive Retaliation: Credibility and Crisis Management in the Taiwan Strait," *International Security* 12, no. 4 (Spring 1988): 124–151. For air force deployments during the crisis, see Jacob Van Staaveran, *Air Operations in the Taiwan Crisis of 1958* (Washington, DC: US Air Force Historical Division Liaison Office, 1962), FOIA release.

73. Quoted in *New York Times*, 17 March 1954. Henry Kissinger used *uncertainty effect* in *The Necessity for Choice: Prospects of American Foreign Policy* (New York: Harper & Brothers, 1961), 52, as though it were a common term at the time. In his biography of Richard Nixon, *One of Us: Richard Nixon and the American Dream* (New York: Random House, 1991), journalist Tom Wicker used the term *uncertainty principle* in reference to some of President Nixon's foreign policy tactics, perhaps as a pun on Heisenberg's Uncertainty Principle regarding quantum physics, which, of course, carried a different meaning. But Wicker was no doubt conjuring up references to nuclear physics and, in general, the atomic age. Wicker was certainly aware of Nixon's debt to Eisenhower and Dulles. For the importance of allied opinion in the crisis, see Jones, *After Hiroshima*, 256–257.

74. News Conference, 16 March 1955, *Public Papers of the Presidents, Eisenhower, 1955*, 332.

75. For a discussion of this latter point, see Tannenwald, *Nuclear Taboo*, 141–148 and 165–175. By 1957, the administration's security policy committed the United States to "place main, but not sole, reliance on nuclear weapons; to integrate nuclear weapons with other weapons in the arsenal of the United States; to consider them as conventional weapons from a military point of view; and to use them when required to achieve national objectives"; "Basic National Security Policy"(NSC 5707/8), 3 June 1957, *FRUS, 1955–1957*, vol. 29, pp. 507–524.

76. *New York Times*, 18 March 1955; Frank, *Ike and Dick*, 105–106.

77. Eisenhower, *Mandate for Change*, 483.

78. William Taubman, *Khrushchev: The Man and His Era* (New York: W. W. Norton, 2003), 359–360; Vladislav Zubok, *A Failed Empire: The Soviet Union in the Cold War from Stalin to Gorbachev* (Chapel Hill: University of North Carolina Press, 2007), 130–131.

79. Wainstein et al., *Evolution*, 34, 257n3; Strategic Air Command, *The SAC Alert Program, 1956–1959*, Historical Study no. 79 (Offutt Air Force Base, NE: Strategic Air Command, 1960), 4 and 27. For "initiative," see Headquarters, US Strategic Air Command, Historial Study 73 A, *SAC Targeting Concepts*, n.d. [ca. 1959], Mandatory Declassification Review (MDR) release.

80. Memo, Lt. Colonel Brian S. Gunderson to General Martin, 2 December 1958, subj: Briefing to Net Evaluation Committee, box 36, OPS 40 (Speeches, Briefings, Presentations) (6 Sep 58–Dec 58), Directorate of Plans, Records for 1958, Records of Headquarters, United States Air Force (Air Staff), RG 341, NARA.

81. Rosenberg, "Origins of Overkill," 55 and 58; Memo, Smith to the Secretary, 25 November 1958, subj: Oral Presentation of the Annual Report of the New Evaluation Subcommittee," *DNSA*.

82. For the problem of nuclear weapons fire effects, see Lynn Eden, *The Whole World on Fire: Organizations, Knowledge, and Nuclear Weapons Devastation* (Ithaca, NY: Cornell University Press, 2003). On pp. 238–242, she discusses the nuclear winter thesis, citing Richard Turco et al., "Nuclear Winter: Global Consequences of Multiple Nuclear Explosions," *Science*, no. 4630 (22 December 1983): 1283–1292.

83. Memo of conference with the President, 15 July 1958, 11:25 a.m., *FRUS, 1958–1960*, vol. 11 (1992), pp. 245–246; Douglas Little, *American Orientalism: The United States and the Middle East since 1945* (Chapel Hill: University of North Carolina Press, 2008), 134–135; Richard Immerman, *John Foster Dulles: Piety, Pragmatism, and Power in US Foreign Policy* (Wilmington, DE: Scholarly Resources, 1999), 165–166; Joint Chiefs of Staff, "Situation Report No. 4 (Middle East), Period Covered: 0800, 17 July 1958–1400, 17 July 1958," Dwight D. Eisenhower Presidential Library (DEPL); "Discussion at the 373rd Meeting of the National Security Council, 24 July 1958," Ann Whitman Files, DEPL.

84. Historical Division, Headquarters Second Air Force, *History of the Second Air Force Jul–Dec 1958*, vol. 1 (Barksdale Air Force Base, LA: Headquarters, Second Air Force, May 1959), 133; Historical Division, Sixteenth Air Force, Strategic Air Command, *Sixteenth Air Force, 1 July–31 December 1958* (Sixteenth Air Force Headquarters, ca. 1959), 66; and Strategic Air Command Historical Study no. 132, *Four Crises: Berlin, Lebanon, Cuba, and Korea* (Offutt Air Force Base, NE: Office of the Historian, Strategic Air Command, 1971). Copies of these three works are available at NSArchive.

85. Van Staaveran, *Air Operations*, 15–16; Memo of Meeting, 22 August 1958, 2:00 p.m., *FRUS, 1958–1960*, vol. 18, doc. 40, pp. 67–68.

86. Van Staaveran, *Air Operations*, 19–24 and 72.

87. Summary of Meeting at White House on Taiwan Straits Situation, 25 August 1958, and Telegram from the Joint Chiefs of Staff to the Commander in Chief, Pacific, 25 August 1958, *FRUS, 1958–1960*, vol. 19, docs. 43 and 44, pp. 73–76, 143; Dwight D. Eisenhower, *Waging Peace, 1956–1961* (Garden City, NY: Doubleday, 1965), 295; Morton H. Halperin, *The 1958 Taiwan Straits Crisis: An Analysis*, RAND Corporation Memo RM-4803-ISA (Santa Monica, CA: RAND Corporation, January 1966), FOIA release; Jones, *After Hiroshima*, 369–377.

88. Van Staaveran, *Air Operations*, 57; Li Xiaobing, Chen Jian, and David Wilson, eds., "Mao Zedong's Handling of the Taiwan Straits Crisis of 1958: Chinese Recollections and Documents," *Cold War International History Project Bulletin*, no. 6–7 (Winter 1995–1996): 208–218.

89. Taubman, *Khrushchev*, 398–399, 401–405; Zubok, *Failed Empire*, 133–134.

90. MemCon, 15 December 1958, subj: Berlin, box 163B, NATO Meeting Paris MemCons, Dec 1958, Conference Files, CF 1196, RG 59, NARA; Memo of

Conference with President Eisenhower, 29 January 1959, *FRUS, 1958–1960*, vol. 8, doc. 149, p. 301; MemCons, 4 February 1959, subj: Secretary's Conversation with General Norstad, 762.0221/2–1259, and Memo for the Record, Livingston Merchant, 27 February 1959, 611.61/2–2759, Decimal Files, 1955–1959, RG 59, NARA.

91. MemCon, 4 February 1959, subj: Subjects Which French May Raise with the Secretary, doc. NH01090, *DNSA*.

92. Memo for the President, 24 December 1958, subj: NATO Atomic Stockpile in Germany, 740.5611/12–2458, RG 59, NARA; US Army Europe, "Field Artillery in the European Theater," *Annual History, USAREUR, 1 July 1958–30 June 1959*, HQ USAREUR, http://www.usarmygermany.com/Sont .htm?http&&&www.usarmygermany.com/Units/FieldArtillery/USAREUR _FieldArty.htm (accessed 6 December 2014).

93. J. C. Hopkins and Sheldon A. Goldberg, *The Development of Strategic Air Command, 1946–1986* (Offutt Air Force Base, NE: Office of the Historian, Headquarters Strategic Air Command, 1986), 55, 59; Rosenberg, "Origins of Overkill," 147; Strategic Air Command, *History of the Strategic Air Command: The B-52—Background and Early Development, 1946–1954*, Historical Study no. 60 (Offutt Air Force Base, NE: Historical Division, Strategic Air Command, 1956), doc. NH00002, pp. 43–44, *DNSA*.

94. Office of Assistant to the Secretary of Defense (Atomic Energy), *History of the Custody and Deployment of Nuclear Weapons, July 1945 through September 1977* (Washington, DC: Department of Defense, 1978), 42, 54, Defense Department FOIA release; Wainstein et al., *Evolution*, 34; Strategic Air Command, *SAC Alert Program, 1956–1959*, Historical Study no. 79 (Offutt Air Force Base, NE: Strategic Air Command, n.d. [ca. 1960]), doc. NH 00018, pp. 80–133, *DNSA*; Strategic Air Command, *The SAC Alert System, 1956–1970*, Historical Study no. 129, 19 September 1973, 30–37, FOIA release; MemCon, 9 March 1959, subj: SAC Overflights, 742.5411/3–959, Decimal Files, RG 59, NARA; Memo of Conference with the President, 9 February 1959, *FRUS, 1958–1960*, vol. 3, doc. 49, pp. 181–182. See also Scott Sagan, *The Limits of Safety: Organizations, Accidents, and Nuclear Weapons* (Princeton, NJ: Princeton University Press, 1993), 167.

95. MemCon, 13 May 1960, subj: Increased Military Readiness, box 219, CF 1664—Summit Paris, May 1960 MemCons, Conference Files, 1949–1963, RG 59, NARA; Scott Sagan, "Nuclear Alerts and Crisis Management," *International Security* 9, no. 4 (Spring 1985): 100–106.

96. Sagan, "Nuclear Alerts and Crisis Management"; Telegrams EC 9–10368 and 977192, USCINCEUR and CJCS to JCS, both 16 May 1960, folder 2, Chairman's Messages (Nov 59 to July 1960), box 32, Records of Nathan Twining, Records of the Joint Chiefs of Staff, RG 218, NARA.

97. For a comprehensive analysis of SIOP-62, see Rosenberg, "Origins of Overkill," 3–8 and 64–69. For casualty estimates, see Fred M. Kaplan, *The Wizards of Armageddon* (Stanford, CA: Stanford University Press, 1991), 269.

98. Letter, Eisenhower to Churchill, 27 April 1956, *Papers of Dwight D. Eisenhower: The Presidency—The Middle Way*, vol. 16, 2139.

99. Rosenberg, "Origins of Overkill," 62.

100. Quoted in ibid., 41 and 42.

101. Note by the Executive Secretary to the National Security Council on US Policy in the Event of War (NSC 5904/1), 17 March 1959, and Memo of Discussion at the 39th Meeting of the National Security Council, 5 March 1959, *FRUS, 1958–1960*, vol. 3, docs. 52 and 55, pp. 207–209 and 288.

102. Tannenwald, *Nuclear Taboo*, 191 and 206–209; Paul, *Tradition of Non-use*, 70–72. See also Philip Nash, "Bear Any Burden? John F. Kennedy and Nuclear Weapons," in *Cold War Statesmen Confront the Bomb: Nuclear Diplomacy since 1945*, ed. John Lewis Gaddis, Ernest May, and Jonathan Rosenberg (Oxford: Oxford University Press, 1999), 120–140.

103. Kaplan, *Wizards of Armageddon*, 278–279; US Air Force, Strategic Air Command, *History of the Joint Strategic Target Planning Staff: Preparation of SIOP-63* (Offutt Air Force Base, NE: Strategic Air Command, 1964) (accessed 7 December 2014); Wainstein et al., *Evolution*, 357n13.

104. Sagan, *Limits of Safety*, 169 and 173; US Strategic Air Command, *History of Headquarters Strategic Air Command 1961*, Historical Study no. 89 (Offutt Air Force Base, NE: Strategic Air Command, n.d.[ca. 1962]), doc. NH00023, pp. 61–63, *DNSA*.

105. For SAC operations during the crisis, see Strategic Air Command, *Strategic Air Command Operations During the Cuban Crisis of 1962*, Historical Study no. 90 (Offutt Air Force Base, NE: Strategic Air Command History and Research Division, n.d. [ca. 1963]), copy at NSArchive; Wainstein et al., *Evolution*, 329–330; Gilpatric handwritten notes, 22 October 1962, FOIA release; LeMay to Taylor, 22 October 1962, subj: Additional Measures, folder: Cuba, box 6, Maxwell Taylor Records, RG 218, NARA.

106. Wainstein et al., *Evolution*, 329–330; Sagan, *Limits of Safety*, 62–67.

107. Taubman, *Khrushchev*, 545–547; Zubok, *Failed Empire*, 143–144. For Kennedy's management of the crisis and the final diplomatic settlement, see Sheldon M. Stern, *Averting "The Final Failure": John F. Kennedy and the Secret Cuban Missile Crisis Meeting* (Stanford, CA: Stanford University Press, 2003); Nash, "Bear Any Burden?," 132–133.

108. Strategic Air Command, *Strategic Air Command Operations during the Cuban Crisis of 1962*.

109. Draft letter, McNamara to James T. Kendall, 30 November 1962, folder: Cuba, box 6: Secret, Taylor, Nov. 1962, Taylor Records, RG 218, NARA.

110. Summary Record of the 517th Meeting of the National Security Council, 12 September 1963, *FRUS, 1961–1963*, vol. 8, doc. 141, pp. 499–507; Oral Report, Net Evaluation Subcommittee, 27 August 1963, FOIA release, copy at NSArchive. In the event of Soviet preemption in 1964, the NESC estimated US

fatalities at 93 million, a number that rose to 134 million in 1968. If the US preempted in 1964, NESC estimated that 63 million Americans would die; in 1968, more than 108 million would die.

111. John Hines, Ellis M. Mishulovich, and John F. Shull, *Soviet Intentions 1965–1985*, vol. 1, *An Analytical Comparison of US-Soviet Assessments during the Cold War* (McLean, VA: BDM Corporation, 1995), FOIA release; Zubok, *Failed Empire*, 151–153; Table of US Ballistic Submarine Forces and Table of USSR Nuclear Warheads, Archive of Nuclear Data, National Resource Defense Council, http://www.nrdc.org/nuclear/nudb/datab5.asp and http://www.nrdc.org/nuclear/nudb/datab10.asp (accessed 7 December 2014).

112. For "mutual deterrence," see, e.g., Lawrence Freedman, *The Evolution of Nuclear Strategy*, 3rd ed. (New York: St. Martin's Press, 2003), 234; Donald G. Brennan, "Mutual Deterrence and Strategic Arms Limitation in Soviet Policy," *International Security* 3, no. 3 (Winter 1978–1979): 193–198.

113. Mitchell B. Lerner, *The Pueblo Incident: A Spy Ship and the Failure of American Foreign Policy* (Lawrence: University Press of Kansas, 2002), 125–130; Strategic Air Command, *Four Crises*.

114. "Airborne Alert Indoctrination Program," 5 December 1965, and "B-52 Airborne Alert," 18 December 1965, docs. NH00924 and NH00925, *DNSA*; Memo for the President, subj: The Strategic Aircraft Program, 11 November 1964, copy at NSArchive; Sagan, *Limits of Safety*, 178–179.

115. Office of the Historian, Headquarters Strategic Air Command, *History of Strategic Air Command, FY 1969*, Historical Study no. 116 (Offutt Air Force Base, NE: Historical Division, Strategic Air Command, 1970) (hereafter cited as *SAC History FY 69*), 117; Strategic Air Command, *SAC Alert System, 1956–1970*.

116. Strategic Air Command, *SAC Alert System, 1956–1970*, 57–58; *SAC History FY 69*, 116–122; US Air Force, Strategic Air Command, *History of Strategic Air Command, FY 1970, Historical Study no. 117* (Offutt Air Force Base, NE: Strategic Air Command Office of the Historian, 1971), 138–140.

117. Tannenwald, *Nuclear Taboo*, 192, 206, and 211–212.

118. JCS, quoted in ibid., 196, and also see 192, 193, 194–195, and 200.

119. William P. Bundy to the Secretary, 26 April 1964, subj: Your April 19 Morning Discussion with Ambassador Lodge, Manila (SEATO) Taipei and Saigon, 20–29 April 1964, vol. 13, box 343, Substantive Miscellaneous, Executive Secretariat Conference Files, RG 59, NARA; MemCon, 18 April 1964, subj: Discussion of Action against the North, folder (1): Special Papers—April–June 1964, box 16, Subject files of the Assistant Secretary of State for East Asian and Pacific Affairs, 1961–1974, RG 59, NARA; Ambassador Thompson to the Secretary, subj: China Study, 15 July 1965, folder: Miscellaneous, box 325, Policy Planning Council Records, Subject and Country Files, 1965–1969, RG 59, NARA; MemCon, 27 August 1965, subj: Meeting on China Study, Pol 1–3 Chicom, box 11, Formerly Top Secret Central Foreign Policy Files, 1965–1966, RG 59, NARA.

120. Tannenwald, *Nuclear Taboo*, 192, 197, 198, 203, 204, 205, and 207.

121. Memo, Ball to Rusk, McNamara, and Bundy, 5 October 1964, subj: How Valid Are the Assumptions Underlying Our Vietnam Policies?, reprinted in *Atlantic Monthly* 230, no. 1 (July 1972): 36–49.

122. Memo, Ball to Johnson, 13 February 1965, subj: Vietnam, 1965, *FRUS, 1964–1968*, vol. 2, doc. 73, p. 255.

123. Memo, CIA Office of National Estimates to the Director, subj: Use of Nuclear Weapons in the Vietnam War, 18 March 1966," CIA FOIA website, http://www.foia.cia.gov/sites/default/files/document_conversions/89801 /DOC_0001166479.pdf (accessed 7 December 2014).

124. Tannenwald, *Nuclear Taboo*, 214–218. Also see "Targeting Ho Chi Minh Trail," at the Nautilus Institute website, http://nautilus.org/essentially -annihilated/essentially-annihilated-targeting-ho-chi-minh-trail/#axzz2tsM8 smfo (accessed 7 December 2014).

125. Tannenwald, *Nuclear Taboo*, 221–227.

Chapter 2. The Madman Theory

1. Quoted in H. R. Haldeman, with Joseph DiMona, *The Ends of Power* (New York: Times Books, 1978), 82–83.

2. "What the President Saw," 49–50. For Nixon's concept of "negative incentives," see, e.g., MemCon, Nixon, Thompson, and Kissinger, 17 October 1969, folder: MemCon—The President, Sir Robert Thompson, et al., 17 October 1969, box 1023, National Security Council Files (NSCF): Presidential/Henry A. Kissinger (HAK) MemCons, RNPL.

3. Nixon, quoted in "What the President Saw," 50–51.

4. Eisenhower, quoted in "President . . . Declines to Rule Out a Nuclear War," *New York Times*, 11 March 1959.

5. A local newspaper obtained a tape recording of Nixon's off-the-record remarks; see "What Dick Nixon Told Southern Delegates," *Miami Herald*, 7 August 1968, 1 and 22A. Nixon continued to allude to this story in public speeches during the 1968 presidential campaign and on other occasions after the war; see, e.g., *New York Times*, 8 October 1968; "What the President Saw," 50; also see Haldeman, *Ends of Power*, 82–83.

6. Oval Office Conversation no. 460-23, Nixon and Henry Brandon, 4:01–5:08 p.m., 26 February 1971, WHT, RNPL.

7. Nixon, *RN*, 129.

8. "What the President Saw," 51. However, in the mid-1980s, when he wanted to ingratiate himself with the Reagan administration, which openly talked about waging nuclear war, Nixon added, "Yet nuclear weapons were safe with him" (i.e., if they were safe with Khrushchev, they are safe with Reagan, who also threatens).

9. Nixon, *RN*, 203, 486.

10. Quoted in Haldeman, *Ends of Power*, 82–83. In addition to Haldeman,

earlier mentions or discussions of the Madman Theory include: Ellsberg, "Call to Mutiny"; Burr and Kimball, "Nixon's Secret Nuclear Alert"; Hersh, *Price of Power*; Raymond L. Garthoff, *Détente and Confrontation: American-Soviet Relations from Nixon to Reagan*, rev. ed. (Washington, DC: Brookings Institution, 1994); Joan Hoff, *Nixon Reconsidered* (New York: Basic Books, 1994); Kimball, "'Peace with Honor': Richard Nixon and the Diplomacy of Threat and Symbolism," chap. 8 in *Shadow on the White House: Presidents and the Vietnam War, 1945–1975*, ed. David L. Anderson (Lawrence: University Press of Kansas, 1993); Kimball, *Nixon's Vietnam War*; Kimball, *Vietnam War Files*; Szulc, *Illusion of Peace*.

11. Richard Whalen, *Catch the Falling Flag: A Republican's Challenge to His Party* (Boston: Houghton Mifflin, 1972), 26–27 (emphasis in original).

12. Herbert G. Klein, *Making It Perfectly Clear* (New York: Doubleday, 1980), 399; William Safire, *Before the Fall: An Inside View of the Pre-Watergate White House* (New York: Doubleday, 1975), 48 and 368; Leonard Garment, *Crazy Rhythm* (New York: Times Books, 1997), 174 and 176–177.

13. Winston Lord, interview by Kimball, 5 December 1994, Washington, DC. Besides Nixon and Kissinger, the three people Lord said would have been in the know about considerations of nuclear weapons use but whom he did not name would probably have been Haig, Robinson, and possibly Haldeman. See also Lord, quoted in Gerald S. and Deborah H. Strober, eds., *Nixon: An Oral History of His Presidency* (New York: HarperCollins, 1994), 178.

14. For more about Nixon's and Kissinger's understanding of ferocity, also see *FRUS, 1969–1976*, vol. 8, docs. 59, 124, and 125, pp. 208, 452, 458, 459, and 463; Memo, Kissinger to Nixon, n.d., subj: Contingency Military Operations against North Vietnam, folder: Vietnam—Operation Pruning Knife [1 of 2], box 123, NSCF: Vietnam Subject Files, RNPL (this memo may have been a draft and not sent to Nixon); MemCon, Ford, Kissinger, Scowcroft, 14 May 1975, subj: Mayaguez, folder: May 14, 1975, box 11, NSA Memoranda of Conversation—Ford Administration, 16 April 1975—Cabinet Meeting, Gerald R. Ford Library (GFL).

15. Harlan K. Ullman and James P. Wade, Jr., with L. A. Edney, Frederick Franks, Jr., Charles Horner, Jonathan Howe, and Keith Brendley, *Shock and Awe: Achieving Rapid Dominance*, prepared by Defense Group, Inc., for the National Defense University, 1996, xxiv, http://www.dodccrp.org/files/Ullman_Shock .pdf (accessed 7 December 2014). The key passages read: "Intimidation and compliance are the outputs we seek to obtain. The intent here is to impose a regime of shock and awe through delivery of instant and nearly incomprehensible levels of massive destruction directed at influencing society writ large. Through very selective, utterly brutal, ruthless, and rapid application of force to intimidate, the aim is to affect the will, perception, and understanding of the adversary. . . . The adversary becomes impotent and entirely vulnerable."

16. See, e.g., Executive Office Building (EOB), Conversation no. 329–42, Nixon and Kissinger, 1:00–2:00 p.m., 15 April 1972, WHT, RNPL; Memo,

Assistant Secretary of Defense for Systems Analysis Gardner Tucker, 10 August 1972, Department of Defense (DOD) MDR release.

17. See, e.g., Lawrence S. Wittner, *Confronting the Bomb: A Short History of the World Nuclear Disarmament Movement* (Stanford, CA: Stanford University Press, 2009).

18. Letter, Eisenhower to Churchill, 27 April 1956, *Papers of Dwight D. Eisenhower: The Presidency—The Middle Way*, vol. 16, p. 2139.

19. Burke, quoted and paraphrased in *Washington Post*, 5 May 1957.

20. McNamara, quoted in *New York Times*, 19 September 1967.

21. Khrushchev, quoted in *New York Times*, 1 June and 5 October 1959 and 17 January 1960. See also "madman" quotes from Georgy Malenkov, Georgy Zhukov, and Henry Cabot Lodge, in *New York Times*, 13 February 1955 and 15 February and 3 and 5 October 1959.

22. Draft memo, McNamara to Johnson, 6 December 1963, *FRUS, 1961–1963*, vol. 8, doc. 151, pp. 554–556. Earlier versions of the memo are dated 31 August and 13 November 1963. Also see Memo, Spurgeon M. Keeny Jr. to McGeorge Bundy, 22 November 1963, *FRUS, 1961–1963*, vol. 8, doc. 147, pp. 534–537. "Actual and credible second-strike capability" is from McNamara's speech to editors of United Press International, 18 September 1967, quoted in *New York Times*, 19 September 1967.

23. For "mutual deterrence," see, e.g., Freedman, *Evolution of Nuclear Strategy*, 234; Donald G. Brennan, "Mutual Deterrence and Strategic Arms Limitation in Soviet Policy," *International Security* 3, no. 3 (Winter 1978–1979): 193–198.

24. "A Nightmare Debate," *New York Times*, 19 September 1967.

25. Robert McNamara, *The Essence of Security: Reflections in Office* (New York: Harper & Row, 1968), 160.

26. Brennan was not so much a critic of nuclear deterrence as a critic of AD as a deterrent doctrine. He wanted "to escape from this MAD posture" by turning to "alternatives" such as putting emphasis on defense—as in the form of antiballistic missiles (ABMs)—and proceeding toward a corresponding reduction in offensive forces through arms control agreements. Critics of ABMs (including McNamara), however, argued that their development and deployment would serve to accelerate the offensive arms race; Donald Brennan, "Strategic Alternatives: I and II," *New York Times*, 24 and 25 May 1971.

27. See, e.g., "Foreign Relations: The Nixinger Report," *Time* 99, no. 8 (21 February 1972): 12–13.

28. The interviewer was historian Joan Hoff. See her chapter entitled "Richard M. Nixon: The Corporate Presidency" in *Leadership in the Modern Presidency*, ed. Fred I. Greenstein (Cambridge, MA: Harvard University Press, 1988), 185–189, and her book *Nixon Reconsidered*, 173–181.

29. Documented examples of this tactic can be found in subsequent chapters of this book.

30. EOB, Conversation no. 329–42, Nixon and Kissinger, 1:00–2:00 p.m., 15

April 1972, WHT, RNPL. For "good courtier," see Henry Kissinger, *White House Years* (Boston: Little, Brown, 1979), 302.

31. See, e.g., Hoff, "Richard M. Nixon," 185–189; Hoff, *Nixon Reconsidered,* 173–181.

32. Hersh, *Price of Power,* 52–53.

33. Haldeman interview, quoted in Walter Isaacson, *Kissinger: A Biography* (New York: Simon & Schuster, 1992), 164. In contrast, Jeremi Suri offers a sanitized version of Kissinger's Vietnam diplomacy in *Henry Kissinger and the American Century* (Cambridge, MA: Belknap Press, 2007), 216. He mentions Nixon's Madman Theory but then contrasts it with Kissinger's Vietnam diplomacy as if there were no relationship between the two.

34. Henry Kissinger, "Military Policy and Defense of the 'Grey Areas,'" *Foreign Affairs* 33, no. 3 (April 1955): 417, 419, 422, 424–425.

35. Henry Kissinger, *Nuclear Weapons and Foreign Policy* (New York: Harper & Brothers, 1957), 224 and 225–226. Kissinger wrote about the projection of uncertainty in this 1957 book, but his use of the phrase *uncertainty effect* may have first appeared in his 1961 book, *Necessity for Choice,* 52.

36. Kissinger, *Nuclear Weapons and Foreign Policy,* 172–173, 178, 182, and 190–194. About "calculated risks," Oskar Morgenstern wrote: "It is little wonder that terms are frequently employed that have the appearance of authority while behind them there is exactly nothing"; Morgenstern, *The Question of National Defense* (New York: Random House, 1959), 5. For critiques of Kissinger's views, see William Kaufman, "Crisis in Military Affairs," *World Politics* 10, no. 4 (July 1958): 579–603, and Morton Halperin, "Nuclear Weapons and Limited War," *Journal of Conflict Resolution* 5, no. 2 (June 1961): esp. 149 and 151–154.

37. Kissinger, *Necessity for Choice,* 40, 45, and 46.

38. Ibid. (emphasis added). Kissinger contradictorily argued that the Soviets were both "rationally" capable of discounting American threats of all-out nuclear war and simultaneously capable of making credible threats of all-out war—presumably because the Americans were more "responsible."

39. Henry Kissinger, "Editor's Introduction," *Problems of National Strategy: A Book of Readings* (New York: Praeger, 1965), 5–6. See also Kissinger, *American Foreign Policy* (New York: W. W. Norton, 1969), 61 and 69. For more on the lives and foreign policy views of Nixon and Kissinger, see Stephen Ambrose, *Nixon: The Education of a Politician, 1913–1962* (New York: Simon & Schuster, 1987), and Ambrose, *Nixon: The Triumph of a Politician, 1962–1972* (New York: Simon & Schuster, 1989); William Burr, ed., "Introduction," *The Kissinger Transcripts: The Top Secret Talks with Beijing and Moscow* (New York: New Press, 1998); Robert Dallek, *Nixon and Kissinger: Partners in Power* (New York: Harper Collins, 2007); Mario Del Pero, *The Eccentric Realist: Henry Kissinger and the Shaping of American Foreign Policy* (Ithaca, NY: Cornell University Press, 2006); Daniel Frick, *Reinventing Richard Nixon: A Cultural History of an American Obsession* (Lawrence: University Press of Kansas, 2008); Garthoff, *Détente and*

Confrontation; David Greenberg, *Nixon's Shadow: The History of an Image* (New York: W. W. Norton, 2004); Jussi Hanhimäki, *The Flawed Architect: Henry Kissinger and American Foreign Policy* (New York: Oxford University Press, 2004); Isaacson, *Kissinger*; Kimball, *Nixon's Vietnam War*; David Landau, *Kissinger: The Uses of Power* (Boston: Houghton Mifflin, 1972); Barbara Keys, "The Emotional Statesman," *Diplomatic History* 35, no. 4 (September 2011): 587–609; Bruce Mazlish, *Kissinger: The European Mind in American Policy* (New York: Basic Books, 1976); Herbert S. Parmet, *Richard Nixon and His America* (Boston: Little, Brown, 1990); Rick Perlstein, *Nixonland: The Rise of a President and the Fracturing of America* (New York: Scribner, 2008); Robert Schulzinger, *Henry Kissinger: Doctor of Diplomacy* (New York: Columbia University Press, 1989); Franz Schurmann, *The Foreign Politics of Richard Nixon: The Grand Design* (Berkeley: University of California Press, 1987); Melvin Small, *The Presidency of Richard Nixon* (Lawrence: University Press of Kansas, 1999); Jeremi Suri, *Henry Kissinger and the American Century*.

40. Isaacson, *Kissinger*, 87.

41. Morgenstern, *Question of National Defense*, 286.

42. Copies of Ellsberg's papers held by the authors. Also see Kimball, "Nixon, Kissinger, and the Madman Theory," chap. 4 in *Nixon's Vietnam War*.

43. See, e.g., Thomas Schelling, *The Strategy of Conflict* (Cambridge, MA: Harvard University Press, 1960). Begun in *Strategy of Conflict* and continuing in other publications, Schelling's work on "game theory as a unifying framework for the social sciences" earned him a Nobel Prize in Economics in 2005. Also see Jeffrey Kimball, "Did Thomas C. Schelling Invent the Madman Theory?," History News Network, 24 October 2005, http://historynewsnetwork.org/article/17183 (accessed 7 December 2014).

44. Voltaire, *A Philosophical Dictionary from the French*, vol. 4 (London: Hunt, 1824), 103.

45. "The Rolling Stone Interview: Dan Ellsberg," *Rolling Stone*, 8 November 1973, 37–38.

46. Hersh, *Price of Power*, 49; Ellsberg repeated the story in *Secrets: A Memoir of Vietnam and the Pentagon Papers* (New York: Viking, 2002), 234–235.

47. Diary entries, 19 April 1969 and 13 May 1971, and Oval Office, Conversation no. 508–13, Nixon and Kissinger, 9:45 a.m.–12:04 p.m., 2 June 1971, WHT, RNPL.

48. William Burr, "The Nixon Administration, the 'Horror Strategy,' and the Search for Limited Nuclear Options, 1969–1972: Prelude to the Schlesinger Doctrine," *Journal of Cold War Studies* 7, no. 3 (Summer 2005): 34–78.

49. Kaplan, *Wizards of Armageddon*, 10.

50. On the book, movie script, motion picture, and real-life models for Dr. Strangelove, see, e.g., Richard Gidd Powers's "new introduction" to Peter George, *Dr. Strangelove: Or, How I Learned to Stop Worrying and Love the Bomb* (Boston:

Gregg Press, 1979); Paul Boyer, "Dr. Strangelove," *Past Imperfect: History Ac-cording to the Movies,* ed. Mark C. Carnes, Ted Mico, John Miller-Monzon, and David Rubel (New York: Henry Holt, 1995), 266–269; Kaplan, *Wizards of Armageddon,* chap. 14; P. D. Smith, *Doomsday Men: The Real Dr. Strangelove and the Dream of the Superweapon* (New York: St. Martin's Press, 2007), 422–435; Grant B. Stillman, "Two of the MADdest Scientists: Where Strangelove Meets Dr. No," *Film History* 20, no. 4 (2008): 487–500; David Bromwich, "Happy Birthday, Dr. Strangelove!," *New York Review of Books,* 3 April 2014, http://www .nybooks.com/articles/archives/2014/apr/03/happy-birthday-dr-strangelove / (accessed 22 December 2014). A rival movie to *Dr. Strangelove,* which was re-leased in late January 1964, was *Fail Safe,* released in early October 1964 and pre-ceded by the book *Fail Safe* (New York: McGraw-Hill, 1962), by Eugene Burdick and Harvey Wheeler. Both *Dr. Strangelove* and *Fail Safe* were roughly based on Peter George's *Red Alert* (New York: Ace Books, 1958). The *Fail Safe* movie character of Walter Grotoschele, played by Walter Matthau, resembled Kissinger in several ways, but Tony Shaw and Denise J. Youngblood, *Cinematic Cold War: The American and Soviet Struggle for Hearts and Minds* (Lawrence: University Press of Kansas, 2010), 147–149, compared Grotoschele to Herman Kahn.

51. See, e.g., Margot Henriksen, *Dr. Strangelove's America: Society and Cul-ture in the Atomic Age* (Berkeley: University of California Press, 1997), xiv–xix; Kaplan, *Wizards of Armageddon,* 231.

52. See Stephen Hilgartner, Richard C. Bell, and Rory O'Connor, *Nukespeak: Nuclear Language, Visions, and Mindset* (San Francisco: Sierra Club Books, 1982).

53. C. Wright Mills, *The Causes of World War Three* (New York: Simon & Schuster, 1958), chap. 13.

54. William Burr, "'Nobody Wins a Nuclear War' but 'Success' Is Possible," NSArchive Electronic Briefing Book no. 336, 19 February 2011, http://www2 .gwu.edu/~nsarchiv/nukevault/ebb336/index.htm (accessed 8 December 2014).

55. E-mail message, Luu Huynh to Kimball, 19 September 2009; Nguyen Vu Tung, interview by Kimball, 2 February 1995, Oslo, Norway.

Chapter 3. The "Big Game" and the Bombing of Cambodia

1. Kissinger, paraphrased by Murray Marder in Conversation, Kissinger and Marder, 14 July 1969, Murray Marder Papers, Background Briefing Files on Vietnam 1969, NSArchive.

2. Nguyen Co Thach, interview by Kimball, 24 September 1994, Hanoi.

3. Nixon's Notes, 15 and 18 February 1972, folder: China Notes, box 7, Presi-dent's Personal File 1969–74, RNPL; Haldeman, *Ends of Power,* 81.

4. Telcon transcript, 8 March 1969, 10:45 a.m., Henry A. Kissinger Telephone Conversation Transcripts, RNPL (also held at the NSArchive; hereafter HAK Telcons); Diary entry, 20 March and 8 October 1969, HRHD; Minutes of NSC

Meeting, 25 January 1969, and Memo, Kissinger to Nixon, 3 April 1969, *FRUS, 1969–1976*, vol. 6, doc. 10, p. 36, and doc. 52, p. 181. Also see Kimball, *Nixon's Vietnam War*, 100–102.

5. Telcon transcript, Kissinger and Nixon, 10:45 a.m., 8 March 1969, HAK Telcons.

6. "Big game" from Telcon transcript, Nixon and Kissinger, 9:45 a.m., 5 April 1969, HAK Telcons. For "game plan," see Memo, Kissinger to Nixon, 8 March 1969, subj: Reflections on De-escalation, folder: March 1969, box 956, NSCF: Alexander M. Haig Chronological Files, RNPL. Fighting while negotiating was yet another strategy—along with the principle of threatening excessive force—with an ancient pedigree. E.g., the Hittites, for whom there are more surviving records than for many other ancients, had the practice of sending an envoy to their enemies with two sets of instructions, a "tablet of war" and a "tablet of peace," one threatening the enemy but the other proposing a deal should the threat fail; Barry Strauss, *The Trojan War: A New History* (New York: Simon & Schuster, 2006), 71.

7. Ellsberg, *Secrets*, 233; Isaacson, *Kissinger*, 162.

8. Ellsberg Options Paper, 27 December 1968 (held by authors) [p. 2]; see also "Vietnam Policy Alternatives," [December 1968], folder 10: Vietnam—RAND, box 3, Henry A. Kissinger Office Files (hereafter HAK Office Files): HAK Staff File—Transition, RNPL. This definition of victory was also reflected in National Security Study Memorandum 1, which represented the Nixon government's understanding; see Revised Summary of Responses to National Security Study Memorandum 1, 22 March 1969, *Documents of the National Security Council: Second Supplement* (Frederick, MD: University Publications of America, 1983), microfilm, reel 3, pp. 2, 24, 27, and 28. See also Minutes, NSC Meeting, 25 January 1969, *FRUS, 1969–1976*, vol. 6, doc. 10, p. 37. Henry Rowen, president of RAND, was also present at the first meeting between Ellsberg, Iklé, and Kissinger; Isaacson, *Kissinger*, 162.

9. Ellsberg Options Paper [p. 6]; see also "Vietnam Policy Alternatives" [December 1968], folder 10: Vietnam—RAND, box 3, Henry A. Kissinger Staff File—Transition, HAK Office Files, RNPL.

10. Ellsberg Options Paper [p. 15].

11. Ibid. [p. 19]. Kissinger expressed similar sentiments and used similar words in Memo, Kissinger to Nixon, 18 September 1971, subj: Vietnam, *FRUS, 1969–1976*, vol. 7, doc. 257, p. 919.

12. Ellsberg Options Paper [p. 18].

13. Memo, Kissinger to Nixon, 24 January 1969, and NSSM 1, *FRUS, 1969–1976*, vol. 6, docs. 8 and 4, pp. 4–5 and 17; Memo, Kissinger to Nixon, 13 January 1969, subj: Vietnam Questions; Memo, Haig to Kissinger, 13 January 1969, subj: Vietnam Questions; and Memo, Haig to Kissinger, 11 March 1969, subj: [misc.]—all in folder: Haig Vietnam File, vol. 1 (Jan.–March 1969), box 1007, NSCF: Alexander M. Haig Special File, RNPL.

14. Telcon transcript, Kissinger and Wheeler, 22 January 1969, HAK Telcons.

15. Minutes, NSC Meeting, 25 January 1969, *FRUS, 1969–1976*, vol. 6, doc. 10, p. 36.

16. Ibid., p. 40.

17. Ibid., p. 41.

18. See, e.g., Revised Summary of NSSM 1, reel 3, p. 27.

19. Memo, Kissinger to Nixon, 8 March 1969, "Reflections on De-escalation," folder: March 1969, box 956, NSCF: Haig Chronological Files, RNPL.

20. Quoted in Whalen, *Catch the Falling Flag,* 202. For Nixon's preinaugural views about Vietnam, see *Nixon Speaks Out: Major Speeches and Statements by Richard Nixon in the Presidential Campaign of 1968* (New York: Nixon-Agnew Campaign Committee, 25 October 1968), 6, 90, 93–100, 103–106, 229–232, and 238–244; Richard Nixon, "Asia after Viet Nam," *Foreign Affairs* 46, no. 1 (October 1967): 111; "What the President Saw"; Whalen, *Catch the Falling Flag,* 12, 25, 28, 29, 31, 76–77, 132–140, 202, and 283–294.

21. Henry Kissinger, "The Viet Nam Negotiations," *Foreign Affairs* 47, no. 2 (January 1969): 218–219; also see Kissinger, *White House Years,* 228.

22. Memo, Kissinger to Nixon, 20 March 1969, subj: Vietnam Situation and Options, folder 7, box 89, NSCF: Vietnam Subject Files, RNPL.

23. Telcon transcript, Nixon and Kissinger, 12 May 1969, 11:30 p.m., HAK Telcons; Kissinger, *White House Years,* 477.

24. Quotations from Minutes, NSC Meeting, 25 January 1969, *FRUS, 1969–1976,* vol. 6, doc. 10, p. 37.

25. The two-, three-, and five-year figures for the desired interval are from MemCon, Kissinger and Boris Sedov, 2 January 1969, *FRUS, 1969–1976.* vol. 12, doc. 1, p. 2; Nixon's comments in a conversation with representatives from Burma, Ceylon, Laos, Malaysia, Nepal, and Singapore, and the US Ambassador to Saigon on 29 July 1969, *FRUS, 1969–1976,* vol. 6, doc. 102, p. 320. "Decent chance" is from MemCon of Kissinger's luncheon with foreign correspondents, 4 November 1972, folder: Press, TV, News, etc., Nov 1972—[2 of 2], box 379, NSCF: Subject Files, RNPL. Documentary excerpts and additional citations of evidence about the decent interval can be found in works by Jeffrey Kimball listed in the bibliography.

26. Nixon, *No More Vietnams,* 211–213.

27. Hersh, *Price of Power,* 47, said that Kissinger had begun writing the article in the summer of 1968. The State Department telegrammed a draft of Kissinger's manuscript to Averell Harriman in Paris on 18 December, which may or may not suggest that Kissinger revised it after Nixon appointed him as national security adviser; Draft article, folder: Henry Kissinger, box 481, Averell Harriman Papers, Manuscript Division, Library of Congress, Washington, DC.

28. Kissinger, "Viet Nam Negotiations," 231–234 (emphasis added).

29. Kissinger, *White House Years,* 470.

30. See the earlier discussion of the RAND study.

31. Kissinger, *White House Years*, 230–234.

32. Paper (by Halperin), "The Value of a Mutual Withdrawal Strategy," 22 June 1968, folder: Vietnam, box 10, Morton Halperin Papers, LBJL. Nixon agreed with this logic; he scribbled this message to his staff concerning similar remarks made by Walt W. Rostow: "[The United States must therefore] withdraw in [a] way Asians can take over their defense, not withdraw in [a] way Asians will collapse. The mistakes this generation makes will be paid for by the next generation"; Note, n.d., folder: Vietnam-Rostow, box 16, WHSF: President's Personal File, 1969–74, RNPL.

33. "Courses of Action in Southeast Asia, 21 November 1964," *FRUS, 1964–1968*, vol. 1, doc. 418, p. 1514.

34. Ellsberg, *Secrets*, 229.

35. Tony Lake, telephone interview by Kimball, 15 October 2001, and Roger Morris, telephone interview by Kimball, 9 February 2007.

36. See, e.g., Allan E. Goodman, *The Lost Peace: America's Search for a Negotiated Settlement of the Vietnam War* (Stanford, CA: Hoover Institution Press, 1978), 81–85 and 167.

37. Unnamed GVN cabinet minister speaking in 1970, quoted in ibid., 84.

38. See, e.g., Luu Van Loi and Nguyen Anh Vu, *Le Duc Tho–Kissinger Negotiations in Paris* (Hanoi: Thê´Giò Publishers, 1996); Ang Cheng Guan, *Ending the Vietnam War: The Vietnamese Communists' Perspective* (London: Routledge-Curzon, 2004).

39. COSVN Resolution no. 9, July 1969, *Vietnam Documents and Research Notes Series: Translation and Analysis of Significant Viet Cong/North Vietnamese Documents* (on microfilm) (Bethesda, MD: University Publications of America, 1991), 12–14. COSVN was the American acronym for Central Office for South Vietnam, which was an American transliteration of the Vietnamese Central Committee Directorate for the South.

40. On the latter point, in mid-1968 Kissinger had secretly passed information to Nixon's presidential election camp about the trajectory of the behind-the-scene talks in Paris that had led to the bombing halt and an agreement to establish formal peace talks between the warring parties. For the historiography of this episode, see Kimball, "Vietnam War Nixonography," *Passport* 43, no. 3 (January 2013): 27. Also see Kimball, *Nixon's Vietnam War*, 56–62, and for a recent account, see Ken Hughes, *Chasing Shadows: The Nixon Tapes, the Chennault Affair, and the Origins of Watergate* (Charlottesville: University of Virginia Press, 2014), especially 4–10 and 45–46.

41. Chronology of US–DRV Negotiations, 1969–1973 (Private Meetings), from *The Foreign Ministry Internal Circulation Chronology on Diplomatic Struggle and International Mobilization in the Anti-American War, 1954–1975* (General Task Force—1987 [Ban Tông Kêt—1987]. Held by the authors). See also the DRV's Four Points (Apr 1965) and the NLF's Ten Points (May 1969) in *Vietnam*

and America: A Documented History, ed. Marvin E. Gettleman, Jane Franklin, Marilyn B. Young, and H. Bruce Franklin (New York: Grove Press, 1995), 276–279 and 430–433; Robert K. Brigham, *Guerrilla Diplomacy: The NLF's Foreign Relations and the Viet Nam War* (Ithaca, NY: Cornell University Press, 1999), chap. 5.

42. For "backstage," see, e.g., Cable, Politburo to Bay Cuong (COSVN Party Secretary), 12 December 1968, in Merle Pribbenow, trans., "North Vietnam's 'Talk-Fight' Strategy and the 1968 Peace Negotiations with the United States," *Cold War International History Project Bulletin*, no. 17 [n.d., ca. 2010]: doc. 13, p. 44.

43. Memo, Kissinger to Nixon, 20 March 1969, subj: Vietnam Situation and Options, folder 7, box 89, NSCF: Vietnam Subject Files, RNPL.

44. See, e.g., Minutes, NSC Meeting, 25 January 1969, *FRUS, 1969–1976*, vol. 6, doc. 10, p. 37.

45. Telcon transcript, Nixon and Kissinger, 11 March 1969, approx. 10:00 p.m., HAK Telcons.

46. Ibid.

47. Memo, Kissinger to Nixon, 20 March 1969, subj: Vietnam Situation and Options, folder 7, box 89, NSCF: Vietnam Subject Files, RNPL.

48. Minutes of NSC Meeting, 12 September 1969, subj: Vietnam, *FRUS, 1969–1976*, vol. 6, doc. 120, p. 400.

49. See, e.g., Minutes of NSC Meeting, 28 March 1969, *FRUS, 1969–1976*, vol. 6, doc. 49, p. 168.

50. Memo for the record, 8 March 1969, subj: Lodge/Thuy meeting, folder 2, box 182, NSCF: Paris Talks/Meetings/Memos, RNPL; Loi and Vu, *Le Duc Tho–Kissinger Negotiations*, 76–78; Telcon, Nixon and Kissinger, 8 March 1969, 6:25 p.m., HAK Telcons.

51. Memo, Kissinger to Nixon, n.d. [ca. 17–20 March 1969], subj: Vietnam Negotiations Papers for the NSC; Minutes of NSC Meeting, 28 March 1969; NSDM 9, 1 April 1969; Memo, Kissinger to Nixon, 3 April 1969, subj: Vietnam Problem—all in *FRUS, 1969–1976*, vol. 6, docs. 46, 49, 51, and 52, pp. 154–161 and 179–184. Also see Memo, Kissinger to Nixon, 8 March 1969, subj: Reflections on De-escalation, folder: March 1969, box 956, NSCF: Haig Chronological Files, RNPL; and Memo, Kissinger to Nixon, 20 March 1969, subj: Vietnam Situation and Options, folder 7, box 89, NSCF: Vietnam Subject Files, RNPL.

52. Memo, Kissinger to Nixon, 27 March 1969, subj: Covert Support, *FRUS, 1969–1976, Nixon: Vietnam*, vol. 6, doc. 47, pp. 161–163.

53. "Viet 3rd Redraft," March 30, 1968, in Whalen, *Catch the Falling Flag*, 284–286.

54. There is a large literature about the indigenous peasant and Communist revolutions in Vietnam; among the most recent works are David W. P. Elliott, *The Vietnamese War: Revolution and Social Change in the Mekong Delta, 1930–1945*,

2 vols. (Armonk, NY: M. E. Sharpe, 2003), and David Hunt, *Vietnam's Southern Revolution: From Peasant Insurrection to Total War* (Amherst: University of Massachusetts Press, 2008).

55. Kissinger, "Viet Nam Negotiations," 219, 220, and 229. Also see Garthoff, *Détente and Confrontation*, 279–281.

56. Garthoff, *Détente and Confrontation*, 32–37. Also see William Bundy, *A Tangled Web: The Making of Foreign Policy in the Nixon Presidency* (New York: Hill and Wang, 1998); Burr, *Kissinger Transcripts*; Michael B. Froman, *The Development of the Idea of Détente: Coming to Terms* (New York: St. Martin's Press, 1991), chaps. 1 and 2; Jussi Hanhimäki and Mary E. Sarotte, in *Nixon in the World: American Foreign Relations, 1969–1977*, ed. Frederik Logevall and Andrew Preston (New York: Oxford University Press, 2008), chaps. 1 and 7; Kimball, *Nixon's Vietnam War*, chap. 3; Keith Nelson, *The Making of Détente: Soviet-American Relations in the Shadow of Vietnam* (Baltimore, MD: Johns Hopkins University Press, 1995). For more on strategic arms control, see David Tal, "'Absolutes' and 'Stages' in the Making and Applications of Nixon's SALT Policy," *Diplomatic History* 37, no. 5 (November 2013): 1090–1116.

57. Garthoff, *Détente and Confrontation*, 33 and 36.

58. Minutes of NSC Meeting, 21 May 1969, *DNSA*.

59. MemCon, Kissinger and Sedov, 2 January 1969, *FRUS: 1969–1976*. vol. 12, doc. 1, pp. 2–3.

60. Ibid.

61. MemCon (USSR), Dobrynin and Kissinger, 14 February 1969, in *Soviet-American Relations: The Détente Years, 1969–1972*, ed. David C. Geyer, Douglas E. Selvage, and Edward C. Keefer (Washington, DC: US Government Printing Office, 2007), doc. 3, p. 5.

62. MemCon (US), Nixon and Dobrynin, 17 February 1969, in ibid., doc. 5, p. 9.

63. MemCon (USSR), Kissinger and Dobrynin, 21 February 1969, in ibid., doc. 8, pp. 22–23.

64. Ibid., p. 23 (emphasis added; in his report, Dobrynin wrote in parentheses: "Kissinger stressed the word 'immediately'").

65. MemCon, Nixon and Dobrynin, 14 May 1969, in ibid., doc. 22, p. 62.

66. Nixon, "Asia after Viet Nam" 121–123; Alexander Haig, *Inner Circles: How America Changed the World: A Memoir* (New York: Warner Books, 1992), 257.

67. Memo, Nixon to Kissinger, 1 February 1969, *FRUS, 1969–1976*, vol. 17, doc. 3, p. 7.

68. Kissinger, *White House Years*, 169 and 179. Also see William Burr, "The Sino-Soviet Border Conflict, 1969: US Reactions and Diplomatic Maneuvers," NSArchive Electronic Briefing Book, 12 June 2011, http://www2.gwu.edu/~nsarchiv/NSAEBB/NSAEBB49/index2.html (accessed 8 December 2014).

69. Paraphrased in Loi and Vu, *Le Duc Tho–Kissinger Negotiations*, 80.

70. For some of the efforts during 1969 to communicate with Beijing, see William Burr, "Sino-American Relations, 1969: The Sino-Soviet Border War and

Steps toward Rapprochement," *Cold War History* 1 (2001): 73–112. For doubts and hesitations, see Minutes of the Senior Review Group Meeting, 15 May 1969, *FRUS, 1969–1976*, vol. 17, doc. 13, pp. 31–39; Garthoff, *Détente and Confrontation*, 243–250.

71. MemCons (USSR), Kissinger and Dobrynin, 21 February, 11 March, and 2 April, and Telegram, Dobrynin to Soviet Foreign Ministry, 13 March 1969, in *Soviet-American Relations*, docs. 8, 11, 14, and 16, pp. 24, 37, 40, and 49.

72. See, e.g., Kissinger, *White House Years*, 261.

73. Memo, Laird to Kissinger, 21 February 1969, subj: Preliminary Draft of Potential Military Actions re Vietnam, DOD MDR (emphasis added); also see folder: Haig's Vietnam File—vol. 1 (January–March 1969), box 1007, NSCF: Haig Special Files, RNPL; President Nixon's Daily Diary, 27 January 1969, RNPL. "Military settlement" was code for a US-DRV negotiated agreement on mutual withdrawal, whereas "political settlement" referred to an RVN-NLF negotiated agreement on political issues, such as the status of government in Saigon.

74. MemCon, 30 January 1969, enclosed in Memo, Haig to Kissinger, 6 February 1969, subj: Actions Resulting from the Meeting at the Pentagon between Dr. Kissinger, Secretary Laird, and General Wheeler, 30 January 1969, folder: 1–15 February, box 955, NSCF: Haig Chronological Files, RNPL (this document is reprinted in *FRUS, 1969–1976*, vol. 6., doc. 12, pp. 44–46).

75. MemCon, 30 January 1969.

76. *New York Times*, 3 November and 15 December 1967. Proposals for escalating US operations in Cambodia and Laos were standard in the discourse of hawkishly inclined policymakers, military strategists, and politicians.

77. See, e.g., question 10 in NSSM 1, *FRUS, Nixon, 1969–1976*, vol. 6, doc. 4, pp. 4–10, and Revised Summary, NSSM 1, 22 March 1969, reel 3, pp. 2, 24, 27, and 28. The Cambodian question was not in a preparatory NSSM memo from Haig to Kissinger, 13 January 1969, subj: Vietnam Questions, folder: Haig Vietnam File, vol. 1 (Jan.–March 1969), box: 1007, NSCF: Haig Special File, RNPL This memo also indicates that the questions in NSSM 1 were drafted based on the mixed results of the RAND survey.

78. Memo, Nixon to Kissinger, 1 February 1969, *FRUS, 1969–1976*, vol. 6, doc 15, p. 52; see also Kissinger, *White House Years*, 240.

79. Memo, Kissinger to Nixon, 19 February 1969, subj: Consideration of B-52 Options against COSVN Headquarters, and Telegram, Dept. of State to Saigon Embassy, 22 February 1969, both in *FRUS, 1969–1976*, vol. 6, docs. 22 and 24, pp. 68–74 and 77n3; William Shawcross, *Sideshow: Kissinger, Nixon and the Destruction of Cambodia*, rev. ed. (New York: Simon & Schuster, 1987), 19–20; William M. Hammond, *The Military and the Media* (Washington, DC: Center of Military History, US Army, 1996), 64–65; Kissinger, *White House Years*, 241.

80. Memo, Kissinger to Nixon, 11 February 1969, subj: Meeting between the President, Secretary Laird, and General McConnell on Vietnam Scheduled for

11 February 1969 at 3:15 p.m., folder 8-F: Reappraisal of Vietnam Commitment, vol. 1, box 64, NSCF: Vietnam Subject Files, RNPL.

81. Kissinger, *White House Years*, 242; for "tasteless," see p. 247. See also Isaacson, *Kissinger*, 172; Hammond, *Military and Media*, 64–65; Kenton Clymer, *The United States and Cambodia, 1969–2000: A Troubled Relationship* (New York: RoutledgeCurzon, 2004), 9–21.

82. Memo, Laird to Kissinger, 21 February 1969 [subj: attachments re potential military actions], DOD MDR (emphasis added). Haig paraphrased these options thus: "1. Actual or feigned airborne/amphibious operations against several objectives in NVN. 2. An actual or feigned airborne/airmobile expedition in force against enemy's [lines of communication] in Laos and Cambodia. 3. Actual or feigned renewed and expanded air and naval operations against NVN. 4. Actual or feigned subversion of the population and preparation for active resistance by the people against the Hanoi regime. 5. A plan for actual or feigned technical escalation of war against [the] North (nuclear) [*sic*]"—Memo, Haig to Kissinger, 2 March 1969, subj: Memorandum from Secretary Laird Enclosing Preliminary Draft of Potential Military Actions re Vietnam, folder: Haig's Vietnam File vol. 1 (Jan.–March 1969), box 1007, NSCF: Haig Special File, RNPL.

83. Memo, Laird to Kissinger, 21 February 1969 [subj: attachments re potential military actions], DOD MDR.

84. Ibid.

85. Memo, Richard C. Steadman (Deputy Asst. Sec. of Defense) to Packard, 6 March 1969, subj: Papers on Possible Retaliation and Enemy Attrition Rates, DOD MDR. COSVN referred to the attacks as the Phase X Spring Offensive; in *White House Years* and elsewhere, Kissinger sometimes referred to the offensive as Mini-Tet and also consistently referred to combined Viet Cong/NVA attacks as "North Vietnamese" attacks. On the Vietnamese offensive and press coverage, see Hammond, *Military and Media*, 65–69.

86. Loi and Vu, *Le Duc Tho–Kissinger Negotiations*, 75.

87. Ibid., 74–76; also see COSVN Resolution no. 9, July 1969; Merle L. Pribbenow, trans., *Victory in Vietnam: The Official History of the People's Army of Vietnam, 1954–1975*, by the Military History Institute of Vietnam (Lawrence: University Press of Kansas, 2002), 244–252.

88. See, e.g., David Burns Sigler, *Vietnam Battle Chronology: US Army and Marine Corps Combat Operations, 1965–1973* (Jefferson, NC: McFarland, 1992), 86–93; David W. P. Elliott, *Vietnamese War*, vol. 2, chap. 20; Clymer, *United States and Cambodia*, 17–18.

89. Memo, Kissinger to Nixon, 6 March 1969, subj: Analysis of Current VC/NVA Offensive, folder 6: Communist Offensive, 22 February 1969, box 68, NSCF: Vietnam Subject Files, RNPL. Also see *Vietnam Documents and Research Notes Series*, doc. 62, p. 1; Philip B. Davidson, *Vietnam at War: The History, 1946–1975* (New York: Oxford University Press, 1988), 591; Kissinger, *White House Years*, 242; Hammond, *Military and Media*, 65–67.

90. Loi and Vu, *Le Duc Tho–Kissinger Negotiations*, 76.

91. "Instincts" and "seething" are in Kissinger, *White House Years*, 242–243, but also see Nixon's comment in *RN*, 380. "Population centers" is in Telcon transcript, Kissinger and Dobrynin, 22 February 1969, 2:45 p.m., HAK Telcons, and *Soviet-American Relations*, 25n4.

92. Kissinger, *White House Years*, 242–243.

93. Ibid.; Hersh, *Price of Power*, 54.

94. Diary entry, 24 February 1969, HRHD; see also Hersh, *Price of Power*, 60.

95. Kissinger, *White House Years*, 243.

96. Nixon, *RN*, 382

97. *The Gallup Poll, 1935–1971*, vol. 3 (New York: Random House, 1971), 2189.

98. Memo, Kissinger to Nixon, 16 March 1969, subj: Breakfast Plan, *FRUS, 1969–1976*, vol. 6, doc. 40, pp. 122–123; Telcon transcript, Kissinger and Nixon, 10:45 a.m., 8 March 1969, HAK Telcons.

99. B-52 crews en masse received the standard premission briefing about their targets in South Vietnam, then selected crews would be taken aside and told that shortly before they reached their objective, ground radar stations in South Vietnam would take over their final bombing run. Receiving special instructions by courier from Saigon, the ground radar crews would know that the targets were in Cambodia, and they and their computers would guide the big bombers to their real targets. After the mission, air crews would report routinely to the air force's command and control center about the success or failure of their missions "inside" South Vietnam. "Sensitive Operations in Southeast Asia, 1964–1973," and "Responses to Senator Harold Hughes," R. B. Furlong Papers, 168.7122–16 and 168.7122–20, Air Force Historical Research Agency (AFHRA), Maxwell Air Force Base, AL.

100. Memo, Kissinger to Nixon, 16 March 1969, subj: Breakfast Plan, *FRUS, 1969–1976*, vol. 6, doc. 40, pp. 122–123. *New York Times* reporter William Beecher broke the story of the secret bombing of Cambodia on 9 May, almost two months after its commencement. There was little follow-up in the press and little public interest in what Beecher had to say because the administration issued a strong denial and also because it appeared to some to be just another American bombing of another Southeast Asian jungle. Beecher, "Raids in Cambodia by US Un-protested," *New York Times*, 9 May 1969. Also see Beecher, "The Secret Bombing of Cambodia," *50 Years in Media: Changes in Journalism*, Harvard University, 2005, http://athome.harvard.edu/programs/fym/fym_video/fym_3 .html (accessed 8 December 2014).

101. Telcon transcript, Kissinger and Nixon, 10:45 a.m., 8 March 1969, HAK Telcons.

102. Kissinger, *White House Years*, 243.

103. Diary entry, 1 March 1969, HRHD; Telcon transcript, Kissinger and Nixon, 8 March 1969, 10:45 a.m., HAK Telcons. Kissinger claimed in *White House Years*, 244, that he had advised postponement because he believed the

timing was unfortunate: coming during the president's European sojourn, the bombing might have aroused antiwar demonstrations and dominated press briefings and private leadership meetings. These concerns may explain what Haldeman meant by "risk otherwise too great," yet "K very disappointed" seems to contradict Kissinger's claims for the advice he gave. See also Nixon, *RN*, 380; Diary entry, 24 February 1969, HRHD.

104. Kissinger, *White House Years*, 243–244; Isaacson, *Kissinger*, 173–174.

105. Memo, Kissinger to Laird, 3 March 1969, subj: Memorandum Enclosing Preliminary Draft of Potential Military Actions re Vietnam, folder 8-F, box 64, NSCF: Vietnam Subject Files, RNPL; MemCon, 30 January 1969, enclosed in Memo, Haig to Kissinger, 6 February 1969, subj: Actions Resulting from the Meeting at the Pentagon between Dr. Kissinger, Secretary Laird, and General Wheeler, 30 January 1969, folder: 1, box 955, NSCF: Haig Chronological Files, RNPL. Also see footnotes to document no. 12 in *FRUS, 1969–1976*, vol. 6, pp. 44–46.

106. Memo, Laird to Nixon, 4 March 1969, subj: Possible Responses to Enemy Activity in South Vietnam, folder 8-F, box 64, NSCF: Vietnam Subject Files, RNPL—also filed in DOD MDR. By psychological, Laird meant "to raise level of US casualties, to increase the level of dissent against the war here, to demonstrate their continued military capability, and to dramatize the inability of allied force to prevent them from striking targets of their choice."

107. Ibid. See also Memo for the Secretary of Defense, 3 March 1969, subj: Situation in Vietnam, DOD MDR.

108. Kissinger, *White House Years*, 245; Diary entry, 9 March 1969, HRHD.

109. News Conference, 4 March 1969, *Public Papers of the Presidents, Nixon: 1969*, 185–186.

110. Kissinger, *White House Years*, 245.

111. Appendix and Annex in Memo, Wheeler to Laird, 15 March 1969, subj: "Indicator" Actions against North Vietnam, DOD MDR.

112. Telcon transcript, Kissinger and Moorer, 7 March 1969, 5:30 p.m., HAK Telcons.

113. Appendix and Annex in Memo, Wheeler to Laird.

114. Memo, Haig to Kissinger, 11 March 1969, subj: [misc.], folder: Haig's Vietnam File, vol. 1 (Jan.–March 1969), box: 1007, NSCF: Haig Special File, RNPL; Annexes A and B in Memo, Wheeler to Laird, 15 March 1969, subj: "Indicator" Actions against North Vietnam; Memo, Wheeler to Laird, 20 October 1969, subj: Movement of Carrier Task Force on YANKEE STATION into Gulf of Tonkin in Connection with Test of Increased Readiness Posture, DOD MDR—with attachments.

115. Telcon transcripts, 8 March 1969, 10:45 a.m. and 6:25 p.m., HAK Telcons. Between these morning and early evening conversations, Nixon and Kissinger were also waiting for reports and assessments of Rogers's meeting with Dobrynin and the US delegation's introductory meeting in Paris with the DRV delegation—both scheduled to take place that day.

Notes to Pages 102-104

116. Ibid. Regarding "six months," Haldeman recalled that Nixon had expected an "acceptable" negotiated solution within the first six months of his presidency; Diary entry, 8 October 1969, HRHD. That would have been July 1969. It appears that the schedule had been extended in March.

117. Telcon transcript, Kissinger and Moorer, 7 March 1969, 5:30 p.m., HAK Telcons. This guess about the connection between canceling the Cambodia bombing and Berlin is based on a parenthetical remark ("Ref activity in Bonn") in Diary entry, 9 March 1969, HRHD (also see 1 March entry); see Paper Prepared by the NSC Staff, 11 March 1969, subj: Soviet Negotiating Interest on Berlin, and Editorial Note—both in *FRUS, 1969–1976*, vol. 40, docs. 18 and 19, pp. 51–57; Angela Stent, *From Embargo to Ostpolitik: The Political Economy of West-German–Soviet Relations, 1955–1980* (New York: Cambridge University Press, 1981), 157–159.

118. Diary entry, 9 March 1969, HRHD.

119. Telcon transcript, Kissinger and Nixon, 15 March 1969, 3:35 p.m., HAK Telcons; Memo for the Record (Nixon), subj: March 16 Rocket Attack on Saigon, 15 March, 1969, *FRUS, 1969–1976*, vol. 6, doc. 39, pp. 120–121. See also Kissinger, *White House Years*, 247. On ship movements, see Memo, Haig to Kissinger, 11 March 1969, folder: Haig's Vietnam File, vol. 1, box: 1007, NSCF: Haig Special File, NSCF, RNPL. In a later summation, the JCS wrote Kissinger that there had not been "any unusual or significant reaction by North Vietnam which could be interpreted as having been in response to the northward positioning of Task Force 77 units"; Memo, Wheeler to Laird, 20 October 1969.

120. Memo, Kissinger to Nixon, 8 March 1969, *FRUS, 1969–1976*, vol. 6, doc. 34, p. 98. Cf. Nixon's and Kissinger's conflicting accounts in Kissinger, *White House Years*, 242–245, and Nixon, *RN*, 380–382.

121. Dale Van Atta, *With Honor: Melvin Laird in War, Peace and Politics* (Madison: University of Wisconsin Press, 2008), 179.

122. Diary entry, 10 March 1969, HRHD; Telcon transcripts, 11 March, 1:00 and 1:30 p.m., HAK Telcons; Kissinger, *White House Years*, 246. The tension between Kissinger and Rogers is an underlying and well-documented factor in Nixon's conduct of foreign policy.

123. Memo for the Record (Nixon), subj: March 16 Rocket Attack on Saigon, 15 March 1969, *FRUS, 1969–1976*, vol. 6, doc. 39, pp. 120–121. See also Telcon transcripts, Nixon and Kissinger, 8 March, 6:25 p.m., and 15 March 1969, 3:35, 3:44, and 3:45 p.m., HAK Telcons.

124. Telcon transcript, Kissinger and Nixon, 10:45 a.m., 8 March 1969, HAK Telcons.

125. Sneider, interview in Hersh, *Price of Power*, 61.

126. Memo, Kissinger to Nixon, 16 March 1969, subj: BREAKFAST Plan, *FRUS, 1969–1976*, vol. 6, doc. 40, p. 121. Also see Memo, Kissinger to Nixon, 20 March 1969, subj: Vietnam Situation and Options, folder 7, box 89, NSCF: Vietnam Subject Files, RNPL.

127. Memo, Kissinger to Nixon, 16 March 1969, subj: BREAKFAST Plan, *FRUS, 1969–1976*, vol. 6, doc. 40, p. 121.

128. Nixon, *RN*, 382.

129. Diary entry, 2 June 1971, HRHD.

Chapter 4. The Vance Ploy and the Mining Ruse

1. Memo, Kissinger to Nixon, 20 March 1969 [sent to president on 22 March], subj: Vietnam Situation and Options, folder 7, box 89, NSCF: Vietnam Subject Files, RNPL.

2. Memo, Robert Pursley to Laird, 28 March 1969, attachment: NSC Ad Hoc Committee on Haiphong Alternatives, subj: Limiting Maritime Imports into NVN, MDR release.

3. See, e.g., *New York Times*, 8, 15, and 18 April 1967; "President Nixon's Record on Vietnam, 1954–68," in *Legislative Proposals Relating to the War in Southeast Asia: Hearings before the Committee on Foreign Relations*, US Senate, 92nd Cong., 1st sess. (Washington, DC: Government Printing Office, 1971), 295–299.

4. Admiral Thomas Moorer told an interviewer that he had visited Washington "sometime" during 1968 in an "attempt to get the Secretary of Defense to agree to mine Haiphong"; Moorer, *Reminiscences of Admiral Thomas H. Moorer (US Navy Ret.)*, vol. 2, *US* (Annapolis, MD: Naval Institute, 1981, 1982), 550, copy at Naval History and Heritage Command, History and Archives Division (HAD), Washington Navy Yard, Washington, DC.

5. Intelligence Memorandum, "Possible Alternatives to the Rolling Thunder Program," 28 May 1968, Directorate of Intelligence, CIA Records Search Tool (CREST), NARA.

6. Ellsberg Options Paper, 27 December 1968 [p. 2]; see also "Vietnam Policy Alternatives" [December 1968], folder 10: Vietnam—RAND, box 3, HAK Staff File—Transition, HAK Office Files, RNPL. For more on the RAND survey and its relationship to NSSM 1, see Kimball, *Nixon's Vietnam War*, chap. 5.

7. Memo, Laird to Kissinger, 21 February 1969 [subj: attachments re potential military actions], DOD MDR.

8. Memo, Steadman to Packard, 6 March 1969, subj: Papers on Possible Retaliation and Enemy Attrition Rates, DOD MDR (see answer to question 6). Cf. "Closing this port would exact the maximum hardship on NVN and would be a determining factor in shaping Hanoi's reaction toward the war," in Memo, Wheeler to Laird, 13 March 1969, subj: Sinking Blocking Craft, Haiphong Channel, DOD MDR.

9. Memo, Steadman to Packard, 6 March 1969; Memo, Packard to Kissinger, 11 March 1969, encls: Memo, McConnell to Acting Secretary of Defense, 11 March 1969, subj: Attack Options, attachments: Memo, Laird to Nixon, n.d., subj: Attack Options—all in DOD MDR.

10. Van Atta, *With Honor*, 151.

11. Memo, Packard to Kissinger, 11 March 1969.

12. Memos, Laird to Nixon, 3 and 4 March 1969, subj for both: Possible Responses to Enemy Activity in South Vietnam; Memo, Steadman to Packard, 6 March 1969—all in DOD MDR.

13. Kissinger, *White House Years*, 245; see also Telcon transcript, Kissinger and Nixon, 8 March, 10:45 a.m., HAK Telcons; Clymer, *United States and Cambodia*, 10–11.

14. Telcon transcript, Kissinger and Moorer, 7 March 1969, 5:30 p.m., HAK Telcons.

15. Telcon transcript, Kissinger and Nixon, 8 March 10:45 a.m.

16. Ibid.

17. Papers sent to Laird's office by Wheeler on 13 and 14 March for sinking blocking craft, mining, and surgical strikes in the Haiphong area referred to previous but unidentified "discussions concerning" these options. The subject could have come up at meetings between Laird, Wheeler, and the president on 5 March, just before the secretary and general left for South Vietnam, or in Kissinger's meeting with Packard, Steadman, and McConnell the following day. Or the "discussions" may refer to earlier talks with planners or between planners in relation to NSSM 1, the indicator action working paper, or retaliatory options.

18. Memo, Haig to Kissinger and Sneider, 19 March 1969, subj: Task Force—Contingency Operations in the Haiphong Area, folder 2, box H-299, Miscellaneous Institutional Files of the Nixon Administration (1969–1974): NSC System, RNPL; Telcon transcript, Kissinger and Laird, 11 April 1969, 3:40 p.m., HAK Telcons.

19. Memo, Pursley to Laird, 28 March 1969, with attachments: JCS memorandum for the NSC Ad Hoc Committee, subj: Limiting Maritime Imports into NVN, DOD MDR. See, e.g., Tab B.

20. Memo, Pursley to Haig, encl: Memo, Wheeler to Laird, 13 March 1969, subj: Mining Plans for Haiphong, and Pursley to Haig, 18 March 1969—both in folder: Mining Haiphong Harbor Plans, 13 March 1969, box 90, NSCF: Vietnam Subject Files, RNPL; Memo, Wheeler to Laird, 13 March, subj: Sinking Blocking Craft, Haiphong Channel, 13 March 1969, DOD MDR.

21. Moorer, *Reminiscences*, 550–553 and 778.

22. Memo, Pursley to Haig, encl: Memo, Wheeler to Laird, 13 March 1969; Memo, Wheeler to Laird, 13 March 1969, subj: Mining Plans for Haiphong, DOD MDR. The JCS also produced a "Surgical Strike" plan for naval bombardment and air strikes in Haiphong. Targeting railway yards, a highway bridge, airfields, and a power plant, the plan was responsive to previous "discussions" of "surgical strikes" (a likely reference to discussions with Kissinger), but the Joint Chiefs did not endorse the plan. In light of the "large effort" that would be needed to suppress North Vietnam's MiG interceptors and other air defenses in order to enable US aircraft to reach just a few targets, they found far more

worthwhile a "sustained bombardment" of 130 military targets located within 5 nautical miles from Haiphong's center; Memo, Wheeler to Laird, 14 March 1969, subj: "Surgical" Strikes and/or Naval Bombardment in the Haiphong Area, 14 March 1969, DOD MDR.

23. Memo, Haig to Kissinger and Sneider, 19 March 1969, subj: Task Force—Contingency Operations in the Haiphong Area, folder 2, box H-299, Misc. Institutional Files of the Nixon Administration (1969–1974): NSC System, RNPL. The task force was probably the same group that Wheeler referred to as the Ad Hoc Committee on Haiphong Alternatives. This committee was apparently neither the Ad Hoc Group on Vietnam, created in February and chaired by William Sullivan to work on negotiation issues, nor the Washington Special Action Group, formed in April, nor the Vietnam Special Studies Group, created in September; Memo, Pursley to Laird, 28 March 1969, attachment: NSC Ad Hoc Committee on Haiphong Alternatives, subj: Limiting Maritime Imports into NVN, DOD MDR.

24. Memo, Wheeler to Laird, 15 March 1969, subj: "Indicator" Actions against North Vietnam (U), DOD MDR.

25. Kissinger said, in *White House Years*, 238, that the summary of the NSSM 1 answers was prepared by his staff; Isaacson, *Kissinger*, 164, said that Ellsberg, still working as a consultant, collated the responses from February to March; Ellsberg, *Secrets*, 240–241, said he and Winston Lord wrote the summary.

26. Summary of Interagency Responses to NSSM 1, 22 March 1949, *FRUS, 1969–1976*, vol. 6, doc. 44, p. 152.

27. Ibid., p. 133.

28. MemCon, Rogers and Dobrynin, 8 March 1969, subj: Viet Nam, *FRUS, 1969–1976*, vol. 6, doc. 32, pp. 94–96; Telcon transcript, Kissinger and Nixon, 8 March 1969, 6:25 p.m., HAK Telcons; Kissinger, *White House Years*, 263–264.

29. Diary entry, 10 March 1969, HRHD.

30. Kissinger, *White House Years*, 265.

31. President's Daily Diary, 18 March 1969, RNPL; Memo, Kissinger to Nixon, 14 March 1969, subj: Your Appointment with Cyrus Vance, Tuesday, 18 March, folder: Memos and Misc./MemCons, vol. 3, box 182, NSCF: Paris Talks/Meetings, RNPL.

32. Telcon transcript, Kissinger and Nixon, 5 April 1969, 9:45 a.m., HAK Telcons.

33. Kissinger, *White House Years*, 263–265; Address by Kissinger at a conference sponsored by the Historian's Office of the US Department of State: "The American Experience in Southeast Asia, 1946–1975," 29–30 September 2010, US State Department Conference Center, Washington, DC. Also see Tal, "'Absolutes' and 'Stages,'" 1098–1099.

34. Telcon transcript, Kissinger and Vance, 19 March 1969, HAK Telcons; "Vance Proposal," n.d., folder: Suspense, box 1006, NSCF: Haig Special File, RNPL. A handwritten version of the memo is in the same file, but it is not in Haig's handwriting.

35. Memo, Kissinger to Nixon, dated 20 March 1969 but sent to president on 22 March, subj: Vietnam Situation and Options, folder 7, box 89, NSCF: Vietnam Subject Files, RNPL. This document can also be found in folder: Vietnam, box 10, Morton Halperin Papers, LBJL; an earlier, 16 March, version is in box 4, which was prepared the day before BREAKFAST was launched. Halperin believes that he drafted these memos; E-mail message, Halperin to Burr, 25 December 2013.

36. Memo, Kissinger to Nixon, 20 March 1969.

37. Ibid.

38. Ibid. (parentheses in original; emphasis added).

39. Regarding the escalation threat, also see Halperin's account, "Lessons Nixon Learned," in *The Vietnam Legacy: The War, American Society, and the Future of American Foreign Policy*, ed. Anthony Lake (New York: NYU Press, 1976), 414–415.

40. On this point, see, e.g., Memo, Kissinger to Nixon, 16 March 1969, subj: Breakfast Plan, *FRUS, 1969–1976*, vol. 6, doc. 40, p. 121; Telcon transcript, Kissinger and Nixon, 20 October 1969, HAK Telcons (also reprinted in *FRUS, 1969–1976*, vol. 12, doc. 94, p. 286).

41. Regarding Soviet ships, see, e.g., MemCon (US), attachment: Memo, Kissinger to Nixon, 15 April 1969, subj: MemCon with Dobrynin, 14 April 1969, in *Soviet-American Relations*, doc. 18, p. 52.

42. Memo, Kissinger to Nixon, 3 April 1969, subj: Vietnam Problem, *FRUS, 1969–1976*, vol. 6, doc. 52, pp. 180–184.

43. Ibid.

44. Telcon transcript, Kissinger and Nixon, 5 April 1969, 9:45 a.m., HAK Telcons. Also see Kissinger, *White House Years*, 265–268.

45. Diary entry, 14 April 1969, HRHD; Memo, Kissinger to Nixon, 12 April 1969, subj: My Talking Points with Dobrynin, *Soviet-American Relations*, doc. 17, p. 50n5. Kissinger met with Dobrynin the same day, but the US and USSR MemCons do not jibe. In his MemCon, Kissinger told Nixon that he was "fairly tough" by saying that in the talks with the DRV, Washington would want to discuss military issues before getting to political matters. By contrast, Dobrynin recorded Kissinger as saying that an "overall political settlement" would come first. The two also discussed the possibility of US escalation, with Kissinger stating that Washington would take countermeasures if Hanoi "dramatically steps up its own military activities." If the administration did escalate, Kissinger told Dobrynin, it would inform Moscow of the "reasons for them [the countermeasures] and of the fact that they are not specifically directed against the Soviet Union." MemCon (US), Kissinger and Dobrynin, 3 April 1969, and MemCon (USSR), 2 April [*sic*] 1969, *Soviet-American Relations*. docs. 15 and 16, pp. 45–47.

46. Memo, Kissinger to Nixon, 3 April 1969, subj: Vietnam Problem, *FRUS, 1969–1976*, vol. 6, doc. 52, pp. 183–184 (emphasis added); Memo, Kissinger to Nixon, 12 April 1969, subj: My Talking Points with Dobrynin, *Soviet-American Relations*, doc. 17, p. 50n5; Kissinger, *White House Years*, 265–266.

47. Memo, Pursley to Laird, 28 March 1969.

48. Ibid.

49. Ibid. A proposed alternative plan involved "the closing of the mouth of the Gulf of Tonkin and the eastern exit of the Hainan Straits."

50. Ibid.

51. Ibid.

52. Ibid.

53. Memo, Taylor to Kissinger, subj: A Course of Action to Avoid a Stalemate in the Paris Negotiations, 7 April 1969, folder: Memos and Misc./MemCons vol. 3, box 182, NSCF: Paris Talks/Meetings, RNPL.

54. Telcon transcript. Kissinger and Laird, 11:25 p.m., 11 April 1969. "War of nerves" was a reference to this 1969 period in telcon transcript, Nixon and Kissinger, 21 September 1971, 11:00 p.m., HAK Telcons.

55. For Robinson's role as liaison, see Moorer, *Reminiscences,* 1316–1317. Rear Admiral Robinson died in a helicopter crash in the Gulf of Tonkin in May 1972.

56. Memo, Moorer to NSC Ad Hoc Committee, 8 April 1969, subj: Mining of Haiphong, with cover memo by Pursley, DOD MDR.

57. Telcon transcript, Kissinger and Laird, 11 April 1969, 3:40 p.m., HAK Telcons.

58. Memo, Laird to Kissinger, 11 April 1969, attachments: Memo, Wheeler to Laird, 11 April 1969, subj: Plan for a Mining Feint of Haiphong Harbor, 11 April 1969, DOD MDR; William Lemnitzer, telephone interview by Burr, 27 March 2007, Arlington, VA. On the original objective of the plan, also see Memo, Wheeler to Laird, 1 July 1969, subj: Mining Readiness Test, folder: White House Memos (1969), box 169, Wheeler Records, RG 218, NARA.

59. Memo, Laird to Kissinger, 11 April 1969. For "trick," see Lemnitzer interview, 27 March 2007.

60. Tom Tompkins, *Yokosuka: Base of an Empire* (Novato, CA: Presidio Press, 1981), 104; communications from Mikio Haruna, September 2007 and December 2013; Allan B. Cole, George O. Totten, and Cecil H. Uyehara, *Socialist Parties in Postwar Japan* (New Haven, CT: Yale University Press, 1966), 221–227 and 316. For "communists," see Lemnitzer interview, 27 March 2007.

61. Memo, Laird to Kissinger, 11 April 1969. "All the way" in Laird's comment is followed by ellipses, then Kissinger's denial in Telcon transcript, Kissinger and Laird, 11 April 1969, 11:25 p.m., HAK Telcons. Kissinger not only had dealt directly with Moorer but also had asked Wheeler for his ideas on contingency plans on 22 January; Telcon transcript, 22 January 1969, a.m., HAK Telcons. Moorer later stated that when Kissinger had set up the NSC system, he had told Laird that the president as commander in chief had the authority to communicate directly with the chairman of the Joint Chiefs—as Kissinger had done on 22 January, two days after Nixon's inauguration; Moorer, *Reminiscences,* 550–553 and 778.

62. Telcon transcript, Kissinger and Nixon, 8 March 1969, 10:45 a.m., HAK Telcons.

63. For Moorer's initial order, see Memo, CNO to CINCPACFLT, 15 April 1969, subj: Mine Readiness, box 122, 7th Fleet Prov Logistics/Ordnance August 1969, Records of 7th Fleet, HAD.

64. Diary entry, 14 April 1969, HRHD (emphasis added).

65. Memo, Kissinger to Nixon, 12 April 1969, subj: My Talking Points with Dobrynin, *Soviet-American Relations*, doc. 17, p. 50nn3 and 5; Telegram (Extremely Urgent), Dobrynin to Soviet Foreign Ministry, 15 April 1969, *Soviet-American Relations*, doc. 19, pp. 53–56.

66. Telegram (Extremely Urgent), Dobrynin to Soviet Foreign Ministry.

67. Ibid.

68. Ibid.

69. Telcon transcript, Nixon and Kissinger, 15 April 1969, 6:30 p.m., HAK Telcons. Although shot down 100 miles from the coast, the plane had earlier flown as close as 15 miles offshore.

70. Telcon transcript, Nixon and Kissinger, 15 April 1969, 5:40 p.m., HAK Telcons; Diary entry, 15 April 1969, HRHD.

71. Laird, paraphrased in Van Atta, *With Honor*, 185 and 187.

72. Briefing for CIA Director Helms for NSC Meeting, 16 April 1969, *FRUS*, *1969–1976*, vol. 19, doc. 11, p. 23.

73. Nixon, *RN*, 382–383; Kissinger, *White House Years*, 312–318.

74. Memo, Laird to Kissinger, 15 April 1969, subj: Air Strikes against North Korean Targets, encl: "Talking Paper for the Chairman, Joint Chiefs of Staff," held by the NSArchive.

75. JCS Paper, 15 April 1969, subj: Analysis of Courses of Action, *FRUS,1969–1976*, vol. 19, doc. 7, pp. 16–17; JCS, "Alternative Courses of Action in Response to Korean Attack on US Aircraft," n.d. [pre–16 April], held by NSArchive; Van Atta, *With Honor*, 185.

76. Memo, Laird to Kissinger, 15 April 1969, subj: Military Operations against North Korean Targets, *FRUS, 1969–1976*, vol. 19, doc. 10, pp. 22–23; Telcon transcripts, Nixon and Kissinger, 15 April 1969, 6:30 p.m. and 10:00 p.m., HAK Telcons, RNPL, and *FRUS, 1969–1976*, vol. 19, docs. 8 and 9, pp. 17–21.

77. Diary entry, 17 April 1969, HRHD.

78. Ibid.; also see briefings, meeting minutes, and memos in *FRUS, 1969–1976*, vol. 19, docs. 11, 12, 13, 14, 15, and 17, pp. 23–26, 28–31, and 14–34.

79. Quoted in Nixon, *RN*, 384. See also Van Atta, *With Honor*, 187.

80. Haldeman, interview by Isaacson, 3 October 1990, quoted in Isaacson, *Kissinger*, 181. Isaacson provides no date for Kissinger's consultation with Ehrlichman and Haldeman except to say "after the NSC meeting" of 16 April 1969 (emphasis added).

81. Telcon transcript, Nixon and Kissinger, 17 April 1969, 8:00 p.m., HAK Telcons (emphasis added).

82. Ibid.

83. Ibid.

84. Ibid. "Piddily thing" is from their 18 April, 9:15 a.m., Telcon transcript, HAK Telcons. (These Telcon transcripts can also be found in *FRUS, 1969–1976*, vol. 19, docs. 15 and 19, pp. 34–37 and 44–45.) Cf. Diary entry, 17 April 1969, HRHD. "Overcoming slothfulness" is from Diary entry, 19 April 1969, HRHD.

85. Diary entries, 18 and 19 April 1969, HRHD; Memo, Kissinger to Nixon, 22 April 1969, *FRUS, 1969–1976*, vol. 6, doc. no. 62, pp. 205–206; Nixon, *RN*, 384. "Coco" was a NATO phonetic alphabet code in the 1950s into the 1960s before "Charlie," a SAC alert code in the 1950s and 1960s, and a reference to control mechanisms regarding bombing-restricted areas in North Vietnam and Laos (Alpha, Bravo, Coco) in late 1960s B-52 bombing.

86. Paraphrased in Diary entries, 18 and 19 April 1969, HRHD (italics in original).

87. Memo, Kissinger to Nixon, 22 April 1969, *FRUS, 1969–1976*, vol. 6, doc. no. 62, pp. 205–206 and 206n1. See also Diary entry, 22 April 1969, HRHD.

88. Diary entry, 19 April 1969, HRHD.

89. Nixon, *RN*, 382–385; Kissinger, *White House Years*, 312–332; Memo, G. Warren Nutter to Kissinger, 26 April 1969, held by the NSArchive; see also Isaacson, *Kissinger*, 180–182.

90. Memo, Laird to Kissinger, 26 June 1969, subj: Review of US Contingency Plans, held by the NSArchive.

91. Kissinger notes on Airborne Command Post, 11 May 1969, folder: Haldeman Notes, Jan–June '69 [May–June 1969], pt. 2, box 40, WHSF: SMOF, HRHPF, RNPL.

92. "Response to Sen. Harold Hughes," Furlong Papers, AFHRA; Thayer, *War without Fronts*, chap. 8; Malvern Lumsden, *Anti-personnel Weapons* (London: Taylor & Francis, 1978), 26–27; Taylor Owen and Ben Kiernan, "Bombs over Cambodia," *Walrus* (October 2006): 65–69, http://walrusmagazine.com /article.php?ref=2006.10-history-bombing-cambodia&page= (accessed 11 August 2011).

93. "Response to Hughes," Furlong Papers; Thayer, *War without Fronts*, chap. 8; Lumsden, *Anti-personnel Weapons*, 26–27; John Prados, *The Blood Road: The Ho Chi Minh Trail and the Vietnam War* (New York: John Wiley & Sons, 1999), chap. 12. A fair number of documents in *FRUS, 1969–1976*, vol. 6, reference the bombing of Laos.

Chapter 5. The Mining Ruse, Threat Diplomacy, Peace Plans, and Withdrawals

1. Telcon transcript, Nixon and Kissinger, 21 September 1971, 11:00 p.m., HAK Telcons.

2. Diary entry, 15 April 1969, HRHD.

3. Msg, CNO to CINPACFLT, 13 April 1969, folder: 7th Fleet Prov Logistics

(Ordnance), April 1969, box 111, 7th Fleet Records, HAD; Memo, Robinson to Kissinger, 14 April 1969, subj: Mine Readiness Test, and Memo, Robinson to Wheeler, 14 April 1969, subj: Mine Readiness Test, folder: White House Memos (1969), box 169, Wheeler Records, RG 218, NARA.

4. Msg, CNO to CINPACFLT, 13 April 1969; Msg, CINCPACFLT to NAVMAG Guam et al., 15 April 1969; and Msg, Admin COMSERVPAC to CNO, 15 April 1969 (3 cables)—all from box 111, 7th Fleet Prov Logistics (Ordnance), April 1969, 7th Fleet Records, HAD. For details of the MK-52, see US Navy Mine Warfare Project (PM-19), *The Mining of North Vietnam 8 May 1972 to 14 January 1973,* 30 June 1973, 2–5 and 3–20, copy at HAD.

5. Msg, Admin COMSERVPAC to CNO, 15 April 1969, box 111, 7th Fleet Prov Logistics (Ordnance), April 1969, 7th Fleet Records, HAD; US Navy Mine Warfare Project, *The Mining of North Vietnam,* 3–19, 3–21, and 3–38. In navy jargon, the lighterage craft were known as Waterborne Logistic Craft.

6. Msg, Admin COMSERVPAC to CNO, 15 April 1969.

7. Memo, Robinson to Wheeler, 22 and 28 April 1969, subj: Mine Readiness Test, folder: White House Memos (1969), box 169, Wheeler Records, RG 218, NARA; Msg, CNO to CINPACFLT, 17 April 1969, box 111, 7th Fleet Prov Logistics (Ordnance), April 1969; Msg, CTF 77 to NAVMAG Subic, 1 May 1969; and Msg, CNO to CINCPACFLT, 19 May 1969, box 114, 7th Fleet Prov Miscellaneous, May 1969, 7th Fleet Records, HAD.

8. MemCon (USSR), Dobrynin and Kissinger, 24 April 1969, in *Soviet-American Relations, 1969–1972,* doc. 20, pp. 56–58. This is Dobrynin's MemCon; no US record of the meeting has been found.

9. Memos, Robinson to Kissinger, 28 May 1969, with attached Memo, Haig to Robinson, 28 April 1969; Robinson to Wheeler, 22 and 29 April 1969; Robinson through Colonel Haig to Kissinger, 16 May 1969—all in subj: Mining Readiness Test, folder: White House Memos (1969), box 169, Wheeler Records, RG 218, NARA.

10. Memo, Robinson to Wheeler, 1 May 1969, and Memo, Robinson to Kissinger, 6 and 16 May 1969, subj: Mining Readiness Test, folder: White House Memos (1969), box 169, Wheeler Records, RG 218, NARA. See also these messages from 7th Fleet Records, HAD: CNO to CINCPACFLT, 30 April 1969, box 111, 7th Fleet Prov Logistics (Ordnance), April 1969 (2 cables); CTF 77 to NAVMAG Subic, 1 May 1969, CTF 77 to NAS Cubi, 1 May 1969; CTF 77 to COMSEVENTHFLT, 7 May 1969, and COMSEVENTHFLT to CINCPAC-FLT, 8 May 1969, box 114, 7th Flt Prov Logistics, May 1969; USS *Bon Homme Richard* to CTF 77, 3 May 1969, and CINCPACFLT to COMSEVENTHFLT, 7 May 1969, and CINCPACFLT to COMSEVENTHFLT, 10 May 1969, 7th Fleet, box 114, 7th Fleet Prov Miscellaneous, May 1969; and COMSEVENTH-FLT to CINCPACFLT, 3 July 1969, 7th Fleet, box 120, 7th Flt Prov Miscellaneous, July 1969.

11. Memo, Robinson to Kissinger, 16 May 1969, subj: Mining Readiness Test, folder: White House Memos (1969), box 169, Wheeler Records, RG 218, NARA; Msg, COMSEVENTHFLT to CTF 77, 12 May 1969; Msg, CTF 77 to CTF 77.4, 13 May 1969, box 114, 7th Fleet Prov Miscellaneous, May 1969; and Msg, COMINEFLOT One to CTG 77.4, 14 May 1969, 7th Fleet, box 114, 7th Fleet Prov Miscellaneous, May 1969, 7th Fleet Records, HAD.

12. Msgs, CTG 77.4 to CFT 77, 20 May 1969; CTF 77 to CTG 77.5, 21 May 1969; COMSEVENTHFLT to CINCPACFLT, 22 May 1969; CTG 77.5 to CTF 77, 22 May 1969; CFT 77.5 to CTF 77, 27 May 1969; and CTF 77 to COM-NAVBASE Subic, 29 May 1969, box 114, 7th Fleet Prov Miscellaneous, May 1969, 7th Fleet Records, HAD.

13. Ilya Gaiduk, citing Soviet documents, in *The Soviet Union and the Vietnam War* (Chicago: Ivan R. Dee, 1996), 207–209; also see Tal, "'Absolutes' and 'Stages,'" 1098–1099.

14. They continued such opposition into 1972; see, e.g., MemCon, Tho and Kissinger et al., 2 May 1972, 10:00 a.m.–1:00 p.m., *FRUS, 1969–1976*, vol. 8, doc. 109, p. 378. Le Duc Tho told Kissinger: "I have pointed out to you that we deal directly with you and vice versa. I have also repeatedly pointed out to you that we don't deal through any intermediary, neither now nor in the previous four years. I told you that."

15. MemCon (USSR), Dobrynin and Kissinger, 14 May 1969, *Soviet-American Relations*, doc. 22, p. 62. The editors of this volume noted that "no American record[s] of Dobrynin's conversation with either Kissinger or Nixon have been found."

16. MemCon (USSR), Dobrynin and Kissinger, 24 April 1969, *Soviet-American Relations*, doc. 20, p. 57n4; Memo, Kissinger to Nixon, 28 May 1969, *FRUS, 1969–1976*, vol. 6, doc. 51, p. 166n1 (emphasis in original); Kissinger, *White House Years*, 144 and 268–269.

17. Address by Kissinger, "American Experience in Southeast Asia, 1946–1975."

18. See, e.g., Memo, Kissinger to Nixon, 3 April 1969, subj: Vietnam Problem, *FRUS, 1969–1976*, vol. 6, doc. 52, pp. 182–184.

19. Regarding the overall game plan, see, e.g., Minutes of NSC Meeting, 25 January 1969, *FRUS, 1969–1976*, vol. 6, doc. 10, p. 40; cf. Kissinger, *White House Years*, 271. For moving forward, see Telcon transcripts, Kissinger and Nixon, 8 March 1969, 10:45 a.m. and 6:25 p.m., and 13 May 1969, 7:30 p.m., HAK Telcons. On 13 May, Kissinger and Nixon discussed revisions in the peace plan speech. About circulating these to his staff, Kissinger remarked, "That is helpful if we want to move the other way [i.e., bombing and mining] before July." Nixon, in a belligerent mood, replied, "July, we are going to move before that."

20. See, e.g., NSSM 37, *FRUS, 1969–1976*, vol. 6, doc. 59, pp. 197–199; Loi and Vu, *Le Duc Tho–Kissinger Negotiations*, 82–84; Editorial Note, *FRUS, 1969–1976*, vol. 6, doc. 68, p. 216; Kissinger, *White House Years*, 270.

21. *Bases for a Settlement of the Viet Nam Problem* (Hanoi: Foreign Languages

Publishing House, 1971), 28–33; "Ten Point Plan," *Washington Post*, 8 May 1969; "Vietcong's 10-Point Program," *New York Times*, 9 May 1969; Loi and Vu, *Le Duc Tho–Kissinger Negotiations*, 82–83; 3 August 1969 entry, Chronology of US-DRV Negotiations, 1969–1973 (Private Meetings); "Declaration of Peace and Progress in Asia and the Pacific," *Public Papers of the Presidents: Lyndon B. Johnson, 1966*, bk. 2, pp. 1262–1263; Minutes of National Security Council Meeting, 25 January 1969, and Memo, Kissinger to Nixon, 10 May 1969, subj: Analysis of the NLF's Ten Points—both in *FRUS, 1969–1976*, vol. 6, doc. 10, p. 35, and doc. 67, p. 215.

22. Memo, Kissinger to Nixon, 10 May 1969, subj: Analysis of the NLF's Ten Points, *FRUS, 1969–1976*, vol. 6, doc. 67, p. 215; Diary entries, 11 and 12 May 1969, HRHD; MemCon (USSR), Dobrynin and Kissinger, 14 May 1969, *Soviet-American Relations*, doc. 22, p. 60; Kissinger, *White House Years*, 270.

23. Address to the Nation, 14 May 1969, *Public Papers of the Presidents: Nixon, 1969*, 374. On the White House understanding of Thieu's position, see, e.g., Memo, Kissinger to Nixon, 4 June 1969, subj: Your Meeting with Thieu, *FRUS, 1969–1976*, vol. 6, doc. 79, pp. 243–246.

24. Telcon transcript, Kissinger and Elliott Richardson, 14 May 1969, 2:40 p.m., HAK Telcons; Address to the Nation, 14 May 1969, *Public Papers of the Presidents: Nixon, 1969*, 374.

25. Telcon transcript, Nixon and Kissinger, 13 May 1969, 7:30 p.m., HAK Telcons.

26. MemCon (USSR), Dobrynin and Nixon, 14 May 1969, *Soviet-American Relations*, doc. 22, p. 61.

27. Quoted in Editorial Note, *FRUS, 1969–1976*, vol. 6, doc. 68, p. 218.

28. Kissinger, quoted in Telegram, DOS to All Diplomatic Posts, 15 May 1969, box 2730, POL 27–14 Viet, Subject-Numeric Files 1967–1969, RG 59, NARA; Laird, quoted in *Los Angeles Times*, 19 May 1969.

29. Telcon transcript, Nixon and Kissinger, 12 May 1969, 11:30 p.m., HAK Telcons. At the Nixon-Thieu meeting on Midway on 8 June, Thieu conceded—rhetorically at least—that "neither side can win militarily"; MemCon, Nixon, Thieu, Kissinger, Nguyen Phu Duc, 8 June 1969, *FRUS, 1969–1976*, vol. 6, doc. 81, p. 249.

30. Conversation (as paraphrased and quoted by Marder), Kissinger and Marder, 29 April 1969, Murray Marder Papers, NSArchive.

31. See discussion of the decent-chance/decent-interval strategy in chapter 3.

32. The DRV/NLF insisted on the Ten Points but might have been willing to agree to withdraw tacitly to the north of the DMZ if both sides agreed to some sort of coalition government or joint electoral commission, whereas the United States agreed to withdraw all of its forces within a year or by the end of 1970. In this way, the American war could have concluded sooner, although this solution probably would not have allowed for a decent interval and was therefore unacceptable to Nixon and Kissinger. Regarding tacit withdrawal, see, e.g., Memo,

Dean Moor to Kissinger, 22 May 1969, subj: Assessment of the 22 May Plenary, and Memo, Kissinger to Nixon, 7 July 1969, subj: *Sequoia* NSC Meeting on Vietnam, *FRUS, 1969–1976*, vol. 6, docs. 72 and 93, pp. 227 and 283n2.

33. COSVN Resolution no. 9, July 1969; also see Military Institute of Vietnam, *Victory in Vietnam*, 240–253.

34. Diary entries, 14 and 18 1969, HRHD.

35. Diary entry, 13 March 1969, HRHD.

36. Jeffrey J. Clarke, *Advice and Support: The Final Years—The US Army in Vietnam* (Washington, DC: Center of Military History, 1988), 346–348. Laird had arrived in Saigon on 5 March.

37. Quoted in ibid., 347.

38. Van Atta, *Melvin Laird in War*, 161–162; Gabriel Kolko, *Anatomy of a War: Vietnam, the United States, and the Modern Historical Experience* (New York: Pantheon Books, 1985), 347–348.

39. Memo, James Fazio to Haig, 21 May 1969; Memo, Laird to Nixon, 21 May 1969, subj: Combat Activity Related to Hill 937; and Alexander Butterfield to Laird and Kissinger, 11 June 1969, subj: Comment by the President—all in folder G: Hamburger Hill, box 67, NSCF: Vietnam Subject Files, RNPL. Also see Hammond, *Military and Media*, 85–89; Samuel Zaffiri, *Hamburger Hill, May 11–20, 1969* (Novato, CA: Presidio Press, 1988).

40. Memo, Laird to Nixon, 21 May 1969, and Telcons, Kissinger and Laird, 20 May 1969, 11:20 a.m., Kissinger and Nixon, 26 May 1969, 10:25 a.m., and Kissinger and Rogers, 3 June 1969, 3:10 p.m.—all in HAK Telcons.

41. Telcon transcript, Kissinger and Nixon, 18 July 1969, 10:15 p.m., HAK Telcons; "Proposed Press Release," folder: Mister "S," vol. 1 [1 of 2], box 106, Country Files–Far East–Vietnam Negotiations, HAK Office Files, RNPL.

42. The home front corollary of de-Americanization included reforms in the Selective Service system, in which the public had lost confidence. On 27 March 1969, Nixon announced the formation of a commission to look into the creation of an all-volunteer force, and on 19 May, he asked Congress to make changes in Selective Service that would reduce draft calls for men who were twenty years old and older while increasing those for eighteen- and nineteen-year-olds, with the purpose, presumably, of muting the former's opposition to the war. Nixon's reforms of the draft system—namely, the lottery (1969) and the all-volunteer system (1973)—came in a period when draft calls were already declining.

43. See, e.g., section D4 in Vietnam Policy Alternatives, July 1969, encl in Memo, Halperin and Lord to Kissinger, 5 August 1969, folder: Misc. Materials—Selected Lord Memos, Director's Files (Winston Lord), 1969–77, Policy Planning Council (S/P), GRDS, RG 59, NARA; Memo, Kissinger to Nixon, 10 September 1969, subj: Our Present Course on Vietnam, folder 2: Tony Lake Chronological File (Jun. 1969–May 1970) [5 of 6], box 1048, NSCF: Lake Chronological Files, RNPL; Lake, telephone interviews by Kimball, 15 October 2001 and 9 December 2005.

44. Memo, Laird to Nixon, 13 March 1969, subj: Trip to Vietnam and CINCPAC, 5–12 March 1969; and Memo, Kissinger to Nixon, n.d., subj: Vietnam Negotiations Papers for the NSC—both in *FRUS, 1969–1976*, vol. 6, doc. 38, pp. 108, 109, and 117, and doc. 46, pp. 156–157. Also see Clarke, *Advice and Support*, 346–348; Kissinger, *White House Years*, 262.

45. *Public Papers of the Presidents, Nixon: 1969*, 215.

46. Minutes of NSC Meeting, 28 March 1969, *FRUS, 1969–1976*, vol. 6, doc. 49, p. 170.

47. On *le jaunissement*, see Spector, *Early Years*, 135–136. On the Wise Men and Johnson policy, see Kolko, *Anatomy of a War*, 320–322; George Herring, *LBJ and Vietnam: A Different Kind of War* (Austin: University of Texas Press, 1994), 60 and 151. On the Johnson and Nixon phases, see Robert K. Brigham, *ARVN: Life and Death in the South Vietnamese Army* (Lawrence: University Press of Kansas, 2006). Regarding Clifford, see his "A Viet Nam Reappraisal: The Personal History of One Man's View and How It Evolved," *Foreign Affairs* 47, no. 4 (July 1969): 614. On the words *de-Americanization* and *Vietnamization*, see, e.g., stories and letters in *New York Times*, 11 August 1967 and 8 December 1968 and in *Washington Post*, 16 March, 14 September, 6 October, and 13 November 1968.

48. NSSM 36, 10 April 1969, *FRUS, 1969–1976*, vol. 6, doc. 58, pp. 195–196; Clarke, *Advice and Support*, 348.

49. Memo, Kissinger to Nixon, 23 June 1969, subj: Vietnamizing the War (NSSM 36), with attachment, Memo, Laird to Nixon, 2 June 1969—both in *FRUS, 1969–1976*, vol. 6, docs. 86 and 87, pp. 260 and 267.

50. Editorial Note, *FRUS, 1969–1976*, vol. 6, doc. 80, p. 247; Kissinger, *White House Years*, 272–273.

51. "Midway toward Peace?," *New York Times*, 10 June 1969.

52. Isaacson, *Kissinger*, 236; Back-channel msg, Kissinger to Bunker, 1 June 1969; MemCon, 8 June 1969, *FRUS, 1969–1976*, vol. 6, docs. 76 and 81, pp. 237–238 and 248–252; Hung and Schecter, *Palace File*, 33.

53. Hung and Schecter, *Palace File*, 33.

54. Ibid., 30–35; Clarke, *Advice and Support*, 351–354.

55. COSVN Resolution no. 9, in *Vietnam Documents and Research Notes Series*, pp. 9 and 17 (italics in original).

56. Nguyen Co Thach, interview by Kimball, 24 September 1994, Hanoi. Thach is quoted making a similar point to Seymour Hersh in *Price of Power*, 134.

57. Loi and Vu, *Le Duc Tho–Kissinger Negotiations*, 88–89. The Communist side announced the formation of the Provisional Revolutionary Government on 10 June 1969.

58. Editorial Note, *FRUS, 1969–1976*, vol. 6, doc. 68, p. 218.

59. See discussion of this point in a similar context in 1972 in Memo of Record, meeting between Kissinger, Moorer, Rush, Haig, and Howe, 5 May 1972, *FRUS, Nixon, 1969–1976*, vol. 8, doc. 124, p. 454.

60. Memo, Robinson to Kissinger, 20 May 1969, subj: Mining Readiness

Test, folder: White House Memos (1969), box 169, Wheeler Records, RG 218, NARA.

61. Memo, Robinson to Kissinger, 20 May 1969, subj: Mining Readiness Test, encls: "STEP FOUR—Supplementary Actions for Further Study and Consideration," n.d., folder: White House Memos (1969), box 169, Wheeler Records, RG 218, NARA. PIRAZ ships were used to identify all aircraft, friendly or hostile, operating in the Tonkin Gulf.

62. Memo, Helms to Kissinger, 25 May 1969, subj: The Possible Quarantine of North Vietnam, with attached report, "The Effects of Imposing a Quarantine on North Vietnam," folder: CIA Jan 69–31 Dec 89, vol. 1, box 297, NSCF: Agency Files, RNPL.

63. Memo, Haig to Kissinger, 29 May 1969, subj: Items to Discuss with Admiral Moorer, folder: Haig, Alexander M. (General), Staff Memos, January 20–November 30, 1969 [2 of 2], box 1001, NSCF: Haig's Special File, RNPL; Memo, Robinson through Haig to Kissinger, subj: Mining Readiness Test, 4 June 1969, folder: White House Memos (1969), box 169, Wheeler Records, RG 218, NARA. Moorer sent an order two days later: Msg, COMSERVPAC to NAVORDFAC Yokosuka, 31 May 1969, box 114, 7th Flt Prov Logistics, May 1969, 7th Fleet, HAD.

64. Msg, COMSTSFE to COMSERVPAC, 16 June 1969, box 117, 7th Flt Prov Logistics, June 1969, and Msg, COMSEVENTHFLT to CINCPACFLT, 3 July 1969, box 120, 7th Flt Prov Miscellaneous, July 1969, 7th Fleet Records, HAD.

65. Memo, Haig to Kissinger, 11 June 1969, subj: Specific Items Raised by the President on the CIA Analysis of the Affects [sic] of Imposing a Quarantine on North Vietnam, folder: Haig Chron June 1969 [2 of 2], box 957, NSCF: Haig Chronological Files, RNPL. Nixon had his own deep-seated animosity toward the CIA, for which he blamed his 1960 defeat because it supposedly had not told candidate John F. Kennedy the full story of the missile gap. This aversion was evident in the tone of Nixon's comments to Haig. For Nixon and the CIA, see Thomas Powers, *The Man Who Kept the Secrets: Richard Helms and the CIA* (New York: Rand House, 1979), 58, 201, and 203.

66. Telcon transcript, Kissinger and Cushman, 2 July 1969, 10:15 a.m., HAK Telcons.

67. MemCon (USSR), Dobrynin and Kissinger, 12 June 1969, *Soviet-American Relations*, doc. 24, pp. 64–70.

68. Ibid.

69. Ibid.

70. Ibid.

71. Memo, Kissinger to Nixon, 26 June 1969, subj: Appointment with Ambassador Lodge, *FRUS, 1969–1976*, vol. 6, doc. 90, p. 275n4.

72. Ibid., p. 275; also see Memo, Kissinger to Nixon, 24 June 1969, folder: CF, FO-6-1, Paris Peace Talks, box 33, WHSF, RNPL.

73. Kissinger, *White House Years*, 271.

74. President's News Conference, 19 June 1969, *Public Papers of the Presidents, Nixon: 1969*, 476.

75. Memo, Robinson to Wheeler, 20 June 1969, folder: White House Memos, box 169, Wheeler Records, RG 218, NARA.

76. Diary entry, 19 June 1969, HRHD.

77. Ibid.

78. Msg, CTF 77 to all TF 77 CDRS, 7 June 1969, box 117, 7th Flt Prov Logistics, June 1969, and Msg, COMSEVENTHFLT to CINCPACFLT, 8 June 1969, box 117, 7th Flt Prov Miscellaneous, June 1969, 7th Fleet Records, HAD.

79. Msg, COMSEVENTHFLT to CINCPACFLT, 3 July 1969, box 120, 7th Flt Prov Miscellaneous, July 1969, 7th Fleet Records, HAD.

80. Memo, Robinson through Haig to Kissinger, 6 and 16 June, subj: Mining Readiness Test, folder: White House Memos (1969), box 169, Wheeler Records, RG 218, NARA.

81. Memo, Wheeler to Laird, 23 June 1969, subj: Mining Readiness Test, CM-4360–69, DOD MDR.

82. Memo, Pursley to Laird, 24 June 1969, subj: Mining Readiness Test Objectives, and Memo, Laird to Wheeler, 27 June 1969, DOD MDR; Memo, Robinson to Wheeler, 1 July 1969, folder: White House Memos (1969), box 169, Wheeler Records, RG 218, NARA. Kissinger and Laird briefly discussed the mine readiness test on the evening of 25 June, although a record of a subsequent conversation on the "secure phone" is not available; Telcon transcript, Kissinger and Laird, 25 June 1969, 6:00 p.m., HAK Telcons.

83. Memo, Haig to Kissinger, 3 July 1969, subj: Mining Readiness Test, folder: Haig Chron July 1969 [2 of 2], box 957, NSCF: Haig Chronological Files, RNPL; Memo, Wheeler to Laird, 1 July 1969, subj: Mining Readiness Test, CM-4393–69, DOD MDR.

84. Memo, Wheeler to Laird, 1 July 1969.

85. Ibid.

86. Robinson to Wheeler, 1 July 1969, folder: White House Memos (1969), box 169, Wheeler Records, RG 218, NARA.

87. See, e.g., chapter 3; Telcon transcripts, Kissinger and Nixon, 8 March 1969, 10:45 a.m. and 6:25 p.m., HAK Telcons; Diary entry, 7 July 1969, HRHD; Memo, Kissinger to Nixon, 7 July 1969, subj: *Sequoia* NSC Meeting on Vietnam, *FRUS, 1969–1976*, vol. 6, doc. 93, pp. 283–288.

Chapter 6. The First DUCK HOOK Plan, the "Nixon Doctrine," and a Deadline

1. Telcon transcript, Kissinger and Laird, 8 July 1969, 10:40 a.m., HAK Telcons.

2. Diary entry, 7 July 1969, HRHD. Haldeman was hoping Kissinger "prevails."

Also see Memo, Kissinger to Nixon, 7 July 1969, subj: *Sequoia* NSC Meeting on Vietnam, *FRUS, 1969–1976*, vol. 6, doc. 93, pp. 283–288.

3. Roger Morris, *Haig: The General's Progress* (New York: Playboy Press, 1982), 135; Haig, conversation with Kimball, 10 March 2006, Kennedy Library.

4. Diary entry, 7 July 1969, HRHD.

5. Memo, Kissinger to Nixon, 7 July 1969.

6. Ibid.; Diary entry, 7 July 1969, HRHD. Kissinger claimed that Nixon changed his mind right after the meeting about altering the mission of US forces, but it was too late, for Laird had already issued orders and leaked to the public; Kissinger, *White House Years*, 276. Cf. Clarke, *Advice and Support*, 358–363, and Hammond, *Military and Media*, 78–85 and 137.

7. Nixon, *RN*, 393.

8. Memo, Robinson to Wheeler, 7 July 1969, folder: White House Memos (1969), box 169, RG 218, NARA.

9. On this point, see Memo, Tony Lake to Kissinger, 17 September 1969, subj: Initial Comments on Concept of Operations, with Attachment, "Vietnam Contingency Planning," 16 September 1969, folder 2, box 1048, NSCF: Lake Chronological Files, RNPL; Memo, Lake and Morris to Robinson, 29 September 1969, subj: Draft Memorandum to the President on Contingency Study, folder 4: Vietnam (General Files) Sep 69–Nov 69 [2 of 2], box 74, NSCF: Vietnam Subject Files, RNPL.

10. Memo, Robinson to Wheeler through Gen. McPherson, 8 July 1969, folder: White House Memos (1969), box 169, Wheeler Records, Records of JCS, RG 218, NARA.

11. Ibid., Telcon transcript, Kissinger and Laird, 8 July 1969 (emphasis in original).

12. MemCon, Sainteny to Nixon, 16 July 1969, and Memo, Sainteny to Kissinger, 20 September 1969, folder: Mister "S," vol. 1 [1 of 2], box 106, HAK Office Files: Country Files—Far East—Vietnam Negotiations, RNPL. Apparently, the original intention was to have Sainteny go to Hanoi in June, but he was told by the leaders in Hanoi that such a trip was "useless," since Xuan Thuy, in Paris, "is entirely responsible for the negotiations with the US"; Memo, Sainteny to Kissinger, 22 July 1969, folder: Mister "S," vol. 1 [1 of 2], box 106, HAK Office Files: Country Files—Far East—Vietnam Negotiations, RNPL; Telcon transcript, Kissinger and Sainteny, 22 May 1969, 3:55 p.m., HAK Telcons. But Sainteny learned later that the real reason was that Ho was "near the end, . . . not capable of sustaining a conversation, and he would not risk that the world know of it."

13. Reprinted in *Public Papers of the Presidents, Nixon: 1969*, 910.

14. MemCon, Sainteny to Nixon, 16 July 1969; the memo can also be found in folder: Sensitive Memoranda, box 1006, NSCF: Haig Special File, RNPL.

15. Ibid.

16. Telcon transcript, Kissinger and Cushman, 2 July 1969, 10:15 a.m., HAK Telcons.

17. Memo, Haig to Mitchell, 19 August 1969, subj: The Effects of the Imposition of a Quarantine on NVN, folder: Haig Chron August 1969, box 958, NSCF: Haig Chronological Files, RNPL.

18. Central Intelligence Agency, "The Effects of the Imposition of a Quarantine on North Vietnam," 16 July 1969, folder: Top Secret Sensitive Vietnam Contingency Planning, Oct. 2, 1969, Henry A. Kissinger [1 of 2], box 89, NSCF: Vietnam Subject Files, RNPL.

19. Ibid.

20. Ibid.

21. Ibid.

22. Ibid.

23. Ibid.

24. Memo, Robinson to Wheeler through Gen. McPherson, 8 July 1969.

25. Memo, Laird to Kissinger, 21 July 1969, encls: Office of the Chief of Naval Operations, "DUCK HOOK," 20 July 1969, and "Summary of Interdiction (Quarantine) Plan for Port of Sihanoukville," n.d., DOD MDR release (also available at RNPL).

26. "DUCK HOOK," 20 July 1969, DOD MDR.

27. Ibid.

28. Ibid.

29. Ibid.

30. Ibid.

31. For the intelligence controversy, see Powers, *Man Who Kept the Secrets*, 216–217; Clymer, *United States and Cambodia*, 10–11; and John Prados, "Port of Entry, Sihanoukville: A Cambodian Munitions Mystery," *VVA Veteran* 25 (November–December 2005), http://www.vva.org/archive/TheVeteran/2005_11 /featureSihanoukville.htm (accessed 10 December 2014).

32. "Summary of Interdiction (Quarantine) Plan."

33. Ibid.

34. Nixon, *RN*, 394; Telcon transcript, Kissinger and Nixon, 5 August 1969, 6:50 p.m., HAK Telcons.

35. "Informal Remarks in Guam with Newsmen, 25 July 1969," *Public Papers of the Presidents, Nixon: 1969*, 548–552.

36. Ibid.

37. Ibid., 553–554.

38. See, e.g., Kissinger, *White House Years*, 224; *New York Times*, 31 July and 3 August 1969, 29 June and 2 July 1970; *Chicago Sun-Times*, 17 September 1970.

39. For "moderate," see, e.g., Telcon transcript, Kissinger and Nixon, 18 July 1969 10:15 a.m., HAK Telcons.

40. See, e.g., MemCon, 30 July 1969, subj: President Nixon's Comments to Chiefs of Mission, Bangkok, attachment to Memo, Marshall Green to Rogers, 12 August 1969, POL 7 US/Nixon, Central Files, RG 59, NARA.

41. Diary entry, 24–25 July 1969, HRHD.

42. Telcon transcript, Kissinger and Nixon, 18 July 1969, 5:45 p.m., HAK Telcons.

43. Clifford, "Viet Nam Reappraisal," 601–622; Carroll Kilpatrick, "Off the Record Interview [with Clark M. Clifford, 2 July 1969]," Murray Marder Papers, NSArchive.

44. Kissinger, *White House Years*, 224.

45. Memo, Lord to Kissinger, 23 January 1970, subj: Issues Raised by the Nixon Doctrine for Asia, folder 2: Misc. Materials—Selected Lord Memos, box 335, Subject-Numeric Files, 1970–73, RG 59, NARA. Cf. Paper, *FRUS, 1969–1976*, vol. 1, doc. 54, pp. 266–278. Also see Memo, Lord to Kissinger, 6 October 1969, *FRUS, 1969–1976*, vol. 6, doc. 130, pp. 424–432, on the question of the Guam Doctrine regarding Laos and whether the "implications" of the analysis "add up to a policy."

46. In his 3 November 1969 address to the nation, e.g., Nixon referred to the Nixon Doctrine as "another plan to bring peace"; as "a major shift in US foreign policy"; and as "a policy which not only will help end the war in Vietnam, but which is an essential element of our program to prevent future Vietnams." For additional analysis, see Jeffrey Kimball, "The Nixon Doctrine: A Saga of Misunderstanding," *Presidential Studies Quarterly* 36, no. 1 (March 2006): 59–74.

47. MemCon, Nixon and Thieu, 30 July 1969, folder: MemCons—The President and President Thieu, 30 July 1969, box 1023, NSCF: Presidential/HAK MemCons, RNPL. By "unorthodox way," Nixon apparently meant the warning would be delivered at a secret diplomatic meeting between Kissinger and Xuan Thuy—after having already issued warnings to Ho by letter and several other warnings to Hanoi through third parties. On 7 August, the White House informed Thieu in "strictest confidence" through Ambassador Bunker that "the message and warning had been passed in Paris" to Thuy with a deadline of 1 November; Msg, Kissinger to Bunker, 7 August 1969 (late p.m.), folder: vol. 1, All Backchannel [1 of 2], box 65, NSCF: Vietnam Subject Files, RNPL.

48. F. S. Aijazuddin, *From a Head, through a Head, to a Head: The Secret Channel between the US and China through Pakistan* (New York: Oxford University Press, 2001), 3; MemCon, Nixon and Ceauşéscu, 3 August 1969, folder: MemCons—The President and President Ceauşéscu, 2 August 1969, box 1023, NSCF: Presidential/HAK MemCons, RNPL.

49. "The Prime Minister's Account of His Conversation with President Nixon at Middenhall on Sunday, 3 August 1969," 5 August 1969, Prime Minister's Office Files (HAK Office Files) 13/3009, British National Archives (copy courtesy of Matthew Jones); Philip Ziegler, *Wilson: The Authorized Life of Lord Wilson of Rievaulx* (London: Weidenfeld & Nicolson, 1993), 325–329. See also Chris Wrigley, "Now You See It; Now You Don't: Harold Wilson and Labour's Foreign Policy, 1964–1970," in *The Wilson Governments, 1964–1970*, ed. R. Coopey, S. Fielding, and N. Tiratsoo (London: St. Martin's Press, 1993), 128–129.

50. "The Prime Minister's Account."

51. See, e.g., Memo to Nixon, subj: Wilson Visit, 16 September 1969, folder 2, box 941, NSCF: Country Files—Europe, RNPL; Mr. Goldstein to Mr. Springsteen, 31 July 1969, subj: British Flag Shipping to North Vietnam, 31 July 1969, STR 12–3 VIET N, Subject-Numeric Files, 1967–1969, RG 59, NARA.

52. Note (no. 734), Thomas L. Hughes (Director of Intelligence and Research) to the Secretary, subj: Shipping to North Vietnam: British Unable to Check Sharp Rise in Hong Kong Shipping under Their Flag, 12 September 1968, and MemCon, 1 August 1969, subj: British Flag Shipping to North Vietnam—both from 31 July 1969, STR 12–3 VIET N, Subject-Numeric Files, 1967–1969, RG 59, NARA.

53. Memo, Kissinger to Nixon, 8 August 1969, subj: Free World Shipping to North Vietnam, folder: Mister "S," vol. 1 [1 of 2], box 106, Country Files—Far East—Vietnam Negotiations, HAK Office Files, RNPL.

54. Kissinger claimed he had wanted to meet with Le Duc Tho, Hanoi's "special adviser" to and actual chief of the North Vietnamese delegation, but Tho had already left Paris for Hanoi; Kissinger, *White House Years*, 277–278.

55. MemCon, Kissinger and Thuy, 4 August 1969, folder: Mister "S," vol. 1 [1 of 2], box 106, Country Files—Far East—Vietnam Negotiations, HAK Office Files, RNPL; see also *FRUS, 1969–1976*, vol. 6, doc. 106, pp. 330–331.

56. MemCon, Kissinger and Thuy, 4 August 1969; and 3 August 1969 entry, Chronology of US-DRV Negotiations, 1969–1973 (Private Meetings).

57. MemCon, Kissinger and Foreign Minister Schumann et al., 4 August 1969, folder: MemCon—Dr. Kissinger and FM Schumann, August 4, 1969, box 1023, NSCF: Presidential/HAK MemCons, RNPL.

58. Leonard Garment, *Crazy Rhythm* (New York: Times Books, 1997), 174 and 176–177, Telcon transcript, Kissinger and Garment, 12 August 1969, HAK Telcons. Another messenger was Kissinger's aide Helmut Sonnenfeldt; see Memo, Sonnenfeldt to Kissinger, 22 September 1969, subj: Message to You from Arbatov, folder: USSR, vol. 5—10/69, box 710, NSCF: Country Files—Europe, RNPL.

59. Msg, CTG 7.6 to COMNAVBASE Subic, 28 July 1969, box 119, 7th Flt Prov Logistics Miscellaneous, July 1969; COMSEVENTHFLT to CINPAC-FLT, 30 July, box 120, 7th Flt Prov Miscellaneous July 1969; Memo, Robinson through Haig to Kissinger, 8 August 1969, subj: Mining Readiness Test, folder: Items to Discuss with the President, 8/8/1969–12/30/1969, box 334, NSCF: Subject Files, RNPL.

60. Msg, CTF 7 to COMSEVENTHFLT, 5 August 1969; Msg, COM-SERVPAC to NAVMAG Subic, 8 August 1969, box 122, 7th Flt Prov Miscellaneous, August 1969; Msg, NAVMAG Subic to COMSEVENTHFLT, 5 August 1969, box 122, 7th Flt Prov Logistics, August 1969; Msg, COMSERVPAC to COMSEVENTHFLT, 6 August 1969, box 122, 7th Flt Prov Logistics/Ordnance, August 1969; Msg, NAVMAG Subic to CTG 7.3, 7 October 1969, and to USS Coral Sea, 30 October 1969, box 128, 7th Flt Prov Mine Warfare, October 1969—all in 7th Fleet Records, HAD.

61. Memo, Robinson through Haig for Kissinger, 8 August 1969 (second of two memos), subj: Mine Readiness Test, folder: Items to Discuss with the President, 8 August 1969–30 December 1969, box 334, NSCF: Subject Files, RNPL; Cable 8452, Embassy Manila to State Department, 8 August 1969, subj: Pincus/Paul Visit, MDR. See also Memo from "Bus" Wheeler to "Mel," 11 August 1969, enclosing memorandum from General McPherson to General Wheeler, 11 August 1969, DOD MDR.

62. Cable 8452, Embassy Manila to State Department. The embassy allowed that the "events recounted may be entirely coincidental" but wanted to "get the facts straight." Pincus may have had this news story in mind: "Nixon Indicates He Seeks Step-Up in War Effort," *New York Times*, 18 April 1967.

63. Memo, Haig to Kissinger, 19 August 1969, subj: Items to Discuss with the President, enclosing message from Fulbright to Laird, folder: Items to Discuss with the President, 8 August 1969–30 December 1969, box 334, NSCF: Subject Files, NPL.

64. See, e.g., *New York Times*, 13 and 17 August 1969.

65. Telcon transcript, Kissinger and Laird, 18 August 1969, 9:30 a.m., HAK Telcons. Rogers "wanted them to be shown in the White House."

Chapter 7. Toward the November Option: DUCK HOOK and PRUNING KNIFE

1. Quoted in Editorial Note, *FRUS, 1969–1976*, vol. 34, doc. 83, p. 283, originally from Memo for the Record, 12 September 1969, folder: Contingency Planning, Sept.–Oct. 1969, box 45: Geopolitical File, Vietnam, Kissinger Papers, MS Div., which is unavailable to researchers.

2. Memo, Robinson to Wheeler, 7 July 1969 folder: White House Memos (1969), box 169, Wheeler Records, RG 218, NARA.

3. See "Vietnam Policy Alternatives" papers for 3 July 1969 and 5 August 1969, both in Misc. Materials—Selected Lord Memos, Policy Planning Staff, Director's Files (Winston Lord), 1969–77, RG 59, NARA. For "'maximum' pressure," see the 5 August 1969 paper, p. 10.

4. "Vietnam Policy Alternatives," 3 July 1969, RG 59, NARA.

5. Telcon transcript, Kissinger and Laird, 2 July 1969, HAK Telcons; Memo, Laird to Nixon, subj: Vietnamizing the War (NSSM 36), *FRUS, 1969–1976*, vol. 6, doc. 114, pp. 358–367.

6. Telcon transcript, Kissinger and Laird, telegram 21 July 1969, 12:55 p.m., HAK Telcons; Memo, Laird to Kissinger, 21 July 1969, encls: Office of the Chief of Naval Operations, "DUCK HOOK," 20 July 1969, and "Summary of Interdiction (Quarantine) Plan for Port of Sihanoukville," n.d., DOD MDR release (also available at RNPL).

7. Memo, Kissinger to Nixon, n.d., subj: Conceptual Plan for Implementation of Operation DUCK HOOK, folder: White House Memos (1969), box 169,

Wheeler Records, RG 218, NARA (emphasis added). The authors' estimate of a July to August date for this memo is based on the reference in the first sentence to the DUCK HOOK aerial mining–only operation. There is no mention of a bombing component against North Vietnam in the document; the bombing component would be added later, but by then, the JCS would have renamed the prospective operation as PRUNING KNIFE.

8. Ibid.

9. Ibid. (emphasis added).

10. Pursley, telephone interview by Burr, 25 July 2001.

11. Memo, Wheeler to Laird, 4 August 1969, and Memo, G. Warren Nutter to Laird, 13 August 1969, subj: Contingency Options for North Vietnam, DOD MDR release; Memo, Halperin to Kissinger, 5 August 1969.

12. Memo, Wheeler to Laird, 4 August 1969; Memo, Nutter to Laird, 13 August 1969.

13. Besides in other documents, this tactic is explained in Memo, Tony Lake to Kissinger, 17 September 1969, subj: Initial Comments on Concept of Operations, with attachment, "Vietnam Contingency Planning," 16 September 1969, folder 2, box 1048, NSCF: Files—Lake Chronological Files, RNPL; the 2 October 1969 DUCK HOOK plan is discussed in the next chapter. For a conveniently accessible executive summary of the plan, see, e.g., Memo, Kissinger to Nixon, 2 October 1969, subj: Contingency Military Operations against North Vietnam ["DUCK HOOK Plan"], *FRUS, 1969–1976,* vol. 6, doc. 129, pp. 418–423.

14. "Vietnam Policy Alternatives," July 1969, encl in Memo, Halperin to Kissinger, 5 August 1969. Groundlessly suspected of leaking, Halperin was on his way out of the NSC staff; Lord, who had worked with Halperin on other options and planning papers, "did most of the drafting" on this one.

15. DeBenedetti and Chatfield, *American Ordeal,* 248–274; Wells, *War Within,* 328–338. The White House was aware of plans for the Moratorium and New Mobilization; see, e.g., Memo, Kissinger to Nixon, 10 September 1969, subj: Our Present Course on Vietnam, *FRUS, 1969–1976,* vol. 6, doc. 117, p. 371.

16. "Vietnam Policy Alternatives" (emphasis in original).

17. Ibid. Halperin and Lord wrote the word *Vietnamization* when referring to de-Americanization, i.e., the withdrawal of US troops and other forces. Concerning the "three basic audiences," Nixon invoked this triad at a 12 September meeting of the NSC, saying, "There are three wars—on the battlefield, the Saigon political war, and US politics"; Minutes, 12 September 1969: subj: Vietnam, *FRUS, 1969–1976,* vol. 6, doc. 120, p. 397.

18. "Vietnam Policy Alternatives."

19. Notes, Richardson-Kissinger discussion, 14 August 1969, folder; Mem-Cons, September 1969, box 97; Memo, Morton Abramowitz to Richardson, subj: Request That You Call in British Ambassador to Discuss British Shipping to North Vietnam, 9 September 1969, folder: Abramowitz, Morton, July–December

1969, box 82—both in Elliot Richardson Papers, and MemCon, subj: British Shipping to North Vietnam, 11 September 1969, folder: STR 12–3 VIET N POL UK, Subject-Numeric Files, 1967–1969 and 1970–73, RG 59, NARA.

20. "Vietnam Policy Alternatives."

21. Ibid.

22. Ibid.

23. See chapter 2 for Kissinger's published remarks about the risks of bluffing.

24. Memo, Halperin to Kissinger, 10 September 1969, subj: Vietnam, folder: Misc. Materials—Selected Lord Memos, Director's Files (Winston Lord), 1969–77, DOS Central Files, RG 59, NARA.

25. Telcon transcript, Kissinger and Nixon, 5 August 1969, 6:50 p.m., HAK Telcons.

26. "Confidential survey conducted for the Republican National Committee in consultation with Dr. David R. Derge," folder: The Public Appraises the Nixon Administration and Key Issues (with Particular Emphasis on Vietnam), August 1969, box 406, WHSF: SMOF, HRHPF, RNPL (hereafter cited as Derge Poll). The authors have not been able to find a record of the May survey.

27. Telcon transcripts, Kissinger and Derge, 14 and 22 July 1969, 4:15 p.m., HAK Telcons; Presidential Daily Diary, 16 July 1969, RNPL.

28. Derge Poll cover letter; Handwritten note, 5 August 1969, folder: H Notes July–Dec '69 [July–Sept. 1969], pt. 1, box 40, WHSP: SMOF, HRHPF, RNPL.

29. Derge Poll, August 1969, pp. v–vii and 18–79.

30. Ibid.

31. Ibid.

32. Ibid. This finding was one of several Nixon underlined.

33. Diary entry, 18 August 1969, HRHD ("hard-core inner circle" is from Diary entry, 21 July 1969); Presidential Daily Diary, 18 August 1969, RNPL; William Watts, who was present in California, is quoted as saying that DUCK HOOK was discussed; Wells, *War Within*, 357.

34. Diary entry, 18 August 1969, HRHD.

35. Diary entry, 28 August 1969, HRHD.

36. Letter, Ho Chi Minh to Nixon, 25 August 1969, folder: Mister "S," vol. 1 [1 of 2], box 106, Country Files—Far East—Vietnam Negotiations, HAK Office Files, RNPL.

37. Memo, Kissinger to Nixon, 5 September 1969, subj: Preliminary Analysis of the Significance of the Death of Ho Chi Minh, *FRUS, 1969–1976*, vol. 6, doc. 116, p. 370.

38. Minutes of NSC Meeting, 12 September 1969, subj: Vietnam, *FRUS, 1969–1976*, vol. 6, doc. 120, p. 400. Also see chapter 5 for a brief discussion of the DRV/NLF Ten Point Plan and Nixon's eight-point plan. In *Hanoi's War: An International History of the War for Peace in Vietnam* (Chapel Hill: University of North Carolina Press, 2012), 144, historian Lien-Hang Nguyen argued that "in reality, it was Le Duan who rejected the offer" and that "Ho Chi Minh might

have been amenable" had he not been "marginalized." But the evidence is scant for the latter claim. In any case, Ho had been ill and at the time of the writing of the letter on the verge of death. Nixon's and Kissinger's "offer" was the eight-point plan of May, which Ho and the leadership in Hanoi had previously rejected. It was also coupled with threats against North Vietnam and a deadline of 1 November, to which no leading party member in Hanoi would likely bend. Also see MemCon, 4 August 1969, Kissinger and Thuy et al., in *FRUS, 1969–1976*, vol. 6, doc. 106, pp. 331–343, and Loi and Vu, *Le Duc Tho–Kissinger Negotiations in Paris*, 95–104.

39. Memo, Kissinger to Nixon, 30 August 1969, subj: Response from Ho Chi Minh, *FRUS, 1969–1976*, vol. 6, doc. 111, pp. 351–352, with Ho's letter attached (emphasis added).

40. Memo, Kissinger to Nixon, 5 September 1969, pp. 369–370 and 390; Nixon, *RN*, 398.

41. "Vietnam Policy Alternatives."

42. Ibid.

43. This assessment is based on the authors' interpretation of events that lay ahead as well as on documents such as Memo, Kissinger to Nixon, 20 July 1970, subj: Alternative Vietnam Strategies, folder: Vietnam, box 148, NSCF: Vietnam Country Files, RNPL. It is reproduced as doc. 347 in *FRUS, 1969–1976*, vol. 6, doc. 347, pp. 1133–1139. Kissinger wrote, e.g., "Our present policy continues to hold open the two options of a negotiated end to the war if possible and a gradual US disengagement from Vietnam in the absence of a settlement" (p. 1134). On the timing of withdrawal, see, e.g., Diary entries, 15 and 21 December 1970, HRHD (cf. Kissinger, *Ending the Vietnam War*, 187 and 300); Oval Office, Conversation 451-23, Nixon and Kissinger, 18 February 1971, WHT, RNPL.

44. Memo, Laird to Nixon, 4 September 1969, subj: Vietnamizing the War (NSSM 36), *FRUS, 1969–1976*, vol. 6, doc. 114, p. 367.

45. Ibid., 358–367; also see Van Atta, *Melvin Laird*, 236–237. Laird's aide Colonel Pursley later recalled that Laird wanted Vietnamization to work, and he also wanted to reduce Soviet support to the DRV so that it would be possible to demonstrate to North Vietnam that the United States and South Vietnam were determined to stay in the field for the long term. Although getting the Soviets to reduce their supplies to the DRV was consistent with Vietnamization, "the last thing he wanted to do was to agitate the hell out of them, because that might cause them to go the opposite way. It was better to handle Soviet aid diplomatically"; Pursley, telephone interview. If this is an accurate description of Laird's views, it indicates that he was not necessarily opposed to exerting military pressure; he was opposed to exerting excessive Madman pressure that would counterproductively agitate Moscow. That perhaps was the basic difference between Laird's policy preferences and those of Nixon and Kissinger. But it exposed the US dilemma: how can you provide Thieu with a decent chance without extending the American war indefinitely? Kissinger wrote in *White House Years*, 476

and 478, that the flaw in Laird's approach was his belief that Hanoi would agree in negotiations to a political solution acceptable to the United States.

46. Memo, John Holdridge to Kissinger, 10 September 1969, subj: Positions of Key US Officials on a Cease Fire in Vietnam, *FRUS, 1969–1976,* vol. 6, doc. 118, p. 374. Also see Kissinger's comments on Rogers's position in *White House Years,* 476.

47. Mueller, *War, Presidents, and Public Opinion,* 93–94.

48. Memo, Haig to Kissinger, 9 September 1969, folder: Items to Discuss with the President, 8/13/69–12/30/69, box 334, Vietnam Subject Files, NSCF, RNPL (emphasis in original).

49. Presidential Daily Diary, 9 September 1969.

50. Msg, Bardshar to Wheeler, 15 September 1969, subj: PRUNING KNIFE Status Report no. 1, box 1969–1970, Creighton Abrams Papers, US Army Military History Research Collection (USAMHRC), Carlisle Barracks, PA.

51. Kissinger, *White House Years,* 284–285; Morris, telephone interview by Kimball, 19 February 2007; Morris, *Haig,* 186. Dates of meetings are mentioned in *FRUS, 1969–1976,* vol. 6, doc. 119, p. 376n3. The 10 September Halperin-Lord paper was briefly summarized earlier in this chapter. In 1970, Lake, Lord, Lynn, Morris, and Watts would oppose the US and South Vietnamese invasion of Cambodia. Watts would resign on 26 April 1970, Lake and Morris on 29 April, and Lynn during the fall of that year. Lord stayed on.

52. Morris, telephone interview; Lemnitzer, telephone conversation with Burr, 27 March 2007.

53. Lemnitzer, telephone conversation with Burr, 27 March 2007; Lake, telephone interview by Kimball, 14 December 2005.

54. Oval Office, Conversation no. 527-16, Nixon, Haldeman, Kissinger, and Ehrlichman, 9:14–10:12 a.m., 23 June 1971, WHT, RNPL.; Watts, interview by Kimball, Washington, DC, 21 April 2007; Kissinger, *White House Years,* 479. Hersh, *Price of Power,* 128, quoted portions of his interview with Lynn, who talked about his analysis of a plan that Kissinger wanted him to criticize, leading Lynn to believe that escalation was Nixon's idea and Kissinger was against it, which of course he was not. In the same interview (which is repeated in Isaacson, *Kissinger,* 246–247, and Wells, *War Within,* 358), he identified the plan as DUCK HOOK, but the plan he analyzed was probably PRUNING KNIFE. In a similar example, Lynn told Kimball in a 31 January 2006 e-mail message that he did not recall Kissinger or Morris mentioning tactical nuclear weapons, even though the issue of their possible use was cited in at least one planning paper and indirectly hinted at in others. In a separate but related example of the isolation of Kissinger's aides from one another or their lack of knowledge about the purpose of things in the White House NSC, Lake told Kimball that he had not been informed about the secret bombing of Cambodia and only discovered it accidently; Lake, telephone interview by Kimball, 15 October 2001.

55. Memo with encl, Kissinger to Nixon, 2 October 1969, subj: Contingency

Military Operations against North Vietnam, folder: Vietnam Contingency Planning Top Secret/Sensitive, Henry A. Kissinger, Oct. 2, 1969 [2 of 2], box 89, NSCF: Vietnam Subject Files, RNPL.

56. Hersh, *Price of Power*, 125, cited Watts's remark. About code names, Morris—who had before September worked on African and United Nations issues—told Kimball in February 2007 that he did not know anything about code name "etymology" but knew of the name DUCK HOOK. Lynn was also a latecomer to the Vietnam group, as was Watts and, to some degree, Lord. Lake did not join Kissinger's staff until June 1969.

57. Memo, Kissinger to Nixon, 11 September 1969, *FRUS, 1969–1976*, vol. 6, doc. 119, pp. 376–390. The September paper contained minor changes in the introduction to bring it up to date. As late as 24 September, Kissinger wrote to Nixon that "we are still faced with the four basic options" outlined in the paper.

58. Msg, Bardshar to Wheeler,15 September 1969, subj: PRUNING KNIFE Status Report no. 1, box 1969–1970, Abrams Papers, USAMHRC. For "on the shelf," see Szulc, *Illusion of Peace*, 152.

59. "Doctrinally pure" regarding PRUNING KNIFE is borrowed from historian Stephen P. Randolph, *Powerful and Brutal Weapons: Nixon, Kissinger, and the Easter Offensive* (Cambridge, MA: Harvard University Press, 2007), 185–189, although he appears not to distinguish between the bombing-and-mining DUCK HOOK concept and PRUNING KNIFE, and his focus is on LINEBACKER.

60. This will be discussed later.

61. Concerning the names DUCK HOOK and November Option, see, e.g., Memo, Haig to Kissinger, 9 September 1969, folder: Items to Discuss with the President, 8/13/69–12/30/69, box 334, NSCF: Vietnam Subject Files, RNPL; Memo, Kissinger to Nixon, 11 September 1969, and Memo, Kissinger to Nixon, 2 October 1969, subj: Contingency Military Operations against North Vietnam, *FRUS, 1969–1976*, vol. 6, docs. 119 and 129, pp. 376n3 and 418n1. "DUCK HOOK Plan" is penciled in at the top of the first page of the original document cited in *FRUS* from the Kissinger papers at the Library of Congress; this is not the case with the version filed at RNPL: Memo with encl, Kissinger to Nixon, 2 October 1969, subj: Contingency Military Operations against North Vietnam, folder: Vietnam Contingency Planning Top Secret/Sensitive, Henry A. Kissinger, Oct. 2, 1969 [2 of 2], box 89, NSCF: Vietnam Subject Files, RNPL.

62. Morris, e-mail message to Burr and Kimball, 19 February 2007; Hersh, *Price of Power*, 126–129; Isaacson, *Kissinger*, 246–247; Szulc, *Illusion of Peace*, 150–151. Colson was quoted by Hersh.

63. Report, "Vietnam Contingency Planning: Concept of Operations," 13 September 1969, folder: Vietnam (General Files), Sep 69–Nov 69 [2 of 2], box 74, NSCF: Vietnam Subject Files, RNPL (emphasis added). Additional papers with direct or indirect references to nuclear weapons are discussed and cited in chapter 8. Regarding the Mu Gia Pass, see chapter 1. Also see "Targeting Ho Chi Minh Trail," http://nautilus.org/essentially-annihilated/essentially-anni

hilated-targeting-ho-chi-minh-trail/#axzz2tsM8smfo (accessed 10 December 2014), and Tannenwald, *Nuclear Taboo*, 214–218.

64. Morris, telephone interview; Lake, telephone interview; Memo, Lake and Morris to Robinson, 29 September 1969, subj: Draft Memorandum to the President on Contingency Study, folder: 4, box 74, NSCF: Vietnam Subject Files, RNPL.

65. Pursley, telephone interview.

66. Laird, interview by Burr, 1 December 2005.

67. Kissinger, *White House Years*, 284–285; Hersh, *Price of Power*, 126 and 129; Szulc, *Illusion of Peace*, 150–151.

68. Quoted in Editorial Note, *FRUS*, *1969–1976*, vol. 34, doc. 83, p. 283 (emphasis added).

69. Kissinger, *White House Years*, 283–284 and 286.

70. Memo, Kissinger to Nixon, 10 September 1969, *FRUS*, *1969–1976*, vol. 6, doc. 117, pp. 370–371.

71. Ibid., 370–374n2–6. Also see Kissinger, *White House Years*, 284–286 and 1482–1483.

72. Minutes of NSC Meeting, 12 September 1969, subj: Vietnam, *FRUS*, *Nixon*, *1969–1976*, vol. 6, doc. 120, pp. 390–404 and nn. 1 and 2 on pp. 390 and 391; Diary entries, 12 and 18 September, HRHD. In attendance were Nixon, Agnew, Rogers, Laird, Mitchell, Wheeler, Helms, Bunker, Abrams, McCain, Habib, Kissinger, and Haig.

73. Diary entries, 12 and 18 September, HRHD; Kissinger, *White House Years*, 264–265; Nixon, *RN*, 398.

74. Telcon transcript, Kissinger and Nixon, 15 September 1969, 7:50 p.m., HAK Telcons.

75. Nguyen Co Thach, interview by Kimball, 24 September 1994, Hanoi.

76. Memo, Kissinger to Nixon, 11 September 1969, subj: Conversations with Professor Joseph Starobin; MemCon, 10 September 1969, Starobin, Kissinger, Lake—both in folder: Joseph Starobin, box 106, NSCF: Country Files—Far East—Vietnam Negotiations, RNPL.

77. MemCon, 10 September 1969, Starobin, Kissinger, Lake. For pressure from the Right to escalate, see Sandra Scanlon, *The Pro-War Movement: Domestic Support for the Vietnam War and the Making of Modern American Conservatism* (Boston: University of Massachusetts Press, 2013), 106, 112–114, and 117–119; Kimball, "Out of Primordial Cultural Ooze: Inventing Political and Policy Legacies about the US Exit from Vietnam," *Diplomatic History* 34, no. 3 (June 2010): 577–587.

78. Memo, Kissinger to Nixon, 11 September 1969, subj: Conversations with Professor Joseph Starobin; MemCon, 10 September 1969, Starobin, Kissinger, Lake—both in folder: Joseph Starobin, box 106, NSCF: Country Files—Far East—Vietnam Negotiations, RNPL.

79. 2 September 1969 entry, Chronology of US–DRV Negotiations, 1969–1973 (private meetings).

80. Translation of Letter Received from Jean Sainteny, 20 September 1969, folder: Mister "S" vol. 1 [1 of 2], box 106, Country Files—Far East—Vietnam Negotiations, NSCF, RNPL.

81. Memo, Kissinger to Nixon, 24 September 1969, box 106, Country Files—Far East—Vietnam Negotiations, NSCF, RNPL.

82. Nixon, *RN*, 398.

Chapter 8. To Escalate or Not to Escalate?

1. Diary entry, 3 October 1969, HRHD.

2. Memo, Kissinger to Nixon, 2 October 1969, subj: Contingency Military Operations against North Vietnam [with attachments], folder: 2, box 89, NSCF: Vietnam Subject Files, RNPL.

3. Report, "Vietnam Contingency Planning: Concept of Operations," 13 September 1969, folder: Vietnam (General Files), Sep 69–Nov 69 [2 of 2], box 74, NSCF: Vietnam Subject Files, RNPL; "Vietnam Contingency Planning: Concept of Operations," 16 September 1969, folder: 2, box 1048, NSCF: Files—Lake Chronological Files, RNPL.

4. Report, "Vietnam Contingency Planning: Concept of Operations."

5. Ibid.

6. Ibid. On "clean," see Toshihiro Higuchi, "'Clean' Bombs: Nuclear Technology and Nuclear Strategy in the 1950s," *Journal of Strategic Studies* 29, no. 1 (August 2006): 83–116; Cecil I. Hudson, "Clean Nuclear Explosive Research Applicable to Tactical Nuclear Weapons," in *Los Alamos Scientific Laboratory, Proceedings of the Tactical Nuclear Weapons Symposium, November 3–6, 1969* (Los Alamos, NM: Los Alamos National Laboratory, ca. 1970), Department of Energy MDR release.

7. Report, "Vietnam Contingency Planning: Concept of Operations." On the railroads to China, see CIA, "The Effects of Imposing a Quarantine on North Vietnam," 23 May 1969, folder: CIA, Jan 69–31 Dec 69, vol. 1, box 297, NSC: Agency Files, RNPL.

8. Memo, Lake to Kissinger, 17 September 1969, subj: Initial Comments on Concept of Operations, with attachment: "Vietnam Contingency Planning," 16 September 1969, folder 2, box 1048, NSCF: Lake Chronological Files, RNPL.

9. Ibid.

10. Memo, Kissinger to Nixon, n.d., subj: Conceptual Plan for Implementation of Operation DUCK HOOK, folder: White House Memos (1969), box 169, Wheeler Records, RG 218, NARA.

11. Msg, Bardshar to Wheeler, 15 September 1969, subj: PRUNING KNIFE Status Report no. 1, box 1969–1970, Abrams Papers, USAMHRC.

12. Memo with encl, Wheeler to Kissinger, 25 September 1969, subj: PRUNING KNIFE Concept, folder: Vietnam—Operation Pruning Knife [2 of 2], box 123, NSCF: Vietnam Subject Files, RNPL. On 30 September, Laird, who must not have known that Kissinger had seen the Saigon-based group's draft, told

him by telephone that the group's messages had at last been received but were "very raw" and that the JCS was "revising them considerably." He added that he "understood that the president didn't want . . . warmed over contingency plans" and instead "wanted a fresh start," but the Joint Chiefs had nonetheless "thrown together the old things." Kissinger, who probably did not want Laird to know he had seen the draft, urged him to get the plans to the White House "fairly quickly" anyway, assuring him that "no decision would be made" and reminding him that "the president needs the input to think about it." Telcon transcript, Kissinger and Laird, 30 September 2012, 5:30 p.m., HAK Telcons.

13. Memo with encls, Moorer to Laird, 1 October 1972, subj: Air and Naval Operations against North Vietnam, DOD MDR release. See also Memo, Kissinger to Nixon, n.d., subj: JCS Concept for Air and Naval Operations against North Vietnam, *FRUS, 1969–1976*, vol. 6, doc. 134, p. 448n5, and Telcon transcript, Kissinger and Laird, 30 September 1969, 5:30 p.m., HAK Telcons.

14. Memo with encl, Moorer to Laird, 1 October 1972, subj: Air and Naval Operations against North Vietnam, DOD MDR release.

15. Ibid.

16. MemCon, 27 September 1969, subj: The Rockefeller Report and General Policy, folder: Governor Rockefeller (1969–1974) [1 of 2], box 831, NSCF: Name Files, RNPL.

17. Memo, Buchanan to Nixon, 18 September 1969, folder: Sep 69–Nov 69 [2 of 2], box 79, NSCF: Vietnam Subject File, RNPL.

18. Nixon followed this declaration with a discussion about how to respond to the Moratorium; Memo to the President's File (by Buchanan), 27 September 1969, subj: Notes of Meeting at Camp David, September 27th of Political Group for 1970, box 79, President's Office Files: President Meeting File, RNPL.

19. Regarding "bug out," see Kimball, *Nixon's Vietnam War*, 202, 286, and 369; Kimball, *Vietnam War Files*, 108, 125, and 131; and *FRUS, 1969–1976*, vol. 8, docs. 43, 142, and 270, pp. 142, 341, and 1009. Spoken among the White House inner circle and in the presence of other conservatives and hawks, it did not necessarily carry the dictionary definition of signifying a disorderly rapid retreat, rout, or debacle. It was hyperbole for an exit that might look like a rout—especially to a hawk.

20. Telcon transcript, Kissinger and Nixon, 27 September 1969, 3:15 p.m., HAK Telcons (emphasis added).

21. Telcon transcript, Nixon and Kissinger, 27 September 1969, 4:40 p.m., HAK Telcons; Briefing Memo, Kissinger to Nixon, 1 October 1969, subj: Conversation with Soviet Ambassador Dobrynin, box 489, Dobrynin and Kissinger 1969 [pt. 1], NSCF: President's Trip Files, RNPL.

22. MemCon (US), Kissinger and Dobrynin, 27 September 1969, *Soviet-American Relations*, doc. 27, p. 77n1.

23. Memo, Kissinger to Nixon, 1 October 1969, subj: Conversation with Soviet Ambassador Dobrynin, attached to MemCon, Kissinger and Dobrynin, 27 September 1969, folder: Dobrynin/Kissinger 1969, box 489, NSCF: President's Trip Files [pt. 2], RNPL (emphasis added); Presidential Daily Diary, 27 September

1969, RNPL; Diary entry, 27 September 1969, HRHD; Telcon transcript, Nixon and Kissinger, 27 September 1969, 4:40 p.m., HAK Telcons.

24. Nixon, *RN,* 399–400; Kissinger, *White House Years,* 304.

25. Memo to the President's File (by Buchanan), 27 September 1969, subj: Notes of Meeting at Camp David, September 27th of Political Group for 1970, box 79, President's Office Files: President's Meeting Files, RNPL; Memo, Haig to Kissinger, 8 October 1969, subj: Buchanan's Memorandum to the President on Vietnam, folder: Sep 69–Nov 69 [2 of 2], box 79, NSCF: Vietnam Subject File, RNPL.

26. See, e.g., Oval Office, Conversations nos. 466-12 and 508-1, 3, Nixon and Kissinger, 11 March 1971 and 2 June 1971, WHT; MemCon, Kissinger and Le Duc Tho, 26 September 1972, folder: SENSITIVE Camp David—vol. 18 [Sep. 1972], box 856, NSCF: For the President's Files (Winston Lord)—China Trip/ Vietnam; Diary entries, 21 February and 7 July 1969, HRHD; MemCon, Nixon, Thompson, and Kissinger, 17 October 1969, folder: MemCon—The President, Sir Robert Thompson et al., 17 October 1969, box 1023, NSCF: Presidential/ HAK MemCons—all at RNPL. Also see Kissinger, *White House Years,* 969; Kimball, *Nixon's Vietnam War,* 364–366; Kimball, *Vietnam War Files,* 278–286; Scanlon, *Pro-War Movement.*

27. Telcon transcript, Nixon and Kissinger, 27 September 1969, 4:40 p.m., HAK Telcons.

28. Rowland Evans and Robert Novak, *Washington Post,* 25 September 1969; DeBenedetti and Chatfield, *American Ordeal,* 253; Scanlon, *Pro-War Movement,* 120–121.

29. Telcon transcript, Nixon and Kissinger, 27 September 1969, 4:40 p.m., HAK Telcons.

30. Nixon, *RN,* 400.

31. Rowland Evans and Robert Novak, *Washington Post,* 8 October 1969.

32. Ibid.

33. Andrew Z. Katz, "Public Opinion and Foreign Policy: The Nixon Administration and the Pursuit of Peace with Honor in Vietnam," *Presidential Studies Quarterly* 27, no. 3 (Summer 1997): fig. 1, p. 298; Small, *Johnson, Nixon, and the Doves,* 188; DeBenedetti and Chatfield, *American Ordeal,* 252; Mueller, *War, Presidents, and Public Opinion,* fig. 3.2, p. 56, tab. 3.3, pp. 54–55, and tab. 4.6, p. 107. Haldeman's meeting notes show that Nixon was following polls closely during this period; see, e.g., entries for 2 and 3 October, folder: H Notes, July–Dec. '69 [Oct.–Dec. 1969], pt. 2, box 40, WHSP: SMOF, HRHPF, RNPL.

34. Telcon transcript, Nixon and Kissinger, 27 September 1969, 4:40 p.m., HAK Telcons; Diary entry, 27 September 1969, HRHD; and Wells, *War Within,* 347–355. "Horrible results" was Nixon's reference to a potential "massive adverse reaction" to his scheduled 3 November speech after he had decided against the November Option, but it accurately reflected his thinking about the effect on the demonstrators of the bombing and mining of North Vietnam had he gone through with these measures; see, e.g., Diary entries, 29 September and 23 October, HRHD, and cf. Nixon, *RN,* 401–402. The words *rioting* and *riots* were

standard White House nomenclature for any and all mass antiwar demonstrations, including the overwhelming majority of nonviolent ones such as the Moratorium and New Mobilization.

35. Telcon transcript, Nixon and Kissinger, 27 September 1969.

36. Handwritten note, 27 September, folder: H Notes July–Dec. '69 [Oct.–Dec. 1969], pt. 2, WHSP: SMOF, HRHPF, RNPL; and Diary entry, 29 September 1969, HRHD.

37. Memo, Kissinger to Nixon, 2 October 1969. A partial copy of this paper from the Kissinger files at the Library of Congress is reproduced in *FRUS, 1969–1976*, vol. 6, doc. 129, pp. 418–423, with a footnote stating that the document was not initialed by Kissinger or seen by Nixon. But see Telcon transcripts, Kissinger and Laird, 30 September 1969, 5:30 and 6:58 p.m., HAK Telcons, in which Kissinger tells Laird that Nixon wants to see the JCS plan (and presumably the DUCK HOOK plan). Also see Diary entry, 3 October 1969, HRHD, in which Haldeman clearly says that Nixon spent several hours with him, Ehrlichman, and Kissinger talking about military and PR plans, including Kissinger's "contingency plans." For attendees at the 2 October White House meeting between Nixon and NSC staff, see Presidential Daily Diary, 2 October 1969, RNPL.

38. For Nixon's views on morality regarding the Vietnam War and World War II, see, e.g., Oval Office, Conversation no. 508-13, Nixon and Kissinger, 2 June 1971, 9:45 a.m.–12:04 p.m., WHT, RNPL; for an excerpt, see Kimball, *Vietnam War Files*, 160–166. Concerning Nixon's infatuation with special ops, see pertinent documents in *FRUS, 1969–1976*, vol. 8.

39. Diary entry, 3 October 1969, HRHD; Handwritten note, 3 October 1969.

40. Diary entry, 3 October 1969, HRHD.

41. Memo, Kissinger to Nixon, 2 October 1969.

42. Ibid.

43. Ibid. The Lake and Morris comments are in Memo, Lake to Kissinger, 17 September 1969; Memo, Lake and Morris to Robinson, 29 September 1969.

44. Memo, Kissinger to Nixon, 2 October 1969.

45. Ibid.

46. Ibid. (emphasis added).

47. Memo, Lake and Morris to Robinson, 29 September 1969 (emphasis added); Morris, telephone interview by Kimball, 19 February 2007; Lake, telephone interview by Kimball, 14 December 2005.

48. Diary entry, 3 October 1969, HRHD; for *bug out* and *cop out*, see, e.g., 3 and 9 October 1969 entries, HRHD.

49. Memo, Laird to Nixon, 8 October 1969, subj: Air and Naval Operations against North Vietnam, DOD MDR release, and Memo, Kissinger to Nixon, n.d., subj: Concept for Air and Naval Operations against North Vietnam, *FRUS, 1969–1976*, vol. 6, doc. 134, pp. 448–450.

50. Memo, Laird to Nixon, 8 October 1969.

51. Diary entry, 8 October 1969, HRHD.

52. Quoted in *New York Times*, 10 October 1968.

53. Quoted in Haldeman, *Ends of Power*, 81.

54. Diary entry, 9 October 1969, HRHD. Compounding Kissinger's deteriorating relationship with Nixon was his own handling of his rivalry with Rogers and Laird. Nixon complained on 9 October, for example, that Kissinger was "obsessed" with wanting their "total compliance." This, along with his insistence on "perfection," led Nixon to tell Haldeman that Kissinger's attitude "needs to be modified somehow." Because his advice for an escalation strategy had been rejected, Kissinger suspected that he was being eased out of the administration. Haldeman's diary entries for 3, 11, and 13 October are also revealing concerning Nixon's thoughts about the November Option.

55. Diary entry, 9 October 1969, HRHD (emphasis in original).

56. Memo, Haig to Kissinger, 9 October 1969, subj: Items to Discuss with the President, folder: Items to Discuss with the President, 8/13/69–12/30/69, box 334, NSCF: Subject Files, RNPL.

57. Oval Office, Conversation no. 713-1, Nixon and Kissinger, 19 April 1972, 3:27–5:01 p.m., WHT, RNPL. The transcript of this conversation in *FRUS, 1969–1976*, vol. 8, doc. 88, does not include this part of the conversation.

58. Ibid., 398–405. A few examples of Nixon's muddled and incomplete account in *RN* are illustrative. He suggested on p. 402 that it was only *after* the 15 October Moratorium had taken place that he thought his warnings to Hanoi had lost their credibility, when in fact the documentary evidence shows that he had expressed this concern to Kissinger at least as early as 29 September (see the discussion of this conversation in a previous section of this chapter). He made no clear distinction between congressional opposition to escalation and the opposition of the antiwar demonstrators in the streets or the populace at large. He did not provide a coherent account of the reasons for the opposition to escalation within the administration, nor did he adequately discuss Hanoi's and Moscow's responses to his threats and how strongly these influenced his decision.

59. Nixon, *No More Vietnams*, 150.

60. See, e.g., Telcon transcript, Nixon and Kissinger, 4:40 p.m., 27 September 1969, HAK Telcons, and Diary entry, 27 September 1969, HRHD, discussed previously.

61. Citing Roger Morris and Tony Lake, Tom Wells's account in *The War Within*, 377–379, is consistent with this assessment. He mentions several of these causes: potential political difficulties on the home front, Laird's opposition, the critical assessments by Kissinger's aides of the military potential of the November Option, and Nixon's mood swings.

62. Diary entry, 3 October 1969, HRHD, and Memo, Robinson to Wheeler, 7 July 1969, folder: White House Memos (1969), box 169, Wheeler Records, RG 218, NARA. Also see chapter 7 in this book.

63. E.g., Draft of a Presidential Speech, 2nd Draft, 27 September 1969, folder: Vietnamese War—Secret Peace Talks (Mister "S" File) (5), 9/1/69–9/30/69,

box 34, National Security Advisor—Kissinger-Scowcroft West Wing Office Files, 1969–1977, GFL. The 2 October draft was probably the third version.

64. Memo, Kissinger to Nixon, 2 October 1969.

65. See, e.g., Diary entry, 4 December 1972, HRHD; Memo, Nixon to Kissinger, 5 December 1972, *FRUS, 1969–1976*, vol. 9, doc. 141, p. 522.

66. Diary entry, 9 October 1969, HRHD.

67. Telcon transcript, Nixon and Kissinger, 10 October 1969, 7;30 p.m., *FRUS, 1969–1976*, vol. 6, doc. 135, pp. 452 and 451.

68. Memo, Nixon to Kissinger, 21 October 1969, folder: Presidential Memoranda 1969, box 228, WHSF: SMOF, HRH, RNPL.; Nixon's yellow-pad notes, 26 October 1969, folder: 3 November 1969, Vietnam Speech [5 of 5], box 53: President's Speech File, 1969–1974 [3 of 5] to 15 December 1969, Vietnam Statement, WHSF: President's Personal File, RNPL; Diary entry, 10 October 1969, HRHD. On Nixon's solicitation of advice regarding the speech, see Editorial note, *FRUS, 1969–1976*, vol. 6, doc. 144, pp. 477–478.

69. Kissinger, *White House Years*, 305.

70. Memo with encl, Kissinger to Nixon, 2 October 1969.

71. Oval Office, Conversation no. 809-2, Nixon, Kissinger, Haldeman, 25 October 1972, WHT, RNPL.

72. Nixon, *RN*, 405.

73. Nixon followed his special-reminder remark with a comment about his meeting with Dobrynin on 20 October. In a talking points memo to Nixon, Kissinger noted that Dobrynin's request for a meeting "comes against the background of several developments, including . . . Moscow's undoubted awareness of unusual military measures on our part," which was a clear reference to the JCS Readiness Test; Memo, Kissinger to Nixon, 18 October 1969, subj: Your Meeting with Ambassador Dobrynin, Monday, 20 October 1969, folder 1: Dobrynin/Kissinger, box 489, NSCF: President's Trip Files, RNPL. See chapter 9 for a discussion of this meeting.

74. See, e.g., Diary entry, 17 October 1969, HRHD, and Memo, Haig to Kissinger, 17 October 1969.

75. Laird, telephone interviews.

76. Pursley, telephone interview.

77. MemCon, Kissinger and Tho, 4 December 1972, folder: Sensitive Camp David—Vol. 22, Minutes of Meetings, Paris, Dec. 4–Dec. 13, box 859, NSCF: For the President's Files (Winston Lord)—China Trip/Vietnam 1972, RNPL.

78. E-mail message, Luu Doan Huynh to Kimball, 19 September 2009.

79. Telcon transcript, Kissinger and Nixon, 10 October 1969, 7:30 p.m., HAK Telcons; also *FRUS, 1969–1976*, vol. 6 doc. 135, p. 453.

80. Note, Robinson to Wheeler, 10 October 1969, folder: White House Memos (1969), box 169, Wheeler Records, RG 218, NARA; Telcon transcripts, Kissinger and Laird, 1 and 7 October 1969, 3:10 p.m. and 9:15 a.m., and Kissinger and Nixon, 7 October 1969, 12:45 p.m., HAK Telcons.

81. For Lynn's analysis of targets, see, e.g., Memo, Kissinger to Nixon, n.d. [probably 10 October], subj: JCS Concept for Air and Naval Operations against North Vietnam, *FRUS, 1969–1976*, vol. 6, doc. 134, pp. 446–450 (emphasis in original). Also see Talking Points [HAK to RN?], 11 October 1969, subj: Meeting with Secretary of Defense and Joint Chiefs of Staff, folder 4: VIETNAM, vol. 11-A, Memos & Misc. [re PRUNING KNIFE], box 139, NSCF: Vietnam Country Files, RNPL, with attachments: Memo, Lynn to Kissinger, 10 October 10, 1969, subj: JCS Concept Plan for Air and Naval Operations against North Vietnam; and Memo, Moorer to Laird, 1 October 1969, subj: Air and Naval Operations against North Vietnam, with Appendixes. Also see Memo, Carver to Lynn, 29 September 1969, subj: North Vietnam Target Inventory, with attachment: "Significant Physical Facilities in North Vietnam," CREST.

82. Memo, Kissinger to Nixon, n.d. [probably 10 October].

83. Ibid.

84. Ibid., 448–450. Laird forwarded his critique of PRUNING KNIFE to Nixon through Kissinger on 8 October.

85. Memo for the Record [by Moorer], 11 October 1969, subj: JCS Meeting with the President, *FRUS, 1969–1976*, vol. 6, doc. 136, pp. 454–460.

86. Ibid.

87. Van Atta, *With Honor*, 237.

88. See, e.g., Memo, Kissinger to Nixon, 20 July 1970, subj: Alternative Vietnam Strategies, folder: Vietnam, box 148, NSCF: Vietnam Country Files, RNPL; see also *FRUS, 1969–1976*, vol. 6, doc. 347, pp. 1133–1139.

89. Memo for the Record [by Moorer], 11 October 1969.

90. Ibid.

91. Ibid.

92. See, e.g., Oval Office, Conversations no. 489-17, Nixon and Kissinger, 2:47–4:12 p.m., 26 April 1971 [Kissinger entered at 3:56 p.m.], and 488-15, Nixon and Kissinger (Haldeman present), 10:19–11:43 a.m., 27 April 1971, WHT, RNPL.; and Memo, Nixon to Kissinger, 11 March 1972, box 230, WHSF: SMOF, Haldeman, RNPL.

93. Memo for the Record [by Moorer], 11 October 1969, subj: JCS Meeting with the President, *FRUS*, 1969–1976, vol. 6, doc. 136, p. 457 (emphasis in original).

94. Ibid.

95. Ibid., 457–458. Moorer quoted Nixon as asking, "What can we do in two weeks?" It is clear from the rest of the conversation that Nixon did not mean attacking North Vietnam in two weeks, i.e., 25 October. He meant: what can we do in a bombing-and-mining operation whose duration is two weeks?

96. Ibid., 460. Moorer, apparently failing to understand what Nixon implied by "tit for tat"—that is, seeking purely military objectives in a US response—parenthetically commented in his MemCon that "the JCS have always thought differently and have never agreed with the previous tit for tat policy."

97. See, e.g., Memo, Kissinger to Nixon, 11 September 1969, subj:

Conversations with Professor Joseph Starobin; MemCon, 10 September 1969, Starobin, Kissinger, Lake—both in folder: Joseph Starobin, box 106, NSCF: Country Files—Far East—Vietnam Negotiations, RNPL; and Memcon (Dobrynin), 20 October 1969, *Soviet-American Relations*, doc. 34, p. 97.

Chapter 9. The Secret Nuclear Alert

1. Nixon, *RN*, 405.

2. Diary entry, 8 October 1969, HRHD.

3. Memo, Haig to Kissinger, 14 October 1969, subj: Significant Military Actions, folder: Haig Chron, October 1–October 15, 1969 [1 of 2], box 958, NSCF: Haig Chronological Files, RNPL. This memo contains a time line, a report on the current status of the alert, and recommendations.

4. Memo, Kissinger to Nixon, n.d., subj: Conceptual Plan for Implementation of Operation DUCK HOOK, folder: World-Wide Increased Readiness Posture, box 109, Wheeler Records, RG 218, NARA. See chapter 7 in this book for a discussion of this plan.

5. Telcon transcript, Kissinger and Laird, 6 October 1969, 11:40 a.m., HAK Telcons; Memo, Haig to Kissinger, 14 October 1969.

6. Telcon transcript, Kissinger/Laird, 7 October.

7. Memo, Haig to Kissinger, 14 October 1969. Suspected by the White House of leaking information, Pursley was then being wiretapped by the FBI on Kissinger's orders.

8. Ibid.

9. See chapter 8.

10. Memo, Kissinger to Nixon, 9 October 1969, subj: Military Alerts, with Pursley memo attached, folder: Schedule of Significant Military Exercises, vol. 1, box 352, NSCF: Subject Files, RNPL.

11. Msg, Holloway to JCS, 9 August 1969, folder: 323.3 CINCSAC, box 80, Wheeler Records, RG 218, NARA; Editorial note, *FRUS, 1969–1976*, vol. 34, doc. 60, pp. 234–235.

12. Memo, Haig to Kissinger, 9 October 1969, subj: Items to Discuss with the President, 10 October, with Pursley memo attached, folder: Items to Discuss with the President, 8/13/69 to 12/30/69, box 334, NSCF: Subject Files, RNPL.

13. Memo, Kissinger to Nixon, 9 October 1969; Memo, Haig to Kissinger, 14 October 1969. A copy with Nixon's initials has not yet surfaced.

14. See chapter 8.

15. Memo, Lemnitzer to Wheeler, 9 October 1969, with attached memoranda, box 109, Wheeler Records, RG 218, NARA (emphasis added). This is yet another of many comments linking the purpose of the alert with Vietnam policy and particularly the November Option.

16. For Wheeler's lack of direct knowledge of specific, official "objectives," see Memo, Wheeler to Laird, 6 November 1969, subj: US Military Readiness Tests—Worldwide, *FRUS, 1969–1976*, vol. 34, doc. 92, p. 296.

17. MemCon (USSR), Dobrynin and Kissinger, 9 October 1969, and Telegram, Dobrynin to Soviet Foreign Ministry, 10 October 1969, *Soviet-American Relations*, docs. 28 and 29, pp. 79–80 and 83. Whether the Soviets connected what Kissinger told Dobrynin about Nixon's displeasure to the alert activities that unfolded in the following weeks can only be determined through closed archives in Moscow.

18. There are two transcripts of this conversation in the record; each is worded slightly differently but does not contradict the other: Telcon transcripts, Kissinger and Laird, 10 October 1969, 11:40 a.m., HAK Telcons, RNPL.

19. Ibid.

20. Ibid. The sentence reads: " . . . much more on L[aird]'s line."

21. Wheeler to Laird, 10 October 1969, subj: Significant Military Actions, with Memo to the President attached, box 109, Wheeler Records, RG 218, NARA.

22. Msgs, CJCS to CINCS, 10 October 1969, subj: Increased Readiness Posture, box 109, Wheeler Records, RG 218, NARA. See also Headquarters, US Strategic Air Command, *Notes on Increased Readiness Posture of October 1969* (Offutt Air Force Base, NE: Strategic Air Command, 1970), prepared by Lynn Peake, SAC History no. 136, January 1970, Air Force FOIA release.

23. For "intensification," see Memo, Wheeler to Laird, 10 October 1969. For "beef up," see US Air Force, 380th Strategic Aerospace Wing, *History of the 380th Strategic Aerospace Wing, October–December 1969, Top Secret Annex* (Plattsburgh Air Force Base, NY: 380th Strategic Aerospace Wing, Strategic Air Command, ca. 1970), prepared by Sgt. Allen McCorstin, copy at NSArchive; Msgs, CINCPAC to JCS, 19 and 20 October 1969, box 109, Wheeler Records, RG 218, NARA. For the navy EMCON programs, see Robert G. Angevine, "Hiding in Plain Sight: The US Navy and Dispersed Operations under ECMCON," *Naval War College Review* 64 (Spring 2011): 80–95.

24. Msg, Wheeler to Holloway, CINCSAC et al., 10 October 1969, box 109, Wheeler Records, RG 218, NARA.

25. Memo, Haig to Kissinger, 14 October 1969.

26. Ibid.; Headquarters, US Strategic Air Command, Office of the Historian, *History of Strategic Air Command, FY 1970*, Historical Study no. 117 (Offutt Air Force Base, NE: Strategic Air Command, 1971), vol. 1, 20 April 1971 (hereafter *SAC History FY 70*), 154; Peake, *Notes on Increased Readiness Posture of October 1969*, 4–5.

27. Laird to the President, 11 October 1969, subj: Test of US Military Readiness, DOD MDR release.

28. Laird, telephone interviews, and Pursley, telephone interview.

29. Memo, Wheeler to Laird, 6 November 1969.

30. Memo, Haig to Kissinger, 13 October 1969, subj: Items to Discuss with the President, folder: Items to Discuss with the President, 8/13/69 to 12/30/69, box 334, NSCF: Subject Files, RNPL.

31. Pursley, telephone interview.

32. *SAC History FY 70,* 151–153; Msg, JCS to CINCEUR et al., 11 October 1969, subj: Increased Readiness Posture, box 109, Wheeler Records, RG 218, NARA.

33. Telcon transcript, Kissinger and Laird, 13 October 1969, 6:50 p.m., HAK Telcons, RNPL; Memo, Haig to Kissinger, 14 October 1969; Memo, Haig to Colonel Behr, 9 September 1969, subj: Military Exercise High Heels 69, folder: Haig Chron, September 1969 [2 of 2], box 958—both in NSCF: Haig Chronological Files, RNPL. The scenario for this HIGH HEELS exercise included "ominous" Soviet and Chinese "threats," US countermeasures, Warsaw Pact seizure of parts of Central Europe and Scandinavia, and the movement of Chinese forces into North Korea. By the second day of the exercise, US strategic forces were at DEFCON 2, close to the brink of nuclear war. See Flag Plot Briefings, Wednesday, 15 October through Friday, 17 October 1969, Smooth Briefs, October 1969, Navy Command Center (NCC), 1958–1998 Collection (COLL/748), HAD.

34. Memo, Wheeler to Laird, 14 October 1969, subj: Plan for Increased Readiness Procedure, with talking points attached, DOD MDR release; Msgs from CINCSAC, CINCLANT, and CINCONAD, 11 October 1969, box 109, Wheeler Records, RG 218, NARA.

35. Memo, Wheeler to Laird, 14 October 1969; Memo, G. C. Brown, Defense Intelligence Agency, to Director J-3 (Operations), subj: Concept Plan to Physically Test US Military Readiness, 11 October 1969—both in DOD MDR release; Telcon, Kissinger and Laird, 13 October 1969. See also CINCAL General Ruegg to Wheeler, 11 October 1969, box 109, Wheeler Records, RG 218, NARA.

36. Memo, Haig to Kissinger, 14 October 1969; Goodpaster and CINCONAD messages to Wheeler, 13 October 1969, DOD MDR release; Msg, Wheeler to Goodpaster, 11 October 1969, box 109, Wheeler Records, RG 218, NARA.

37. Telcon, Secretary Laird, 13 October 1969, 6:50 p.m. (emphasis added).

38. Memo, Jackson to General Wheeler, 13 October 1969, box 109, Wheeler Records, RG 218, NARA; Memo, Haig to Kissinger, 14 October 1969 (emphasis added).

39. Memo, Haig to Kissinger, 14 October 1969, subj: Items to Discuss with the President, 14 October 1969, folder: Items to Discuss with the President, 8/13/69 to 12/30/69, box 334, NSCF: Subject Files, RNPL.

40. Memo, Dean Axene to Vice Chief of Naval Operations, 28 October 1969, subj: High Heels '69, folder: 3500 Training and Readiness, box 32, Immediate Office Files of the Chief of Naval Operations, HAD; Memo, Wheeler to AIG, 14 October 1969, subj: High Heels 69, box 123, Wheeler Records, RG 218, NARA.

41. Msg, Wheeler to Spivy, Brussels; Msg, Wheeler to Holloway et al., 14 October 1969, box 109, Wheeler Records, RG 218, NARA.

42. Memo, Wheeler to Holloway et al., 14 October 1969, subj: Increased Readiness Posture, box 109, Wheeler Records, RG 218, NARA.

43. US Air Force, 305th Bombardment Wing, *History of 305th Bombardment*

Wing (Medium), October–December 1969, Annex 1 (Grissom Air Force Base, IN: 305th Bombardment Wing, Strategic Command, ca. 1970), copy at NSArchive; *SAC History FY 1970,* 151; Peake, *Notes on Increased Readiness Posture of October 1969,* 12.

44. Msg, COMSEVENTHFLT to CFT 71 et al., 18 October 1969, subj: Increased Readiness Posture, 18 October 1969, folder: Soviet Fleet Operations, October 1969, box 128, 7th Fleet Records, HAD; Lemnitzer memorandum, 15 October 1969, subj: Additional Actions for US Military Readiness Tests—Worldwide, box 109, Wheeler Records, RG 218, NARA.

45. Telcons, Kissinger and Laird, 13 and 14 October 1969, 12:05 and 9:30 a.m., HAK Telcons, RNPL; "Private Diary," entry for 17 October 1969, box 201, Wheeler Records, RG 218, NARA.

46. Msg, CINCSAC to commanders, 12 October 1969, copy at NSArchive; *SAC History FY 1970,* 117, 123, 126, and 153; US Air Force, 15th Air Force, *History of the 456th Strategic Aerospace Wing, Heavy, and 456th Combat Support Group, 1 October–31 December 1969* (Beale Air Force Base, CA: 456th Strategic Aerospace Wing, ca. 1970), 28, copy at NSArchive.

47. *SAC History FY 1970,* 153; *Top Secret Annex to the October–December 1969 History.*

48. US Air Forces in Europe, Headquarters, *History of United States Air Forces in Europe, Fiscal Year 1970* (Ramstein Air Force Base, Germany: US Air Forces in Europe, ca. 1971), vol. 1, excerpts, FOIA release. For Goodpaster's directive to army, air, and naval forces in Europe, see Goodpaster to CINCUSAFE et al., 13 October 1969, subj: Increased Readiness Posture, box 109, Wheeler Records, RG 218, NARA.

49. Msgs, SSO Strike to General Wheeler, 13 October 1969, and JCS to CINCSTRIKE, 10, 13, and 14 October 1969, subj: Increased Readiness Posture, box 109, Wheeler Records, RG 218, NARA; US Tactical Air Command, *History of the Tactical Air Command, 1 July 1969–30* (Langley Air Force Base, VA: Tactical Air Command, 1970), 237; E-mail msg from Daniel Harrington (Air Combat Command Historical Office) to Burr, 26 August 2002, regarding CINC-STRIKE-TAC relationship.

50. Msgs, JCS to CINCAL and CINCONAD, 10 October 1969, box 109, Wheeler Records, RG 218, NARA. For descriptions of the Aerospace Defense Command and Alaska Air Command force structures, see *Air Force and Space Digest* 52 (September 1969): 110–119 and 152–157. Bomarc is an acronym for the Boeing-Michigan Air Research Center.

51. *History of the 380th Strategic Aerospace Wing*; L. Douglas Keeney, *15 Minutes: General Curtis LeMay and the Countdown to Nuclear Armageddon* (New York: St. Martin's Press, 2011), 176. According to the 380th's official historian, McCorstin, the "crux was to not let the Soviets know *why*" US forces were on higher alert, but even SAC did not know the answer.

52. Telcon, Kissinger and Rockefeller, 14 October 1969, 4:50 p.m., HAK Telcons, RNPL; Memo, Wheeler to Laird, 17 October 1969, subj: US Military Readiness Tests—Worldwide, box 109, Wheeler Records, RG 218, NARA; CIA, "Possible Communist Reactions to US Military Readiness Test," 27 October 1969, State Department MDR release. Rockefeller had been in Washington a few days earlier, and the implication of the Telcon transcript is that Kissinger had then briefed him on the readiness test.

53. DIA Special Intelligence Report, "Final Summary of Soviet Reactions to US Operations," 6 November 1969, folder: Vietnam—Operation Pruning Knife [2 of 2], box 123, NSCF: Vietnam Subject Files, RNPL. That this report and others can be found in a Vietnam War contingency planning file is further evidence on the central importance of the Vietnam connection in the White House's readiness test decision.

54. *SAC History* FY 1970, 151; Peake, *Notes on Increased Readiness Posture*, 12.

55. See Msgs, CINCs to JCS, 11 and 12 October 1969, box 109, Wheeler Records, RG 218, NARA. CINCEUR Goodpaster's suggestions remain classified.

56. Msg, McCain to Wheeler, subj: Military Readiness, 12 October 1969, box 109, Wheeler Records, RG 218, NARA.

57. Msg, Ruegg to Wheeler, 11 October 1969, box 109, Wheeler Records. RG 218. NARA.

58. Msg, Vice Admiral Nels Johnson, Joint Staff, to Wheeler, 15 October 1969, subj: Additional Actions for US Military Readiness Tests—Worldwide, and Jackson to Wheeler, 17 October 1969—both in box 109, Wheeler Records, RG 218, NARA; Wheeler to Laird, 17 October 1969, subj: Additional Actions for US Military Readiness Tests—World-Wide, DOD MDR release.

59. Msg, Vice Admiral Nels C. Johnson to Wheeler, 17 October 1969, subj: US Military Readiness Tests—Worldwide, with attached messages, DOD MDR release.

60. *SAC History FY 1970*, 155; US Air Force, Second Air Force, *The October 1969 Readiness Test and Second Air Force: Supplement to Headquarters Second Air Force Barksdale Air Force Base, Louisiana, 1 July 1969–30 June 1970* (Barksdale Air Force Base, LA: Second Air Force, 1970), prepared by Louis Herzberg; Peake, *Notes on Increased Readiness Posture*, 5.

61. *SAC History FY 70*, 155. For background on SEAGA and GIANT LANCE, see Office of the Historian, Headquarters Strategic Air Command, *History of Strategic Air Command, FY 1969*, Historical Study no. 116 (Offutt Air Force Base, NE: Strategic Air Command, 1970), 116–122.

62. Msgs, JCS to CINCS, 17 October 1969, box 109, Wheeler Records, RG 218, NARA.

63. Ibid.

64. Ibid.

65. Msg, CINCPAC to JCS, 12 October 1969; Msg, JCS to CINCPAC, 17 October 1969, box 109, Wheeler Records, RG 218, NARA.

66. Memo, Wheeler to Laird, 20 October 1969, subj: Movement of Carrier Task Force on YANKEE STATION, with attached memo to Kissinger, box 109, Wheeler Records. RG 218, NARA.

67. Msgs, JCS to CINCAL and CINCONAD, 17 October 1969, box 109, Wheeler Records, RG 218, NARA.

68. Memo, Wheeler to Laird, 17 October 1969; Memo, Lemnitzer to Wheeler, 15 October 1969, subj: Additional Actions for US Military Readiness Tests—Worldwide, box 109, Wheeler Records, RG 218, NARA.

69. Telcon transcripts, Kissinger and Dobrynin, 17 October 1969, 4:40 p.m., and Kissinger and Laird, 18 October 1969, 5:15 p.m., HAK Telcons, RNPL; CIA, "Possible Communist Reactions."

70. Diary entry, 17 October 1969, HRHD (emphasis added).

71. MemCon, Nixon, Thompson, and Kissinger, 17 October 1969, folder: MemCon—The President, Sir Robert Thompson, et al., 17 October 1969, box 1023, NSCF: Presidential/HAK MemCons, RNPL.

72. Memo, Haig to Kissinger,17 October 1969, subj: Items to Discuss with the President, folder: Items to Discuss with the President, 8/13/69 to 12/30/69, box 334, NSCF: Subject Files; Memo, Kissinger to Nixon, 18 October 1969, subj: Your Meeting with Ambassador Dobrynin, Monday, 20 October 1969, folder 1: Dobrynin/Kissinger, box 489, NSCF: President's Trip Files (emphasis in original); Diary entry, 17 October 1969, HRHD—all at RNPL.

73. Telcon transcripts, Kissinger and Rockefeller, 20 October 1969, 11:10 a.m., and Kissinger and Kraemer, 20 October 1969, 12:30 p.m., HAK Telcons, RNPL.

74. MemCon (US) and MemCon (USSR), 20 October 1969, *Soviet-American Relations*, doc. 31, p. 86, and doc. 34, p. 91. The shorter US MemCon barely mentions Dobrynin's report of the views of the Soviet leadership. The two MemCons are mostly consistent with one another; Kissinger's emphasizes Nixon's tough statements, but Dobrynin's is more detailed on all counts and indicates that Dobrynin was tough in his own way.

75. MemCon (USSR), 20 October 1969, *Soviet-American Relations*, doc. 34, p. 93.

76. Ibid., and MemCon (US), 20 October 1969, *Soviet-American Relations*, doc. 31, pp. 95 and 87.

77. MemCon (US), 20 October 1969, *Soviet-American Relations*, doc. 31, p. 87.

78. MemCon (USSR) and Note from Soviet Leadership to President Nixon, 20 October 1969, *Soviet-American Relations*, doc. 34, p. 93, and doc. 32, p. 89 (emphasis added).

79. Ibid.

80. MemCon (USSR), 20 October 1969, *Soviet-American Relations*, doc. 34, pp. 94–95.

81. Ibid., 97.

82. Ibid., 95–97.

83. Ibid., 96–97 (emphasis added).

84. Telcon, Nixon, 20 October 1969, 8:25 p.m., HAK Telcons, RNPL.

85. Kissinger, *White House Years*, 305. In n. 4 on p. 87 of *Soviet-American Relations*, the editors wrote that Kissinger met with Dobrynin in the morning of 21 October and gave Dobrynin the "plain slip of paper," although "no record of the [21 October Kissinger-Dobrynin] conversation has been found."

86. Diary entry, 20 October 1969, HRHD; Memo, Kissinger to Nixon, 21 October 1969, subj: Dobrynin's Message, folder 2: Dobrynin/Kissinger, box 489, NSCF: President's Trip Files, RNPL (emphasis in original); Kissinger, *White House Years*, 305. Perhaps Kissinger's riverboat gambler metaphor was consciously or unconsciously satirical, suggesting that like some riverboat or casino gamblers, Nixon did not have many cards to play, as Haig had pointed out eleven days earlier.

87. Msg, COMSEVENTHFLT to CTF 71 et al., 18 October 1969, subj: Increased Readiness Posture, folder: Soviet Fleet Operations, October 1969, box 128, Records of 7th Fleet, HAD; Flag Plot Briefs, Tuesday, 7 October 1969, and Monday, 20 October 1969, Coll/748, HAD; and Commander-in-Chief US Pacific Fleet, *Fleet Operations Review*, October 1969 (8 December 1969), pp. 11 and 35, Records of CINCPACFLT, 1941–1975, series 6; "Fleet Air Reconnaissance Squadron ONE Command History for 1969," 28 February 1970, HAD. Stationed on the *Constellation* were nuclear-capable A-7A Corsair fighter jets. Rene J. Francillon, *Tonkin Gulf Yacht Club: US Carrier Operations off Vietnam* (Annapolis, MD: Naval Institute Press, 1988), 125 and 191.

88. Msg, COMSEVENTHFLT to CFT 71 [et al.], 18 October 1969.

89. COMSEVENTHFLT to CTG 20 October 1969, subj: Surveillance of Sov Mership, 20 October 1969; COMSEVENTHFLT to CTF, 20 October 1969, subj: Mership Location Increased Readiness Posture, 20 October 1969, folder: Soviet Fleet Operations, October 1969, box 128, 7th Fleet Records, HAD.

90. Msg, CTF to CINPACFLT, n.d. [ca. 21–22 October 1969], subj: Increased Readiness Posture Sitrep Four; USS *Orleck*, 22 October 1969 to CTG, 22 October 1969, subj: Surveillance of Sov Mership, folder: Soviet Fleet Operations, October 1969, box 128, 7th Fleet Records, HAD.

91. Msg, COMESDIV to CTG, 23 October 1969, subj: Surveillance of Sov Mership Uzghorod Sitrep Nr Ten, folder: Soviet Fleet Operations, October 1969, box 128, 7th Fleet Records, HAD; "Deck Log Book of the USS *Ozbourn* (DD 846) [1 October 1969 to 31 October 1969]," "Deck Log Book of the USS *Orleck* (DD-886) [1 October 1969 to 31 October 1969]"—all in Logs of US Naval Ships and Stations, 1969, Records of the Bureau of Naval Personnel, RG 24, NARA.

92. COMSEVENTHFLT to CTG, 25 October 1969, subj: Increased Readiness Posture; CTG to CINCPACFLT, 29 October 1969, subj: Readiness Sitrep; CTG to COMSEVENTHFLT, 2 November 1969, subj: Increased Readiness Posture, folder: Soviet Fleet Operations, October 1969, box 128, 7th Fleet Records, HAD; "Deck Log Books" of the USS *Hamner* (DD 718) and the USS *Everett F. Larson* (DD 830) [1 October to 31 October 1969]—both in RG 24, NARA.

93. "Executive Secretariat Operations Center Duty Officer Log Sheet, 20 October 1969, Shift I," folder: Operation Center Watch Logs, October 1969, box 30, Office of Secretariat Operations Watch Logs, RG 59, NARA.

94. Hersh, *Price of Power*, unnumbered footnote on pp. 124–125. Urgo could not remember whether he had called the Associated Press or United Press International.

95. US Air Force, Fifteenth Air Force, *History of 22nd Bombardment Wing (Heavy), October–December 1969* (March Air Force Base, CA: 22nd Bombardment Wing, ca. 1970), 38, copy at NSArchive; Telcon transcripts, Kissinger and Laird, 13 October 1969, 12:05 p.m., and 14 October 1969, 5:35 p.m., HAK Telcons, RNPL.

96. Headquarters, US Strategic Air Command, *SAC History FY 1970*, 152.

97. John Greenbacker, "The Carrier Readiness Test," *Virginia Pilot*, 26 October 1969, enclosed with memo from Robinson to Haig, 19 December 1969, box 109, Wheeler Records, RG 218, NARA.

98. *Washington Post*, 19 and 20 October 1969; *New York Times*, 20 October 1969. For "heroic job," see Telegram, US Embassy Netherlands to State Department, 20 October 1969, subj: Press Guidance for Early Departure of US Naval Vessels, folder: Def 7 US, box 1661, Subject-Numeric Files 1967–1969, RG 59, NARA; Msg, CINCLANT to JCS, 20 October 1969, box 109, Wheeler Records, RG 218, NARA.

99. Greenbacker, "Carrier Readiness Test."

100. Telegram, US Embassy Netherlands to State Department, 20 October 1969, and Telegram, Embassy Rabat to State Department, 18 October 1969, subj: Press Guidance for Early Departure of US Naval Vessels, folder: Def 7 US, box 1661, Subject-Numeric Files 1967–1969—both in RG 59, NARA; CINCLANT to JCS Chairman, 18 October 1968, subj: Increased Readiness Posture, and CINCLANT to JCS, 3 November 1969, subj: Increased Readiness Posture, box 109, Wheeler Records, RG 218, NARA.

101. *SAC History*, FY 1970, 155; SAC cable, 23 October 1969, subj: Incrased Readiness Posture, copy at NSArchive.

102. *SAC History, FY 1970*, 155; SAC cable, 23 October 1969. The two wings received earlier notification of the GIANT LANCE implementation orders on 20 October; see US Air Force, Fifteenth Air Force, *92nd Strategic Aerospace Wing (Heavy) and 92nd Combat Support Group, 14 September–31 December 1969*, (Fairchild Air Force Base, WA: 92nd Strategic Aerospace Wing, 1970) (copy courtesy of Scott Sagan), 43.

103. *SAC History FY 70*, 155; *68th Bombardment Wing (Heavy) Annex to October–December 1969 History*.

104. US Air Force, *92nd Strategic Aerospace Wing (Heavy)* 44–45, US Air Force, *History of 22nd Bombardment Wing (Heavy) October–December 1969* (March Air Force Base, CA: 22nd Bombardment Wing, ca. 1970), 49–50. For the accident at Thule, see Scott Sagan, *The Limits of Safety: Organizations,*

Accidents, and Nuclear Weapons (Princeton, NJ: Princeton University Press, 1993), 156–203. For more than four nuclear weapons, see Memo, Martin J. Hillenbrand to Under Secretary, 2 June 1970, subj: Strategic Nuclear Balance Briefing for the NATO Nuclear Planning Group (NPG), untitled folder, box 11, General Files on NSC Matters, RG 59, NARA.

105. US Pacific Air Forces, *Annual History, 1 July 1969–30 June 1970* (Hickam Air Force Base, HI: US Pacific Air Forces, ca. 1970), 157, FOIA release at NSArchive. For PACAF's arsenal, see "1969 PACAF Review," provided by PACAF Historical Office.

106. Msg, SAC to JCS, 4 November 69, copy at NSArchive; Msgs, CINCEUR to JCS, CINCLANT to JCS, and CINCONAD to JCS, 3 and 4 November 1969, subj: Increased Readiness Posture, box 109, Wheeler Records, RG 218, NARA. See also Headquarters, Tactical Air Command, *History of the Tactical Air Command, 1 July 1969–30 June 1970*, attachment 20, subj: Increased Readiness Posture Test Final Report, n.d., copy at NSArchive.

107. Cable, CINCEUR to JCS, 4 November 1969, subj: Increased Readiness Posture; and Msg, SAC to JCS, 4 November 69, copy at NSArchive.

108. *History of the Tactical Air Command, 1 July 1969–30 June 1970*; Memo, Wheeler to Laird, 6 November 1969, subj: US Military Readiness Tests—Worldwide, *FRUS, 1969–1976*, vol. 34, doc. 92, p. 297. It should be noted that Colonel Cesar J. Martinez, director of operations at the 479th Tactical Fighter Wing, had a more positive evaluation: the readiness test permitted the "most realistic exercise in a number of years." Msg 050615, 5 November 1969, subj: Increased Readiness Posture Summary, attachment to *History of the Tactical Air Command, 1 July 1969–30 June 1970.*

109. Memo, Haig to Kissinger, 14 October 1969. The information on DEFCONs is in e-mail msg, Bruce Blair to Burr, 22 March 2002. See also Scott Sagan, "Nuclear Alerts and Crisis Management," in Lynn-Jones, Miller, and Van Evera, *Nuclear Diplomacy and Crisis Management*, 160–197.

110. Memo, Wheeler to Laird, subj: US Military Readiness Tests—Worldwide, 6 November 1969, *FRUS, 1969–1976*, vol. 34, doc. 92, pp. 296–297.

111. Hersh, *Price of Power*, 124.

112. Memo, Wheeler to Laird, 22 October 1969, subj: US Military Readiness Tests—Worldwide, box 109, Wheeler Records, RG 218, NARA. The CIA believed, however, that Moscow may have associated the presence of the US ships with the assassination of Somalia's president on 15 October and a coup d'état six days later; CIA Report, "Possible Communist Reactions."

113. Flag Plot Brief, Tuesday, 21 October 1969, Seventh Fleet Records, NCC, COLL/748, HAD.

114. Telcon transcripts, Kissinger and Laird, 21 October 1969, 6:23 p.m., and Laird, 22 October 1969, 8:25 a.m., HAK Telcons.

115. CIA Report, "Possible Communist Reactions."

116. Roderick MacFarquhar and Michael Schoenhals, *Mao's Last Revolution* (Cambridge, MA: Harvard University Press, 2006), 313–319.

117. Memo, Wheeler to Laird, 25 October 1969, subj: US Military Readiness Tests—Worldwide, box 109, Wheeler Records, RG 218, NARA and MDR release.

118. Ibid.

119. Defense Intelligence Agency, Special Intelligence Report, "Summary of Soviet Reactions to US Operations No. 5," 22 October 1969, folder: Vietnam—Operation Pruning Knife [2 of 2], box 123, NSCF: Vietnam Subject Files, RNPL; Editorial note, *FRUS, 1969–1976*, vol. 34, doc. 88, p. 291.

120. CIA, "Possible Communist Reactions."

121. Memo, Kissinger to Nixon, 1 December 1969, subj: Soviet Reactions to US Operations during October, *FRUS, 1969–1976*, vol. 34, doc. 93, pp. 300–301.

122. DIA Special Intelligence Report, "Final Summary of Soviet Reactions to US Operations," 6 November 1969, folder: Vietnam—Operation Pruning Knife [2 of 2], box 123, NSCF: Vietnam Subject Files, RNPL.

123. DIA Special Intelligence Report, "Summary of Soviet Reactions to US Operations No. 5," 28 October 1969, folder: Vietnam—Operation Pruning Knife [2 of 2], box 123, NSCF: Vietnam Subject Files, RNPL.

124. Ibid.

125. Ibid.

126. Memo, Westmoreland to Laird, 28 October 1969, subj: US Military Readiness Tests—Worldwide, box 109, Wheeler Records, RG 218, NARA.

127. Msg, JCS to CINCs, 28 October 1969, box 109, Wheeler Records, RG 218, NARA; *SAC History FY 70*, 256; *History of the 380th Strategic Aerospace Wing, October–December, Top Secret Annex 1969*.

128. Laird, interview by Burr, 6 September 2001.

129. Memo, Kissinger to Nixon, 1 December 1969, subj: Soviet Reactions to US Operations during October, enclosing DIA Special Intelligence Report, "Final Summary of Soviet Reactions to US Operations," 6 November 1969, box 123, Vietnam—Operation Pruning Knife [2 of 2], NSCF: Vietnam Subject Files, RNPL; also see *FRUS, 1969–1976*, vol. 34, doc. 93, pp. 300–301.

130. E-mail message, Luu Huynh to Kimball, 19 September 2009; Merle L. Pribbenow, "The Soviet-Vietnamese Intelligence Relationship during the Vietnam War: Cooperation and Conflict," *Cold War International History Project: Working Paper*, no. 73 (11 December 2014): 13, http://www.wilsoncenter.org/sites/default/files/CWIHP_Working_Paper_73_Soviet-Vietnamese_Intelligence_Relationship_Vietnam_War_0.pdf (accessed 11 December 2014).

131. The NSA was eavesdropping on the radiotelephone conversations of Soviet leaders as they traveled in their limousines, but whether it produced any useful intelligence on reactions to the alert is unknown. For the GAMMA GUPPY program, see James Banford, *The Puzzle Palace: Inside the National Security*

Agency—America's Most Secret Intelligence Organization (New York: Penguin, 1983), 359–360.

Epilogue: Aftermaths and Assessments

1. Diary entries, 15 and 16 October 1969, HRHD.

2. Diary entry, 23 October 1969, HRHD.

3. "The President's Pursuit for Peace," *Public Papers of the Presidents, Nixon: 1969*, 901–909; Nixon, *RN*, 409–412.

4. For the demonstrations and administration reactions, see DeBenedetti and Chatfield, *American Ordeal*, 262–274; Small, *Johnson, Nixon, and the Doves*, 190; Wells, *War Within*, 379; Kimball, *Nixon's Vietnam War*, 171–176; Diary entries for October and November, HRHD.

5. See analysis in Hammond, *Military and the Media*, 157–159 and 165–169; Kimball, *Nixon's Vietnam War*, 171–176.

6. Nixon, *In the Arena*, 332; Nixon, *No More Vietnams*, 115.

7. Diary entry, 16 December 1969, HRHD.

8. Oval Office, Conversation no. 471-2, Nixon and Kissinger, 19 March 1971, 7:03–7:27 p.m., WHT, RNPL.

9. These two options contained elements of Options A, B, and C in the August and September 1969 policy alternatives pages; see chapter 7.

10. Memo, Kissinger to Nixon, 20 July 1970, subj: Alternative Vietnam Strategies, folder: Vietnam, box 148, NSCF: Vietnam Country Files, RNPL. This document is reprinted in *FRUS, 1969–1976*, vol. 6, doc. 347, pp. 1133–1139. For an important example of Kissinger's advocacy of a negotiated settlement, see, e.g., Memo, Kissinger to Nixon, 18 September 1971, subj: Vietnam, reproduced in *FRUS, 1969–1976*, vol. 7, doc. 257, p. 919.

11. Memo, Kissinger to Nixon, 20 July 1970, subj: Alternative Vietnam Strategies, *FRUS, 1969–1976*, vol. 6, doc. 347, p. 1136n2.

12. Ibid., pp. 1134–1135.

13. For instances of Nixon's and Kissinger's talk of bombing the *bejeezus* out of them (as well as similar oaths and expletives), see, e.g., *FRUS, 1969–1976*, vol. 8, doc. 14, pp. 76 and 78, doc. 19, p. 88, doc. 50, p. 168, doc. 85, p. 283, doc. 88, p. 291, doc. 91, p. 299, and doc. 270, p. 1009.

14. *FRUS, 1969–1976*, vol. 8, doc. 224, p. 786; Kissinger, *White House Years*, 470.

15. Diary entry, 21 December 1970, HRHD.

16. Memo, Nixon to Kissinger, 24 November 1969, folder 12, box 1, WHSF: President's Personal File, Memoranda from the President, 1969–74, RNPL.

17. MemCon, Dobrynin and Kissinger, 9 January 1971, *Soviet-American Relations*, doc. 110, p. 262.

18. Memo, Soviet Ambassador Ilya S. Scherbakov to Prime Minister Pham Van Dong, quoted in Loi and Vu, *Le Duc Tho–Kissinger Negotiations*, 165–166.

19. Background book for HAK's July 1971 trip POLO I, box 850, NSC: For the President's Files (Winston Lord)—China Trip/Vietnam, RNPL. "Objective

realities" was a reference to the balance of forces in South Vietnam after the US exit.

20. Memo, Nixon to Kissinger, 30 April 1972, *FRUS, 1969–1976*, vol. 8, doc. 103, pp. 339 and 341.

21. MemCon, Nixon and Kissinger, 29 September 1972, *FRUS, 1969–1976*, vol. 8, doc. 270, p. 1009.

22. Oval Office, Conversation no. 760-6, Nixon and Kissinger, 3 August 1972, WHT, RNPL.

23. EOB, Conversation no. 371-19, Nixon/Haig, 23 October 1972, WHT, RNPL (*not* included in *FRUS, 1969–1976*, vol. 9, but cf. docs. 19 and 59 in that volume).

24. Kissinger was responding to a question posed by historian Thomas A. Schwartz at a conference organized by the US Department of State, Office of the Historian, 29–30 September 2010, Washington, DC, http://history.state .gov/conferences/2010-southeast-asia/videos-transcripts (accessed 13 December 2014).

25. Oval Office, Conversation no. 527-16, Nixon, Haldeman, Kissinger, and Ehrlichman, 23 June 1971, 9:14 a.m.–10:12 a.m., WHT, RNPL. The plan, DUCK HOOK/PRUNING KNIFE, had not really been "ready," but the "concept plan" had been, along with many of the operational elements that would have comprised one or the other "plan."

26. The authors have examined PRUNING KNIFE plans for early 1970 but not beyond. In *Powerful and Brutal Weapons*, 185–188, Randolph argues that the original PRUNING KNIFE plan served as the basis for LINEBACKER plans.

27. Murray Marder, "US Diplomacy Paying Diplomatic Price for Cambodia Military Gain," *Washington Post*, 10 May 1970.

28. To some immeasurable degree, Nixon also launched these operations because by this time, May 1972, he regretted not having mined and bombed North Vietnam in 1969. See, e.g., Oval Office, Conversation no. 721-11, Nixon, Kissinger, and John Connally, 8 May 1972, sometime between 12:13–1:15 p.m., WHT, RNPL.

29. Oval Office, Conversation no. 466-12, Nixon and Kissinger, 11 March 1971, after 4:00 p.m., WHT, RNPL.

30. MemCon, Nixon and Kissinger, 19 April 1972, *FRUS, 1969–1976*, vol. 8, doc. 88, pp. 290–291.

31. During a conversation a year earlier, for example, as Nixon and Kissinger were discussing how to play it tough in the Paris negotiations, Kissinger suggested that he could talk to Xuan Thuy alone for five minutes and tell him: "This president is extremely tough." "[If you do not accept our offer,] he will stop at nothing." Nixon interjected: "That's right." Kissinger continued: "And imply that you might do it . . . use nuclear weapons. . . . Do the Dulles ploy." Nixon added that Kissinger could also say: "I cannot control him." Oval Office, Conversation no. 487-7, 23 April 1971, *FRUS, 1969–1976*, vol. 7, doc. 190, p. 581.

During a White House meeting with a small group of antiwar activists on 6 March 1971, Kissinger, when pressed, refused to take the nuclear option off the table with respect to Vietnam; see Betty Medsger, *The Burglary: The Discovery of J. Edgar Hoover's Secret FBI* (New York: Knopf, 2014), 77–78.

32. E.g., see Nixon's position on using atomic weapons in Vietnam during the Dien Bien Phu crisis, as well as his enthusiasm for brinkmanship, discussed in chapter 1; also see Nixon's 1967 remarks to Whalen, quoted in chapter 2.

33. EOB, Conversation no. 332-35, Nixon and Kissinger, 25 April 1972, WHT, RNPL (transcribed by Kimball and Ken Hughes). "A nuclear bomb, you wouldn't do it anyway" is the best and most likely interpretation of an unclear portion of the conversation.

34. Memo for the President's Files, "National Security Council Meeting," 8 May 1972, *FRUS, 1969–1976*, vol. 8, doc. 131, p. 491; also see EOB, Conversation no. 332-35, Nixon and Kissinger, 25 April 1972, between 12:00 and 12:28 p.m., WHT, RNPL; "Transcripts of Secretary Roger's Testimony before the Senate Foreign Relations Committee," *New York Times*, 19 April 1972; Murray Marder, "Rhetoric Escalates over Vietnam War," *Washington Post*, 19 April 1972.

35. In a conversation with Xuan Thuy on 31 May 1971, a month after the Oval Office discussion in which Nixon made a nuclear threat (see discussion in note 31), Kissinger made such an open-ended threat: "You must judge whether prolonged fighting against those who pose no long-term threat to you might face you with more real dangers later on and jeopardize your long-term future"; *FRUS, 1969–1976*, vol. 7, doc. 207, p. 654.

36. For the negotiations, see, e.g., Kimball, *Nixon's Vietnam War*, chap. 13, and Kimball, *Vietnam War Files*, chap. 6; Loi and Vu, *Le Duc Tho–Kissinger Negotiations in Paris;* chaps. 8–11; Ang Cheng Guan, *Ending the Vietnam War*, chap. 5; and Randolph, *Powerful and Brutal Weapons*, 331–335. Select documents on the negotiations for the Nixon period are reproduced in *FRUS*, vols. 6 through 9.

37. On the contested question of which side wanted to settle in October, see discussion and citations in Kimball, *Vietnam War Files*, 241–246.

38. Telcon transcript, Kissinger and Nixon, 1 December 1972, 10:03 a.m., HAK Telcons.

39. Kimball, *Nixon's Vietnam War*, 348–368, and Kimball, *Vietnam War Files*, 262–269.

40. Memo, Negroponte to Kissinger, 23 October 1972, subj: Some Thoughts on Where We Go from Here, folder: Sensitive Camp David—vol. 21, box 857, NSCF: For the President's Files (Winston Lord)—China Trip/Vietnam, RNPL. For "strategic success," see David W. P. Elliott, "NLF-DRV Strategy and the 1972 Spring Offensive," International Relations of East Asia Project, Interim Report no. 4 (Ithaca, NY: Cornell University, 1974).

41. See, e.g., Diary entries, 5–7 December 1972, HRHD; Msgs, Nixon to

Kissinger [via aides], 4–6 December, folder: HAK Paris Trip 3–13 Dec. 1972 TOHAK 1–100 [2 of 2], box 27, HAK Trip Files; Msgs, Kissinger to Nixon [via aides], 4–7 December 1972, folder: HAK Paris Trip 3–13 Dec. 1972 HAKTO— both in HAK Office Files, RNPL, with some reproduced in *FRUS, 1969–1976*, vol. 9, pp. 521–538. Also see Nixon, *RN*, 728–730; Kissinger, *White House Years*, 1428–1446.

42. Msgs, Kissinger to Nixon, 12 and 13 December 1972, *FRUS, 1969–1976*, vol. 9, docs. 163 and 171, pp. 592–596 and 621–623; Kissinger, *White House Years*, 1439; Nixon, *RN*, 733.

43. MemCon, Kissinger and Tho, 13 December 1972, folder: Sensitive Camp David—vol. 22, Minutes of Meetings, Paris, 4–13 Dec. 1972, box 859, For the President's Files (Winston Lord)—China Trip/Vietnam, NSCF, RNPL—also available on *DNSA*.

44. Msg, Kissinger to Nixon via Haig, 13 December 1972, *FRUS, 1969–1976*, vol. 9, doc. 171, pp. 621–625.

45. Diary entries, 13 and 15 December 1972, HRHD; Msg, Haig to Kissinger, 12 December 1972, and Memo, Haig to Kissinger, 13 December 1972, subj: Items to Discuss with the President's Meeting at 10:00 a.m., 14 December, *FRUS, 1969–1976*, vol. 9, docs. 158 and 173, pp. 566 and 627–630.

46. Kimball, *Nixon's Vietnam War*, 364–366; Kimball, *Vietnam War Files*, 272–287. Also see Randolph, *Powerful and Brutal Weapons*, 339.

47. For their comments on bombing, see conversations between Nixon and Haig, 12 December 1972, and among Nixon, Kissinger, and Haig, 14 December 1972, *FRUS, 1969–1976*, vol. 9, docs. 159 and 175, pp. 577–578, 656, and 661–662.

48. See, e.g., MemCon, Ford, Kissinger, and Congressional Delegation, 5 March 1975, box 9, folder: Memoranda of Conversations—Ford Administration, 30 January 1975, National Security Advisor: Memorandum of Conversations, 1975–1977, GFL. On a related note, a retired DRV Ministry of Public Security general said in an interview after the war that in 1975, Public Security had deciphered (probably with Soviet assistance) an encoded message from the Saigon embassy of a US ally that yielded definitive evidence showing that the United States would not reintervene militarily to save South Vietnam; Pribbenow, "Soviet-Vietnamese Intelligence Relationship," 6.

49. MemCon, Graham Martin, Lawrence Eagleburger, W. R. Smyser, Kissinger, 19 July 1974, subj: [situation in South Vietnam], box 9: July 1974 NODIS MemCons, Records of Henry Kissinger, 1973–1977, RG 59, NARA.

50. Minutes of WSAG Meeting, 2 April 1975, subj: Vietnam, *FRUS, 1969–1976*, vol. 9, doc. 202, p. 738.

51. See, e.g., Jeffrey Kimball, "The Stab-in-the-Back Legend and the Vietnam War," *Armed Forces and Society* 14 (Spring 1988): 433–458; a more recent article is Kimball, "Out of Primordial Cultural Ooze: Inventing Political and Policy Legacies about the US Exit from Vietnam," *Diplomatic History* 34, no. 3 (June 2010):

577–587. For a recent example of the enduring myth, see the opinion piece by Richard Cohen, "Internationally, Obama Must Be Feared as Well as Admired," *Washington Post,* 13 October 2014, and reply by Merle Pribbenow, "Debating Presidential 'Weakness,'" *Washington Post,* 16 October 2014.

52. See, e.g., Kimball, "Out of Primordial Cultural Ooze," 581, and for 1972, Kimball, *Nixon's Vietnam War,* 368–369; Kimball, *Vietnam War Files,* chap. 7.

53. Oval Office, Conversation no. 721-11, Nixon, Kissinger, and John Connally, 8 May 1972, sometime between 12:13 and 1:15 p.m., WHT, RNPL. See analysis of this and other conversations in Kimball, *Vietnam War Files,* 218–220.

54. Quoted in Safire, *Before the Fall,* 368.

55. Nixon, *RN,* 398 and 414.

56. Nixon, *No More Vietnams,* 150. About holding the country together, cf. Diary entry, 3 October 1969, HRHD.

57. Nixon, *RN,* 405 and 404.

58. In *The Soviet Union and the Vietnam War,* chap. 10, the late Ilya Gaiduk drew on then available documents indicating that Moscow advised Hanoi to compromise but also indicating that the bombing, from Hanoi's and Moscow's point of view, was an obstacle to restarting the negotiations. Also see John Dumbrell, *Rethinking the Vietnam War* (New York: Palgrave Macmillan, 2012), 130; Loi and Vu, *Le Duc Tho–Kissinger Negotiations in Paris,* chap. 10; Ang Cheng Guan, *Ending the Vietnam War,* 120–126; and Kimball, *Vietnam War Files,* chap. 10, which draws on US, Vietnamese, and Soviet documents concerning the issue.

59. Quoted in Hersh, *Price of Power,* 134.

60. For details of ship movements and other alert measures, see *FRUS, 1969–1976,* vol. 24, docs. 254, 256, 264, and 274, pp. 17, 18, 19, 704–707, 717, 739, and 765. For useful background on the crisis, published before this *FRUS* volume became available, see Nigel J. Ashton, "Pulling the Strings: King Hussein's Role during the Crisis of 1970 in Jordan," *International History Review* 28, no. 1 (March 2006): 94–118.

61. Lisagor, quoted by Hedrick Smith in the *New York Times,* 19 September 1971. Except for notes taken by journalists and government officials, the original *Sun-Times* article seems lost to history because microfilm records preserve only final editions. James F. Hoge, Jr.—then editor in chief of the *Sun-Times*—and present at the meeting with Nixon—confirmed Lisagor's notes in e-mails to Kimball, 30 July 2004. For a fuller account of this affair, see Kimball, *Vietnam War Files,* 57–59.

62. Richard Harwood, "The Anatomy of a 'Backgrounder' with the President," *Washington Post,* 20 September 1970; also see discussion and sources in Kimball, *Vietnam War Files,* 57–59.

63. Telcon transcript, Nixon and Kissinger, 17 September 1970, *FRUS, 1969–1976,* vol. 24, doc. 262, p. 730.

64. Memo for the record by Tucker, subj: Kissinger, 10 August 1972, DOD MDR release from Tucker's Pentagon files.

65. Memo, A. W. Marshall to NSC Intelligence Committee Working Group, subj: Study of the Jordanian Crisis, 8 March 1973, CREST.

66. Richard N. Lebow and Janice G. Stein, *We All Lost the Cold War* (Princeton, NJ: Princeton University Press, 1994), 248–250; Garthoff, *Détente and Confrontation*, 420–433. Msg, US Embassy Soviet Union to Dept. of State, 21 October 1973, in William Burr, ed., "The October War and US Policy," Document 51, NSArchive Electronic Briefing Book 98, 7 (October 2003) http://www2.gwu.edu/~nsarchiv/NSAEBB/NSAEBB98/index.htm#VI (accessed 13 December 2014).

67. Memo for the Record, 24/25 October 1973, *FRUS, 1969–1976*, vol. 25, doc. 269, pp. 737–742. DEFCON III was higher than the usual force readiness level, although not as intense as the DEFCON II maintained during the Cuban missile crisis.

68. Ibid.

69. MemCon by Marder, 20 November 1973, subj: Kissinger on Air Force Plane between Tokyo and Washington, 16 November 1973, Background Only, Background Briefing File, Marder Collection, RNPL; Lebow and Stein, *We All Lost the Cold War*, 254–255.

70. Lebow and Stein, *We All Lost the Cold War*, 251–259 and 266–269.

71. Ibid., 488n37.

72. The long-standing nuclear taboo itself may have been a factor in North Vietnam's leaders' resistance to implied nuclear threats insofar as their awareness of US concerns about Asian opinion may have emboldened them to resist US nuclear threats; E-mail message, Luu Huynh to Kimball, 19 September 2009.

73. Memo, Zbigniew to Carter, 8 April 1977, subj: Weekly National Security Report #8, folder: Weekly Reports (to the President), 1–15 [2/77–6/77], box 41, Zbigniew Brzezinski Collection, Jimmy Carter Presidential Library, Atlanta, GA.

SELECTED BIBLIOGRAPHY

Unpublished Material

Archives

Gerald R. Ford Library (GFL), Ann Arbor, MI
    General Subject File
        Vietnam
        Vietnam—Correspondence from Richard Nixon to Nguyen Van Thieu
    National Security Advisor
        Kissinger-Scowcroft West Wing Office Files, 1969–1977
        Memoranda of Conversations
        Presidential Country Files for East Asia and the Pacific, 1974–1977
Library of Congress, Manuscript Division, Washington, DC
    Leonard Garment Papers
    W. Averell Harriman Papers
    J. Robert Oppenheimer Papers
    Elliot L. Richardson Papers
    Glenn Seaborg Papers
    Hedrick Smith Papers
National Archives and Records Administration (NARA), College Park, MD
    C[entral] I[ntelligence] A[gency] Records Search Tool (CREST)
        General Records of the Department of State, Record Group (RG) 59
    Records of the Bureau of Naval Personnel, RG 24
    Records of Headquarters, United States Air Force (Air Staff), RG 341
    Records of the Joint Chiefs of Staff, RG 218
    Records of Chairman Maxwell Taylor
    Records of Chairman Nathan Twining
    Records of Chairman Earle Wheeler, including files declassified for this project
National Security Archive, George Washington University, Washington, DC
    Declassified air force histories and other government studies (see Government Documents, Reports, Histories, and Collections)
    ProQuest/National Security Archive, *Digital National Security Archive (DSNA)*, online subscription service

Files of declassified secretary of defense records (1969) requested under mandatory declassification review (MDR)

Murray Marder Papers, Background Briefing Memoranda on Vietnam, 1969

Naval History and Heritage Command, History and Archives Division (HAD), Washington Navy Yard, Washington, DC

Immediate Office Files of the Chief of Naval Operations

Navy Command Center (NCC), 1958–1998 Collection (COLL/748), Records of US Seventh Fleet

Records of Commander-in-Chief, Pacific Fleet (CINCPACFLT), 1941–1975

Richard M. Nixon Presidential Library (RNPL), Yorba Linda, CA

Henry A. Kissinger (HAK) Office Files

Country Files—Europe—USSR

Country Files—Far East—Vietnam Negotiations

HAK Administrative and Staff Files

HAK Trip Files

Henry A. Kissinger Telephone Conversation Transcripts

Institutional Files: Minutes of Meetings (1969–1974)

Journals and Diaries of Harry Robbins Haldeman (HRHD)

Miscellaneous Institutional Files of the Nixon Administration (1969–1974)

National Security Council Files (NSCF)

Agency Files

Country Files—Europe

Alexander M. Haig Chronological Files

Alexander M. Haig's Special File

Name Files

Paris Talks/Meetings

Presidential/HAK Memcons

President's Press Conferences

President's Trip Files

Staff Files—Tony Lake Chronological Files

Subject Files

Vietnam Country Files

Vietnam Subject Files

National Security Council Institutional Files (NSCIF)

National Security Decision Memoranda (NSDM)

National Security Study Memoranda (NSSM)

Presidential Daily Diary

President's Office Files: President's Meeting File

White House Special Files (WHSF): Staff Member and Office Files (SMOF),

H. R. Haldeman Personal Files

White House Tapes (WHT)

US Air Force Historical Research Agency, Maxwell Air Force Base, AL
US Army Military History Research Collection, Carlisle Barracks, PA (USA-MHRC) Creighton Abrams Papers

Documents in Authors' Personal Collections

Chronology of US-DRV Negotiations, 1969–1973 (Private Meetings). From *The Foreign Ministry Internal Circulation Chronology on Diplomatic Struggle and International Mobilization in the Anti-American War, 1954–1975*. Hanoi: General Task Force—1987 (Ban Tông Kêt—1987).

Ellsberg, Daniel. "The Incentives to Preemptive Attack"; "The Political Uses of Madness"; "Presidents as Perfect Detonators"; "The Theory and Practice of Blackmail"; "The Threat of Violence." Lecture transcripts. 1959.

———. Options Paper (RAND). 27 December 1968.

Hughes, Thomas L. Personal notes.

Interviews, Letters, Communications, Conversations, and Q and As

Habiger, General Eugene (ret.). Conversation with "The Bulletin of the Atomic Scientists' Third Annual Doomsday Clock Symposium." 9 January 2012, Washington, DC (W. Burr).

Haig, Alexander M. 10 March 2006. John F. Kennedy Library, Boston (J. Kimball).

Hoge, James, Jr. 30 July 2004, e-mail (J. Kimball).

Kissinger, Henry A. 11 March 2006. John F. Kennedy Library, Boston (question posed by J. Kimball).

———. 29 September 2010. US State Department, Washington, DC (question posed by Thomas. A. Schwartz, Vanderbilt University).

———. 13 February 2013. Conversation with Prof. David Holloway (Stanford University) (as reported by Holloway to Burr, 18 October 2013, Austin, TX).

Laird, Melvin. 18 June and 6 September 2001, telephone; 15 July 2002, e-mail (W. Burr).

Lake, Anthony. 15 October 2001 and 14 December 2005, telephone (J. Kimball).

Lemnitzer, William. 27 March 2007, telephone (W. Burr).

Lord, Winston. 5 December 1994, Washington, DC; 20 July 2001, Washington, DC (J. Kimball).

Luu Doan Huynh. 12 January 2000, Hong Kong; 13 May 2008, Paris; September 2009, e-mail (J. Kimball).

Luu Van Loi. 26 September 1994. Hanoi (J. Kimball).

Lynn, Lawrence, Jr. 31 January 2006, e-mail (J. Kimball).

Morris, Roger. 19 February 2007, telephone (J. Kimball); 19 February 2007 e-mail (W. Burr and Kimball).

Nguyen Co Thach. 17 January 1988, Ho Chi Minh City; 24 September 1994, Hanoi (J. Kimball).

Nguyen Vu Tung. 2 February 1995. Oslo (J. Kimball).

Pursley, Robert E. 25 July 2001 and 14 May 2002, telephone (W. Burr).

Smith, Howard K., and Benedicte Smith. 16 and 24 August 2001, telephone (J. Kimball).
Watts, William. 21 April 2007. Washington, DC (J. Kimball).

Published Material

Government Documents, Reports, Histories, and Collections

Burr, William. "'Nobody Wins a Nuclear War' but 'Success' Is Possible." National Security Archive Electronic Briefing Book no. 336. 19 February 2011. http://www2.gwu.edu/~nsarchiv/nukevault/ebb336/index.htm.

———. "The October War and U.S. Policy." Document 51, National Security Archive Electronic Briefing Book no. 98. 7 October 2003. http://www2.gwu.edu/~nsarchiv/NSAEBB/NSAEBB98/index.htm#VI.

———. "The Sino-Soviet Border Conflict, 1969: U.S. Reactions and Diplomatic Maneuvers." National Security Archive Electronic Briefing Book. 12 June 2011. http://www2.gwu.edu/~nsarchiv/NSAEBB/NSAEBB49/index2.html.

———. "60th Anniversary of Castle BRAVO Nuclear Test, the Worst Nuclear Test in U.S. History." National Security Archive Electronic Briefing Book no. 459. 28 February 2014. http://www2.gwu.edu/~nsarchiv/nukevault/ebb459/.

Burr, William, and Jeffrey P. Kimball. "Nixon White House Considered Nuclear Options against North Vietnam, Declassified Documents Reveal: Nuclear Weapons, the Vietnam War, and the 'Nuclear Taboo.'" National Security Archive Electronic Briefing Book no. 195. 31 July 2006. http://www.gwu.edu/~nsarchiv/NSAEBB/NSAEBB195/index.htm.

Elliott, David W. P. "NLF-DRV Strategy and the 1972 Spring Offensive." Interim Report no. 4. International Relations of East Asia Project. Cornell University, Ithaca, NY, 1974.

Geyer, David C., Douglas E. Selvage, and Edward C. Keefer, eds. *Soviet-American Relations: The Détente Years, 1969–1972.* Washington, DC: US Government Printing Office, 2007.

Military History Institute of Vietnam. *Victory in Vietnam: The Official History of the People's Army of Vietnam, 1954–1975.* Trans. Merle L. Pribbenow. Lawrence: University Press of Kansas, 2002.

The Papers of Dwight D. Eisenhower. Vols. 12 and 16. Ed. Louis Galambos. Baltimore, MD: Johns Hopkins University Press, 1970.

The Pentagon Papers: The Defense Department History of United States Decision-Making on Vietnam. Senator Gravel Edition. Boston: Beacon Press, 1971.

"President Nixon's Record on Vietnam, 1954–68." *Legislative Proposals Relating to the War in Southeast Asia: Hearings Before the Committee on Foreign Relations.* US Senate, 92nd Cong., 1st sess. Washington, DC: Government Printing Office, 1971.

Public Papers of the Presidents of the United States. For Harry S. Truman, Dwight D. Eisenhower, John F. Kennedy, Lyndon B. Johnson, and Richard M.

Nixon. Washington, DC: Government Printing Office, various years. http://quod.lib.umich.edu/p/ppotpus/.

Thompson, Wayne. *To Hanoi and Back: The United States Air Force and North Vietnam, 1966–1973.* Washington, DC: Air Force History and Museum Program, 2000.

US Air Force. Eighth Air Force. *History of the 68th Bombardment Wing (Heavy) Top Secret Annex, October–December 1969.* Seymour Johnson Air Force Base, NC: 68th Bombardment Wing, n.d. [ca. 1970]. FOIA release.

———. Fifteenth Air Force. *History of the 22nd Bombardment Wing (Heavy), October–December 1969.* March Air Force Base, CA: 22nd Bombardment Wing, n.d. [ca. 1970]. FOIA release.

———. Fifteenth Air Force. *History of the 92nd Strategic Aerospace Wing (Heavy) and 92nd Combat Support Group, 14 September–31 December 1969.* Fairchild Air Force Base, WA: 92nd Strategic Aerospace Wing, 1970. FOIA release.

———. Fifteenth Air Force. *History of the 456th Strategic Aerospace Wing, Heavy, and 456th Combat Support Group, 1 October–31 December 1969.* Beale Air Force Base, CA: 456th Strategic Aerospace Wing, ca. 1970. Copy at NSArchive.

———. Second Air Force. *The October 1969 Readiness Test and Second Air Force: Supplement to Headquarters Second Air Force Barksdale Air Force Base, Louisiana, 1 July 1969–30 June 1970.* Prepared by Louis Hertzberg. Barksdale Air Force Base, LA: Second Air Force, n.d. [ca. 1971]. FOIA release.

———. Strategic Air Command. *Four Crises: Berlin, Lebanon, Cuba, and Korea.* Historical Study no. 132. Offutt Air Force Base, NE: Strategic Air Command, 1971. FOIA release.

———. Strategic Air Command. *History of Strategic Air Command, FY 1969.* Historical Study no. 116. Offutt Air Force Base, NE: Office of the Historian, Strategic Air Command, 1970. FOIA release.

———. Strategic Air Command. *History of Strategic Air Command, FY 1970.* Historical Study vol. 1, no. 117. Offutt Air Force Base, NE: Strategic Air Command, 1971. FOIA release.

———. Strategic Air Command. *Notes on Increased Readiness Posture of October 1969.* SAC History no. 136. Prepared by Lynn Peake. Offutt Air Force Base, NE: US Strategic Air Command, 1970. Air Force FOIA release.

———. Strategic Air Command. *SAC Targeting Concepts.* Historical Study 73A. Offutt Air Force Base, NE: Strategic Air Command, n.d. [ca. 1959]. MDR release.

———. Tactical Air Command, Headquarters. *History of the Tactical Air Command, 1 July 1969–30 June 1970.* Langley Air Force Base, VA: Tactical Air Command, n.d. [ca. 1970].

———. 305th Bombardment Wing. *History of 305th Bombardment Wing (Medium), October–December 1969, Annex 1.* Grissom Air Force Base, IN: 305th Bombardment Wing, n.d. [ca. 1970]. FOIA release.

————. 380th Strategic Aerospace Wing. *History of the 380th Strategic Aerospace Wing, October–December 1969, Top Secret Annex.* Prepared by Sgt. Allen Mc-Corstin. Plattsburgh Air Force Base, NY: 380th Strategic Aerospace Wing, Strategic Air Command, n.d. [ca. 1970]. FOIA release.

————. United States Air Forces in Europe, Office of the Chief of Staff. *History of United States Air Forces in Europe Fiscal Year 1970.* Vol. 1. Ramstein Air Force Base, Germany: US Air Forces in Europe, n.d. [ca. 1971]. FOIA release.

US Department of State. *Foreign Relations of the United States Series.* Various date ranges and volume numbers for the presidential terms of Harry S. Truman, Dwight D. Eisenhower, John F. Kennedy, Lyndon B. Johnson, Richard M. Nixon, and Gerald R. Ford. Washington, DC: Government Printing Office, various years. http://history.state.gov/historicaldocuments/frus1969–76v21.

Wainstein, L., C. D. Cremeans, J. K. Moriarty, and J. Porturo. *The Evolution of U.S. Strategic Command and Control and Warning, 1945–1972.* Institute for Defense Analyses Study S-467, June 1975.

Weathersby, Kathryn, trans. "New Evidence on the Korean War: New Russian Documents on the Korean War." *Cold War International History Project Bulletin,* nos. 6–7 (Winter 1995–1996): 30–93. http://www.wilsoncenter.org/sites/default/files/CWIHPBulletin6-7_p2.pdf.

Books, Articles, Dissertations, and Essays

Aijazuddin, F. S. *From a Head, through a Head, to a Head: The Secret Channel between the U.S. and China through Pakistan.* New York: Oxford University Press, 2001.

Alperovitz, Gar. *Atomic Diplomacy: Hiroshima and Potsdam—The Use of the Atomic Bomb and the American Confrontation with Soviet Power.* New York: Simon & Schuster, 1965.

Ambrose, Stephen E. *Nixon: The Education of a Politician, 1913–1962.* New York: Simon & Schuster, 1987.

————. *Nixon, the Triumph of a Politician, 1962–1972.* New York: Simon & Schuster, 1989.

Anderson, David L. *Trapped by Success: The Eisenhower Administration and Vietnam, 1953–1961.* New York: Columbia University Press, 1991.

Ang Cheng Guan. *Ending the Vietnam War: The Vietnamese Communists' Perspective.* New York: Routledge & Curzon, 2004.

Angevine, Robert G. "Hiding in Plain Sight: The U.S. Navy and Dispersed Operations under ECMCON." *Naval War College Review* 64 (Spring 2011): 80–95.

Banford, James. *The Puzzle Palace: Inside the National Security Agency—America's Most Secret Intelligence Organization.* New York: Penguin, 1983.

Barlow, Jeffrey. *From Hot to Cold War: The U.S. Navy and National Security Affairs, 1945–1955.* Stanford, CA: Stanford University Press, 2009.

Batchelder, Robert C. *The Irreversible Decision, 1939–1950.* Boston: Houghton Mifflin, 1962.

Beecher, William. "The Secret Bombing of Cambodia." *50 Years in Media: Changes in Journalism.* Harvard University. 2005. http://athome.harvard. edu/programs/fym/fym_video/fym_3.html.

Bernstein, Barton J. "The Atomic Bombings Reconsidered." *Foreign Affairs* 74, no. 1 (January–February 1995): 135–152.

Betts, Richard. *Nuclear Blackmail and Nuclear Balance.* Washington, DC: Brookings Institution, 1987.

Bidault, George. *Resistance: The Political Autobiography of Georges Bidault.* Trans. Marianne Sinclair. New York: Praeger, 1967. First published in French in 1965.

Blair, Bruce G. *The Logic of Accidental Nuclear War.* Washington, DC: Brookings Institution, 1993.

Bowie, Robert R., and Richard H. Immerman. *Waging Peace: How Eisenhower Shaped an Enduring Cold War Strategy.* New York: Oxford University Press, 1998.

Boyer, Paul. "Dr. Strangelove." In *Past Imperfect: History According to the Movies.* Edited by Mark C. Carnes, Ted Mico, John Miller-Monzon, and David Rubel. New York: Henry Holt, 1995.

Brandon, Henry. *The Retreat of American Power.* Garden City, NY: Doubleday, 1973.

Brands, H. W. "Testing Massive Retaliation: Credibility and Crisis Management in the Taiwan Strait." *International Security* 12, no. 4 (Spring 1988): 124–151.

Brennan, Donald G. "Mutual Deterrence and Strategic Arms Limitation in Soviet Policy." *International Security* 3, no. 3 (Winter 1978–1979): 193–198.

Brigham, Robert K. *ARVN: Life and Death in the South Vietnamese Army.* Lawrence: University Press of Kansas, 2006.

———. *Guerrilla Diplomacy: The NLF's Foreign Relations and the Viet Nam War.* Ithaca, NY: Cornell University Press, 1999.

Bromwich, David. "Happy Birthday, Dr. Strangelove!" *New York Review of Books,* 3 April 2014. http://www.nybooks.com/articles/archives/2014/apr/03 /happy-birthday-dr-strangelove/.

Bundy, William. *A Tangled Web: The Making of Foreign Policy in the Nixon Presidency.* New York: Hill & Wang, 1998.

Burdick, Eugene, and Harvey Wheeler. *Fail Safe.* New York: McGraw-Hill, 1962.

Burr, William. "The Complexities of Rapprochement." In *The Harmony and Prosperity of Civilizations: Selected Papers of Beijing Forum.* Beijing, 2005.

———, ed. *The Kissinger Transcripts: The Top Secret Talks with Beijing and Moscow.* New York: New Press, 1998.

———. "The Nixon Administration, the 'Horror Strategy,' and the Search for Limited Nuclear Options, 1969–1972: Prelude to the Schlesinger Doctrine." *Journal of Cold War Studies* [China] 7, no. 3 (Summer 2005): 34–78.

———. "Sino-American Relations, 1969: The Sino-Soviet Border War and Steps toward Rapprochement." *Cold War History* 1 (2001): 73–112.

Burr, William, and Jeffrey P. Kimball. "New Evidence on the Secret Nuclear Alert of October 1969: The Henry A. Kissinger Telcons." *Passport: The Society for Historians of American Foreign Relations* 36, no. 1 (April 2005): 12–14. http://www.shafr.org/passport/2005/april/burrkimball.htm.

———. "Nixon's Nuclear Ploy," *Bulletin of the Atomic Scientists* 59, no. 1 (January–February 2003): 28–37 and 72–73.

———. "Nixon's Nuclear Ploy." National Security Archive Electronic Briefing Book no. 81, 23 December 2002. http://www.gwu.edu/~nsarchiv/NSAEBB /NSAEBB81/index2.htm.

———. "Nixon's Secret Nuclear Alert." *Cold War International History Studies* 2 (June 2006): 34–78.

———. "Nixon's Secret Nuclear Alert: Vietnam War Diplomacy and the Joint Chiefs of Staff Readiness Test, October 1969." *Cold War History* 3 (January 2003): 113–156.

Buttinger, Joseph. *Vietnam: A Dragon Embattled*, vol. 2, *Vietnam at War*. New York: Praeger, 1967.

Calingaert, Daniel. "Nuclear Weapons and the Korean War." *Journal of Strategic Studies* 11 (June 1988): 177–202.

Chang, Gordon, and He Di. "The Absence of War in the U.S.-China Confrontation over Quemoy and Matsu in 1954–1955: Contingency, Luck, Deterrence?" *American Historical Review* 98, no. 5 (December 1993): 1500–1524.

Chen, Jian. *Mao's China and the Cold War*. Chapel Hill: University of North Carolina Press, 2001.

Chen, Jian, and David Wilson, eds. "Mao Zedong's Handling of the Taiwan Straits Crisis of 1958: Chinese Recollections and Documents." *Cold War International History Project Bulletin*, no. 6–7 (Winter 1995–1996): 208–218.

Clarke, Jeffrey J. *Advice and Support: The Final Years—The U.S. Army in Vietnam*. Washington, DC: Center of Military History, 1988.

Clifford, Clark. "A Viet Nam Reappraisal: The Personal History of One Man's View and How It Evolved." *Foreign Affairs* 47, no. 4 (July 1969): 601–622.

Clymer, Kenton. *The United States and Cambodia, 1969–2000: A Troubled Relationship*. London: Routledge & Curzon, 2004.

Dallek, Robert. *Nixon and Kissinger: Partners in Power*. New York: Harper-Collins, 2007.

"Dan Ellsberg." Interview. *Rolling Stone*, 8 November 1973, 1–39.

Davidson, Philip B. *Vietnam at War: The History, 1946–1975*. New York: Oxford University Press, 1988.

DeBenedetti, Charles, and Charles Chatfield. *An American Ordeal: The Antiwar Movement of the Vietnam Era*. Syracuse, NY: Syracuse University Press, 1990.

Del Pero, Mario. *The Eccentric Realist: Henry Kissinger and the Shaping of American Foreign Policy*. Ithaca, NY: Cornell University Press, 2006.

Dingman, Roger. "Atomic Diplomacy during the Korean War." *International Security* 13, no. 3 (Winter 1988–1989): 56–65.

Drews, Robert. *The End of the Bronze Age: Changes in Warfare and the Catastrophe ca. 1200 B.C.* Princeton, NJ: Princeton University Press, 1993.

Duke, Simon. *U.S. Defense Bases in the United Kingdom: A Matter for Joint Decision?* New York: Macmillan, 1987.

Dulles, John Foster. "The Evolution of Foreign Policy." *Department of State Bulletin* 30 (January 1954): 107–110.

———. "Policy for Security and Peace." *Foreign Affairs* 32, no. 3 (April 1954): 353–364.

Dumbrell, John. *Rethinking the Vietnam War.* New York: Palgrave Macmillan, 2012.

Eden, Lynn. "Capitalist Conflict and the State: The Making of United States Military Policy in 1948." In *Statemaking and Social Movements.* Edited by Charles Bright and Susan Harding. Ann Arbor: University of Michigan Press, 1984.

———. "The Contingent Taboo." *Review of International Studies* 36, no. 4 (October 2010): 831–837.

———. *The Whole World on Fire: Organizations, Knowledge, and Nuclear Weapons Devastation.* Ithaca, NY: Cornell University Press, 2003.

Elliott, David W. P. *The Vietnamese War: Revolution and Social Change in the Mekong Delta, 1930–1945.* 2 vols. Armonk, NY: M. E. Sharpe, 2003.

Ellsberg, Daniel. "Call to Mutiny." *Monthly Review* 33, no. 4 (September 1981): 1–26.

———. *Secrets: A Memoir of Vietnam and the Pentagon Papers.* New York: Viking, 2002.

Fall, Bernard. *Hell in a Very Small Place: The Siege of Dienbienphu.* Philadelphia: J. B. Lippincott, 1967.

Foot, Rosemary. *The Wrong War: American Policy and the Dimensions of the Korean Conflict—1950–1953.* Ithaca, NY: Cornell University Press, 1985.

"Foreign Relations: The Nixinger Report," *Time* 99, no. 8 (21 February 1972): 12–13.

Francillon, Rene J. *Tonkin Gulf Yacht Club: U.S. Carrier Operations off Vietnam.* Annapolis, MD: Naval Institute Press, 1988.

Frank, Jeffrey. *Ike and Dick: Portrait of a Strange Political Marriage.* New York: Simon & Schuster, 2013.

Frick, Daniel. *Reinventing Richard Nixon: A Cultural History of an American Obsession.* Lawrence: University Press of Kansas, 2008.

Froman, Michael B. *The Development of the Idea of Détente: Coming to Terms.* New York: St. Martin's Press, 1991.

Gaddis, John Lewis, Philip H. Gordon, Ernest R. May, and Jonathan Rosenberg. *Cold War Statesmen Confront the Bomb: Nuclear Diplomacy since 1945.* Oxford: Oxford University Press, 1999.

Gardner, Lloyd. *Approaching Vietnam: From World War II through Dienbienphu, 1941–1954.* New York: W. W. Norton, 1988.

Garment, Leonard. *Crazy Rhythm.* New York: Times Books, 1997.

Garthoff, Raymond L. *Détente and Confrontation: American-Soviet Relations from Nixon to Reagan.* Rev. ed. Washington, DC: Brookings Institution, 1994.

George, Peter. *Dr. Strangelove: or, How I Learned to Stop Worrying and Love the Bomb.* Boston: Gregg Press, 1979.

Goodman, Allan E. *The Lost Peace: America's Search for a Negotiated Settlement of the Vietnam War.* Stanford, CA: Stanford University Press, 1978.

Greenberg, David. *Nixon's Shadow: The History of an Image.* New York: W. W. Norton, 2004.

Haig, Alexander. *Inner Circles: How America Changed the World—A Memoir.* New York: Warner Books, 1992.

Haldeman, H. R., with Joseph DiMona. *The Ends of Power.* New York: Times Books, 1978.

Halperin, Morton. "Lessons Nixon Learned." In *The Vietnam Legacy: The War, American Society, and the Future of American Foreign Policy.* Edited by Anthony Lake. New York: New York University Press, 1976.

———. "Nuclear Weapons and Limited War." *Journal of Conflict Resolution* 5, no. 2 (June 1961): 146–166.

Hammond, William. *Public Affairs: The Military and the Media, 1968–1973.* Washington, DC: US Army Center of Military History, 1996.

Hanhimäki, Jussi. *The Flawed Architect: Henry Kissinger and American Foreign Policy.* New York: Oxford University Press, 2004.

Harper, John Lamberton. *American Visions of Europe: Franklin D. Roosevelt, George F. Kennan, and Dean G. Acheson.* New York: Cambridge University Press, 1996.

Henriksen, Margot. *Dr. Strangelove's America: Society and Culture in the Atomic Age.* Berkeley: University of California Press, 1997.

Herring, George. *LBJ and Vietnam: A Different Kind of War.* Austin: University of Texas Press, 1994.

Hersh, Seymour. *The Price of Power: Kissinger in the Nixon White House.* New York: Summit Books, 1983.

Higuchi, Toshihiro. "'Clean' Bombs: Nuclear Technology and Nuclear Strategy in the 1950s." *Journal of Strategic Studies* 29, no. 1 (August 2006): 83–116.

———. "Radioactive Fall-Out, the Politics of Risk, and the Making of a Global Environmental Crisis, 1954–1963." Ph.D. diss., Georgetown University, 2011.

Hilgartner, Stephen, Richard C. Bell, and Rory O'Connor. *Nukespeak: Nuclear Language, Visions, and Mindset.* San Francisco: Sierra Club Books, 1982.

Hoff, Joan. *Nixon Reconsidered.* New York: Basic Books, 1994.

———. "Richard M. Nixon: The Corporate Presidency." In *Leadership in the Modern Presidency.* Edited by Fred Greenstein. Cambridge, MA: Harvard University Press, 1988.

Hughes, Ken. *Chasing Shadows: The Nixon Tapes, the Chennault Affair, and the Origins of Watergate.* Charlottesville: University of Virginia Press, 2014.

——. "Fatal Politics: Nixon's Political Timetable for Withdrawing from Vietnam." *Diplomatic History* 34, no. 3 (June 2010): 497–506.

Hunt, David. *Vietnam's Southern Revolution: From Peasant Insurrection to Total War.* Amherst: University of Massachusetts Press, 2008.

Immerman, Richard. *John Foster Dulles: Piety, Pragmatism, and Power in U.S. Foreign Policy.* Wilmington, DE: Scholarly Resources, 1999.

Isaacson, Walter. *Kissinger: A Biography.* New York: Simon & Schuster, 1992.

Jones, Matthew. *After Hiroshima: The United States, Race, and Nuclear Weapons in Asia, 1945–1965.* New York: Cambridge University Press, 2011.

Joy, C. Turner. *How Communists Negotiate.* New York: Macmillan, 1955.

Kaplan, Fred M. *The Wizards of Armageddon.* New York: Simon & Schuster, 1983.

Kaplan, Lawrence S., Denise Artaud, and Mark R. Rubin, eds. *Dien Bien Phu and the Crisis of Franco-American Relations, 1954–1955.* Wilmington, DE: Scholarly Resources, 1990.

Katz, Andrew Z. "Public Opinion and Foreign Policy: The Nixon Administration and the Pursuit of Peace with Honor in Vietnam." *Presidential Studies Quarterly* 27, no. 3 (Summer 1997): 496–513.

Kaufman, William. "Crisis in Military Affairs." *World Politics* 10, no. 4 (July 1958): 579–603.

Keefer, Edward. "President Dwight D. Eisenhower and the End of the Korean War." *Diplomatic History* 10 (July 1986): 267–289.

Keeney, L. Douglas. *15 Minutes: General Curtis LeMay and the Countdown to Nuclear Armageddon.* New York: St. Martin's Press, 2011.

Keys, Barbara. "The Emotional Statesman." *Diplomatic History* 35, no. 4 (September 2011): 587–609.

Kimball, Jeffrey P. "The Case of the 'Decent Interval': Do We Now Have a Smoking Gun?" *SHAFR Newsletter* 32, 3 (September 2001): 35–39.

——. "Decent Interval or Not? The Paris Agreement and the End of the Vietnam War." *Passport: The Society for Historians of American Foreign Relations Review* 34, 3 (December 2003): 26–31.

——. "The Nixon Doctrine: A Saga of Misunderstanding." *Presidential Studies Quarterly* 36, no. 1 (March 2006): 59–74.

——. *Nixon's Vietnam War.* Lawrence: University Press of Kansas, 1998.

——. "Out of Primordial Cultural Ooze: Inventing Political and Policy Legacies about the U.S. Exit from Vietnam." *Diplomatic History* 34, no. 3 (June 2010): 577–587.

——. "The Panmunjom and Paris Armistices: Patterns of War Termination." In *America, the Vietnam War, and the World: Comparative and International Perspectives.* Edited by Andreas W. Daum, Lloyd Gardner, and Wilfried Mausbach. New York: Cambridge University Press, 2003.

―――. "'Peace with Honor': Richard Nixon and the Diplomacy of Threat and Symbolism." In *Shadow on the White House: Presidents and the Vietnam War, 1945–1975*. Edited by David L. Anderson. Lawrence: University Press of Kansas, 1993.

―――. "Response to Review No. 21." 17 April 2013. http://www.h-net.org /~diplo/FRUS/PDF/FRUS21-Response.pdf.

―――. "The Stab-in-the-Back Legend and the Vietnam War." *Armed Forces and Society* 14 (Spring 1988): 433–458.

―――. *The Vietnam War Files: Uncovering the Secret History of Nixon-Era Strategy*. Lawrence: University Press of Kansas, 2004.

―――. "Vietnam War Nixonography." *Passport: The Society for Historians of American Foreign Relations* 43, no. 3 (January 2013): 25–33. http://www.shafr .org/wp-content/uploads/2013/03/Passport-January-2013.pdf.

Kissinger, Henry. *American Foreign Policy*. New York: W. W. Norton, 1969.

―――. "Force and Diplomacy in the Nuclear Age." *Foreign Affairs* 34, no. 3 (April 1956): 349–366.

―――. "Military Policy and Defense of the 'Grey Areas.'" *Foreign Affairs* 33, no. 3 (April 1955): 416–428.

―――. *The Necessity for Choice: Prospects of American Foreign Policy*. New York: Harper and Brothers, 1961.

―――. *Nuclear Weapons and Foreign Policy*. New York: Harper & Brothers, 1957.

―――. *Problems of National Strategy: A Book of Readings*. New York: Praeger, 1965.

―――. "The Viet Nam Negotiations." *Foreign Affairs* 47, no. 2 (January 1969): 211–234.

―――. *White House Years*. Boston: Little, Brown, 1979.

Klein, Herbert. *Making It Perfectly Clear*. New York: Doubleday, 1980.

Knebel, Fletcher. "We Nearly Went to War Three Times Last Year." *Look*, 8 February 1955.

Kuznik, Peter. "The Decision to Risk the Future: Harry Truman, the Atomic Bomb and the Apocalyptic Narrative." *Japan Focus*. http://japanfocus.org /products/details/2479.

Landau, David. *Kissinger: The Uses of Power*. Boston: Houghton Mifflin, 1972.

Lebow, Richard N., and Janice G. Stein. *We All Lost the Cold War*. Princeton, NJ: Princeton University Press, 1994.

Lee, Lorraine M. *Keeping Tito Afloat: The United States, Yugoslavia, and the Cold War*. University Park: Pennsylvania State University Press, 1997.

Leffler, Melvyn P. *A Preponderance of Power: National Security, the Truman dministration, and the Cold War*. Stanford, CA: Stanford University Press, 1992.

Lerner, Mitchell B. *The "Pueblo" Incident: A Spy Ship and the Failure of American Foreign Policy*. Lawrence: University Press of Kansas, 2002.

Lien-Hang Nguyen. *Hanoi's War: An International History of the War for Peace in Vietnam*. Chapel Hill: University of North Carolina Press, 2012.

Little, Douglas. *American Orientalism: The United States and the Middle East since 1945*. Chapel Hill: University of North Carolina Press, 2008.

Logevall, Frederik, and Andrew Preston. *Embers of War: The Fall of an Empire and the Making of America's Vietnam*. New York: Random House, 2012.

———, eds. *Nixon in the World: American Foreign Relations, 1969–1977*. New York: Oxford University Press, 2008.

Lumsden, Malvern. *Anti-personnel Weapons*. London: Taylor & Francis, 1978.

Luu Van Loi and Nguyen Anh Vu. *Le Duc Tho–Kissinger Negotiations in Paris*. Hanoi: Thê´Giớ Publishers, 1996.

Lynn-Jones, Sean M., Steven E. Miller, and Stephen Van Evera, eds. *Nuclear Diplomacy and Crisis Management*. Cambridge: Massachusetts Institute of Technology Press, 1990.

Malloy, Sean. *Atomic Tragedy: Henry L. Stimson and the Decision to Use the Atomic Bomb against Japan*. Ithaca, NY: Cornell University Press, 2008.

Marolda, Edward J. *By Sea, Air, and Land: An Illustrated History of the U.S. Navy and the War in Southeast Asia*. Washington, DC: US Department of the Navy, 1994.

Mazlish, Bruce. *Kissinger: The European Mind in American Policy*. New York: Basic Books, 1976.

McClintock, Robert. *The Meaning of Limited War*. Boston: Houghton Mifflin, 1967.

Medsger, Betty. *The Burglary: The Discovery of J. Edgar Hoover's Secret FBI*. New York: Knopf, 2014.

Metzger, H. Peter. *The Atomic Establishment*. New York: Simon & Shuster, 1972.

Mills, C. Wright. *The Causes of World War Three*. New York: Simon & Schuster, 1958.

Moody, Walton S. *Building a Strategic Air Force*. Washington, DC: Air Force History and Museums Program, 1996.

Morgenstern, Oskar. *The Question of National Defense*. New York: Random House, 1959.

Morris, Roger. *Haig: The General's Progress*. New York: Playboy Press, 1982.

Nelson, Keith. *The Making of Détente: Soviet-American Relations in the Shadow of Vietnam*. Baltimore, MD: Johns Hopkins University Press, 1995.

Nguyen Tien Hung, and Jerrold L. Schecter. *The Palace File*. New York: Harper & Row, 1986.

Nixon, Richard M. "Asia after Viet Nam." *Foreign Affairs* 46, no. 1 (October 1967): 111–125.

———. *Leaders*. New York: Simon & Schuster, 1982.

———. *No More Vietnams*. New York: Arbor House, 1985.

———. *RN: The Memoirs of Richard Nixon*. New York: Simon & Schuster, 1978.

Owen, Taylor, and Ben Kiernan. "Bombs over Cambodia." *Walrus* (October 2006): 65–69. http://walrusmagazine.com/article.php?ref=2006.10-history -bombing -cambodia&page=.

Parmet, Herbert S. *Eisenhower and the American Crusades.* New York: Macmillan, 1972.

———. *Richard Nixon and His America.* Boston: Little, Brown, 1990.

Paul, T. V. *The Tradition of Non-use of Nuclear Weapons.* Stanford, CA: Stanford University Press, 2009.

Perlstein, Rick. *Nixonland: The Rise of a President and the Fracturing of America.* New York: Scribner, 2008.

Powers, Thomas. *The Man Who Kept the Secrets: Richard Helms and the CIA.* New York: Knopf, 1979.

Prados, John. *The Blood Road: Ho Chi Minh Trail and the Vietnam War.* New York: John Wiley & Sons, 1999.

———. "Port of Entry, Sihanoukville: A Cambodian Munitions Mystery." *VVA Veteran* 25 (November–December 2005). http://www.vva.org/archive/The Veteran/2005_11/featureSihanoukville.htm.

———. *The Sky Would Fall: Operation Vulture, the Secret U.S. Bombing Mission to Vietnam, 1954.* New York: Dial Press, 1983.

———. *Vietnam: The History of an Unwinnable War, 1945–1975.* Lawrence: University Press of Kansas, 2009.

Pribbenow, Merle, trans. "North Vietnam's 'Talk-Fight' Strategy and the 1968 Peace Negotiations with the United States." E-dossier no. 33. *Cold War International History Project Bulletin,* no. 17, n.d. (ca. 2010). http://www .wilsoncenter.org/publication/north-vietnams-talk-fight-strategy-and-the -1968-peace-negotiations-the-united-states.

———. "The Soviet-Vietnamese Intelligence Relationship during the Vietnam War: Cooperation and Conflict." *Cold War International History Project: Working Paper* no. 73 (11 December 2014): 1–17. http://www.wilsoncenter.org /sites/default/files/CWIHP_Working_Paper_73_Soviet-Vietnamese_Intel ligence_Relationship_Vietnam_War_0.pdf.

Randolph, Stephen P. *Powerful and Brutal Weapons: Nixon, Kissinger, and the Easter Offensive.* Cambridge, MA: Harvard University Press, 2007.

Rosenberg, David Alan. "The Origins of Overkill: Nuclear Weapons and American Strategy, 1945–1960." *International Security* 7, no. 4 (Spring 1983): 3–71.

———. "'A Smoking Radiating Ruin at the End of Two Hours': Documents on American Plans for Nuclear War with the Soviet Union, 1954–1955." *International Security* 6, no. 3 (Winter 1981–1982): 3–38.

Roy, Jules. *The Battle of Dienbienphu.* New York: Harper & Row, 1963.

Ryan, Mark A. *Chinese Attitudes toward Nuclear Weapons: China and the United States during the Korean War.* Armonk, NY: M. E. Sharpe, 1989.

Safire, William. *Before the Fall: An Inside View of the Pre-Watergate White House.* New York: Doubleday, 1975.

Sagan, Scott. *The Limits of Safety: Organizations, Accidents, and Nuclear Weapons* (Princeton: Princeton University Press, 1993).

———. "Nuclear Alerts and Crisis Management." *International Security* 9, no. 4 (Spring 1985): 99–139.

———. "Proliferation, Pessimism, and Emerging Nuclear Powers." *International Security* 22, no. 2 (Fall 1997): 185–207.

———. "SIOP-62: The Nuclear War Plan Briefing to President Kennedy." *International Security* 12, no. 1 (Summer 1987): 22–51.

Sagan, Scott, and Jeremi Suri. "The Madman Nuclear Alert: Secrecy, Signaling, and Safety in October 1969." *International Security* 27, no. 4 (Spring 2003): 150–183.

Scanlon, Sandra. *The Pro-War Movement: Domestic Support for the Vietnam War and the Making of Modern American Conservatism.* Boston: University of Massachusetts Press, 2013.

Schaffer, Ronald. *Wings of Judgment: American Bombing in World War II.* New York: Oxford University Press, 1985.

Schelling, Thomas. *Arms and Influence.* New Haven, CT: Yale University Press, 1966.

———. *The Strategy of Conflict.* Cambridge, MA: Harvard University Press, 1960.

Schulzinger, Robert. *Henry Kissinger: Doctor of Diplomacy.* New York: Columbia University Press, 1989.

Schurmann, Franz. *The Foreign Politics of Richard Nixon: The Grand Design.* Berkeley: University of California Press, 1987.

Shaw, Tony, and Denise J. Youngblood. *Cinematic Cold War: The American and Soviet Struggle for Hearts and Minds.* Lawrence: University Press of Kansas, 2010.

Shepley, James. "How Dulles Averted War." *Life,* 16 January 1956, 70–80.

Sherry, Michael S. *Preparing for the Next War: American Plans for Postwar Defense, 1941–1945.* New Haven, CT: Yale University Press, 1977.

———. *Rise of American Air Power: The Creation of Armageddon.* New Haven, CT: Yale University Press, 1987.

Sigler, David Burns. *Vietnam Battle Chronology: U.S. Army and Marine Corps Combat Operations, 1965–1973.* Jefferson, NC: McFarland, 1992.

Small, Melvin. *Johnson, Nixon, and the Doves.* New Brunswick, NJ: Rutgers University Press, 1988.

———. *The Presidency of Richard Nixon.* Lawrence: University Press of Kansas, 1999.

Smith, P. D. *Doomsday Men: The Real Dr. Strangelove and the Dream of the Superweapon.* New York: St. Martin's Press, 2007.

Spector, Ronald H. *Advice and Support: The Early Years, 1941–1960.* United States Army in Vietnam series. Washington, DC: Center of Military History, 1983.

Stent, Angela. *From Embargo to Ostpolitik: The Political Economy of West-German–Soviet Relations, 1955–1980.* New York: Cambridge University Press, 1981.

Strober, Gerald S., and Deborah H., eds. *Nixon: An Oral History of His Presidency*. New York: HarperCollins, 1994.

Stueck, William. *The Korean War: An International History*. Princeton, NJ: Princeton University Press, 1995.

Suri, Jeremi. *Henry Kissinger and the American Century*. Cambridge, MA: Belknap Press, 2007.

———. "The Nukes of October: Richard Nixon's Secret Plan to Bring Peace to Vietnam." *Wired Magazine* 16, no. 3 (25 February 2008): 1–5.

Szulc, Tad. *The Illusion of Peace: Foreign Policy in the Nixon Years*. New York: Viking, 1978.

Tal, David. "'Absolutes' and 'Stages' in the Making and Applications of Nixon's SALT Policy." *Diplomatic History* 37, no. 5 (November 2013): 1090–1116.

Tannenwald, Nina. *The Nuclear Taboo: The United States and the Non-use of Nuclear Weapons since 1945*. New York: Cambridge University Press, 2007.

———. "Nuclear Weapons and the Vietnam War." *Journal of Strategic Studies* 29, no. 4 (August 2006): 675–722.

Taubman, William. *Khrushchev: The Man and His Era*. New York: W. W. Norton, 2003.

Thayer, Thomas. *War without Fronts: The American Experience in Vietnam*. Boulder, CO: Westview Press, 1985.

Tompkins, Tom. *Yokosuka: Base of an Empire*. Novato, CA: Presidio Press, 1981.

Uyehara, Cecil H. *Socialist Parties in Japan*. New Haven, CT: Yale University Press, 1966.

Vo Nguyen Giap. *Dien Bien Phu*. 6th ed. Hanoi: Thê´Gió Publishers, 1999.

Wall, Irwin. "France and the North Atlantic Alliance." In *NATO: The Founding of the Atlantic Alliance and the Integration of Europe*. Edited by Francis H. Heller and John R. Gillingham. New York: Palgrave Macmillan, 1992.

Wampler, Robert. "Ambiguous Legacy: The United States, Great Britain, and the Foundations of NATO Strategy, 1948–1957." Ph.D. diss., Harvard University, 1991.

Wells, Tom. *The War Within: America's Battle over Vietnam*. Berkeley: University of California Press, 1994.

Whalen, Richard. *Catch the Falling Flag: A Republican's Challenge to His Party*. Boston: Houghton Mifflin, 1972.

"What the President Saw: A Nation Coming into Its Own," *Time*, 29 July 1985, 48–53.

Wicker, Tom. *One of Us: Richard Nixon and the American Dream*. New York: Random House, 1991.

Wittner, Lawrence S. *The Struggle against the Bomb*, vol. 1, *One World or None: A History of the World Nuclear Disarmament Movement through 1953*. Stanford, CA: Stanford University Press, 1993.

Wrigley, Chris. "Now You See It, Now You Don't: Harold Wilson and Labour's

Foreign Policy, 1964–1970." In *The Wilson Governments, 1964–1970.* Edited by R. Coopey, S. Fielding, and N. Tiratsoo. London: St. Martin's Press, 1993.

Young, Ken. "U.S. 'Atomic Capability' and the British Forward Bases in the Early Cold War." *Journal of Contemporary History* 42, no. 1 (January 2007): 117–136.

Ziegler, Philip. *Wilson: The Authorized Life of Lord Wilson of Rievaulx.* London: Weidenfeld & Nicolson, 1993.

Zubok, Vladislav. *A Failed Empire: The Soviet Union in the Cold War from Stalin to Gorbachev.* Chapel Hill: University of North Carolina Press, 2007.

Newspapers

Chicago Sun-Times
Des Moines Star-News
Los Angeles Times
Miami Herald
New York Times
Washington Post
Washington Star-News

INDEX